The Greenwood Encyclopedia of American Institutions

Labor Unions

editor-in-chief GARY M FINK

GREENWOOD PRESS
Westport, Connecticut • London, England

Library of Congress Cataloging in Publication Data

Main entry under title:

Labor unions.
  (The Greenwood encyclopedia of American institutions ; 1)
  Includes index.
  1. Trade-unions—United States—History. I. Fink, Gary M.
  II. Series.
HD6508.L234   331.88'0973   76-8734
ISBN 0-8371-8938-1

Library of Congress Catalog Card Number: 76-8734
ISBN: 0-8371-8938-1

First published in 1977

Greenwood Press, Inc.
51 Riverside Avenue, Westport, Connecticut 06880

Printed in the United States of America

Contributors

Elaine Ross Cline
  Unaffiliated (formerly Archival Assistant, Southern Labor Archives)

Robert C. Dinwiddie
  Assistant to the Archivist, Southern Labor Archives

Nuala McGann Drescher
  Associate Professor, State University College at Buffalo

Joseph Y. Garrison
  Ph.D. Candidate, George State University

Carl S. Matthews
  Assistant Professor, George State University

David L. Nass
  Associate Professor, Southwest Minnesota State College

Merl E. Reed
  Professor, George State University

Donald G. Sofchalk
  Professor, Mankato State College

Marie Tedesco
  Ph.D. Candidate, George State University

William G. Whittaker
  Staff, United States House of Representatives

Robert E. Zeigler
  Assistant Professor, San Antonio College

Consultants[†]

Albert A. Blum, Director, Lyndon B. Johnson School of Public Affairs, University of Texas, Austin

David Brody, Professor of History, University of California, Davis

Louis Cantor, Associate Professor of History, Indiana University at Fort Wayne

Marten Estey, Associate Professor of Industry, Wharton School, University of Pennsylvania

John Hevener, Associate Professor of History, The Ohio State University, Lima

Morris A. Horowitz, Professor of Economics, Northeastern University

Elmer T. Kehrer, Southern Director, AFL-CIO Civil Rights Department

Melton A. McLaurin, Associate Professor of History, University of South Alabama

Leon Stein, Editor, *Justice*

†The individuals listed above read selected sketches in various areas. Their invaluable assistance is deeply appreciated.

FOR LISA, JEFFREY, KAREN, AND KRISTEN

Contents

PREFACE

This book contains historical sketches of more than two hundred national unions† and labor federations that have been part of the American labor movement. The nature and composition of these unions vary considerably. Some are industrial unions composed of all the workers in a particular industry; others are craft unions of specialized workers or associations of highly skilled artists and professionals. Many nearly approximate a cross-section of the American labor force, while a small number are composed predominantly of women, blacks, or Chicanos. Most of them have earned favorable reputations as honest, constructive organizations; yet a few are more noted for corruption, mismanagement, and the abuse of their trust. To some degree, success has characterized the experience of most of these unions, but a few are more significant for what they failed to accomplish than for any successes they may have had.

Although the unions vary significantly in size, power, age, character, and historical significance, each exercised a degree of sovereignty over a particular group of workers. But there are more steelworkers than siderographers, more carpenters than granite cutters; thus, while the unions have approximately the same significance to the individual workers they represent, some unions obviously have had a much larger impact than others on the national economy and the national labor movement. The historical importance of each union, then, is to some extent dependent upon the perspective from which it is viewed. I hope that the following sketches will prove useful to all students of the labor movement, regardless of their perspective.

During the planning stage of this project, it was hoped that sketches of most

---

†"National unions" and "international unions" are used synonymously in this volume. The term *international* was usually adopted with the addition of Canadian locals. It has little other significance.

national unions associated with the American labor movement could be included. It soon became obvious, however, that anything approaching comprehensive coverage would be impossible in a single volume. The American Federation of Labor alone chartered nearly 250 unions between 1886 and 1955, the Congress of Industrial Organizations another sixty-three during its brief existence, and, despite the great wave of union mergers and amalgamations in recent years, the AFL-CIO still had 111 affiliates in 1975. Moreover, hundreds of national unions never affiliated with any of the above federations.

Because of the large number of national unions, several loose and rather subjective criteria were developed to facilitate the selection process. Among the more important criteria, any one of which could qualify a union for inclusion, were longevity, historical significance, size and economic power, and the influence a particular union had in the development of organized labor in America. An effort was also made to include unions representative of most minority groups, trades and industries, chronological time periods, and ideological movements.

Distinguishing between professional associations and national labor unions presented a difficult problem. Local units of organizations, such as the Fraternal Order of Police, the National Education Association, the American Association of University Professors, and the American Nurses' Association, have assumed many of the functions of labor unions, including collective bargaining; the criteria employed here revolved around the organization's self-image. Professional societies (such as the Screen Actors Guild and the American Federation of Teachers) that clearly identify with the labor movement were included. Those professional groups that have resisted identification with organized labor were omitted.

The emphasis in the sketches is historical. Although not completely neglected, there has been no sustained effort to include such basic information as membership qualifications, apprenticeship regulations, and work rules; initiation fees, dues, and financial structure; collective bargaining procedures, strike policy, and agreements; or pension and welfare plans. Much of this information is available in the publications of the Bureau of Labor Statistics in the U.S. Department of Labor. The emphasis in the following sketches centers upon the circumstances surrounding the formation of national unions, the early formative years during which they gradually adopted the policies and practices that would influence their mature development, and the radical structural changes and leadership characteristics that had some impact on the growth and/or decline of the particular union. Although some effort was made to maintain conformity in sketch length, sketches on unions having an especially significant historical impact on the labor movement may be longer than those on smaller, highly specialized unions whose primary significance was their longevity.

Unfortunately, the sketches vary in quality as well as length. The availability of sound, scholarly analyses greatly strengthened the sketches of particular unions. Informative secondary sources exist for nearly half of the unions discussed. Information for the remainder of the unions had to be secured from union publications, data accumulated by the Bureau of Labor Statistics, random comments in the secondary literature, and a variety of other sources. The bibliographic references at the end of each sketch often reflect the sources from which the material for the sketch was drawn. An asterisk (*) following a union title indicates that there is a sketch of that union elsewhere in the volume.

This volume is the first in a projected multivolume *Greenwood Encyclopedia of American Institutions*. Future volumes will describe political parties and ancillary organizations, business and employer associations, charitable and welfare groups, fraternal societies, and other key American institutions, from the colonial era to the present.

Whatever merit this volume has is due in large part to those diligent and resourceful scholars who have produced so much of value in the field of labor history. It has become vogue in recent years to question the value of institutional history. Certainly institutional history has its limitations, and obviously there are other ways of approaching the study of labor history. Nevertheless, 20 million American workers belonged to labor organizations in 1975, and it would be foolish to suggest that unions had no influence in determining the conditions of their employment. Labor historiography would be much the poorer without Robert Christie's analysis of the Brotherhood of Carpenters, David Brody's history of the Amalgamated Meat Cutters, or Vernon Jensen's volumes on metal miners and lumber workers. Studies such as these and a host of others need no defense; they need only to be read.

On a more personal level, I would like to thank those contributors identified on the title page, and the scholars listed on the consultants' page who read selected sketches and offered valuable suggestions. They, of course, bear no responsibility for any errors that may appear in the published sketches. Numerous national unions responded generously to requests for assistance. Donald G. Sofchalk and Merl E. Reed, colleagues past and present, as usual have been especially helpful. Both contributed sketches and read portions of the final manuscript. It is the presence of friends and scholars such as these that makes work in the field of labor history so enjoyable and rewarding. Nearly every morning for over a year, my wife Mary arose at 5:30 to read, critique, edit, and proofread sketches. There is scarcely a page in the volume that fails to reflect her influence. Jane Hobson and the reference department staff at the Georgia State University Library exhibited their usual resourcefulness and diligence in locating source materials. Finally, James T. Sabin of the Greenwood Press not only conceived the project but has been instrumental in guiding the development of the volume.

Gary M Fink
  Atlanta, Ga.   February 1976

NATIONAL UNION HISTORICAL SKETCHES

ACTORS AND ARTISTES OF AMERICA, ASSOCIATED (AAAA). Nineteenth-century actors and artists suffered a variety of abuses instigated by unscrupulous managers and booking agents. This, along with the casual nature of employment, the necessity of travel to acquire work, and the financial instability of many producers, encouraged the early unionization of performing artists. The American Federation of Labor* (AFL) chartered its first actors' union—the Actors National Protective Union—on January 4, 1896. In 1909 the union changed its title to Actors International Union, and the following year it amalgamated with the White Rats of America to form the White Rats Actors Union of America.

The White Rats Actors Union had been organized in 1900 and was much more activist than the Actors International Union, which confined itself largely to publishing a list of approved, as well as unreliable or dishonest, managers. At the time of the merger the Actors International had about 1,000 members and the White Rats 8,000. The charter issued to the White Rats Union of American by the AFL in 1910 granted the union a broad jurisdiction covering "all parts of theatrical production occurring behind the footlights and in front of the scenery after the same has been placed in position by stage mechanics . . . and any form of entertainment known as either legitimate, variety or vaudeville."

This extensive jurisdictional grant created a dilemma for AFL leaders when the Actors' Equity Association* (AEA) organized in 1913 and steadily grew in membership and prestige. Not only was the AEA anxious to affiliate with the AFL, but AFL president Samuel Gompers reciprocated the enthusiasm. Gompers's efforts to effect a merger between the two actors' unions failed, however, and a resolution introduced in the 1917 annual AFL convention to cancel the White Rats' charter met a similar fate. A compromise broke the deadlock in 1919 when the White Rats Union turned in its charter under a stipulation that the charter would be reissued as the Associated Actors and Artistes of America. On August 28, 1919, the AFL executive council approved the title and chartering of the new organization, which included the AEA.

The new AFL union's jurisdiction included "all actors and actresses, either legitimate, lyceum, circus, cabaret, vaudeville, chautauqua, burlesque, motion picture, stage managers, or any other entertainers of the public." Despite its broad jurisdictional grant, the AAAA is a figurehead organization having virtually no real function or authority. It serves as an umbrella organization encompassing several autonomous branches representing different types of artists in the field of the performing arts. It provides a forum to discuss matters of mutual interest, a necessary channel of communications, and the machinery to resolve jurisdictional conflicts and regulate the activities of affiliated branches during strikes.

The AAAA, which maintains its headquarters in New York City, holds biennial conventions. The AAAA has no full-time officials. The limited functions of the association are carried on by a part-time secretary in a one-room New York City office. Elective officers include a president and executive secretary. The international board is comprised of delegates representing each of the affiliated branches. In 1973 the AAAA had a membership of 63,000 located in eight branches: AEA, American Federation of Television and Radio Artists,* American Guild of Musical Artists,* American Guild of Variety Artists, Italian Actors Union, Hebrew Actors Union, Screen Actors Guild,* and Screen Extras Guild.

For further information, see the sketches of AAAA branch unions in this volume. See also, Michael H. Moskow, *Labor Relations in the Performing Arts: An Introductory Survey* (1969); Alfred Harding, *The Revolt of the Actors* (1929); and Murray Ross, *Stars and Strikes: Unionization of Hollywood* (1941).

ACTORS' EQUITY ASSOCIATION (AEA). The acting profession in the United States during the last quarter of the nineteenth century underwent a fundamental change as the theater increasingly came under the control of business-oriented production managers more interested in profits than artistic excellence. As a result actors suffered increasing exploitation with little control over such factors as salaries, working conditions, and employment security.

Exhibiting the same reaction as other groups of workers experiencing similar difficulties in urbanizing and industrializing America, actors responded to their deteriorating situation by organizing. One of the more important of these early, ephemeral organizations was the Actors' Society of America, founded in 1896. Although the society failed to gain enough strength to protect actors, it inspired the organization of a permanent actors' association. In 1912 it created a "Plan and Scope Committee" to draft the constitution and bylaws of a new organization. Resulting from this initiative, 112 actors met in New York City on May 26, 1913, and formally organized the Actors' Equity Association.

With the objective of negotiating a standard contract and claiming jurisdiction over all actors, the new union immediately set about the task of gaining recognition as the bargaining agent for actors. After four years of hard bargaining, the Equity finally achieved recognition and a contract from the United Managers' Protective Association. The victory proved illusory, however: a majority of theatrical managers refused to recognize the legitimacy of either the agreement or the Managers' Association.

The Equity had a membership of 2,700 by 1919, and under the auspices of the Associated Actors and Artists of America* (AAAA), of which it was the largest component, the AEA received an American Federation of Labor* char- ter on July 18, 1919. Meanwhile, during World War I the working conditions of actors had further deteriorated as conflicts among producers complicated actors' lives, and a new producer organization, the Production Managers Association, determined to eliminate the neophyte actors' union from the theatrical field.

The producers' actions resulted in the historic strike of 1919, beginning on August 7 and ending on September 6. Theaters in eight cities closed, thirty- seven plays closed, and sixteen scheduled plays failed to open. The major issue in the thirty-day strike was recognition of the Equity as bargaining agent for actors. With the aid and assistance of the International Alliance of Theatrical Stage Employees* and the American Federation of Musicians,* the AEA won a remarkable victory. Not only did it gain its major negotiating demands, but membership jumped to 14,000, and despite the expenses of the strike, the Equity's treasury increased over $100,000. Moreover, the Chorus Equity Asso- ciation, organized during the strike to support the actors, virtually amalga- mated with the AEA shortly after the strike.

After negotiating a five-year contract with the Producing Managers Asso- ciation, the AEA began a concerted drive to win a closed shop agreement. The Equity shop was achieved after a threatened strike in 1924. Thereafter, the Equity won a number of concessions, including bonding agreements to guar- antee actors' salaries and transportation, protection from the importation of alien actors, control of commission charges by theatrical representatives, and a minimum wage.

During the 1920s, the AEA, which had been given jurisdiction over screen actors by the AAAA, made several attempts to organize Hollywood motion picture actors; however, internal divisions, rivalries between stage and screen actors, technological changes in the motion picture industry, and the resist- ance of motion picture producers who organized an employee-representation group (the Academy of Motion Picture Arts and Sciences) frustrated the Equity's efforts. Following an unsuccessful strike of Equity-affiliated screen actors in 1929, the AEA largely abandoned its efforts to enroll screen actors. Nevertheless, the Equity threat forced producers to make major otherwise un- obtainable concessions to screen actors. The AEA surrendered its jurisdiction over screen actors to the AAAA in 1934 with the understanding that the juris- diction would be given the newly organized Screen Actors Guild.*

Following its turbulent early years, the AEA entered into a period of relative stability after the mid-1930s. Pursuing its original commitment to arbitrate all disputes arising from contract disagreements, the AEA had usually found it possible to attain its bargaining objectives without striking until the "Broad- way blackout" of 1960 closed all New York City theaters for thirteen days in June. As a result of the strike, the AEA won a welfare fund and a pension plan for its members.

The AEA made one of its more important contributions in the area of civil rights. In 1947 the Equity ordered its members to refuse employment with the National Theatre in Washington, D.C., because of its racial discriminatory policies. Several years later, the AEA negotiated an agreement with the League of New York Theatres enabling Equity members to refuse to perform in any theater practicing racial or ethnic discrimination against either performers or patrons. In 1964 an Afro-American, Frederick O'Neal, was elected president of AEA; he served until 1973.

The AEA has its national headquarters in New York City with branch offices located in Los Angeles, Chicago, San Francisco, and Toronto. The AEA holds annual conventions and is governed by a non-salaried elected council of sixty-five in addition to the president, four vice-presidents, a treasurer, a recording secretary, and an executive secretary. In 1971 AEA reported a membership of 16,000.

For further information, see Murray Ross, *Stars and Strikes: Unionization of Hollywood* (1941), which contains a good discussion of the AEA's efforts to organize screen actors. Alfred Harding, the official AEA historian, tells the story of the early years of the union in *The Revolt of the Actors* (1929). Ralph Bellamy also has a short history of the Equity in the *AFL-CIO American Federationist* (June 1963). See also Robert E. Faulkender, "Historical Development and Basic Policies of the Actors' Equity" (Ph.D. dissertation, University of Pittsburgh, 1954).

AIRLINE PILOTS ASSOCIATION; INTERNATIONAL (ALPA). Militant union activity among airplane pilots began shortly after World War I and centered around pilots hired by the airmail division of the U.S. Post Office Department. The emphasis by Post Office officials on completed flights, regardless of weather conditions, and their refusal to buy and equip planes suitable for bad-weather flying, caused a series of crashes in the first half of 1919. Consequently, on July 22 of that year, two veteran pilots, supported by other pilots, refused to fly because of poor weather conditions. Their immediate dismissal inspired a strike of airmail pilots and a confrontation with the Post Office Department. As public and congressional criticism of the Post Office Department grew, officials became more conciliatory, and a compromise settlement was reached. The Air Mail Pilots of America grew from the strike, but it was largely a social organization with no permanent staff.

When the government turned over airmail deliveries to private contractors, desire for an effective pilots' organization increased. In response a California-based group enrolling only a few pilots was organized in 1926 as the Professional Pilots Association. More significant was the organization in 1928 of the National Air Pilots Association (NAPA), a successor of the older Air Mail Pilots of America. The NAPA, although more coherently organized and professionally directed than its predecessor, was an inclusive organization with membership open to any flier. The growing group of airline pilots, which provided much of the NAPA's finances, became increasingly restive as the association failed to adequately represent their interests.

Threatened wage cuts and lengthened flying hours during the early years of the depression increased interest in forming a commercial airline pilots' organization. The final step came in Chicago in 1930 when David Behncke, a pilot for United Air Lines, led a group of well-organized pilots in negotiations with United. The success of the Chicago group stimulated interest among pilots on other lines. On July 27, 1931, a meeting attended by pilot representatives of most major airlines convened in Chicago to discuss the creation of a national association. Their labor resulted in the formation of the Air Line Pilots Association, which received an American Federation of Labor* charter on August 10, 1931.

Shortly after its organization, the ALPA was confronted with its first major crisis when pilots struck the Chicago-based Century Air Lines. Due in part to the crass arrogance of Century's owner, E. L. Cord, the ALPA gained much valuable publicity enabling it to prevent Century from receiving a government airmail contract plus the accompanying lucrative subsidies. Although not entirely successful, the strike established the ALPA as a force in the airline industry with considerable influence in Washington, an important recruiting argument for the controversial new union.

Between 1932 and 1938, the ALPA devoted most of its energies to lobbying in Washington for federal legislation to protect airline pilots. The union's first substantial victory in this endeavor came when it successfully gained exemption of pilot labor from the National Recovery Administration's Air Transportation Code, which proposed low minimum wages and long maximum hours for pilots. With this decision, the question of regulating the wages and hours of pilots remained in the hands of the U.S. Department of Commerce, where the pilots had more influence. The airlines subsequently declared their intention to cut wages by switching from the mileage system of pay to an hourly wage. After threatening a national strike, the ALPA appealed the case to the National Labor Board and received a favorable ruling, Decision 83, stating that pilots should accept a basic hourly pay system, but they should also receive a mileage increment. This assured pilots of a substantial share of the productivity gains associated with technological advances in the airline industry. Moreover, the ALPA succeeded in incorporating Decision 83 in the Air Mail Act of 1934, the Civil Aeronautics Act of 1938, and the Federal Aviation Act of 1958. In 1947 the pay formula was supplemented by the addition of gross weight pay associated with the introduction of larger four-engine aircraft. During the mid-1930s, the ALPA also had succeeded in gaining the inclusion of air transportation in the collective bargaining provisions of the Railway Labor Act.

Having firmly established collective bargaining procedures in federal law, after 1938 the ALPA turned to the neglected area of negotiating collective bargaining agreements. In May 1939 it concluded a national contract with American Airlines and within two years had reached agreements with most other major airlines. The ALPA called its first national strike against Trans World Airlines in 1946. During the post-World War II period, the ALPA also inspired the organization of the International Federation of Air Line Pilots, a worldwide association of pilot organizations, and ALPA president Behncke served as its first president.

As principal founder and seminal figure in the early history of the ALPA, David Behncke guided the union effectively through the 1930s and 1940s. But in the post-World War II period, Behncke's domineering and autocratic personality and his inability to delegate authority created increasing tensions and frictions among lower-echelon union leaders. Moreover, technological changes in the aviation industry alienated the aging and uncompromising Behncke from the growing corps of rank-and-file pilots who had no roots in the older barnstorming days of American aviation. The effort to remove the irascible Behncke disrupted the union for over a year before Clarence W. Sayen finally assumed office in 1952 and brought order to union affairs. In 1960 the Airline Employees Association affiliated with the ALPA.

The ALPA, which maintains its national headquarters in Washington, D.C., holds biennial conventions. A president, six vice-presidents, a secretary, and a treasurer comprise the principal executive officers. The ALPA has a complex organization structure consisting of three divisions: Pilot Division, Association of Flight Attendants, and Air Line Employees Association. All three are "fiscally separate and self-sustaining and separately make and implement their separate policies." The ALPA is divided into five geographical divisions, each headed by a vice-president. The line of authority extends downward from the biennial convention to the board of directors, executive committee, executive board, master executive councils, and local councils. In 1973 the Pilot Division reported a membership of 27,639 located in 108 local unions; the Association of Flight Attendants reported 12,900 members in sixty local unions; and the Air Line Employees Association reported 9,200 members in sixty-five local unions.

For further information, see the *Air Line Pilot* issued monthly by the ALPA since 1932. Three books document the history and occupational concerns of the well-studied ALPA: George E. Hopkins, *The Airline Pilots: A Study in Elite Unionization* (1971); Oscar Leiding, *A Story of the Origin and Progression of the Air Line Pilots Association and of Its Key Figure and Organizer, 1930-1944* (1945); and Harold M. Levinson et al., *Collective Bargaining and Technological Change in American Transportation* (1971).

ALLIED INDUSTRIAL WORKERS OF AMERICA; INTERNATIONAL UNION (AIW). Efforts to organize automobile workers are almost as old as the industry itself, but they accomplished little until the 1930s. After the enactment of the National Industrial Recovery Act, the American Federation of Labor* (AFL) revived its campaign to organize workers in the automobile industry into federal labor unions, and in 1934 it organized the National Council of Automobile Workers. A year later, on August 26, the United Automobile Workers of America (UAW) received an industrial union charter from the AFL, one of the few unions at that time to receive such a charter.

Evidencing its dissatisfaction with, and independence of, the AFL leadership, within a year the UAW cast aside its AFL-appointed leaders and elected Homer W. Martin as union president. Shortly thereafter, it joined the Congress of Industrial Organizations* (CIO). The AFL responded by suspending the UAW charter on September 5, 1936, and officially revoking it a year later.

Martin spent three turbulent years at the UAW helm before the union's executive board replaced him with Rolland J. Thomas. Impulsive and temperamental, Martin had exacerbated already existing factional conflicts and rivalries within the union, which, along with his own administrative deficiencies, led to his downfall. (For a more extended discussion of this period of UAW history, see the UAW sketch in this volume.)

Shortly after his ouster in 1939, Martin led several locals out of the renamed United Automobile, Aircraft and Agricultural Implement Workers of America* (UAW) back into the AFL. The AFL then reissued the original UAW charter to the Martin group. The UAW-AFL, however, had little success in challenging the UAW-CIO in the automobile industry, and, after losing several National Labor Relations Board representational elections, Martin resigned the union presidency in 1946. Thereafter the UAW-AFL devoted its energies to the organization of industrial workers in a variety of trades, such as appliances, cookware, electrical components, motorcycles, and leather goods. Organizing efforts were confined largely to the Midwest.

As a result of the merger between the AFL and CIO in 1955, the UAW-AFL was renamed the International Union, Allied Industrial Workers of America on May 1, 1956. Nevertheless, the AIW retained its jurisdictional claim to

all branches of the industry engaged in the manufacture of automobiles, motor trucks, aircraft, tractors, farm implements, and all related or allied industries, including the manufacture of parts, tools, and dies, etc., and the assembly of such parts into completed products and shall embrace all employees engaged in such manufacture and also in the office work, sales, distribution and maintenance divisions of such industries, and the affiliated or allied industries to which charters may be granted by the International Executive Board.

Although the AIW retained its jurisdictional claim in the automobile industry, the new title much more accurately reflected the nature of the organization. Following the mid-1940s, the AIW organized successful locals and negotiated contracts with such corporations as Eaton Industries, Essex International, Fruehauf Trailer, and Sheller-Globe.

The AIW, which holds biennial conventions, maintains its national headquarters in Milwaukee. Elected officers include a president, a secretary-treasurer, an executive board member elected at large, and board members elected from each geographical region. The international executive board is composed of the above officials. In 1973 the AIW reported a membership of 86,000 located in 430 local unions.

For further information, see the *Allied Industrial Worker* published monthly by the AIW. The early history of the UAW has been well depicted in two books by Sidney Fine, *The Automobile Under the Blue Eagle: Labor, Management, and the Automobile Manufacturing Code* (1963), and *Sit-Down: The General Motors Strike of 1936-1937* (1969). Very little published information exists on either the UAW-AFL or the AIW. The AIW now publishes a "Report to Members" following each biennial convention, but its emphasis, of course, is contemporary rather than historical.

ALUMINUM WORKERS INTERNATIONAL UNION (AWIU). The early American aluminum industry, which was dominated by the Aluminum Company of America (ALCOA), began to reach maturity during the late 1920s and early 1930s. As a consequence, the American Federation of Labor* (AFL) launched an effort in 1932 to bring workers of the major ALCOA aluminum plants under the cloak of trade unionism by organizing workers in the industry into directly affiliated federal labor unions. Organizing success resulted in the chartering of a growing number of federal locals in the industry, and in 1936 the AFL created the International Council of Aluminum Workers' Union (ICAWU), the first national union organized in the aluminum industry.

Divisions within the national labor movement resulting in the organization of the Congress of Industrial Organizations* (CIO) soon spread to workers in the aluminum industry. Several federal locals chartered by the ICAWU withdrew from the AFL Council and affiliated with the CIO in 1937 as the Aluminum Workers of America (AWA). The new CIO affiliate inaugurated a major organizing drive in the industry and rapidly surpassed the ICAWU in membership, but the AWA had less success in gaining union recognition from major aluminum producers and in negotiating collective bargaining agreements. Consequently the AWA's early organizing surge subsided, and in 1944 the United Steelworkers of America* (USWA) absorbed the AWA's membership and trade jurisdiction.

The AWA, which maintained its national headquarters in New Kensington, Pennsylvania, held biennial conventions. Full-time officers included a president, vice-president, and secretary-treasurer. The executive board was composed of the full-time officers, three auditors, and five district board members. At the time of the USWA merger, the AWA paid per-capita taxes to the CIO on 25,000 members.

- Meanwhile, in competing with the powerful USWA, the ICAWU expanded its original organizing base among the workers of ALCOA to include workers of such other industry giants as Reynolds Metals and Kaiser Aluminum. On February 26, 1953, the AFL finally extended an international charter to the ICAWU, converting the directly chartered council into an independent international affiliate, the Aluminum Workers International Union. After the merger of the AFL and the CIO in 1955, the AWIU shared jurisdiction in the aluminum industry with the USWA. In competing with the Steelworkers, the much smaller AWIU maintained its own membership, although it organized fewer workers in the industry than its giant rival.

The AWIU, which maintains its national headquarters in St. Louis, holds biennial conventions. Principal officers include a president, an assistant to the president, thirteen vice-presidents, and a secretary-treasurer. The executive council is comprised of the above officials. In 1973 the AWIU reported a membership of 29,500 located in ninety-one local unions.

For further information, see the *Aluminum Light* published bimonthly by the AWIU. Published accounts of AWIU history were not located.

AMERICAN FEDERATION OF LABOR (AFL). Concerned about the encroachments of the then powerful industrial-oriented Knights of Labor* (KofL) and the inability of the weak and disorganized Federation of Organized Trades and Labor Unions* to cope with labor's pressing problems, thirteen national unions founded the American Federation of Labor in 1886. Under Samuel Gompers, who served as president until 1924 (with the exception of one year), the AFL experienced slow but steady growth. By 1892 there were forty national unions, and the KofL was rapidly declining. Based upon the principle of autonomy for member unions, the AFL was at first meagerly supported by a small per-capita tax. The AFL mediated jurisdictional differences among member unions; brought dispersed locals together into national unions; made the organizing talents of older unions available to new ones; aided its member unions in employer negotiations; heard complaints from individual union members; established new locals for its international unions; encouraged joint organizing campaigns with full-time AFL organizers (after 1900); and made loans and donations to member unions. The AFL also chartered federal labor unions (FLUs) for the unskilled, who were unwelcome in the craft organizations. As the number of member unions grew, the AFL in 1908-1909 established three departments: building trades, metal trades, and railway employees.

After the decline of the KofL, the AFL faced its most serious challenge to the principle of "pure and simple" unionism from Socialists, both inside and outside its ranks. In 1894 the AFL leadership narrowly averted the adoption of a Socialist plank calling for collective ownership of all means of production and distribution. That same year, the AFL did endorse compulsory education, the eight-hour day, employer liability laws, abolition of contract and sweating systems, municipal ownership of utilities, and the nationalization of transportation and communications. In 1903 AFL leaders defeated the Socialists again by rejecting independent political action as a means of achieving its ends. Instead, the AFL adopted a nonpartisan approach, urging its members to support candidates favorable to labor, but it officially refrained from endorsing parties or candidates.

The end of the first decade of the twentieth century saw the defeat of the Socialists and the end or decline of other challenges from the left, such as the Western Federation of Miners (later the International Union of Mine, Mill and Smelter Workers),* the American Labor Union,* and the Industrial Workers of the World.* The AFL then settled firmly on a policy of "voluntarism," rejecting any role in labor-management affairs by a distrusted government and stressing collective bargaining free from outside interference. During this period the AFL opposed proposals for minimum and maximum wages except for marginal groups, health and social insurance except accident and annuities for the aged, and unemployment insurance. State federations, central city unions, and FLUs frequently disagreed with these AFL policies and others that followed in later decades.

Initially the craft union principle emphasizing business unionism helped ensure survival. The AFL grew rapidly in membership, increasing from 264,000 in 1897 to 1,676,200 by 1904. Its position thereafter was one of relative decline, however. As the number of organizable workers increased by 50 percent between 1910 and 1930, AFL membership rose only about 9 percent, leaving the great majority of the labor force outside any union influence. Although AFL leaders blamed the unorganized themselves for this condition, the real causes lay elsewhere. A vigorous open-shop campaign begun in 1904 by several business associations successfully stressed employer and community anti-union action. Employers were buttressed by the liberal use of injunctions and by court decisions unfavorable to such vital labor concerns as the boycott, child labor, and yellow-dog contracts. But the policies of the AFL itself, stressing craft hegemony over industrial organization, especially in the mass production industries, also contributed to its own failures. Although industrial unionism had roots in the early AFL movement, the crafts dominated and insisted that their jurisdiction be respected in organizing large industries. Ironically, the craft principle that initially ensured survival later contributed to decline. FLUs of the unskilled comprised a maximum of 7 percent of AFL membership between 1897 and 1910 but only 1.3 percent in 1910. Meanwhile, AFL leaders, fearing the unskilled would dilute the power and influence of the crafts in the AFL structure, refused to charter national unions of unskilled workers. With technology and machines modifying and destroying skills, this AFL approach to organizing the mass production industries, questionable before 1920 and totally obsolete thereafter, gave employers the upper hand in collective bargaining.

Under William Green, who became AFL president in 1924, craft domination continued. Green also sought cooperation with business, a futile policy begun at the turn of the century by Gompers and other AFL leaders who joined the National Civic Federation, an employer-dominated group. AFL membership, at 2,865,000 in 1924, remained stable until 1930 although the economy expanded considerably as new mass production industries in automobiles, rubber, chemicals, and utilities sprang up. When the depression struck, the AFL lost 850,000 members between 1930 and 1933. However, with the passage of the Norris-LaGuardia anti-injunction legislation and Section 7(a) of the National Industrial Recovery Act (NIRA) in 1932-1933, possibilities for organizing the mass production industries seemed better than ever before.

As the NIRA spurred enthusiasm for union organization, the metal and building trades unions insisted vehemently on preserving their "exclusive jurisdiction" in the large industries, regardless of workers' majority wishes for one big union. The conflict over industrial versus craft unionism intensified throughout 1934 and was hardly mitigated by a craft concession that enlarged the AFL executive council to include additional industrial union spokesmen, who still remained a decided minority. Meanwhile, by the spring of 1935, organizing campaigns in steel, automobiles, aluminum, cement, and rubber failed because the FLUs received only limited jurisdiction from the executive committee while craft unions withheld crucial support.

Spurred by the intransigence of the AFL craft unions, John L. Lewis and eight other AFL union presidents formed the Committee for Industrial Organization* (CIO) in 1935 to push forward this type of unionism. The AFL executive council responded with charges of dual unionism, and in August 1936 it suspended the CIO unions, although the AFL constitution granted the council no such power. Efforts at reconciling the differences between the two groups failed until 1955.

Although eventual expulsion of the CIO unions in 1938 resulted in a membership loss of 561,000, the AFL experienced a significant spurt of growth during the early New Deal—from 2,126,000 to 3,422,000 members between 1933 and 1936. Spurred by CIO competition, the AFL began preparing a defense and counterattack, which increased its membership to over 4 million by 1939. It succeeded in holding back CIO penetration into existing areas of AFL hegemony while entering and organizing new fields in competition with the CIO.

As times changed, the AFL still adhered closely to its traditional policy of political nonpartisanship (which it officially abandoned only once, during the presidential election of 1924). By 1944, however, AFL members were serving as delegates to the Democratic national convention, and in 1947 the AFL created a "nonpartisan" League for Political Education following the passage of the anti-labor Taft-Hartley Act. The league compiled the voting records of political candidates for dissemination to union members. Meanwhile the AFL's legislative committee, organized in an earlier period, increased its activity, closely observing congressional committees and lobbying directly with congressmen.

Even before abandoning its opposition to unemployment insurance in 1932, the AFL began developing a more progressive record on other economic and social issues. In the 1920s it opposed a federal sales tax and later supported graduated income and inheritance taxes, credit control, and federal licenses for corporations. During the World War II period, the AFL opposed the oil depletion allowance and general or manufacturers' sales taxes while it supported corporation income taxes and the income withholding feature; it also opposed a wartime proposal to limit individual incomes to $25,000. In the postwar years, the AFL favored enactment of laws to lower tax rates and to give more exemptions to low income people; to fully tax capital gains; to close loopholes in estate and gift taxes; to supply free textbooks and more money for public education; to create a stronger federal housing program; and to improve social security benefits.

In other areas of social concern, the AFL in its earlier years often had a less enviable record. The plight of the less fortunate—particularly the unskilled, immigrants, blacks, and women—was often of little concern. Those without skills were sometimes regarded as rivals more dangerous than employers. Immigrants, allegedly difficult to organize, were also potentially unskilled adversaries. Although in 1900 the AFL rejected immigration restrictions, many leaders made no secret of their preference for the "old" immigrants (North Europeans) compared to the "new" immigrants from eastern and southern Europe.

The AFL constitution prohibited racial discrimination, and in the 1890s the federation refused admission to unions whose constitutions violated this principle. However, once discriminatory phrases were removed, AFL leaders quietly countenanced the exclusion of blacks through union ritual. Throughout its history, AFL craft unions remained largely closed to blacks except for a few segregated auxiliary unions and FLUs. The AFL and its unions also had little concern for women workers, whose place ideally was considered to be in the home, and attitudes toward Oriental workers remained ignoble.

With a change of leadership in 1952, the AFL under President George Meany began to exercise stronger resistance to its overweening crafts and also made headway toward a merger with the CIO. Under a formula recognizing craft and industrial unionization, with membership open to all national, international, federal labor, and local industrial unions, the AFL merged with the CIO in 1955, seventy-five years after its founding. (For a further discussion of the merger, see the AFL-CIO sketch in this volume.)

The AFL, which maintained its national headquarters in Washington, D.C., held annual conventions. Principal officers included a president, sixteen vice-presidents, and a secretary-treasurer. The above officials constituted the executive council. At the time of the merger, the AFL received per-capita taxes from 10,593,100 members located in 110 affiliated national unions.

For further information, see the *AFL News-Reporter* and the *American Federationist*. The standard history of the AFL consists of two volumes by Philip Taft, *The A.F. of L. in the Time of Gompers* (1957) and *The A.F. of L. from the Death of Gompers to the Merger* (1959). Although largely superseded by Taft's volumes, Lewis L. Lorwin's *The American Federation of Labor: History, Policies, and Prospects* (1933) still has value. In volumes 2 (1955) and 3 (1964) of his *History of the Labor Movement in the United States*, Philip S. Foner provides a Marxist critique of AFL activities. For biographies of AFL leaders, see Bernard Mandel, *Samuel Gompers* (1963); Stuart B. Kaufman, *Samuel Gompers and the Origins of the American Federation of Labor, 1848-1896* (1973); Max Danish, *William Green* (1952); and Joseph C. Goulden, *Meany* (1972). The conflict over industrial unionism is discussed in James O. Morris, *Conflict within the AFL: A Study of Craft Versus Industrial Unionism, 1901-1938* (1958); and Walter Galenson, *The CIO Challenge to the AFL: A History of the American Labor Movement, 1935-1941* (1960).

Merl E. Reed

AMERICAN FEDERATION OF LABOR-CONGRESS OF INDUSTRIAL ORGANIZATIONS (AFL-CIO). Continual frustration characterized early efforts to effect a reunification of the American labor movement following the Congress of Industrial Organizations'* (CIO) break with the American Federation of Labor* (AFL) during the mid-1930s. For several years thereafter leaders of both the AFL and CIO paid lip-service to the objective of labor unity and appointed committees to study and discuss the feasibility of a merger, but due to a variety of circumstances, few serious efforts were made to heal the fissure in the labor movement.

The Republican party's success in the 1946 congressional elections and the enactment of the anti-labor Taft-Hartley Act, however, rekindled interest in labor unity. The growing trend toward cooperative action was accelerated following the congressional elections of 1950 and the formation of the United Labor Policy Committee, a committee composed of AFL, CIO, and independent unions to look after labor's interest during the Korean War mobilization effort. Effective merger discussions did not occur until 1952, after the deaths of the presidents of the two rival organizations, William Green, AFL, and Philip

Murray, CIO. Their long years of bitter rivalry had resulted in hardened attitudes and mutual suspicion.

The new leaders of the AFL and CIO, George Meany and Walter Reuther, exhibited a much stronger commitment to labor unity and refused to permit minor disagreements to undermine the larger objective. More than anyone else, George Meany was responsible for the success of the merger effort. Devoting almost singular attention to the reunification effort, Meany employed his considerable leadership talent and his knowledge of internal labor politics to accomplish the task. The Republican party's success in the 1952 general elections, especially after the disastrous experience with the anti-labor Eightieth Congress, gave both Meany and Reuther added leverage in their efforts to bring affiliated unions in their respective organizations into line.

Before organic unity could be achieved, however, the highly divisive practice of raiding the membership of rival unions had to be resolved. Consequently, in June 1953, the AFL and CIO executive councils approved a proposal under which affiliates of both organizations agreed to refrain from organizing raids in cases where a union had already been certified by the National Labor Relations Board as the collective bargaining agent or where such status had been recognized by employers. The agreement became effective in July 1954 and was not binding on individual unions refusing to sign the agreement, but both AFL and CIO officials exerted considerable pressure to gain voluntary compliance.

The significant progress toward resolution of the raiding issue spurred the merger drive. The executive councils of the AFL and CIO quickly ratified (February 1955) the basic merger agreement reached by the joint unity committee. By May the committee had published a proposed constitution for the new federation. At its final meeting, held on July 20, 1955, the unity committee agreed to recommend that the new federation be named the American Federation of Labor-Congress of Industrial Organizations.

Under the terms of the merger, all AFL and CIO affiliates were granted membership in the new federation. Existing organizing jurisdictions were recognized, but international unions with identical or overlapping jurisdictions were encouraged to merge. AFL state-city federations and comparable CIO industrial union councils were given two years to arrange a merger. The AFL's well-developed department structure was retained, and a new department—the industrial union department—was established to serve CIO and AFL industrial unions.

Delegates to the national conventions of the AFL and CIO during the fall of 1955 accepted the agreement with little opposition, and the first national convention of the AFL-CIO met on December 5, 1955. Under the terms of the agreement, George Meany became president and William Schnitzler secretary-treasurer. Walter Reuther assumed the presidency of the industrial union department.

Although the merger created numerous internal problems, especially involving the efforts to integrate such important committees as education, research, and foreign affairs, the exposure of corrupt union practices absorbed much of the time and attention of AFL-CIO leaders during the years immediately following the merger. Even before the merger, leaders of both organizations recognized the existence of serious problems within the administration of various international union health and welfare funds. The AFL-CIO ethical practices committee, established at the time of the merger, opened investigations of the financial practices of the International Union of Allied Industrial Workers of America* (AIW), Distillery, Rectifying, Wine and Allied Workers International Union of America* (DRWAWIUA), and the Laundry, Dry Cleaning and Dye House Workers International Union* (LDC&DHWIU).

In the midst of efforts to rectify their own affairs, AFL-CIO leaders confronted the specter of a special Senate investigating committee chaired by Senator John L. McClellan of Arkansas, a legislator whose antipathy toward the labor movement was well known. The McClellan committee, organized to investigate labor-management racketeering, immediately began a probe into the affairs of the International Brotherhood of Teamsters, Chauffeurs, Warehousemen and Helpers of America* (IBT). Further investigation also revealed widespread misuse of funds by officials of the United Textile Workers of America* (UTWA) and the Bakery and Confectionery Workers' International Union of America* (BCWIUA).

The AFL-CIO leadership responded to these exposures by launching its own investigation of the IBT, BCWIUA, and the UTWA. Meanwhile, the AIW, DRWAWIUA, and LDC&DHWIU were suspended for failing to comply with the reforms ordered by the ethical practices committee. The IBT and UTWA were suspended in the fall of 1957, and the AFL-CIO gave the BCWIUA ninety days to adopted required reforms. After reviewing the progress made by various international unions in reforming their administrative practices, in December 1957 the AFL-CIO expelled the IBT, BCWIUA, and the LDC&DHWIU, and eventually restored the other suspended unions to full autonomy. After the expulsion of the BCWIUA and the LDC&DHWIU, the AFL-CIO chartered two new unions to contest the expelled unions for membership in their trade jurisdictions, the American Bakery and Confectionery Workers Union and the Laundry and Dry Cleaning International Union.* The AFL-CIO, however, did not attempt to challenge the IBT. As a result of the exposures, Congress enacted the Welfare and Pension Plan Disclosure Act of 1958 (which the AFL-CIO supported) and the Labor Management Reporting and Disclosure Act of 1959, which contained some adjustments of the Taft-Hartley Act long sought by organized labor but was generally considered anti-labor legislation.

Throughout its history the AFL-CIO has devoted much time, attention, and considerable financial resources to political affairs. Although rhetorically pursuing the traditional nonpartisan political policy, under the guidance of its committee on political education, the AFL-CIO assumed considerable power and influence within the councils of the national Democratic party organization. From its founding until 1972, it endorsed Democratic presidential candidates exclusively. During these years the AFL-CIO strongly supported the social and labor reforms sought by the John F. Kennedy and Lyndon B. Johnson administrations and consistently supported U.S. foreign policy, including the war in Southeast Asia. Breaking precedent in 1972, the AFL-CIO executive council refused to endorse the Democratic party candidacy of George S. McGovern. Nevertheless, several AFL-CIO affiliated unions ignored the injunction and supported the Democratic ticket. Beginning in 1973, the AFL-CIO executive council, under the resolute leadership of George Meany, launched a major effort to impeach President Richard M. Nixon, a campaign inspired at least partially by the Republican president's economic policies as well as his malfeasance in office.

During the early 1960s, the Negro American Labor Council,* an organization led by A. Philip Randolph which sought to end racial discrimination within the labor movement, brought pressure on the AFL-CIO leadership to eliminate discrimination in employment, to increase the advancement of blacks, and to encourage their entry into trades controlled by the AFL-CIO's various affiliated unions. Although they made consistent progress in these areas, AFL-CIO leaders encountered considerable criticism from reformers for failing to act quickly and forcefully enough. Nevertheless, the AFL-CIO leadership exhibited its commitment to racial justice through consistent support of the many civil-rights measures enacted during the 1960s.

The principal proponents and supporters of the AFL-CIO merger had hoped that the merged federation would lead a reinvigorated organizing drive, especially among the growing numbers of unorganized white-collar workers. Although it created an organizing department and led a major unionizing campaign, the AFL-CIO had only limited success among these workers, and, in fact, it lost almost as many workers to automation as it added to union rolls. AFL-CIO leaders also supported the organization of migratory and farm workers and contributed large sums of money to the United Farm Workers' Union* in its jurisdictional struggles with the powerful IBT.

Arguing that the AFL-CIO leadership was making neither a determined nor effective effort to organize either office workers or the workers in traditionally nonunion industries, the United Automobile, Aerospace and Agricultural Implement Workers of America* (UAW), the largest AFL-CIO affiliate, withdrew from the federation on July 1, 1968. A year later, on May 26, 1969, the UAW joined with the IBT to establish the Alliance for Labor Action, an organization designed to correct the organizational and political shortcomings of the AFL-CIO. But the concord between the UAW and the IBT was at best an improbable affair, and except for an organizing effort in Atlanta, Georgia, the alliance accomplished little and disintegrated shortly after Reuther's death in 1970. The alliance was formally dissolved in 1972.

More than any other single influence or personage, George Meany has dominated the first two decades of AFL-CIO history. Although he has little institutional power, Meany, through the force of personality, shrewd judgments of human character, and a gift for persuasion, quickly established himself as the unrivaled leader of the American labor movement, the first since the heyday of Samuel Gompers.

The AFL-CIO, which maintains its national headquarters in Washington, D.C., holds biennial conventions. Principal officers include a president, thirty-three vice-presidents, and a secretary-treasurer. The executive council is composed of the above officials. In 1973 the AFL-CIO reported a membership of 13,407,000 members located in 114 affiliated unions.

For further information, see the *AFL-CIO News* issued weekly and the *American Federationist* published monthly by the AFL-CIO. Accounts of the AFL-CIO merger can be found in Arthur Goldberg, *AFL-CIO Labor United* (1956); Philip Taft, *Organized Labor in American History* (1964), and the *A.F. of L. from the Death of Gompers to the Merger* (1959); and Joseph G. Rayback, *A History of American Labor* (1966). The best account of racketeering and corruption in the labor movement is John Hutchinson's *The Imperfect Union: A History of Corruption in American Trade Unions* (1970). Joseph C. Goulden's *Meany* (1972) provides many insights into the background and character of the controversial AFL-CIO president.

AMERICAN LABOR UNION (ALU). Developments in the American Labor movement following the formation of the American Federation of Labor* (AFL) in 1886 gradually convinced labor leaders in the West that their interests and needs were being ignored. Eastern trade unionists, who dominated and controlled the AFL and most of its major international union affiliates, seemed to have little understanding or concern about the problems encountered by the labor movement in the West. Such an attitude led the State Trade and Labor Council of Montana to withdraw from the AFL and suggest the organization of a separate federation. Meeting in the fall of 1897, the Montana labor council adopted resolutions calling for the creation of a western federation, and a short time later, delegates attending the Western Federation of Miners'* (WFM) national convention endorsed the proposal. After canvassing other labor unions in the West to ascertain their feelings on the proposal, the WFM issued a call for a convention to meet in Salt Lake City on May 10, 1898; 119 delegates responded, and before adjourning, they founded the Western Labor Union (WLU).

The WLU was not conceived as a dual union movement, and affiliated unions were encouraged to maintain their membership in international labor unions and the AFL. But WLU leaders clearly disliked the AFL's dedication to craft unionism and its failure to organize unskilled workers. Officials hoped that the WLU would overcome these deficiencies by organizing the unorganized through industrial unionism. Within six months of the Salt Lake City conference, the WLU had sixty-five affiliated unions, the largest and most influential of which was the WFM.

The AFL responded to this perceived threat to its hegemony by first sending President Samuel Gompers to the Salt Lake City conference in an attempt to abort the projected western federation. When that failed, the AFL branded the WLU a dual union and tried to destroy it. AFL organizers in the West attempted to detach local unions from the WLU and to create dual unions when circumstances, such as a strike, made such action feasible. Finally the AFL sent two emissaries to the WLU's third national convention meeting in Denver in June 1902. The AFL representatives bluntly ordered the WLU to disband in six months or the AFL would establish rival unions in all western states. The AFL representatives were further discredited in the eyes of WLU sympathizers when it was discovered that they were actively assisting an AFL organizer who was attempting to crush a Denver building trades strike led by the WLU.

Confronted with this declaration of war by the AFL, delegates to the WLU convention responded to the advice of Eugene V. Debs and others by changing the organization's name to the American Labor Union and challenging the AFL claim to national labor leadership. The ALU endorsed industrial unionism, direct economic action, syndicalism, and the Socialist Party of America. The AFL initiated hostilities by launching a major organizing drive in the West, which westerners had been urging for years, but the primary objective was to destroy the ALU rather than to organize the unorganized. AFL representatives in the area seemed more intent on breaking ALU strikes than on creating strong, legitimate unions of their own. These tactics served the AFL cause poorly. Western trade unionists, even those sympathetic to the AFL, refused to excuse such tactics as a necessary expedient to eliminate the Socialist menace.

The AFL campaign had little immediate effect on the ALU. At its first national convention, ALU leaders claimed a membrership of 100,000, which, although undoubtedly exaggerated and composed largely of WFM members, still represented a significant growth. It also added two international unions to its roster, the United Brotherhood of Railway Employees and the United Association of Hotel and Restaurant Employees. The ALU made few inroads in the East and continued to exhibit its greatest strength in Colorado, Montana, Idaho, Washington, California, and British Columbia, all areas in which the WFM was strong. ALU leaders respected the jurisdiction of AFL national unions actively attempting to organize the workers in their trade but declared their intention to unionize workers who were not being organized. This declaration was especially directed toward those national unions discriminating against women, blacks, and unskilled workers.

Nevertheless, the ALU's promising prospects were not fulfilled. To a considerable extent the union remained the creation of the WFM, and when the WFM suffered a series of defeats in Colorado in 1903 and 1904, the ALU declined precipitantly. Besides its overdependence on the WFM, the ALU also suffered from divisions within the Socialist party. The large, influential right wing of the party had adopted a "boring from within" strategy and saw the emergence of the ALU as a major threat to the hopes of converting AFL unions to the Socialist cause. Consequently the right-wing Socialist press was almost as vitriolic as the AFL in its denunciation of the western movement. Besides this major schism in the ranks of those opposed to the existing leadership of the AFL, the ALU's effectiveness was increasingly limited by a severe financial strain precipitated by its commitment to a low dues structure. Finally the ALU's decision to become a national union left little doubt concerning its role as a dual union, thus compromising its prestige in the national labor movement by violating the cardinal sin of trade unionism.

The short-lived ALU, however, had a significant impact on the American labor movement. It dramatized the western trade unionists' unhappiness with the AFL and forced it and its national unions to pay more attention to the neglected western union movement. It also dramatized the debate over organizing strategy, which planted the seeds of industrial unionism that bore fruit in the growth of the Industrial Workers of the World* (IWW) and later the Congress of Industrial Organizations.* On June 27, 1905, representatives of the ALU participated in the organization of the IWW, and the ALU disbanded.

The ALU, which maintained its headquarters in Butte, Montana, until 1904 and Chicago thereafter, held annual conventions. Full-time officers included a president and a secretary-treasurer. At the height of its power and influence, the ALU claimed a membership of 100,000 located in 276 local unions in twenty-four states, territories, and provinces.

For further information, see the *American Labor Union Journal* published weekly until the summer of 1904 and monthly thereafter. See also Philip S. Foner, *History of the Labor Movement in the United States*, vol. 3 (1964), a sympathetic account; Melvyn Dubofsky, *We Shall Be All: A History of the Industrial Workers of the World* (1969), more balanced and judicious; and Philip Taft, *The A.F. of L. in the Time of Gompers* (1957), the AFL version.

ASBESTOS WORKERS; INTERNATIONAL ASSOCIATION OF HEAT AND FROST INSULATORS AND (IAHFIAW). The organization of heat and frost insulator workers began under the auspices of the Knights of Labor* (KofL) during the late years of the nineteenth century. Many of these KofL local assemblies eventually joined the American Federation of Labor* (AFL) as directly chartered and affiliated federal labor unions. By 1904 organization had succeeded to the point that AFL officials called a national conference of such federal locals. On September 22, 1904, the AFL issued a national union charter to the National Association of Heat, Frost, General Insulators and Asbestos Workers of America. The addition of Canadian locals a few years later resulted in the substitution of "International" for "National" in the union title. The present title was adopted in 1910.

The new international union was organized to advance the economic interests and increase the job security of its members and claimed jurisdiction over all workers engaged in the

> practical mechanical application, installation, or erection of heat and frost insulation such as magnesia, asbestos, hair felt, wool felt, cork, mineral wool, infusorial earth, mercerized silk, flax fiber, fire felt, asbestos paper, asbestos curtain, asbestos millboard, or any substitute for these materials, or engaged in any labor connected with the handling or distributing of insulating materials on job premises.

Membership was restricted to those applicants capable of demonstrating proficiency in the trade through successful performance on a comprehensive examination. "Improver" membership and apprentices, among other requirements, needed to demonstrate the ability "to read, write, and understand English."

The new national union functioned in a relatively restricted trade jurisdiction and was established at an extremely inopportune time in the history of the American labor movement—just as employers launched a major open-shop offensive. Within a year, the IAHFIAW's original membership of 700 fell to 300. While it started to climb again in 1906, the Asbestos Workers did not reach 1,000 members until 1914, a figure that doubled before the end of World War I. Although falling sharply during the early years of the Great Depression of the 1930s, IAHFIAW membership generally has risen slowly but with great consistency since World War I.

The IAHFIAW has functioned predominately as an instrument to establish and maintain an acceptable scale of wages. Union leaders traditionally have used control over the supply of labor through a strict apprenticeship program as the principal weapon in accomplishing this objective. Subcontractors, employed by highly competitive steam fitting and plumbing contractors, performed much of the work in the trade. In their efforts to reduce costs to meet competition, semiskilled workers were employed extensively. Hoping to improve the quality of craftsmanship and to restrict the use of so-called poor mechanics, IAHFIAW officials cooperated closely with contractors in an effort to gain direct contracts from architects and owners.

Much of IAHFIAW history is closely intertwined with Joseph A. Mullaney's career in the American labor movement. Mullaney, who before the end of his career had acquired the affectionate title "Mr. Asbestos," began work as an apprentice asbestos worker in 1888. He soon joined the local union in his trade and in 1912 was elected national president of the IAHFIAW. He served in that capacity until his death in 1954. In 1937 he was elected to a life term as president, an honor in recognition of his years of service and contributions to the union he had helped create and which he was to serve for over fifty years.

The IAHFIAW, which maintains its national headquarters in Washington, D.C., holds quinquennial conventions. Principal officers include a president, seven vice-presidents, and a secretary-treasurer. The above officials constitute the international executive board. In 1973 the IAHFIAW reported a membership of 18,833 located in 120 local unions.

For further information, see *The Asbestos Worker* issued quarterly by the IAHFIAW. Although the Asbestos Workers have not received much attention from students of the labor movement, fragmented information can be found in Lewis L. Lorwin, *The American Federation of Labor: History, Policies, and Prospects* (1933); *The American Federationist* (February 1955); and *Bulletin No. 618*, Bureau of Labor Statistics, U.S. Department of Labor (1936).

AUTOMOBILE, AEROSPACE AND AGRICULTURAL IMPLEMENT WORKERS OF AMERICA; INTERNATIONAL UNION, UNITED (UAW). The first efforts to organize automobile workers began at the turn of the century when the Carriage and Wagon Workers International Union added "automobile" to its union title. The expanded jurisdiction, however, soon resulted in numerous jurisdictional conflicts with other American Federation of Labor* (AFL) metal trades' unions, and on April 1, 1918, it was suspended by the AFL. The union was then renamed the Automobile, Aircraft and Vehicle Workers of America. Although acquiring a membership of nearly 40,000 by 1920, the union all but disappeared during the 1920s, and its few remaining members were absorbed by the Communist-controlled Auto Workers Union. Unemployment, numbering in excess of 200,000 automobile workers during the Great Depression, further retarded unionism in the industry. Nevertheless, the passage of the National Industrial Recovery Act (NIRA) in June 1933 encouraged AFL leaders to initiate organizing drives in several mass-production industries, including the automobile industry.

Confronting seasonal layoffs that drastically reduced annual incomes, "speed-ups" that forced workers to produce at accelerated rates, and unsafe and unhealthy shop conditions, automobile workers responded enthusiastically to organizing initiatives. Within a year of the enactment of NIRA, the AFL had chartered 106 federal labor unions in the industry; twelve months earlier there had been none. As a consequence of the successful organizing initiatives, delegates from several federal locals met in Detroit on June 23, 1934, and organized the National Council of Automobile Workers' Unions.

The organization of the council, however, did not halt growing demands for the chartering of an international union of automobile workers. Moreover, unsuccessful strikes during the summer of 1934, the hostility of automobile manufacturers who began organizing company unions on a large scale, and the unwillingness of the Roosevelt administration to enforce effectively the collective bargaining provisions of NIRA halted earlier organizing initiatives. In an effort to reverse this trend, AFL president William Green, despite objections from several craft union leaders, issued a limited industrial union charter to the United Automobile Workers of America at a conference held in Detroit on August 26, 1935.

Although pleased by the chartering of the UAW, industrial union advocates objected to the limitations on the UAW organizing jurisdiction, which specifically excluded the workers in job and contract shops, as well as the employees of die, tool, and machinery manufacturers. Automobile workers also opposed a proviso accompanying the charter declaring that "the American Federation of Labor shall for a provisional period direct the policies, administer the business, and designate the administrative and financial officers" of the new union. As a result of these objections to the conditions of the charter, a second UAW national convention met within nine months of the founding convention, and the AFL-appointed president, Francis Dillon, was ousted and replaced by Homer Martin. The UAW further alienated the AFL in July 1936 by joining the Committee for Industrial Organization* (CIO). Shortly thereafter the AFL executive council suspended the UAW charter and on May 2, 1938, revoked it.

Encouraged by the UAW's affiliation with the militant CIO and the passage of the National Labor Relations Act, unorganized automobile workers joined UAW locals in growing numbers. At its inception, the membership of the UAW stood between 20,000 and 30,000. By 1937 this figure had increased tenfold, and by 1941 there were approximately 650,000 organized automobile workers.

Within two years of its founding, the UAW faced its first great challenge from automobile manufacturers. In December 1936 UAW local officials felt the union was numerically strong enough to demand recognition by the "big three" automobile companies: General Motors, Chrysler, and Ford. General Motors was picked as the test case because it had defied federal law by refusing to discuss collective bargaining or even recognition of the UAW. "Quickie" strikes occurred at the Atlanta, Cleveland, Toledo, and Flint, Michigan, plants. Despite personal reservations, UAW president Martin finally declared a nationwide strike against General Motors in January 1937. The sitdown strike quickly became the UAW's most effective weapon. Automobile workers in the Flint plant employed the sitdown tactic with great success. Flint police attempting to storm the plant were driven off with a barrage of soft-drink bottles, bolts, and water from fire hoses, an event that became known in labor circles as the "Battle of the Running Bulls." The strike continued, and in February 1937 General Motors was compelled to recognize the UAW. Subsequently, a short sitdown strike forced Chrysler Motors to accept the UAW as bargaining agent for their employees. These successes generated substantial increases in UAW membership.

Despite its organizing success, factional disputes within the UAW grew, resulting in a split between a group led by Homer Martin, which reaffiliated with the AFL in the spring of 1939, and a larger faction, which remained faithful to the CIO. During the following year, the rival unions fought for the allegiance of automobile workers. Due to successful strikes, National Labor Relations Board recognition elections, and successful membership drives, by 1940 the UAW-CIO had almost completely vanquished the UAW-AFL.

After an unsuccessful strike at the Ford Motor Company plant at River Rouge, which culminated in the infamous "Battle of the Overpass" during which UAW organizers Walter Reuther and Richard Frankensteen were severely beaten by Henry Ford's private police, the UAW leadership curtailed organizing efforts at Ford. Two years later, after the UAW-CIO had defeated the UAW-AFL, thereby becoming the sole spokesman for automobile workers, union leaders resumed the task of organizing the workers of the Ford Motor Company. A work stoppage called at the River Rouge plant in May 1941 was quickly concluded when Henry Ford, under considerable government pressure, recognized the UAW. With this success, the UAW represented almost all workers in the automobile industry.

From its inception, the UAW had been plagued by factional struggles within its ranks. One of the most acrimonious involved a left-wing group led by George P. Addes and a moderate faction headed by the director of the General Motors department, Walter Reuther. Chiefly through the support of locals in his department, Reuther ousted UAW president R. J. Thomas in 1946. Once established, the so-called Reuther caucus consolidated its power by removing opposition within the ranks, thereby bringing to an end nearly a decade of internecine warfare, which had seriously threatened the foundations of UAW strength.

Under Reuther's leadership, the UAW engaged in a number of postwar strikes culminating in 1948 with a General Motors agreement that included an "escalator clause" bound to the U.S. Bureau of Labor Statistics' cost-of-living index. During the 1950s, the functions of the national convention and the international executive board were rationalized, and the UAW's organizing jurisdiction expanded.

UAW president Reuther, who also had assumed the CIO presidency in 1952, played a leading role in merger discussions with the AFL; and after the organization of the AFL-CIO* in 1955, he became the president of the newly

organized industrial union department. But as a result of a growing estrangement between himself and AFL-CIO president George Meany, primarily concerning social issues and organizing activities, Reuther led the UAW out of the
AFL-CIO in 1968.

Along with Frank Fitzsimmons, acting president of the International
Brotherhood of Teamsters,* Reuther inaugurated the Alliance for Labor
Action on May 26, 1969. The alliance was founded to organize office workers
along with workers in industries only sparsely unionized. Reuther's death in
May 1970 seriously curtailed organizing activities, and the alliance was dis-
solved in 1972.

The UAW, which maintains its national headquarters in Detroit, holds
biennial conventions. Full-time executive officers include a president, three
vice-presidents, and a secretary-treasurer. The twenty-six-member international executive board consists of the above officers in addition to eighteen
regional directors and three members at large. In 1973 the UAW reported a
membership of 1,393,501 located in 1,575 local unions.

For further information, see *Solidarity* published monthly by the UAW. The
early history of the UAW can best be studied in the extensive publications of
Sidney Fine, including "The Origins of the United Automobile Workers,
1933-35," *Journal of Economic History* (September 1958), *The Automobile
Under the Blue Eagle: Labor, Management, and the Automobile Manufac-
turers Code* (1963), and *Sit-Down: The General Motors Strike of 1936-1937*
(1969). See also Jack Stieber, *Governing the UAW* (1962), the standard
account of its subject; Walter Galenson, *The CIO Challenge to the AFL: A
History of the American Labor Movement, 1933-1941* (1960); Philip Taft, *The
A.F. of L. from the Death of Gompers to the Merger* (1959); William J. Eaton,
Reuther (1970); and Jean Gould and Lorena Hickok, *Walter Reuther: Labor's
Rugged Individualist* (1972).

Joseph Y. Garrison

AUTOMOBILE WORKERS OF AMERICA; UNITED (UAW). *See* International Union, Allied Industrial Workers of America.

BAKERY AND CONFECTIONERY WORKERS' INTERNATIONAL
UNION OF AMERICA (BCWIUA). Bakers in various cities throughout the
United States began organizing during the last quarter of the nineteenth century, but the resulting organizations were never deeply rooted and disappeared
soon after resolution of the particular issue bringing them into existence. One
such union in New York City conducted a successful strike in 1880, but, following the usual pattern of such unions, it began to disintegrate shortly after
the strike. The union secretary, however, refused to allow the New York orga-

nization to die, and with a few other interested members, he began publication of the *Deutsch-Amerikanische Bäker-Zeitung*, a German-language trade journal that soon acquired a large circulation among German bakers throughout the country. Editors of the journal constantly extolled the virtues of collective action and agitated for trade union organization. Considerable success rewarded their efforts; defunct and moribund local unions reorganized as the labor movement among bakery workers surged forward. Finally, on January 13, 1886, twenty-five delegates representing local bakers' unions in fifteen cities met in Pittsburgh and organized the Journeymen Bakers' National Union of North America (JBNUNA).

The new national union received an American Federation of Labor* (AFL) charter on February 23, 1887, and followed the usual pattern of union growth in the United States. It grew steadily until the depression of the 1890s depleted local union ranks and brought organizing initiatives to a halt. During the 1897-1904 period, the JBNUNA grew steadily, increasing its membership from 2,000 to 16,000. The employers' open-shop offensive temporarily reversed the union's growth curve from 1904 to 1910, but thereafter successful union organizing resulted in almost 30,000 members by the end of World War I. To some extent, an expanded trade jurisdiction promoted this union growth. In 1903, the AFL gave the JBNUNA jurisdiction over candy and ice cream makers, and the union title was changed to Bakery and Confectionery Workers' International Union of America.

A growing dispute over organizing strategy presented BCWIUA leaders with a serious problem during this period. A faction within the union, centered among Jewish bakers in New York City, strongly advocated industrial organization. When international officers failed to satisfy these dissidents, a secessionist movement began among New York locals in 1913. In 1921 several of these unions met in New York City in conjunction with a small independent union, the Hotel, Restaurant and Caterer Workers' Federation, and organized the International Workers in the Amalgamated Food Industry. Two years later the union title was changed to Amalgamated Food Workers of America (AFWA). The new rival union organized on an industrial basis and claimed jurisdiction over "the manufacture, packing, preparing, distributing, and serving of foodstuffs of all descriptions." Although the AFWA claimed a membership of 12,000 by 1929, its strength was largely confined to the Northeast, especially the New York City metropolitan area.

As a result of economic pressures and declining membership during the Great Depression, merger discussions between the rival unions produced an agreement by which AFWA locals were either absorbed by BCWIUA locals or entered as separate units. The merger agreement also provided for the full acceptance into the BCWIUA of the industrial workers in large mass-production bakeries organized by the AFWA. The merger served as an important stimulant to the BCWIUA whose membership had declined steadily during the early years of the Great Depression. Membership turned upward in 1935 and increased steadily until mid-century when the figure stabilized at about 150,000.

The BCWIUA, which had contained a large Socialist element in its earlier years, acquired an enviable record of honest administration and democratic governance through the years. The McClellan committee's investigation of corrupt practices in the labor movement during the late 1950s, however, besmirched the BCWIUA's reputation. The BCWIUA president and two vice-presidents were convicted on a variety of charges involving bribery and corruption. The AFL-CIO* expelled the BCWIUA on December 12, 1957, after union leaders refused to institute the reforms demanded by the AFL-CIO ethical practices committee, and it then chartered a new international union in the trade, the American Bakery and Confectionery Workers International Union, which quickly began cutting into the older union's membership. Within ten years of its organization, the new AFL-CIO union surpassed the BCWIUA in membership and collective bargaining agreements. As a result of changes in BCWIUA leadership and practices, on December 4, 1969, the two rival unions merged under the historic BCWIUA title.

The BCWIUA, which maintains its national headquarters in Washington, D.C., holds quadrennial conventions. Principal officers include a president, an executive vice-president, seven regional vice-presidents, and a secretary-treasurer. The general executive board is comprised of the above officials, in addition to two board members elected from each geographical region. In 1973 the BCWIUA reported a membership of 145,836 located in 217 local unions.

For further information, see the *Deutsch-Amerikanische Bäcker-Zeitung*, the *Bakers' Journal*, the *Bakers' and Confectioners' Journal*, and the *B&C News* published consecutively by the BCWIUA, as well as the *ABC News* published by the American Bakery and Confectionery Workers International Union. See also *Bulletins No. 420, 506,* and *618*, Bureau of Labor Statistics, U.S. Department of Labor (1926, 1929, 1936). Discussions of corruption in the BCWIUA are included in Philip Taft, *Corruption and Racketeering in the Labor Movement* (1970), and John Hutchinson, *The Imperfect Union* (1970).

BARBERS, HAIRDRESSERS, COSMETOLOGISTS AND PROPRI-ETORS INTERNATIONAL UNION OF AMERICA; JOURNEYMEN (JBHCIU). Organization among barbers began during the early years of the nineteenth century; however, these short-lived groups were usually social or beneficial in character. After the Civil War, organizing activities increased, and several barber associations affiliated with the Knights of Labor.* The first permanent organization of barbers came into existence in Buffalo, New York, on December 5, 1887, when five delegates representing barber organizations in Toledo, Ohio, Muskegon, Michigan, New York City, Detroit, and Buffalo founded the Journeymen Barbers' International Union of America (JBIU). On April 10, 1888, the new union received a charter from the American Federation of Labor* (AFL). The Journeymen Barbers was a weak organization operating in a widely diffused trade, but it grew steadily during the remaining years of the nineteenth century. A founding membership of fifty increased to 1,300 in 1891, 1,800 in 1896, and 6,900 in 1900.

The early years of the national barbers' union were uneventful; nevertheless, the union made important strides in the evolution of a governing structure, the determination of an organizing strategy, and the formulation of policy objectives. In 1894 the JBIU revamped its financial system. Per-capita dues were raised, and it was stipulated that they be forwarded directly to the international union. At the same time, the International took over the sickness and death benefit system previously administered by local unions. The JBIU established a national defense fund and appointed its first full-time, salaried organizer in 1909. Meanwhile, membership continued to grow, reaching a peak of 54,762 in 1927 before declining precipitantly during the Great Depression.

In its efforts to unionize the trade, the JBIU confronted a variety of difficulties. Barbers located in the small towns of rural areas presented one problem. Few small towns had enough barbers to organize a local, and efforts to form groups encompassing larger geographic areas never succeeded. Large cities proved a second difficult area to organize because of intense competition among barbers and the presence of diverse ethnic groups. In the South racial antagonisms led to the formation of segregated locals of black and white barbers. The JBIU's success in organizing barbers was largely dependent upon the strength of the labor movement in a particular area; the stronger the labor movement, the easier it was to unionize.

The JBIU's original AFL charter covered only the barber's trade, but gradually it was broadened. In 1924, the JBIU jurisdiction included "shampooing the hair, shaving the beard, trimming the hair, bobbing women's or children's hair, or massaging." Later in the same year, the JBIU claimed jurisdiction over "hairdressers, wavers, marcellers and cosmeticians." Manicurists were added in 1929. The potential membership of the JBIU more than doubled as a result of these jurisdictional claims.

The International's constitution was amended in 1935 to permit the establishment of a separate organization of beauticians within the JBIU, and in 1941 beauty workers acquired a vice-presidency and permanent representation on the international executive board. Reflecting these changes, the organization was renamed The Journeymen Barbers, Hairdressers and Cosmetologists' International Union of America.

During the first half-century of its existence, the JBHCIU avoided the frustrating jurisdictional conflicts common to so many other American trade unions. A number of independent local organizations did emerge from time to time, primarily in larger cities, but they were usually short-lived and never attempted to organize a rival body. The first national union to challenge the JBHCIU, the Barbers and Beauty Culturists Union of America, was chartered by the Congress of Industrial Organizations* (CIO) in 1943; however, it never acquired a large membership, and after the AFL-CIO* merger, it was absorbed by the JBHCIU on July 1, 1956.

Because of the decentralized nature of the trade it was attempting to organize, the JBHCIU took an active interest in politics, especially on the local and state level. Consequently, local members of the International participated in the affairs of the various state federations of labor and city central unions chartered by the AFL. These central unions were highly involved in state and local politics and in lobbying activities during sessions of the state legislature. Working in conjunction with state labor bodies, barbers in most states gained laws establishing state licensing standards for new barbers and regulating barber and beauty schools. In many states barber union leaders played a major role in administering these regulations.

The JBHCIU maintains its national headquarters in Indianapolis, where it also has operated a nonprofit barbers' and beauticians' school since 1933. Conventions are held every five years. The president is the only full-time officer. The general executive board is comprised of the president and eleven vice-presidents. In 1973 the JBHCIU reported a membership of 50,000 located in 732 local unions.

For further information, see the *Journeyman Barber and Beauty Culture* published monthly by the JBHCIU. The early history and organizational structure of the union is briefly described in W. Scott Hall's *The Journeymen Barbers International Union of America* (1936). See also Richard A. Plumb and Milton V. Lee, *Ancient and Honorable Barber Profession* (1968), published by the JBHCIU.

BASEBALL PLAYERS ASSOCIATION; MAJOR LEAGUE (MLBPA).

Major league baseball, like most other professional athletic ventures, remains one of the last lingering vestiges of what might be termed a feudal tradition in the American entertainment industry. The manor, represented by the club franchise, is ruled by a lord (owner) and administered by a group of vassals (coaches, managers, and front-office personnel). At the bottom are the serfs (players) securely bound to the manor by a reserve rule. Although the accuracy of this analogy has diminished significantly in recent years, it still contains a degree of validity.

Efforts to reform this anachronistic system began almost as early as the development of the sport as a professional enterprise. But lacking unity and easily intimidated, the players lacked a sense of common purpose, and their efforts were easily crushed by the barons who controlled major league baseball. The first significant change in existing player-owner relations accompanied Jorge Pasquel's efforts in the spring of 1946 to establish the Mexican League as a rival to the established American leagues. The well-financed Mexican League, which offered higher salaries and other economic concessions, successfully raided the American clubs until Commissioner of Baseball A. B. Chandler announced a five-year ban against any ballplayer taking a "Mexican holiday." Three years later the Mexican League folded.

Competition for established baseball players, the first since 1903, stimulated a growing restiveness among the performers. Recognizing this unhappiness, Robert Murphy, a former legal examiner for the National Labor Relations Board, established the American Baseball Guild, the first bona fide labor union of major league baseball players. During the spring of 1946, Murphy attempted to sell his new union to the players on the sixteen major league team rosters. The new union demanded a pension system, a minimum wage, and compensation for spring training expenses. Before the beginning of the regular season, Murphy had gained the support of a majority of the players on six clubs; the strongest came from the Pittsburgh Pirates. Consequently he sought to use the Pirates as a lever to establish the precedent of union recognition and collective bargaining. The Pirates' management refused, and the players voted to strike unless the club agreed to conduct a representation election. Management again adamantly refused, and melting under their employer's withering counterattack, the players took a second vote on the issue and reversed the strike decision. Before the end of the summer, the guild had collapsed.

In response to the threat of outside unionism, the owners developed baseball's version of the company union, an employee-representation plan. The owners invited the players on each club to select a representative (in fact, the representatives were usually selected by the owners) to confer on an irregular basis with the owners. The Major League Baseball Players Association grew from this arrangement. The owners also created a pension system, established a $5,000 minimum wage, and compensated players at a rate of twenty-five dollars per week for spring training expenses.

As occasionally happened with comparable organizations established by American industry, the MLBPA did not remain a creature of management but gradually evolved into an independent, hard-bargaining labor union. The character and financing of the pension system remained the issue of greatest concern to the players. In 1953 MLBPA leaders hired a lawyer, J. Norman Lewis, to represent them in discussions with the owners. It was the first significant display of independence since 1946, and the owners responded in typical fashion, incredulous at the ingratitude of their chattel.

Although advances were made under Lewis's guidance, he found his association with the MLBPA extremely time-consuming and financially unrewarding. Consequently, when the owners refused to consider his appointment as legal consel for the pension fund, he resigned and was replaced by Robert C. Cannon of the Wisconsin Circuit Court. Cannon was clearly more sympathetic to management's point of view.

The final conversion of the MLBPA into an independent, legitimate labor union came in 1966 when the owners, anticipating Cannon's election, enthusiastically endorsed the proposal to establish a permanent MLBPA office and to appoint a full-time executive director. Cannon, however, declined the appointment, and the players then secured the services of Marvin J. Miller, who had a long association with organized labor and was then serving as chief economic adviser and assistant to the president of the United Steelworkers of America.* The owners bitterly opposed Miller's appointment and launched a major campaign to discredit him. Nevertheless, exhibiting increased militancy, the players ratified the choice by an overwhelming vote in a player referendum.

Miller quickly welded the MLBPA into a unified, democratically organized, collective bargaining unit. The employers' threat to undermine the financial basis of the pension fund was effectively countered, and in 1968 the first written agreement was signed by the owners. The agreement, which contained concessions long sought by the MLBPA, was renegotiated two years later with further concessions. During the following years, the MLBPA won one important court decision but lost another. In 1971 it successfully appealed the case of Alex Johnson, who had been suspended without pay for allegedly failing to play with sufficient vigor, but in 1972 it lost an even more significant case when the Supreme Court dismissed a challenge to the reserve rule initiated by Curt Flood.

The climax to the MLBPA's activities came in the spring of 1972 when it called the first general strike in baseball history. After an eleven-day strike, resulting in the cancellation of eighty-six games, a settlement was reached under which the owners agreed to increase their annual contribution to the pension fund by approximately $1 million. A year later an arbitrational system was established permitting players to submit salary disputes to professional arbitration.

The MLBPA, which maintains its national headquarters in New York City, meets semiannually. Principal officers include an executive director and general counsel. The executive board consists of the league player representatives, the club player representatives, and the pension committee representatives. In 1973 the MLBPA reported a membership of 1,000 located in twenty-four local units.

For further information, see *Sport* (October 1972) and *Sports Illustrated* (February 24, 1969). Curt Flood tells his story and provides historical perspective in *The Way It Is* (1971). Information on Marvin Miller can be found in *Current Biography* (May 1973).

BILL POSTERS, BILLERS AND DISTRIBUTORS OF THE UNITED STATES AND CANADA; INTERNATIONAL ALLIANCE OF (IABPBD). Delegates from several American Federation of Labor* (AFL) federal labor unions of bill posters and billers assembled in New York City in January 1903 and organized the National Alliance of Bill Posters and Billers of America. When locals were chartered in Canada, the union title was changed to International Alliance of Bill Posters and Billers of America (IABPBA) on January 7, 1908.

Although never destined to be one of the larger or more influential unions in the American labor movement, the IABPBA grew slowly but quite steadily during the years following its chartering. An initial membership of 1,000 in 1903 increased to 1,400 in 1910 and 1,600 by 1920, but membership stabilized there and remained virtually unchanged for the next twenty years.

The IABPBA jurisdiction was slightly enlarged in 1940 to include distributors, but because of protests from the International Printing Pressmen and Assistants' Union of North America* (IPPAU), the AFL withdrew the new charter pending an agreement with the IPPAU. Such an agreement was reached in 1955, and the AFL then sanctioned a title change to International Alliance of Bill Posters, Billers and Distributors of the United States and Canada. The IABPBD reached its peak membership of over 3,000 during World War II, but during the succeeding years, membership shrank to less than a thousand. Finally, on October 31, 1971, it surrendered its charter to the AFL-CIO* and disbanded.

The IABPDB, which maintained its headquarters in New York City, held triennial conventions. The union had no full-time officers but elected a president, nine vice-presidents, and a secretary-treasurer by majority vote during regular conventions. The above officials also constituted the union's executive board. Shortly before disbanding, the IABPBD paid per-capita taxes to the AFL-CIO on 400 members.

For further information, see Florence Peterson, *Handbook of Labor Unions* (1944). Other published information on the IABPBD was not located.

BLACKSMITHS, DROP FORGERS AND HELPERS; INTERNATIONAL BROTHERHOOD OF (IBBDFH). Blacksmiths organized on a local basis during the first half of the nineteenth century. As a result of the depression following the panic of 1857, blacksmith locals joined with similar organizations of machinists to organize the National Union of Machinists and Blacksmiths (NUMB). Although it played an influential role in the early, formative years of the modern American labor movement, the NUMB failed to survive the depression precipitated by the panic of 1873.

Blacksmiths joined local assemblies of the Knights of Labor* (KofL) and participated in the spectacular railroad strikes igniting both its rise and fall during the 1880s. The unsuccessful Southwest railroad strike of 1886 revived interest in the creation of a national union. In 1889 the first local of such a union, the International Brotherhood of Blacksmiths (IBB), appeared in

Atlanta, a rapidly growing railroad center. Composed of railroad blacksmiths, the Atlanta union joined similar unions of machinists and boilermakers also appearing in Atlanta at about the same time. Disillusionment with the organizing structure of the KofL and a desire to become disassociated from the unfavorable publicity accompanying the Haymarket Square riot and the Southwest railroad strike appears to have motivated the creation of these new unions.

As was true of both the International Association of Machinists* and the International Brotherhood of Boilermakers, Iron Ship Builders and Helpers of America* (IBBISBHA), the IBB spread from Atlanta through the South and then nationally, although it remained predominantly a railroad union. On October 30, 1897, the American Federation of Labor* (AFL) confirmed the evolving national structure of the IBB by conferring a charter upon the organization granting it exclusive jurisdiction over the trade.

During the first five years of the twentieth century, the IBB grew rapidly, reaching a membership in excess of 10,000 by 1904. The vigorous open-shop offensive initiated in that year, however, halted organizing advances, and IBB membership remained fairly constant for several years thereafter. The next significant organizing breakthrough came during the World War I period when two developments greatly stimulated the IBB's organizing successes. First was a merger with an independent union of drop forgers, which not only increased the IBB's membership but also enlarged its trade jurisdiction. As a consequence, the union title was expanded to International Brotherhood of Blacksmiths, Drop Forgers and Helpers. The second development resulted from government operation of the railroads during the war. The government-appointed railroad managers accepted union organization of the railroad work force, and the favorable climate for union organizing was reflected in the IBBDFH membership figures, which jumped from 18,000 in 1918 to 50,000 in 1921. That much of this membership came from the railroad industry was evidenced by the disastrous strike of railroad shopmen in 1922. Before the strike officially ended, IBBDFH membership fell to 5,000.

Resulting from the open-shop offensive of the 1920s, the Great Depression of the 1930s, and a constantly shrinking trade jurisdiction caused by technological change, the IBBDFH never recovered its World War I membership. Although the union made a small comeback during World War II, membership at the end of the war only slightly exceeded the 10,000 mark. Finally, on May 16, 1951, the IBBDFH relinquished its separate identity and merged with the IBBISBHA, creating the International Brotherhood of Boilermakers, Iron Shipbuilders, Blacksmiths, Forgers and Helpers of America* (IBB).

The IBBDFH, which maintained its headquarters in Chicago, held quadrennial conventions. Full-time officers included a general president, five vice-presidents, and a secretary-treasurer. The general executive board was composed of the president, a secretary-treasurer, and seven members elected by delegates at quadrennial conventions. At the time of the merger with the IBB, the IBBDFH had a membership of 10,000 located in 328 local unions.

For further information, see *The American Federationist* (July 1949), and Florence Peterson, *Handbook of Labor Unions* (1944).

BOILERMAKERS, IRON SHIPBUILDERS, BLACKSMITHS, FORGERS AND HELPERS; INTERNATIONAL BROTHERHOOD OF (IBB). The beginnings of labor organization among boilermakers and associated workers antedated the Civil War; as early as 1842 a well-organized union of boiler-makers in Pittsburgh conducted a strike in opposition to wage reductions. Strikes of boilermakers in Pittsburgh occurred again in 1845 and 1850. Boiler-maker unions conducted a successful strike in New York City in 1853, and achieved a shorter workday in New Orleans after a strike in 1866. During the 1860s, a boilermaker and blacksmiths' union functioned in Pennsylvania for several years.

A group of organized boilermakers requested affiliation as a national trade assembly with the Knights of Labor* in 1874, but it was not until 1878 that the Knights acted positively. By this time the boilermakers had resolved to form an independent union. Unions of boilermakers had been founded in many American cities by 1880, and a year later, the unions in Chicago, Detroit, and St. Paul, Minnesota, agreed to sponsor an organizing trip into several cities by the president of the Chicago union, Thomas P. Dwyer. Dwyer's successful efforts resulted in the convening of a national meeting in Chicago on August 6, 1881, and the organization of the National Boilermaker and Helpers Protective and Benevolent Union. At the third annual convention in 1883 the organization was renamed the International Brotherhood of Boilermakers and Iron Ship Builders, Protective and Benevolent Union of the United States and Canada. The ten local lodges that formed the nucleus of the boilermakers' union in 1881 had expanded to fifty-nine lodges by 1889, a period during which various lodges conducted a number of inconclusive strikes.

A second national union of boilermakers came into existence in Atlanta in 1888 when several lodges in that city combined to form the National Brotherhood of Boilermakers. During the ensuing years, the southern-based association of boilermakers expanded rapidly into the Midwest, and by the time of its national convention in Topeka in 1893, it had 108 affiliated lodges.

During the summer of 1893, the International Brotherhood of Boilermakers and Iron Ship Builders, Protective and Benevolent Union of the United States and Canada and the National Brotherhood of Boilermakers appointed committees to study the feasibility of a merger between the two unions. The discussions resulted in a consolidation proposal agreed to by representatives of both organizations, and on November 1, 1893, the two boilermaker unions met in convention in Chicago and organized the International Brotherhood of Boilermakers and Iron Ship Builders of America.

The IBB received an international charter from the American Federation of Labor* (AFL) in 1897. The union became an affiliate of the AFL metal trades department in 1908, the railway employees department in 1912, the building and construction trades department in 1931, and the union label trades department in 1945.

There were many disruptions for the IBB during its early years. Frequent changes in national officers caused confusion as did a constitutional provision requiring referral for membership approval of all constitutional, bylaw, or policy changes adopted by annual conventions. Year after year, almost every proposed change was rejected, regardless of merit, creating general confusion and dissatisfaction. The ensuing factionalism resulted in the brief disaffiliation of several lodges in the Pittsburgh area in late 1903. The 1906 convention rescinded the referendum law, declaring that it had been illegally adopted, and revised and reformed the bylaws to provide for an effective and efficient governing system. Considerable stability was brought to the IBB by these structural changes and by the election in 1908 of J. A. Franklin, who led the union for the following thirty-six years.

The 1912 convention also changed the name of the union to the International Brotherhood of Boilermakers, Iron Ship Builders and Helpers of America. A helpers' division had been created in 1902, and its rapid growth in the following decade led to its incorporation into the parent body. The 1912 convention also reorganized the financial structure of the union by levying increased assessments for a defense fund and for larger death and disability benefits.

The IBB, which had a steady, if slow, growth since the turn of the century, experienced a great increase of membership during World War I. By 1919 over 180,000 workers held IBB membership cards. In the postwar period, however, the loss of the export market, the contraction of the shipbuilding industry, and an employer open-shop offensive combined to eliminate many of the wartime gains. The unsuccessful national strike of railroad shopmen in 1922, which included nearly 30,000 IBB members, further debilitated the union. Thereafter the IBB experienced a period of reasonable stability until the Great Depression.

New Deal labor legislation and World War II created a second great membership expansion in the IBB's history. By the end of the war, the union had organized nearly a half-million workers. In 1944 Charles J. MacGowan succeeded the retiring J. A. Franklin as president. Upon assuming office, MacGowan sponsored several important structural changes. The first involved the creation of a unit for tank builders to handle the affairs of workers in that industry, and the second, the establishment of a research unit to provide informational and communicative services to the union. Later the IBB created a building and construction trades unit and an organizing unit. In 1951 the IBB merged with the International Brotherhood of Blacksmiths, Drop Forgers and Helpers* to create the International Brotherhood of Boilermakers, Iron Shipbuilders, Blacksmiths, Forgers and Helpers of America.

Following World War II, membership in the IBB began a slow decline, caused in part by the contraction of the ship building industry following the war and by technological changes in the fabrication of iron and steel. Membership declined to about 150,000 by the time of the AFL-Congress of Industrial Organizations* merger in 1955.

The IBB, which maintains its national headquarters in Kansas City, Kansas, holds quadrennial conventions. Principal officers include a president, an assistant president, ten vice-presidents, and a secretary-treasurer. The executive council consists of all of the above except the secretary-treasurer. In 1973 the IBB reported a membership of 132,000 located in 395 local unions.

For further information, see the *Boilermakers Journal*, a monthly published by the IBB since its founding in 1893. See also *The American Federationist* (August 1950).

BOOKBINDERS; INTERNATIONAL BROTHERHOOD OF (IBB). *See* Graphic Arts International Union.

BOOTS AND SHOE WORKERS' UNION (BSWU). Boot and shoe workers were among the first skilled craftsmen to begin organizing in the United States. Organizations of cordwainer societies date back to the eighteenth century, and the famous cordwainer conspiracy cases of the early 1800s are one of the landmarks of American labor history. Nevertheless, other than a short-lived effort during the 1830s when cordwainers discussed the creation of a national union, organization of the trade remained localized and fragmented until the Civil War. Following the brief but spectacular career of the Knights of St. Crispin* during the 1860s, unionism in the trade reverted to the antebellum condition.

Boot and shoe workers flocked into the Knights of Labor* (KofL) during the late 1870s and early 1880s, but the geographical organizing method the Knights emphasized discouraged the development of national unions. Nevertheless, leaders of the KofL encountered growing pressures to permit the organization of national assemblies in particular trades. By 1884 the KofL's general assembly conceded permission to the general executive board to grant charters to national trade assemblies.

Responding to the 1885 rules, a national assembly of shoeworkers, National Trades Assembly No. 216, was organized, but the great rush of unskilled workers into the Knights following the historic victory over the Gould-controlled railroads persuaded leaders of the KofL to revert to the older organizing methods. The decision antagonized the shoemakers and led to a growing feud between KofL president Terence V. Powderly and Assembly No. 216 leader Harry J. Skeffington. The dispute erupted into open warfare during the 1888 general assembly of the Knights when Powderly unsuccessfully sought to expel Skeffington and, failing that, to suspend him.

If the differences with the KofL's general executive board could not be resolved, delegates to the national convention of Assembly No. 216, meeting in Rochester, New York, in June 1888, adopted resolutions authorizing district officers to withdraw from the Knights and organize an independent union. Pursuant to those instructions, on February 19, 1889, Skeffington issued a circular calling upon all local assemblies affiliated with Assembly No. 216 to return their KofL charters and reorganize as local unions of the Boot and Shoe Workers' International Union (BSWIU). By the date of the BSWIU's first national convention, June 3-5, 1889, forty-seven affiliated local unions sent delegates. A few weeks earlier the American Federation of Labor* (AFL) had issued a charter to the new union.

By 1894 three different national organizations of shoe workers existed: the remnants of National Trade Assembly No. 216, the Lasters' Protective Union, chartered by the AFL in 1887, and the BSWIU. On April 13, 1895, these three organizations merged and received an AFL charter as the Boot and Shoe Workers' Union.

The history of the BSWU has been characterized by internal dissension, dual unionism, and a general failure to organize workers within its jurisdiction. BSWU officers adopted an organizing strategy of attempting to convince manufacturers to adopt the union label, thus turning the workers over to the union; others advocated the more traditional method of organizing the work force from the bottom up. These and other disagreements came to a climax in the much disputed union elections of 1906, which the insurgents appeared to have won; however, the issue was resolved in favor of the existing leadership, and many dissident locals seceded, taking with them a substantial proportion of BSWU members. In 1909 most of these seceding locals amalgamated at a convention in Lynn, Massachusetts, creating the United Shoe Workers of America. Until its 1923 merger with the Shoe Workers' Protective Union, another independent union of shoemakers, the United Shoe Workers provided the BSWU with a formidable challenge in its organizing field.

Membership in the BSWU had slowly dwindled from 1897 to 1900, but an organizing surge during 1901-1904 increased membership from less than 5,000 to over 32,000. Although increasing slightly during World War I, BSWU membership remained at the 1904 figure until the early years of the Great Depression. Depression losses were gradually recovered, and by the end of World War II, BSWU membership approximated the World War I total of 40,000; it has remained fairly constant since.

A variety of circumstances prevented the BSWU from fully organizing workers in its jurisdiction. The great geographical dispersion of the industry, especially into traditionally anti-union areas, inhibited organization. Union organizing in the shoe industry was also especially susceptible to the infamous

"Mohawk Valley formula" technique, which resulted in the phenomenon of the runaway factory. These runaway factories continued despite proscriptions against the practice in federal law. Finally, the many unions competing for membership in the industry confused and fragmented organizing efforts.

The BSWU, which maintains its national headquarters in Boston, holds quadrennial conventions. Principal officers include a general president-secretary-treasurer and a general vice-president. The general executive board is composed of the above officers and nine members elected at national conventions. In 1973 the BSWU reported a membership of 35,000 located in 145 local unions.

For further information, see the *Shoe Workers Journal* published bimonthly by the BSWU. Although few studies of trade unionism in the shoe industry have been published recently, there are a number of older monographs, including Augusta E. Galster, *The Labor Movement in the Shoe Industry with Sepcial Reference to Philadelphia* (1924); Horace B. Davis, *Shoes: The Workers and the Industry* (1940); and Edward B. Burt, *The Shoe-Craft: Its Organization* (1917).

BREWERY, FLOUR, CEREAL, SOFT DRINK AND DISTILLERY WORKERS OF AMERICA; INTERNATIONAL UNION OF UNITED (UBW). Although there had been sporadic efforts to organize workers in breweries as early as the 1850s through the creation of mutual aid organizations in St. Louis and Cincinnati and later through the activities of the Knights of Labor* in New York City, the first genuine union in the industry was formed in Cincinnati in 1879. Its life was short, as was that of a similar New York City organization created in 1881 as a result of agitation among workers for the eight-hour day.

The institution that was to successfully organize and represent the workers in brewing was founded at a Baltimore convention in August 1886. Calling itself the Brewery Workers National Union, it represented five locals from Newark, New Jersey, New York City, Philadelphia, Detroit, and Baltimore. The local from St. Louis, unable to send delegates to the four-day session, gave its proxy to New York City. In four months, the new organization had a membership of more than 4,000, ample testimony to the degrading and exploitative conditions characteristic of the industry. An American Federation of Labor* (AFL) charter was issued on March 4, 1887, authorizing the new group to "proceed with the organization of the trade."

At the annual convention that year, delegates wrestled with a fundamental question of structure, finally determining to open membership to all persons employed in breweries, regardless of craft. This historic decision made the United Brewery Workers Union the first real industrial union in the organized labor movement in the United States. It also involved the organization in a series of prolonged and bitter jurisdictional disputes plaguing its history to the recent merger with the International Brotherhood of Teamsters* (IBT).

Devotion to the principle of industrial unionism was consistent; members were convinced that only through the complete organization of each plant in a single union could their objectives be realized. Brewing was an industry requiring very little skill beyond that of the brewmaster and the "first men," which meant that management could train new workers in just a few days to replace men on strike. As a result of this approach to organization, the UBW became involved in serious, often violent conflicts, particularly with the Teamsters (organized with the assistance of Charles Bechtold of the Brewery Workers in 1898), the firemen, and the stationary engineers. Efforts were made within the craft-oriented AFL to force the UBW to surrender men engaged in these occupations, and a referendum of the membership was held on the issue in 1904. The vote was overwhelmingly hostile to the proposal, 34,612 to 367, but agitation continued until, against the advice of Samuel Gompers, the AFL executive council revoked the UBW charter in 1907. The failure of this tactic became quickly apparent, and the charter was restored one year later, largely because of the strength and wealth of the organization. Fully 95 percent of all eligible brewery workmen then belonged to the UBW.

At the second convention, the uniform union label was adopted, its historic form to be decided in 1896. The label was an important ingredient in the organizing efforts in the brewing industry because it permitted the successful use of the boycott. Beer was the beverage of the working class, and the UBW depended very heavily on support from both the Knights of Labor and the AFL for "fair" beer.

In its early years, the organization was very heavily German, although it had successfully organized English and Irish ale and porter workers. Indeed, the UBW remained a bilingual organization until World War II. Close ties were maintained with brewery workers in Germany, Switzerland, and Austria, and membership cards were exchangeable. These relationships reinforced the predilection of the members toward a socialist ideology, which profoundly influenced the structure of the organization, its political philosophy and activities, and its position on class struggle and racism throughout its history. Quite clearly, this commitment to socialism served to strengthen devotion to industrial unionism and tended to preserve democracy within the ranks.

Statutory Prohibition absorbed a major portion of the organization's resources and energies from the turn of the century through repeal and virtually destroyed both the union and its socialist commitment. It proved to be almost impossible to maintain a militant position to the "class struggle" when the better part of its resources was devoted to saving the assets of the "bosses." Although the organization devoted considerable time to a continuing nationwide campaign to educate the public to a moderate use of alcoholic beverages, it was to little avail as over 1,100 brewery employees were thrown out of work by the adoption of the Eighteenth Amendment. In an effort to preserve the life of one of its earliest and most loyal affiliates, the AFL extended its jurisdiction to include flour, cereal, and later soft drink workers, but the heart of the UBW was in brewing. The organization languished until the restoration of the industry in 1933.

Although the UBW recovered to a large degree after repeal, it never again regained the strength and prestige it had enjoyed before Prohibition. The most telling evidence of this lies in the fact that while the UBW had been almost uniformly successful in defending itself in the heated disputes with the IBT prior to Prohibition, after repeal it was only occasionally able to protect its jurisdiction.

As the organization struggled to recover its position in the labor movement, the IBT, then among the largest and most powerful affiliates of the AFL, held firm to its commitment to organize beer drivers. It began a successful attack on the UBW, designed to organize "inside workers" as well, arguing that the loyalty of these workers was essential to the welfare of the drivers. The strategy for this effort was designed by Dave Beck and operated successfully first in Seattle and then was applied elsewhere in the nation. The conflict was bitter, resulting in the suspension of the UBW from the AFL in 1941 and such incidents as the extremely violent "Pittsburgh beer war" from 1944 to 1946.

The UBW continued to function as an independent union until 1946 when, following a referendum vote of the membership, it affiliated with the Congress of Industrial Organizations* (CIO). The CIO expanded its jurisdiction to include distillery and wine workers. When the AFL and CIO merged in 1955, Karl Feller, president of the UBW, was named a vice-president of the united organization and was reelected to that position in 1957 by the same convention that expelled the IBT. Conflict between the two organizations continued unabated until 1972 when negotiations were successfully completed to allow the IBT to absorb the UBW, bringing an end to the seventy-five year old struggle between them. The UBW is now a department of the IBT.

The UBW, which maintained its national headquarters in Cincinnati, held triennial conventions. The organizational structure of the old Brewery Workers Union is eloquent testimony to its commitment to the socialist ideology and places heavy emphasis on the brotherhood of all men. Unlike other organizations in the labor movement, the UBW declined to elevate any of its number to a position of special prestige. It operated without a president until 1942. Governance was conducted by a general executive board, democratically elected by written ballot of all members. The key leader in its history was Joseph Obergfell who was elected to the general executive board in 1907, became general recording secretary in 1915, general secretary-treasurer (prime officer of the union) in 1924, and first general president in 1942 when that office was created. Obergfell remained in this position until his death in 1945. Karl Feller was elected international president in 1949 and continued in that office until the merger with the IBT. He remains head of the brewery department and is a vice-president of the IBT. Shortly before the IBT merger, the UBW claimed a membership of 47,304 located in 211 local unions.

For further information, see *The Brewery Worker* published monthly by the UBW. See also *Union with a Heart: International Union of United Brewery, Flour, Cereal, Soft Drink and Distillery Workers of America, 75 Years of a Great Union, 1886-1961* (1961), published by the UBW, and *AFL-CIO American Federationist* (August 1961). Hermann Schlütter, *The Brewing Industry and the Brewery Workers' Movement in America* (1910), has valuable information on the early history of the industry, and Nuala McGann Drescher discusses opposition to Prohibition in "Organized Labor and the Eighteenth Amendment," *Labor History* (Fall 1967). A good discussion of the conflicts over industrial unionism is contained in James O. Morris, *Conflict Within the AFL: A Study of Craft Versus Industrial Unionism, 1901-1938* (1958). References pertaining to the Teamsters can be found following the IBT sketch in this volume.

Nuala McGann Drescher

BRICK AND CLAY WORKERS OF AMERICA; UNITED (UBCWA). A Knights of Labor* (KofL) organizer created the first effective union of brick and terra-cotta workers in Chicago in 1885. Thereafter the Chicago union, Local Assembly No. 1771, gradually expanded its organization into adjacent areas and after the demise of the KofL applied for an American Federation of Labor* (AFL) charter. On May 18, 1894, the AFL extended a federal labor union charter under the title Illinois Brickmakers Alliance. Two years later the AFL converted the federal locals into a national union, the National Brick Makers' Alliance, with jurisdiction over the brickmaking trade. Meanwhile, the AFL also organized terra-cotta workers into federal labor unions, and on October 17, 1901, the brickmakers and terra-cotta workers amalgamated to form the International Alliance of Brick, Tile, and Terra Cotta Workers.

The new union adopted the eight-hour day as its first priority, and by 1901, all its members under contract worked the shorter hours. Relatively few workers in the industry were organized, and alliance officials confronted a problem of extending their control over the work force throughout the industry. While continuing its efforts to organize in the Midwest, especially in Illinois, Indiana, and Kentucky, the alliance conducted intensive, and largely successful, organizing campaigns in Pennsylvania, the Pacific Northwest, and the Hudson River valley of New York. As a result membership expanded from 1,700 in 1901 to 7,300 by the end of 1904.

As happened to so many other American trade unions, the increased use of restrictive court injunctions and the employers' open-shop offensive not only halted but reversed the alliance's growth. Moreover, organizing problems were further complicated during the period immediately prior to World War I by a growing internal conflict that ultimately resulted in the loss of alliance members and the creation in 1915 of a rival union, the United Brick and Clay Workers. After two years of dual union rivalry, the two organizations, with the assistance and encouragement of the AFL, amalgamated under the title United Brick and Clay Workers of America. On December 28, 1917, the AFL extended a new charter to the reunited union, which included jurisdiction over

> all building, sewer, paving, fire and ornamental brickmakers; all building-tile, drain-tile, and sewer-pipe workers, all plain, ornamental, and architectural terra-cotta workers; stoneware and art pottery workers; and clay miners.

The UBCWA thrived during World War I and the immediate postwar years. Although it lost costly strikes in the refractory industry in Kentucky and Pennsylvania, it succeeded in a hard-fought campaign to organize the clay workers in Brazil, Indiana, reputed to be the "clay capital of the world." Unlike most other national unions, the boom in the building industry following the war enabled the UBCWA to maintain the gains it made during the war, although it failed to expand upon its 1920 membership of slightly over 5,000.

The Great Depression was especially severe in the building trades industry and severely tested the UBCWA. By 1932 it paid per-capita taxes to the AFL on only 2,000 members and four years later on fewer than half that number. Enactment of the National Labor Relations Act of 1935, an improving economy, and an extensive organizing campaign combined to reverse the UBCWA's fortunes. After years of frustration, the refractory industry in Colorado, Pennsylvania, Ohio, Kentucky, and Alabama finally succumbed to organization in 1938. Two years later the union broke a long-standing open-shop alliance of clay manufacturers in southern California and won collective bargaining rights for most clay workers in that area. Finally, in 1942, the National War Labor Board issued a directive providing for joint national bargaining in the refractory industry. As a result of these initiatives, UBCWA membership grew steadily, surpassing the 10,000 figure by the end of World War II.

After the war, the union launched a major campaign to organize its jurisdiction in the Southwest and Southeast. Although the campaign in the Southeast made little headway, most southwestern employers reached an accommodation with the union after long, costly strikes at Elgin, Texas, and Malvern, Arkansas. The UBCWA continued to grow until 1957, reaching a membership in excess of 25,000 before new production techniques, changing building methods, and new materials precipitated a slow decline in employment. In an effort to reverse membership losses, in 1959 the UBCWA expanded its trade jurisdiction to include new products developed from plastics, textile and hospital supplies, and metaltronics. It also accelerated its organizing activities in the South, the only section of the nation containing substantial numbers of unorganized workers in the industry.

The UBCWA, which maintains its national headquarters in Columbus, Ohio, holds quinquennial conventions. General officers include a president, not more than eight vice-presidents, numbered consecutively, and a secretary-treasurer. Two of the vice-presidents are selected and designated by the general executive board as the executive vice-president and vice-president of legislation. The above officers constitute the general executive board. In 1973 the UBCWA reported a membership of 16,160 located in 265 local unions.

Little published information exists on the UBCWA. Some information is contained in Florence Peterson's *Handbook of Labor Unions* (1944). Information can also be found in *Bulletins No. 420, 506,* and *618*, Bureau of Labor Statistics, U.S. Department of Labor (1926, 1929, 1936).

BRICKLAYERS, MASONS AND PLASTERERS' INTERNATIONAL UNION OF AMERICA (BMPIUA). The first known strike in the masonry trade in the United States occurred in New York City in 1823 when journeymen stonecutters struck for a ten-hour day. During the following decade other organizations of masons appeared in the larger cities of the United States, most of them agitating for the ten-hour day. Although the panic of 1837 and the following depression destroyed many of these unions, they later reorganized. In the spring of 1850 the organization of the Bricklayers and Plasterers Protective Association, a central union functioning primarily in the New York City area, reflected the further development of union organization in the trade. Again, depression, this one accompanying the panic of 1857, halted union activity.

A permanent national union of bricklayers emerged at the end of the Civil War. During the late years of the war, bricklayer unions in Philadelphia and Baltimore agreed to an informal plan of mutual assistance. After the war, they decided to bring other cities into the agreement and establish a permanent national union. Consequently, on October 16, 1865, five delegates from Baltimore and four from Philadelphia met in Painters Hall, Philadelphia, and organized the Bricklayers International Union of the United States of North America. Within a year locals from Brooklyn, New York City, St. Louis, Jersey City, Cincinnati, and Richmond, Virginia, added more than 1,000 members to the national union.

The bricklayers' union grew in strength and numbers during the remaining years of the decade. It adopted as its primary objective the winning of an eight-hour day and between 1866 and 1870 cooperated closely with leaders of the National Labor Union* to that end. A slump in construction beginning in 1870, however, reversed the growth pattern of the renamed National Union of Bricklayers of the United States of America. Adding to existing problems, a debate raged through 1873 and 1874 concerning the adoption of a secret oath and ritual. The rejection of secrecy led to the secession of most New York City and Brooklyn locals and the formation of a rival organization, the United Order of American Bricklayers. Resulting from these setbacks, the union, numbering nearly 7,000 at the beginning of the decade, shrank to 1,700 by 1875, and by the end of the decade, only three affiliated locals remained, with a combined membership of 229.

Unlike most national unions, however, the renamed Bricklayers and Masons International Union of America (BMIU) survived the 1870s decade and revived during the following years. The BMIU continued to grow until the 1893-1897 depression and the defection of several stonemason locals that organized the rival Stonemasons International Union. Nevertheless, it managed to survive this period of hard times much more easily than it had the 1870s depression; by the end of the decade, losses had been recovered and membership reached an all-time high.

Despite the open-shop offensive launched by employers in 1904, the BMIU continued to grow, reaching a membership of nearly 70,000 by 1910. In successfully resisting the attacks of open-shop employers, the BMIU developed a number of highly successful tactics. For example, open-shop contractors in small towns were brought to heel when the union established rival contracting firms that took jobs on a cost basis. This action not only provided employment for union bricklayers but took jobs from open-shop contractors. In another instance, the union established its own brickyard in El Paso, Texas, when employers in that city refused to sell bricks to union contractors. This action also had the desired effect; the boycott ended abruptly.

Changes in building methods and materials caused increasingly serious problems. A large faction in the union had traditionally opposed extending membership to associated workers in the masonry trade, but the increased use of hollow tile, cement, and plaster along with varying types of stone cut into the work usually done by bricklayers. Moreover, as a result of the BMIU's continuing refusal to affiliate with the American Federation of Labor* (AFL), unions such as the American Brotherhood of Cement Workers were chartered with jurisdictions overlapping those claimed by the BMIU. After a favorable arbitration decision in 1904 and in an effort to strengthen its position, the BMIU reached an agreement with the Stonemasons International Union for the reaffiliation of stonemason locals. In 1910 the union signaled a renewed interest in organizing plasterers when the union title became Bricklayers, Masons and Plasterers' International Union of America. This action came after a series of disputes with the Operative Plasterers International Association* with which the BMPIUA had traditionally shared jurisdiction over plasterers. To further protect its jurisdiction, the BMPIUA finally affiliated with the AFL in 1916.

The BMPIUA made gains during World War I and sustained those advances during the hectic 1920s, claiming a membership in excess of 130,000 in 1928. But the Great Depression had a crushing impact on the building trades, and BMPIUA membership fell to 35,000 in 1933 before again turning upward. Not until the late 1940s did the union regain its 1928 enrollment. By 1955 membership had stabilized at approximately 140,000, where it remains.

The BMPIUA, which maintains its headquarters in Washington, D.C., holds biennial conventions. Principal officers include a president, ten vice-presidents, a secretary, and a treasurer. The executive board is composed of the president, first vice-president, secretary, and treasurer. In 1973 the BMPIUA reported a membership of 149,000 located in 850 local unions.

For further information, see the *Bricklayers, Masons & Plasterers Journal* issued monthly by the BMPIUA. See also Harry C. Bates, *Bricklayers' Century of Craftsmanship: A History of the Bricklayers, Masons and Plasterers' International Union of America* (1955), an account written by a former BMPIUA president, and *The American Federationist* (May 1955).

BROADCAST EMPLOYEES AND TECHNICIANS; NATIONAL ASSO-CIATION OF (NABET). American corporations found that one of the easiest and most effective methods of avoiding the collective bargaining provisions of the National Industrial Recovery Act of 1933 was to organize company unions. This appears to have been the inspiration for the organization of the Association of Technical Employees (ATE), the first union composed exclusively of broadcasting technicians in the emerging radio industry. During its early years, the ATE was dominated and controlled by the National Broadcasting Company (NBC) with which it signed a network contract in 1934. Fearing that its employees would be swayed by the large and powerful International Brotherhood of Electrical Workers* (IBEW), NBC officials organized the company union. The ATE, however, indicated early that it would not long remain under the company yoke. During the late 1930s it launched a vigorous organizing campaign, and in 1940 changed its title to the National Association of Broadcast Engineers and Technicians.

NBC originally owned two national networks, known as the Red and Blue Networks, but during the early 1940s, the Federal Communications Commission ordered NBC to divest itself of one of its transcontinental chains. As a consequence, the Blue Network was sold and later became the American Broadcasting Company (ABC). Meanwhile, NABET contracts with the local stations of the Blue Network remained in effect; thus the association became the recognized bargaining agent for the technicians of both NBC and ABC.

During the 1940s decade, NABET found itself involved in a continual jurisdictional war with the IBEW. In seeking allies in its fights with the powerful American Federation of Labor* (AFL) union, in 1951 the one-time company union joined the Congress of Industrial Organizations* (CIO). The new CIO affiliate received an industrial union charter conferring jurisdiction over the entire broadcasting industry and was renamed the National Association of Broadcast Employees and Technicians. Substitution of "Employees" for "Engineers" in the union title reflected the NABET's commitment to organize nonprofessional as well as professional employees of the radio industry.

Shortly after its affiliation with the CIO, the NABET became embroiled in a major controversy with the IBEW over the organization of technicians employed by the Columbia Broadcasting System, but the IBEW prevailed in a National Labor Relations Board representational election. NABET later lost control over television lighting crews to the International Alliance of Theatrical Stage Employees and Moving Picture Machine Operators of the United States and Canada.*

As NABET became more militant and then affiliated with the CIO, its previous relationship to NBC and ABC changed drastically. During the 1950s, NABET was involved in a number of bitter disputes with ABC and NBC, one resulting in a three-week strike against NBC in 1959. Because of a contract dispute, the NABET also struck ABC in 1967 and gained important concessions in a new four-year agreement.

An abortive strike against KABC-TV in Hollywood, California, in January 1967 signaled another major problem for NABET officials. Led by the Hollywood and New York City locals, a growing internal dispute over local autonomy nearly destroyed the NABET. The controversy resulted in major constitutional changes, which had the effect of greatly increasing the power and influence of network locals.

The NABET, which maintains its national headquarters in Washington, D.C., holds triennial conventions. Full-time officers include a president and secretary-treasurer. In 1973 the NABET reported a membership of 8,900 located in eighty-eight local unions.

For further information, see the *NABET News* issued bimonthly. See also Allen E. Koenig, ed., *Broadcasting and Bargaining: Labor Relations in Radio and Television* (1970), and Morris Gelman, "The Above-the-Line-Unions," *Television* (November 1967).

BROOM AND WHISK MAKERS UNION; INTERNATIONAL (IBWMU). Several American Federation of Labor* (AFL) federal labor unions composed of broom makers met in Chicago in the spring of 1893 and organized the International Broom Makers Union. In 1905 the union title was changed to International Broom and Whisk Makers Union, and the union's trade jurisdiction was expanded to include "all broom or whisk tiers and sewers (hand or power), broom corn sorters, sizers, bunchers, scrapers, operators on patent broom machines, nailers or metal case brooms, feather duster makers, all workers engaged in the preparation of material for brooms or whisks, all workers on articles made for sweeping, whether made of broom corn or other material."

The IBWMU, which had an original membership of 100, grew very slowly during the following years, reaching a peak of 1,400 in 1920. In its effort to organize the workers in the broom making trade, the IBWMU carried on a long struggle against prison labor contractors who operated at a great competitive advantage as compared to free labor. It faced similar competition from blind workers in charitable institutions and handicapped workshops. The union label became the IBWMU's chief organizing weapon, and much of its membership was confined to union shops that displayed the union label.

As a result of technological change and the Great Depression, the IBWMU's potential organizing jurisdiction, never very large, shrank drastically. By 1936 it paid AFL per-capita taxes on only 200 members. Nevertheless, the small union exhibited great perseverance before finally succumbing in August 1962 and surrendering its charter.

The IBWMU, which maintained its national headquarters in Chicago, held quadrennial conventions. Principal officers included a president, vice-president, secretary-treasurer (the only full-time officer), and eight district representatives. The above officers constituted the general executive board. Shortly before disbanding, the IBWMU paid per-capita taxes on 100 members.

For further information, see *The Broom Makers* published monthly by the IBWMU. See also Florence Peterson, *Handbook of Labor Unions* (1944), and *Bulletin No. 618*, Bureau of Labor Statistics, U.S. Department of Labor (1936).

BUILDING SERVICE EMPLOYEES' INTERNATIONAL UNION (BSEIU). *See* Laborers' International Union of North America.

BUTCHER WORKERS OF AMERICA; HEBREW (HBWA). On the evening of November 15, 1908, twenty-five men met in the Mills Hotel in New York City and agreed to organize a union of kosher butcher workers. Long hours (up to 100 hours per week), low wages (twenty-five cents a day), debilitating physical labor, and employer abuse characterized the working conditions giving rise to discontent. The unhappy butcher workers turned to the United Hebrew Trades (UHT) for assistance in organizing a union and were assigned a full-time organizer. Although employer intimidation restrained most butcher workers from associating with the effort, on July 13, 1909, an organizing meeting was held, and the Hebrew Butcher Workers of America organized. On August 17, 1909, the UHT extended a charter to the new union.

Later the same year, the HBWA called its first strike shortly before Rosh Hashana, the Jewish New Year. As butcher workers not previously identified with the union joined the striking workers, the conflict quickly evolved into a general strike in the New York kosher meat trade. The strike was a stunning success; wages were raised considerably and hours of work substantially reduced. Successful strikes again in 1910 and 1911 gained further concessions, but these early victories created an exaggerated sense of strength. Meanwhile, vowing to resist further concessions, employers organized their own association and imported thugs to harrass and intimidate union members and pickets. Confronted by this increased employer militancy, the union lost strikes in 1912 and 1913. When it was discovered that during the latter strike a union official had hired gangsters for picket duty, the union was further discredited, and membership declined to the small nucleus of union organizers responsible for its creation four years earlier. Nevertheless the union survived, and a successful strike in 1915 restored much of the confidence lost as a consequence of the disastrous strike of 1913.

The HBWA grew steadily during World War I and managed to hold its members during the postwar years. In 1921 the HBWA successfully applied for membership in the Amalgamated Meat Cutters and Butcher Workmen of North America* (AMCBWNA), becoming Local 234. Although the HBWA briefly left the AMCBWNA during the late 1920s, Local 234 proved a sturdy, effective union capable of resisting racketeer influences, left-wing "boring from within" tactics, and the attacks of the rival Progressive Butcher and Poultry Union created by the Communist Food Workers' Industrial Union in 1928. Reflecting the influence of Local 234, its secretary, Joseph Belsky, was elected an AMCBWNA vice president in 1936.

The HBWA maintained its headquarters in New York City. Principal officers included a manager, president, vice-president, and secretary-treasurer. The executive board was composed of eight members elected at large by the membership. At the time of its affiliation with the AMCBWNA, the HBWA had approximately 4,000 members.

For further information, see Joseph Belsky, *I, The Union; Being the Personalized Trade Union Story of the Hebrew Butcher Workers of America* (1952); David Brody, *The Butcher Workmen: A Study of Unionization* (1964); and Melech Epstein, *Jewish Labor in the U.S.A., 1914-1952*, 2 vols. (1953).

CANNERY, AGRICULTURAL, PACKING AND ALLIED WORKERS OF AMERICA; UNITED (UCAPAWA). *See* Food, Tobacco, Agricultural and Allied Workers Union of America.

CARPENTERS AND JOINERS OF AMERICA; UNITED BROTHERHOOD OF (UBC). On August 8, 1881, thirty-six delegates, representing carpenters in eleven cities, met in Chicago and organized the Brotherhood of Carpenters and Joiners. Although organizing activities among carpenters dated back to the colonial period, it was not until the Chicago meeting that a permanent national organization was formed. Under the devoted and watchful supervision of its founder and principal administrator, Peter J. McGuire, the brotherhood grew slowly but steadily during the remaining years of the nineteenth century. A membership of slightly over 2,000 in 1881 increased to nearly 70,000 by the turn of the century. Although discontent with the piecework system had inspired the early organization of the Carpenters, the eight-hour day movement became the seminal issue to which the union devoted its energies and resources during its formative years. When the Knights of Labor* (KofL) refused to endorse the movement, McGuire convinced the Federation of Organized Trades and Labor Unions* to champion the cause in 1884. Two years later the federation was reorganized into the American Federation of Labor* (AFL) and the brotherhood became a charter member.

The brotherhood effectively established its supremacy over rival carpenter organizations during the 1880s. The Progressive Carpenters' Union, sponsored by the KofL, failed to withstand its challenge, and the independent United Order of Carpenters, which had established its hegemony in New York City, was forced into amalgamation, thus creating the United Brotherhood of Carpenters and Joiners of America in 1888.

By 1890 the UBC was one of the largest, most successful, and secure unions affiliated with the AFL. Consequently, when national labor leaders attempted to revitalize the eight-hour day movement, which had deteriorated after the 1886 Haymarket Square bombing, they selected the UBC to lead the movement. The UBC, with the support of the AFL, struck for the eight-hour day in the spring of 1890, hoping to establish a successful example that could be followed by other unions. An unprecedented success, the strike further heightened the UBC's already influential role in the AFL and the national labor movement.

A dramatic transition took place during the following two decades, altering the nature and organizational structure of the UBC. Despite McGuire's determined resistance, a group of professional organizers gradually transformed the loosely organized confederation of local unions into a highly centralized federation. During the same period pure and simple business unionism replaced the broad commitment to radical change that had previously characterized the union's social philosophy. The ouster of McGuire from office in 1901, on contrived charges of embezzling union funds, marked the key date in this transition.

The emergence of the pure and simple trade union philosophy profoundly altered the UBC's jurisdictional policy. Under the leadership of the reformist McGuire, the brotherhood had not contested the chartering of either the Amalgamated Wood Workers' Union* or the International Furniture Workers' Union. But with McGuire's disgrace, the new leadership claimed a jurisdiction that included "all that's made of wood," and a few years later "or that was ever made of wood;" moreover, the UBC successfully foisted this policy of jurisdictional laissez-faire on the AFL. Thereafter the UBC virtually ceased organizing, depending instead on union label contractors to force union membership and on jurisdictional raids on other unions previously organizing workers now claimed by the UBC. Although these tactics kept the UBC locked in constant jurisdictional wars with other unions, it was a highly successful tactic. UBC membership soared from 68,000 in 1900 to 232,000 in 1910 and to 350,000 in 1924.

William L. Hutcheson assumed the union presidency in 1915 and accelerated the trend toward centralized authority, as he crushed all opposition to his growing executive power. During the first two decades of his presidency, Hutcheson carried on a volatile relationship with other unions in the building trades department of the AFL. Despite gaining firm control of the department in 1934, he was forced to gradually accept limitations on UBC jurisdiction following the enactment of the National Labor Relations Act and the Taft-Hartley Labor Act.

Under Hutcheson's leadership, the UBC bitterly opposed the Congress of Industrial Organizations* (CIO) and violently contested the CIO-chartered International Woodworkers of America* (IWA), which challenged the UBC in the organization of lumber workers. Although the UBC failed to crush the IWA, it prevented further erosion of its jurisdiction and continued its opposition to the CIO until the 1955 AFL-CIO* merger. Meanwhile William Hutcheson retired in 1952 and was succeeded by his son Maurice, who served until 1972. During this period, total membership first grew to a peak of more than 800,000 in 1958, and then declined to 700,000 in 1972.

The UBC, which maintains its national headquarters in Washington, D.C., holds quadrennial conventions. Full-time executive officers include a general president, first and second vice-presidents, a general secretary, and a general treasurer. The executive board consists of the above officers, with the exception of the second vice-president, and representatives of seven geographical divisions. The national office assumes full authority to define jurisdictional boundaries and resolve jurisdictional conflicts, while local unions have considerable autonomy in collective bargaining. In 1973 the UBC reported a membership of 820,000 located in 2,435 local unions.

For further information, see *The Carpenter*, a monthly journal published by the UBC since 1881. See also Robert A. Christie, *Empire in Wood* (1956), a brilliant account of the early history of the UBC. Morris A. Horowitz, *The Structure and Government of the Carpenters' Union* (1962), is the best account of the topic. Maxwell C. Raddock's *Portrait of an American Labor Leader, William L. Hutcheson* (1955), is a UBC-sponsored biography that deals uncritically with its subject.

CEMENT, LIME AND GYPSUM WORKERS INTERNATIONAL UNION; UNITED (UCLGWIU). Efforts to organize cement workers began early in the twentieth century. Between 1911 and 1923, the American Federation of

Labor* (AFL) directly chartered at least twenty different federal labor unions of cement workers. These unions consisted primarily of unskilled workers, and few survived the decade in which they were organized. By 1923 all these cement worker federal unions had disappeared, and it was more than a decade before effective labor unions again appeared in the industry.

One of the labor provisions contained in Section 7(a) of the National Industrial Recovery Act of 1933 guaranteed the right of collective bargaining. But early attempts by cement workers to take advantage of the legislation were frustrated by employers who found numerous ways to avoid bargaining in good faith with their employees. The favorite employer tactic during the National Recovery Administration period was the formation of employee representation plans or employee protective associations to avoid recognizing legitimate, independent unions. Meanwhile, organizing activities were conducted by the AFL through its traditional tactic of organizing directly affiliated federal labor unions. Eventually the organization of cement workers was placed under the general supervision of William Schoenberg, who was serving as midwestern organizer for the AFL. Under Schoenberg's leadership and with the enactment of the National Labor Relations Act, union membership among cement workers expanded rapidly.

By the late summer of 1936, twenty-three federal locals had been organized. In September these unions sent delegates to a meeting in St. Louis where the National Council of United Cement Workers was formed; Schoenberg served as director of the new AFL council. Shortly thereafter the AFL broadened the council's jurisdiction to include lime and gypsum workers.

The organization of cement and allied workers proceeded steadily after the organization of the National Council, and at the 1938 council convention, delegates instructed their officers to petition the AFL executive council for an international charter. Although encountering some resistance from established building trades' unions interested in absorbing organized cement workers, on May 10, 1939, the executive council voted to extend the charter.

St. Louis hosted the founding convention of the new international union, and on September 12, 1939, AFL president William Green presented the charter to the United Cement, Lime and Gypsum Workers International Union. The new union received a jurisdictional grant including workers engaged in manufacturing, producing, processing, and quarrying materials used in the production of cement, lime, and gypsum. This made the UCLGWIU one of the few industrial unions to be chartered by the AFL to that time.

Organizing activities accelerated in the period immediately following the chartering but slowed during World War II as many cement plants considered unessential to the war effort closed. When normal production resumed in the postwar period, the UCLGWIU launched a vigorous organizing drive to unionize the industry. During this campaign the union also made significant inroads into Canada where by 1948 enough local unions had been organized to establish a district council.

Despite its organizing successes, UCLGWIU unions encountered great employer resistance during collective bargaining negotiations. Hoping to strengthen its negotiating position and to create a unified system of bargaining, delegates to the third international convention meeting in 1946 enacted several far-reaching reforms. As a result the UCLGWIU's financial situation was strengthened, a strike fund established, and an international policy committee created to coordinate negotiating activities and to develop a single collective bargaining program.

The UCLGWIU, which maintains its national headquarters in Chicago, Illinois, has ten full-time officers, including a president, a secretary-treasurer, and eight vice-presidents. These officers also constitute the international executive board. The union is divided into eleven district councils, nine in the United States and two in Canada. The UCLGWIU, which had a 1971 membership of 35,509, holds biennial conventions.

For further information, see *The Voice*, a monthly published by the union. The UCLGWIU has also published *A Brief History of the United Cement, Lime and Gypsum Workers International Union* (1973).

CHEMICAL WORKERS UNION; INTERNATIONAL (ICWU). Union organization of chemical workers might actually be said to have begun in Philadelphia where a soap boilers' and tallow chandlers' union existed as early as 1836. Much later a salt workers' union appeared in Michigan's Saginaw Valley, but it was a victim of the famous 1885 lumber workers' strike in the area. By the turn of the century, the American Federation of Labor* (AFL) made some effort to organize chemical workers into federal labor unions, and one such union, the Explosive Powder Workers Union, had 400 members in 1902. Most chemical workers organized by the AFL, however, were assigned to the National Association of Heat, Frost, General Insulators and Asbestos Workers of America,* chartered in 1904.

Growth of the chemical industry during and immediately following World War I provided great organizing opportunities, but through the use of welfare capitalism and company unionism, the industry maintained an open shop throughout the decade of the 1920s. Until the enactment of the National Industrial Recovery Act in 1933, there were no extensive efforts to organize chemical workers, but during the 1930s, the federal labor union device was again used by the AFL to unionize these workers. Organization was most successful in the Midwest where a council was established in Chicago in 1937 to coordinate area activities of the various federal locals and to direct an organizing campaign.

The AFL initiated the first effort to establish a national union of chemical workers on September 7, 1940, when the International Council of Chemical and Allied Industries Union was founded in Akron, Ohio. Fifty-four delegates, representing forty-two federal labor unions and 9,910 members in nineteen

states, attended the founding convention. H. A. Bradley, an AFL staff organizer who had been given the assignment to organize the council, was elected
president.

By 1944, the council had a membership of 28,993 enrolled in 161 locals,
twelve of which were located in Canada. In September of that year, AFL president William Green extended an international charter to the Council as the International Chemical Workers Union. Unfortunately for the young union, it
was not without competitors in its field of organization. District 50* of the
United Mine Workers* was actively organizing chemical workers, and in 1942
the Congress of Industrial Organizations* (CIO) chartered a rival union, the
United Gas, Coke and Chemical Workers* (UGCCW).

Although the ICWU did well in the triangular competition and reached a
membership of 50,000 by 1947, the confused organizing activities in the industry had a detrimental effect on collective bargaining. It was not unusual, for
example, for various plants in the same company to be organized by different
unions. As a consequence, company-wide bargaining, which characterizes
negotiating patterns in most mass-production industries, was the exception
rather than the rule in the chemical industry. The only major company-wide
settlement the ICWU negotiated was with Lever Brothers Company in 1946,
an agreement that continues in existence. During the 1950s and 1960s, the
ICWU negotiated master agreements for its units in many other companies.

The ICWU's progress was temporarily stalled by a serious internal union
dispute lasting from 1953 until 1957. A bitter controversy erupted between
President H. A. Bradley and a majority of board members concerning the constitutional authority of the executive board between conventions. The dispute
was carried to the 1954 convention, where the delegates sided with the executive board and elected Edward R. Moffet to the union presidency, a position
held by Bradley since 1940. Bradley's supporters then organized a rival organization, the Emergency Reorganization Committee, and encouraged locals to
leave the ICWU. The rump organization had little success, and the ICWU lost
fewer than 1,000 members. Moffet's election failed to end factional conflicts,
however, and in 1956 he was defeated by Walter L. Mitchell who finally ended
the internal divisions.

Meanwhile, merger discussions were opened with the UGCCW shortly after
the establishment of the AFL-CIO.* Although a merger was never consummated, the two unions established a close working relationship, and in many
instances, units of the two unions carried on unified collective bargaining
negotiations with the same company. To further strengthen its collective bargaining negotiating position, the ICWU changed its constitution to include the
creation of company-wide councils and established a strike fund to provide assistance to striking members. In 1966 the international president was given authority to decide the acceptability of contracts negotiated by local unions or
company-wide councils, and two years later a separate collective bargaining
department was established.

Hoping to revitalize its organizing and political activities, the ICWU affiliated with the Alliance for Labor Action, a loose federation of unions sponsored by the United Automobile Workers* and the International Brotherhood of Teamsters* in 1968. As a result of this indiscretion, the AFL-CIO revoked the ICWU charter on October 3, 1969, but it was reinstated on May 12, 1971.

The ICWU, which holds biennial conventions, maintains its national headquarters in Akron. Full-time officers include a president, nine vice-presidents, and a secretary-treasurer. The above officers also constitute the international executive board. In 1971 the ICWU reported a membership of 100,597 located in 428 local unions.

For further information, see *The International Chemical Worker* published monthly by the international union. The ICWU also has produced "A Brief History of the International Chemical Workers Union," and "Questions and Answers About ICWU," both of which contain valuable information. See also *The American Federationist* (January 1951), and Melvin Rothbaum, *The Government of the Oil, Chemical, and Atomic Workers Union* (1962).

CIGARMAKERS' INTERNATIONAL UNION OF AMERICA (CIU). During the Civil War, the National Union of Cigar Makers was established with twenty-one locals and held its first convention in 1864. The impetus was the transformation of the industry from the one-man shop to the large shop, making independent workers into employees. Establishment of the large shop was necessitated by wartime taxes on cigars and by regulations involving government permits to, and the bonding of, employers, workers, and shops. The union, which shortly became the Cigarmakers' International Union to accommodate Canadian workers, immediately adopted strict rules excluding migrant cigarmakers from membership unless admitted to a union "from whence" they came, and forbade members from working in places employing workers outside the shop (in tenement sweatshops). The CIU grew rapidly, with eighty-seven locals and 5,800 members by 1869.

Even as the CIU prospered, technological change—in particular, the mold, invented in 1867—began to threaten the well-being of its members by dividing the trade into bunch breakers and rollers. With cigarmaking easier and faster, women and children entered the trade and wages declined. Although Cincinnati cigarmakers, supported by CIU funds, waged a successful strike in 1869 for an increase in piece rates, the victory proved illusory since manufacturers everywhere began utilizing the mold, enforcing wages below subsistence. By 1870 the CIU resolved that "no local union shall allow its members to work with a filler breaker [mold]." This stand proved ill conceived since it defied progress and could not be enforced. It was violated by many locals under the leadership of the New York City cigarmakers who formed the United Cigarmakers (later CIU Local 144) and admitted to membership rollers, bunch breakers, and tenement workers. Led by Local 144, the CIU had reversed itself by 1873; union men could work in shops with filler breakers but not in conjunction with them. Two years later, new CIU rules prohibited local discrimination because of the "system of work" and set apprenticeship requirements at three years. The mold and the depression of 1873 together decimated the CIU as the industry moved from the large shop to tenement sweatshops. By 1877 a general strike of cigarmakers against the tenements failed miserably, and union membership declined to 1,016.

The CIU's fortunes began to turn upward as President Adolph Strasser, supported by Samuel Gompers of Local 144, began rebuilding the International, following the British model of "pure wage-conscious" unionism, which involved higher dues, central authority over the locals, and "equalization of funds," an organizational pattern eventually followed by most other craft unions. Other changes included loans for members who had to move to get employment; sick, death, jobless, and strike benefits; and central control over strikes. Reorganization, along with economic recovery, brought CIU membership to 7,931 by 1881. With its treasury replenished, the CIU in 1884 and 1885 could expend $184,000 in strike funds for an unsuccessful thirteen-month struggle against Cincinnati cigar manufacturers. The establishment of centralized control over the affairs of locals also strengthened it against socialists in Local 144, whose elected officers were unconstitutionally suspended by Strasser during a struggle for power that nearly wrecked this important New York union.

Strasser's socialist opponents in Local 144 formed the Cigarmakers' Progressive Union (CPU) in 1882, which lowered dues, admitted tenement workers, and began recruiting members outside the city. When Strasser rejected their bid for cooperation with the CIU, the Progressives received support in 1883 from District Assembly (DA)49 of the Knights of Labor* (KofL), which sought to organize the New York City trades into one large labor organization. In 1885 the CIU and CPU arranged a merger agreement involving some local autonomy for the Progressives, although their funds would be controlled by the CIU. The two groups pledged to avoid separate negotiations with the New York cigar manufacturers who had instituted a general layout of all cigarmakers following a wage reduction, but in February 1886, the Progressives unilaterally accepted a wage scale lower than that of the CIU. DA 49 then organized all returning cigarmakers into Local Assembly 2814, concluded a wage settlement at the lower rate, and issued a white union label (the CIU cigar label was blue), which the CIU immediately boycotted.

As this inter-union struggle spread outside New York, both sides scabbed, while negotiations between top CIU officers on the one hand, and Terence Powderly and the executive board of the Knights on the other, brought a refusal to discipline the aggressive DA 49. Thus encouraged, DA 49 made a bold attempt to gain control of the entire industry. Ignoring the CPU, the Knights offered to supply the cigar manufacturers with workers in return for a closed-shop agreement. Faced with the loss of their craft union, the Progressives supported by the CIU went on strike, forcing the manufacturers to reinstate all workers regardless of membership in the KofL. With the CIU-Progressive victory over the Knights complete, the Progressives immediately rejoined the CIU, and in 1887 a united CIU spearheaded the adoption of an AFL boycott of the KofL's white label—ending forever that union's influence in cigarmaking. In that year CIU membership reached 20,566 and climbed to 24,624 by 1890.

These were the golden years, for the CIU soon began a decline, partly because of its resistance to the machine and its blind preoccupation with narrow craft exclusiveness. Even as membership climbed in 1887, Strasser, with Gompers's support, sought to keep manufacturers with machines from using the union label. The CIU held to this rigid policy until 1923 when it ended opposition to organizing workers where machines were used. However, by this time other forces had long been at work. In 1895 the Tobacco Workers International Union* began organizing outside of cigarmaking. By 1940 this union claimed 18,000 members compared to the CIU's 7,000. In gradual decline after 1900, the CIU maintained influence in the AFL partly through its famous vice-president, Samuel Gompers, and his close ally and friend, CIU president George W. Perkins, who replaced Strasser in 1891. With the demise or eclipse of these two leading figures by 1924, the CIU played a minor, if not insignificant, role in the labor movement thereafter. On June 1, 1974, the CIU merged with the Retail, Wholesale and Department Store Union* (RWDSU).

The CIU, which maintained its national headquarters in Washington, D.C., held quadrennial conventions. The international president was the only full-time officer. The international executive board was composed of the president and seven vice-presidents. Shortly before the merger with the RWDSU, the CIU paid per-capita taxes to the AFL-CIO on less than 2,000 members.

For further information, see the *Cigar Makers Official Journal* published quarterly by the CIU. See, also, John R. Commons et al., *History of Labour in the United States*, vol. 2 (1918); Bernard Mandel, *Samuel Gompers* (1963); John R. Commons, *Labor and Administration* (1913); Carroll R. Daugherty, *Labor Problems in American Industry* (1941); Samuel Gompers, *Seventy Years of Life and Labor* (1925); and Philip Taft, *The A.F. of L. in the Time of Gompers* (1957).

Merl E. Reed

CLOTHING WORKERS OF AMERICA; AMALGAMATED (ACWA). Delegates representing sixty-eight local unions in the men's and children's clothing industry met in Webster Hall, New York City, on December 26, 1914, and established the Amalgamated Clothing Workers of America. Although organizing activity among men's clothing workers dates back to the post-Civil War period, no permanent union had been created until the establishment of the United Garment Workers* (UGW) in 1891.

A large segment of the UGW workers, primarily foreign born, radical, and quick to strike, became dissatisfied with the conservative, native-born, craft-union-oriented leaders of the UGW. Differences between the two groups became especially heated during a Hart, Schaffner, and Marx strike in Chicago, lasting from September 22, 1910, to January 14, 1911. The more radical locals calling the strike lost the support of UGW leaders, but they gained concessions from plant managers that in the years ahead proved to be of paramount importance. Management agreed to abide by the decisions of an arbitration committee of three men (later reduced to one), which would adjust all disputes between the clothing workers and the owners within a particular geographical region. The impartial chairman of the committee was to be well versed in the complexities of the industry and was expected by both sides to render fair decisions.

Success in the Hart, Schaffner, and Marx strike encouraged the more radical locals to challenge their conservative colleagues for control of the union. The struggle came to a head in October 1914 at the national convention of the UGW held in Nashville. A rump session of representatives from immigrant locals formed their own version of the UGW, and it was this group that formed the Amalgamated in December 1914. They selected as their first president Sidney Hillman, who had been bargaining representative at the Hart, Schaffner, and Marx plant in Chicago and was chief clerk of the New York Cloak Workers. At its inception, membership in the ACWA stood between 40,000 and 50,000. By 1920 it had grown to 177,000. Seasonal layoffs, long hours, and low wages were the chief grievances of the clothing workers. Members of the Amalgamated were also dedicated to the concept of industrial unionism.

Once established, the ACWA challenged the UGW for the allegiance of the unorganized clothing workers. Hillman's innovative ideas brought success to his union against both recalcitrant managers and the UGW until the United States entered World War I. Pressured by the needs of the government for uniforms, employers again resorted to sweatshop tactics. But the results were somewhat modified by the Board of Control and Labor Standards, an agency whose position was usually favorable to the worker. By the end of the war, the ACWA had eclipsed the UGW; wages, hours, and working conditions had been substantially improved, and the Hart, Schaffner, and Marx arbitration system had been extended to other markets in the industry.

The postwar depression and the red scare, however, effected the Amalgamated adversely. Men's clothing plant owners compounded the problems of the ACWA by calling an industry-wide lockout in December 1920. Hillman countered by using the skills of his well-developed central organization, which distributed relief supplies and kept the locals constantly informed by calling mass meetings of the workers. Faced with such organized resistance, managers ended the lockout in June 1921.

Throughout the 1920s, the Amalgamated encountered many threats, none more detrimental to the cause of organized labor than the infiltration of the union by organized crime. Racketeers, who demanded "protection" money from the members of the Cutters' Union, an Amalgamated subsidiary, came to the attention of the ACWA leadership. Through the quick and decisive action of Hillman and other union officials, the ACWA succeeded in expelling the racketeers from the union, thereby removing a parasitic menace to effective organization.

Rejecting the assumption, implicit in the open-shop movement of the 1920s, that the interests of labor and management were antithetical, the ACWA attempted to maintain financially troubled clothing factories through loans, cooperative management of facilities, and efficiency studies. Employment exchanges were also created to bring unemployed workers to available jobs.

Ancillary to its "pure and simple" functions, the ACWA branched out into areas not usually associated with organized labor. An Amalgamated-sponsored insurance plan was inaugurated in 1923. ACWA banks, which provided personal loans at low interest rates to union members, were established in Chicago and New York City. Low-cost housing cooperatives were constructed. Medical clinics, recreational facilities, and even union-owned restaurants were provided for the benefit of the workers. Politically, the ACWA supported Robert M. La Follette in the 1924 presidential elections. Although containing a strong socialist element, the ACWA did not support the total Communist rejection of capitalism; in fact, Communists within the ranks of the ACWA found little support and were summarily expelled.

During the 1920s, the functions of the joint board were rationalized. The board represented all locals in a given region. Management, therefore, dealt with only one organization rather than a proliferation of various local officials. The national office of the ACWA also regularized its control of joint boards and locals. By 1929 the Amalgamated had become a complex and diverse organization.

The depression made great inroads into the achievements of the ACWA, as well as those of other unions. In order to meet the challenge of high unemployment, the ACWA and other independents joined the AFL in the hope that by combining the organized work force, the worst effects of the depression could be offset. Franklin Roosevelt's National Recovery Administration (NRA) had a salutory effect on ACWA membership, for it seemed to many unorganized workers that the president was encouraging labor organization. Sidney Hillman added his prestige by becoming a member of the NRA advisory board and the National Industrial Recovery Board. By the mid-1930s, Hillman, long an advocate of industrial unionism, came to the conclusion that the AFL leadership would never break with its craft orientation; therefore, he supported the newly formed Committee for Industrial Organization. When that committee evolved into the Congress of Industrial Organizations* (CIO), the

ACWA became a charter member. Through his involvement with government agencies, Hillman brought the Amalgamated into political affairs, and he was influential in the establishment of Labor's Non-Partisan League. From this point onward, Hillman became increasingly removed from ACWA affairs as more of his time and talent were commanded by the CIO and its Textile Workers Organizing Committee, which he led.

During the turbulent 1930s, the Amalgamated rationalized its contract negotiation procedures. Until 1937 ACWA contracts had been negotiated at the regional level, but by 1941 the industry-wide contract had replaced most regional contracts, furthering the process of centralization of authority in the national board.

Throughout the war and during the immediate postwar period, the Amalgamated worked closely with the various government agencies created to facilitate the defeat of nazism. In addition, the ACWA broadened its jurisdiction and continued its various ancillary and social welfare functions. The bright prospects after the war were dimmed by the passing of Sidney Hillman in 1946. Hillman's contributions to the labor movement and the nation were substantial. He was succeeded by Jacob S. Potofsky in July 1946.

The great fears spawned by the Taft-Hartley Act of 1947 infected the ACWA, but, like many other American unions, the Amalgamated found ways in which it could accommodate its program to the requirements of the act. During the 1950s and 1960s, the ACWA continued the program Sidney Hillman had begun in the 1920s. This was so successful that 95 percent of the workers in the men's clothing industry were ACWA members by 1970. The ACWA had also broadened its jurisdiction to include retail sales personnel, laundry workers, and cleaning and dying workers. Like many of its contemporary unions, the ACWA, in effect, had become a conglomerate whose interests included day-care centers for working mothers and scholarships for children of clothing workers, as well as the more traditional functions of organizing and collective bargaining.

The ACWA, which maintains its national headquarters in New York City, holds biennial conventions. Full-time officers include a general president, a vice-president, a secretary-treasurer, and fifteen regional directors. The executive board is composed of the above officials. In 1973 the ACWA reported a membership of 365,000 located in 797 local unions.

For further information, see *The Advance* published triweekly by the ACWA. The ACWA is noted for its "in-house" histories, which include: Jacob Hardman, ed., *The Amalgamated—Today and Tomorrow* (1959); Hyman H. Bookbinder et al., *To Promote the General Welfare: The Story of the Amalgamated* (1950); Elden LaMar, *The Clothing Workers of Philadelphia; History of Their Struggle for Union and Security* (1940); and *The Clothing Workers in Chicago, 1910-1922* (1922). Good biographies of Sidney Hillman include: Jean Gould, *Sidney Hillman, Great American* (1952); George H. Soule, *Sidney Hill-*

man, Labor Statesman (1959); and Matthew Josephson, *Sidney Hillman, Statesman of American Labor* (1952).

Joseph Y. Garrison

COMMUNICATIONS ASSOCIATION; AMERICAN (ACA). Trade union organization among radio operators on passenger and freight vessels in the maritime industry began during the early years of the Great Depression. Especially hard hit by the depression, marine radio operators found themselves working longer hours for lower wages. Typically, the radio operator worked a twelve-hour day for wages ranging from fifty dollars to one hundred dollars a month. As a result of such conditions, thirteen radio operators met at the Hotel Monterey in New York City on August 17, 1931, and organized the American Radio Association. Shortly thereafter it was renamed the American Radio Telegraphists Association. A similar group, the Commercial Radiomen's Protective Association, had been organized on the West Coast, and on April 8, 1932, the two groups merged under the title American Radio Telegraphists Association (ARTA).

ARTA officials spent their first year establishing an administrative structure and publicizing the new union, and they soon demonstrated their determination to militantly pursue the objectives of improved wages and working conditions by conducting an eight-month strike against the American Merchant Line during the fall and winter of 1933-1934. Although the ARTA could not claim victory in the strike, the solidarity of radio operators during the strike illustrated their determination to alter the conditions under which they labored. During the following two years, the ARTA engaged in more than thirty strikes, which resulted in considerable additions to the paychecks of radio operators.

In 1935 the ARTA negotiated a merger agreement with the Commercial Telegraphers Union (CTU) under which the ARTA would become the radio department of the CTU. The agreement was later approved by a membership referendum, but before the merger could be consummated, it was destroyed. Disagreements arose concerning the ARTA's boycott of Mackay Radio, an affiliate of the Postal Telegraph Company with which the CTU had good working relations, and its affiliation with the Maritime Federation of the Pacific, which the American Federation of Labor* had branded a dual union.

In February 1937 the ARTA requested a charter from the newly organized Congress of Industrial Organizations* (CIO), and on April 14, 1937, a charter was received with a broad jurisdictional grant that, in effect, made it a full-scale rival of the CTU. Cooperating closely with the CIO-affiliated National Maritime Union, the ARTA made major advances in the organization of maritime radio operators. It also began organizing its "land" jurisdiction, choosing as its major objective the employees of the Postal Telegraph Company. CIO

president John L. Lewis assigned ten organizers to assist the ARTA in its organizing drives. The effort brought hundreds of Postal Telegraph employees into
the ARTA while at the same time ARTA won National Labor Relations Board
(NLRB) representational elections among the communication employees of
Globe Radio and the Radio Corporation of America.

Reflecting its expanded jurisdiction, the union title was changed in 1937
to the American Communications Association. The newly named union redoubled its campaign among Postal Telegraph employees in 1938, and in a
series of bold steps ordered "stop work meetings" in several strategic locations.
By December 1938 the Postal Telegraph Company agreed to negotiations. In
January of the following year, after an NLRB representational election in
which Postal employees voted overwhelmingly for the ACA, Postal signed a
national closed-shop agreement with the ACA.

The ACA then turned to Western Union, which had resisted union orga-
nization for over seventy-five years and had a well-established company union,
the Association of Western Union Employees (AWUE), organized in 1918. In
January 1938, ACA filed unfair labor practices charges against Western
Union, and on November 1, 1939, the NLRB's trial examiner adjudged the
AWUE a company union in violation of the National Labor Relations Act.

The ACA won a great victory with the disestablishment of the AWUE, but
the spoils were destined to go not to the victor but to the CTU. Both unions
made a vigorous drive to enroll the employees of Western Union, but the CTU
effectively used the issue of the ACA's alleged Communist domination and
proved most successful in representational elections. The next blow came in
1943 when Western Union absorbed the Postal Telegraph Corporation. During January 1945 a series of NLRB elections of Western Union employees (including the employees of Postal Telegraph whom the ACA had represented)
resulted in large CTU majorities in all areas except the New York metropolitan
area. The ACA's hold on New York City also was weakened by unsuccessful
strikes in 1946 and 1948. Even more important, the provisions of the Taft-
Hartley Act requiring union leaders to sign a non-Communist affidavit as a
condition for using NLRB representation procedures debilitated the union
whose officials refused to sign such statements. Moreover, the CIO charged the
ACA with being a Communist-dominated union and expelled it in 1950. After
the CIO expulsion, the ACA remained a small, independent union until affiliating with the International Brotherhood of Teamsters* in 1966.

The ACA, which maintained its national headquarters in New York City,
held annual conventions. Full-time officers included a president, a secretary-
treasurer, and a vice-president representing each department in the international union. The general executive board was composed of all full-time officers and two members elected at large from each department. The ACA's
membership at the time of its expulsion from the CIO was 10,000.

For further information, see the *ARTA News*, 1933-1937, the *ACA News*,

1937-1949, and Vidkunn Ulriksson, *The Telegraphers: Their Craft and Their Unions* (1953).

COMMUNICATIONS WORKERS OF AMERICA (CWA). Within twenty years of the patenting of Alexander Graham Bell's telephone in 1876, labor organizing of telephone workers had begun. During the late nineteenth century and the early years of the twentieth century, the International Brotherhood of Electrical Workers* (IBEW) did much of the organizing work among these workers, although several federal labor unions of telephone operators were organized and directly affiliated with the American Federation of Labor* (AFL). The Commercial Telegraphers' Union also exhibited an interest in organizing telephone operators.

Because of opposition to the admission of female operators to full IBEW membership, in 1918 the union established an autonomous division, the Telephone Operators Department. The organization of telephone workers expanded dramatically during World War I, but when the government returned the telephone companies to private control after the war, an employer anti-union offensive and the use of employer representation plans (company unions) destroyed much of the previous progress. Moreover, when the IBEW refused to create an autonomous department of male telephone workers in 1920, a group of New England telephone workers seceded and established the International Brotherhood of Telephone Workers, which eventually assumed a role resembling a company union in the New England Bell Telephone Corporation. With the exception of Montana and Chicago, independent organizations of telephone operators virtually disappeared during the decade beginning in 1923.

Enactment of the labor provisions of the National Industrial Recovery Act of 1933 and, more specifically, the National Labor Relations Act (NLRA) of 1935 revived organizing activities among telephone workers. Ironically, the employee representation associations organized by the companies in the Bell Telephone system became the basis for the organization of a national union of telephone workers. Complying with the provisions of the NLRA, by 1937 employee's associations had officially severed their relationship with the telephone companies. A series of meetings between representatives of these associations commenced in 1937 and ultimately resulted in the creation of the National Federation of Telephone Workers (NFTW) in Chicago on June 5, 1939. The NFTW, however, was more a confederation, a union of unions, than a federation of local unions. A high degree of decentralization and local autonomy made the NFTW a weak and ineffective organization; nevertheless, in terms of membership growth, the NFTW thrived. An original 1939 membership of 45,000 grew to 170,000 by 1945.

Many of the early efforts of NFTW officers were directed toward gaining adjustments in the telephone companies' pension systems. Indeed, the inability to gain effective reform of the pension plan had been one of the major motivations for the creation of a national organization. A second objective was to gain recognition as the representative of telephone workers not only from the telephone companies but also from government agencies and the labor movement. Progress was made in all these areas by the end of World War II.

During the immediate postwar period, many strikes by telephone workers occurred in various sections of the nation, most resulting in favorable terms for the strikers. The climax to this militant activity came in the spring of 1946 when NFTW president Joseph Beirne, despite considerable disunity within the union, threatened a national strike of telephone workers. This was averted when for the first time in its history the American Telephone and Telegraph Company (AT&T) committed itself and its associated companies to an agreement with a national union of telephone workers. At that time, it was the NFTW's greatest collective bargaining triumph. A year later, however, AT&T adamantly refused the NFTW's demand for industry-wide bargaining, and despite a national telephone strike, defeated the union on the issue, although most telephone workers did receive substantial wage increases resulting from the strike.

Assuming the 1947 strike was lost by a structural defect, the NFTW leadership proposed a fundamental reorganization of the administrative structure to create a national union of telephone workers rather than a confederation of autonomous locals. Criticism of the decentralized structure of the NFTW had been voiced since its organization in 1939, but it was not until 1947 that the reorganization finally occurred. At that time the union was renamed the Communications Workers of America.

The end of the bitter 1947 strike and the organization of the CWA did not end the union's troubles. Occurring almost simultaneously with the organization of the CWA, the CIO established the Telephone Workers' Organizing Committee (TWOC). The CIO's motivation for this action is unclear although it seems likely that CIO officials hoped to pressure the CWA into affiliation. The NFTW previously had survived jurisdictional disputes with the IBEW, the CIO-chartered American Communications Association, and the United Electrical, Radio, and Machine Workers of America, but the new challenge, backed by the considerable resources of the CIO, was a serious threat to the continued survival of the CWA, especially because some of the union's strongest affiliates and most effective leaders left the CWA to join the TWOC.

As its status as an independent union became increasingly untenable, the CWA faced the choice of joining the AFL by becoming an affiliate of the IBEW or affiliating with the CIO, which had established the rival TWOC as an independent national union. The 1948 convention of the CWA instructed the executive board to make a recommendation on the affiliation question and to institute a membership referendum on the board's decision. On February 12, 1949, the executive board recommended affiliation with the CIO, and in a membership referendum held in the spring of 1949, it carried by a large margin. As a consequence, on May 9, 1949, the CWA formally joined the CIO. At that time the TWOC and CWA merged into one organization, the Communications Workers of America as it is presently constituted.

During the years following the CIO affiliation, the CWA gradually strengthened its collective bargaining position, expanded its membership, and increased the power and authority of the national union office, A CWA membership of 180,000 in 1950 increased to 260,000 in 1960 and 420,000 ten years later. Besides the growing influence in the labor movement that accompanied the CWA's increased membership, under the farsighted leadership of Joseph Beirne, the union also became an influential supporter of social and economic reforms in American society.

The CWA, which maintains its national headquarters in Washington, D.C., holds annual conventions. Principal officers include a president, three executive vice-presidents, nine district vice-presidents, and a secretary-treasurer. The above officers constitute the executive board. In 1973 the CWA reported a membership of 443,278 located in 861 local unions.

For further information, see the *CWA News* (monthly) and the *CWA Newsletter* (weekly). See also Jack Barbash, *Unions and Telephones* (1952), which provides an interesting account of telephone unionism through the founding of the CWA. Joseph A. Beirne, long-time CWA president, wrote two books, *New Horizons for American Labor* (1962) and *Challenge to Labor: New Roles for American Trade Unions* (1969), which contain some information on the CWA, although their scope is the national labor movement.

CONGRESS OF INDUSTRIAL ORGANIZATIONS (CIO). Enactment of the National Industrial Recovery Act (NIRA) of 1933 with provisions for union recognition and collective bargaining greatly stimulated a virtually dormant labor movement in the United States. For more than a decade the trade union movement had floundered haplessly, seemingly overwhelmed by open-shop employers, the accelerated decline of nineteenth-century standards of craftsmanship, welfare capitalism and company unionism, political ineptitude, racketeering and corruption, and the catastrophic economic consequences of the Great Depression. Yet a huge reservoir of latent union sentiment lay just beneath the surface, and, stimulated by early New Deal programs and Franklin Roosevelt's rhetoric, a great resurgence of trade union activity occurred. Thousands of American workers rushed to join the unions of their trade, and where unions did not already exist, they organized them. Many new union members came from the expanding industrial labor force of unskilled and semiskilled workers. These mass production workers had been largely neglected by the established labor unions, and the American Federation of Labor* (AFL) organized them into directly chartered federal labor unions.

Ultimately the AFL leadership planned to distribute these new unionists to pertinent craft unions.

Although conforming to past custom and tradition, the practice of dismantling the federal locals met with a growing chorus of criticism from union leaders favoring the industrial organization of mass production workers. Arguing that the craft union structure was unsuited to the organization of mass production workers, these critics assumed that the success with which employers evaded the labor provisions of the NIRA and subdued their rebellious employees simply documented their argument. Responding to mounting pressures, delegates to the 1934 national AFL convention meeting in San Francisco instructed the AFL leadership to charter industrial unions of automobile, rubber, cement, radio, and aluminum workers and to launch a major organizing drive in the steel industry. Nevertheless, no new industrial union charters were issued and no major drive to organize steel was initiated. Consequently, as delegates assembled in Atlantic City, New Jersey, for the 1935 AFL convention, a frustrated and angry group of industrial union advocates arrived determined to rebuke the AFL's old guard leadership and commit the federation to a broad program of industrial unionism.

But the conservatives, led by AFL president William Green, William Hutcheson of the United Brotherhood of Carpenters and Joiners* (UBC), and Daniel Tobin of the International Brotherhood of Teamsters* (IBT), firmly controlled the convention. After a bitter three-day debate, a resolution supporting the principle of industrial organization was defeated by nearly two to one. John L. Lewis of the United Mine Workers of America* (UMWA) quickly emerged as the leading spokesman of the industrial union cause. Lewis headed one of the few industrial unions chartered by the AFL and had great faith in the efficacy of industrial unionism. He had recently conducted a ruthless and often violent campaign to consolidate his control over the UMWA, a campaign that nearly destroyed the union before the organizing opportunities created by the NIRA revived the historic old union. To further stimulate the revival, Lewis was especially anxious to see the steel industry organized to ensure the stability of the recently unionized captive mines owned by various steel companies.

Determined to reverse the unfavorable vote on industrial unionism, Lewis met with the presidents of several other international unions and formed the Committee for Industrial Organization (CIO), an extralegal committee organized to promote industrial unionism and to convert the AFL to that principle. The original membership of the CIO included Sidney Hillman (Amalgamated Clothing Workers*), David Dubinsky (International Ladies' Garment Workers*), Charles Howard (International Typographical Union*), Thomas McMahon (United Textile Workers*), Max Zaritsky (United Hatters*), Thomas Brown (Mine, Mill and Smelter Workers*), and Harvey Fremming (Oil Field, Gas Well and Refining Workers*).

Ignoring Green's aggrieved objections to the CIO, Lewis resigned his AFL vice-presidency, laid plans for a massive organizing drive in the steel industry, and brashly requested industrial union charters for workers in the steel, automobile, radio, and rubber industries. Incredulous at the audacity of their antagonist, members of the AFL executive council rejected the appeal and ordered the dissolution of the CIO. Thereafter, as Lewis completed plans for the steel drive, relations between the two rival groups further deteriorated, and in August 1936 the executive council suspended the ten unions affiliated with the CIO.

The steel organizing drive began in June 1936 under the auspices of the newly created Steel Workers Organizing Committee (SWOC), largely financed by the UMWA and led by Lewis's chief lieutenant Philip Murray. Suddenly hundreds of union organizers appeared in steel centers across the nation. Steelworkers responded enthusiastically, and by the end of the year, SWOC claimed more than 100 locals and 100,000 workers. The anticipated confrontation with the giant of the industry, the notoriously anti-union U.S. Steel Corporation, however, never materialized. Lewis and U.S. Steel board chairman Myron Taylor held a series of secret meetings and in March 1937 announced an agreement under which SWOC won recognition as the collective bargaining agent for workers of U.S. Steel's largest subsidiary, Carnegie-Illinois Steel. The agreement also included significant wage and hour concessions. Other subsidiaries of the giant steel company soon followed suit. The victory had a symbolic significance far beyond any immediate and palpable result. In a few weeks the brash, young CIO had accomplished what the AFL had failed to do over the course of nearly a half-century. The very citadel of union resistance in the United States had been breached. The victory converted the CIO from a highly speculative enterprise into a hard reality in inter-labor and labor-management relations in the United States.

Soon after the capitulation of U.S. Steel, General Motors Corporation, the giant of the automobile industry, succumbed after a series of bitter strikes to another CIO union, the United Automobile Workers Union.* The development of the sitdown strike during the automobile organizing campaign proved one of the most effective tactical weapons available to CIO organizers in their efforts to extend union organization to other mass production industries. Inspired by the success in the steel and automobile industries, workers in the rubber, glass, textile, electrical appliance, and numerous other industries employed the sitdown tactic to gain union recognition from reluctant employers. The organizing effort was also greatly stimulated by the U.S. Supreme Court's favorable decision on the constitutionality of the National Labor Relations Act.

While its victories were numerous and in many cases highly significant, the bitterness of defeat sometimes accompanied the sweetness of victory. The SWOC's campaign to organize "little steel" after the capitulation of U.S.

Steel, for example, failed badly as did the effort to organize the Ford Motor Company. Success in organizing these companies awaited the application of government pressure during the World War II mobilization effort. Despite occasional defeats, the CIO grew spectacularly. Within eighteen months of the first organizing initiatives in the steel campaign, the CIO claimed a membership of nearly 4 million (although only about half of that number paid per-capita taxes) and approached equity with the AFL.

The CIO's success confounded and startled the AFL leadership. To avoid being left behind in the great surge of trade unionism sweeping the nation during the late 1930s, the AFL had to meet the CIO challenge. Although the conflicts between the AFL and CIO had centered upon the organizing issue—craft versus industrial unionism—in fact, resulting from technological change, the most powerful AFL craft unions had ceased to be pure craft unions of skilled workers. Older AFL craft unions, such as the Brotherhood of Carpenters, opposed closely defined jurisdictional boundaries and claimed the right to organize whomever they chose; in effect, they advocated a policy of jurisdictional laissez-faire. Although this policy had served the interests of a few powerful AFL craft unions, it could no longer be tolerated if the AFL were to counter the CIO threat. Moreover, the introduction of National Labor Relations Board representational elections largely removed the issue of jurisdictional supremacy from the councils of the AFL or the individual international unions and placed the decision in the hands of the workers. Led by such unions as the International Association of Machinists* and the Brotherhood of Teamsters, the AFL unions ultimately responded to the CIO challenge by becoming semi-industrial unions of multiple crafts and skills. Thus even before the end of the 1930s, advocates of industrial unionism had won an overwhelming victory.

Even as the AFL leadership moved slowly toward the final expulsion of the CIO unions in the fall of 1938, reconciliation efforts occurred. In October 1937 delegates from the AFL and CIO met in Washington, D.C., to discuss the possibilities of labor unity. Personal ambitions and rivalries and the early AFL insistence that several CIO unions be dismantled and their membership absorbed by existing AFL unions caused these negotiations to fail as did later unity discussions, the most significant inspired by Franklin Roosevelt's call for labor harmony in 1939.

Nevertheless unity was still a possibility until the summer of 1938. At that time the Committee for Industrial Organization became the Congress of Industrial Organizations and projected itself as a national rival of the AFL. Soon thereafter, a full-scale jurisdictional raiding war erupted. Rival unions, both craft and industrial, were chartered by both federations in most organizing jurisdictions, resulting in bitter and often violent confrontations, which, with the radical sitdown tactic, began to turn public opinion against organized labor. But for the arbitrational role of the NLRB and the partial suspension of inter-union hostilities accompanying American intervention in World War II, the organizing war could well have been even more devastating.

After the war the CIO never regained its prewar organizing initiatives, and during the postwar years the AFL rapidly outstripped the CIO in membership. The AFL's relative success during these years was the product of varied circumstances. Before the end of the war the CIO had succeeded in organizing the vast majority of the work force in the mass production industries, the foundation upon which the early, dramatic success of the CIO was built. Moreover, the defection of the UMWA after John L. Lewis resigned the CIO presidency in 1940 meant the loss of not only hundreds of thousands of members but also of the union that had formed the very backbone of the early CIO.

A general change in the political atmosphere in the United States also worked to the detriment of the CIO. The developing cold war following World War II worked to the advantage of the AFL, which had cultivated a much more conservative image than the CIO had. Furthermore, the enactment of the Taft-Hartley Act by the Republican-controlled, anti-labor Eightieth Congress accelerated already existing ideological divisions among CIO international unions. The Taft-Hartley Act required union leaders to sign non-Communist affidavits as a necessary precondition for using NLRB representational election machinery. Several CIO union leaders refused to sign the affidavits, thus exposing their unions to AFL raids. Ideological divisions within the CIO were further exacerbated when several union leaders endorsed the presidential candidacy of Henry Wallace on the Progressive party ticket in 1948. The CIO leadership had officially endorsed the Democratic party's candidate, Harry Truman, and generally assumed the Wallace movement to be under Communist influence, if not Communist control. Ultimately ten "Communist-dominated" unions were expelled from the CIO. As a result of the intense ideological conflicts that transfixed the CIO during the postwar years, organizing suffered and the AFL profited.

Circumstances existing during the early 1950s converted leaders of both the AFL and CIO to the cause of labor unity. On December 5, 1955, a merger of the two organizations resulted in the formation of the AFL-CIO.* (For a discussion of the merger, see the AFL-CIO sketch in this volume.) Under terms of the merger, all AFL and CIO international unions were automatically eligible to become members of the new federation with no prior conditions.

Although similar in many respects, significant differences separated the AFL and CIO, especially during the early years of the rivalry. The CIO contained a more socially and politically conscious leadership than the conservative, business unionists who directed the affairs of the AFL. The early CIO had proven a haven for a variety of displaced radicals, and although later a source of debilitating internal conflicts, the radicals nevertheless instilled a social consciousness and a fervent dedication to organizing that for several years had been largely absent in the American labor movement. Moreover, partially because of the industrial organizing tactic, CIO unions proved much more hospitable to black workers than the older AFL unions, many of which still openly practiced racial discrimination.

Politically, the CIO early rejected the anti-statist voluntarism that had served as the basic AFL political doctrine for much of its history. CIO leaders assumed that political power was as important as economic power, and they became strong advocates of progressive labor legislation, such as the Fair Labor Standards Act of 1938, beneficial to unorganized as well as organized labor. The CIO also played a much more activist role in electoral politics. Through the creation of Labor's Non-Partisan League, as early as 1936 the CIO took an active role in the reelection of President Franklin Roosevelt. But nonpartisanship was largely rhetoric as the CIO increasingly committed itself to the Democratic party. When John L. Lewis attempted to reverse that trend in 1940 by endorsing the Republican party candidacy of Wendell Willkie, CIO leaders and members repudiated their president, the individual most responsible for the formation of the CIO. Fulfilling a pre-election pledge, Lewis resigned his CIO presidency and a short time later took the UMWA out of the CIO. After substantial Republican gains in the congressional elections of 1942, the CIO's political activity became more formalized and centralized under the direction of the newly organized political action committee.

The AFL leadership responded to the CIO's social and political initiatives in much the same way it had responded to its rival's organizing initiatives. Older shibboleths were pushed aside as the AFL reformed its traditional doctrines and strategies to meet new challenges. As a consequence, by the time of the 1955 merger few differences remained between the old rivals. There could be little doubt that the CIO had effected a radical transformation of the American labor movement.

The CIO, which maintained its national headquarters in Washington, D.C., held annual conventions. Principal officers included a president, ten vice-presidents, and a secretary-treasurer. The executive council was comprised of the above officials. The general council was composed of the presidents of each affiliated national union. At the time of the merger with the AFL, the CIO received per-capita taxes from 4,608,000 members located in thirty-two affiliated national unions.

For further information, see the *CIO News* published weekly. The debate over industrial unionism is discussed in James O. Morris, *Conflict within the AFL: A Study of Craft Versus Industrial Unionism, 1901-1938* (1958). In two major books, Walter Galenson discusses rival unionism in the United States; see *Rival Unionism in the United States* (1940) and *The CIO Challenge to the AFL: A History of the American Labor Movement, 1935-1941* (1960). There are several popular histories of the early CIO years, including Herbert Harris, *Labor's Civil War* (1940), Edward Levinson, *Labor on the March* (1938), Rose Pesotta, *Bread upon the Waters* (1945), and Benjamin Stolberg, *The Story of the CIO* (1938). The only book to treat the entire CIO period is Art Preis, *Labor's Giant Step: Twenty Years of the CIO* (1964), a book taken largely from the pages of *The Militant* and marred by ideological rigidity. The Communist influence is discussed in Max M. Kampelman, *The Communist Party vs. the C.I.O.: A Study in Power Politics* (1957), and David J. Saposs, *Communism in American Unions* (1959). Joseph G. Rayback, in his *History of American Labor* (1966), does an exceptional job of placing the CIO into the larger context of American labor history. The CIO's political activity is treated in Fay Calkins, *The CIO and the Democratic Party* (1952); Joseph Gaer, *The First Round: The Story of the CIO Political Action Committee* (1944); and James C. Foster, *The Union Politic: The CIO Political Action Committee* (1975). Arthur J. Goldberg, a participant, discusses the AFL-CIO merger in *AFL-CIO: Labor United* (1956).

CONFEDERACIÓN INTERAMERICANA DE TRABAJADORES (CIT). On January 10, 1948, the founding conference of the CIT convened at Lima, Peru, with delegations representing trade union bodies from the United States, Chile, Peru, Mexico, Brazil, Costa Rica, Colombia, Dutch Guiana, Puerto Rico, El Salvador, Panama, Bolivia, and Cuba. Venezuela and the Dominican Republic were represented by fraternal delegates; Ecuador, by an observer; Argentina, in absentia, by a delegation from the anti-Perónista unions. Notably absent from the centrist gathering were representatives of the American Congress of Industrial Organizations* (CIO), the Argentine Confederación General del Trabajo (CGT) and the several major Mexican federations. Elected to lead the CIT were : president, Bernardo Ibañez of Chile, and vice-presidents, George Meany and Bert Jewell of the United States, Arturo Sabroso of Peru, Enrique Rangel of Mexico, Juan C. Lara of Colombia, Francisco Aguirre of Cuba, C. Cabral Mello of Brazil, Luis Alberto Monge of Costa Rica, Leo E. Eleazer of Dutch Guiana, with a seat left vacant for a delegate from Venezuela. Named as special assistants to the president were Isidoro Godoy of Chile, Eusebio Mujal of Cuba, Serafino Romualdi of the United States and, later, Arturo Jauregui of Peru. Headquarters were established at Lima; they were moved almost immediately to Santiago, Chile, and in 1949 to Havana.

In 1925 William Green succeeded Samuel Gompers as president both of the AFL and of the Pan-American Federation of Labor (PAFL). The decline of the latter was swift, and by the 1930s, it existed only as a paper organization. Then, at Mexico City in September 1938, Vicente Lombardo Toledano convoked the founding conference of a new hemispheric trade union body, the Confederación de Trabajadores de America Latina (CTAL)—left leaning and anti-PAFL. Among those attending were Bernardo Ibañez of Chile and John L. Lewis of the United States. Lombardo Toledano had broken away from the AFL-oriented Confederación Regional Obrero Mexicano (CROM) to found the rival Confederación de Trabajadores de Mexico (CTM); Lewis had broken with the AFL to found the CIO. The CROM and the AFL had provided the substantive core of the PAFL and, indeed, Green and CROM leader Luis Morones remained, respectively, president and vice-president of the PAFL.

Fear of a Lewis-Lombardo Toledano alliance (and its prospect) sparked a momentary flurry of activity. The CIO established an advisory committee on Latin American affairs. Chester M. Wright, one of the founders of the PAFL, and Matthew Woll of the AFL executive council were dispatched to Mexico to confer with Morones and to size up the new CTAL. In May of 1939, the PAFL was revitalized with Green, Morones, Woll, and Santiago Iglesias of Puerto Rico as the executive committee. Iglesias, then resident commissioner of Puerto Rico in the United States Congress, was dispatched on a goodwill tour of the Americas, but his death in December 1939, while on an organizational mission, dashed all hopes for rebuilding the PAFL.

Growing turbulence in Europe produced a change in Pan-American trade union patterns. Nelson Rockefeller was appointed coordinator of the Office of Inter-American Affairs at the Department of State. In order to neutralize Axis influence among the workers of Latin America, Rockefeller created a division of labor relations and attached Italian-born Serafino Romualdi of the New York International Ladies' Garment Workers' Union* (ILG) to his staff. Rockefeller worked closely with Meany and Robert Watt of the AFL, and with CIO leaders as well. Romualdi moved easily through the Americas, often representing both labor and the interests of the American government. Ibañez was wooed away from the CTAL. In 1944 and again in 1945, Meany visited Mexico in behalf of trade union solidarity, opening communications between the AFL and the CTM. These successes, however, were offset by growing tension between Romualdi, the AFL, and the Perónista unions of Argentina.

Meanwhile, two other figures entered the international trade union scene. One was Jay Lovestone of the ILG, a "cold warrior" who would become the leading theoretian of American labor's international policy for the next three decades. The other was Ernesto Galarza, in charge of labor affairs at the Pan American Union. Mexican-born, with a doctorate from Columbia University, and associated with the New York Foreign Policy Association, Galarza was intense, angry, and brilliant. While Galarza was willing to challenge "the system" and the Department of State in defense of inter-American labor, Lovestone and Romualdi appeared to work from within. That control of AFL inter-American policy fell to the Meany-Lovestone-Romualdi faction rather than to Galarza (or to persons of his persuasion) was decisive for the future.

The Lima conference was convened by Ibañez at the urging of the AFL and with at least covert support from the Department of State. Arturo Sabroso of Peru served as host, the sessions being held in the Peruvian capitol building itself. Nicholas Nogueras Rivera of Puerto Rico presented the bylaws and declaration of principles but, throughout, the key figure was Serafino Romualdi. Headquarters for the CIT were established in Lima. No sooner had the delegates departed, however, than the Peruvian government declared war upon organized labor, imprisoned or exiled Peruvian trade union leaders, and expelled the CIT. Ibañez set up interim headquarters in Santiago. In September 1949 the first regular convention of the CIT met in Havana, restructured the entire CIT, created vast secretarial powers, and established the CIT's permanent headquarters in the Cuban capital. Ibañez remained as president, but General Secretary-Treasurer Francisco Aguirre of Cuba possessed the administrative authority. Associated with him were Romualdi, Jauregui of Peru, and Augusto Malava Villalba of Venezuela—all three of growing stature.

Just as Gompers had ignored the Industrial Workers of the World* (IWW) when establishing the PAFL, so the Meany-Lovestone-Romualdi group had ignored the CIO when creating the CIT. Meanwhile, in Europe, the cold war had divided the old World Federation of Trade Unions (WFTU) and, by 1949, both the CIO and the British Trade Union Congress had withdrawn to create the International Confederation of Free Trade Unions (ICFTU), a new anti-communist and anti-fascist world labor body. In the Americas, the CIT found itself assaulted from the right by the Perónista unions and from the left by the CTAL. Clearly, it was time for a general reordering of the Western Hemisphere trade union movement to bring it into line with the ICFTU and to heal old wounds at the same time. At Mexico City in January 1951, the CIT transformed itself into the Organización Regional Interamericana de Trabajadores* (ORIT), which included the CIO.

The best background study of the CIT is Henry W. Berger, "Union Diplomacy: American Labor's Foreign Policy in Latin America, 1932-1955" (Ph.D. dissertation, University of Wisconsin, 1966). See also Robert Mellon, *Vicente Lombardo Toledano, Mexican Marxist* (1966); Romualdi's autobiography, *Presidents and Peons: Recollections of a Labor Ambassador in Latin America* (1967); Harvey Levenstein's *Labor Organizations in the United States and Mexico: A History of their Relations* (1971); and Ronald Radosh's more critical *American Labor and United States Foreign Policy* (1969). *The American Federationist* is another valuable source of information.

William G. Whittaker

COOPERS' INTERNATIONAL UNION OF NORTH AMERICA (CIU). Organization of coopers in the United States began during the colonial period, but these groups were primarily fraternal and benevolent. Legitimate trade unions did not appear until the 1830s with the agitation for the ten-hour day. Unions of coopers then arose in several cities, including strong organizations in New York City, Baltimore, and Philadelphia, Most of these unions succumbed to the depression signaled by the panic of 1837, but a few survived, including the Coopers' Protective Union No. 1 of New York City, and played a role in the future development of labor organization in the trade.

During the Civil War and the immediate postwar years, the demand for all types of cooperage increased dramatically. Although temporarily beneficial to workers in the trade, the increased demand encouraged the development of machinery to replace hand labor. Barrel producers were especially interested in perfecting barrel-making machinery, and while the early machine-made barrels were crude and often leaked, experimentation in mechanization continued because producers (who were also consumers) could afford to use inferior products while awaiting machinery refinements. As the machines improved and made greater inroads in the trade, wages fell and coopers organized in self-defense.

Led by Martin A. Foran, Cleveland coopers conducted a long and bitter but successful strike during the early weeks of 1870. This struggle was almost lost when coopers in nearby cities supplied the struck shops with barrels. To remedy this situation, Foran issued a national call to coopers to meet in Cleveland and organize a national union. Thirteen delegates representing approximately 1,500 coopers in New York, Pennsylvania, Ohio, and Maryland responded and organized the Coopers International Union (CIU). Foran was elected president of the new national union.

The CIU grew rapidly, attaining a membership of 3,350 in forty-one affiliated locals within six months of its organization. Within a year membership jumped to 8,371, making the CIU one of the larger unions in the United States. The CIU played a leading role in the organization of the Industrial Congress following the breakup of the National Labor Union in 1873, and its president, Robert Schilling, was elected president of the short-lived new federation. The Industrial Congress and many of the CIU's early achievements evaporated when the depression initiated by the panic of 1873 struck the nation. Only eleven delegates representing 1,110 members attended the CIU's fifth annual convention in Rochester, New York, in 1876. Although represented at the founding conference of the Federation of Organized Trades and Labor Unions in 1881, the CIU was then largely a paper organization. Shortly thereafter, the remaining cooper locals apparently affiliated with local assemblies of the emerging Knights of Labor.

The American Federation of Labor* (AFL) chartered a short-lived Coopers National Union on January 16, 1888, but it surrendered its charter in November. A permanent union of coopers was organized two years later at Titusville, Pennsylvania, on November 10, 1890. The following year the AFL granted a charter to the Coopers' International Union of North America, conferring jurisdiction over "the manufacture and fabrication of cooperage of every description."

The coopers finally gave up their opposition to machine-made barrels, after experimenting with cooperative ventures during the 1880s, and they began organizing machine workers during the late 1890s. The CIU grew steadily until 1903, reaching a membership of approximately 8,000, but increased mechanization, the employers' open-shop offensive, and jurisdictional conflicts with the International Union of United Brewery Workers* reversed the CIU's growth, and it began a slow decline, only temporarily halted by World War I. The CIU lost more than half of its 1903 membership by 1920. The introduction of Prohibition during the 1920s and the depression of the 1930s reduced the CIU to a skeleton organization of 600 members by 1932. The end of Prohibition and favorable governmental policies, however, combined to revive the small national union which enrolled nearly 3,000 members by the end of the depression decade and almost doubled that figure in the years following World War II. Technological advances and the increased use of substitutes for wooden barrels during the 1950s and 1960s combined to again depress the ancient trade.

The CIU, which maintains its national headquarters in Louisville, Kentucky, holds biennial conventions. The president-secretary-treasurer is the only full-time officer. The general executive board is composed of the above official and four vice-presidents, all elected by majority vote at biennial conventions. In 1973 the CIU reported a membership of 1,824 located in twenty-five local unions.

For further information, see the *Coopers' Journal* published quarterly. See also *The American Federationist* (October 1947); John R. Commons et al., *History of Labour in the United States*, vol. 2 (1918); Norman J. Ware, *The Labor Movement in the United States, 1860-1895: A Study in Democracy* (1929), and Philip Taft, *Organized Labor in American History* (1964).

DISTILLERY, RECTIFYING, WINE AND ALLIED WORKERS' INTERNATIONAL UNION OF AMERICA (DRWAWIUA). As a result of favorable labor legislation during the 1930s and the emergence of the CIO as a rival to the AFL, union organizing was greatly stimulated, especially among semiskilled and unskilled workers, and jurisdictional lines became increasingly clouded. Such was the case when the AFL combined several previously organized federal labor unions to create a national council of distillery, rectifying, and wine workers in 1938. Two years later, on December 20, 1940, the council was chartered as an international union, the Distillery, Rectifying and Wine Workers International Union (DRWW). The new union organized in a trade jurisdiction paralleling and sometimes overlapping that of another AFL affiliate, the International Union of United Brewery, Flour, Cereal, Soft Drink and Distillery Workers of America.* After the AFL suspended the Brewery Workers on October 16, 1941, because of a jurisdictional dispute with the International Brotherhood of Teamsters, Chauffeurs, Warehousemen and Helpers of America,* the DRWW remained the only AFL union in its trade jurisdiction. The Brewery Workers later affiliated with the CIO.

The new AFL union grew slowly, reaching a membership of 10,000 before the end of World War II and 25,000 by mid-century. The discovery that the

DRWW secretary had embezzled hundreds of thousands of dollars from the union's health and welfare funds during the early 1950s, however, threatened the continued existence of the international. The AFL-CIO* suspended the DRWW after an investigation conducted by its ethical practices committee and threatened expulsion if the DRWW failed to take action immediately to eliminate corrupt influences within the union. The DRWW complied and after serving a probationary period regained complete autonomy. In 1962 the DRWW adopted the listed title.

The DRWAWIUA, which maintains its national headquarters in Englewood, New Jersey, holds biennial conventions. Principal officers include a president, seven vice-presidents, and a secretary-treasurer. The executive board is comprised of the above officials. In 1973 the DRWAWIUA reported a membership of 33,000 located in ninety-five local unions.

For further information, see the *DWU Journal* issued periodically by the DRWAWIUA. See also John Hutchinson, *The Imperfect Union* (1970), a study of corruption in American trade unions, and Florence Peterson, *Handbook of Labor Unions* (1944).

DISTRICT 50, ALLIED AND TECHNICAL WORKERS OF THE UNITED STATES AND CANADA; INTERNATIONAL UNION OF. In the 1930s anthracite coal was being replaced as a domestic fuel by coke, a major source of manufactured gas in the eastern United States. The market for such gas was in decline, but new coking methods in the steel industry retained valuable gases and tars for the expanding by-product industries. In 1935 only a few thousand coke and gas workers were organized, members of several federal unions chartered by the American Federation of Labor* (AFL); these locals were affiliated with the National Council of Gas and By-Product Coke Workers. Transformation of the Council into District 50 of the United Mine Workers of America* (UMWA) resulted from the warfare between the AFL and the newly formed Committee for Industrial Organization* (CIO). When the AFL ignored the National Council's request for a national industrial union charter, UMWA president John L. Lewis offered the gas and coke workers the opportunity to join his union. At a joint conference in August 1936, the UMWA amended its constitution in order to take over the National Council as a "national department." Lewis appointed the National Council's executive secretary, James Nelson, president of the new District 50, UMWA, and Martin Wagner, a former Illinois coal miner, became vice-president. Thus Lewis not only recouped the loss in anthracite but created a jurisdiction that could be used for expansion and organizing raids. Meanwhile, the gas and coke workers gave up any chance of having autonomy within the labor movement.

Unlike other UMWA districts, District 50 had no specific geographical basis, although most of its locals were in the East. In 1937 the CIO expanded

District 50's jurisdiction to include most of the chemical industry, giving it a potential membership of 250,000. With some UMWA financial aid, Nelson and Wagner conducted an organizing drive, which by 1939 increased total membership to 17,000, including the employees of a few major chemical firms. Due to the complicated structure of the chemical and allied industries, however, District 50, with its membership scattered in small locals, was becoming a catchall rather than an industrial-type union.

From the outset, the UMWA international office dominated the affairs of District 50. Its president and secretary-treasurer were appointed by the UMWA, which also determined basic organizational policies for District 50. Its membership was not represented in UMWA conventions. With only minor changes, this relationship lasted for twenty-five years.

During the 1940s John L. Lewis used District 50 to intimidate his adversaries within and outside the labor movement. In 1941 he replaced Nelson with Ora Gasaway, a UMWA functionary, and appointed Kathryn Lewis, his daughter, secretary-treasurer. To offset the expanding CIO (from which the UMWA soon withdrew) and to restore his prestige, Lewis sought new organizational achievements. Early in 1942 the UMWA announced a campaign to organize the dairy farmers through District 50. In fact, it became a front for organizing a hodgepodge of unaffiliated workers and for raiding vulnerable CIO or AFL unions. Large UMWA funds were poured into the drive. Although the dairy effort never materialized, District 50 increased its membership, especially in chemicals and gas utilities, and by 1943 it had 48,000 members. Meanwhile, the UMWA's ill-fated United Construction Workers Organizing Committee was conveniently absorbed by District 50.

Lewis appointed his brother, Alma D. Lewis, president in 1946, and Elwood S. Moffett, presidential assistant in 1948. Hampered by its inability to file for NLRB elections because Lewis refused to comply with the Taft-Hartley anti-Communist affidavit, District 50 took advantage of its nonexistent jurisdictional lines and the jurisdictional battles of the AFL and CIO. By the mid-1950s the union had expanded to, or acquired a foothold in, public utilities, construction, lumber, pulp, shipping, light manufacturing, chemicals, retail and service trades, and a variety of previously nonunion occupations. District 50 often organized in the shadow of its founder, taking in, for example, the construction crews of UMWA hospitals and employees of businesses in which the UMWA president had invested. Significantly, however, almost half the District's membership was concentrated in chemicals, pulp, and paper. When the AFL-CIO* merged in 1955, it launched a raiding campaign against District 50. After a few initial victories, it lost momentum. In 1960 District 50 stepped up its organizing, making effective use of NLRB procedures. In a period of general union lethargy, it projected the image of a dynamic organization, and, organizing under the aegis of John L. Lewis, it made inroads in the AFL-CIO chemical unions and even in some construction unions.

As required by the Landrum-Griffin Act, District 50 held its first convention in February 1961. A. D. Lewis and Elwood Moffett were *elected* president and vice-president. According to UMWA officials, District 50 was now an "independent" but "fully affiliated" organization. Accordingly, District 50 offices remained in the UMWA's Washington, D.C., headquarters. With A. D. Lewis's death in 1962, Moffett assumed the presidency. Ambitious and capable, he made several innovations, primarily gaining financial independence from the UMWA (largely by reducing District 50's per-capita payment). Moffett also worked for industry-wide bargaining in chemicals. By this time, moreover, with membership approaching 200,000, the stepchild had grown larger than the guardian.

When in 1968 District 50 officials endorsed the production of nuclear energy and began organizing in that industry, UMWA president W. A. "Tony" Boyle castigated the catchall union as a "thankless child" and announced that it would be expelled. Subsequently the UMWA executive board also drummed the top District 50 officers out of the miners' union amidst charges of their having brought "discredit and disgrace to the International Union." The UMWA then instituted a damage suit against District 50, UMWA, for continuing to use that designation. The catchall union simply changed its name to District 50, Allied and Technical Workers of the United States and Canada.

Beset with financial difficulties, harassed by UMWA lawsuits, and, above all, aware that as an independent union District 50 could not easily achieve consolidated bargaining in chemicals and utilities, District 50 officers started negotiations in 1969 for merger of their 230,000 member organization with the United Steelworkers of America* (USWA). After defeating a UMWA attempt to prevent a referendum on the merger pact with the USWA, Moffett in 1972 recommended it to the District 50 membership. They voted approval, and on August 9, 1972, the merger was accomplished, thus terminating the existence of one of the most unusual and fascinating national unions in the history of the American labor movement.

District 50, which maintained its national headquarters in Washington, D.C., held quinquennial conventions. Full-time officers included a president, vice-president, and secretary-treasurer. Shortly before its merger with the USWA District 50 reported a membership of 210,000 located in 1,475 local unions.

For further information, see *District 50 News* published semimonthly. There is no adequate history of District 50. James Nelson's *The Mine Workers' District 50* (1955) is a self-serving but informative document that does not go beyond the author's presidency. Walter Galenson, *The CIO Challenge to the AFL: A History of the American Labor Movement, 1935-1941* (1960), has the best scholarly account of District 50's origins. Saul Alinsky, *John L. Lewis, An Unauthorized Biography* (1949) has interesting comments. *Business Week,* the *New York Times,* and the *Wall Street Journal* contain useful articles and analyses. For the relationship between District 50 and the UMWA, see the *United Mine Workers Journal.*

Donald G. Sofchalk

ELECTRICAL, RADIO AND MACHINE WORKERS; INTERNATIONAL UNION OF (IUE). Delegates attending the annual convention of the Congress of Industrial Organizations* (CIO) on November 1, 1949, declared they would "no longer tolerate within the family of the CIO the Communist Party masquerading as a labor union." Approval of Resolution 2 provided for the expulsion of the United Electrical, Radio and Machine Workers of America* (UE) from CIO membership. Twenty-four hours later CIO president Philip Murray issued a charter for a new union in the industry, the International Union of Electrical, Radio and Machine Workers. James B. Carey, a founder and former president of the UE, who had been deposed by a left-wing coup in 1941, became the new union's leader.

Within days of its chartering the IUE started challenging the UE for members and began to petition the National Labor Relations Board (NLRB) for representation elections. The union had considerable success in attracting members of the Communist-tainted UE during the early 1950s, a period when the phenomenon of McCarthyism dramatically illustrated the anti-Communist hysteria sweeping the country. By its first national convention in November 1949, the IUE had already issued charters to sixty-eight locals, and by the end of the year, it represented more than 200,000 workers. Within a few years the IUE had become the dominant union in the electrical industry; nevertheless, the UE exhibited remarkable tenacity and continued to retain a substantial number of loyal workers.

During the intense intra-industry union rivalry throughout the 1950s and early 1960s, the IUE's affiliation with the CIO and later the AFL-CIO provided much greater immunity from jurisdictional raids. Members of the outcast UE were considered fair game by many international unions. The IUE leadership, moreover, exhibited a determination to avoid the expensive and debilitating jurisdictional conflicts that had plagued the UE during the postwar years. Consequently, IUE leaders sought to reach an accommodation among the organizations of workers in the electrical industry with such traditional rivals as the United Automobile Workers Union,* the International Association of Machinists,* and the International Brotherhood of Electrical Workers.*

The IUE's success in the interunion rivalry also depended upon its ability to win concessions at the bargaining table. The union pioneered in establishing severance pay benefits, won the first guaranteed annual wage from a major electrical corporation, negotiated increased wage rates, and improved pension, insurance, and health benefits. These gains often came only after lengthy and bitterly contested strikes. Among the more dramatic was a successful 156-day nationwide strike against Westinghouse during in 1955 and 1956.

One of the most frustrating bargaining (or non-bargaining) tactics union negotiators encountered in the elctrical industry involved the General Electric Corporation (GE), which developed the tactic of "Boulwarism," named after GE vice-president Lemuel R. Boulware. Under this policy, GE offered the unions a non-negotiable, "take-it-or-leave-it" package, which was announced in conjunction with an intensive public relations campaign justifying the company's position. On December 17, 1964, the NLRB decided that this GE procedure did not constitute bargaining in good faith. Under terms of the National Labor Relations Act, the propaganda barrage accompanying publication of the corporation's terms was also considered an unfair labor practice.

In addition to the end of Boulwarism, the decade of the 1960s was a significant period for the IUE. Paul Jennings assumed the presidency in a much disputed election in which the incumbent, James Carey, was originally declared the winner. After an investigation of the election results by the U.S. Department of Labor, Jennings was recognized as the winner. Forgetting many past enmities, the IUE and the UE finally joined with twelve other unions to present a unified bargaining front in negotiations with GE and Westinghouse. Success in a 101-day nationwide strike against GE in 1969 and 1970 illustrated the potential strength of the bargaining alliance.

The IUE, which holds biennial conventions, maintains its national headquarters in Washington, D.C. Principal officers include a president, seven vice-presidents, and a secretary- treasurer. The executive board is composed of the above officers and a varying number of additional representatives from the various geographical districts. In 1973 the IUE reported a membership of 290,000 located in 600 local unions.

For further information, see the *IUE News* published every third week. Information can also be found in James J. Matles and James Higgins, *Them and Us: Struggles of a Rank and File Union* (1974), and Max M. Kampelman, *The Communist Party vs. the C.I.O.: A Study in Power Politics* (1957).

ELECTRICAL, RADIO, AND MACHINE WORKERS OF AMERICA; UNITED (UE). The origin of the United Electrical, Radio, and Machine Workers of America began with the organization of radio workers at the Philadelphia Philco plant in July 1933, when Philco signed an agreement with the newly formed American Federation of Radio Workers led by James B. Carey. Workers secured an eight-hour day, a forty-hour work week, time-and-a-half for overtime, and a minimum hourly wage of forty-five cents for men and thirty-six cents for women. Subsequently, on August 3, 1933, the American Federation of Labor* (AFL) chartered the union as the Radio and Television Workers Federal Local 18386.

Unionization spread rapidly to other companies, and in December 1933, AFL federal locals and independent unions formed the Radio and Allied Trades National Labor Council. A proponent of industrial unionism, the council desired to obtain a national charter from the AFL, but in 1933 the AFL denied this request. In 1935 it deferred the council's request but recognized the council as an official AFL body. In 1936, however, the AFL again denied a request for a national charter and instead ordered all federal locals in the field transferred to the jurisdiction of the International Brotherhood of Electrical Workers* (IBEW). Radio worker representatives meeting in Washington, D.C., in February 1936 then decided to launch a national union without AFL sanction and to invite the independent Electrical and Radio Workers Union, which claimed 25,000 members, to join the new union. The United Electrical and Radio Workers of America was finally formed in March 1936 at Buffalo, New York. James Carey was elected president and Julius Emspak, from the independent General Electric Local, Schenectady, New York, was elected secretary-treasurer. The AFL reacted to the formation of the UE by revoking the charters of all federal locals affiliated with the new organization.

During the UE's first convention in September 1936 at Fort Wayne, Indiana, unions affiliated with the Committee for Industrial Organization* (CIO) were suspended from the AFL. UE immediately applied for and received a charter from the CIO, thus becoming the first non-AFL union to be admitted to the CIO.

Growth of UE throughout 1936 was relatively slow, but it gathered momentum later that year and in early 1937. In 1937 a group of locals affiliated with the International Association of Machinists* (IAM) broke with that union and joined UE. Led by James J. Matles, these locals, claiming 15,000 members, previously belonged to the Communist-dominated Federation of Metal and Allied Unions. Also in 1937 jurisdiction over machine workers was inserted into UE's constitution and "machine workers" was added to the union's name. By 1937 UE claimed 275 locals and approximately 125,000 members.

Throughout 1936 and 1937 UE ran into bitter opposition from IBEW, particularly in utility plants. The AFL and the corporations cooperated with IBEW to prevent UE from unionizing plants, and in 1939 the IBEW intensified its anti-UE drive. UE responded by instituting federal suit under the National Labor Relations Act (NLRA) against IBEW, charged IBEW with conspiracy to deprive UE members of their rights under the NLRA, and brought complaints against companies that had conspired with IBEW against UE.

Communist infiltration and domination of UE, an issue that plagued the union for the next two decades, reached a crisis between 1939 and 1941. Julius Emspak and James Matles, director of organization, became the focus of much controversy. In 1941 Carey launched an offensive against Communists in the union by introducing a resolution at the 1941 convention to permit locals to bar Communists and fascists from union office. Emspak, Matles, and Albert J. Fitzgerald, chairman of the resolutions committee, successfully opposed Carey on the issue. At the same convention, Carey lost the presidency of UE to Fitzgerald, who, although not a Communist, agreed with Matles and Emspak. The Communist issue and the 1941 convention fight did not affect UE's ability to attract new members, however, and by the end of 1941 paid membership rose to 180,000.

In the post-World War II years, UE determined to improve wage scales in the larger plants; consequently, the union struck Westinghouse, General Electric (GE), and the electrical division of the General Motors Corporation (GMC) in January 1946. Although UE originally demanded a 19½ cent per hour raise, it settled with GMC and GE in March 1946 for 18½ cents and later in May with Westinghouse for 19 cents. Meanwhile, the United Automobile Workers Union* (UAW), also on strike against GMC for the same 19½ cent increase, was forced to settle for less. Walter Reuther, then vice-president of UAW, blamed the UE settlements for the UAW failure to gain the larger wage. The 1946 settlement helped precipitate a two-decade split between UAW and UE.

The passage of the Taft-Hartley Act in 1947 further exacerbated the Communist issue. Initially the CIO and UE boycotted the section of Taft-Hartley requiring union officers to sign affidavits disavowing Communist party membership. But eventually in 1948-1949, the CIO, and later in the 1950s UE, acceded to the Taft-Hartley requirements.

During 1948 and 1949 the United Steelworkers* and UAW constantly raided UE. In September 1949 UE sought to obtain a no-raiding agreement from the CIO, but delegates to the November 1949 CIO convention refused to grant this concession. Consequently, UE ceased paying dues and refused to send delegates to the CIO convention. The CIO responded by expelling UE and chartering a new union, the International Union of Electrical, Radio, and Machine Workers* (IUE), headed by James Carey.

The McCarthyism of the 1950s hurt UE as it increasingly came under attack for being a Communist-dominated union. In 1955 the Subversive Activities Control Board convinced the Justice Department to file proceedings against UE, charging the union with Communist infiltration. Four years later the Justice Department asked for federal court permission to drop the charges. UE then asked the court to dismiss the charges so they could not be used against the union in the future. The court agreed to UE's request.

Increasingly in the 1960s it became evident that UE and IUE would have to cooperate if they hoped to secure favorable contracts from the conglomerates. Although the 1966 strike against GE witnessed one of the first attempts at cooperation between the two unions, it was not until the 1969-1970 GE strike that the unions engaged in coordinated bargaining, along with the International Brotherhood of Teamsters,* to defeat GE. The February 1970 strike settlement with GE marked the first time in twenty years that the company agreed to a negotiated settlement.

The UE, which maintains its national headquarters in New York City, holds annual conventions. Principal officers include a president, a secretary-treasurer, and a director of organization. The general executive board is comprised of the above officials in addition to the president and secretary of each UE district. In 1973 the UE reported a membership of 165,000 located in 189 local unions.

For further information, see *UE News* published biweekly. See also James J. Matles and James Higgins, *Them and Us: Struggles of a Rank-and-File Union* (1974), and Walter Galenson, *The CIO Challenge to the AFL: A History of the American Labor Movement, 1935-1941* (1960).

Marie Tedesco

ELECTRICAL WORKERS; INTERNATIONAL BROTHERHOOD OF (IBEW). Organizing activities among electrical workers began shortly after the Civil War, but it was not until 1880 that modern trade unions began to appear in this field. In that year a group of telegraph linemen formed a local assembly of the Knights of Labor.* After the organization of other locals, a district council was established, but an unsuccessful general strike against telegraph companies in 1883 crushed the movement. The following year the United Order of Linemen, a secret organization with headquarters in Denver, gained some success in organizing linemen in the western states.

The impetus for the organization of a permanent national association grew directly from a St. Louis exposition of "electrical wonders" in 1890. The exposition, which employed large numbers of workers, attracted electricians from cities throughout the nation. Inevitably the workers began discussing working conditions in various cities as well as the long hours and low wages in St. Louis. The resulting dissatisfaction led to the organization of Federal Local Union 5221 of the American Federation of Labor* (AFL). Shortly thereafter a national convention of electrical workers convened in St. Louis on November 21, 1891. Ten delegates representing 300 members attended the meeting, and the National Brotherhood of Electrical Workers resulted. Henry Miller, a St. Louis lineman, was elected president, and he attended the AFL convention meeting in Birmingham a few days later and secured a national charter issued by the AFL on December 7, 1891.

During the first few years of its existence, membership in the electrical workers grew steadily, but the national economic depression of 1893 threatened the survival of the young union. By 1894 only eleven delegates representing eight locals attended the national convention in Washington, D.C. Nevertheless, the union not only survived the depression but by the end of the decade was making substantial membership gains. Organization of the

first Canadian local in 1899 inspired a name change to International Brotherhood of Electrical Workers.

The early years of the new century were difficult ones for the IBEW. The
absence of a full-time, paid leadership, a rash of unauthorized strikes, and a
constitutional provision requiring all convention decisions to be submitted to a
membership referendum all served to disrupt the effective operation of the
organization. The election of Frank J. McNulty in 1903 and the provision to
pay him a full-time salary resolved the first two problems, and a constitutional
amendment adopted in 1918 making the convention the supreme legislative
authority solved the third. The most difficult problem during these years,
however, was a five-year period of dual unionism in the electrical industry,
occurring between 1908 and 1913.

The split in the IBEW climaxed a long period of antagonism between linemen and wiremen, sectional differences, and personal jealousies. Two conventions met in 1908, one by the established McNulty-Collins faction and the
other by the Reid-Murphy faction, a secessionist group originally including
approximately three-quarters of the IBEW membership. The AFL attemped
to mediate the dispute, but when the Reid-Murphy faction refused to carry out
the recommendations of a special AFL committee, the executive council recognized the McNulty-Collins group as the legitimate officials of the IBEW. After
considerable acrimony, especially during strikes on the West Coast in 1912
and 1913, and a 1912 court decision favoring the McNulty group, AFL
president Samuel Gompers arranged a settlement between the two factions
under which seceding locals were permitted to reenter the IBEW without
penalty.

Along with conditions arising from World War I, reconciliation sparked a
large growth in membership. During this period, the IBEW established a separate department for telephone operators. The brotherhood had begun
organizing telephone operators as early as 1892, and in 1896 a woman served
as one of its two national organizers. By 1919 the IBEW had 148,072 members
as compared with 23,500 in 1913.

As it was for the labor movement nationally, postwar America was a period
of trial for the IBEW. The employers' open-shop drive, restrictive legislation,
frequent anti-labor injunctions, and the depression of 1920-1921 all took their
toll on IBEW membership, which declined to 56,349 in 1925. Nevertheless, the
decade of the 1920s was one of the most significant periods in IBEW history. In
1920 the Council on Industrial Relations came into existence by mutual agreement of the IBEW and the National Electrical Contractors Association. The
council, composed of an equal number representing employers and the IBEW,
provided a highly effective method of resolving industrial disputes in the electrical construction industry. In 1922 the Electrical Workers' Benefit Association, which provided a death benefit for union electricians, was reorganized on
a sound basis, and five years later a pension plan was adopted. The pension
plan was placed on a firm financial footing in 1946 when the members of the

National Electrical Contractors Association agreed to put 1 percent of their payroll into a special pension fund.

Although the brotherhood suffered during the early years of the Great Depression, New Deal labor legislation and World War II stimulated great union growth. The major problem confronting the IBEW during the 1930s resulted from the Congress of Industrial Organizations* (CIO)-chartered United Electrical, Radio, and Machine Workers of America* (UE), which challenged the IBEW in the organization of industrial workers in the electrical manufacturing field. In an effort to meet the challenge, the IBEW created a class "B" membership permitting the organization of workers in utility and manufacturing plants at low initiation and per-capita tax rates. "B" members were not eligible for death or pension benefits, and their voting rights were limited to one vote per local as opposed to one vote per member for "A" members. Because of the stigma of "second-class membership" and the vigorous organizing effort of the UE, the IBEW never enrolled large numbers of industrial workers in the electrical manufacturing industry.

Despite its shortcomings in the organization of unskilled industrial workers, the IBEW continued to grow and in the postwar period became one of the largest international unions in the United States. A 1941 membership of 200,000 jumped to 360,000 in 1946, 460,000 in 1955, and nearly 800,000 by 1970, making it the second largest AFL-CIO affiliate.

The IBEW, which maintains its national headquarters in Washington, D.C., holds quadrennial conventions. Principal officers include an international president, a secretary, a treasurer, and twelve vice-presidents elected by geographical district. The international executive committee consists of members elected from eight prescribed districts and a chairman elected at large. In 1973 the IBEW reported a membership of 956,579 located in 1,647 local unions.

For further information, see *The Electrical Workers' Journal* published monthly by the IBEW since 1893. Michael Mulcaire tells the story of the early years of the IBEW in *The International Brotherhood of Electrical Workers: A Study in Trade Union Structure and Functions* (1923). In *The CIO Challenge to the AFL: A History of the American Labor Movement, 1935-1941* (1960), Walter Galenson describes the conflicts between the UE and the IBEW.

ELEVATOR CONSTRUCTORS; INTERNATIONAL UNION OF (IUEC). Eleven delegates representing elevator construction workers in six cities met in Pittsburgh on July 18, 1901, and organized the National Union of Elevator Constructors. Two years later, delegates to the national convention voted to provide financial assistance to striking elevator constructors in Ottawa, Canada, and at the same time changed the name of the organization to the International Union of Elevator Constructors. During the same year, on June 1, the IUEC affiliated with the American Federation of Labor* (AFL).

The new international union, which sought "to bind together and unite the locals of which it is composed for mutual interest and protection," grew steadily during its early years. In 1909 membership reached the 2,000 figure, expanded to 5,000 in 1923, and surpassed 10,000 by 1930. Membership remained stable at the latter figure for nearly thirty years. This unusual stability, which encompassed years of depression and war, resulted from the development of a nationwide standard collective bargaining agreement (known as the Atlantic City plan) with major American elevator construction companies. The agreement not only provided for union recognition but established procedures for determining the basic economic terms of employment.

From its organization the IUEC confronted almost constant jurisdictional conflict, primarily with the International Association of Machinists,* the International Brotherhood of Electrical Workers,* and the United Association of Plumbers and Steam Fitters.* At the 1914 AFL national convention, the IUEC won a hard-fought, landmark jurisdictional decision confirming its right to organize all classes of elevator constructors. After another long jurisdictional dispute—this time with the Building Service Employees' International Union*—the IUEC won another significant award when the AFL gave it jurisdiction over elevator operators and starters.

Following the adoption of the Atlantic City plan, nearly fifty years of relative peace and harmony characterized relations between workers and employers in the elevator construction industry. This atmosphere of amicability ended in 1966 when the IUEC and employers party to the standard agreement failed to reach a settlement on union demands for better fringe benefits, especially concerning welfare and pension programs. A nationwide fifty-three day strike resulted in which the IUEC won major concessions. A 101-day national strike in 1972 brought further modifications of the standard agreement. During the same years, primarily as a result of increased building activity, the IUEC experienced its first significant membership gains since the 1920s.

The IUEC, which maintains its national headquarters in Philadelphia, holds quinquennial conventions. Principal officers include a general president, an assistant to the general president, eight vice-presidents, and a general secretary-treasurer. The general executive board is composed of the above officials. In 1973 the IUEC reported a membership of 17,683 located in 109 local unions.

For further information, see *The Elevator Constructor* issued monthly by the IUEC. Unfortunately, little published information exists on the IUEC, but basic information can be found in *Bulletins No. 420, 506*, and *618*, Bureau of Labor Statistics, U.S. Department of Labor (1926, 1929, 1936), and Florence Peterson, *Handbook of Labor Unions* (1944).

ENGINEERS; INTERNATIONAL UNION OF OPERATING (IUOE). Creation of the first national union of steam engineers occurred nearly a century after the development of the steam engine. The National Association of Stationary Engineers (NASE), a self-help society that specifically rejected trade union activities, was originally organized in 1880 on a local basis in Providence, Rhode Island, and in 1882, it became a national organization. Becoming disillusioned with the meager results of self-help, many NASE members established local organizations with a trade union orientation. Meanwhile, the Brewery Workers Union* actively organized stationary engineers in its jurisdiction, and local unions of hoisting engineers appeared. Many local unions affiliated directly with the American Federation of Labor* (AFL) as federal labor unions, and on December 7, 1896, six of them formed the National Union of Steam Engineers in Cincinnati, Ohio. The new union received an AFL charter on May 7, 1897. After the affiliation of Canadian locals the following year, the name was changed to the International Union of Steam Engineers (IUSE).

The early history of the IUSE was characterized by serious internal and external challenges. The IUSE was essentially a loosely organized association of autonomous local unions, and conflicts between national and local leaders retarded union growth for nearly fifty years. Local and national officers disagreed about apprenticeship policy, traveling cards, and collective bargaining issues. More seriously, local autonomy led to continual jurisdictional conflicts between geographical units and various branches of the IUSE. Finally, dual unions, technological change, and an unstable market structure plus the scattered labor force and diverse occupational interests retarded centralized policy making.

Consequently, the IUSE grew only slowly during its first six years; by 1902 membership approached 8,000. While the establishment of full-time, salaried officers and the initiation of an organizing drive added many new members, the vigorous open-shop offensive launched by employers in 1904 sharply reduced membership gains that a more stable administrative structure and active organizing drives should have produced.

Responding to changes in technology, the organization was renamed the International Union of Steam and Operating Engineers (IUSOE) in 1912. The internal combustion engine, water turbines, and electricity gradually replaced steam power, and the IUSOE expanded its jurisdictional grasp to include workers operating from these new energy bases. The years following 1912 produced other significant changes in the IUSOE. Prior to 1912 stationary engineers constituted the overwhelming majority of union membership and controlled much of the IUSOE's executive leadership. Although the stationary engineers retained numerical superiority until 1940, between 1912 and 1927 the hoisting and portable engineers assumed an increasingly important role in the union.

IUSOE membership grew dramatically during World War I, reaching a figure of over 40,000 in 1920, but the renewal of the open-shop offensive after the war, the weak financial position of the union, and the generally hostile attitude of government at various levels eliminated many of the membership gains. By 1924, IUSOE membership declined to 27,000.

The most significant development in this transitional period for the IUSOE was the merger with the International Brotherhood of Steam Shovel and Dredgemen (IBSSD). The IBSSD had been organized by steam shovel operators in Chicago in 1896. Although most steam shovel operators had originally worked on railroad construction, excavation projects such as the Chicago drainage canal, the Soo Locks, and the Welland and Panama canals not only opened new employment opportunities but also brought many steam shovel operators from diverse locations together on one job. Later strip mining of copper and coal served the same function.

The early history of the IBSSD was characterized by internal divisions, continual warfare with the IUSOE, and, between 1903 and 1915, dual union-ism. The IBSSD affiliated with the AFL on January 13, 1915, but its charter was suspended on March 1, 1919, when it refused to amalgamate with the IUSOE. After years of bitter conflict, the IBSSD finally merged with the IUSOE on April 1, 1927. Under terms of the merger, the IBSSD districts were chartered as IUSOE locals, and Steam Shovel and Dredgemen officials were integrated into the IUSOE bureaucracy. More as a result of changing technology than the merger, the union was renamed the International Union of Operating Engineers in September 1927.

The merger with the IBSSD and the increased employment of operating engineers for building and highway construction projects opened important new organizing opportunities to the IUOE. Nevertheless, the effects of the Great Depression, especially in the building trades, and the acceleration of internal conflicts between local and national officers prevented the IUOE from taking advantage of these opportunities. Despite its problems during the depression, through the use of direct international supervision of rebellious locals and the amalgamation of small local unions into market-wide and state-wide organizations, the IUOE was in a strong position to take advantage of the organizing opportunities resulting from the United States' entry into World War II and the revived economy.

Under the skillful leadership of William E. Maloney, who took office in 1940, the IUOE became financially secure for the first time in its history. Moreover, Maloney not only continued his predecessor's policy of negotiating national agreements but made the national agreement standard IUOE policy. The return of economic prosperity, expanded employment opportunities for operating engineers, and the consolidation of centralized authority in the IUOE resulted in tremendous membership gains during the 1940s and 1950s. A membership of 58,000 in 1940 increased to over 160,000 in 1950 and 300,000 in 1960. While growing in wealth and power, however, the IUOE's public image suffered from accusations of corruption and labor racketeering. The hearings of the Senate Select Committee on Improper Activities in the Labor or Management Field did much to give these charges national publicity. Instances of corruption undoubtedly did occur, but given the conditions of the industry and the decentralized nature of the organization, remarkably few charges of corruption were ever proven.

The IUOE, which maintains its national headquarters in Washington, D.C., holds quadrennial conventions. Full-time officers include a general president, a secretary-treasurer, and ten vice-presidents. The above officers also constitute the general executive board. In 1973 the IUOE reported a membership of 401,537 located in 260 local unions.

For further information, see *The International Operating Engineer* published monthly by the IUOE. See also Garth L. Mangum's excellent study, *The Operating Engineers: The Economic History of a Trade Union* (1964).

FARM EQUIPMENT AND METAL WORKERS OF AMERICA; UNITED (FE). Union efforts to organize the labor force of farm equipment manufacturers was a long, violent, and, until the World War II period, largely frustrating experience. Prior to 1886 there had been some collective bargaining in the industry, but efforts to initiate the eight-hour day at the McCormick Harvester plant in Chicago precipitated the historic Haymarket Square riot. Thereafter, McCormick resolutely determined to avoid unionization. Vigorous open-shop drives in 1904 and 1921 eliminated union gains made at the turn of the century and during World War I. Like such other open-shop bastions as steel and automobiles, farm equipment manufacturers, led by McCormick Harvester, instituted elaborate employee representation plans in a determined effort to avoid independent unionism.

Favorable legislation, sympathetic governmental policies, and the inauguration of the Congress of Industrial Organizations* (CIO) combined to revive interest in bringing farm equipment manufacturers under union contract. The largest firm in the industry, the International Harvester Company (IH), provided the focal point of organizing efforts. Union activity began under the auspices of the farm equipment branch of the Steel Workers Organizing Committee, which gained control of the employer-sponsored Works Council at McCormick's Chicago Tractor Works in 1938. Later the same year, an independent Farm Equipment Workers Organizing Committee (FE) was established, but initial successes were not soon repeated. Resulting from its own anti-union traditions, the extensive and long-lived company union structure, and the 1937-1938 economic recession, by 1941 IH remained one of the few large companies to withstand union organizing efforts.

As a result of charges filed by the FE in 1938, the National Labor Relations Board (NLRB) announced a decision on February 8, 1941, branding the former Works Councils (then designated independent unions) as company-dominated organizations and ordering their dissolution. Assuming they could not win an NLRB representational election in key IH plants, FE officials nevertheless decided to strike IH in hopes of gaining union recognition and/ or wage increases useful in enhancing FE's prestige among the workers before a representational election. Meanwhile, the American Federation of Labor* (AFL) organized several federal labor unions in the industry and requested an immediate NLRB election.

Despite a small minority of enrolled workers, FE succeeded in closing IH. Hoping to conciliate the dispute, Secretary of Labor Frances Perkins then intervened. Battle lines and strategies were clearly drawn. Officials at IH, AFL headquarters, and in the federal bureaucracy clearly assumed the AFL would win a representational election. FE and CIO leaders also projected an AFL victory and desperately wanted to avoid an election until concessions could be wrung from IH, thus giving them a campaign issue. FE lost the bureaucratic skirmish; IH plants reopened, and a representational election was scheduled for the early summer of 1941. To the surprise of everyone, including FE officials, FE won four of the six contested plants. The victories gave FE control of the major plants in the McCormick empire.

Negotiations between the union and IH soon reached an impasse, and the conflict was once again in the hands of federal agencies. This time the FE received a more sympathetic hearing, and the recommendations of the National War Labor Board (NWLB), including the union's much desired maintenance of membership provision, were reluctantly accepted by IH.

For FE, chartered by the CIO as the United Farm Equipment and Metal Workers of America in 1942, the postwar years revealed how little IH's antiunion disposition had changed. The company immediately cancelled the maintenance of membership agreement and demanded adjustments in other NWLB concessions won by the union. As a result strikes almost inevitably accompanied contract negotiations. In only one instance between 1946 and 1954 was a contract (1949) negotiated without a strike.

Three somewhat related circumstances explain the extended period of conflict in industrial relations at IH. First, and probably least important, was the FE's left-wing leadership. Union leaders actively cooperated with Communist elements in the labor movement, supported the Soviet Union's foreign policy line, and supported Henry Wallace's 1948 presidential candidacy. It could be argued that FE officials refused to recognize the legitimacy of management and had no desire for peaceful relations; yet the turbulent nature of labor relations at IH was not confined to FE but characterized relations with non-Communist and anti-Communist unions as well.

Second, an intense inter-union rivalry disrupted labor relations. As early as 1939 the United Automobile Workers* (UAW) began organizing workers manufacturing farm implements and secured contracts with Allis-Chalmers and J. I. Chase plus a few IH plants. Throughout the 1940s and early 1950s, the two unions bitterly contested each other for the loyalty of the farm equipment labor force. Concessions wrought from employers represented useful propaganda weapons in these skirmishes.

Finally, and perhaps most important, IH owners and managers clearly failed to recognize or accept the new reality of industrial relations in the United States. The company adopted an anti-union policy making the peaceful resolution of grievances virtually impossible; it attempted to play off the rival unions against each other and quickly took advantage of the so-called employers free speech provision of the Taft-Hartley Act to launch an attack on the union. More than anything else, company intransigence disrupted labor relations at IH.

Because of the overlapping jurisdictions claimed by FE and the UAW, as early as 1940 CIO officials recommended an amalgamation of the FE and the larger, more conservative UAW. The FE rejected these suggestions and during the postwar years successfully withstood UAW raids on FE membership in key IH plants. Finally, in 1949 the CIO expelled the FE after it ignored orders to merge with the UAW. Instead, it merged with the United Electrical Workers* (UE), which the CIO also expelled a few months later as a "Communist-dominated" union. Thereafter, FE became the UE-FE. Although UE-FE continued to defend its membership from UAW raids, a strike in 1952 signaled the demise of the maverick union. In their continuing rivalry with the UAW, UE-FE leaders sought in 1952 to negotiate a contract much more favorable than the UAW's existing five-year contract. After a disastrous thirteen-week strike, the UE-FE accepted terms less favorable than either those existing before the strike or the provisions of the UAW contract. Moreover, the settlement required union members to request the checkoff of union dues and eliminated procedures permitting union stewards to handle grievances during working hours. These provisions undermined the union's financial stability (only 50 percent of the workers signed dues deduction requests) and antagonized staff members who viewed the UAW's grievance procedure with growing envy. In 1954 several UE-FE locals opened negotiations with the UAW, and shortly thereafter, UAW officials decided to again challenge the UE-FE in representational elections. The UAW's success marked the final demise of the UE-FE.

The FE, which maintained its headquarters in Chicago, held biennial conventions. Principal officers included a president, vice-president, and secretary-treasurer. The international executive board consisted of full-time officers and five district vice-presidents. At the time of the merger with UE, FE was paying per-capita taxes to the CIO on 43,000 members.

For further information, see the *Farm Equipment News* published semi-monthly by FE. See also Robert Ozanne's *A Century of Labor-Management Relations at McCormick and International Harvester* (1967), a brilliant analysis, and Max M. Kampelman's *The Communist Party vs. the C.I.O.: A Study in Power Politics* (1957), a hard-line, anti-Communist study.

FARM WORKERS' UNION; UNITED (UFW). The United Farm Workers' Union began in April 1962 when Cesar Chavez formed the National Farm Workers' Association (FWA) at Delano, California. Building from the grass roots, FWA at first eschewed large monetary contributions and stressed total worker involvement, including relatively high union dues of $3.50 per month. The organization also avoided emotional mass meetings and strikes, concentrating on home visits and developing leadership. Its initial followers were Mexican-Americans, although Filipinos, Anglos, and Negroes also comprised part of the labor force. By the summer of 1964 the FWA became self-supporting, with more than fifty local organizations and about 1,000 dues-paying members. Although more a social movement than a labor union at this time, FWA conducted two small strikes in the summer of 1965, which brought higher wages and rehiring of discharged workers.

More important activity followed in the fall. The impetus came with repeal of Public Law 78, which ended the bracero program, continuation of the program under another name by the U.S. Department of Labor, and the resulting discontent among Filipino farm workers led by Larry Itliong of the Agricultural Workers' Organizing Committee (AWOC) of the American Federation of Labor-Congress of Industrial Organizations* (AFL-CIO). Receiving twenty cents less than the government-established $1.40 hourly wage of the bracero, Filipino workers walked out of the Delano grape fields on September 8. Weak and short of resources, the FWA nevertheless honored the Filipino picket lines and soon joined the strike. Undeterred by hostile local police and grower appeals to the courts, FWA expanded the strike in December to a consumer boycott, particularly of the products of Schenley Industries. By the spring of 1966 help had come from the United Automobile Workers,* which pledged $5,000 a month support, and from political figures such as Senator Robert Kennedy. Toward the end of the Lenten season, Chavez led the FWA on a 230-mile *peregrinaciones* (pilgrimage) to Sacramento to request action on farm worker collective bargaining rights from Governor Edmund "Pat" Brown, Sr. As a result, Schenley recognized the FWA and eventually signed contracts for a wage of $1.75, a union hiring hall, and fringe benefits previously unheard of for farm workers. The DiGiorgio Corporation also responded to the *peregrinaciones*, calling for representative elections, but it shortly urged its workers to join the International Brotherhood of Teamsters* (IBT), which had organized truck drivers and cannery and packinghouse workers. At an election on August 30, Chavez's union, having that month merged with Itliong's AWOC to form the United Farm Workers Organizing Committee (UFWOC), won two-thirds of the votes at DiGiorgio. Other victories followed, and by 1967 UFWOC represented the farm workers of the major California wineries.

UFWOC immediately began concentrating on the growers of table grapes, a more difficult assignment because of the absence of brand names and the standardized character of the product, which invited nonunion growers to surreptitiously use the boxes of union-approved growers. Consequently, UFWOC eventually boycotted all California table grapes. By summer 1969 many growers faced bankruptcy and began bargaining with UFWOC, but negotiations floundered over the use of pesticides, an issue Chavez took up in 1968 because of the poisonous effects on nearly all farm workers. The "great grape boycott" finally ended in the summer of 1970, and UFWOC signed three-year contracts with the major California growers.

The UFWOC, soon to become the United Farm Workers, AFL-CIO, moved quickly into the California lettuce and strawberry fields and into the citrus groves of Florida, where in February 1972 the Minute Maid Division of the Coca Cola Company, the state's largest grower, signed a three-year contract. In that year, the UFW claimed 55,000 members and over 200 contracts. Wages were higher in areas the union controlled, and union hiring halls replaced the infamous labor contractors. In addition, farm workers had toilets in the field, rest periods, ice water, health benefits, and a pension fund. On each ranch five-man committees elected by the workers supervised day-to-day implementation of the contract in California, while four UFW service centers performed similar tasks in Florida, administered the Robert F. Kennedy health program, made work referrals, provided legal services, trained union stewards, and engaged in community development work.

In the spring of 1973, UFW's fortunes dramatically changed with the entrance of the Teamsters into the lettuce fields. Although the two union rivals formed a "no-raiding" agreement in 1967 and again in 1970, the Teamster power and presence continued ominously as the UFW edged toward its triumph over the grape growers. But the Teamsters violated their agreements, and by 1971 UFW negotiations with the lettuce growers were stalemated. The Teamsters' motives for continued meddling with the farm workers were best expressed by William Grami, head of the farm workers' division of the Western Conference: "It enhances our bargaining power for the rest of the workers." The Teamsters also opposed many farm worker strikes, which put their permanent members out of work.

There were few UFW gains throughout 1971, and in 1972 UFW had to divert precious resources to a battle against Proposition 22, a grower-sponsored proposal on the California ballot outlawing secondary boycotts, in effect, a union-destroying device. In an address to the American Farm Bureau Federation Convention in December 1972, Frank Fitzsimmons, IBT president, urged an alliance between the Teamsters and American agribusiness. Fitzsimmons later announced a renegotiation of the lettuce contracts and warned the UFW to stay away from the lettuce fields or the Teamsters would retaliate by organizing the grape growers. The UFW understood the seriousness of the threat but rejected it defiantly. When the first of the UFW grape contracts came up for renewal in the spring of 1973, growers abandoned the UFW and signed with the Teamsters.

Called a "sweetheart deal" by Chavez and "disgraceful union busting" by AFL-CIO president George Meany, the Teamster raid brought to UFW a $1.6 million strike fund from the AFL-CIO and other aid from the UAW. But the assault unleashed an unprecedented wave of violence and brutality against UFW pickets by imported Teamster "guards" and Los Angeles freight handlers, referred to as "the animals" even by their union brothers, resulting in two deaths and more than 300 injuries, sixty by gunshot wounds. In addition, more than 3,000 UFW pickets were jailed by hostile law officers. Forced to abandon picketing, the UFW returned to the boycott and later to "submarine" or spy tactics, which sought to lower quality and slow the pace of Teamster workers. With the strike fund exhausted by the end of 1973, the UFW retained only twelve contracts, and its membership soon dropped below 5,000.

The Teamster victory returned the corrupt contract labor system and union control from above. There were no membership meetings or elections in the Teamster Farm Workers Union, Local 1973, and a figurehead Mexican-American, David B. Castro, became the local's appointed secretary-treasurer as a counterpart to Chavez. With over 350 contracts by 1974, the Teamsters abandoned some of their "sweetheart" practices. They negotiated an hourly wage only ten cents below that of the UFW, with a medical plan and pensions, but most benefits went to permanent farm workers. Despite worker gains and increasing costs, growers preferred Teamster contracts, which preserved their control over the work force, the basic issue in the controversy, which had ended with the establishment of UFW hiring halls and local committees. Although these UFW institutions operated ineptly at first, they became instruments for community change bitterly resented by the growers who also opposed UFW restrictions on the use of pesticides, a matter of no concern to the Teamsters.

As 1975 approached, the struggle continued, but the California political climate significantly changed with the election of Edmund "Jerry" Brown, Jr., as governor. After weeks of labor strife in 1975, the California legislature, in an emergency session called by the governor, passed a law in May providing for balloting within seven days after workers on a farm petitioned for union representation. A newly created Agricultural Labor Relations Board would supervise elections to be held only during the season of high employment. Secondary boycotts of distributors and retailers were prohibited, although the union duly certified as winning the election could appeal to consumers to boycott certain products. Effective on August 28, the law would test UFW claims of solid support from a majority of farm workers while prohibiting one aspect of the secondary boycott so effective in previous UFW struggles.

The UFW maintains its national headquarters in Keene, California. Full-time officers include a director, a secretary, and a treasurer. In 1973 the UFW reported a membership of 20,000.

For further information, see *El Malcriado* issued biweekly. Several books have been published that discuss UFW activities. Among the better ones are:

Joan London and Henry Anderson, *So Shall Ye Reap: The Story of Cesar Chavez and the Farm Workers' Movement* (1970); Peter Mathiessen, *Sal Si Peudes Cesar Chavez and the New Revolution* (1969); Mark Day, *Forty Acres* (1971); John E. Dunne, *Delano: The Story of the California Grape Strike* (1967); and George D. Horwitz, *La Causa: The California Grape Strike* (1970).

Merl E. Reed

FARMERS UNION; SOUTHERN TENANT (STFU). In July 1934, near Tyronza in eastern Arkansas, eighteen sharecroppers, black and white, met to discuss their deteriorating economic situation. At the suggestion of H(arry) L(eland) Mitchell and Clay East, Tyronza Socialists and small businessmen to whom the sharecroppers had appealed for leadership, they agreed to form what became the Southern Tenant Farmers' Union (STFU). The group opened union membership to both races.

The impetus for STFU was the cotton program of the Agricultural Adjustment Administration (AAA). The lot of the sharecropper, never enviable, worsened under the AAA program of scarcity during 1933 and 1934, which squeezed agricultural workers beyond endurance. Federal funds received for taking cotton land out of production went entirely to the landlords who had to share with the tenants only the parity payments on the reduced crop. Even this money often went to the landlords who handled it as they desired. While landowner income rose, sometimes doubling, tenant income declined. The economic destruction of the sharecroppers continued when planters began shifting to wage work, an illegal practice tolerated by the AAA's Cotton Section in Washington, D.C.

The STFU began organizing locals in eastern Arkansas, and at the union's first annual convention in January 1935, delegates adopted a constitution and elected officers representing both races. Meanwhile, planter resistance to union activity stiffened, and arrests, beatings, threats, and intimidation of STFU organizers became usual. In spite of such deep planter hostility, STFU leaders urged their members to pursue passive resistance while union officials gathered evidence to prove that landlords were violating their cotton contracts by evicting sharecroppers. Although carefully documented, the STFU charges were rejected by the planter-oriented AAA Cotton Section. Nevertheless, the STFU struggled on, developing tenant farmer leadership and forming a workable race policy. Mitchell, himself a former sharecropper, became executive secretary and provided strong, stable administrative guidance. The presidency and vice-presidency of the STFU eventually went to a white and to a black sharecropper, J. R. Butler and Edward B. McKinney. The resolution of the race question ultimately depended on local conditions. In some instances, the two-local pattern was followed, with separate locals for white and black members; in other situations, integrated locals and leadership prevailed.

During 1935 the STFU could well have drifted into oblivion had not planter violence brought the desperation of the sharecroppers into the national limelight. A "reign of terror" in eastern Arkansas, which continued from late March to May, was carried out by local police officers, plantation hirelings, and landowners themselves. In response, a host of prominent people and organizations began voicing support for the embattled sharecroppers, including Norman Thomas and the Socialist party, theologians and various Protestant denominations, national magazines, the National Association for the Advancement of Colored People, and the American Civil Liberties Union. Many solicited funds to aid the STFU; among them was Gardner Jackson, formerly with the AAA Consumers' Council, who also contributed heavily from his family fortune.

Although such philanthropy was welcome, Mitchell believed the STFU must become "a real union" to succeed. Expansion was important, and by summer STFU locals were spreading beyond the delta region to Oklahoma. By August 1935 STFU members, nearly 12,000 strong, voted overwhelmingly to strike for a one dollar pay rate for 100 pounds of cotton. The strike precipitated new landowner terrorism, but succeeded in raising the pay rate from forty and sixty cents to seventy-five cents when it was called off by the union in October. It was a stunning STFU success, arousing renewed nationwide interest and spurring union expansion into southeast Missouri—the bootheel area. Despite these successes, STFU efforts for recognition were rebuffed at the Atlantic City convention of the American Federation of Labor* (AFL) in October 1935.

But worse setbacks awaited the STFU in Arkansas. With the approach of the new year and contract renewal, many sharecroppers were evicted. When Mitchell advised his organizers to set up tent colonies along the highway to publicize cropper misery, infuriated delta planters blacklisted all union tenants, forcing thousands to leave, and supported a new wave of brutal attacks against union meetings and individual organizers. In this new crisis, Gardner Jackson in Washington became practically a one-man lobby for STFU, successfully persuading Works Progress Administration (WPA) leaders to authorize government relief for evicted tenants; however, local WPA officials, controlled by the landowners, refused to carry out federal WPA policies. Also, partly through Jackson's efforts, the La Follette Civil Liberties Committee was created, but it never investigated civil liberties in Arkansas because powerful southern senators denied it the funds.

As weeding time arrived in the spring of 1936, Mitchell turned again to "real union" activity. The STFU voted to strike for higher wages during chopping season. In response, the usual pattern of terrorism resumed and continued with increasing ferocity into the summer and fall. The strike failed, but STFU leaders and their allies succeeded in turning every incident of brutality into a rising groundswell of nationwide indignation at a time when a presidential election approached. President Roosevelt's attitude began to change. The

Federal Bureau of Investigation, instead of the AAA, began investigating complaints in Arkansas, and federal grand juries handed down indictments against lawless Arkansas lawmen. The administration became convinced that the farm tenancy problem had to be remedied. The Bankhead-Jones Tenant Act followed in the summer of 1937 along with the creation of the Farm Security Administration, although both fell far short of the need.

By 1937, the STFU began seeking affiliation with the Congress of Industrial Organizations* (CIO), but the response was lukewarm. Then in July 1937 the United Cannery, Packing, and Allied Workers of America* (UCAPAWA) was created as a CIO international union under the leadership of Donald Henderson, a Communist. The easiest way to the CIO for STFU was by affiliation with UCAPAWA. Receiving promises of autonomy from Henderson, STFU delegates voted to join that CIO union in September 1937. But trouble soon erupted over Henderson's insistence that dues of fifty cents a month be paid directly to UCAPAWA, a moot point since most STFU members were too poor to pay dues. Other STFU-UCAPAWA hostilities involved disagreements over STFU autonomy. In August 1938, schisms appeared within the STFU leadership itself over an alleged Communist takeover, the secession of the Oklahoma locals, and the discontent of former Vice-President E. B. McKinney, who leaned toward black separatism. With STFU wracked by internal dissension, UCAPAWA voted down a proposal for STFU autonomy at its December 1938 convention and succeeded in capturing the allegiance of some STFU locals, including those in the Missouri bootheel under the shrewd black organizer, Reverend Owen Whitfield, who led a Missouri highway demonstration of evicted tenants early in 1939.

The STFU executive council withdrew from UCAPAWA in March 1939. The break marked the end, effectively, of the farm union movement in the 1930s. It also completely alienated Gardner Jackson and other financial contributors, many of whom deplored Mitchell's public anti-Communist attacks on UCAPAWA's leadership. Thereafter, STFU could count only forty locals among its membership. After unsuccessful attempts at affiliation with the AFL, the International Ladies' Garment Workers,* and the National Farmers' Union in 1939 and 1940, the STFU faded from existence by 1943. The STFU probably had a greater impact as a pressure group than in organizing sharecroppers and would take considerable credit for creating the climate leading to changes in government policies as well as making contributions to the content of some legislative enactments. Also, the origins of the La Follette committee can be traced directly to outrages against STFU members in Arkansas.

The STFU, which maintained its national headquarters in Memphis, held annual conventions. Principal officers included a president, vice-president, secretary, and legal investigator. Composition of the executive council varied between seven and eleven members, including officers.

For the early history of STFU, see David E. Conrad, *The Forgotten Farmers: The Story of the Sharecroppers in the New Deal* (1965), who sympathizes with the sharecroppers but places blame for the AAA schism on the "impracticality" of its Legal Division; Donald H. Grubbs, *Cry from Cotton: The STFU and the New Deal* (1971), who stresses the "public relations" features of STFU and castigates the AAA Cotton Section for partiality to the landowners; and Louis Cantor, *A Prologue to the Protest Movement: The Missouri Sharecropper Roadside Demonstration of 1939* (1969), who tells that dramatic story well.

Merl E. Reed

FEDERACIÓN LIBRE DE LOS TRABAJADORES DE PUERTO RICO. Established on June 18, 1899, at San Juan, Puerto Rico, the Federación Libre was for many years the American Federation of Labor* (AFL) affiliate on the island. It still maintains offices in San Juan and ties with the international trade union community.

Under Spanish rule, Puerto Rican labor had not organized, at least not until the closing months of the Spanish colonial period. There had been workingmen's societies, but these had been social and religious, generally guided by local ecclesiastical or military authorities. These brotherhoods (or *gremios*) did not bargain collectively, and there was no tradition of working-class cooperation or initiative upon which a trade union movement might be built. Spanish Puerto Rico was quiet, provincial, dominated largely by appointive Spaniards and an insular aristocracy, an imperial backwash.

Santiago Iglesias Pantín (1872-1939) chief architect of the Puerto Rican trade union movement and one of the leading advocates of hemispheric trade union solidarity, was born in Coruña, Spain. As a carpenter's apprentice, he was introduced to the theories of Marx and Bakunin and of the Spanish republicans. In the mid-1880s, Iglesias resettled in Cuba where he became an activist in the Cuban trade union movement. In 1896, when the Cuban revolution broke out, labor organizing became a dangerous and subversive calling, and Iglesias moved into exile in San Juan. There, after a few months of quiet agitation, a labor paper, *Ensayo Obrero*, was launched (May 1, 1897) and a small body of labor activists, largely new recruits, assembled around its offices. Almost at once, a split developed over the role of labor in the political sphere. Iglesias, leading a generally "pure and simple" trade union group, established the Centro de Estudios Económicos-Sociales. On March 25, 1898, the Centro sponsored a rally at the Teatro Municipal in San Juan, the first mass meeting called by the Puerto Rican workers at their own initiative. About 3,000 attended, complaining of arbitrary and vicious harassment of labor by the government. But as had happened at Tompkins Square and in the Haymarket, a detachment of police was dispatched, the meeting was broken up, and, through the next several days, leaders of the local Socialist and trade union communities, including Iglesias, were arrested.

The coming of the Americans marked a new era in insular labor history. In October 1898, the *Porvenir Social* replaced the defunct *Ensayo Obrero* and, shortly thereafter, the Federación Regional de los Trabajadores de Puerto Rico was created. This new body vowed cooperation with the American authorities and moved to dispatch a delegation to the mainland to establish relations with the AFL and with the Socialist Labor party (SLP). But the Federación Regional split into two factions—in part, the result of general conditions under the occupation and, in part, due to the temporary illness of Iglesias, which created a leadership vacuum. The Federación Regional became the labor wing of the insular Republican party.

On June 18, 1899, Iglesias called a meeting of the "nonpolitical" trade unionists, and the Federación Libre was founded along lines similar in Iglesias' judgment to the AFL. The same meeting established the Partido Obrero Socialista. Although the two organizations were technically separate, it appears that the membership was largely the same, and the *Porvenir Social* was proclaimed the official organ both of the party and of the federation. This interrelationship continued through the years as did repercussions of the clash between the Federación Libre and the Federación Regional.

An indigenous movement, both trade unionist and political, had thus been established within Puerto Rico, largely the result of the work, ideas, and personality of Santiago Iglesias, prior to the first direct contacts with the American mainland trade union or Socialist communities. During the summer of 1899, the Partido Obrero Socialista moved to affiliate with the American SLP. Before affiliation occurred, however, the SLP split into two factions: the regulars led by Daniel DeLeon and the dissident "kangaroo" faction led by Morris Hillquit. The Puerto Rican Socialists associated themselves with the latter group. When the AFL met in convention in Louisville, in 1900, it was confronted with an appeal from the Federación Libre for affiliation and assistance. Iglesias was invited to Washington to confer with AFL president Samuel Gompers and the AFL executive council. A charter was issued to the insular trade union body, $3,000 was authorized from the AFL treasury for organizational purposes and, on November 2, 1901, Iglesias traveled to Puerto Rico as the general organizer for the AFL.

For over forty years Iglesias remained the principal spokesman for the AFL in Puerto Rico and for the Federación Libre on the mainland. The insular federation was consistent in its advocacy of closer ties with the mainland and a permanent relationship. It championed constitutional reform and a place for labor within the insular government—fighting vigorously for better education, housing, and diet for the Puerto Rican masses, for a broadening of the voting franchise, for the creation of an insular department of labor, and for laws to protect child and women workers. Of special concern was the condition of agricultural labor. Led by Santiago Iglesias the Federación Libre argued continuously for a more effective campaign through which to organize the Spanish-speaking workers, not just in Puerto Rico, but in Cuba, Florida, New

York, the American Southwest, and broadly throughout the Americas. From 1925 until his death in 1939, Iglesias served as secretary of the Pan-American Federation of Labor, with which the Federación Libre was affiliated.

The Federación Libre was supported by an active labor press. Aside from *Ensayo Obrero* and *El Porvenir Social*, noted above, and *Justicia*, all associated with or edited by Iglesias, and the later *Boletin del Trabajo*, journals designed to promote the work of the federation appeared in most of the insular towns; unfortunately, few copies have survived.

With the death of Iglesias in 1939, followed shortly by that of Rafael Alonso Torres, a continuing force within the Federacion Libre and in insular politics, factions began to develop and fragmentation followed. Changing political attitudes, the rise of the Congress of Industrial Organizations,* and Communist and other radical agitation played a part. In the early 1950s, growing tensions between the Federación Libre and the national AFL resulted in a transfer of the insular charter to the rival Federación del Trabajo de Puerto Rico.

For further information, see Santiago Iglesias Pantín, *Luchas Emancipadoras, Cronicas de Puerto Rico* (1958), and Ráfael Alonso Torres, *Cuarenta Años de Lucha Proletaria* (1939). The most comprehensive treatment of the early years of the Federación Libre is *El Obrerismo en Puerto Rico, Época de Santiago Iglesias, 1896-1905* (1973) by Igualdad Iglesias de Pagan. See also William G. Whittaker, "The Santiago Iglesias Case, 1901-1902: Origins of American Trade Union Involvement in Puerto Rico," *The Americas* (April 1968), and Clarence Senior, *Santiago Iglesias, Labor Crusader* (1972).

William G. Whittaker

FEDERAL EMPLOYEES; NATIONAL FEDERATION OF (NFFE). At the beginning of the twentieth century, little systematic organization characterized employment in the federal civil service. There were relatively few career appointments, no systematic classification of duties, no retirement system, and great variations in the personnel administration of the various agencies and departments of the federal government. Although the Pendleton Act of 1883 had created a civil service system, patronage remained the fastest and easiest way to gain federal employment.

In addition to the above conditions, civil service employees were concerned about the failure of the U.S. Congress to effect a general pay increase for nearly fifty years. General unhappiness over low wages became more intense when the cost of living rose rapidly during the inflationary spiral accompanying World War I. Oblivious to the growing discontent in the civil service, Congressman William P. Borlund of Missouri attached an amendment to an appropriation bill increasing the minimum daily hours of government employees. Instead of complacently accepting this measure as they so often had done previously, federal workers vigorously protested, and the American Federation of Labor* (AFL), long interested in organizing federal workers, supported the protesting government workers. When the Borlund amendment lost by a margin of 282 to 67, many observers credited organized labor with defeating the measure.

Agitation over the Borlund amendment and the AFL's vigorous activities in behalf of government workers led to the organization of several federal labor unions directly affiliated with the AFL. The organization of government employees spread rapidly, and by the late summer of 1917 more than fifty federal locals existed. As a consequence, on September 24, the AFL chartered the National Federation of Federal Employees with jurisdiction over workers employed in the U.S. civil service. The new national union had a chartering membership of nearly 10,000.

Organizing effectively, the NFFE grew to nearly 40,000 by 1920, but membership fluctuated erratically during the 1920s, and by the end of the decade, the union had lost about 20 percent of the 1920 figure. Union officials, however, could find satisfaction in other developments during the decade. In 1920 the U.S. Congress enacted a retirement plan for federal employees, and three years later the first federal classification act went into effect.

One of the NFFE's more important watersheds occurred on December 1, 1931, when it withdrew from the AFL. Events leading to this action began when the AFL, supporting several of its craft union affiliates, opposed the report of the U.S. Personnel Classification Board, which recommended that the civil service classification system be extended to include the skilled crafts. The NFFE strongly favored the extension of the classification principle and protested the AFL's stand by withdrawing from the federation.

Approximately 500 NFFE members in twelve locals objected to this action, and they became the nucleus of the American Federation of Government Employees* (AFGE), chartered by the AFL on August 18, 1932, and given the NFFE's old jurisdiction. The NFFE did well in its competition with the new AFL affiliate until the mid-1950s when AFGE began a period of rapid growth at the expense of the declining NFFE. Although claiming a much larger membership, by 1964 the NFFE was the exclusive bargaining representative of only 8,828 federal employees as compared to over 120,000 by the AFGE.

The NFFE's failure to keep pace with its AFL-CIO* rival resulted in part from its isolation from the established labor movement. Beyond that, NFFE policies were highly influenced by the large number of management personnel in the organization and appeared inconsistent, reflecting some confusion regarding the character and objectives of the federation. Specifically NFFE leaders seemed uncertain whether the organization was a professional association or a collective bargaining unit. Reflecting this confusion, the NFFE challenged the constitutionality of Executive Order 10988 issued by President John F. Kennedy on January 17, 1962, which provided for the recognition of, and commitment to bargain collectively with, unions of civil service employees. Conversely, the AFGE welcomed the executive order and used it to greatly extend its organizing activities.

The NFFE, which maintains its national headquarters in Washington,

D.C., holds biennial conventions. Principal officers include a president, nine vice-presidents, and a secretary-treasurer. The above officials constitute the NFFE executive council. In 1973 the NFFE reported a membership of 85,000 located in 1,200 local unions.

For further information, see the *Federal Employee* published monthly by the NFFE. See also Sterling D. Spero, *Government as Employer* (1948); J. Joseph Loewenberg and Michael H. Moskow, *Collective Bargaining in Government: Readings and Cases* (1972); and Daniel H. Kruger and Charles T. Schmidt, Jr., *Collective Bargaining in the Public Service* (1969).

FEDERAL WORKERS OF AMERICA; UNITED (UFWA). *See* United Public Workers of America.

FEDERATION OF ORGANIZED TRADES AND LABOR UNIONS OF THE UNITED STATES AND CANADA (FOTLU). Twenty-one trade unionists, many of them disillusioned members of the Knights of Labor* (KofL), met in Terre Haute, Indiana, on August 2, 1881, to discuss the possibilities of forming a new national federation of labor. The most significant action taken by the group was to issue a call for an international trades' union congress to be held in Pittsburgh on November 15, 1881. According to the convention call, the primary objective of the prospective new national federation would be to look after organized labor's legislative interests. Neither the promotion of trade unionism nor the organization of labor was greatly emphasized.

Eight national and international unions, three district assemblies and forty-six local assemblies of the KofL, eleven city trades councils, and forty-two local trade unions sent 107 representatives to the Pittsburgh convention. After resolving conflicts over representation and the election of permanent officers, the Federation of Organized Trades and Labor Unions of the United States and Canada was formed. Convention delegates adopted a platform that included most of the traditional objectives of labor reform: abolition of child and convict labor, compulsory school attendance, the legal incorporation of trade unions, a national bureau of labor statistics, uniform apprentice laws, enforcement of the national eight-hour law, abolition of conspiracy laws as applied to labor unions, and a protective tariff.

The protective tariff plank was removed during its second annual convention held in Cleveland, Ohio, in November 1882. This action led to the withdrawal of the Amalgamated Association of Iron and Steel Workers of America* whose president, John Jarret, had pushed the tariff proposal through the 1881 convention. The delegates also voted favorably on Ira Steward's eight-hour principle and resolved to study Henry George's single-tax proposal.

The following three conventions of the FOTLU were similar in format to the first two. However, the adoption of reform platforms and debates over resolutions did not substitute for effective action, and few positive initiatives were taken. Hampered by the continual lack of funds and limited support from national trade unions, the FOTLU accomplished little. At best it kept alive the idea of a national federation of labor and in this respect can be considered the forerunner of the American Federation of Labor* (AFL). Perhaps the most significant act of the FOTLU occurred during the waning hours of the 1884 convention, when members voted for a resolution "that eight hours shall constitute a legal day's work from and after May 1, 1886." Although the FOTLU did nothing to support the proposal and quickly became extraneous (if not forgotten) to the May Day Movement, this action had far-reaching ramifications.

In 1886 a trade union committee, which had been negotiating with the KofL, issued a call for a convention of national trade unions to meet in Columbus, Ohio, on December 8, 1886. Upon the issuance of this call, Samuel Gompers, who had presided over the preceding convention of the FOTLU, immediately changed the date and place of the FOTLU's convention to correspond with the committee's call. After meeting on December 7, the FOTLU dissolved and as a group joined the new labor conference that created the AFL.

The FOTLU was not a highly organized national group. It had no national headquarters, no president, and no executive staff. The only regularly constituted authority was a legislative committee of five members. This committee was later expanded to nine members, including the federation's secretary. Delegates attending the 1884 convention of the FOTLU represented approximately 50,000 trade unionists.

For further information, see John R. Commons et al., *History of Labour in the United States*, vol. 2 (1918); Norman J. Ware, *The Labor Movement in the United States, 1860-1895: A Study in Democracy* (1929); and Stuart Bruce Kaufman, *Samuel Gompers and the Origins of the American Federation of Labor, 1848-1896* (1973).

FIRE FIGHTERS; INTERNATIONAL ASSOCIATION OF (IAFF). Fire fighters first began organizing fraternal and social organizations during the nineteenth century. Gradually these societies took an increasing interest in work-related problems encountered by firemen, and by the turn of the nineteenth century, many were functioning as trade unions. In 1901 the American Federation of Labor* (AFL) chartered one such organization in Washington, D.C., as a federal labor union. Two years later members of the Pittsburgh Fire Department formed a union and affiliated with the AFL, and by 1906 seven such unions held AFL charters. Delegates to the 1904, 1912, and 1913 annual conventions of the AFL instructed their officials and organizers to launch and continue a national campaign to unionize firemen. These efforts met with considerable success, and by 1917, sixty-six firemen's unions had affiliated with the AFL as federal labor unions.

Because of the growth of union organization among firemen, a resolution calling for the organization of a national union of firemen was submitted to delegates attending the Thirty-seventh Annual AFL Convention meeting in Buffalo in 1917. The International Brotherhood of Teamsters,* which claimed jurisdiction over drivers, and the Union of Steam and Operating Engineers, claiming steam pump operators, voiced opposition to the resolution. In one of the few instances in which it refused to support craft autonomy, the AFL rejected the claims of the two protesting unions and approved the resolution.

In compliance with the convention's instructions, AFL president Samuel Gompers invited firemen's unions to send representatives to an organizing convention in Washington, D.C., on February 26, 1918. Delegates representing twenty-four local unions responded, and their labors gave birth to the International Association of Fire Fighters.

Internal disputes and difficulties in gaining union recognition characterized the early years of the IAFF. The internal problems centered around the activities of Thomas G. Spellacy, an unfortunate choice as first president of the association. Spellacy proved an arrogant and autocratic leader who ignored constitutional restrictions and responsibilities and neglected financial niceties in the disposition of IAFF funds. As a result of repeated violations of constitutional provisions, Spellacy was recalled from office during the summer of 1919 by a membership referendum. Later the same year, Fred W. Baer, who later guided the IAFF's fortunes for over a quarter century, assumed the presidential office.

The second problem the IAFF encountered during its early, formative years arose from the reluctance of city officials to grant union recognition. Cincinnati set the precedent for this resistance. Members of a delegation representing union firemen approached the chief of the Cincinnati Fire Department in 1918 to discuss recognition and were immediately discharged under a department rule prohibiting firemen "from joining any association which would interfere with the discipline, organization, or good order of the fire department." When other Cincinnati firemen protested, they too were summarily dismissed. Despite vigorous protests, the city refused to compromise on the issue, and the union disintegrated as several firemen lost their jobs.

The famous Boston police strike of 1919 further compromised the growth and stability of the IAFF. After the much-publicized strike, public opinion turned against the organization of public service employees, and municipalities throughout the nation passed ordinances prohibiting city employees from joining trade unions.

The successes and failures of the IAFF are reflected in the capricious nature of its organizing efforts. Between 1918 and 1926, for example, the IAFF chartered 219 new locals, but during the same period, 109 locals withdrew from the association due either to nonpayment of per-capita taxes or to restrictive legislation forcing locals to disband.

By the end of the 1920s, much of the public hysteria concerning the organization of public employees had dissipated. Although it did not include provisions for the organization of public employees, the enactment of the National Industrial Recovery Act of 1933 created a favorable climate for trade unionism. Many cities rescinded their restrictive measures, and the IAFF quickly took advantage of new opportunities to extend its organizational reach. Membership began a slow but steady upward trend that has continued since 1928 with only minor fluctuations. At the beginning of the period, the IAFF counted fewer than 20,000 members, but that figure increased to 35,000 by 1935, to nearly 50,000 by the end of World War II, and to more than 130, 000 by 1970.

The IAFF, which holds biennial conventions, maintains its international headquarters in Washington, D.C. Principal officers include a president, a secretary-treasurer, and thirteen vice-presidents representing geographical divisions. The executive committee is composed of the above officers. In 1973 the IAFF reported a membership of 160,258 located in 1,658 local unions.

For further information, see the *International Fire Fighter* published monthly by the IAFF. See also James J. Gibbons, *The International Association of Fire Fighters* (1944); Emma Schweppe, *The Firemen's and Patrolmen's Unions in the City of New York* (1948); and Richard L. Lyons, "The Boston Police Strike of 1919," *New England Quarterly* (June 1947).

FIREMEN AND OILERS; INTERNATIONAL BROTHERHOOD OF (IBFO). Five delegates representing independent unions and American Federation of Labor* (AFL) federal locals met in Kansas City, Missouri, on December 18, 1898, and organized the International Brotherhood of Stationary Firemen (IBSF). Wages averaging seventeen cents an hour, a twelve-hour day and six-day week, and exhausting physical labor characterized the working conditions calling the new national union into existence. The IBSF experienced a typical pattern of union growth and decline during its first twenty years. The Stationary Firemen grew steadily until the initiation of the employers' open-shop offensive in 1903-1904. Beginning with fewer than a thousand members, the IBSF enrolled nearly 20,000 members by 1904; it declined thereafter, bottoming at 8,000 in 1911 before again turning upward, reaching a new peak of more than 35,000 members in 1921.

Meanwhile, the IBSF had affiliated with the AFL on January 11, 1899, receiving a charter limiting its trade jurisdiction to stationary firemen. In 1919 the charter was expanded to include oilers and helpers in the boiler rooms, and, reflecting this expanded jurisdiction, the union was renamed the International Brotherhood of Firemen and Oilers. As a result of a decision by the Railroad Labor Board during the 1920s, the IBFO's jurisdiction was further expanded to include roundhouse and railroad shop laborers. Recognizing this new trade jurisdiction, the AFL on June 24, 1931, issued the IBFO a new charter including jurisdiction over "boiler firemen, retort firemen, water tenders, boiler washers, boiler washers helpers, oilers, ash handlers, coal passers, stoker firemen, stoker helpers, roundhouse and railroad shop helpers and laborers, utility men and maintenance laborers when employed in and around the boiler and engine room."

Because a large percentage of its membership came from the railroad industry, the IBFO early exhibited an interest in attempting to gain improved working conditions through political action as well as economic trade unionism. The IBFO largely concentrated its early political efforts at the state level, but after World War II, the federal government commanded much attention from union leaders. The brotherhood also placed great emphasis on the union label and was an active member of the AFL union label trades department, as well as the departments of railway employees and metal trades.

Resulting from the public nature of the railroad industry and the brotherhood's emphasis on political action, the IBFO rarely resorted to strikes to win concessions from employers; one instance in which it did so, the historic railroad shopmen's strike of 1922, proved an unmitigated disaster for the union. By the time the strike officially ended, the IBFO had lost nearly three-quarters of its 1921 membership. Moreover, the union continued to decline until 1928 when it enrolled about 8,000 members. Despite the severe economic depression that wracked the nation during the 1930s, an expanded jurisdiction, plus the Railroad Labor Act of 1926 and favorable labor legislation during the New Deal years, reversed the direction of the IBFO's membership curve.

The IBFO membership surpassed 20,000 by 1936 and at the end of World War II, it had risen to nearly 50,000. It continued to grow until the mid-1950s when a slow decline began as a result of technological changes, the increased substitution of oil and gas for coal, and the consolidation and rationalization of railroads, all of which reduced employment within the IBFO's trade jurisdiction.

The IBFO, which maintains its national headquarters in Washington, D.C., holds quinquennial conventions. Principal officers include a general president, six vice-presidents, and a secretary-treasurer. These officials also constitute the IBFO general executive board. In 1973 the IBFO reported a membership of 44,000 located in 520 local unions.

For further information, see the IBFO *Journal* published bimonthly. See also *The American Federationist* (December 1949), and Florence Peterson, *Handbook of Labor Unions* (1944).

FOOD, TOBACCO, AGRICULTURAL AND ALLIED WORKERS UNION OF AMERICA (FTA). The United Cannery, Agricultural, Packing and Allied Workers of America (UCAPAWA) was organized at Denver in July 1937 under a charter from the Committee for Industrial Organization* (CIO). This new union drew its leaders and members from a variety of groups organizing in agricultural and allied industries during the earlier 1930s at the height of the Great Depression. These included the Communist Trade Union Unity League* (TUUL) and its Cannery and Agricultural Workers Industrial Union, a dual union operating mainly in California; independent agricultural unions; and federal labor unions (FLUs) of the American Federation of Labor* (AFL).

With the abolishment of the TUUL in 1935, left-wing unionists began calling for labor unity and the organization of an international union of agricultural and allied workers under the AFL, which for business reasons had hitherto been satisfied to leave this area of activity mostly to others. By 1936 seventy-two locals had been formed with a total of 7,500 dues-paying members. Their leadership, supported by a few state federations of labor and central labor councils, began pressuring the AFL to issue an industrial union charter. Rebuffed at the 1936 AFL convention, in the spring of 1937 the group, led by Donald Henderson, a Communist, turned to the CIO. Henderson charged that the FLUs paid large per-capita taxes to the AFL for which they received few benefits because the AFL had never hired organizers in agriculture. But more importantly, an industrial union structure possible under the CIO was superior to the AFL craft organization in this field of activity. The organization of UCAPAWA in Denver, with Henderson as president, followed shortly.

Supported by CIO funds, UCAPAWA in 1937 and 1938 undertook a costly campaign to organize agricultural workers. According to Henderson, the union made astounding gains, and by December 1938 he claimed to have 300 locals with 124,750 voting members. The facts, however, indicated a much different situation. Despite partial UCAPAWA victories in some areas, in California AFL-Teamster* opposition left the union with only fifteen locals and a net loss in membership by the end of 1938. Restricting its strike activities for a year, UCAPAWA in 1940 announced another California campaign aimed at agricultural workers but faltered when the Filipino Agricultural Laborers Association, with which UCAPAWA had at times cooperated, joined the AFL because of its control over the trucks. By February 1941 UCAPAWA completely abandoned its West Cost efforts in the fields.

Initially UCAPAWA's prospects seemed bright among the sugar beet workers of the mountain states. By spring 1938 the union's District III reported forty-seven locals with over 10,000 members. During that year, however, beet acreage declined, forcing the union to abandon its spring objectives. By October, when a strike threatened, UCAPAWA was so weak that only pressure from Washington on the growers forestalled a humiliating union defeat. In 1939, as wages for beet workers dropped 4 percent, UCAPAWA membership declined drastically.

In the Rio Grande Valley a few minor strikes were won, but union locals could not be maintained, while efforts to organize shed workers and crate makers also failed. In Florida UCAPAWA faced opposition from the Ku Klux

Klan and the American Legion, in addition to the growers and law officials. With thirteen locals organized by late 1937, sporadic strikes were conducted with mixed success until a general citrus strike in Winter Haven broke the union in the fall of 1938. As elsewhere, UCAPAWA organizers in Florida tried to cover a wide area when they should have concentrated on a vital center of activity, such as Polk County.

UCAPAWA's District VII in the Northeast conducted a few small strikes in agriculture but achieved its only significant success among several processors in New Jersey, particularly the Campbell Soup Company. In Connecticut attempts to organize Negro workers from the South in the "shade" tobacco plantations around Hartford had to be abandoned. Only in the Midwest, where strong CIO unions already existed, did UCAPAWA achieve the closed shop and make important gains in wages and hours. By the end of 1940, about twenty-four midwestern locals existed; however, an attempt that year to organize the Wisconsin dairy industry failed in the face of AFL-Teamster opposition.

Finally, in the southern cotton fields, success also eluded UCAPAWA because of an unsuccessful struggle with the Southern Tenant Farmers Union* (STFU), a group originally affiliated with UCAPAWA but which withdrew in 1939 over issues of communism and the payment of dues. The STFU-UCAPAWA schism contributed to the failure of both unions among the tenant farmers, and for the STFU, led directly to its demise. By 1940 UCAPAWA officially abandoned its efforts among most agricultural workers and began concentrating upon food processing as the backbone of the organization. Here, the work force was more stable and enjoyed federal protection under the National Labor Relations Act of 1935.

When the UCAPAWA was reorganized in 1946 as the Food, Tobacco, Agricultural and Allied Workers Union of America, it was one of several internationals in the CIO under Communist leadership. These unions comprised 15 percent of the CIO membership. Although as a disciplined minority, the Communists were able to define union policies, they could not count on rank-and-file support. As the cold war heightened in intensity and emotion, FTA's position became increasingly controversial since its president had opposed the Marshall Plan. In addition, during the election of 1948, Henderson and his allies on the CIO executive board attempted to take that organization into the Henry Wallace camp.

When the CIO convention met in December 1948, President Philip Murray threatened to take action against the FTA, whose membership at that time stood at 24,000. Meanwhile, William Steinberg, president of the American Radio Association* and a member of the CIO executive board, charged the FTA and nine other international unions with policies "consistently directed toward the achievement of the program or the purposes of the Communist Party rather than the objectives and policies set forth in the Constitution of the

CIO." A committee appointed by Murray later heard charges and gathered evidence and testimony against the FTA. It found that the international consistently followed the Communist line and that Henderson had concealed his Communist party membership from union members and from the CIO. On March 1, 1949, the FTA was expelled from the CIO. A short time later the remaining remnants of the once-promising union merged with the Distributive, Processing and Office Workers of America, an amalgamation of several Communist-dominated unions expelled from the CIO.

The FTA, which maintained its national headquarters in Philadelphia, held biennial conventions. Principal officers included a president, an executive vice-president, eight vice-presidents, and a secretary-treasurer. The above officers constituted the international executive board. At the time of its expulsion from the CIO, the FTA claimed a membership of 22,590.

For further information, see the semimonthly *UCAPAWA News* and the monthly *FTA News*. See also David E. Conrad, *The Forgotten Farmers: The Story of the Sharecroppers in the New Deal* (1965); Donald H. Grubbs, *Cry from Cotton: The STFU and the New Deal* (1971); and Stuart M. Jamieson, *Labor Unionism in American Agriculture* (1945), an especially valuable source of information on the FTA.

Merl E. Reed

FOOTBALL LEAGUE PLAYERS ASSOCIATION; NATIONAL (NFLPA). The first step toward union organization of professional football players occurred in 1956 when players in the National Football League (NFL) formed the NFL Players Association. Several years later players in the American Football League formed a similar association. On January 8, 1970, representatives of the two associations met and organized the National Football League Players Association, which was designed primarily as a collective bargaining unit. Membership was open to any person employed as a professional football player by a member club in the NFL, including those players on club active, move, future, reserve, injured reserve, and military service lists, and players actively seeking employment as professional football players.

The first task confronting officials of the new union involved gaining recognition as the bargaining agent for professional football players in the NFL and securing a collective bargaining agreement. After hard, often acrimonious negotiations and a short strike, NFL owners recognized the NFLPA as the exclusive bargaining agent for professional football players and signed a four-year contract effective February 1, 1970. The contract included nearly $20 million in player benefits over the agreement's four-year term.

Following the expiration of the 1970 contract, negotiations between the NFLPA and the NFL Management Council for a new contract collapsed when association bargainers insisted upon the right of players to move from one team to another after the expiration of their contracts. The "freedom issue" involved the legitimacy of the so-called Rozelle rule instituted by NFL commissioner Peter Rozelle after David Parks of the San Francisco 49ers played out his option and signed a contract with the New Orleans Saints. When owners of the two clubs failed to agree upon just compensation, Rozelle ordered the Saints to relinquish to the 49ers their first-round choice in the college draft for the following two years. The severe penalty was seen as an effort (largely successful) to restrict the movement of players between clubs.

Resulting from the breakdown of negotiations, the NFLPA called the longest strike in professional sports history, which lasted through much of the 1974 exhibition season. By a vote of twenty-five to one on August 27, the player representatives rejected the owners' final offer, but voted to end the strike and to play the 1974 season without a contract. Consequently the players continued to perform under provisions of the 1970 contract.

After the collapse of contract negotiations in the fall of 1974, NFL owners exhibited little interest in renewed discussions with the NFLPA. The stalemate continued until September 1975 when Randy Vataha, a wide receiver and player representative for the New England Patriots, announced the decision of players on the New England roster to boycott the last game of their preseason schedule and continue the strike until contract discussions resumed. Shortly thereafter players on the New York Jets, Washington Redskins, Detroit Lions, and New York Giants joined the strike. But players on eleven teams refused to strike. The strike ended when federal mediator W. J. Usery, Jr., after discussions with the NFL Management Council, assured the striking players that the owners would bargain in good faith.

Nevertheless, recognizing and exploiting the disunity within the NFLPA, the owners refused to modify their position on contract issues separating them and the NFLPA. The discord within the NFLPA generally revolved around the personality and policies of the NFLPA executive director, Edward Garvey. There was opposition to Garvey's militancy and arguments that he had emphasized the wrong issues and had been generally ineffective in contract negotiations. One team, the Minnesota Vikings, voted to withhold dues payments until Garvey was replaced.

Another source of discord involved differences between younger and older players. Veterans argued that too much emphasis had been placed by the association on freedom issues and too little attention was given the pension plan, insurance programs, and the expansion of the player roster beyond the forty-three player limit. Finally, elements of racial separation (if not division) existed over vital issues concerning the NFLPA. Black players, generally more militant, placed greater emphasis on freedom issues and strongly supported Garvey. White players were more likely to question the emphasis placed on the freedom issue and more often crossed the picket line during the 1974 strike.

Any complacency that NFL owners felt as a result of the players' disunity was shattered on December 30, 1975, when the federal district court in Minneapolis ruled that the Rozelle rule violated federal antitrust laws. The decision removed the issue that had proven a major source of conflict within the NFLPA, as well as the major obstacle to substantive collective bargaining negotiations between the owners and players. Moreover, the ruling placed the owners in the position of needing the cooperation and support of the NFLPA, an ironic development for the myopic curmudgeons who controlled professional football. Nevertheless, a lengthy list of unfair labor practice charges before the National Labor Relations Board and a number of lawsuits promised to keep professional football in litigation for some time.

The NFLPA, which maintains its national headquarters in Washington, D.C., holds annual meetings. Principal officers include a president and a vice-president and two representatives from each conference. The board of representatives, the governing body of the NFLPA, consists of the president and one player representative from each club. The executive council is composed of the president, vice-presidents, and conference representatives. The executive director, the only full-time officer, serves as an ex officio member of the board of representatives and the executive council. In 1973 the NFLPA reported a membership of 1,160 located in twenty-six local clubs.

For further information, see *The Audible* published monthly by the NFLPA. See also the *Membership Booklet* (1972-1973), issued by the association, and *Sports Illustrated* (August 5, 1974).

FOREMAN'S ASSOCIATION OF AMERICA (FAA). The spread of union organization in the mass production industries of the United States during the late 1930s and early 1940s resulted in higher wages, improved working conditions, and greater job security for thousands of industrial workers. By comparison the relative position of unorganized, lower-echelon supervisory personnel deteriorated. In the words of Robert H. Keys, one of the early leaders in the movement to organize foremen, "While the ordinary worker was gaining concessions, we foremen have been getting conversation, banquets, picnics, and promises." Although the organization of supervisors had a long tradition in the craft trades, trade unionism of such employees in the mass production industries awaited the successful organization of production workers. By the time the United States entered World War II, this had been largely accomplished.

In November 1941, 1,200 foremen employed by the Ford Motor Company in Detroit met at Fordson High School and organized the Foreman's Association of America. The new union claimed jurisdiction over "foremen for any employers of labor" but specifically excluded from membership any "foreman or supervisor who is an employer of labor, or individual in a position to act as negotiator in the interests of employer policy." The FAA constitution also prohibited any discrimination in membership based on "race, religion, nationality, sex or political views or opinions."

Within six months the FAA had increased its membership to 5,000, but the Ford Motor Company refused to recognize or bargain with the union. Moreover, the company began to systematically discharge foremen active in the union movement. By the time the FAA celebrated its first anniversary, a strike had forced the reinstatement of all discharged foremen and a signed agreement.

Despite their broad jurisdictional claim, FAA founders, envisioning the new organization only as a union of Ford foremen, had no particularly grandiose design. But the FAA's success in signing an agreement with the notoriously anti-union Ford Motor Company stimulated requests for membership from foremen in other companies, many of them outside Detroit. As a consequence, the FAA quickly became a national organization.

A National Labor Relations Board (NLRB) ruling in 1943 dangerously jeopardized the FAA's initial successes. In the Maryland Drydock case, the NLRB declared that supervisory personnel were not an appropriate unit for collective bargaining under the provisions of the National Labor Relations Act (NLRA). As a result of the decision the Ford Motor Company withdrew its recognition of the FAA. Having no status under the NLRA and finding employers unwilling to bargain voluntarily, the FAA used the only weapon at its disposal—the strike. During 1944 over thirty foremen strikes idled thousands of workers. Although rebuked by the National War Labor Board and other government officials, the strikers accomplished what months of supplication had failed to achieve—union recognition and collective bargaining. Perhaps most notable, the Ford Motor Company signed a new agreement with the FAA in May 1944.

In the spring of 1945, the NLRB reversed its previous position and in the Packard Motor Company decision recognized foremen as an appropriate collective bargaining unit. Thereafter the FAA grew rapidly. In 1945 the association reported a membership of 28,000 located in 245 chapters. The FAA continued to grow until the enactment of the Taft-Hartley Act in 1947. Section 2(3) specifically excluded supervisors from the provisions of existing labor legislation. The results for the FAA were catastrophic. Many employers immediately withdrew recognition, and within a few years the association disintegrated. Although the FAA hung on for several years in Detroit, the enactment of the Taft-Hartley Act marked its demise as a national organization.

The FAA, which maintained its national headquarters in Detroit, held annual conventions. Full-time officers included a president, secretary-treasurer, and membership director. A twelve-member executive board was elected at each annual convention. At the time of the enactment of the Taft-Hartley Act, the FAA had a membership of approximately 30,000.

For further information, see *The Supervisor* published monthly by the FAA. See also J. Carl Cabe, *Foremen's Unions: A New Development in Industrial*

Relations (1947); Ernest Dale, *The Development of Foremen in Management* (1945); and "The American Foremen Unionizes," *The Journal of Business* (January 1946); Frank P. Huddle, *Unionization of Foremen* (1944); Charles P. Larrowe, "A Meteor on the Industrial Relations Horizon: The Foreman's Association of America," *Labor History* (Fall 1961); and H. R. Northrup, "The Foreman's Association of America," *Harvard Business Review* (Winter 1945).

FUR AND LEATHER WORKERS UNION; INTERNATIONAL (IFLWU). Organizing among American fur workers dates back to 1849 when a group of German immigrants in New York established a furriers' union, which throughout the remainder of the century was associated with such movements as the eight-hour day, reform of working conditions, and protection of worker civil liberties. Membership in the fur workers' unions was slow to increase until an unusually rapid expansion of the fur industry after 1907 and a revolt among workers in many American clothing industries against harsh sweatshop working conditions combined to provoke a sharp upsurge in organizing among fur workers. A general strike in the fur industry was called on June 12, 1912. It lasted until September 8 and resulted in an overwhelming union victory, laying the ground work for an international union of fur workers. On June 16, 1913, twenty delegates representing 14,000 workers organized in eight American Federation of Labor* (AFL) federal labor unions in five cities met in Washington, D.C. and formed the International Fur Workers Union of the United States and Canada. This union, officially chartered by the AFL on July 1, 1913, was authorized to organize workers in every branch of the fur industry into craft-type locals. Albert W. Miller was elected president and general organizer. By 1916 the union had organized twenty-seven locals. Even as the union was reaching these organizing heights, however, corruption, mismanagement, and political factionalism eroded its strength.

Leaders of the fur workers, chiefly Isadore Cohen, manager of the New York Joint Board, became enmeshed in corrupt practices by accepting bribes from fur processors who then could ignore their signed contracts with the fur workers' union. When faced with protests from the rank and file, Cohen hired "enforcers" to stifle discontent, but he was ultimately expelled. This did not relieve the problem, however, and gangsterism was a perennial threat to the union for the next generation. President Miller proved too weak to rid the union of corruption. This, plus his cautious stance when dealing with management, lost him support at the grass-roots level. Miller eventually resigned in the face of growing resentment toward him and was replaced by Morris Kaufman who served through the years of World War I. During this period, the fur workers were plagued by internal dissent concerning American involvement in the war. Old-line Socialists and a more conservative wing within the union also disagreed over the issue of supporting the 1917 bolshevik revolution. Ben Gold, a former fur cutter who had proved a successful union organizer, led the left-wing Socialist faction. Gold and his followers militated strongly against corruption and gangsterism within the union and also pressed for recognition of the newly created Soviet government in Russia. The Gold-Kaufman struggle was not resolved by the end of the war, and it continued into the 1920s.

After the war, the fur trade became a dangerously speculative venture. In April 1920 the fur market crashed, and thousands of fur workers lost their jobs. To save what few jobs remained, a general strike was called on May 27, but from the beginning, it was doomed to disaster. Anti-labor sentiment in government and anti-radical feelings within the community combined to support the managers against the workers. Gangsterism within the union shattered what little strength remained. Violence against the strikers was rampant, from both company-hired goons and union hoodlums hired to keep strikers in line. The outcome was complete failure. Kaufman became the scapegoat for the disaster, and Gold took the opportunity to strengthen his position within the union. The Kaufman-Gold feud continued until early 1924, when Kaufman expelled Gold from the union. Kaufman's action incited the more progressive element within the ranks to rise up against him. Gold was reinstated in November 1924 and subsequently was appointed manager of the New York Joint Board. Here, he fought an almost singlehanded battle against corruption and gangsterism. In recognition of his efforts in behalf of the union, Gold was given control of a strike called in 1926 against the Fur Manufacturers Association for the institution of a forty-hour week. The strike lasted seventeen weeks and was largely unsuccessful. In its wake, Gold was expelled from the union.

For the next decade the fur workers fought a desperate war against organized crime. By the early 1930s, leaders of the criminal element, Louis (Lepke) Buchalter and Jacob (Gurrah) Shapiro, forced their way into the New York garment and fur industries with a protection racket that netted millions of dollars a year. To obtain absolute control over the operation and profits of the garment industry, the unions holding contracts with the various garment and fur processors would have to be controlled. Sidney Hillman of the Amalgamated Clothing Workers* had already moved with great speed and success to rid his union of this influence. The fur workers followed suit and fought the Lepke-Gurrah mobsters in violent and sometimes bloody conflicts, which eventually resulted in the purging of gangsterism from the union.

When President Roosevelt signed the National Industrial Recovery Act (NIRA) into law on June 13, 1933, he paved the way for vast organizing campaigns among workers in all branches of American industry. While numbers of unorganized fur workers embraced the union as a result of NIRA, the major thrust of the law in the fur industry was directed at the creation of National Recovery Administration (NRA) codes. Throughout the life of NRA, ideological groups within the union squabbled with each other for official recognition as the representative of the fur workers. As a result, union membership was polarized into left- and right-wing elements. These factions reunited in the summer of 1935 and not only reinstated Ben Gold but elected him international president at the Eleventh Biennial Convention held in May 1937, just in time to sponsor affiliation with the Congress of Industrial Organizations* (CIO), whose industrial unionism was more in keeping with the philosophy of the fur workers than the craft unionism of the AFL. CIO affiliation also broadened the membership of the international. In May 1939 the National Leather Workers Association, formerly the United Leather Workers International Union of America, joined the fur workers to form the International Fur and Leather Workers Union.

Both fur and leather workers had taken strong anti-fascist positions during the 1930s and were among the first to pledge their support in the struggle against Hitler. Like so many others in the American labor movement, they made no-strike pledges for the duration of the war. Shortly after the conclusion of hostilities, the international launched an industry-wide drive for wage increases, which would have been more successful had it not been confronted by a growing anti-union sentiment in the country, which culminated in the Taft-Hartley Act. The union had a long history of radicalism and was hit hard by the anti-radical provisions of the act. In response to pressures from right-wing elements, the CIO expelled the Fur and Leather Workers in 1950 as a Communist-dominated union. As a former member of the Communist party, Gold resigned in order to comply with the non-Communist provision of Taft-Hartley. Nevertheless, the strength of the union waned in the face of conservative pressures, and in 1955 the union was finally forced to merge with the Amalgamated Meat Cutters and Butcher Workmen of North America* (AMCBWNA).

The IFLWU, which maintained its national headquarters in New York City, held biennial conventions. Principal officers included a president and secretary-treasurer. The executive board included the above officers in addition to thirty-six members elected by convention delegates. At the time of the merger with the AMCBWNA, the IFLWU had approximately 40,000 members.

For further information, see the *Fur and Leather Worker* issued monthly by the IFLWU. See also Philip Foner, *The Fur and Leather Workers Union: A Story of Dramatic Struggles and Achievements* (1950), an account very sympathetic to the IFLWU's left-wing leadership. Max M. Kampelman provides a much different perspective in *The Communist Party vs. the C.I.O.: A Study in Power Politics* (1957).

Joseph Y. Garrison

FURNITURE WORKERS OF AMERICA; UNITED (UFWA). The schism in the American labor movement during the 1930s, resulting in the formation

of the Congress of Industrial Organizations* (CIO) to contest the American
Federation of Labor* (AFL) for labor leadership, encouraged similar
secessionist movements among national unions in several industries. One such
industry involved the manufacture of furniture. Until the mid-1930s, furniture
workers had been organized by local units of the Upholsterers' International
Union of North America* (UIU). But because of ideological political conflicts
and differences over organizing tactics, leaders of several UIU locals broke
with the old AFL union and led their membership into the CIO. In December
1937 delegates from these locals met in Washington, D.C., with representatives of several CIO local industrial unions and a number of independent
unions to organize the United Furniture Workers of America.

The new CIO affiliate received a broad jurisdictional grant including "all
employees working in or about the plants of manufacturers of furniture and
kindred products." Membership was open to all workers in the industry "regardless of craft, age, sex, nationality, race, creed, and political belief." Beginning with a founding membership of about 10,000, the UFWA grew steadily,
reaching a membership of 20,000 in 1940 and 30,000 by the end of World War
II. Vigorous organizing drives, improved economic circumstances, and favorable government policies contributed significantly to the UFWA's success during the early 1940s.

The greatest threat to the union's continued success revolved around
potential political conflicts growing from the UFWA's Communist-influenced,
left-wing leadership. During the unity years of World War II, this threat
remained largely dormant, but after the war, the increasingly bitter antagonism between the United States and the Soviet Union soon had repercussions in
union affairs. In 1946 UFWA president Morris Muster, who had served in that
office since the union's founding in 1937, won reelection after a vigorous anti-
Communist campaign. Although Morris won easily, the other candidates on
his slate were defeated due to factionalized bloc voting. Muster, who had previously served as president of the Eastern Seaboard Council of the UIU and
had been a leader of the secessionist movement that resulted in the creation of
the UFWA, had had a long flirtation with the Communist party; nevertheless,
he obviously underwent a political conversion. After the election returns
became known, Muster suddenly resigned his office with the explanation that
"Communist intrigue and chicanery have captured our international. . . . My
record as a trade unionist will not permit me to remain head of a Communist-
controlled organization." There could be little doubt that his analysis of Communist influence had merit. UFWA secretary-treasurer Max Perlow, a self-
admitted member of the Communist party, and a majority of the members of
the UFWA executive board supported the Communist cause.

After the war, ideological conflict absorbed much of the time and attention
of both left- and right-wing union leaders. During these years organizing suffered, and the UIU, which had fallen far behind the UFWA in membership,

regained its dominant position in the industry. Enactment of the Taft-Hartley Act with provisions for non-Communist affidavits intensified internal political conflicts, and open rebellion by several locals appeared a real possibility. At this point, the UFWA's left-wing leadership suffered a further setback when the CIO launched a campaign to purge the organization of Communist-controlled affiliates. The UFWA was high on the list.

Ultimately, Morris Pizer, who had succeeded Muster after his resignation in 1946, broke with the Communists and led a successful anti-Communist slate in the union elections of 1950. Not only were the Communists swept from international union office, but by a four-to-one vote UFWA members adopted a resolution "supporting the program, policies and principles of the CIO." Thereafter, the CIO dropped the charges against the UFWA.

The ideological conflict was a costly one for the UFWA. It never recovered the earlier organizing initiatives of the late 1930s and early 1940s and remained a relatively small union with a membership fluctuating between 30,000 and 40,000. After the AFL-CIO* merger in 1955, the UFWA and the UIU formed "a confederation for common union action" under which both unions retained their autonomy but agreed to establish a joint board to coordinate organizing drives, political activities, research, and union label promotions.

The UFWA, which maintains its national headquarters in New York City, holds biennial conventions. Principal officers include a president, secretary-treasurer, and director of organization. The general executive board is composed of representatives from eleven geographical districts and eight major branches of the industry. In 1973 the UFWA reported a membership of 30,503 located in 110 local unions.

For further information, see the *Furniture Workers Press* issued monthly by the UFWA. The Communist influence is discussed in Max M. Kampelman, *The Communist Party vs. the C.I.O.: A Study in Power Politics* (1957), and David J. Saposs, *Communism in American Unions* (1959).

GARMENT WORKERS OF AMERICA; UNITED (UGW). The character of the American needle trades industry and the composition of the labor force employed in it changed dramatically during the beginning of the twentieth century. The custom tailor in the early nineteenth century was a highly skilled craftsman, but during the course of the century, the developing special order trade involving clothing made to measure but factory produced and the increased popularity of ready-made clothing drastically altered the nature of the trade and the conditions of employment. More specialized divisions of labor continually reduced the skill level of most employees in the industry.

Meanwhile, the composition of the labor force also changed. Early nineteenth-century custom tailors were typically of English or Scottish stock. By mid-century, German, Austrian, and Irish immigrants were entering the labor force of the garment industry, and a few years later large numbers of East European Jews and a lesser number of Italians secured employment in the industry.

Trade union organization in the industry had begun during the closing years of the eighteenth century, and in 1865 a first, short-lived, national union was organized—the Journeymen Tailors' National Trades Union. Although local union organization flourished during the last half of the nineteenth century, the first permanent national union in the industry, the Journeymen Tailors' Union of America* (JTUA), was not organized until 1883. The ethnic diversity of the labor force and the changes in production methods plagued trade union organizers in the industry.

The JTUA was composed primarily of conservative, native-stock custom tailors and excluded less-skilled factory workers and shop tailors who often were East European Jews of a more radical ideological persuasion. The latter group first joined the Knights of Labor* (KofL) in large numbers and later organized a national union of their own, the Tailors' National Progressive Union (TNPU). Thus, cultural and ethnic differences, ideological conflicts, and craft separatism prevented the organization of a single national union in the clothing industry. The JTUA's craft exclusivism and ideological conservatism continually frustrated efforts to effect a merger of the various unions in the industry.

This situation existed when forty-seven delegates representing workers in eighteen local unions in four cities met in New York City in April 1891 and organized the United Garment Workers of America. The new union, which was chartered by the American Federation of Labor* (AFL) on May 1, 1891, represented an effort to combine into one union the diverse labor force in the men's ready-made clothing industry. The UGW included native-born, skilled cutters of German and Irish stock, Jewish shop tailors, disillusioned KofL elements, AFL federal labor unions, and remnants of the TNPU.

The skilled cutters who assumed control of the UGW made some concessions to the socialist proclivities of the Jewish tailors, and a period of uneasy harmony prevailed during the union's first few years. Moreover, UGW leaders adopted an aggressive posture as they sought to extend the original membership base of 3,000. In 1893 the union withstood a major effort by employers to break the union, and a year later it led a successful strike of 16,000 cloakmakers in New York City. The early militancy and harmony ended when the UGW suffered a series of reverses during strikes in 1896. Thereafter the innately conservative union leadership discouraged strikes and placed greater emphasis on organizing the work clothing industry, using the union label as an effective instrument in pressuring manufacturers to reach an accommodation with the union. This new strategy drew immediate opposition from the more radical Jewish shop tailors who gained little from the tactic.

The years between 1896 and 1910 witnessed a growing conflict between the skilled, craft-conscious cutters who controlled the union and the less skilled, class-conscious cutters. During the struggle, UGW officers continually sought to centralize power in the national office, while their critics advocated greater local autonomy. A general strike of New York tailors in 1907 dramatically illustrated the divisions within the union. Because the strike affected union label shops, UGW officials declared it illegal and ordered workers in those shops back to work; their failure to comply resulted in suspensions, further aggravating already tense divisions within the union.

The internal conflict reached a climax in Chicago during a Hart, Schaffner, and Marx strike beginning in September 1910. The struggle gradually evolved into a local general strike in the industry. National UGW officers who had reluctantly supported the strike quickly negotiated an agreement, but it was vetoed in a referendum by the striking workers. The Hart, Schaffner, and Marx strikers thereafter refused to accept UGW leadership, and the strike was finally resolved in January 1911 with more favorable terms than those negotiated by UGW officials. Much to the annoyance of many local strikers and their leaders and with little prior consultation, UGW officials called off the general strike three weeks later.

UGW officers took similar action during a general strike of New York clothing workers in 1912. As a result disillusionment and frustration continued to grow, and it became increasingly obvious that the UGW's 1914 national convention would become a battlefield between the opposing groups in the union. The expected conflict never materialized, however. Through a series of dubious parliamentary maneuvers, UGW leaders maintained control of the union by disqualifying large numbers of dissident New York delegates. Those objecting to the established leadership withdrew from the regular convention and held their own meeting, which they contended represented the legitimate UGW. The insurgents, however, lost the legal battle for the union name, offices, and funds; and as a consequence, they met in New York City in December 1914 to organize the Amalgamated Clothing Workers of America* (ACWA).

The ACWA quickly became the dominant union in the men's clothing industry, leaving the UGW little more than its base in the work clothing industry. After the revolt, UGW membership fell to about 45,000 where it remained amazingly stable through the 1920s, the Great Depression, and World War II. Beginning in the mid-1950s, however, UGW membership began a slow but consistent decline.

The UGW, which maintains its headquarters in New York City, holds quinquennial conventions. Full-time officers include a president and a secretary-treasurer. The executive board is composed of the above officers and a varying number of vice-presidents. In 1973 the UGW reported a membership of 25,000 located in 166 local unions.

For further information, see *The Garment Workers* published monthly by the UGW. See also the JTUA and ACWA sketches in this volume. Information can also be found in Joel Seidman, *The Needle Trades* (1942), and Philip Taft, *Organized Labor in American History* (1964).

GARMENT WORKERS' UNION; INTERNATIONAL LADIES' (ILG). New York City cloakmakers issued a call for a convention in March 1900 in hopes of organizing a union of all crafts within the ladies' garment industry. Eleven delegates representing seven local unions with 2,000 members met on June 3, 1900, in New York City in response to the call and organized the International Ladies' Garment Workers' Union. On June 23, 1900, the American Federation of Labor* (AFL) issued a charter to the new union. Prior to 1900, especially in the years 1890-1900 when the garment industry grew at a tremendous pace, attempts had been made to form an international union of ladies' garment workers. Initiative for organizing an international came particularly from cloakmakers in Philadelphia and New York, but these early endeavors had been doomed by personal factionalism and rivalry between cloakmakers' unions disagreeing about their relationship to Daniel DeLeon's Socialist Trades and Labor Alliance.

The ILG, which expanded rapidly during the early years of its existence, developed a liberal and progressive outlook advocating independent political action for labor and endorsement of the Socialist party. In part its stance could be attributed to the high percentage of Jewish and East European immigrants comprising the union's membership. Radicalism in the ILG centered in the Jewish Cloakmakers' locals and in the predominantly female dressmakers' locals. Cutters, usually native-born Scots-Irish or Irish, and pressers, generally unskilled Italian immigrants, tended to be more conservative. Although male workers dominated the cloak and suit trades, female workers controlled shirtwaist and underwear manufacturing and dominated the ladies' garment industry overall.

From 1900 to 1904 the ILG concentrated on supporting boycotts and unionizing firms by means of its label. This strategy, however, largely failed; consequently, prodded by its general secretary, John Dyche, the ILG embarked on the course of centralizing authority. While the union attempted to effect this structural reform, it also encountered a threat from the Industrial Workers of the World* (IWW), which had organized four locals in New York City in 1905, but the IWW effort proved abortive when a restrictive court injunction signaled the failure of a 1906-1907 strike against Beller & Co. in New York City.

By the end of World War I, the ILG was one of the strongest and best-known international unions in the nation. To a considerable extent two successful strikes permanently established the union: the 1909 New York City shirtwaist makers' strike—the famous "uprising of the 20,000"—and the 1910 New York City cloakmakers' strike. The historic "Protocol of Peace" grew from the cloakmakers' strike. The protocol abolished home work and inside subcontracting, established a six-day week of fifty-four hours, allowed the preferential union shop, and created the machinery for arbitrating disputes and grievances. Although the arbitration features of the protocol largely failed to promote long-range industrial peace, union membership increased significantly. By 1912, for example 90 percent of the New York City cloak trade was under union control.

In the decade after World War I, left-wing agitation in the ILG, centered in New York City, increased, particularly in Local 25, waist and dressmakers, which established soviet-type delegates' leagues. In early 1921 the general executive board (GEB) declared the delegates' leagues unconstitutional, and in an attempt to isolate the more radical shirtwaist makers, Local 25 was divided into two unions. But the radicals quickly seized control of Local 22, which was organized as a result of the division. Radicalism and factionalism in the union increased after 1921 when the Comintern dropped its dual union policy and adopted a "boring from within" strategy. Communist membership rose, but at the same time ILG anarchists broke with the Communists, and the Socialists also split, some siding with the Communists and others supporting efforts to drive the Communists from the union.

Morris Sigman, who replaced Benjamin Schlesinger as president in 1923, determined to rid the union of Communists, and in August 1923, the GEB ordered the disbanding of left-wing groups on the grounds that they were cells of the Communist party. In addition Sigman charged the Communist leaders of Local 22 with conspiracy and expelled them from office. But the battle was not over. In 1925 radicals formed the Joint Action Committee, an alliance of left-wing locals against the parent union.

The ill-fated 1926 cloakmakers' strike proved much more successful than the efforts of union leaders in effecting the removal of Communists from the ILG ranks. On July 1, 1926, 30,000 cloakmakers struck, protesting an agreement allowing employers the right to discharge up to 10 percent of their work force annually. Because the Communist leadership consistently advised against tentative agreements that could have settled the strike, the Sigman faction seized control of the Joint Board in December and settled the strike on January 12, 1927. Due to flagrant mismanagement of strike funds by radicals, the ILG found itself over $800,000 in debt. By 1928 most Communists were driven from the union, but union membership had declined to 40,000 with thousands behind in dues' payments.

The union leadership's main task was to regain financial stability and increase union membership. Benjamin Schlesinger, elected president again in 1928, and David Dubinsky, elected in 1932 upon Schlesinger's death, concentrated on these goals. The National Industrial Recovery Act aided the drive to increase membership. By 1934 ILG membership soared to over 200,000, and the union's debts were almost liquidated.

Dubinsky and the ILG played an important part in encouraging industrial unionism and in forming the Committee for Industrial Organization in 1935. The union remained with the Committee until 1938 when it became the Congress of Industrial Organizations,* a separate association of unions. From 1938 until reaffiliating with the AFL in 1940, the ILG remained an independent union.

Under Dubinsky's leadership, the union focused both on reforming the garment industry and upon providing union members with more fringe benefits. Always at the forefront of social welfare reform, the ILG was the first union to formulate an employer-contributed unemployment compensation plan (1919) and to establish union health centers (1913). Beginning in the New Deal era, the ILG became less radical and more moderate, increasingly seeking to rationalize the industry by including efficiency clauses in its contracts and conducting studies under the auspices of its management engineering department.

Since World War II the ILG has concentrated on increasing wage levels in an industry that typically has been behind other American industries in this regard. A high percentage of unskilled workers, together with a tendency for many manufacturers to move South to take advantage of lower wages has exacerbated this problem. Moreover the union has had to fight competition from countries with much lower wage levels.

During the postwar years the ethnic and racial composition of the union has altered markedly. In the New York City area more blacks and Puerto Ricans entered the labor force, while in California, Mexican-Americans and persons of Chinese ancestry became garment workers. Females continue to dominate the union, comprising 80 percent of the ILG membership as of 1970.

The ILG, which maintains its national headquarters in New York City, holds triennial conventions. Principal union officers include a general president, secretary-treasurer, first vice-president, and executive vice-president. The union contains eleven geographical divisions within the United States and Canada headed by a supervisor and general manager. The general executive board is comprised of full-time officers in addition to members elected at national conventions. In 1973 the ILG reported a membership of 427,568 located in 486 local unions.

For further information, see *Justice* (semimonthly), *Giustizia* (monthly), and *Justicia* (monthly) issued by the ILG. Louis Levine, *The Women's Garment Workers: A History of the International Ladies' Garment Workers' Union* (1924), and Benjamin Stolberg, *Tailor's Progress: The Story of a Union and the Men Who Made It* (1944), contain valuable information on the early history of the union. Although his scope is much larger, Joel Seidman's *The Needle Trades* (1942) is still useful. See also Leon Stein, *The Triangle Fire* (1962), a valuable account of that tragic event; Max D. Danish and Leon Stein, eds., *ILGWU News—History, 1900-1950* (1950); and Harry Haskel, *Leader of the Garment Workers: The Biography of Isidore Nagler* (1950). Biographical material on David Dubinsky can be found in Max D. Danish, *The World of David Dubinsky* (1957), and "David Dubinsky, the ILGWU and the American Labor Movement," Special Supplement, *Labor History* (Spring 1968).

Marie Tedesco

GAS, COKE AND CHEMICAL WORKERS OF AMERICA; UNITED. *See* Oil, Chemical and Atomic Workers International Union.

GLASS BOTTLE BLOWERS ASSOCIATION OF THE UNITED STATES AND CANADA (GBBA). Union organization among glass bottle blowers began during the first half of the nineteenth century when a group of bottle blowers organized a union in 1842 at the Wistarburg Glass Works in Alloway, New Jersey. After several other unions had been organized by 1846, they banded together to form the Glass Blowers League. On June 22, 1846, the new national union negotiated one of the first industry-wide collective bargaining agreements in American history; however, the young trade union failed to survive the panic and depression of 1857.

The direct predecessor of the Glass Bottle Blowers Association of the United States and Canada was the Independent Druggists' Wares League, which was organized in Pittsburgh, Pennsylvania, in 1868. A weak organization, the league responded enthusiastically to the appearance of the Noble Order of the Knights of Labor* (KofL). Bottle blowers west of the Allegheny Mountains organized National Trade Assembly No. 143, with headquarters in Pittsburgh, and bottle blowers east of the mountains organized National Trade Assembly No. 149. The United Green Glass Workers Association was organized at a joint 1890 convention of the two assemblies in Baltimore, and the following year, it withdrew from the KofL. The GBBA, which adopted its present name in 1895, remained independent until 1899, when it affiliated with the American Federation of Labor* (AFL) and attained a jurisdiction including "all men and women employed in and around glass factories and component parts thereof."

Perhaps no group of workers underwent more technologically necessitated changes in production methods than glass blowers. During the nineteenth century glass blowing was a specialized, highly skilled craft, and the early organization of the craft ensured rigid standards of training and excellence. As a result of their control of apprenticeship, recruitment, and training and the high skill level required for handblown glass, workers in the industry attained a relatively high standard of living and had remarkably good employer relations.

The introduction of a glass blowing machine at the Atlas Glass works in Washington, Pennsylvania, in the fall of 1896, however, presaged a revolution in the production of glass containers that soon made the handblown glass artisan obsolete. Under the farsighted leadership of Denis A. Hayes, the GBBA decided against fighting the introduction of machine work and instead endeavored to enroll machine workers and to gain employment for GBBA members on the new machines. By 1916 the GBBA had gradually evolved from an exclusive craft union to an industrially organized union that included semiskilled and unskilled workers in the bottle trade.

The GBBA's decision to organize machine workers opened up a new era in industrial relations in the glass making industry. The security that the workers in the highly skilled craft had enjoyed evaporated with the introduction of machine production. Consequently, employers, no longer dependent on highly skilled workers, exhibited a growing belligerence. Nevertheless, membership figures of the GBBA evidence the union's success in organizing machine workers; an 1890 membership of 2,423 increased to 3,789 in 1900 and to 7,305 in 1907.

As it was for so many other unions, World War I was a period of substantial growth for the GBBA. Developments evolving from the war and postwar period, however, eventually confronted the GBBA with challenges far exceeding those inspired by the introduction of machines. The glass industry in the United States experienced severe reductions in exports while imports increased, and this, along with the employers' open-shop drive, the introduction of the feed and flow manufacturing process, and the increased use of plastics, disrupted the traditional work force in the glass industry. Even more devastating was Prohibition's disastrous impact on the glass container industry and those employed therein. The GBBA responded to the challenge by further expanding its jurisdiction and by joining the United Brewery Workers* in the campaign to repeal Prohibition, but union membership declined precipitantly. When James Maloney assumed the union presidency in 1924, the GBBA received dues from only 1,000 members.

If the decade of the 1920s was fraught with dangers and hardships for the GBBA, the decade that followed contained years of promise. The repeal of Prohibition, the glass container code of the National Recovery Administration, and New Deal labor policies stimulated a sharp revival of unionism in the glass industry. Moreover, the Owens and Illinois Glass companies, which merged in 1929, recognized the GBBA and the American Flint Glass Workers' Union* as bargaining agents for their employees. By late 1938, the GBBA had organized over 85 percent of the workers in the glass bottle industry, and by 1945 it had nearly 35,000 members.

The most serious problem confronting the association during the 1930s involved the effort to protect its jurisdiction from encroachment by the unions of the Congress of Industrial Organizations* (CIO). The Glass Bottle Blowers had survived jurisdictional disputes in the past, especially with the American Flint Glass Workers' Union, but the CIO and its affiliates, with their vast resources, represented a much more serious threat. Nevertheless, during the

1930s and 1940s, the GBBA successfully defended its jurisdiction against the International Longshoremen's and Warehousemen's Union,* the CIO Federation of Flat Glass Workers, the International Union of Mine, Mill and Smelter Workers,* and the United Mine Workers.* In the post-World War II period, the GBBA, again responding to technological change, extended its jurisdictional reach to include the employees of the new glass fiber industry. Following the AFL-CIO* merger, the GBBA began a long but frustrated effort to arrange a merger of all American glass unions.

The GBBA, which maintains its national headquarters in Philadelphia, holds quadrennial conventions. Principal officers include a president, three vice-presidents, a secretary, a treasurer, and eleven executive officials. The executive board is comprised of the above officers. In 1973 the GBBA reported a membership of 78,883 located in 232 local unions.

For further information, see *GBBA Horizons*, a monthly publication, and *Flame and Heart: A History of the Glass Bottle Blowers Association of the United States and Canada* (1961), written by Lee W. Minton, a long-term president of the union.

GLASS AND CERAMIC WORKERS OF NORTH AMERICA; UNITED (UGCW). The organization of workers involved in such varied occupations as glass gatherers, blowers, flatteners, and cutters extends back to the nineteenth century. In the early 1880s these four distinct craft trades were organized into Local Assembly 300 of the Knights of Labor,* but the combination was a volatile one. By 1900 it had splintered into three independent organizations: the Cutters and Flatteners Protective Association, the Cutters and Flatteners Association, and the Window Glass Cutters League.

As mechanization rapidly changed methods of production in the glass industry, pressures for amalgamation again grew. In 1917 the three craft unions merged into the Window Glass Cutters League of America, but the new unity once again was destined to be short-lived. Following the enactment of the National Industrial Recovery Act and its provision for collective bargaining contained in Section 7(a), a mass influx of unskilled workers led to increasing tensions between skilled and industrial workers. Hoping to overcome these difficulties, a constitutional convention was called in Columbus, Ohio, in March 1934. The convention dominated by industrial flat glass workers, ultimately resolved a plan to organize industrial workers and skilled cutters into two separate divisions under the same executive officers. The cutters, however, rejected the proposal, and the two groups split.

The industrial workers who had met in Columbus organized the Federation of Flat Glass Workers of America (FFGW), and on August 7, 1934, the American Federation of Labor* (AFL) granted a charter to the new national union. Glen W. McCabe was elected the first president of the union and Irwin

L. DeShetler executive board member at large (later secretary-treasurer and president).

Shortly after its organization, the young union entered into contract discussions with the largest producers in the flat glass industry—Libbey-Owens-Ford, Pittsburgh Plate Glass, American Window Glass, and Fourcault Window Glass. Before the end of the year, the FFGW had gained recognition from these companies, which assured its survival. By the end of 1935, the Flat Glass Workers had added nearly 12,000 members to the small cadre of workers who had organized the union in the previous year.

With its membership of semiskilled and unskilled industrial workers, the FFGW had a natural bond with those elements in the AFL pressing for the industrial organization of mass production industries. When an industrial organizing resolution was debated and voted upon during the AFL's 1935 convention, the FFGW cast its votes for the minority report supporting industrial organization. The Flat Glass Workers joined the Committee for Industrial Organization* (CIO) in November 1935, and a year later, along with other unions suspended by the AFL, affiliated with the newly established CIO. Under the charter issued by the CIO, the FFGW received an expanded jurisdiction including "all those employed in and around factories engaged in the business of manufacturing, processing and/or marketing of glass and allied products, also the mining and quarrying of silica sands, and the making and processing of ceramic or plastic products."

Resulting from its new jurisdictional base, the FFGW grew rapidly as it began organizing ceramic and plastics workers. A new name adopted in 1940—the Federation of Glass, Ceramic and Silica Sand Workers of America—symbolized the changes in the union. The renamed union reported a membership of 29,500 in 1944 and 46,600 in 1956. The Federation of Glass, Ceramic and Silica Sand Workers chartered its first Canadian local in 1954, thus necessitating another name change. The union became the United Glass and Ceramic Workers of North America.

The UGCW, which maintains its national headquarters in Columbus, Ohio, holds quadrennial conventions. Principal officers include a president, six district presidents, four vice-presidents, and a secretary-treasurer. The international executive board is comprised of the above officials. In 1973, the UGCW reported a membership of 42,943 located in 196 local unions.

For further information, see *The UGCWNA in Pictures: United Glass and Ceramic Workers of North America, AFL-CIO-CLC* (1956), a pictorial record prepared by Leland Beard, director of the union's department of research and education, and *Glass Workers News* published monthly by the UGCW.

GLASS CUTTERS LEAGUE OF AMERICA; WINDOW (WGCLA). The large-scale organizing activities of the Knights of Labor* (KofL) during the

1870s greatly accelerated the unionization of glass workers, which had begun during the second half of the nineteenth century. In 1880 Local Assembly No. 300, KofL, organized as a powerful industrial union of glass workers, including cutters, blowers, flatteners, and gatherers. Local Assembly 300 controlled the labor force in the glass industry for nearly twenty years. Operating on a union-shop basis, it gained company recognition and, through the negotiation of national agreements with employers, controlled wages and working conditions in the industry.

Bitter internal political conflicts and the movement toward craft separatism, reflected by the organization and growth of the American Federation of Labor* (AFL), however, plagued Local Assembly 300 as the cutters, and shortly thereafter the flatteners, initiated a secessionist movement that eventually destroyed the once powerful Local Assembly. The cutters created their own national union in 1894, the Window Glass Cutters' League. On May 24, 1898, the new national union received an AFL charter. A month earlier, on April 27, 1898, the AFL had chartered the secessionist flatteners as the Window Glass Flatteners Association of North America.

Both new AFL affiliates found their greatest organizing opportunities among the skilled machine workers in cylinder-machine plants. Local Assembly 300 had neglected these workers in favor of organizing flatteners and cutters in hand processing plants. The two small unions amalgamated in 1902, creating the Window Glass Cutters and Flatteners' Association of America, Inc. (WGC&FAA). But the AFL never recognized the merger and suspended the two small unions in 1904 for failing to pay per-capita taxes.

The WGC&FAA organized in an industry characterized by rival unionism and complicated by accelerated technological change. The AFL chartered several short-lived national unions in the industry, including the Amalgamated Glass Workers International Association of America, 1900-1915; Window Glass Snappers National Protective Association of America, 1902-1908; International Association of Glass House Employees, 1903-1907; and the Amalgamated Window Glass Workers of America, 1906-1908. The WGC&FAA also encountered competition from independent organizations, such as the Window Glass Cutters and Flatteners' Protective Association, which represented the employees of the American Window Glass Company.

One of the most significant technological changes in the industry was introduced by Libbey-Owens in 1917. The earlier development of cylinder machinery had displaced gatherers and blowers, but the cylindrical glass still needed to be hand flattened before cutting. The introduction of the sheet-drawing machine, however, also signaled the demise of hand glass flattening, leaving the cutters as the only skilled hand workers in the flat glass industry.

Meanwhile, the AFL rechartered the WGC&FAA on November 6, 1925. On April 14, 1928, the AFL issued a charter to the Window Glass Cutters League of America, which had been organized in 1917 and was composed almost exclusively of the sheet-drawing machine workers employed by Libbey-Owens Company. The two AFL unions in the trade jurisdiction, the WGC&FAA and the WGCLA, merged under the title of the latter on April 22, 1930. Three years later the union of American Window Company employees, the Window Glass Cutters and Flatteners' Protective Association, also merged with the WGCLA, leaving it the only national union in its trade jurisdiction for the first time in several decades.

Continuing technological change in the flat glass industry greatly reduced the employment of skilled workers; consequently, the WGCLA organized in a shrinking trade jurisdiction. Nevertheless, the small union maintained an average membership of about 1,500 workers for several years before beginning a gradual decline during the 1960s. In 1974 the WGCLA merged with the Glass Bottle Blowers Association of the United States and Canada* (GBBA).

The WGCLA, which maintained its national headquarters in Columbus, Ohio, had no constitutional provisions for national conventions. The principal officer was a president-secretary-treasurer. The executive board was composed of the above official in addition to representatives from each geographical district. Shortly before merging with the GBBA, the WGCLA reported a membership of 602 located in nine local unions.

For further information, see *The Glass Cutters*, a monthly issued irregularly by the WGCLA for several years. See also *Bulletins No. 420, 506, 618*, Bureau of Labor Statistics, U.S. Department of Labor (1926, 1929, 1936).

GLASS WORKERS' UNION OF NORTH AMERICA; AMERICAN FLINT (AFGWU). Highly skilled glass workers from New York City, Pittsburgh, Wheeling, West Virginia, Bellaire and Steubenville, Ohio, Philadelphia, and St. Louis met in Pittsburgh on July 1, 1878, and organized the United Flint Glass Workers. The new union adopted its current title in 1912 and originally confined its organizing activities to skilled workers, making no effort to organize either the semiskilled or unskilled workers in the industry.

Although represented at the founding convention of the Federation of Organized Trades and Labor Unions* (FOTLU), many AFGWU locals were affiliated with the Knights of Labor,* and did not affiliate with the FOTLU but did join the American Federation of Labor* (AFL) shortly after its organization in 1886. Resulting from a dispute with the Glass Bottle Blowers Association,* however, the AFGWU withdrew from the AFL on January 30, 1903. It remained independent until October 21, 1912, when it renounced its previous claims to jurisdiction over workers involved in the production of bottles and fruit jars.

The AFGWU became one of the first trade unions to bargain on an industry-wide basis when, in 1888, it negotiated a collective bargaining agreement with the National Association of Manufacturers of Pressed and Blown Glassware

(NAMPBG), an organization encompassing many of the nation's leading manufacturing concerns. In 1903 the AFGWU and the NAMPBG began a series of annual wage conferences under the provisions of what came to be known as the "Star Island agreement." Acquiring its title from a series of conferences held on Star Island, Michigan, the agreement provided:

> If a dispute arises in any factory and said dispute cannot be settled locally, it shall be referred to the joint conference for final adjustment and, pending the settlement of the matter, there shall be no change in the working conditions; that is, work shall be continued just as if no cause for a controversy or dispute had arisen and, pending a final settlement of the matter, there shall be no strike, lockout or cessation of work by either the employer or employes, and the decision of the joint conference shall be final and binding on each party.

This long-lived agreement, negotiated at a time when most employers were making plans for a national open-shop campaign, produced an aura of industrial harmony quite out of tune with the experience of most other industries of that day. Moreover many of the independent glass manufacturers established collective bargaining plans and procedures similar to those employed by the AFGWU and the NAMPBG.

Because of the amicable labor-management relations in the industry, the AFGWU's membership figures did not exhibit the great fluctuations characteristic of so many other trade unions during the first two decades of the twentieth century. Starting in the early twentieth century, the AFGWU steadily increased its membership until reaching 10,000 in 1920. Thereafter AFGWU membership fell below 4,000 by 1932 as a result of mechanization, technological change, the Great Depression, and its own myopic organizing strategy.

After the enactment of the National Industrial Recovery Act of 1933 and its provisions for collective bargaining, the AFGWU expanded its jurisdiction to include workers who performed semiskilled and unskilled operations in the industry. In September 1933 it inaugurated an organizing campaign among these workers, but the results were disappointing, and at its annual convention in 1935, the AFGWU voted to transfer to the AFL all locals composed of semiskilled and unskilled workers.

The disdain with which AFGWU leaders had traditionally viewed unskilled workers in the industry began to change after the inauguration of the Congress of Industrial Organizations* (CIO). In a dramatic turnabout, the AFGWU began to actively recruit the workers it had previously ignored. After a successful organizing drive, the AFGWU opened negotiations with the NAMPBG, and on January 4, 1937, a uniform agreement was signed covering the semiskilled and unskilled workers in the industry.

With its expanded jurisdiction, the AFGWU grew rapidly during the following years. Membership reached 20,000 during World War II, and by the time of the AFL-CIO merger in 1955, over 30,000 flint glass workers held AFGWU membership cards.

The AFGWU, which maintains its headquarters at Toledo, Ohio, holds biennial conventions. Full-time officers include a president, three vice-presidents, a secretary-treasurer, and an assistant secretary. The AFGWU is split into an industrial and a skilled division, each with its own executive board. The industrial division board consists of fifty-five members and the skilled division council forty-eight members selected from the various departments within each division. In 1973 the AFGWU reported a membership of 36,000 located in 235 local unions.

For further information, see the *American Flint* published monthly. See also *The American Federationist* (February 1948 and August 1954); Lloyd Ulman, *The Rise of the National Trade Union: The Development and Significance of Its Structure, Governing Institutions, and Economic Policies* (1966); and Lee W. Minton, *Flame and Heat: A History of the Glass Bottle Blowers Association of the United States and Canada* (1961).

GLOVE WORKERS UNION OF AMERICA; INTERNATIONAL (IGWUA). At the American Federation of Labor* (AFL) convention on December 17, 1902, twenty-eight glove workers' locals formed the International Glove Workers Union of America, which, a few days later, received an AFL charter. Prior to 1902, unionization in the glove industry consisted of scattered locals organized on a craft basis and sometimes, as in the table cutters' locals, by nationality groups. In the nineteenth century unionization first took place in Gloversville and Johnstown (Fulton County), New York, the original home of the glove industry in the United States; it then spread to the Midwest. By the time of the IGWUA founding, seventeen locals, located primarily in the Midwest, already had been chartered by the AFL.

Long anti-union, glove manufacturers often refused to recognize the IGWUA and frequently locked out union workers. Shortly after the founding of the IGWUA, table cutters in Fulton County were locked out when manufacturers refused to grant a closed shop. This resulted in defeat and the virtual destruction of the Fulton County union. Because Fulton County workers in part blamed their defeat on the lack of AFL support, they refused to affiliate with the AFL when they reorganized their locals in 1907, and it was not until 1911 that these workers reaffiliated. Another consequence of the disastrous 1903-1904 lockout was the transferral of IGWUA headquarters from Gloversville to Chicago in 1906. Thereafter, leadership in the union came primarily from midwestern locals.

The 1913 convention most clearly expressed the glove workers' goals. Condemning home work, it demanded that all gloves be made in the factory and carry the union label. Further, the convention supported the establishment of uniform working hours and wages; however, the union failed to achieve these demands and had to rely on piecemeal state legislation to correct such abuses. (A minimum wage for the industry was not established until 1942 when the Glove Industry Commission, authorized under the Fair Labor Standards Act of 1938, granted a forty-cent minimum hourly rate.) The 1913 convention additionally approved affiliation with the national Women's Trade Union League* (WTUL). Unable to afford its own organizer, the IGWUA accepted the WTUL's offer to pay Agnes Nestor as an organizer for one year. Seldom did the IGWUA have sufficient funds for organizing and consequently relied on either the WTUL or the AFL for help in this area.

Because the glove industry was particularly sensitive to foreign competition, both manufacturers and the IGWUA opposed the reduction of the tariff on gloves provided by the Underwood-Simms Tariff Act (1913). With the beginning of World War I, the European glove industry declined, and American manufacturers prospered from increased orders; yet glove workers did not receive a significant wage increase during the war years.

The post-World War I years, however, witnessed a depression that plagued the glove industry from 1920 to 1932. Glove workers' locals suffered as membership declined during these years, and manufacturers took advantage of the situation by reducing wages and refusing to grant the closed shop. Strikes, such as the one undertaken by employees of the United States Glove Co., Marion, Indiana, often were broken when the manufacturer simply transferred production to other plants. But the National Recovery Administration aided unionization in the IGWUA, and from 1933 to 1935, organization began anew, resulting not only in the unionization of many midwestern plants but also in the reorganization of the long dormant Fulton County locals.

In 1936 conflict within the union surfaced over the many strikes undertaken by locals. The table cutters' branch of Local 69, Fulton County, maintained that too much money was being spent in the work glove field where costly strikes often occurred, and it resented providing support from the large Fulton County fund. In protest table cutters withdrew their affiliation from the International in March 1936. That summer the operator's branch of Local 69 also withdrew its affiliation, leaving only the unemployed affiliated with the IGWUA. In the midst of this conflict, officers of the union at the 1936 convention endorsed a proposed merger suggested by Sidney Hillman of the Amalgamated Clothing Workers of America* (ACWA). The proposal passed by a small margin, primarily with support from eastern locals. Generally midwestern locals were unwilling to relinquish their independence to the ACWA and desired to remain apart from the industrial unionism of the Congress of Industrial Organizations;* thus in 1937 these locals held their own convention and reorganized the AFL-affiliated IGWUA. The cutters and operators in Fulton County, however, remained independent.

Throughout the late 1930s and during the 1940s, the IGWUA and the

ACWA clashed over jurisdictional claims. The Amalgamated adopted a policy of organizing glove workers and employees in plants manufacturing items of clothing other than gloves. The IGWUA claimed that these workers formed a separate unit and therefore should be organized into the IGWUA. Generally, the ACWA succeeded in organizing those workers in factories that were not predominantly glove-manufacturing plants.

Perhaps because it perpetually lacked funds, the International did little in the area of welfare unionism. Not until 1940, for example, was a death benefit established. Officers frequently were women, which was unusual even for a union dominated by female workers. The IGWUA not only elected Agnes Nestor as the first female president of an international union in 1913 but also elected numerous women to the general executive board. On December 6, 1961, the IGWUA merged with the ACWA, thus ending the International's fifty-nine years of existence as an independent union.

At the time of the merger, the IGWUA, which held biennial conventions, maintained its national headquarters in Kewanee, Illinois. Principal officers included a president, seven vice-presidents, and a secretary-treasurer. The above officers constituted the general executive board. At the time of the merger with the ACWA, the IGWUA had a membership of 2,212 located in twenty-one local unions.

For further information, see the *Glove Workers' Monthly Bulletin* issued by the IGWUA. See also Agnes Nestor, *Brief History of the International Glove Workers Union* (1943), and *Woman's Labor Leader: An Autobiography of Agnes Nestor* (1954).

Marie Tedesco

GOVERNMENT EMPLOYEES; AMERICAN FEDERATION OF (AFGE). The U.S. Personnel Classification Board issued a report in 1931 recommending that skilled craft workers be included in the civil service classification system. Responding to objections from many of its craft union affiliates, leaders of the American Federation of Labor* (AFL) immediately protested the extension of the classification system. While this action pleased craft union leaders, officers of the AFL's largest national union of federal employees, the National Federation of Federal Employees* (NFFE), bitterly objected. The NFFE leadership envisioned an industrial union encompassing all federal workers and had strongly supported the extension of the classification system. In a referendum sponsored by its leaders, NFFE members voted 16,335 to 11,406 against continued affiliation with the AFL. The NFFE then withdrew from the federation on December 1, 1931, and has since remained an independent national union.

The decision to withdraw from the AFL, however, was not popular among several Washington area federal workers. As a consequence twelve locals with a membership of 562 withdrew from the NFFE and petitioned the AFL for federal labor union charters. The AFL agreed and assisted the locals in conducting a successful organizing campaign. As a result of this growth, in August 1932 the AFL issued a charter to the American Federation of Government Employees with jurisdiction over the executive branch of the United States government.

Although it was some years before the AFGE overtook the older NFFE, it grew rapidly as it successfully organized workers in the Veterans Administration, the Department of Justice, the Weather Bureau, and other government departments and agencies. Within three years of its chartering, the AFGE grew to a union of over 20,000 with 211 affiliated locals. In 1935 the AFGE's jurisdiction was expanded to include the employees of state, county, and municipal governments, but a year later when the AFL chartered the American Federation of State, County, and Municipal Employees,* the AFGE was again restricted to federal workers.

The AFGE came into existence during the depths of the Great Depression, an especially bad time for underpaid federal workers. Moreover, the inauguration of Franklin D. Roosevelt signaled another setback for the civil service. One of the first measures Roosevelt sent to Congress was an economy measure proposing a substantial reduction in the civil service and a $100 million slash in pay for federal employees. In addition to recouping these losses, AFGE officials lobbied for an extension of the job classification system to the clerical field services, establishment of a five-day week, and employee representation on executive bodies dealing with employment policies and working conditions throughout the government service, including an employee representative on the Civil Service Commission. Under the direction of "Super Lobbyist" Charles E. Stengle, who had served one term as AFGE president, union lobbyists had considerable success in getting congressional action in these matters.

The AFGE's early years were not free of conflict and discord, however. One of the its more controversial positions involved a strict no-strike policy, a provision written into the organization's constitution. During the late 1930s, a growing group of critics within the AFGE organized the "Committee Against False Economy" which chastised the national officers for their lack of militancy and their failure to take a stronger stand against the administration. Rejecting pleas of the discontented members, the AFGE expelled them from the union. These dissidents then joined the newly organized Congress of Industrial Organizations* (CIO) and founded a rival national union, the United Federal Workers of America.* The new CIO affiliate, however, never proved as formidable a rival as the independent NFFE.

After growing rapidly in the years immediately following its chartering, the AFGE's growth rate increased more slowly during the 1940s and 1950s, especially considering the large increases in government employees. Membership increased from 25,000 in 1935 to 35,000 at the end of World War II, to

50,000 by the time of the AFL-CIO* merger, and to nearly 80,000 by 1960, when the AFGE reached approximate parity with its old rival, the NFFE.

As a result of two unrelated but almost simultaneous occurrences during the early 1960s, however, membership virtually exploded, and the AFGE became the fastest growing union in the United States. One reason for this growth was the election to the AFGE presidency of the dynamic John F. Griner in 1962. When Griner took office, AFGE membership stood at 83,767; eight years later more than 325,000 government workers held membership cards, and the AFGE represented nearly a half-million workers in collective bargaining negotiations. In leading the AFGE during this tremendous period of growth, Griner took full advantage of the other new circumstance, Executive Order 10988 issued by President John F. Kennedy in January 1962. The order provided for the recognition of and collective bargaining with unions of civil service employees. The management-dominated NFFE challenged the constitutionality of the order and was left behind as the AFGE enrolled more employees and negotiated more contracts than all of its competitors combined. By 1970 AFGE was the largest union in the entire federal service sector, including the long-established postal unions, and it was rapidly emerging as one of the AFL-CIO's largest and most influential affiliates. Moreover, despite the union's great growth during the 1960s, large numbers of federal workers, especially white-collar employees, remained unorganized, thus leaving the AFGE a large jurisdiction in which to further expand its control and influence.

The AFGE, which maintains its national headquarters in Washington, D.C., holds biennial conventions. Full-time officers include a president, executive vice-president, and secretary-treasurer. The national executive council consists of the above officers and fifteen vice-presidents representing geographical districts. In 1973 the AFGE reported a membership of 292,809 located in 1,458 local unions.

For further information, see *The Government Standard* issued monthly by the AFGE. See also Albert A. Blum et al., *White-Collar Workers* (1971); J. Joseph Loewenberg and Michael H. Moskow, *Collective Bargaining in Government: Readings and Cases* (1972); and Sterling D. Spero, *Government as Employer* (1948).

GRAIN MILLERS INTERNATIONAL UNION; AMERICAN FEDERATION OF (AFGM). The organization of an international union of grain millers resulted from the Great Depression. Prior to the enactment of the National Industrial Recovery Act (1933) with its provisions for collective bargaining, little progress had been made in organizing workers employed in the milling industry. The first international union to attempt to organize workers in the industry was the International union of Flour, Feed, Cereal, Soft Drink and Bakery Workers, but the most effective organization resulted from the formation of federal labor unions directly affiliated with the American Federation of Labor* (AFL).

During the 1933-1936 period, several informal attempts were made to establish communication between the scattered locals of grain milling workers. Little was accomplished until AFL president William Green appointed William Schoenberg (then AFL midwestern director of organization) to organize a council of grain milling locals. As a result the Grain Processors Council was organized in Toledo, Ohio, in July 1936. Schoenberg served as president of the council until the fall of 1936, when he was replaced by Meyer Lewis.

The council, renamed the National Council of Grain Processors, became a self-governing organization after a national conference held in Wichita, Kansas, in 1939, at which Samuel P. Ming was elected president. It negotiated agreements with such large milling companies as General Mills, Pillsbury, Russell Miller Milling, and International Milling and grew steadily during its early years, attaining a membership of 25,000 by the mid-1940s.

Shortly after the Grain Processors Council acquired independent status in 1939, its leaders began agitating for an AFL international charter. AFL craft unions, however, strongly opposed the chartering of the Grain Processors Council as an international union until the maintenance workers it had organized were assigned to their respective craft unions. President Ming and Secretary-Treasurer Harold Schneider strongly resisted such a division or fragmentation of their organization, and in 1948 the AFL executive council finally voted to issue an international charter to the Grain Processors without detaching any of the so-called craftsmen from the union. The charter, officially granted to the American Federation of Grain Millers International Union on July 26, 1948, gave the new union a jurisdiction including "workers engaged in the milling of raw grains, such as wheat, corn, rye, barley, flax, soybeans, rice and seeds, where such raw materials are milled for human consumption or for feeding of poultry, livestock or any other animal, in the processing or manufacture of cereals, the handling or processing of potatoes and similar food, feed or seed."

The new international union immediately increased its per-capita tax in order to put several full-time organizers in the field. The resulting organizing campaign produced substantial membership gains. AFGM also met with considerable success in collective bargaining negotiations with grain milling companies. Meanwhile, the AFGM early took an active interest in local, state, and national politics and played an active role in the AFL's Labor's League for Political Education and its successor, the AFL-CIO* committee for political education.

The AFGM, which maintains its national headquarters in Minneapolis, holds biennial conventions. Full-time officers include a general president, an executive vice-president, a secretary-treasurer, and ten vice-presidents who represent geographic districts. The general executive board is comprised of the above officers. In 1973 the AFGM reported a membership of 36,000 located in 203 local unions.

The AFGM does not issue an official journal, and no published sources were located.

GRANITE CUTTERS' INTERNATIONAL ASSOCIATION OF AMERICA; THE (GCIAA). The year 1877 climaxed a turbulent period in the history of the American labor movement. The severe economic depression signaled by the panic of 1873 wrecked havoc with trade unions, many of which ceased to exist by 1877. Two years earlier the Molly Maguires had captured unfavorable public attention, and this, along with the violent railroad strike of 1877, created an unfavorable public image of organized labor. It was under these inauspicious circumstances that a small group of granite cutters met at Rockland, Maine, in the spring of 1877 to organize the National Union of Granite Cutters (NUGC).

Deplorable as they were, the working conditions bringing about the need for the NUGC were not atypical of many other occupations at that time. Daily working hours varied between ten and twelve depending upon the season, and company-owned stores and boardinghouses usually absorbed the small wages paid the workers. Because these conditions pervaded in the industry, granite cutters throughout the country responded enthusiastically to the initiatives taken at Rockland.

Renamed The Granite Cutters' International Association of America in 1905, this union played a significant role in the national labor movement. It was a charter member of both the Federation of Organized Trades and Labor Unions* in 1881 and the American Federation of Labor* (AFL) in 1886. The GCIAA has been a continuous affiliate of the AFL and the AFL-CIO,* except between 1890 and 1895 when AFL support was withdrawn in a dispute over a special assessment levied in support of the eight-hour strike by the United Brotherhood of Carpenters and Joiners.*

Although temporarily checked during the depression of the 1890s, the GCIAA grew steadily during the last quarter of the nineteenth century and the early years of the twentieth century, reaching a peak membership of approximately 15,000 in 1911. Membership stabilized there for several years before beginning a slow decline. By 1911 the GCIAA had organized virtually all workers in its trade jurisdiction; consequently, membership fluctuations thereafter were caused by circumstances over which the union had little control.

Membership advances and collective bargaining achievement were not gained without employer opposition. In 1892 employers locked out union members in an unsuccessful effort to destroy the union. The GCIAA not only prevailed but succeeded in eliminating many of those conditions that originally necessitated the organization of the union. The eight-hour day and a half-day on Saturday were won, and the company store and piecework were eliminated. The GCIAA also increased the minimum daily wage in the industry from $2.50 during the 1890s to $3.00 at the turn of the century, $4.00 in 1916, and $8.00 in 1920. In 1940 the GCIAA won a five-day week and a minimum wage of $9.00.

The GCIAA also clashed with employers in 1909 over the introduction of pneumatic tools in the industry. Although raising no objections to the use of the new machinery, the GCIAA argued that dust raised by the tools created a serious health hazard and demanded the introduction of safety and ventilation measures. The GCIAA also objected to the use of a heavy pneumatic hammer called the "boomer," whose four-pointed drill created great clouds of dust. After a strike lasting several months and exhausting the GCIAA treasury, employers agreed to discontinue use of the objectionable tool.

A major clash between the union and employers occurred again in the years following World War I. During the 1920-1921 economic recession, employers determined to lower the minimum wage from $8.00 to $6.50. The GCIAA resisted and, after a strike lasting over a year, prevailed; the $8.00 wage rate was retained.

Despite its success in maintaining wage rates and winning concessions from employers, GCIAA membership continued to decline. The large-scale introduction of machinery during the 1920s and 1930s constantly reduced employment in the trade, and union membership suffered accordingly. A 1920 membership in excess of 10,000 fell to 6,000 in 1932, 4,000 by the end of World War II, and 3,000 shortly after the AFL-CIO merger in 1955.

The GCIAA, which maintains its headquarters in Quincy, Massachusetts, holds quinquennial conventions. The union president, the only full-time official, is joined on the executive council by four members elected by GCIAA districts and one member each from the polishers and tool sharpeners. In 1973 the GCIAA reported a membership of 3,033 located in twenty-two local unions.

For further information, see *The Granite Cutters' Journal* published quarterly. See also *The American Federationist* (January 1947); Philip Taft, *The A.F. of L. in the Time of Gompers* (1957); and Norman J. Ware, *The Labor Movement in the United States, 1860-1895: A Study in Democracy* (1929).

GRAPHIC ARTS INTERNATIONAL UNION (GAIU). After several months of negotiations, two of the oldest unions in the American labor movement, the Amalgamated Lithographers of America (ALA) and the International Photoengravers Union of North America (IPUNA), merged on September 7, 1964, to form the Lithographers and Photoengravers International Union* (LPIU). The merger was designed to unify all unions in the graphic arts industry, to eliminate inter-union rivalries and "to accomplish the organization of all workers within its authority, to advance the economic and other interests of all members, to safeguard, enhance, and insure their job security, to enlarge upon their job opportunities, and to provide in every respect their continuing full share of reward in the growth and expansion of the graphic arts industry to which they contribute so substantially in the commitment of their working lives."

Consolidation within the graphic arts industry was further promoted on September 4, 1972, when the LPIU and the International Brotherhood of Bookbinders (IBB) merged to form the Graphic Arts International Union. This merger, like the previous merger between the ALA and the IPUNA, was designed to increase the bargaining power of the unions involved, to facilitate organization in the industry, and to eliminate costly jurisdictional conflicts arising from the rapidly changing technology in the industry.

International Brotherhood of Bookbinders. The bookbinding art was a handicraft skill dating back to the period in which the parchment roll gave way to books composed of several sheets. Catholic monks developed bookbinding into a highly skilled trade, but in the nineteenth century new technology and increasingly complex machinery eventually resulted in the mechanization of the trade.

The rapid technological change in the industry soon produced insecurities in the labor force. Skill levels provided less protection from unemployment or economic exploitation by employers, and by the mid-nineteenth century, bookbinders became increasingly susceptible to trade union organization. During the early years of union activity, bookbinders joined the International Typographical Union* (ITU), which accepted membership from most skilled craftsmen in the printing industry.

After four decades of membership in the ITU, the bookbinders withdrew in 1892 and joined with a few independent unions to form the International Brotherhood of Bookbinders. Two years later the ITU disclaimed any jurisdictional rights to the organization of these craftsmen and released its remaining bookbinder members to the IBB. On March 24, 1898, Samuel Gompers, president of the American Federation of Labor* (AFL), confirmed the new union's full acceptance in the labor community by extending a charter granting the IBB exclusive jurisdiction in the bookbinding trade.

From the date of its founding until the end of World War I, the IBB exhibited a steady and substantial membership growth. Unlike most other unions, this was not interrupted by the national open-shop campaign launched by employers in 1904. At the time of its AFL chartering, the IBB had 2,500 members; by 1904, 6,500 bookbinders had enrolled, and a decade later membership stood at 11,000. The IBB reached its early membership peak in 1920 when 20,700 bookbinders held union cards.

Two decades of frustration and decline followed the IBB's comparable period of success and accomplishment. A disastrous nationwide strike for the forty-four-hour week in 1921 signaled its changing fortunes. The strike came at an extremely unpropitious time during a short but severe economic recession accompanying reconversion to peacetime production. Before the strike ended, the IBB lost thousands of members and faced financial bankruptcy. The slow, difficult recuperation the IBB realized during the remainder of the decade ended, and as the Great Depression exposed a near fatal malignancy in the national economy, it suffered a relapse.

Gradual economic recovery and New Deal legislative cures held great promise for a healthy IBB recovery. To a considerable extent the IBB realized that promise during the World War II and postwar periods. By 1950 the IBB had organized well over 75 percent of the eligible workers in its trade jurisdiction, including employees in the special editions and magazine fields whose employers had proven especially resistant to trade unionism. Meanwhile the IBB won collective bargaining concessions comparable to those achieved by other unions in the printing industry. While willing to strike if necessary, the IBB developed amicable relations with most employers in the industry and emphasized the principles of mediation, conciliation, and arbitration in resolving contract disputes.

The IBB, which maintained its national headquarters in Washington, D.C., held biennial conventions. Principal officers included a president, five vice-presidents, and a secretary-treasurer. The executive council was composed of the above officers. Shortly before the merger creating the GAIU, the IBB reported a membership of 62,480 located in 199 local unions.

The GAIU, which maintains its national headquarters in Washington, D.C., holds triennial conventions. Principal officers include a president, eight vice-presidents, a recording secretary, a financial secretary, and a secretary-treasurer. The above officials also constitute the international executive board. In 1973 the GAIU reported a membership of 106,441 located in 316 local unions.

For further information, see the *Graphic Arts Unionist* issued nine times annually by the GAIU. Information on the IBB can be found in *The International Bookbinder* published bimonthly, and *The International Bookbinder* (n.d.) produced by the IBB. See, also, the references listed in this volume for the ALA, IPUNA, and LPIU.

HATTERS, CAP AND MILLINERY WORKERS INTERNATIONAL UNION; UNITED (UHCMW). Twenty-one workers representing 1,200 cap and hat makers met in New York City on December 27, 1901, and formally organized the United Cloth Hat and Cap Makers of North America (UCHCM). Their actions marked the climax of a long and frustrating effort to create a permanent union of cap makers. Local unions in the industry emerged during the first half of the nineteenth century, but it was not until 1878 that a union with national pretensions, the Cap Finishers' Union, appeared. This union, however, disintegrated after losing a strike in 1884. The Cap Finishers' fate was duplicated by the Joint Council of Cap Makers Union, 1886; Cloth Hat and Cap Operators No. 1, 1887-1891; and Cloth Hat and Cap Operators Union No. 2, 1893-1901. These early organizatioris succumbed to militant employer resistance, general economic conditions in the industry, and considerable internal antagonism between the native-born Americans, Irish, and German Jews who comprised the labor force in the industry. Rather than declining as Jewish workers began to dominate the work force, these antagonisms accelerated. Conflicts between German and Russian Jews and between left- and right-wing Socialists further retarded the organization of an effective union.

These internal problems immediately confronted the leadership of the newly organized UCHCM in 1901. One example was the question of whether to affiliate with the American Federation of Labor* (AFL) or Daniel DeLeon's Socialist Trade and Labor Alliance. Although originally resisting affiliation with either group, the advantages of an AFL affiliation became increasingly apparent, and on June 12, 1902, the UCHCM requested a charter. It was granted five days later. During its early years the new union made important forward strides. Union membership grew, and a series of successful strikes raised wages and improved working conditions.

The first serious challenge to the UCHCM occurred at the end of 1904 when an open-shop campaign was initiated by twenty New York manufacturers, backed by the National Association of Manufacturers and other anti-union employers. A three-month strike ensued in which the national labor movement came to the aid of the young and vulnerable UCHCM. The strike was ended by a compromise under which employers accepted a preferential union shop. Although far from a victory, the UCHCM survived the assault, and the open-shop drive in the cap industry was blunted. Moreover the strike vaulted Max Zuckerman into a leadership position in the union; Zuckerman was to be the central figure in the formative period of UCHCM history.

The recession of 1907 depressed both the industry and the union, but despite losing half its membership, the UCHCM survived and took advantage of the industry's upsurge in the following years. By the end of World War I, approximately 75 percent of the cap makers had been organized. During the same period the UCHCM made significant advances in the organization of millinery workers. In 1915 the first collective bargaining agreement of its kind in the industry was signed between millinery workers Local 24 and several New York manufacturers. A disastrous strike in 1918 eliminated many of these gains, however, and unionization of millinery workers was retarded for several years. Reflecting the interest in millinery workers, the union name was changed to Cloth Hat, Cap and Millinery Workers' International Union (CHCMW).

In a perverse way, the years of the 1920s were years of triumph for the CHCMW. The union survived the decade despite many obstacles: an open-shop offensive in the early 1920s; a decade-long depression in the cloth cap in-

dustry; a bitter jurisdictional war with the United Hatters of North America*
(UH), which resulted in the CHCMW's suspension from the AFL from 1918 to
1923; a violent struggle to prevent racketeers from taking over the millinery
industry; and a bitter intra-union conflict for control of the union between
moderates and Communists. The CHCMW survived all of these challenges,
but its triumph was costly. Union membership of cloth cap workers declined
from 4,233 in 1925 to 755 in 1932, and general union membership shrank
drastically from its 1920 level. The most hopeful development took place in the
millinery industry where the struggle against racketeers eventually led to an
unprecedented spirit of cooperation between manufacturers and union
leaders. This, along with militant organizing activities, stimulated unionization even during the depths of the Great Depression. The 3,987 millinery
workers organized in 1929 increased to 7,236 in 1933 and 12,647 a year later.

After the struggles of the 1920s, the CHCMW looked optimistically toward
the 1930s. One of the more significant achievements was the merger of the
CHCMW and the UH after years of bitter conflict. A merger was finally approved on January 17, 1924, creating the United Hatters, Cap and Millinery
Workers International Union with a membership of 19,375. Taking advantage
of its new unification and the favorable labor policies of Franklin D. Roosevelt's New Deal, the UHCMW moved to organize the entire industry. Within a
decade 70 percent of the men's hat workers, 80 percent of millinery workers,
and 90 percent of the cap workers had been organized. Meanwhile, UHCMW
membership rose to 30,000 in 1938 and 40,000 in 1944. Although favoring
industrial organization, the UHCMW was not immediately involved in the
struggle between the AFL and the Congress of Industrial Organizations,* and
Max Zaritsky's efforts to mediate the dispute were unsuccessful.

The bitter industrial relations that characterized the headwear industry
during the first three decades of the twentieth century changed dramatically
during the 1930s and 1940s. UHCMW leaders cultivated a spirit of labor-
management cooperation to protect the health and stability of the hat, cap,
and millinery industry, an important consideration to both workers and employers. Reflecting its cooperative approach to manufacturers, the UHCMW
conducted advertising campaigns to promote the industry, provided technological assistance to producers, made loans to manufacturers, and in a few
cases invested in or purchased companies threatened with bankruptcy. Nevertheless both the industry and the union were highly susceptible to fashion
trends, and when the popularity of hats waned following World War II, the
industry gradually declined.

The UHCMW, which maintains its national headquarters in New York
City, holds triennial conventions. Full-time officers include a president and
secretary-treasurer. The general executive board is composed of the above officers and twenty-four vice-presidents. In 1973 the UHCMW reported a
membership of 15,000 located in fifty-nine local unions.

For further information, see *The Hat Worker* published bimonthly by the

UHCMW. See also Donald B. Robinson, *Spotlight on a Union: The Story of the United Hatters, Cap and Millinery Workers International Union* (1948), a valuable account of both union organization and industrial trends in the headwear industry, and Charles H. Green, *The Headwear Workers* (1944), an account published by the UHCMW.

HATTERS OF NORTH AMERICA; UNITED (UH). The decade of the 1820s witnessed the first great wave of union organization in the United States, and employees of the well-established American hat industry fully participated in the movement. As early as 1822 a group of New York journeymen hatters attempted to establish a closed shop, and by 1833 at least three hatters' unions existed in New York City. Associations of hatters are also known to have existed in Philadelphia, Cincinnati, Baltimore, Schenectady, New York, and Newark, New Jersey. Although these local hatters' unions often informally cooperated and supported city-wide association of laborers, no attempt was made to organize a national association of hatters' unions.

The panic of 1837 and the following depression destroyed much of this early labor organization. Trade unionism, however, revived during the 1850s, and this time hatters formed a national association, the United States Hat Finishers Trade Organization. Inspired by the rapid mechanization of the hat-making industry during the second quarter of the nineteenth century, the new organization was founded in Philadelphia on June 5, 1854, by twenty-seven delegates representing twelve unions throughout the nation. Delegates at the founding convention elected Robert J. Tiffany president. During the years before the Civil War, locals of the new national engaged in a number of successful skirmishes with employers, and union membership grew rapidly during and immediately following the war. A membership of 879 in 1862 increased to 1,322 in 1866 and 2,100 in 1868.

A long-smoldering dispute over apprenticeship rules favoring a strict and exclusionist craft policy, however, divided the Hat Finishers Trade Association in 1868. Those favoring highly restrictive craft policies broke with the national organization and organized the Silk Hatters Union of America. The remainder, consisting primarily of felt hat finishers, adopted liberalized apprenticeship rules in 1869 after a constitutional revision. The reorganized national hatters' union was one of the few to survive the depression that began in 1873.

A second major national union in the men's hat industry appeared in 1883 when the National Hat Makers Association of the United States was founded in Norwalk, Connecticut. Cordial relations between the Hat Finishers and Hat Makers facilitated a coordinated campaign against contract convict labor and the establishment of a joint union label. The two unions affiliated with the Knights of Labor* in 1886 as District Assembly 128. The years between 1886 and 1893 were successful years for the men's hat industry and those employed therein. Much of the industry was organized, and relations between the unions and manufacturers were friendly.

The good times and harmony in the hat industry ended with the industrial depression beginning in 1893. Union resistance to wage reductions led to an employer offensive against the unions. The conflict was a costly one for unions in the industry and led to an increased interest in a long-discussed merger of the Hat Finishers and Hat Makers. The amalgamation was accomplished on January 18, 1896, in New York City, thus creating the United Hatters of North America.

In an effort to recoup its 1893 losses and taking advantage of the upsurge of union organization at the turn of the century, the new union launched a vigorous organizing drive. The campaign was marked by a series of successes until the UH confronted D. E. Loewe & Co., of Danbury, Connecticut. Seeking a total of $240,000 in damages, Loewe initiated suit against 248 members of the Danbury Hatters' Union under the provisions of the Sherman Anti-trust Act. The UH lost a lengthy court fight in which the American Federation of Labor* (AFL) fully participated, and the legality of its major weapon, the union boycott, was severely challenged. The Danbury case consumed the attention of union officials and virtually bankrupted the UH. This, along with an aggressive employer open-shop offensive, eliminated most of the gains the union had made since 1896.

The UH broadened its jurisdictional reach in 1911, and in the following years, trimmers, wool hatters, and millinery workers were eligible for membership. Nevertheless, the union decline precipitated by the historic Danbury struggle continued through World War I, when most unions prospered, and persisted throughout the 1920s. The UH suffered for many reasons: a general decline in the men's hat industry; its resistance to the introduction of machinery; a general lack of initiative and vigor; and a costly jurisdictional struggle with the United Cloth Hat, Cap and Millinery Workers Union.*

Conflicts with the Cap Workers began in 1915 as a result of the UH's decision to organize millinery workers, an area in which the Cap Workers were already active. The jurisdictional dispute was placed before the 1916 AFL convention, where the UH received a favorable ruling, but the Cap Workers ignored the decision, and a long jurisdictional struggle ensued. A temporary compromise in 1923 introduced a period of amicable relations between the two unions lasting until 1931. At that time, the UH laid claim to workers in the women's felt hat industry, which the Cap Workers had organized by default. An intense and bitter jurisdictional war raged until the fall of 1932 when the presidents of the UH and Cap Workers, Michael Greene and Max Zaritsky, met and agreed to an amalgamation of the two unions. On June 22, 1933, a merger proposal was agreed upon; the merger took place on January 17, 1934.

The UH, which maintained its national headquarters in New York City, held biennial conventions. Principal officers included a president, vice-president, and secretary-treasurer. The joint executive board consisted of the above officials, a board of directors, and representatives of the two unions that had merged at its birth. By the time of the merger with the Cap Workers, the UH's membership had fallen below 10,000.

For further information, see the *Journal of the United Hatters of North America*, 1898-1905, and *The Hatter*, 1926-1927. See also Donald B. Robinson, *Spotlight on a Union: The Story of the United Hatters, Cap and Millinery Workers International Union* (1948), and Charles H. Green, *The Headwear Workers* (1944).

HOCKEY LEAGUE PLAYERS' ASSOCIATION; NATIONAL (NHLPA). In December 1966 players employed by the Springfield Indians hockey team struck to protest several grievances. The strike reflected a growing restiveness among the hockey players performing in the National and American Hockey leagues. The Springfield players engaged R. Alan Eagleson, a Toronto lawyer and member of the Ontario legislature, to represent them. Eagleson, who had previously represented individual National Hockey League (NHL) players as legal counsel, had established a reputation as an effective negotiator. Consequently, on December 28, 1966, players of the Boston Bruin club arranged a meeting with Eagleson in Montreal, where he was retained to explore the possibilities of establishing a hockey players' association. Because the NHL planned a large expansion in 1967 bringing many new players into the league, Eagleson found it necessary to meet not only with the players in the NHL but also with the American and Western Hockey League teams. Eagleson's inquiries met with an overwhelmingly favorable response.

With these initiatives already taken, player representatives from six NHL clubs attended the annual meeting of NHL owners in Montreal in June 1967, and at a player-owner council meeting, they informed the owners of the formation of the National Hockey League Players' Association and of the retention of Alan Eagleson as counsel and spokesman. After a short time, the owners agreed to recognize the association as the representative of the NHL players. The resulting negotiations resolved such issues as pay for exhibition games, meal allowances, and a recognition agreement.

During its first year, the NHLPA encountered two major problems. Resulting from a misunderstanding growing from the June 1967 negotiations, several NHL players refused to report to training camp. The NHL players believed the owners had agreed that all NHLPA members would be signed prior to the opening of training camps, but the owners argued that no such understanding had been reached. After several meetings with owners and players, the NHLPA arranged an acceptable adjustment. The second problem involved the management of the Toronto franchise, which seemed determined to break the association. This irritant ended when all but three members of the Toronto club applied for NHLPA membership, although the association's first president, Bob Pulford, a member of the Toronto Maple Leafs, resigned because not all the players on his team joined the NHLPA.

Early collective bargaining negotiations were concerned primarily with the NHL pension plan, which was eventually adjusted to the satisfaction of the NHLPA. During subsequent bargaining sessions, other adjustments were made in the pension system, compensation for exhibition games was increased, and the NHLPA was granted the right to meet each NHL team at training camp. The NHLPA's financial stability was assured when its officials signed an agreement with the Licensing Corporation of America. The arrangement involved the use of the NHLPA logogram on commercial products and provided enough money to make the association self-supporting.

The NHLPA, which maintains its national headquarters in Toronto, holds semiannual meetings. The principal official of the NHLPA is an executive director appointed by the executive board, which is composed of the association's president, vice-president, and player representatives from each NHL club. In 1973 the NHLPA had a membership of 320 located in sixteen local clubs.

For further information, see "Background and History of the Association" (n.d.), a brief, unpublished history produced by the NHLPA.

HOD CARRIERS, BUILDING AND COMMON LABORERS UNION OF AMERICA; INTERNATIONAL. *See* Laborer's International Union of America.

HORSESHOERS OF THE UNITED STATES AND CANADA; INTERNATIONAL UNION OF JOURNEYMEN (IUJH). Delegates from several local unions met on April 27, 1874, and organized the Journeymen Horseshoers' National Union of the United States of America. The present title was adopted in 1893 when organizing activities were extended into Canada. On July 1, 1893, the IUJH received a charter from the American Federation of Labor* (AFL) conferring exclusive jurisdiction over horseshoeing.

From its founding, the IUJH operated on strict trade union principles. A four-year apprenticeship was established as a requirement for membership, but allowances were made for apprentices who exhibited exceptional proficiency before they completed the regular apprenticeship. Local unions conducted collective bargaining negotiations, but agreements had to be approved by the international executive board.

The IUJH grew steadily from its founding until the depression of the 1890s, when membership declined precipitantly. During the early years of the twentieth century, the IUJH once again experienced considerable organizing success as membership grew from 2,000 in 1900 to nearly 8,000 a decade later. The demise of the horse as the primary means of local transportation, however, resulted in reduced employment in the IUJH trade jurisdiction. With the growing utilization of automobiles after World War I, the IUJH, although exhibiting considerable tenacity, evolved into a very small, specialty union with a declining membership.

The IUJH, which maintains its national headquarters in Miami, holds biennial conventions. Principal officers include a president, a secretary-treasurer (the only full-time officer), and three vice-presidents. The above officials constitute the international executive council. In 1973 the IUJH reported a membership of 390 located in twenty-four local unions.

For further information, see the *International Horseshoer* published periodically by the IUJH. Information can also be found in *Bulletins No. 420, 506,* and *618,* Bureau of Labor Statistics, U.S. Department of Labor (1926, 1929, 1936), and Florence Peterson, *Handbook of Labor Unions* (1944).

HOSIERY WORKERS; AMERICAN FEDERATION OF (AFHW). The organization of the United Textile Workers of America* (UTWA) in 1901 stimulated the organization of various associated workers. The unionization of hosiery workers, one such group of textile operatives, lagged until the development of the silk stocking industry added hundreds of new workers to the craft. The first permanent dues-paying union of hosiery workers, Local 706, was established in Philadelphia in 1909. Thereafter, locals sprang up all over the nation.

By 1913 the hosiery locals, which organized and constituted themselves as the American Federation of Full Fashioned Hosiery Workers (AFFFHW), felt sufficiently strong to request that the UTWA grant them independent status as a federation within the UTWA. The AFFFHW also asked that the UTWA order every affiliated hosiery local to enroll with it, and in turn the federation would require all of its members to affiliate with the UTWA. Delegates to the annual UTWA convention in 1913 acted favorably on a resolution encompassing these proposals, but when the AFFFHW attempted to push the UTWA even further toward craft autonomy the following year, their efforts met with resistance. During the 1915 convention, the AFFFHW proposed a sharing of the per-capita tax between the UTWA and the federation. When this proposal was rejected, the AFFFHW (with the exception of Philadelphia Local 706) withdrew from the UTWA.

During the following five years, Local 706, which had approximately the same membership as the combined total of those unions withdrawing, spearheaded the UTWA's attacks on the secessionist unions. Faced with UTWA hostility on one side and a growing employer offensive on the other, the

AFFFHW began searching for allies. The first approach was to the newly organized Amalgamated Textile Workers of America* (ATW), which proposed to establish joint boards in all cities where ATW and AFFFHW locals existed. The failure to establish a textile council in Philadelphia to replace the defunct UTWA council, however, forced the AFFFHW to reconsider its decision to affiliate with the ATW. Once again Local 706 had remained faithful to the UTWA, and when it refused to affiliate with the proposed textile council, other hosiery locals, feeling that they had to stick together, rescinded their favorable vote on affiliation with the ATW. Similarly, the AFFFHW also attended the preliminary meetings leading to the formation of the Federated Textile Unions of America, a loose association of independent textile unions, but were again deterred by the absence of Local 706.

Ultimately leaders of the AFFFHW looked to the UTWA, and as a result of a series of conferences with UTWA officials, agreed to reaffiliate as a semiautonomous federation. Under the terms of the agreement, which added more than 2,000 hosiery workers to the UTWA membership rolls, the AFFFHW was to retain its authority in all matters not directly affecting the interests of the UTWA.

During the 1920s, the hosiery worker locals played a significant role in the UTWA. Unlike most other unions, the AFFFHW grew steadily throughout the decade, reaching a membership of 5,000 by 1925, 8,000 a year later, and 12,000 by 1932. By the latter date, the hosiery workers constituted over one-third of the UTWA's membership and contributed at least that percentage to its financial support. The AFFFHW also made significant contributions to the UTWA organizing efforts, especially in the South.

When the Congress of Industrial Organizations* (CIO) launched the Textile Workers Organizing Committee under the auspices of the UTWA in 1937, the AFFFHW vigorously participated in the organizing drive, and a year later affiliated with the Textile Workers Union of America* (TWUA). When the UTWA split, one group returned to the American Federation of Labor* (AFL) and the other joined the CIO. In April 1948 the AFHW was expelled from the TWUA and thereafter remained independent until August 8, 1951, when it received an AFL charter. On April 15, 1965, the AFHW reaffiliated with the TWUA, now an affiliate of the AFL-CIO.*

The AFHW, which maintained its national headquarters in Philadelphia, held annual conventions. Full-time officers included a president, two vice-presidents, and a secretary-treasurer. The AFHW national executive board was composed of full-time officers and fourteen members elected at national conventions. At the time of the merger with the TWUA, the AFHW had a membership of 5,000.

For further information, see *The Hosiery Worker*, a monthly published by the AFHW. Robert R. R. Brooks, "The United Textile Workers of America" (Ph.D. dissertation, Yale University, 1935), also contains valuable information. See also Laurence Rogin, *Making History: The Story of the American Federation of Hosiery Workers* (1938), and George W. Taylor, *The Full-Fashioned Hosiery Worker: His Changing Economic Status* (1931).

HOTEL AND RESTAURANT EMPLOYEES AND BARTENDERS INTERNATIONAL UNION (HREBIU). Organization in the bartending and catering trades dates back to 1866 when waiters and bartenders in Chicago formed a local union. In 1880 this union affiliated with the Knights of Labor* (KofL), but later it conflicted with the Knights, which desired to exclude bartenders from the organization. Dissatisfaction with the KofL led to affiliation with the American Federation of Labor* (AFL) in 1890. Several more waiters and bartenders locals were organized, and in April 1891, a national union, the Waiters and Bartenders National Union, was founded. Subsequently at the first national convention held in New York City, in 1892, the union's name was changed to the Hotel and Restaurant Employees National Alliance. In 1898 the name changed again to the Hotel and Restaurant Employees' International Alliance and Bartenders' International League of America.

Divisions in the union developed early between a Chicago faction headed by W. C. Pomeroy and the rest of the union led by Jere Sullivan of St. Louis. Sullivan objected to Pomeroy's use of the union as a springboard for his political ambitions. At the 1896 convention Sullivan charged Pomeroy with misuse of funds, failure to honor cards of members from other cities, and unlawful expulsion of opponents from the general executive board. It was not until 1899 when Sullivan was elected general secretary-treasurer that he ousted Pomeroy from control and assumed leadership of the national union.

Sullivan embarked upon a program of reorganization. Gompers and the AFL supported Sullivan and, thus, when Pomeroy was expelled from the union in 1900, the AFL did nothing. Sullivan implemented craft organization based upon the unionization of the bartenders. Between 1902 and 1914 the HREBIU concentrated on unionizing bartenders, which created friction between bartenders and waiters, cooks, and other restaurant employees who desired union affiliation. This antagonism not only plagued the HREBIU for many years but also led to the formation of rival restaurant unions.

Although the Sullivan-controlled HREBIU was basically conservative and craft oriented in approach, the San Francisco and Rocky Mountain locals were primarily industrial organizations. Members in these two areas always displayed a more militant outlook and succeeded in unionizing large numbers of unskilled and semiskilled workers; moreover, the western locals retained an autonomy that effectively prevented Sullivan from meddling in their affairs.

In the first two decades of the twentieth century, the luxury hotel business boomed, opening many jobs for waiters, cooks, bellhops, and other hotel personnel, but because Sullivan refused to organize the unskilled and foreign-born, the HREBIU did not invade the hotel trade. This was particulary true in New York City and Chicago. Workers then often joined more radical unions such as the Hotel Workers International Union, which the Industrial Workers of the World* infiltrated, or later the Food Workers Industrial Union (FWIU).

The onset of Prohibition in 1920 came at the end of a three-year period of declining HREBIU enrollment and further eroded union membership. As a result of the enactment of the Eighteenth Amendment, the HREBIU lost approximately one-third of its members almost immediately. Although the number of cafeteria workers increased significantly in the 1920s, HREBIU leaders, composed mainly of former bartenders, failed to organize these workers. In addition a vigorous open-shop campaign waged by employers during the decade contributed to the declining fortunes of the union.

Forced to reassess their policies as a result of continual union decline, many HREBIU leaders openly criticized Sullivan's craft-unionist orientation and his despotic control over the union. At the 1927 convention anti-Sullivan sentiment came to a head when HREBIU president Edward Flore charged the secretary-treasurer with neglect of duties, especially regarding aid to locals for organizational drives. Flore had the union constitution amended to enable the president rather than the secretary-treasurer to appoint organizers, but he had to wait until Sullivan's death in 1928 to overhaul union leadership. At that time Flore responded to the demands for organizing the unskilled by bringing more industrial-oriented western leaders into the International's bureaucracy. More importantly, Flore undertook a drive to organized long-neglected New York City. A new local (16) was chartered to cover the theater district, while Local 302 was given jurisdictional rights over cafeteria workers. Local 302, however, faced competition from the left-wing Amalgamated Food Workers Union, as well as conflict from Local 1, which claimed jurisdiction over cafeteria workers.

Still, the HREBIU did not fully commit itself to industrial organization until 1932 when the international convention passed a resolution endorsing the organization of busboys, porters, housemaids, and other unskilled workers. From 1934 to 1937, the union concentrated upon organizing the unskilled. The 1934 convention supported amalgamated unions that ignored craft distinctions, but the convention refused to endorse a resolution authorizing delegates to be sent to the next AFL convention supporting John L. Lewis and the pro-industrial union faction in the AFL. Undoubtedly the most significant action undertaken by Flore toward the organization of the unskilled was the merger with the FWIU in 1935 and 1936. As a result approximately 9,000 new members, mostly unskilled, were brought into the HREBIU.

Meanwhile, in the 1930s and 1940s gangsterism plagued the union. In New York City and Chicago it was alleged that HREBIU officials consorted with racketeers who had gained control of key locals, and Locals 6 and 302 in New York were especially dominated by gangsters. The problem came to a head in

1936 with the murder of Harry Koenig of Local 6 at the HREBIU national convention, which met in Rochester, New York. Subsequent investigation by the Special Commission on Crime headed by Thomas Dewey revealed a flourishing restaurant racketeering business in New York City and Chicago. In 1937 three HREBIU officials were convicted, Locals 16 and 302 were suspended, and those members associated with criminal activities expelled.

Inspired by the example of the drive by the Congress of Industrial Organizations* in coal and steel, the HREBIU began its own massive organizational drives from 1937 to 1941. Finally, service workers were brought into the union and to facilitate their organization, a new local, Hotel Service Workers Local 283 (San Francisco), was chartered. Because jurisdictional claims of this local often conflicted with the Building Service Employees International Union* (BSEIU), the AFL executive board ruled that only workers in apartment and hotel buildings with eating establishments could be organized by the HREBIU; all others would remain under BSEIU control.

In the late 1930s and early 1940s attention was focused on hotel workers. The HREBIU San Francisco strike of 1937 resulted in agreements with most of the city's hotels and firmly established the power of the union in that city. Hotel organization in New York City also progressed. The solution of jurisdictional disputes and the ouster of gangsters made this task easier. In 1938 Jay Rubin and Gertrude Lane led a drive to organize hotel workers and additionally provided the impetus for the formation of the New York Hotel Trades Council. Subsequently in December 1938 the New York Hotel Association, representing sixty-two large hotels, entered into a comprehensive agreement with the eleven locals of the council.

Like many other unions, the HREBIU experienced post-World War II conflicts over the issue of Communist membership. Locals 1, 6, and 89 in New York City were accused of being Communist infiltrated. These locals long had been left wing, and radical elements had played an important role in leading organizational drives. Still, in 1946 a union committee empowered to investigate Communist activities in the New York locals ordered all Communist affiliation severed, upon threat of expulsion from the International. The Communist problem erupted again in 1949 and 1950, resulting in the reorganization of Local 6 and the removal of its Communist and left-wing members.

Although membership in the late 1940s and early 1950s remained consistently near 400,000, the HREBIU succeeded in securing the eight-hour day and in passing health and welfare legislation. The union also became more centralized as international officers were allowed to intervene directly in the affairs of its locals. The 1949 decision to hold conventions every four years reflects this centralization.

The HREBIU, which maintains its national headquarters in Cincinnati, holds quinquennial conventions. Principal officers include a president, eleven vice-presidents elected by geographical district, three vice-presidents elected at large, and a secretary-treasurer. The above officials constitute the general executive board. In 1973 the HREBIU reported a membership of 458,029 located in 441 local unions.

For further information, see the *Catering Industry Employee* published monthly by the HREBIU. See also Matthew Josephson, *The History of the Hotel and Restaurant Employees and Bartenders International Union, AFL-CIO* (1956); Jay Rubin and Michael Obermeier, *Growth of a Union: The Life and Times of Edward Flore* (1943); and Morris A. Horowitz, *The New York Hotel Industry: A Labor Relations Study* (1960).

                                                          Marie Tedesco

INDUSTRIAL WORKERS OF THE WORLD (IWW). The failure of the American Labor Union* (ALU) to effectively challenge the hegemony of craft unionism and its principal sponsor and defender, the American Federation of Labor* (AFL), led numerous advocates of industrial unionism to contemplate the organization of a new national organization they hoped would be more effective. At a Chicago meeting held late in 1904, several AFL critics, all strong proponents of the Socialist cause, met to discuss the founding of a new labor federation. As a result of their deliberations, a secret call was issued for a conference to meet in Chicago on January 2, 1905.

Twenty-two labor reformers responded to the invitation. The delegates included William Haywood, Charles Moyer, and John O'Neill of the Western Federation of Miners* (WFM), the only union of any significance represented at the conference; Daniel MacDonald, Clarence Smith, and Thomas Hagerty, representing the ALU; and the famous Mary "Mother" Jones, the only woman in attendance. The conferees, most self-appointed representatives of the working class, agreed on several basic principles, including the necessity of creating a general industrial union incorporating all industries and the inevitability of class conflict. The delegates then adopted the famous "Industrial Union Manifesto" condemning craft unionism and issued a call for a conference to meet in Chicago on June 27, 1905, to create a new national organization based on the principles of Marxist class conflict and industrial unionism.

The convention call was answered by 203 delegates. Again, the only substantial organization represented was the WFM. Besides the union faction dominated by the WFM, two other significant groups attended the conference. One followed the lead of Daniel DeLeon and hoped to commit the new organization to the Socialist Labor party (SLP). The other faction consisted of supporters of the Socialist party of America (SPA) who saw in such an organization a potential source of new voter support.

Although representing an amalgam of varied radical causes, the delegates were united by their hatred of Samuel Gompers and the AFL and exhibited an unusual degree of harmony. The two most divisive issues confronting the conferees revolved around the questions of political action and the general administrative structure of the proposed organization. While refusing to endorse either Socialist party, the delegates, many of whom viewed any political activity as a waste of time, agreed upon a vague commitment to socialist political action as a concession to the political radicals. The structural arguments centered upon Hagerty's elaborate and confusing "Wheel of Fortune." The general administration was located at the center of the wheel, and radiating out were five departments at the circumference and thirteen industrial divisions in between. Although unenthusiastic, the delegates ultimately accepted the Wheel. Finally, it was decided to name the organization the Industrial Workers of the World, and Charles O. Sherman and William Trautmann were elected president and secretary-treasurer.

Any exaggerated hopes that the IWW would explode upon the labor scene, leaving the AFL leaders to ponder their failure, quickly proved illusory. Instead the early years of the IWW were fraught with discord, frustration, and failure. Worried about the influence of DeLeon and concluding that the AFL offered much better opportunities for political education, most SPA leaders soon disassociated themselves from the IWW. The WFM was next to defect. During the second national convention of the IWW, a split developed between a conservative, trade unionist faction, which advocated increased concentration on industrial unionism and less emphasis on revolutionary principles, and a radical faction led by Secretary-Treasurer Trautmann, DeLeon, and Vincent St. John. When the radicals won, President Sherman and many of the WFM delegates left the convention. A legal struggle then ensued for control of IWW properties and finances, and again the radicals won. As a result there were two IWWs, one led by Sherman, which included the WFM, and the other following the more radical pronouncements of Trautmann and DeLeon. The Sherman-IWW failed to build any significant support and soon disintegrated, and the WFM returned to the AFL in 1911.

Although reduced to a small cadre of hard-core radicals, the Trautmann faction meanwhile launched an organizing offensive among the disaffected agricultural, lumber, and dock workers who had been ignored by the AFL unions. Although achieving only limited success, the campaign revived the IWW, but this soon produced further discord. Uninterested in revolutionary theory or political ideology, the new recruits demanded more action and less rhetoric and clashed with the pedantic DeLeon. Soon each was hurling verbal broadsides at the other, and when the rhetorical smoke cleared, DeLeon had been expelled. He then organized yet another IWW, the "Detroit" IWW; but largely a figment of DeLeon's ego and imagination, it was never much more than a SLP publicity organ.

The legitimate IWW that emerged from the 1908 convention quickly made its presence felt on the national scene. Beginning in Spokane, Washington, in 1909, it launched a series of free-speech fights that soon spread to a number of cities. During these dramatic confrontations, IWW members and sympathizers filled city jails until embattled city officials recognized that the freedom of the press also applied to IWW members as did the right to assemble peacefully and to distribute their publications to the public.

An equally spectacular series of strikes and organizing campaigns startled the nation. In the East the IWW concentrated on depressed textile workers and won a dramatic strike in Lawrence, Massachusetts, which resulted in higher wages for employees in most of the city's mills. A year later, however, an equally dramatic strike of silk workers in Paterson, New Jersey, failed, leaving the IWW's eastern organizing effort in disarray. A short time later, scattered locals of midwestern agricultural workers banded together into the Agricultural Workers Organization (AWO), perhaps the most successful IWW venture. Demanding higher wages, shorter hours, and improved living conditions, the AWO managed to gain effective control over migratory harvest labor by the fall of 1916 and acquired a membership approaching 18,000. Another area of intense IWW involvement was the Pacific Northwest, where the IWW concentrated on the organization of lumber workers. During this campaign, punctuated by the infamous Everett massacre of 1916, the IWW developed the "strike-on-the-job" or slowdown tactic during a 1917 lumber strike. The IWW also led a major strike in the copper mining industry of the Southwest, broken by the illegal deportation of hundreds of strikers, including friends and relatives, from the mining centers of Jerome and Bisbee, Arizona.

Although its successes were limited and its membership small, the IWW remained a viable organization as the United States drifted toward war in 1917. But after the United States declared war, the full weight of oppressive federal, state, and local governments plus the vigilante activities of local defenders of American liberty, fell upon the shoulders of the rather hapless band of radical agitators who had transversed the country singing "Hallelujah I'm a Bum!" Upset by the revolutionary rhetoric, the violence that accompanied IWW strikes, and, most of all, the IWW's opposition to the war effort, agents of the federal government determined to exterminate the IWW menace. In the fall of 1917, agents of the Justice Department conducted raids on IWW offices and the homes of IWW members in several cities. Thousands were arrested, including William Haywood and the entire IWW executive board.

In the spring of 1918, 105 of those arrested were brought to trial in Chicago and charged with a variety of offenses associated with the conduct of war; 91 were convicted. Moreover, arrests, trials, and convictions continued in both federal and state courts during the months that followed until virtually all capable IWW leaders were either awaiting trial, in prison, or in exile. Although the IWW refused to die, it largely ceased to be an active organization after the government purges. Through the years, it gradually enrolled a number of student radicals, romantic revolutionaries perhaps well within the tradition of the martyred heroes of the halcyon years.

The IWW indulged in a flaming, revolutionary rhetoric that made its essentially conservative economic objectives difficult, if not impossible, to attain. While its dedication to the improvement of the working and living conditions of depressed workers cannot be questioned, the IWW seldom left workers they assisted in strikes across the nation any better off than they found them. Few IWW organizers appeared willing or able to undertake the time-consuming, patient, and disciplined effort required to build strong, stable unions. Moreover, little or no effort was expended on negotiations that might have avoided the strikes so devastating to the workers involved. Instead, there appears to have been an obsession with confrontation—confrontations in which the strikers became pawns soon forgotten as their leaders moved on to challenge the establishment at another time and another place.

Nevertheless, the IWW served the labor movement and the nation well. By comparison, for many employers, the AFL became an acceptable, conservative alternative to the IWW. The IWW also demonstrated the ability to organize unskilled workers in the factory and on the farm, new immigrants, black workers, and the miners, lumberjacks, and dock workers so long neglected by the establishment labor movement. While seldom successful, the spectacular IWW strikes dramatically exposed the deplorable working and living conditions of a desperate class of unskilled industrial workers. Finally, the repression of the IWW revealed in clear and unmistakable ways the close relationship existing between business and government and the lengths to which this partnership was willing to go to protect its presumed prerogatives.

The IWW, which maintained its national headquarters in Chicago, held annual conventions. Principal officers included a general organizer, chief administrative officer from 1906 until replaced by the secretary-treasurer in 1915. The executive board was comprised of representatives of each industrial department. Although accurate membership figures are not available, the IWW claimed a membership ranging from 58,000 to 100,000 during the 1919-1924 period.

For further information, see the *Industrial Worker* published biweekly by the IWW. The most comprehensive study of the much-studied IWW is Melvyn Dubofsky, *We Shall Be All: A History of the Industrial Workers of the World* (1969). See also Paul F. Brissenden, *The I.W.W.: A Study of American Syndicalism* (1920), and *The Launching of the Industrial Workers of the World* (1913); John Gambs, *The Decline of the I.W.W.* (1932); Patrick Renshaw, *The Wobblies: The Story of Syndicalism in the United States* (1967); and Philip S. Foner, *History of the Labor Movement in the United States*, vol. 4 (1965). IWW activities in the Northwest are analyzed by Robert L. Tyler, *Rebels of the Woods: The I.W.W. in the Pacific Northwest* (1967). The most famous IWW leader, William Haywood, has written his autobiography, *Bill Haywood's Book: The Autobiography of William D. Haywood* (1929), and he is treated in Joseph H. Conlin, *Big Bill Haywood and the Radical Union Movement* (1969).

INSURANCE WORKERS INTERNATIONAL UNION (IWIU). Organization of insurance workers began as early as the last quarter of the nineteenth century. In 1895 the national convention of the American Federation of Labor* (AFL) seated an insurance delegate from the American Agents Association. The American labor movement, however, viewing the insurance industry with considerable suspicion, if not hostility, and, tending to associate the agents with the companies, showed little interest in organizing insurance workers. Indeed, the AFL in 1900 not only refused to seat the delegate from the Agents Association but enacted a resolution prohibiting the chartering of unions of insurance agents. Nevertheless organizations of insurance workers continued to appear in the nation's major insurance centers.

The most influential union to enroll insurance workers was New York City "Bookkeepers, Stenographers and Accountants' Union" (BSAU), chartered directly by the AFL as Federal Labor Union 12646. Because of a strong left-wing element in its leadership, the federal union had carried on a volatile relationship with the AFL. In 1927 the BSAU resolved to organize insurance workers and unsuccessfully attempted to unionize Metropolitan Life Insurance Company employees in New York City.

Year after year the AFL had refused to issue a national charter for a union of white-collar workers and continued to do so during the 1930s even though white-collar unionism had grown dramatically during the Great Depression. As BSAU demands for such a charter became more strident during the mid-1930s, the AFL responded by threatening suspension. The BSAU then reorganized as United Office and Professional Workers of America, International* (UOPWA), and sought a charter from the Congress of Industrial Organizations* (CIO); it was granted on June 1, 1937.

Responding to the CIO challenge, the AFL leadership suddenly reversed its position and established a union of insurance agents and issued an international charter to office and professional workers. In 1938 the AFL created the Industrial and Ordinary Insurance Agents Council and the Office Employees International Council with jurisdiction over white-collar workers.

The UOPWA concentrated its early efforts on organizing the Metropolitan and John Hancock insurance companies. On October 9, 1940, the UOPWA gained certification as the bargaining agent for Hancock's debit agents in the New York City metropolitan area, but, through a series of legal maneuvers, the company avoided collective bargaining for a time. The UOPWA's most significant success came on February 1, 1943, when the Prudential Life Insurance Company signed a national agreement with the UOPWA covering a thirty-one-state area.

Although the UOPWA had considerable success in organizing insurance workers and in winning collective bargaining elections, the internal affairs of the union were in almost constant turmoil. The left-wing faction in the union, which had always been strong, gained complete control of the UOPWA in

1942. Ideological conflicts, however, were subdued during World War II, but after the war the emerging cold war between the United States and the Soviet Union fueled the dispute, especially as the UOPWA leadership conformed more closely to the official Communist party line. Internal conflict reached a climax in 1948 when UOPWA leaders refused to take the non-Communist oath required by the Taft-Hartley Act, thus endangering the union's ability to use the representational election machinery of the National Labor Relations Board (NLRB). Despite the CIO's support of Harry Truman, the UOPWA's endorsement of Henry Wallace's presidential candidacy also rankled many members. At the UOPWA convention in 1948, a group of right-wing insurgents attempted to oust the UOPWA leadership; failing that, many left the UOPWA and joined the United Paperworkers of America,* which had created an autonomous insurance division to accommodate them.

Meanwhile, seeing an opportunity to take advantage of the disruption and unhappiness in the union, the AFL breathed new life into its nearly moribund Industrial and Ordinary Insurance Agents Council, renamed it the National Federation of Insurance Agents' Council, and challenged the CIO union in representation elections. Its greatest success came in 1949, when it dealt the UOPWA a devastating defeat in an NLRB election of Prudential agents, whom the UOPWA had represented since 1943.

The loss of the Prudential workers was just one of a number of hammer blows that signaled the imminent demise of the UOPWA. At the CIO's national convention in 1948, the UOPWA was officially charged with being Communist-dominated and two years later was expelled. Shortly thereafter, the UOPWA merged with the Distributive Workers Union and the Food, Tobacco, Agricultural and Allied Workers* to create the Distributive, Processing and Office Workers of America.

After the expulsion of the UOPWA, the CIO initiated the Insurance and Allied Workers Organizing Committee and three years later issued it a national charter as the Insurance Workers of America. The AFL National Federation of Insurance Agents Council, beneficiary of many of the UOPWA Prudential defections, was rechartered in 1951 as the Insurance Agents International Union. The two rival unions agreed to the 1953 no-raiding agreement negotiated between the national leaders of the AFL and CIO. After an extended period of negotiations, a merger of the two unions was effected on May 27, 1959, creating the Insurance Workers International Union.

The IWIU holds biennial conventions and maintains its national headquarters in Washington, D.C. Principal officers include a president, four vice-presidents, and a secretary-treasurer. The executive board consists of the above officials in addition to eighteen other members elected at biennial conventions. In 1973 the IWIU reported a membership of 23,556 located in 235 local unions.

For further information, see *The Insurance Worker* issued monthly by the IWIU. See also Harvey J. Clermont, *Organizing the Insurance Worker: A His-*

tory of Labor Unions of Insurance Employees (1966), a solid monograph, especially good for the 1940s and early 1950s, and *The American Federationist* (August 1950, December 1954, and June 1957).

INTERNATIONAL LABOR UNION (ILU). Delegates to the 1877 convention of the Workingmen's party of the United States, the American branch of the Red International, met in Newark, New Jersey, and made several far-reaching decisions. Most significantly, they changed the name of the party to the Socialist Labor Party and adopted a program almost exclusively political. Several members of the International, primarily from New York and the East Coast, raised objections to these decisions and withdrew from the party to devote their energies solely to the economic organization of labor. The dissenters followed two distinct lines of thought: one group joined with Ira Steward, George McNeill, and other eight-hour advocates in an attempt to organize the unskilled, and the other group, led by Adolph Strasser of the cigarmakers' union, hoped to rebuild the existing unions of skilled workers. The former organized the International Labor Union, and the latter eventually created the Federation of Organized Trades and Labor Unions.*

The ILU was founded in Boston in February 1878 when George McNeill and J. P. McDonnell organized a provisional central committee with members from eighteen different states. Despite the seemingly broad representation, however, the new union predominantly represented an amalgamation of Steward's eight-hour advocates in Massachusetts and the New York City trade unionist faction of the International. Although both groups advocated a radical solution to the exploitation of labor, they differed regarding the means. The eight-hour advocates assumed that the reduction in the hours of labor would inevitably increase the material wants of the worker. As a result irrepressible pressures for increased wages would eventually absorb employer profits. The trade unionists placed their emphasis on the economic organization of labor, which would eventually lead to the creation of a labor party controlled by the trade union movement.

Borrowing selectively from both sources, the founders of the ILU adopted the eight-hour theory of wages and the International's commitment to trade unionism. The program emphasized such economic objectives as shorter hours, higher wages, relief for the unemployed, factory and mine inspection, restrictions on convict and child labor, improved employer liability, and the creation of state and national bureaus of labor statistics. It was hoped that agitation for these reforms would serve to radicalize the working class, increase class consciousness, and precipitate the socialist revolution. The methods adopted to achieve these objectives were:

1st. The formation of an Amalgamated Union of Labourers so that members of any calling can combine under a central head, and form a part of the Amalgamated Trade Unions.

2nd. The establishment of a general fund for benefit and protective purposes.

3rd. The Organization of all workingmen in their Trade Unions, and the creation of such Unions where none exist.

4th. The National and International Amalgamation of all Labor Unions. [*Labor Standard*, October 12, 1878.]

The ILU's major organizing effort centered in the Northeastern textile industry. In June 1878 the ILU came to the assistance of striking cotton mill operatives protesting a wage reduction in Paterson, New Jersey, and Fall River, Massachusetts. When these strikes were resolved successfully, the reputation of the ILU was greatly enhanced, and its membership grew proportionately. In the following two years, however, the union became involved in a large number of textile strikes, particularly at Passaic, New Jersey, and Clinton and Cohoes, New York. Most ended in failure. Thereafter the ILU declined rapidly, and by 1881 it was reduced to a single branch at Hoboken, New Jersey, which existed until 1887.

Although confined primarily to the Northeastern textile industry and never markedly successful, the ILU did play a significant role in the development of the American labor movement. It represented the first concerted effort to organize unskilled laborers on a comprehensive scale. As such, it anticipated the strategy later adopted by the Knights of Labor* and, to a lesser extent, the Congress of Industrial Organizations.*

The ILU held annual conventions in various cities. It was governed by a president, a seven-member executive board, and a variably numbered central committee. The ILU reached its largest membership in late 1878 when it enrolled approximately 8,000 workers.

For further information, see John R. Commons et al., *History of Labour in the United States* (1918); Stuart B. Kaufman, *Samuel Gompers and the Origins of the American Federation of Labor, 1848-1896* (1973); Samuel Bernstein, *The First International in America* (1962); and George E. McNeill, ed., *The Labor Movement: The Problem of Today* (1887).

IRON, STEEL, AND TIN WORKERS; AMALGAMATED ASSOCIATION OF (AA). Unionization of the iron industry first began in the Pittsburgh area during the 1850s. As the center of the nation's heavy iron trade, Pittsburgh attracted skilled workers already experienced in trade unionism from the iron centers of the British Isles. The panic of 1857 stimulated an existing desire for collective labor action, and on April 12, 1858, a local union of iron puddlers, named the Iron City Forge of the Sons of Vulcan, was organized in Pittsburgh.

A secret organization with a small membership, it engaged in little trade union activity. The revival of the iron trade during the Civil War, however, revitalized the Sons of Vulcan, and on September 8, 1862, it reorganized as a national union—The Grand Forge of the United Sates, United Sons of Vulcan.

Few employer-labor conflicts erupted during the war, but immediately after the war, the effort to reduce wages precipitated a long eight-month strike. The Sons of Vulcan enjoyed some advantages in the struggle; the highly skilled iron puddlers were difficult to replace, and the centralization of the iron trade in the Pittsburgh area facilitated their organization. As a result of the strike, the union signed a trade agreement with an employers' association in February 1865, which contained a sliding scale of wages based on the selling price of bar iron. The settlement lasted for two years after which a new trade agreement, lasting until 1873, satisfied worker demands for higher wages.

The Sons of Vulcan grew slowly during the 1860s. In 1870 the national organization assumed authority over calling strikes and levying and collecting strike assessments. Thereafter the union grew rapidly, reaching nearly 3,500 members in seventy-one forges in 1873.

Workers in other branches of the industry had begun organizing about the same time as the puddlers. The first permanent local unions of workers employed in the furnaces and rolls of finishing departments appeared in Chicago in 1861. In August 1872 several lodges combined to form the Associated Brotherhood of Iron and Steel Heaters, Rollers and Roughers of the United States. By 1873 the new national union had organized twenty-two lodges in seven states and had a paid membership of 480. Rollers, roughers, catchers, hookers, straighteners, and buggymen also formed a national organization in Springfield, Illinois, on June 2, 1873—The National Union of Rollers, Roughers, Catchers and Hookers of the United States. Renamed the Iron and Steel Roll Hands Union in 1874, it had fifteen lodges and 473 members at its founding.

The panic of 1873 and the following depression accelerated an existing interest in the amalgamation of all these trade unions into one national iron trade union. It was a period of frequent strike activity precipitated by efforts to lower wages, and the unions had failed in many of these strikes, leading many unionists to the conclusion that the lack of trade union unity was responsible for the reverses. After a period of extended negotiations, the Amalgamated Association of Iron and Steel Workers of the United States was founded in Pittsburgh on August 3, 1876.

The early accomplishments of the AA seemed to justify the optimism of those involved in its founding. It had considerable success in its conflicts with employers, and the number of lodges and members grew steadily, although at no time was 25 percent of the iron and steel industry organized. By 1891 membership had reached a peak of 24,068, and the union had 290 locals organized in eight districts. Within a few years of its organization, the AA had become one of the leading trade unions in the United States and played an influential role in the emerging national labor movement. The AA president presided over several of the meetings preliminary to the formation of the Federation of Organized Trades and Labor Unions* in 1881 and also was influential in the creation of the American Federation of Labor* (AFL) in 1886. The AA disaffiliated briefly from the AFL in 1887, however, because of the federation's refusal to support the high tariff policy favored by the AA.

The AA met its first great crisis in 1892 when it decided to oppose wage cuts instituted by the Carnegie Steel Company at its Homestead, Pennsylvania, plant. The result was the historic Homestead strike. The confrontation, which included a pitched battle between strikers and an army of Pinkerton detectives, ended in disaster for the AA. Declaration of marshal law and the intervention of the state militia crushed the strike, and few of the strikers gained re-employment in the Carnegie mills.

Failure of the strike reversed the AA's previous growth pattern. Membership fell below 10,000 by 1894, and a year later, the number of active lodges fell to 125. It was not until 1900 that the AA began rebuilding its membership. The revival, however, was destined to be short-lived. At its 1901 convention, the AA enacted a constitutional amendment stating: "Should one mill in a combine or trust have a difficulty, all mills in such combine or trust shall cease work until such grievance is settled." The issue almost immediately came to the fore when the AA entered into contract negotiations with mills and subsidiaries of the newly incorporated United States Steel Company (USS). The AA demanded a contract including all USS mills. The company countered with a proposal that, while not meeting AA's demands for total unionization, would have substantially expanded AA's contracts in the industry. In retrospect it is clear that the AA should have accepted the compromise; instead, it resolved to strike in an effort to gain its original demands. The AA's defeat in the strike greatly weakened its foothold in USS, by far the largest producer in the industry. The coup de grace came in 1909 when USS announced that it would no longer recognize or bargain with the union. In the resulting strike the giant steel company once again persevered. Thereafter, USS operated on the open-shop basis until 1937.

The AA, which had made some advances during World War I, participated in the ill-fated National Committee for Organizing Iron and Steel Workers in 1918. The organizing campaign, which was remarkably successful, resulted in the great steel strike of 1919, but its failure meant that the AA remained locked out of the major steel companies of the nation. After 1919 the AA slowly disintegrated into a helpless, hapless little union with neither the resources nor the will to once again attack the giants of the steel industry. After the establishment of the National Recovery Administration in 1933, the AA conducted a perfunctory organizing campaign, but within eighteen months it did not have a single full-time organizer in the field. By 1935 the union had fewer than 10,000 members, and in that year alone it suffered a new loss of eighty local lodges.

When the 1934 convention of the AFL directed its executive council to inaugurate an organizing campaign in the steel industry, AA president Michael F. Tighe refused to wave the association's jurisdiction and demanded that the campaign be conducted by his union. The AA then submitted an organizing plan to the AFL executive council noteworthy primarily for its petty interest in dues and the preservation of its death benefit fund. The executive council rejected the plan and directed AFL president William Green to draw up a new plan for a one-year campaign to organize steelworkers. Meanwhile, under the leadership of John L. Lewis, the Congress of Industrial Organizations* (CIO) made plans to launch a major organizing offensive in the steel industry.

The CIO initiatives confronted the AA leadership with a dilemma. The CIO promised an enlarged jurisdiction, a large corps of organizers, and $500,000 to organize the steel industry. On the other hand, the AFL once again promised much but refused to take any concrete steps to fulfill its long-neglected commitments. Nevertheless AA officers cherished their long association with the AFL and worried about their independence if they aligned with the awesome John L. Lewis. Ultimately, however, rank-and-file pressures pushed AA leaders into the Lewis camp and on June 4, 1936, the AA joined the CIO. The CIO immediately established the Steel Workers Organizing Committee (SWOC) to conduct the campaign in the steel industry and assigned the AA only a nominal role in the campaign. As many AA leaders had feared, the small, old union was quickly swallowed up by the SWOC. The AA reluctantly relinquished its charter to the CIO in 1942, and in its place the CIO established a new national union, the United Steelworkers of America.*

The AA held annual conventions and maintained its national headquarters in Pittsburgh. Full-time officers included a president, two vice-presidents, and a secretary-treasurer. The national executive board consisted of the above officers and the assistant secretary, managing editor of the *Amalgamated Journal*, residing trustee, and insurance secretary. At the time of its dissolution, the AA had approximately 8,500 members.

For further information, see the *Amalgamated Journal* issued by the AA during the period 1899-1942. See also Jesse S. Robinson, *The Amalgamated Association of Iron, Steel and Tin Workers* (1920), an account of the early history, structure, and government of the union. David Brody's *Labor in Crisis: The Steel Strike of 1919* (1965), is the standard account of the 1919 steel strike, and Walter Galenson, *The CIO Challenge to the AFL: A History of the American Labor Movement, 1935-1941* (1960), covers the AA in the 1930s.

IRON WORKERS; INTERNATIONAL ASSOCIATION OF BRIDGE, STRUCTURAL AND ORNAMENTAL (IABSOIW). Structural iron was first used in constructing steel bridges during the second half of the nineteenth century. Much of this early iron work was done by laborers who originally had worked as bridge carpenters. As steel began to replace timbers in bridge build-ing, however, these workers became the nation's first structural steelworkers. The uses of structural steel in the building industry, first experimented with extensively in Chicago, made possible the construction of steel skyscrapers, which increased employment opportunities for bridgemen who readily adapted their skills to building construction.

Trade union organization of ironworkers first began among bridgemen in various sections of the nation, and the first local of ironworkers involved pri-marily in the building construction industry was organized in Chicago in 1891. It was not until 1896, however, that the first national organization of structural ironworkers appeared. The national union was formed in Pittsburgh on February 4, 1896, when delegates representing local unions in New York City, Buffalo, Boston, Pittsburgh, and Chicago organized the International Asso-ciation of Bridge and Structural Ironworkers (IA).

During its early years the IA was more an idea than a reality. It had little power or influence; union affairs were conducted on a local level, and there was little coordination of efforts among the various locals. It was not until 1901 that the IA began to function as a national union; two years later it affiliated with the American Federation of Labor* (AFL).

To a large extent, the early history of the IA revolved around its volatile rela-tionship with the American Bridge Company, an affiliate of the United States Steel Company and the nation's largest employer of ironworkers. The IA signed its first national agreement with the American Bridge Company in 1902, which among other concessions provided for union recognition and a closed shop. Due to the strength of local autonomy and local rivalries, how-ever, the contract was rejected by most of the larger IA locals. Because Ameri-can Bridge was generally recognized as the trend setter in the industry, rejec-tion of the contract was a major setback to the national organization of iron-workers.

As a result of numerous local grievances, a national strike was called against the American Bridge Company in the spring of 1903. After a month-long strike, a new national agreement was signed between the company and IA. Although less favorable than the previously rejected contract, the settlement did constitute something of a union victory. Upon expiration of the contract, lengthy negotiations failed to resolve conflicts over the expanded unionization of ironworkers, and a second national strike was called.

As a result of the strike, the American Bridge Company and other firms in the structural iron trade launched an open-shop offensive on May 1, 1906, under the leadership of the National Erectors' Association, which had been organized in New York City in the spring of 1903. It soon became clear that the companies comprising the Erectors' Association intended nothing less than the total destruction of trade unionism in the structural steel industry. The open-shop campaign soon halted trade union advances and succeeded in eliminating some previous union gains. To ironworkers, for example, New York City virtually became an open-shop city.

Clearly, the open-shop campaign was a well-organized, well-financed effort by the National Erectors' Association to destroy the IA. As their situation became increasingly critical, a number of IA officers under the general direction of John J. McNamara, the general secretary-treasurer, launched a series of dynamite attacks on construction work done by members of the Erectors' Association and by nonunion independent contractors. Between 1908 and 1911 seventy explosions occurred; no lives were lost and little property damage was reported. The series of bombings culminated in the *Los Angeles Times'* explosion that took the lives of twenty people. Ultimately John McNamara and his brother James confessed to placing the explosives. Thereafter, forty IA officials were indicted in federal courts on charges of conspiracy in the series of bombing incidents. Thirty-eight were found guilty, including IA president Frank Ryan, who was given a seven-year prison sentence.

Although the convictions and the public outrage that accompanied them severely undermined the effectiveness of the IA, it did not destroy the union. Instead, between 1908 and 1914, IA membership increased from 9,600 to 13,200. Nevertheless, the IA not only failed to expand its control over structural steel erection work but in reality lost ground. The added membership came primarily from ancillary workers who had not previously been organized.

Like many other unions the IA prospered during World War I, but its gains were ephemeral, and by 1932 IA membership was approximately the same as it had been in 1910. It was not until the unionization of the basic steel industry in the late 1930s and early 1940s that the IA succeeded in organizing its trade jurisdiction. Once the open shop in structural steel was breached, union organization proceeded rapidly. By 1944, the IA had a membership of nearly 150,000, and by the end of the decade it had succeeded in enrolling most of the potential membership within its jurisdiction. By the 1960s it was one of the strongest unions affiliated with the AFL-CIO.* The listed union title was adopted in 1957.

The IABSOIW, which maintains its national headquarters in St. Louis, holds quadrennial conventions. Principal officers include a general president, nine vice-presidents, a secretary, and a treasurer. The executive council consists of the above officers. In 1973 the IABSOIW reported a membership of 175,611 located in 324 local unions.

For further information, see *The Ironworker* (formerly *The Bridgemen's Magazine*) published monthly by the IABSOIW. See also Luke Grant, *The National Erectors' Association and the International Association of Bridge and Structural Ironworkers* (1915).

JEWELRY WORKERS' UNION; INTERNATIONAL (IJWU). The American Federation of Labor* (AFL) began recruiting jewelry workers during the late nineteenth century. These workers were organized into federal labor unions, and as their numbers grew, the AFL combined the federal unions to form a national union, the International Jewelry Workers' Union of America (IJWUA), which it chartered on September 17, 1900. Beginning with an original membership of fewer than 1,000, the IJWUA took advantage of the favorable organizing conditions existing in the early years of the new century to expand its membership, organizing nearly 3,000 members by the end of 1904. Approximately 300 workers were added when a merger between the IJWUA and the International Watch Case Makers union, chartered by the AFL on February 15, 1901, was consummated on September 15, 1908.

Despite its early successes, the IJWUA suffered the fate of numerous other unions when employers launched a national open-shop offensive in 1904; the IJWUA steadily lost members until 1913 when it surrendered its AFL charter and disbanded. At the time of the union's dissolution, the surviving locals re-affiliated with the AFL as federal labor unions. Three years later representatives of those federal labor unions met in New York City and organized a new national union, the International Jewelry Workers' Union, which received an AFL charter on September 28, 1916. In an attempt to avoid the circumstances leading to the demise of its predecessor, the new jewelry workers' union organized along industrial lines.

The expanded trade jurisdiction claimed by the IJWU inevitably created jurisdictional conflicts with AFL craft unions. One such conflict arose when the IJWU organized diamond polishers and cutters claimed by the Diamond Workers' Protective Union of America (DWPUA). This dispute was adjusted in 1918 when the IJWU agreed to release those craft workers to the DWPUA. A short time later, a dispute with the Metal Polishers International Union* (MPIU) resulted in the IJWU's suspension from the AFL when it refused to release all metal workers in the jewelry trade to the MPIU. After the AFL began chartering new federal labor unions of jewelry workers, the IJWU retreated from its earlier position and agreed to assign the disputed workers to the MPIU; thereupon, the AFL reinstated the IJWU on May 11, 1922.

Jurisdictional disputes and the AFL suspension cost the IJWU dearly. Membership in excess of 8,000 in 1920 shrank to 1,000 in 1924 and 600 in 1927 before again turning upward. New Deal legislation and an active organizing campaign stimulated an IJWU recovery, and by the end of World War II, membership of the small specialty union exceeded its previous 1920 high. The IJWU continued to grow after the war, reaching nearly 25,000 in the mid-1950s. Thereafter, a slow decline began, resulting from decreasing employment in the IJWU's trade jurisdiction.

On December 2, 1955, the IJWU merged with its old rival, the Diamond Workers' Protective Union. The DWPUA had been organized in New York City on September 16, 1902, under the title Diamond Polishers' Protective Union of America. A year later it also began organizing cutters and setters, and the title was changed to Diamond Workers' Protective Union of America. The AFL chartered the DWPUA on April 12, 1912, extending jurisdiction over diamond polishing, cutting, and sawing. At the time of the merger with the IJWU, the DWPUA had fewer than 500 members.

The IJWU, which maintains its national headquarters in New York City, holds triennial conventions. Principal officers include a president-secretary-treasurer and eleven vice-presidents. The general executive board is composed of the above officials. In 1973 the IJWU reported a membership of 12,500 located in thirty-six local unions.

For further information, see *The Gem* published biannually. Information can also be found in *Bulletin No. 618*, Bureau of Labor Statistics, U.S. Department of Labor (1936), and Florence Peterson, *Handbook of Labor Unions* (1944).

KNIGHTS OF LABOR; NOBLE ORDER OF THE (KofL). Concerned about wages and working conditions during the Civil War, a group of garment cutters met in Philadelphia in 1862 and organized the Garment Cutters' Association of Philadelphia (GCA). The association successfully resisted a proposed wage reduction but lost its effectiveness as a result of extensive blacklisting during the 1866-1868 recession and gradually evolved into a beneficial society. On December 9, 1869, members of the GCA voted to dissolve the organization and divide its assets. Nevertheless, a few members anticipating the association's demise held a series of meetings to plan a new society. In Philadelphia on December 28, 1869, they organized Local Assembly No. 1 of the Noble Order of the Knights of Labor. A few days later officers were elected, and Uriah S. Stephens became the first master workman.

Founders of the new union rejected the wage labor system and emphasized cooperation and education as the cardinal principles of their order. Resulting from their study of the GCA's failure, organizers of the new union concluded that the association had failed largely because its members were too well known and thus too susceptible to the blacklist; consequently a policy of strict secrecy was adopted. New members took an oath not to reveal the name, object, or activities of the order or the name of any member. Founders of the new union also believed that labor organizations divided into craft units lacked the unity and strength to withstand employer attacks; therefore they decided to organize all workers regardless of craft of skill. The only requirement for membership was that prospective members "gain their bread by the sweat of their brow."

The basic organizing unit of the KofL was a local assembly composed of workers in a single trade or craft. Mixed assemblies were introduced where a group lacked enough members to constitute a trade assembly. The KofL was organized on a geographical basis, and when five local assemblies (later ten) existed in a particular area, they could organize a district assembly. Despite official displeasure, increasingly after 1879 national trade assemblies were organized under the guise of local assemblies.

During its first few years, the KofL remained largely a local union confined to the Philadlephia area. Local Assembly No. 2, also in Philadlephia, did not exist until July 18, 1872, and the first district assembly was not organized until Christmas Day, 1873. The organization of District Assembly No. 3 in Pittsburgh in the summer of 1875 was the first significant expansion beyond the original Philadelphia base.

Profiting from the collapse of many trade unions during the depression of the 1870s, the KofL quickly outgrew its original organizational structure. Moreover, as it expanded, conflict between the Philadelphia and Pittsburgh assemblies erupted. Although minor disagreements over politics and organizing strategy occurred, the major issue dividing the two factions involved the commitment to secrecy. The Roman Catholic church opposed secret oaths and secret organizations, and this proved a major obstacle to the Pittsburgh Knights who were organizing large numbers of Catholic workmen. The notorious exploits of the secretive Molly Mcguires further poisoned public attitudes toward secrecy in western Pennsylvania. The growth of the order and the emergence of conflicting ideas about tactics and objectives necessitated the formation of a national organization. Tentative steps were taken toward such an arrangement in 1876 and 1877, but it was not until the Reading convention of January 1, 1878, that a representative assembly of both eastern and western groups gathered. The Reading convention was called "for the purpose of creating a central resistance fund, bureau of statistics, providing revenue for the work of the organization, establishment of an official register giving the number, place of meeting of each assembly, etc."

Although delegates to the Reading meeting voted to continue operating as a secret society and elected Uriah Stephens grand master workman, sentiment on secrecy changed rapidly, and by January 1882 it was largely abandoned. Although reelected grand master workman at the second national convention in 1881, Stephens resigned shortly thereafter to devote his time to politics; he was replaced by Terence V. Powderly. Powderly, who would direct the affairs of the KofL for over a decade, opposed secrecy but endorsed the Knights' commitment to cooperative ventures. He opposed strikes as a meaningless waste of resources that might be better used to establish cooperatives and bring the eventual end of wage labor. Of a more immediate nature, Powderly strongly advocated arbitration as a substitute for strikes, but rank-and-file sentiment forced him to revise his position, and he reluctantly endorsed the creation of a strike fund. The strike issue reflected the organization's growing schism between the reformist element and trade union advocates. In 1881 the Knights' claim to national labor leadership was challenged when representatives of several national trade unions met and formed the Federation of Organized Trades and Labor Unions of the United States and Canada* (FOTLU).

Between 1881 and 1885, local assemblies of the Knights were involved in a number of only moderately successful strikes, but in 1885 the Knights persevered in a dramatic confrontation with the Jay Gould-controlled Wabash Railroad. The victory had a profound effect on the KofL. Although its membership had steadily increased from the original 9,000 at the time of the creation of a national union in 1878, reaching 19,000 by 1881 and 111,000 in 1885, organizing virtually exploded after the successful Wabash strike. Within a year membership exceeded 700,000. The great membership boom, however, proved to be disastrous. Thousands of undisciplined, unskilled workers with little or no experience in labor unionism joined and immediately began agitating for long overdue changes in wages, hours, and working conditions. A false sense of power gripped many rank-and-file members. This optimism was quickly dispelled by Jay Gould's defeat of the Knights in a strike on the Southwestern railroad system in 1886. The reputation of the Knights further suffered when its leaders refused to endorse or participate in the eight-hour movement sweeping the country. Finally although not involved in the Haymarket Square riot, the general anti-labor hysteria following the incident served to further discredit the KofL.

The year 1886 was a poor one for the Knights in other ways. An unsuccessful strike in the Chicago stockyards further weakened the once-powerful order. Then in December, unable to reach an agreement with KofL leaders on the vital issue of dual unions, a group of trade union leaders reorganized the moribund FOTLU into the American Federation of Labor* (AFL), which quickly proved a major threat to the Knights' leadership position in the American labor movement. Resulting from the series of defeats, membership in the Knights declined almost as dramatically as it had grown. By the summer of 1887 membership was down to 250,000, and the decline continued, reaching 100,000 in 1890 and 75,000 in 1893. In the latter year, an alliance between western agrarian elements and Socialists controlling District Assembly 49 in New York (also known as the Home Club) seized control of the KofL, and James R. Sovereign, an Iowa farm editor, replaced Powderly. A short time later the Socialists broke with Sovereign and left the order, which thereafter rapidly disintegrated. By the end of the century, the KofL ceased to be an effective trade union organization.

The general assembly of the Knights of Labor, which maintained its national headquarters in Philadelphia, met annually. Principal officers included a master workman, worthy foreman, worthy inspector, almoner, financial secretary, recording secretary, worthy treasurer, and statistician.

For further information, see the *Journal of the Knights of Labor*, 1889-1904, 1905-1917, and *Journal of United Labor*, 1880-1889. The most comprehensive account of the Knights of Labor is found in Norman J. Ware, *The Labor Movement in the United States, 1860-1895* (1929). Valuable accounts of the KofL can also be found in John R. Commons et al., *History of Labour in the United States*, vol. 2 (1918); Philip S. Foner, *History of the Labor Movement in the*

168 /LABOR UNIONS

United States, vol. 2 (1955); and Joseph G. Rayback, *A History of American Labor* (1959). The activities of the Knights in the South are described well by Melton A. McLaurin, *Paternalism and Protest: Southern Cotton Mill Workers and Organized Labor, 1875-1904* (1971).

KNIGHTS OF ST. CRISPIN; THE (KSC). Mechanization of the shoe and textile industries anticipated changes in production methods destined to affect virtually all industrial activity in the United States. Large-scale factory production in the shoe industry began in 1852 with the utilization of the sewing machine, invented six years earlier, for stitching on the upper portions of boots and shoes. But it was the introduction of power pegging machinery in 1862 that inspired the large-scale replacement of skilled workers by unskilled and semi-skilled employees. The large market for boots and shoes, combined with labor scarcity during the Civil War, greatly accelerated the introduction of new machinery.

The postwar period was a difficult one for both employers and labor. After the war the demand for boots and shoes contracted, and manufacturers with growing inventories responded by cutting both prices and wages. Many smaller producers failed to survive the economic dislocations. The impact of these changes on workers in the industry was even more painful. As returning soldiers reentered the work force, a labor surplus developed, and as wage rates declined and unemployment and underemployment grew, the security evaporated that the shoemakers' skill had previously provided. This, along with rapid technological changes in the trade, made the shoemaker particularly susceptible to any proposal promising employment security, regular wages, and acceptable working conditions.

Newell Daniels and six associates meeting in Milwaukee, Wisconsin, on March 1, 1867, offered one such solution when they organized the Knights of St. Crispin. In responding to the chaotic conditions prevalent in the postwar shoe industry, the KSC dedicated its major effort to gaining control of the labor supply in the industry through exclusive control of apprenticeship programs and working conditions. The importance of this objective is evidenced in a constitutional provision requiring that "no member of this order shall teach, or aid in teaching, any part or parts of boot and shoe making, unless the lodge shall give permission by a three-fourths vote of those present and voting thereon, when such permission is first asked." Moreover the constitution stipulated that international grand lodge strike funds could be expanded only for the defense of the KSC and the support of its apprenticeship reform program. Although many of its affiliated lodges opposed the introduction of machines entirely, the KSC leadership accepted mechanization but stipulated that skilled shoemakers would operate the machines and share in the benefits of the increased labor productivity growing from machine production.

The organization of the KSC struck a responsive chord among shoemakers, and it grew rapidly during its first three years. Before the first national convention of the KSC convened at Rochester, New York, in July 1868, eighty-seven lodges had been organized, and by the spring of 1870, 327 lodges had affiliated with it.

Numerous strikes characterized the short history of the KSC. From 1868 to 1870, the organization experienced considerable success in industrial disputes, but from 1871 to 1874, it almost inevitably failed. As noted above, control of apprenticeship was the primary objective of the KSC, but most of the strikes involved wage disputes. Many workers who joined the order were unwilling to wait for the long-term benefits that would ensue from control of the supply of labor; they were more interested in immediate benefits. Strikes in Lynn, Massachusetts, in 1870 and 1872, in San Francisco in 1869, and in Philadelphia and Worcester, Massachusetts, in 1870 were among the more significant strikes conducted by KSC lodges. Other than wage disputes, the recognition and defense of the KSC were the most frequent causes of conflict.

Although the KSC devoted much of its energy and resources to the effort to control entry into the shoemaking trade, its ultimate objective involved the elimination of the wage labor system and its replacement by producer cooperatives. Such cooperatives and a large number of consumer cooperatives were organized in most towns and cities where the Knights had strong lodges. If they had not failed previously, most of these ventures succumbed during the panic and depression of 1873.

An unsuccessful strike in Lynn in 1872 presaged the KSC's downfall. The Lynn lodge was one of the most powerful and successful in the order. Two years previously it had forced manufacturers to sign a wage agreement for the ensuing year. The agreement was renewed a year later, but facing severe competition, manufacturers, in 1872, repudiated the agreement and withstood the resulting strike. Within a few years, the KSC was a moribund organization. Its failure resulted from a variety of circumstances: the failure to control entry into the trade, severe competition among manufacturers, a large pool of native labor and contract immigrant labor, and the failure of the KSC to either control or support the numerous strikes of its affiliated lodges.

A reorganized KSC appeared in 1875, but it espoused different principles than the original order had and never had a significant impact on the industry. It disappeared by 1878.

The KSC held annual conventions between 1869 and 1873. The principal officers of the grand lodge included an international grand sir knight, deputy grand sir knight, grand scribe, grand treasurer, three grand knights, and three grand trustees. The executive board consisted of the grand sir knight, deputy grand sir knight, and the three grand knights. Membership estimates of the order range from 30,000 to 80,000 workers, but they are distorted by the KSC practice of carrying inactive members on the rolls; those who joined virtually remained members for life.

For further information, see Don D. Lescohier, *The Knights of St. Crispin, 1867-1874* (1910), the only detailed account of the KSC. Brief accounts of the order also appear in Philip Taft, *Organized Labor in American History* (1964), and John R. Commons et al., *History of Labour in the United States*, vol. 2 (1918).

LABORERS' INTERNATIONAL UNION OF NORTH AMERICA (LIU). Hoping to organize a national union of building laborers, twenty-five delegates representing 8,000 workers in seventeen cities met in Washington, D.C., on April 13, 1903, in response to an invitation by American Federation of Labor* president Samuel Gompers. Most unions represented at the organizing convention were directly chartered AFL federal labor unions of hod carriers and building laborers. Before adjourning, the delegates created the International Hod Carriers and Building Laborers' Union of America (IHCBLUA). As stated in the Declaration of Principles adopted by the new national union, an effort to extend organization throughout its trade jurisdiction, increased wages, the eight-hour day, and the establishment of a system of conciliation and arbitration were among the more notable objectives.

Discontinuities in both leadership and the location of national headquarters, jurisdictional conflict, and union growth and expansion characterized the IHCBLUA's first decade. By 1908 the new union had had five presidents and had moved its national headquarters four times. During the decade, the IHCBLUA confronted two independent unions attempting to organize on a national basis within its trade jurisdiction: the Building Laborers' International Protective Union of America headquartered at Lowell, Massachusetts, and the Laborers' Protective Union of America based in Dayton, Ohio. In its competition with these rivals, the new AFL national union gained a powerful ally when the independent Bricklayers' and Masons' International Union* endorsed the IHCBLUA as the only bona fide union in its jurisdiction. Meanwhile, by the end of its first decade, the IHCBLUA could boast a 300 percent increase in membership, as the 8,000 of 1903 approached 25,000 in 1913.

Because of changes in technology and expanded jurisdictional claims, name changes are not uncommon among American national unions, but the IHCBLUA established an unusual record by changing its title twice within three months. On September 24, 1912, the organization became the International Hod Carriers' and Common Laborers' Union of America, and in December it adopted the name International Hod Carriers', Building and Common Laborers' Union of America (IHCB&CLUA). These changes reflected the expanding organizing scope of the union. Originally it had been exclusively a building trades' union, but as organization was extended to include common laborers outside the building trades area, a name change was necessitated.

Due primarily to the organizing opportunities during World War I, the

IHCB&CLUA grew steadily during the second decade of the twentieth century, reaching nearly 100,000 members by the end of 1920. Membership declined sharply between 1921 and 1922, however, leveling at about 70,000 before moving upward again, it continued to increase until the Great Depression settled upon the nation.

The union's growth and increased stability owed much to the enlightened and far-sighted leadership of Domenico D'Alessandro, who served as president from 1908 to 1926, and his successor, Joseph V. Moreschi, who guided the affairs of the IHCB&CLUA for the following forty-two years. The absorption of, or merger with, smaller national unions also stimulated union growth during these years. After the dissolution of the American Brotherhood of Cement Workers, also chartered by the AFL in 1903, the Hod Carriers absorbed the cement laborers organized by the Brotherhood. In 1918 the IHCB&CLUA merged with the Compressed Air and Foundation Workers' International Union (chartered by the AFL in 1904), and in 1929 the Tunnel and Subway Constructors' International Union (chartered by the AFL in 1910) joined the IHCB&CLUA.

The Great Depression proved almost as disastrous to the IHCB&CLUA as it did to the national economy. Membership, which had approached 100,000 before the depression, fell to the 1913 figure of approximately 25,000 by 1933. In addition to pervasive unemployment during the 1930s, especially in the building trades, the IHCB&CLUA also confronted serious infringements on its jurisdiction, especially from the United Mine Workers,* Mine, Mill and Smelter Workers,* the Brotherhoods of Electrical Workers* and Carpenters,* Cement Workers,* Boilermakers,* State, County and Municipal Employees,* and the International Union of Pavers, Rammermen, Flag Layers, Bridge and Stone Curb Setters and Sheet Asphalt Pavers. Long-standing problems with the last union were resolved by an amalgamation effected on February 9, 1937.

New Deal legislation and national economic recovery sparked a remarkable surge in IHCB&CLUA membership, which peaked at 430,187 in 1942. While much of this artificially inflated figure was lost during the remaining war years, clearly the union's hard times had ended. IHCB&CLUA membership climbed steadily after World War II and reached the half-million mark during the 1950s. One of the more significant developments during these years involved the negotiation of national agreements with such employers as the National Pipeline Association, Association of Railway Track Contractors of America, Inc., Associated General Contractors of America, National Constructors' Association, Building Trades Employers' Association, and General Contractors' Association. On September 20, 1965, the union title was changed to Laborers' International Union of North America to more accurately reflect the organizing scope of the union.

The LIU, which maintains its national headquarters in Washington, D.C., holds quinquennial conventions. Principal officers include a president, six vice-presidents, and a secretary-treasurer. The general executive board is composed of the above officers. In 1973 the LIU reported a membership of 600,000 located in 890 local unions.

For further information, see *The Laborer* issued monthly and *The Leader* published quarterly by the LIU. The best source on the LIU is Arch A. Mercey, *The Laborers' Story, 1903-1953: The First Fifty Years of the International Hod Carriers', Building and Common Laborers' Union of America* (1954), an account sponsored by the LIU.

LACE OPERATIVES OF AMERICA; AMALGAMATED (ALOA). A small group of textile workers specializing in the lace-making trade met in Philadelphia in 1892 and organized the Amalgamated Lace Curtain Operatives of America. On November 28, 1894, the new union affiliated with the American Federation of Labor* (AFL). Several years later the Amalgamated sought and received AFL jurisdiction over the entire lace-making trade. As a consequence, on August 31, 1912, the AFL approved a new union title, the Charter Society of Amalgamated Lace Operatives of America. The name was later shortened to the listed title.

Although organizing in a limited trade jurisdiction, the ALOA grew steadily during the first two decades of the twentieth century. The small union's continued existence as a national union, however, was severely challenged in 1919. The AFL ordered the ALOA and another small textile union, the International Mule Spinners (IMS), to merge with the United Textile Workers of America* (UTWA) or their charters would be revoked. The ALOA had a charter predating that of the UTWA, and both the IMS and the ALOA defied the AFL; on December 31, 1919, both were expelled from the federation. Since that time, the ALOA has continued to function as an independent union. Through the years, the ALOA has developed a rather amicable relationship with the UTWA and has attained a relatively stable membership ranging between 2,000 and 3,000 members.

The ALOA, which maintains its national headquarters in Philadelphia, holds quinquennial conventions. The union has no full-time officers but elects a president, eight vice-presidents, and a secretary-treasurer. The above officers also constitute the international advisory board. In 1973 the ALOA reported a membership of 2,450 located in eleven local unions.

For further information, see the *American Lace Worker* published bimonthly by the ALOA. See also Robert R. R. Brooks, "The United Textile Workers of America" (Ph.D. dissertation, Yale University, 1935), and *Bulletin No. 618*, Bureau of Labor Statistics, U.S. Department of Labor (1936).

LATHERS INTERNATIONAL UNION; WOOD, WIRE AND METAL (WWMLIU). The introduction of metal lathing as a base for plaster in 1839 greatly refined the ancient building craft of lathing. Local unions of lathers began to appear shortly thereafter, but effective trade unionism awaited the organization of the American Federation of Labor* (AFL) in 1886. A growing number of locals directly chartered as AFL federal labor unions were organized by the new national union.

AFL president Samuel Gompers called these various locals into conference in Detroit on December 15, 1899, to discuss the creation of an international union. Four delegates, representing locals in Columbus and Cleveland, Ohio, Scranton, Pennsylvania, and Marion, Indiana, responded to the conference call. Resulting from their deliberations, the AFL issued a charter to the Wood, Wire and Metal Lathers International Union (WWMLIU) on January 15, 1900.

By its second national convention in November 1900, leaders of the WWMLIU had secured the affiliation of most existing lather locals. Although finding its membership drive temporarily slowed by the open-shop offensive initiated by employers in 1904, the WWMLIU grew steadily during the early years of the twentieth century, expanding from 600 in 1900 to 8,000 by the end of World War I. Defying the experience of most trade unions during the 1920s, the WWMLIU doubled its membership during the decade; however, the depression of the 1930s sharply reversed the growth rate of the lathers' union as it lost more than half its membership. For several years the WWMLIU's membership hovered around 8,000 before gradually climbing to 16,000, where it stabilized during the early 1950s.

The WWMLIU currently claims jurisdiction over the following work:

erecting, constructing, installing and completing of all light iron construction, furring; making and erecting of brackets, clips, and hangers; wood, wire and metal lath; plaster board or other material which takes the place of same to which plastic or acoustical material is adhered; corner beads, all floor construction; arches erected for the purpose of holding plaster, cement, concrete or any other plastic or acoustical material.

Although technological changes in materials and construction methods have forced the WWMLIU to periodically revise its jurisdictional claims, the union has been able to avoid many jurisdictional conflicts characterizing the history of so many other unions in the building trades industry.

Much of the first half-century of the WWMLIU's history is associated with the career of William J. McSorley, who, with one brief exception, served as general president from 1904 to 1955. McSorley not only served the WWMLIU in several capacities but also played an influential role in the national labor movement. He was involved in a variety of AFL affairs and served as a delegate to AFL annual conventions for over fifty years. He helped organize the AFL building trades department and from 1926 to 1929 served as its president.

Over the years the WWMLIU developed a variety of welfare plans and fringe benefits including a funeral benefit trust fund and a general pension fund to supplement the retirement payments of Social Security. Moreover, most union contracts have included such items as health and welfare, pensions, vacations, and travel and subsistence pay.

The WWMLIU, which holds triennial conventions, maintains its national headquarters in the AFL-CIO Building in Washington, D.C. Principal officers include a general president, seven vice-presidents, and a secretary-treasurer. The executive council consists of the seven vice-presidents. In 1973 the WWMLIU reported a membership of 13,767.

For further information, see *The Lather* published monthly by the WWMLIU, and "The Wood, Wire and Metal Lathers International Union: History and Founding," an unpublished, undated essay prepared by the union. Florence Peterson's *Handbook of Labor Unions* (1944) also contains information on the WWMLIU.

LAUNDRY, DRY CLEANING AND DYE HOUSE WORKERS' INTERNATIONAL UNION (LDC&DHWIU). Working hours in excess of sixty per week, low wages, and a sweatshop environment characterized working conditions in the nation's laundries at the start of the twentieth century. Conditions such as these inspired laundry workers in Troy, New York, to organize a local union of laundry workers, which the American Federation of Labor* (AFL) chartered as a federal labor union in 1898. Two years later organization had expanded to the extent that on November 19, 1900, the AFL issued a charter to the Shirt, Waist and Laundry Workers International Union. The new union's original charter included jurisdiction over the making and laundering of shirts and collars, but in 1909, the AFL withdrew the original charter, gave the United Garment Workers of America* exclusive jurisdiction over shirt manufacturing, and rechartered the laundry workers with a jurisdiction limited to "all employees employed in laundries, towel and linen supply companies and rag shops and all employees employed in cleaning and dyeing establishments run in connection with laundries." As a result of the revised jurisdiction, the union was renamed the Laundry Workers International Union (LWIU).

Neither the changed title nor the revised jurisdiction had much impact on the frustrating efforts to organize the thousands of depressed laundry workers in the United States. The LWIU's original membership of 2,000 grew to only 3,500 by 1909. Even with the favorable conditions existing during World War I. The union still enrolled only a fraction of the workers employed in the laundry industry. Moreover, a peak LWIU membership of 7,000 in 1921 gradually declined during the 1920s, dipping to 5,500 in 1924 before stabilizing and eventually turning upward again in 1936.

Although the LWIU originated in the East, it increasingly became a West Coast organization as the vast majority of its members resided between San Francisco and Seattle. The emergence of the Congress of Industrial Organizations* (CIO), enactment of the National Labor Relations Act, and election of a new LWIU leadership combined to drastically alter the fortunes of the union. The LWIU launched a nationwide organizing campaign in 1939 that not only doubled its membership but extended union organization throughout the nation.

World War II slowed the organizing effort and increased the turnover problem that had always plagued union organizing among laundry workers, but nevertheless the LWIU continued to grow, attaining a membership in excess of 50,000 by the end of the war. In the postwar years, the LWIU initiated a vigorous organizing effort in the South but was only partially successful in organizing workers there. During this period, the LWIU also experimented with arbitrational agreements to eliminate strikes and lockouts, while providing workers with adequate wages, better ventilated and more sanitary working conditions, and a forty-hour week. Although many laundry workers remained unorganized at the time of the AFL-CIO merger, the LWIU continued to grow, reaching a membership of nearly 80,000 by 1955.

On May 1, 1956, the LWIU merged with the International Association of Cleaning and Dye House Workers (IACDHW) to create the Laundry, Dry Cleaning and Dye House Workers' International Union. The IACDHW had received an AFL charter on January 21, 1937, and was given jurisdiction over "all dry cleaners, dry cleaning spotters, dry cleaning pressers, dry cleaning checkers, dry cleaning markers, dry cleaning packers, dry cleaning washers and dryers employed in dry cleaning establishments, and all other persons employed in dry cleaning establishments who work on dry cleaned garments." The new union quickly expanded its original membership of 4,800 to nearly 20,000, where it remained largely unchanged until the LWIU merger.

The IACDHW, which held quinquennial conventions, maintained its national headquarters in Cleveland. Full-time officers included a president and a secretary-treasurer. The general executive board was composed of the above officials and seven vice-presidents. At the time of the merger with the LWIU, the IACDHW reported a membership of 20,000 located in fifty-nine local unions.

Shortly after the merger, the LDC&DHWIU attracted the attention of the McClellan committee investigating corrupt practices in the American labor movement. It was discovered that an LWIU insurance agent, in collusion with a union officer, had stolen over $900,000 from the LWIU insurance fund. As a result of this exposure, the AFL-CIO ethical practices committee demanded a number of reforms as a prerequisite for continued AFL-CIO affiliation. The LDC&DHWIU refused to make the necessary reforms and was summarily expelled from the AFL-CIO in December 1957. The AFL-CIO then chartered a new international union in the industry, the Laundry and Dry Cleaning International Union,* which received the old LDC&DHWIU trade jurisdiction. After its expulsion from the AFL-CIO and the chartering of a rival union, the LDC&DHWIU lost a number of its affiliated local unions and thousands of its members. Hoping to gain some security in its battle with the powerful AFL-CIO, in March 1962 the LDC&DHWIU became a subordinate division of the International Brotherhood of Teamsters, Chauffeurs, Warehousemen and Helpers of America,* which had also been expelled from the AFL-CIO for corrupt practices.

The LDC&DHWIU, which maintains its national headquarters in Chicago, holds quinquennial conventions. Full-time officers include a president and a secretary-treasurer. The general executive board is composed of the above officers and seven vice-presidents elected by convention delegates for five-year terms. In 1973 the LDC&DHWIU reported a membership of 37,354 located in fifty-five local unions.

For further information, see the *International Laundry Worker* issued quarterly by the LDC&DHWIU. See also *The American Federationist* (May 1946), and John Hutchinson, *The Imperfect Union* (1970), an important study of labor racketeering.

LAUNDRY AND DRY CLEANING INTERNATIONAL UNION (L&DCIU). Investigators for the Select Committee on Improper Activities in the Labor or Management Field (McClellan committee), which was appointed by the U.S. Senate in 1957 to investigate corrupt practices in the American labor movement, soon unraveled major scandals involving the administration of an insurance fund maintained by the Laundry, Dry Cleaning and Dye House Workers' International Union* (LDC&DHWIU). As a result of these exposures, the American Federation of Labor-Congress of Industrial Organizations* (AFL-CIO) ethical practices committee launched its own investigation of corruption in the LDC&DHWIU. Following the AFL-CIO investigation, the offending union was ordered to discharge union officials involved in illegal and unethical activities and to adopt several reforms recommended by the ethical practices committee. When the LDC&DHWIU failed to comply, it was expelled from the AFL-CIO in December 1957.

Under the direction of Peter M. McGaven, an assistant to AFL-CIO president George Meany, the AFL-CIO immediately initiated a campaign to detach local unions from the LDC&DHWIU and to recharter them as directly affiliated federal unions. Shortly after Local 3008 in Milwaukee disaffiliated, the LDC&DHWIU initiated legal proceedings in an effort to seize control of the local and prevent its defection. The courts refused to intervene, however, and several other LDC&DHWIU locals reaffiliated with the AFL-CIO as federal unions. Within a month of the LDC&DHWIU's expulsion, nearly twenty locals had left the discredited international. Because of its success in separating laundry workers and locals from the LDC&DHWIU, the AFL-CIO, in an effort to establish a more formal organization, sponsored a national conference of laundry worker locals in Milwaukee on January 25, 1958. The AFL-CIO-affiliated Laundry and Cleaning Trades International Council was established as a result of the conference. Seventeen former LDC&DHWIU locals chartered by the AFL-CIO as federal unions formed the nucleus of the new council.

Raids on the membership and locals of the LDC&DHWIU continued, increasing the membership and stability of the council. As a consequence, the AFL-CIO converted it into an international union, chartered as the Laundry and Dry Cleaning International Union after a constitutional convention held in Washington, D.C., on May 12, 1959. One hundred fifteen delegates representing forty-one local unions participated in the organizing convention of the new international union. During the early years of the rivalry between the L&DCIU and the LDC&DHWIU, the AFL-CIO union had considerable success and within a few years the L&DCIU approached parity with the older, outcast union. But after the LDC&DHWIU affiliated with the International Brotherhood of Teamsters* as a subordinate division, the L&DCIU's raids lost momentum, and its membership stabilized at a figure fluctuating around 25,000.

The L&DCIU, which maintains its national headquarters in Pittsburgh, holds quadrennial conventions. Principal officers include a president, nine vice-presidents, and a secretary-treasurer. The international executive board consists of the above officers. Three trustees are also elected at national conventions. In 1973 the L&DCIU reported a membership of 22,556 located in thirty-eight local unions.

For further information, see the *AFL-CIO Laundry and Dry Cleaning Worker* published annually by the L&DCIU. Other published sources were not located.

LEATHER GOODS, PLASTICS AND NOVELTY WORKERS UNION; INTERNATIONAL (ILGPNWU). Handbag, luggage, and personal leather goods workers first began organizing in New York City, where, on February 1, 1886, German and Jewish workers joined in the organization of the Pursemakers Union of New York City. Instability characterized trade unionism in the industry; work was seasonal and union organizations tended to follow the same pattern. The labor force was quite young, containing large numbers of children, and the turnover was high. Sweatshop conditions, long hours, and low wages precipitated numerous strikes, but employers usually managed to maintain strict control over the conditions of employment.

In an effort to alter this situation, the American Federation of Labor* (AFL) chartered the Travelers' Goods and Leather Novelty Workers International Union of America (TGLNWIUA) on April 3, 1915. The AFL had previously chartered the Trunk and Bag Workers International Union on August 4, 1898, but it had made little headway in organizing workers in its jurisdiction. Shortly after the formation of the TGLNWIUA, the New York City local called a general strike, but workers received little help from the new international union, and the strike was broken.

On July 24, 1917, the TGLNWIUA amalgamated with the United Brotherhood of Leather Workers on Horse Goods to create the United Leather Workers' International Union* (ULWIU). Meanwhile, pocketbook workers organized federal labor unions directly affiliated with the AFL. In 1918 Ossip Walinsky, a local official in the International Ladies' Garment Workers' Union,* assumed leadership of the pocketbook worker unions. After organizing a Joint Board of the East composed of fancy leather goods, pocketbook, luggage, and personal leather goods workers, Walinsky ordered a series of selected shop strikes that resulted in the negotiation of the first collective bargaining agreement in the specialty leather industry. The agreement, signed on August 23, 1918, covered all pocketbook and personal leather goods workers in New York City. A similar agreement was reached in August 1920 with employers of New York suitcase, bag, and portfolio workers.

In 1928 the AFL pocketbook workers' federal labor unions amalgamated with the ULWIU as an autonomous unit. The marriage was short-lived, however, and on March 5, 1937, the AFL chartered the International Ladies' Handbag, Pocketbook and Novelty Workers Union. Changes in the union title reflected the growth of the new union's jurisdiction. In 1942, "Luggage" and "Belt" were added, and four years later "Ladies" was dropped from the union title. Then, in 1955, "Plastics" was added, and the union became the International Leather Goods, Plastics and Novelty Workers Union.

A variety of problems largely peculiar to the specialty leather trade disrupted trade unionism in the industry. Unlike so many other American industries, small, highly competitive manufacturers continued to dominate the industry in the twentieth century, complicating collective bargaining and giving rise to the phenomenon of runaway shops. Small manufacturing plants in the industry could be moved easily and inexpensively to anti-union communities that promised a cheap, docile labor supply, tax concessions, and free land or rent-free accommodations. The trade continued to be seasonal, with retail sales highest during major holidays; over one-third of all retail sales in the industry occurred during November and December. Finally, high luxury taxes, jurisdictional conflicts, and foreign competition complicated labor relations in the industry.

The ILGPNWU succeeded in ameliorating many of these problems. Luxury taxes were reduced, and runaway shops occurred with less frequency as the union aggressively pursued the shops and made vigorous efforts to organize the new labor force. Moreover, the ILGPNWU negotiated contracts prohibiting the relocation of shops during the life of the contract. Jurisdictional disputes were adjusted more peacefully after the AFL instituted its internal disputes plan and signed a no-raiding agreement with the Congress of Industrial Organizations.* A slow but steady membership growth in the post-World War II years and steadily increasing control over labor conditions in the industry reflected the International's success in coping with the problems in the industry.

The ILGPNWU, which maintains its national headquarters in New York City, holds quinquennial conventions. Principal officers include a president, two vice-presidents, and a secretary-treasurer. In addition to the above officers, the international executive board is comprised of several board members elected at national conventions. In 1973 the ILGPNWU reported a membership of 9,200 located in 100 local unions.

For further information, see the *Union News Bulletin* published monthly by the ILGPNWU. Early organizing efforts in the leather industry are described in Leo C. Brown, *Union Policies in the Leather Industry* (1947). See also Ossip Walinsky, ed., *Industrial Peace in Action: Thirty Years of Collective Bargaining in the Pocketbook Industry of New York* (1948), and *The American Federationist* (August 1955).

LEATHER WORKERS INTERNATIONAL UNION; UNITED (ULWIU). The American Federation of Labor* (AFL) first chartered a national union in the leather industry, the National Association of Saddle and Harness Makers of America, on August 12, 1889. Thereafter, the AFL chartered several other unions of leather workers: the United Brotherhood of Leather Workers on Horse Goods (1896); United Brotherhood of Harness and Saddle Makers of America (1896); Trunk and Bag Workers' International Union (1898); Amalgamated Leather Workers of America (1901); and the Travelers' Goods and Leather Novelty Workers International Union of America (1915).

As the chartering of all these unions suggests, instability and confused jurisdictional lines characterized trade union organization in the industry. Most of these organizations were essentially local unions, which never succeeded in organizing their national jurisdiction. The first permanent organization in the industry did not emerge until July 24, 1917, when the Travelers' Goods and Leather Novelty Workers International Union of America and the United Brotherhood of Leather Workers on Horse Goods merged to create the United Leather Workers International Union.

Although the new union thrived during World War I, reaching a membership of nearly 12,000 by 1920, the ULWIU disintegrated rapidly during the following decade. By 1932 the union had lost approximately 90 percent of this membership. The ULWIU, whose organizing successes are confined primarily to the Northeast, never succeeded in launching a national organizing campaign. Besides its own deficiencies, which were considerable, the ULWIU's failure to organize the leather industry was the product of two associated circumstances. First, small, highly competitive companies widely scattered throughout the country characterized the industry, making organization very difficult. Second, these small manufacturers proved very hostile and resistant to trade unionism.

The second and more important problem confronting the ULWIU was the great competition within its trade jurisdiction. Small, independent organizations, such as the Independent Leather Workers of Fulton County (New York), dominated organization in several localities. More importantly, a number of national and international unions organized in the ULWIU's jurisdiction. The Amalgamated Meat Cutters and Butcher Workmen of North America,* Amalgamated Clothing Workers of America,* United Shoe Workers,* International Fur Workers Union of the United States and Canada,* and the International Leather Goods, Plastics and Novelty Workers Union* all encroached upon the ULWIU's jurisdiction, although in most instances they were simply organizing where the ULWIU had failed to organize.

The ULWIU's greatest challenge, however, came in May 1937 when the National Leather Workers' Association received a charter from the Congress of Industrial Organizations* (CIO). The new CIO union quickly established its hegemony over its AFL rival, and when it merged with the Fur Workers to create the International Fur and Leather Workers Union,* the ULWIU was relegated to the status of a small, minor union with a pretentious title. The ULWIU, which had never really recovered from the great Depression, merged with the Amalgamated Meat Cutters in 1951.

The ULWIU, which maintained its national headquarters in Philadelphia, held triennial conventions. Full-time officers included a president, two vice-presidents, and a secretary-treasurer. The president, vice-presidents, and six members elected at national conventions constituted the general executive council. At the time of its merger with the Amalgamated Meat Cutters, the ULWIU had a membership of approximately 5,000 located in twenty-four local unions.

For further information, see Leo C. Brown, *Union Policies in the Leather Industry* (1947), and Philip S. Foner, *The Fur and Leather Workers Union* (1950).

LETTER CARRIERS OF THE UNITED STATES OF AMERICA; NATIONAL ASSOCIATION OF (NALC). Abraham Lincoln, on March 3, 1863, signed a bill providing for free city delivery of mail. Residential deliveries began on July 1. This action brought a large number of new employees—mail carriers—into public service. During the early years, employment conditions experienced by these new federal employees were characterized by low wages and, as a result of political patronage, little job security. Improvements were gained through wage legislation in 1877, the Pendleton Civil Service Act of 1883, and the enactment of an eight-hour law for federal employees in 1888. But many problems still remained.

The spectacular appearance of the Noble Order of the Knights of Labor* (KofL) attracted many letter carriers who joined the order in many cities despite the hostility of postal officials. This experience with organized labor inevitably led to an interest in the formation of a national organization of letter carriers. Because many letter carriers were veterans, William H. Wood, a Detroit letter carrier, clandestinely circulated a proposal to form such an organization during a Grand Army of the Republic encampment in Milwaukee, Wisconsin, in 1889. With delegates from several cities in attendance, the meeting resulted in the formation of the National Association of Letter Carriers on August 29, 1889. After electing Wood president, the new union established a priority list of wage and benefit demands. Although originally viewed with some suspicion by letter carriers, the NALC quickly gained support, especially after the affiliation of the influential New York Letter Carriers' Association.

The most divisive issue confronting the NALC leadership in its early years revolved around its relationship to the Knights of Labor. Many letter carriers belonged to KofL assemblies and strongly urged affiliation with the order. The national NALC leadership, however, correctly foresaw the decline of the Knights and successfully opposed affiliation. Their action created a fissure in the organization, and the faction loyal to the KofL formed a rival national union.

A Post Office Department decision shortly after the rupture effectively reunified the quarreling letter carriers. In an effort to reduce costs, post office officials reinterpreted the eight-hour law to mean that an eight-hour day constituted a fifty-six-hour work week. Consequently, if letter carriers worked a nine-hour day, six days a week, they would still owe the department two hours of work per week. The department's ruling clearly violated the intent and spirit of the legislation, and the NALC challenged the action in the courts, eventually winning its case before the Supreme Court. The NALC's victory, along with an appropriation of $3.5 million to settle overtime claims, was a momentous event in the history of the Association. It had demonstrated its ability to act effectively in the interests of letter carriers despite the obstinacy of the Post Office Department, and recruitment of new members became much easier.

Because of the public nature of their employment, letter carriers did not have access to strikes, boycotts, or collective bargaining available to private employees. Conditions of employment, working conditions, and wages were largely determined by Congress. Consequently, improvement in these areas could only be achieved through legislative lobbying. On January 31, 1902, President Theodore Roosevelt challenged even this bargaining method with his famous (or infamous) "gag rule" forbidding federal employees from "either directly or indirectly, individually or through association, to solicit an increase of pay or to influence or attempt to influence in their own interest any other legislation whatever, either before Congress or its Committees, or in any way, save through the heads of the Department in or under which they serve, on penalty of dismissal from the Government service."

Although the gag rule was essentially unenforceable, it provided a valuable weapon that postal officials could use to discipline employees. The most notable case involved the president of the NALC, James C. Keller, who was dismissed after opposing the reelection of the anti-labor chairman of the House Post Office Committee. The NALC lost a measure of its previous prestige and respect when it failed to go to the assistance of its occasionally indiscreet leader.

The gag rule ended with the Lloyd-La Follette Act of 1912, although strikes of postal or federal employees were still specifically prohibited. Despite the enactment of other measures liberalizing postal employment, the following years were difficult for postal employees. Woodrow Wilson's postmaster general, Albert S. Burleson, deeply offended postal workers by his anti-union behavior, severe economy measures, authoritarian manner, and callous dismissal of "super-annuated" employees. Burleson's insensitive behavior, however, also offended both the public and the Congress, thus inadvertently strengthening the postal unions. Congress repudiated Burleson's policies in 1920 and enacted legislation reclassifying postal employees and providing a substantial increase in the wage scale, a fifteen-day annual leave, and ten days sick leave. On May 22, 1920, Congress also enacted the Civil Service Retirement Act.

After 1920 the NALC devoted much of its time to lobbying for improved working conditions and increased wages. The major objective of the NALC was to achieve wages and benefits for letter carriers comparable to those received by similar types of employees in private industry. Following World War II, the wages of letter carriers reached near parity, but inefficiencies in the administration of the post office and the economy measures of the Eisenhower administration again resulted in comparatively lower pay for postal workers. This situation remained during the 1960s even though the rhetoric became more liberal.

When Lawrence T. O'Brien, on April 3, 1967, first proposed the creation of a semi-autonomous postal corporation, the NALC adamantly opposed the idea. But after several features of the proposed legislation were eliminated at a conference between President Richard M. Nixon and NALC president James H. Rademacher, the NALC gave its support to the Postal Reform Act of 1970.

Meanwhile a series of unprecedented wildcat strikes, particularly in New York City, illustrated the need for reform and demonstrated to Congress and postal officials the extent of employee dissatisfaction. When entering into negotiations with the newly established U.S. Postal Service, the NALC joined with seven other postal unions to form the Council of American Postal Employees. After six months of hard bargaining, an agreement was signed, which did not satisfy all demands but did provide for substantial increases in pay.

The NALC, which maintains its national headquarters in Washington, D.C., holds biennial conventions. Full-time officers include a president, executive vice-president, vice-president, secretary-treasurer, and assistant secretary-treasurer. The executive council includes the above officers and national business agents, the board of trustees, and the directors and assistant directors of the life insurance and the health benefits plan. In 1973 the NALC reported a membership of 220,000 located in 5,500 local unions.

For further information, see *The Postal Record* published monthly by the NALC since 1893. See also *Mailman U.S.A.* (1960), an account written by the influential William C. Doherty, president of the NALC from 1941 to 1962, and Gerald Cullinan, *The Mail Man: A Short History and Appraisal* (1967).

LETTER CARRIERS' ASSOCIATION; NATIONAL RURAL (NRLCA). Delegates representing rural letter carriers throughout the U.S. Post Office Department met in Chicago in 1903 and organized the National Rural Letter Carriers' Association. Their action resulted from the refusal of urban letter carriers to admit them to membership until they came under the provisions of the civil service merit system. Membership in the NRLCA was open to all regular, substitute, or retired rural letter carriers, but only white members could serve as delegates to conventions or hold office. Despite the serious economic problems affecting postal employees at the time, during its early years the NRLCA stressed fraternal and professional objectives. The NRLCA was essentially a national federation of state and county organizations and as such had only a limited degree of authority over its affiliated units.

One of the unique features of the NRLCA's early history was the seminal role the *R.F.D. News* played in the organization. The editor of the journal took a leading role in the organization of the association, and the *News* was designated the NRLCA's official organ. Yet the paper was privately owned, and the editor was not responsible to union officials for editorial policy. Wisdom D. Brown, an attorney unaffiliated with the NRLCA, acquired the *News* in 1910 and immediately determined to gain control of the association; to a considerable extent, he succeeded.

Post office officials responded to the organization of rural letter carriers with the same hostility with which they had greeted the organization of urban letter carriers. Shortly after the NRLCA began agitating for increased wages, postal officials placed severe restrictions on the political activities of rural carriers and dismissed several NRLCA officials, including its president, from the postal service. Nevertheless, the rural letter carriers had an unusual degree of political influence. Well-known figures among the rural patrons along their routes, they exercised considerable influence in the districts of rural congress-men. Consequently, such congressmen were hesitant to offend such potentially influential members of their constituencies.

The NRLCA grew at a remarkable rate during its early years. By 1914 it had enrolled over two-thirds of all rural letter carriers employed by the U.S. Post Office. This period of growth, however, came to an abrupt end during Post-master General Albert S. Burleson's eight hectic years in office between 1913 and 1921. Burleson launched an intensive campaign against the unions in the post office in an effort to eliminate obstacles to his plans for large-scale postal service economies. While most unions functioning in the Post Office Depart-ment not only survived Burleson's blustering anti-union campaign but grew stronger and more unified, the NRLCA almost collapsed. By 1917 member-ship had fallen from 68 percent of the rural carriers to 15 percent. The Post Office Department's success among rural letter carriers was primarily the product of the rural carrier's lack of contact with other association members. Isolated and alone, they found it much more difficult to withstand the pres-sures emanating from the Post Office Department.

Besides the anti-union policies of the post office, other circumstances con-tributed to the NRLCA's decline. Chief among them was a growing internal conflict revolving largely around Wisdom Brown's role in the organization. As the association's membership declined, criticism of Brown grew, and distinct pro- and anti-Brown factions appeared. These factional conflicts accelerated after the National Association of Letter Carriers* and the Railway Mail Asso-ciation affiliated with the American Federation of Labor* (AFL) in 1917. The question of joining the AFL became an important issue in the NRLCA councils. Brown opposed affiliation, and his vehement objections reflected an increasingly hostile attitude toward the labor movement generally. Although Brown persevered, a disaffected group centered primarily in the Pennsylvania branch of the NRLCA withdrew from the association, founded their own orga-nization (the National Federation of Rural Letter Carriers), and secured an AFL national charter. The AFL affiliate never became a major element in the postal labor movement, however, and on October 23, 1946, it amalgamated with the NALC.

After Burleson left office in 1921, a degree of regularity returned to labor relations in the Post Office Department. Yet the NRLCA failed to regain its previous high membership percentage among rural letter carriers. Enrollment climbed to approximately 40,000, and, although it fluctuates annually, it re-mains near that figure. Through the years the NRLCA has increased the per-centage of rural letter carriers it represents, but changes in the organization of the postal service have reduced the number of rural carriers; hence member-ship gains are offset by losses in employment, and total NRLCA membership remains fairly constant.

The NRLCA, which maintains its national headquarters in Washington,

D.C., holds annual conventions. Principal officers include a president, vice-president, and secretary-treasurer. The executive committee consists of four members elected by the delegates at national conventions. The NRLCA also has a national board comprised of the principal executive officers and the executive committee. In 1973 the NRLCA reported a membership of 46,300 located in 2,000 local unions.

For further information, see the *National Rural Letter Carrier* issued weekly. See also Sterling D. Spero, *Government as Employer* (1948), a fine study of public service unions. Information can also be found in *Bulletin No. 618*, Bureau of Labor Statistics, U.S. Department of Labor (1936), and Florence Peterson, *Handbook of Labor Unions* (1944).

LITHOGRAPHERS OF AMERICA; AMALGAMATED. *See* Lithographers and Photoengravers International Union.

LITHOGRAPHERS AND PHOTOENGRAVERS INTERNATIONAL UNION (LPIU). On September 7, 1964, the Amalgamated Lithographers of American (ALA) and the International Photo Engravers Union of North America (IPEUNA) merged to create the Lithographers and Photoengravers International Union. The two small merging unions had acquired considerable longevity in the American labor movement.

Amalgamated Lithographers of America. Trade union organization in the lithographic industry began prior to the Civil War. Before being destroyed by the panic of 1857, local organizations of lithographers existed in most of the larger cities in the United States. Although trade union organization in the industry revived after the Civil War, a permanent national union did not exist until 1886. This union, the Lithographers' International Protective and Beneficial Association of the United States and Canada (LIPBA), first organized as a national assembly of the Knights of Labor* and included most skilled workers in the industry, including artists, designers, engravers, provers, transferrers, and pressmen. In 1890 most artists and engravers withdrew, forming their own organization, the International Lithographic Artists' and Engravers' Insurance and Protective Association of the United States and Canada (ILAE).

The ILAE conducted the first major industrial strike of lithographic workers in 1896. It called a general strike in New York after negotiations with the Lithographers' Association of the Metropolitan (New York City) District failed to satisfy the union. The dispute eventually was resolved by arbitration in which most of the union's demands were met, including the abolition of piecework and the establishment of a minimum wage.

Because the LIPBA and ILAE refused to admit press feeders into their organizations, a third national union in the industry, the International Protective

Association of Lithographic Apprentices and Press Feeders of the United States and Canada, was established in 1898. Also organized in the following years were the Poster Artists' Association of America (1899), the International Association of Lithographic Stone and Plate Preparers of the United States and Canada (1900), and the Paper Cutters Union (1900). The proliferation of independent unions in the industry and the inevitable jurisdictional conflicts accompanying such organization weakened the trade union movement among lithographers at the same time that employers were creating their own centralized organization, the Lithographers' Association.

On March 15, 1904, the Lithographers' Association declared a national lockout of its union employees. Although employers failed to impose their will on labor during the conflict, the unions lost ground in the compromise agreement accepted by both the association and the unions in April 1904. Two years later, a much stronger, newly organized employers' association, the National Association of Employing Lithographers, launched a successful open-shop campaign that ended over two decades of collective bargaining in the industry.

Defeated by the unified, collective power of employers, all trade unions in the lithographic industry except the Poster Artists' Association and the Press Feeders' Union agreed to a merger consummated in 1915 under the title of the Amalgamated Lithographers of America. Later the Press Feeders (1918) and the Post Artists' Association (1942) also affiliated with the ALA.

Although collective bargaining briefly revived on a limited basis in 1919, employer strength, an unsuccessful strike in 1922, and technological changes in the industry combined to retard the growth of ALA. It failed to surpass 10,000 members until the years of World War II.

The LIPBA and its successor, the ALA, carried on a volatile relationship with the American Federation of Labor* (AFL). The LIPBA affiliated with the AFL in 1906, but resulting from jurisdictional conflicts with the IPEUNA and especially the International Printing Pressmen and Assistants' Union* (IPPAU), the AFL recognized neither the merger of the lithographic unions in 1915 nor the ALA label. Officially the AFL leadership continued to recognize the LIPBA even though it no longer existed. In 1916 the AFL ordered the lithographic unions to merge with either the IPEUNA or the IPPAU. The ALA refused, and the conflict simmered until 1946 when AFL headquarters actively intervened on the side of the IPPUA in an attempt to raid ALA membership in Atlanta. In response, the ALA withdrew from the AFL and affiliated with the Congress of Industrial Organizations* (CIO). The merger of the AFL and CIO appeared to extend to the ALA the legitimacy that the AFL had formerly denied. Nevertheless, the ALA soon found itself again confronted with jurisdictional disputes with its old rival, the IPPAU, and was again outvoted in national conventions. Consequently, in 1958 the ALA withdrew from the AFL-CIO and remained independent until the 1964 merger with the IPEUNA.

The ALA, which maintained its national headquarters in Chicago, held triennial conventions. Principal officers included a president, a secretary-treasurer, four vice-presidents, and a journal editor. The international council was composed of the above officials and a representative of each department in the industry. At the time of the merger with the IPEUNA, the ALA had a membership of 38,000.

International Photo Engravers Union of North America. Efforts to organize photoengravers began as early as 1886, but while local organizations sprang up periodically in larger American cities, it was not until 1894 that photoengravers organized in a systematic way. In 1894 the International Typographical Union* (ITU) issued a charter to a group of New York City photoengravers and thereafter welcomed engravers into the ITU. By 1899 nineteen locals, composed primarily of newspaper workers, were affiliated with the ITU. Meanwhile commercial engravers had organized their own unions. Thus the early period of unionization in the trade was characterized by numerous dual organizations.

Much of the jurisdictional chaos in the photoengraving trade ended on May 19, 1904, when the AFL issued a charter to the International Photo Engravers of North America. The new union, which absorbed the former ITU locals and many independent unions, was given a trade jurisdiction that included "all workers engaged in producing engravings, images, and characters of every description by the means of photography, or any other method or process for printing purposes of every type and form."

Beginning with a membership of 2,000, the IPEUNA gradually extended its control over the labor force within its jurisdiction. Unlike many other trade unions, the IPEUNA did not greatly expand its membership during World War I, but under the leadership of Matthew Woll and Edward Volz, the IPEUNA grew steadily during the 1920s and the years of the Great Depression. A 1920 membership of 5,900 grew to 8,900 in 1932 and 9,100 in 1937. By the 1950s, the IPEUNA had organized well over 90 percent of the potential membership in its jurisdiction.

Labor-management relations in the photoengraving industry were much less volatile than those of many other trades. The highly skilled photoengravers maintained an amicable relationship with employers, many of whom retained their membership in the IPEUNA after becoming plant owners. Through effective collective bargaining the IPEUNA was one of the pioneer American unions in gaining for its members major improvements in working conditions, the five-day week, paid vacations and holidays, and health and welfare benefits.

The IPEUNA, which maintained its national headquarters in St. Louis, held annual conventions. Principal officers included a president, a secretary-treasurer, and five vice-presidents. The general executive council was composed of the above officials. At the time of the merger with the ALA, the IPEUNA had approximately 20,000 members.

On September 4, 1972, the LPIU merged with the International Brother-hood of Bookbinders* (IBB) to create the Graphic Arts International Union.* It was hoped that the merger would further eliminate jurisdictional disputes in the industry, increase bargaining power, and facilitate organizing efforts.

The LPIU maintained its national headquarters in Washington D.C., and held biennial conventions. Principal officers included a president, secretary, treasurer, and a varied number of vice-presidents. The general executive council included the aforementioned officials. Shortly before the merger with the IBB, the LPIU reported a membership of 60,000 located in 140 local unions.

For further information, see *The American Photo-Engraver* published monthly by the IPEUNA, *The Lithographers' Journal* published monthly by the ALA, and the *Graphic Arts Unionist* issued nine times a year by the LPIU. See also Fred C. Munson, *Labor Relations in the Lithographic Industry* (1963) and *History of the Lithographers Union* (1963); Henry E. Hoagland, *Collective Bargaining in the Lithographic Industry* (1917); and Charles Leese, *Collective Bargaining Among Photo-Engravers in Philadelphia* (1929).

LOCOMOTIVE ENGINEERS; BROTHERHOOD OF (BLE). Angered over changes in wages and working hours, thirteen engineers of the Michigan Central Railroad issued a call to all engineers to meet in Detroit on March 17, 1893, to discuss their grievances. From this meeting came the establishment of Division Number One, Brotherhood of the Footboard (BOF). By August ten subdivisions of the brotherhood existed, and the Grand National Division, BOF, was formed on August 18, with William D. Robinson as grand chief engineer.

During the following year numerous wildcat strikes caused dissatisfaction with the ineffective Robinson, and he was ousted at the first annual convention in 1864. He was replaced by Charles Wilson, who adopted a very conservative trade union policy. Under Wilson's leadership the organization became the Grand International Division of the Brotherhood of Locomotive Engineers with membership specifically limited to locomotive engineers. Following a policy of appeasement toward employers, the BLE avoided alliances with such reformist unions as the National Labor Union* and the Knights of Labor.*

By 1873 the BLE had a membership of 9,500. In that year, however, a severe depression, which had a devastating effect on railroads, swept the country. At this crucial juncture some members of the BLE began to question the con-servative, no-strike philosophy of Grand Chief Wilson, and ultimately this dis-satisfaction led to his replacement by Peter M. Arthur in 1874. Faced with the problem of railroads' reducing wages and employment, Arthur was pushed to adopt a more militant policy. In 1876 and 1877, two unsuccessful strikes weak-ened the BLE, and although the brotherhood was not involved in the great railroad strike of 1877, the failure of that violence-ridden strike contributed to the BLE's decline. After the disasters of 1876 and 1877, the brotherhood reverted to its earlier conservatism, even rejecting the "pure and simple" trade unionism developing nationally in the late 1870s and 1880s.

The brotherhood gradually recovered its lost membership and prestige, and by 1886 the 20,000-member BLE had become one of the most powerful unions in the country, and Arthur had acquired the status of a national labor leader. The stability of the union, however, was threatened once again by the loss of a major strike. Upset by what they considered an unfair pay classification system and other abuses, engineers called a strike against the Burlington Railroad in 1888. The easy availability of strikebreakers, some from other labor organizations, as well as internal dissension among the engineers themselves, ensured the company an easy victory. The Burlington strike severely damaged the status and prestige previously enjoyed by the BLE, requiring the union to engage once more in a rebuilding effort. After 1888 the BLE attempted to avoid strikes and continued its policy of independence, thus rebuffing efforts on the part of the American Railway Union,* Knights of Labor, and the American Federation of Labor* to achieve closer unity. Shortly after Arthur's death in 1903, the grand officers elected Warren S. Stone as grand chief engineer. Stone served in the position until 1924. Like Arthur, Stone followed an independent, conservative policy, but this did not interfere with the development of increased cooperation between the brotherhood and other railway unions in grievance settlement and collective bargaining. Partially due to this cooperation, the BLE helped secure passage of the Locomotive Inspection Act in 1911 and, a few years later, the Adamson Act, which established an eight-hour day for rail-operating employees. Legislation and regulation later brought such innovations as electric headlights, power reverse gears, automatic fire doors, and mechanical stokers. The BLE's greatest legislative failure derived from its inability to secure the enactment of the Plumb plan of government ownership of the railroads following World War I.

By 1920 membership had climbed to over 86,000, and the union had developed sophisticated machinery for dealing with the increasingly complex problems of grievance settlement and collective bargaining. Also, by 1920, the BLE had established a system of work rules covering all the nation's major railroads. Although it considered abandoning its independent policy during the 1920s, the BLE ultimately elected to retain its autonomy. It made an effort to involve itself in investment banking and real estate in the 1920s but abandoned these unsuccessful ventures by the end of the decade. It also formed political alliances with farm and labor groups, which resulted in its support of the Progressive party presidential candidacy of Robert M. La Follette in 1924. Third-party politics, however, lost favor after La Follette's defeat.

After the 1920s increased competition from other forms of transportation, changes brought by technological advances, and deterioration of the railroads during the depression years of the 1930s reduced the demand for engineers, but that demand revived dramatically during World War II. In the years following the war, management became less tolerant of union-required work rules and wage demands, and the labor-management bargaining relationships became much more volatile.

Resulting from those changes in the industry appearing before World War II, the inflated wartime membership declined during the postwar years. By 1960 membership had fallen to 68,000. Despite this numerical decline, the BLE remains active in insurance and benevolent activities and in lobbying through legislative committees (a practice that has become increasingly important as the industry has become quasi-public) as well as the continuing concern with contract and work rules negotiation.

The BLE, which maintains its national headquarters in Cleveland, holds quinquennial conventions. Principal officers include a grand chief engineer, first assistant grand chief engineer, sixteen assistant grand chief engineers, and a secretary-treasurer. The executive committee is comprised of the grand chief engineer, first assistant grand chief engineer, and the secretary-treasurer. In 1973 the BLE reported a membership of 37,600 located in 811 local unions.

For additional information, see the *Locomotive Engineers Journal*, a monthly journal begun shortly after the founding of the BLE. In 1956 a newspaper, the *Locomotive Engineer*, was started and has since replaced the *Journal*. See also the excellent work by Reed C. Richardson, *The Locomotive Engineer, 1863-1963: A Century of Railway Labor Relations and Work Rules* (1963), and the brief monograph, *A Contemporary Analysis of a Labor Union*, by Miles E. Hoffman. Beginning in March 1969, the *Locomotive Engineer* ran an informative series of articles tracing the history of the BLE.

Robert E. Zeigler

LOCOMOTIVE FIREMEN AND ENGINEMEN; BROTHERHOOD OF (BLFE). Eleven Erie Railroad firemen met at Port Jervis, New York, on December 1, 1873, and organized the Brotherhood of Locomotive Firemen (BLF). Although delegates to the first grand lodge convention (held in Cornellsville, New York, the following year) created the BLF Life Insurance Association to provide sickness and funeral benefits for locomotive firemen, the BLF did not long remain simply an insurance or beneficial society. At its second annual convention, meeting in Indianapolis in 1875, the BLF had 900 members in twenty-nine lodges. The forty-six delegates attending the convention clearly established the BLF as a labor union when they committed the organization to "protection of members in industrial relations, as well as a life insurance organization."

The BLF grew steadily until 1877, but the great railroad strikes of that year, an anti-union employer offensive, and growing unemployment precipitated declines in membership and financial resources lasting for several years. The extent of the BLF's decline, however, was checked in 1879 by a merger with the International Firemen's Union, a loosely knit organization formed several years before the founding of the BLF. During the early 1880s, BLF organizing revived, and the union began a steady growth. Meanwhile, the brotherhood became increasingly involved in negotiations with railroads to improve working conditions and wages and in lobbying for a variety of measures to improve safety conditions.

By the time of the fourth biennial and seventeenth national convention in 1894, the BLF had a membership of nearly 26,000, but the depression of the 1890s and the great railroad strike precipitated by the Pullman boycott halted the BLF's progress, although it did not result in any significant membership losses. By the turn of the century, the brotherhood was growing steadily once again. As early as 1902 the BLFE had amended its constitution to permit the enrollment of locomotive engineers, and in 1906 the name of the union was changed to the Brotherhood of Locomotive Firemen and Enginemen. Also in 1906 the BLFE joined with the other three railroad train service labor organizations in joint wage negotiations with several western railroads, which substantially increased the wages of 81,000 railroaders.

The second decade of the twentieth century was a period of great progress for the BLFE. Membership grew steadily, reaching a peak of nearly 126,000 by 1920. The brotherhood also made steady advances in collective bargaining, and after a threatened nationwide railroad strike, the eight-hour day for railroad workers was guaranteed by the Adamson Act of 1917. Moreover, after the government assumed control of the railroads during World War I, the railroad brotherhoods won two wage increases.

After 1920 the BLFE entered a period of slow decline. Determined to check the growing power of the railroad brotherhoods, railroad managers found a faithful ally in the federal government. The U.S. Railroad Labor Board created under the Transportation Act of 1920 proved so unfavorable to employees that the unions eventually disregarded it and resumed direct negotiations with the railroads. Another problem the BLFE encountered in the immediate postwar years was the creation of a rival union, the United Enginemen's Association, which attracted many brotherhood members and some lodges. Before the internecine war ended, BLFE officers revoked the charters of sixty lodges with a total membership of nearly 16,000.

The BLFE's problems grew even more serious later during the 1920s and when the Great Depression struck the nation and continued for nearly a decade. During these years, most of the BLFE's achievements came as the result of legislative lobbying, the Railway Labor Act of 1926, safety legislation, and the Railroad Retirement Act of 1934 were all considered legislative victories by BLFE officials.

Like World War I, World War II proved a period of full employment and growth for the BLFE. During the decade beginning in 1941, the brotherhood won major wage increases, a five-day week for yardmen, and an agreement that firemen would be retained in the cabs of all diesel locomotives used in passenger service. The issue of retaining firemen plagued the BLFE for several years, however, and ultimately led to a strike in 1962, temporarily resolved by arbitration that resulted in the removal of firemen-helpers from many freight and yard jobs. The manning issue remained a heated controversy, which at one point led to the jailing of several BLFE officers as a 'result of a 1966 strike.

After several unsuccessful attempts to negotiate a merger with the Brotherhood of Locomotive Engineers,* the BLFE entered merger discussions with the Order of Railroad Conductors and Brakemen,* the Brotherhood of Railroad Trainmen,* and the Switchmen's Union of North America* in 1968. A unity agreement resulted, and on January 1, 1969, the United Transportation Union* was created.

The BLFE, which held quadrennial conventions, maintained its national headquarters in Cleveland. Principal officers included a president, an assistant president, three executive and thirteen regional vice-presidents, and a secretary-treasurer. The brotherhood also had a five member-board of directors elected by majority vote of convention delegates. At the time of the merger with UTU, the BLFE had a membership of 67,750.

For further information, see the *Locomotive Firemen's Magazine* published by the BLFE since 1876, and the "Historical Sketch of the Brotherhood" published in the convention proceedings of the BLFE's thirty-third convention which met in Milwaukee in June 1937. See also Morris A. Horowitz, "The Diesel Firemen Issue on the Railroads," *Industrial and Labor Relations Review* (July 1960).

LONGSHOREMEN'S ASSOCIATION; INTERNATIONAL (ILA). Militant strike actions among American dockworkers began as early as 1836, but it was not until 1864 that a formal union of such workers came into existence. In that year the New York State legislature issued a charter to the Alongshoremen's Union Protective Association (LUPA). The new union prospered in the years immediately following the Civil War; five locals were begun in New York City, and organization spread along the coast. The initial success, however, ended with the panic of 1873 and the depression that followed. When shipowners further reduced already depressed wages in the fall of 1874, longshoremen revolted; on November 16, they struck the Port of New York. It was not a propitious time to call a strike; the depression had created large-scale unemployment, and this, along with the absence of any trade union unity, doomed the strike from the beginning. Within thirty days the strike ended in total defeat for the workers.

With the failure of the strike, unionism along the waterfront virtually disappeared, although the LUPA did manage to survive the strike. It was not until the Knights of Labor* (KofL) entered the field during the mid-1880s that unionism revived. The KofL was particularly successful in organizing the previously unorganized longshoremen handling the coastal trade. A group of such workers walked off their jobs after a 20 percent wage reduction, and when the grievances of a group of New Jersey coal handlers became involved in the dispute, a general strike gradually evolved on the New York and New Jersey waterfronts. Exhibiting unexpected solidarity, the waterfront workers closed the Port of New York, but when the KofL leadership negotiated a settlement of the coal handlers' dispute without reference to the dockworkers' grievances, the strike collapsed and, with it, trade unionism among longshoremen. In this case not even the resilient LUPA survived the debacle.

In the following years, the British Dockers' Union sent a representative, Edward McHugh, to the United States to organize an American division of a projected worldwide union of longshoremen. McHugh's initial efforts met with considerable success, and at a convention in New York City in January 1897, the American Longshoremen's Union (ALU) was organized. Growing rapidly, the new union recruited a membership of 15,000 in twenty-one branches by 1898. During a strike in Philadelphia late in 1898, however, it was discovered that the ALU general secretary had absconded with the union's funds. In the recriminations and accusations that followed the disclosure, the ALU was destroyed. In its place a new union emerged that adopted the old LUPA's name. Repeating the experience of previous dockworker organizations, the LUPA disintegrated after an unsuccessful strike in 1907.

Despite the long history of organizing attempts on the East Coast, the first permanent union of longshoremen was destined to emerge in the unlikely setting of the Great Lakes. A local union of longshoremen first appeared in Chicago in 1877. Led by Dan Keefe, an energetic union entrepreneur who carried the union message to other ports on the Great Lakes, the Chicago local took the initiative in a movement to create an association of longshoremen unions. As a result, a meeting was held in Detroit in 1892 at which the National Longshoremen's Association of the United States was founded. Following the affiliation of Canadian locals, the name was changed in 1895 to the International Longshoremen's Association. On November 9 of the following year, the ILA received a charter from the American Federation of Labor* (AFL).

The early ILA exhibited an expansionist tendency that soon aroused the suspicions of the craft-oriented leaders of the AFL. The ILA's drift toward industrial unionism became explicit in 1902 when the union title was changed to the International Longshoremen, Marine and Transport Workers' Association of North and South America and the Island Possessions. The actions of the ILA provoked an immediate confrontation with the International Seamen's Union of America* and the AFL. After four years of futile negotiations, the AFL, threatening expulsion, ordered the ILA to drop "Marine and Transport Workers" from its title. After stalling for a year, the ILA complied with the directive.

By guaranteeing employers against work stoppages and promising them an adequate and steady labor supply, the ILA succeeded in establishing a closed shop on the Great Lakes. In order to preserve the closed shop, however, the ILA eliminated local autonomy and ruthlessly crushed wildcat strikes. The problem of controlling the waterfront labor force was solved by drastically raising or lowering initiation fees to encourage or discourage casual laborers from entering the work force.

However dubious its tactics, the ILA grew spectacularly. By 1905 it had a membership of over 100,000, half of which was on the Great Lakes and the remainder scattered throughout the country. The ILA avoided the fate of other maritime unions on the Great Lakes during the open-shop offensive of 1908 but did so at the expense of its reputation in labor circles. When the ILA refused to join the strike against the shippers banded together in the Lake Carriers' Association, it was immediately branded a company union by other maritime unions and blamed for the success of the open-shop drive.

ILA policies changed significantly after T. V. O'Connor replaced Keefe in the presidency in 1908. O'Connor did not share Keefe's grandiose designs and restricted organizing activities to longshoremen, thus avoiding jurisdictional conflicts and the AFL hostility that had characterized the Keefe years. Prior to World War I, the ILA made important strides in organizing the Gulf Coast ports, carried on a volatile relationship with Pacific Coast locals, and made important inroads on the Atlantic Coast. During these years, the ILA faced competition from the Industrial Workers of the World* (IWW) in some East Coast ports, especially Philadelphia and Baltimore, but government repression of the IWW during the war removed that potential competitor for the loyalties of longshoremen, although the IWW survived for several years on the Philadelphia waterfront. Nevertheless, the postwar years were not good ones for the ILA. The vigorous open-shop offensive during the early 1920s nearly destroyed seagoing maritime unionism, and the ILA's strength on the Great Lakes and along the Gulf Coast was seriously eroded.

When Joseph Ryan ascended to the ILA presidency in 1927, it marked the completion of a trend beginning as early as 1912, the gradual transferral of ILA power and leadership from the Great Lakes to the Atlantic Coast. Ryan's long presidency, however, was destined to be filled with bitterness, acrimony, and controversy.

The Great Depression nearly smothered the ILA until the enactment of the National Industrial Recovery Act, which precipitated a remarkable recovery. But the resurgence ultimately caused the ILA leadership great problems on the Pacific Coast. The Pacific Coast Division of the ILA had been organized in 1912 and after achieving some organizing success was rendered ineffective by unsuccessful strikes in 1916 and 1919. During the 1920s, waterfront organization was controlled by employer-sponsored, company unions. With the revival of ILA organizations in 1933, the employers' unions collapsed. In the spring of 1934, the western district longshoremen presented their demands to the Waterfront Employers Association, a coastwise organization: a union hiring hall, a six-hour day and thirty-hour week, and a wage increase. When these demands were rejected, a strike, postponed several times at the request of federal mediators and President Franklin Roosevelt, was called. The strike began on May 9 and eventually involved most West Coast maritime unions. It lasted eleven weeks and was climaxed by the San Francisco general strike of July 1934. Eventually both sides agreed to submit the dispute to the presidentially appointed National Longshoremen's Board for arbitration, and in time the unions won most of their demands.

The strike catapulted Harry Bridges, who headed the Joint Marine Strike Committee, into national union prominence. In 1935 he was elected president of the San Francisco ILA local, and the following year he became president of the Pacific Coast District. Bridges, an alleged supporter of the Communist party and a fervent advocate of industrial unionism, disagreed with Ryan and other ILA leaders on virtually every policy issue. Consequently after the organization of the Congress of Industrial Organizations* (CIO), Bridges moved quickly to secure a charter for the Pacific Coast District as the International Longshoremen's and Warehousemen's Union* (ILWU). In 1938 the National Labor Relations Board (NLRB) recognized the ILWU as the bargaining agent for longshoremen on the Pacific Coast. Following the split, both organizations grew steadily, especially during Worl War II, but neither had any significant success in jurisdictional raids on the other.

In the years following World War II, rank-and-file members of the ILA became increasingly restive as a result of dissatisfaction with union contracts. Finally, in the fall of 1951, a series of unauthorized strikes was climaxed by a twenty-one day wildcat strike in the Port of New York. This time the strikers included several high-ranking ILA officials and a future president, Thomas Gleason. The strike ended when a board of inquiry to investigate the strikers' grievances was appointed by Edward Corsi, the New York industrial commissioner. The so-called Corsi board uncovered several irregularities, including numerous fradulent votes in the contract referendum. Shortly after this incident, the New York State Crime Commission hearings on the New York waterfront produced many sensational charges of corruption and racketeering against ILA officials, many of which were unproven. Nevertheless, bothered and embarrassed by the charges and assuming the accuracy of the Crime Commission's findings, the AFL demanded a variety of reforms from ILA officials. When lengthy negotiations failed to produce a satisfactory agreement, the AFL suspended the ILA on September 22, 1953. Three days later the AFL issued a charter covering the old ILA jurisdiction to the International Brotherhood of Longshoremen (IBL). In an NLRB representational election in December 1953, the ILA won by a comfortable majority. Thereafter, the IBL remained a factor on the waterfront but did not seriously challenge the ILA's hegemony. On November 17, 1959, the IBL merged with the ILA, which, in turn, reaffiliated with the AFL-CIO.*

The ILA, which maintains its national headquarters in New York City, holds quadrennial conventions. Principal officers include a president, secretary-treasurer, and vice-presidents representing each geographical district. The executive committee is composed of the above officials. In 1973 the ILA reported a membership of 60,000 located in 212 local unions.

For further information, see the ILA's monthly *Longshore News and Longshoremen's Voice*. Charles P. Larrowe has firmly established himself as the preeminent authority on American waterfront unionism. See his *Shape-Up and Hiring Hall: A Comparison of Hiring Methods and Labor Relations on the New York and Seattle Waterfronts* (1955), *Maritime Labor Relations on the Great Lakes* (1959), and *Harry Bridges: The Rise and Fall of Radical Labor in the U.S.* (1972). See also Joseph H. Ball, one of the architects of the Taft-Hartley Act, who has a somewhat hostile account in *The Government-Subsidized Union Monopoly: A Study of Labor Practices in the Shipping Industry* (1966), and Maud Russell, who has a sympathetic view in *Men Along the Shore* (1966).

LONGSHOREMEN'S AND WAREHOUSEMEN'S UNION; INTERNATIONAL (ILWU). Longshoremen's unions on the Pacific Coast had traditionally carried on a volatile relationship with the International Longshoremen's Association* (ILA). During the early years of the twentieth century, a group of West Coast locals opposing the autocratic policies of ILA president Dan Keefe seceded from the national union and formed a loosely knit confederation of largely autonomous branches called the Longshoremen's Union of the Pacific Coast. The estrangement was not long-lived. Shortly after T. V. O'Connor replaced Keefe as ILA president, the western locals reaffiliated, and in 1912 most joined with the ILA's newly constituted Pacific Coast District Council.

After failing in a campaign for the ILA presidency in 1915, Thomas Herring led San Francisco longshoremen's unions out of the ILA and into an employer-dominated "blue book" union (derived from the blue membership books, which provided the holder preferential treatment in employment). Then in 1919 the Pacific Coast District, ILA, conducted an unsuccessful strike on the West Coast that ended effective trade unionism in the area for over a decade. Employers banded together into the Waterfront Employers Association, which dominated industrial affairs on the West Coast waterfront between World War I and the mid-1930s.

Capitalizing on the labor provisions of the National Industrial Recovery Act, Pacific Coast organizers quickly revived ILA locals in western ports. Within a few months the blue book unions collapsed, and by the spring of 1934, leaders of the ILA's Pacific Coast District felt strong enough to present their demands to the Waterfront Employers Association. Union demands included coastwise bargaining, union hiring halls, a six-hour day and thirty-hour week, in addition to wage increases.

Meanwhile, ILA president Joseph Ryan, who had hoped to institute unified bargaining on all three coasts, traveled to the Pacific Coast in an attempt to resolve the dispute. A traditional craft unionist, Ryan neither understood nor sympathized with the leaders of the Pacific Coast locals who demanded unified bargaining for all West Coast maritime unions. He argued (correctly, as later events were to prove) that the policies established by the National Recovery Admininstration did not permit such bargaining. Subjected to a torrent of abuse in Seattle, Portland, and San Francisco, Ryan returned to New York convinced that the Pacific locals were dominated by a Communist leadership more interested in radical politics than in the legitimate interests of longshoremen.

Despite the political complications and several delays at the request of federal mediators and President Franklin Roosevelt, the strike began on May 9. It lasted eleven weeks and was climaxed by the historic San Francisco general strike of July 16-19, 1934. Eventually both sides accepted the National Longshoremen's Board as an impartial arbitrator, thus ending the long and violent strike, which, although settled on terms similar to those proposed by Ryan months earlier, included the much-desired union hiring hall. The strike served to entrench the leadership of western militants led by Harry Bridges, however, and in 1935 Bridges was elected president of the San Francisco ILA local and a year later president of the Pacific Coast District, ILA.

The conflict between Ryan and the West Coast leaders continued into 1936. During the summer of that year, the Pacific, Atlantic, and Gulf Coast districts reached a general agreement on bargaining demands, but Bridges destroyed the apparent unity by announcing that Pacific longshoremen would not sign a contract until all maritime unions on the West Coast had agreed to terms. Assuming that Bridges was attempting to use the ILA to bolster weak, Communist-dominated maritime unions, Ryan informed Bridges that neither the Atlantic nor Gulf Coast districts would support a West Coast strike, the settlement of which depended on the terms Bridges outlined. Later Ryan informed Bridges that the other districts of the ILA would sign new contracts on October 1, 1936, and advised him to follow suit. Instead, the Pacific Coast District struck and tied up Pacific Coast ports for ninety-eight days. On February 5, 1937, the strike ended on terms similar to those other ILA districts had attained in October. Without questioning their own judgment, western leaders blamed Ryan's treachery for the failure of the strike; Ryan was equally convinced that they were little more than puppets of what he considered the "international Communist conspiracy."

The growing hostility between the two leaders and their differing trade union philosophies made a split in the organization inevitable. The formation of the Congress of Industrial Organizations* (CIO) precipitated the break that came in August 1937 when the Bridges-led dissidents received a CIO charter for the International Longshoremen's and Warehousemen's Union. In June 1938 the National Labor Relations Board certified the new union as the collective bargaining agent for all longshoremen on the Pacific Coast.

Neither the ILA nor the ILWU made significant inroads in the territorial jurisdiction of the other, and both unions grew stronger during World War II. Nevertheless, the postwar years were chaotic for the longshoremen's unions. ILA leaders faced a growing rank-and-file revolt, and this, along with widespread charges of corruption on the New York waterfront, led to the union's expulsion from the American Federation of Labor.* The opportunities that these events should have provided the ILWU were qualified by its own equally serious problems. Throughout the 1940s and well into the 1950s, ILWU president Harry Bridges was involved in almost constant legal battles—first to avoid deportation and later to avoid imprisonment for perjury. Bridges's union confronted equally serious problems. The provisions of the Taft-Hartley Act outlawing the closed shop challenged the legitimacy of the ILWU's highly prized union hiring hall, and the refusal of ILWU officials to sign the non-Communist affidavits required by the labor act made the union's warehouse division very vulnerable to the raids of rival unions. In order to use NLRB election machinery to protect itself from raids on ILWU warehousemen by the International Brotherhood of Teamsters,* ILWU officials ultimately signed the affidavits. The CIO's expulsion of the ILWU in 1950 because of its alleged Communist domination further isolated the West Coast union.

Despite its problems and unlike most other unions expelled by the CIO, the ILWU remained a strong, stable trade union. As a result of a ninety-five-day strike in the autumn of 1948, the ILWU maintained its control over hiring and convinced employers that it would not succumb to either red-baiting or the provisions of the Taft-Hartley Act. Consequently, a "New Look" developed in relations between the ILWU and Pacific Coast employers. The new atmosphere of company-union cooperation virtually ended strike activities on the West Coast waterfront from 1948 to 1971, although numerous independent job action strikes still occurred. In 1960 the ILWU signed a mechanization and modernization agreement with the Pacific Maritime Association that suspended previous ILWU-negotiated work rules, permitted a reduction in the work force, and provided a multimillion dollar trust fund to be used for retirement pensions and no-layoff guarantees. The industrial harmony ended in the fall of 1971 when the ILWU, abandoning the mechanization and modernization agreement, struck in favor of traditional collective bargaining demands. Under the threat of federal intervention, the 135-day strike ended on terms similar to those first offered by the Pacific Maritime Association.

The ILWU, which holds biennial conventions, maintains its national headquarters in San Francisco. Full-time officers include a president, two vicepresidents, and a secretary-treasurer. The executive board is composed of the above officers in addition to members elected from six geographical areas. In 1973 the ILWU reported a membership of 58,000 located in seventy-seven local unions.

For further information, see *The Dispatcher* published biweekly by the ILWU. Charles P. Larrowe has two important books containing valuable material on the ILWU: *Shape-Up and Hiring Hall: A Comparison of Hiring Methods and Labor Relations on the New York and Seattle Waterfronts* (1955), and *Harry Bridges: The Rise and Fall of Radical Labor in the U.S.* (1972), See also Joseph H. Ball, *The Government-Subsidized Union Monopoly: A Study of Labor Practices in the Shipping Industry* (1966); Maud Russell, *Men Along the Shore* (1966); and Betty V. H. Schneider and Abraham Siegel, *Industrial Relations in the Pacific Coast Longshore Industry* (1956).

LOWELL FEMALE LABOR REFORM ASSOCIATION (LFLRA). Founded in Lowell, Massachusetts by five mill girls in December 1844, the Lowell Female Labor Reform Association was one of the few mid-nineteenth century associations that organized women workers outside a local area. Primarily begun to better working conditions for female operatives in the textile mills, the LFLRA originally was to serve as an auxiliary of the Lowell Mechanics and Laborers Association, but it early established its independence and began to function as a separate entity. The association grew rapidly, and within a year it had approximately 600 members. Throughout 1845 and 1846 branches of the LFLRA were established in the mill towns of Waltham and Fall River, Massachusetts and Nashua, Dover, and Manchester, New Hampshire.

The constitution of the association, devised at the January 1846 meeting, reflected the desires to improve factory conditions and upgrade the quality of life for female workers. It pledged to work for the ten-hour day and for improvements in sanitary and lighting conditions in the textile factories. The constitution prohibited strikes except in instances where pacific measures had failed. According to the constitution, an increase in leisure time, and hence a shorter working day, would allow the working woman to "cultivate her mind" and improve her morals, and all society would benefit from a more educated, enlightened female working class. The January 1846 meeting also established the executive structure of the LFLRA by providing for a president, two vicepresidents, a secretary, a treasurer, and a board of eight directors. Sarah Bagley, a mill operative from New Hampshire, became the first president.

Bagley led the association's drive for the ten-hour day, and in 1845 when the Massachusetts House of Representatives' Committee on Manufacturing held hearings on the proposition, the association blanketed mill towns with petitions favoring the shorter day. After the committee failed to support the ten-hour day, the LFLRA, in conjunction with the New England Workingmen's Association (NEWA), again circulated petitions and held meetings, hoping to gain support for the demand.

The LFLRA held separate meetings but also conducted joint meetings with the NEWA and sent delegates to the NEWA conventions. At the 1846 and 1847 NEWA conventions, LFLRA delegates became increasingly involved in discussions on slavery and utopianism. At the same time, the publication of the NEWA and the LFLRA, the *Voice of Industry*, began devoting more space to slavery and utopian reform schemes. The operatives, however, opposed this shift and wanted the *Voice* to continue emphasizing wage and hour demands.

Members of the LFLRA initiated only one strike during the association's existence. In 1846 operatives at the Massachusetts Mills walked out in protest of a new rule requiring them to operate four looms instead of one and to accept one cent less per piece. Although the strike was successful, the LFLRA's leadership denied any responsibility for its success.

In 1846 Mary Emerson replaced Sarah Bagley as president of the association, and at the September 1846 NEWA convention, the LFLRA changed its name to the Labor Reform League of New England. By late 1846 the league began to drift from labor reform toward mutual aid, which in part was designed to recoup a falling membership. The league again changed its name in January 1847 to the Lowell Female Industrial Reform and Mutual Aid Society. An initiation fee of fifty cents, weekly dues of not less than six cents, together with fines for nonattendance of meetings provided the resources for a sickness benefit fund. Mary Emerson continued as president of the society until it disbanded in March 1848.

The LFLRA utilized the *Voice of Industry*, the NEWA's organ, as its official publication. The journal contained a female department directly under the control of the LFLRA. The association exercised much control over the *Voice* as Sarah Bagley, and later Mehitable Eastman, a Manchester factory operative, served as editors. In late 1845 or early 1846, the LFLRA bought the press and type of the *Voice*.

For further information, see Hannah Josephson, *The Golden Threads: New England's Mill Girls and Magnates* (1949); Eleanor Flexnor, *Century of Struggle: The Women's Rights Movement of the United States* (1959); and John B. Andrews and W. D. P. Bliss, "History of Women in Trade Unions," *Report on Conditions of Women and Child Wage Earners in the United States*, vol. 10 (1911).

Marie Tedesco

LUMBERMEN; LOYAL LEGION OF LOGGERS AND. *See* Timber Workers; International Union of.

MACHINISTS AND AEROSPACE WORKERS; INTERNATIONAL AS-
SOCIATION OF (IAM). On May 5, 1888, a group of nineteen railroad machinists in Atlanta, Georgia, founded the Order of United Machinists and
Mechanical Engineers, the first local of the modern International Association
of Machinists. The leader of the new organization, Thomas W. Talbot, had belonged to the Knights of Labor* (KofL) as had most of the original founders.
Talbot and his followers wanted to disassociate themselves from the floundering KofL and its concept of inclusiveness. Also among the original aims of the
association was the desire to improve the quality of the machinist trade and to
provide unemployment, illness, and accident insurance for its members.
Initially the union limited membership to white, free-born, practicing machinists.

The union grew rather rapidly; by 1891, there were 189 lodges comprised of
railroad machinists located primarily in the South and Midwest. The establishment of a rival American Federation of Labor* (AFL) affiliate caused increased organizational activity in the Northeast bringing many Irish shop machinists into the order. Thus, cultural solidarity declined, and the binding
element for most members became economic rather than social or fraternal.

At the first convention of the union in 1889, Talbot was unanimously elected
grand master machinist, and the name of the organization was changed to the
National Association of Machinists. The association went on record as opposing strikes, but two years later, it rejected its own original anti-strike position.
At the 1891 convention northerners and midwesterners were elected to leadership positions, further weakening the waning southern influence. The association again changed its name and became the International Association of
Machinists (IAM).

In 1893 James O'Connell became grand master machinist. O'Connell, reflecting the northern influence in the organization, attempted to make the
IAM a true trade union with control over all jobs filled by skilled machinists.
He also urged affiliation with the AFL, but a major block to this goal was the
union's adherence to the white-only policy. The offending anti-black clause
was omitted from the union constitution, thus pacifying Samuel Gompers and
the AFL, but against O'Connell's wishes it was inserted into the IAM's secret
ritual. Nevertheless, the IAM affiliation with the AFL became official in 1895.
In that year O'Connell influenced the AFL to revoke the charter of the rival International Machinists Union. O'Connell also worked to build the union and
traveled extensively to revive floundering local lodges and to help in local contract negotiations. He was able to transform the grand lodge (the central body)
into an efficient record-keeping unit, a step that he felt would aid in bargaining.

O'Connell also wanted to cooperate with other national leaders in the hope
of converting industrialists to the idea of collective bargaining. He had some
success and in 1900 was able to effect the so-called Murray Hill agreement with

the principal employer group, the National Metal Trades Association (NMTA). The agreement covered matters such as collective bargaining, over-time and a nine-hour day, a definition of the trade, apprentice training, and arbitration. By 1901 membership had reached 32,500, and O'Connell's craft union program seemed to be succeeding beyond expectations. However, in that same year the Murray Hill agreement floundered on the nine-hour day issue, creating an enmity between the IAM and the NMTA lasting thirty-five years. Another problem that plagued the O'Connell administration was a growing disagreement between supporters of O'Connell's brand of pure and simple unionism and advocates of socialism who urged more local autonomy and encouraged industrial unionism.

The failure of the Murray Hill agreement and the growing opposition to O'Connell's leadership led to his defeat in 1911 in a close race with a Socialist-sponsored candidate, W. H. Johnston. Despite his supporters' interest in local autonomy, after gaining power, Johnston moved to increase the strength of the grand lodge. The association agreed to admit all unskilled workers employed in the machine industry but stopped short of enrolling all members of the metal trades.

In 1912 an unsuccessful general strike against all the western railroads and several other strike failures prior to 1915 hurt the IAM. Despite these prob-lems wartime prosperity aided the union, and between 1916 and 1919 member-ship increased from 107,444 to 331,449. In 1920 a major strike against the American Can Company to combat anti-union activity failed; in 1922 an im-portant walkout by all railroad shop craftsmen over the issues of overtime pay, contracting out, and wage cuts also ended in failure. As a result membership fell drastically. By 1923 it was down to 111,677. Also during the 1920s the IAM became involved, largely unsuccessfully, in various business ventures. It also entered politics and supported Progressive party presidential candidate Robert La Follette in 1924; his defeat, however, ended union interest in third-party efforts. Throughout his presidency Johnston had been unable to con-solidate his control over the union, and the decline in membership with its accompanying financial losses further weakened his position. In 1926 he re-signed and was replaced by Arthur O. Wharton.

Under Wharton, who became a vice-president of the AFL in 1928, the IAM developed better relations with other AFL unions than had previously existed. Wharton was reluctant to authorize strikes and preferred to negotiate with em-ployers. Partially due to this approach and to legislation passed during the New Deal period, many IAM-employer problems were solved during the latter part of Wharton's administration. A serious blow to the union came in 1938 when the Congress of Industrial Organizations* (CIO) defected and carried with it 8,000 IAM members, representing a financial loss of $13,000. This was merely a continuation of a trend of declining membership that had started in the Johnston administration and continued through the depression years of the early 1930s. In 1932 membership was down to 58,900. Realizing the need to expand, union leaders initiated an organizing effort in the airframe industry and extensively used the machinery of the National Labor Relations Board.

During the late 1930s and early 1940s, the union's scope and jurisdiction were expanded. This led to jurisdictional conflicts with the United Brotherhood of Carpenters* (UBC) and the International Union of Operating Engineers,* which ultimately resulted in the IAM's withdrawal from the AFL. There was also an attempt to assert greater control over locals evidencing dissident attitudes.

The IAM reaffiliated with the AFL in 1951 and began to work out jurisdictional agreements with other unions, including the United Automobile Workers,* UBC, Bridge, Structural and Ornamental Iron Workers,* and the International Air Line Pilots Association.* Membership grew and reached 860,200 in 1957. In 1964 the name of the organization was changed to the International Association of Machinists and Aerospace Workers.

The IAM, which maintains its national headquarters in Washington, D.C., holds quadrennial conventions. Principal officers include an international president, nine vice-presidents (one of whom must be from Canada), and a secretary-treasurer. The executive council is composed of the above officials. In 1973 the IAM reported a membership of 757,564 located in 1,929 local lodges.

For further information, see *The Machinist* issued weekly by the IAM. See also two excellent works by Mark Perlman: *The Machinists: A New Study in American Trade Unionism* (1961) and *Democracy in the International Association of Machinists* (1962). The Socialist influence is discussed in *Labor and the Left: A Study of Socialist and Radical Influences in the American Labor Movement, 1881-1924* (1970) by John H. M. Laslett.

Robert E. Zeigler

MACHINISTS AND BLACKSMITHS; NATIONAL UNION OF (NUMB). The panic of 1857 and the following depression destroyed most of the trade unions that had previously been organized. In an effort to survive the depression, unions representing workers in similar crafts found it advantageous to combine in order to establish national unions for mutual assistance and protection. Such was the case of the National Union of Machinists and Blacksmiths. The first combined union of the two professions appeared in Philadelphia in the Spring of 1858. Growing rapidly, an April membership of fourteen grew to 300 by the end of the summer, and within a year similar organizations had appeared in four other cities. Consequently, on March 3, 1859, twenty-one delegates met in Philadelphia and organized the NUMB. By its first annual convention in November 1860, the promising new union had fifty-seven affiliated local unions and 2,828 members.

The Machinists and Blacksmiths soon exhibited the volatile growth and decline that would characterize its history. The successful beginning of 1860 was followed by a rapid decline as the nation drifted into civil war the following year. NUMB not only lost several of its strong locals when southern affiliates withdrew, but also lost many northern members who volunteered for military service. During 1861 the number of locals shrank from eighty-seven to thirty, and membership fell from 2,717 to 1,898. At its national convention in the fall of 1861 only four states sent delegates—Massachusetts, Missouri, Wisconsin, and Kentucky. NUMB regained its 1861 losses during the wartime prosperity, yet the revival proved ephemeral, and again NUMB fell into a state of decline and disintegration as a postwar depression struck the nation.

The instability of the NUMB was, in part, the product of a highly capable but overly idealistic and theoretical leadership. NUMB produced such prominent labor figures as Jonathan Fincher, Ira Steward, and Terence Powderly, but these leaders worried more about the state of the general movement for labor reform than about the daily problems of their small union.

Early endorsement of Ira Steward's eight-hour theory reflects the reform orientation of the union. Moreover, in 1863 NUMB was one of the unions in the forefront of the movement calling for the organization of a national labor federation to more effectively promote labor reform. As a result of this agitation, the National Labor Union* (NLU) was formed in 1866, but the Machinists and Blacksmiths broke with the NLU in the early 1870s when it turned almost exclusively to politics. In conjunction with the Iron Molders* and Coopers'* international unions, NUMB launched a new Industrial Congress in 1873. It was designed exclusively as a trade union organization similar in character to the American Federation of Labor,* which organized the following decade. Nevertheless, along with the depression of the 1870s, the same internal divisions that had plagued the NLU destroyed the new national federation.

During the prosperity of the early 1870s, NUMB experienced its most rapid growth, increasing its membership from 1,500 in 1870 to nearly 18,000 by 1873. But the panic of 1873 and the severe depression that followed again resulted in a drastic reduction in the NUMB's membership. By the end of the decade only a skeleton organization remained, and during the following decade machinists and blacksmiths drifted into local assemblies of the Knights of Labor.* The organization of a permanent national union in the trade awaited the founding of the International Association of Machinists* and the International Brotherhood of Blacksmiths, Drop Forgers and Helpers* in 1889.

For further information, see *Fincher's Trades' Review*, edited by Jonathan Fincher. See also John R. Commons et al., *History of Labour in the United States*, vol. 2 (1918); Norman J. Ware, *The Labor Movement in the United States, 1860-1895: A Study in Democracy* (1959); and David Montgomery, *Beyond Equality: Labor and the Radical Republicans, 1862-1872* (1967).

MAINTENANCE OF WAY EMPLOYES: BROTHERHOOD OF (BMWE). Like so many other unions of railroad workers, the Brotherhood of Mainte- nance of Way Employes began primarily as a fraternal and insurance society. The first union of maintenance of way workers appeared in Demopolis, Alabama, in 1887, and in June of that year it was chartered under the laws of the state of Alabama as the Order of Railroad Trackmen. Despite the valiant efforts of its founder and principal organizer, John T. Wilson, the new union encountered both employer resistance and worker apathy. Growing very slowly, by 1890 the order's membership numbered only 628.

Meanwhile, a second organization of maintenance of way employees, the Brotherhood of Railway Section Foremen of North America, was organized in La Porte City, Iowa. Like the Alabama group, the Iowa union's organizing efforts were hampered by hostile employers, apathetic or intimidated employ- ees, and the restriction of membership to white foremen.

The obvious advantages of amalgamation for both small organizations led to a joint meeting in St. Louis on October 13, 1891, and a resulting merger agreement effective January 1, 1892. The new union assumed the title of Brotherhood of Railway Track Foremen of America. With seven organizers in the field, membership jumped from 863 to 2,000 within nine months, and the future of the organization looked promising. The encroachments of Eugene Debs's American Railway Union* and the economic depression of the mid- 1890s soon modified the early optimism.

Despite the brotherhood's relatively dormant state during much of the 1890s, important decisions greatly affecting the future of the organization were made. During the decade the brotherhood gradually shifted its emphasis from insurance to broad economic issues. Reflecting this change the conven- tion delegates meeting in St. Louis in 1896 voted to establish system grievance committees and modified the anti-strike clause in the preamble to their con- stitution. A second significant development occurred when the brotherhood decided to make membership available to track laborers on the same basis as foremen, although a "whites only" policy continued. With this change the organization was renamed the Brotherhood of Railway Trackmen of America (BRTA) in 1896.

At the time the brotherhood was struggling to survive in the closing years of the nineteenth century, significant events transpired in Canada. In 1892 Canadian railroad workers organized the United Brotherhood of Railroad Trackmen. Although the Canadian union experienced many of the same prob- lems as its American counterpart, it won some economic concessions from the railroads. The advantages of an amalgamation of the American and Canadian unions were obvious, and after two years of frustrating and unproductive nego- tiations, Canadian railroad workers transferred their membership to the BRTA, thereby effecting the merger their leaders had failed to accomplish. In February 1900 the BRTA affiliated with the American Federation of Labor* (AFL) and was granted a jurisdiction that included white employees "in the

Track, Bridge and Building, Water Supply and Fuel Departments, and Signal and Interlocking Service on all Railways of America.''

Increased rank-and-file pressure to exercise its potential economic power accompanied the rapid growth of the BRTA during the early years of the twentieth century. Responding to this pressure, the brotherhood's first authorized strike occurred on the Maine Central Railroad in the summer of 1901, but the lack of preparation, organization, and unity shattered the effort. The BRTA's defeat in Maine, however, was more than compensated for by its successful strike against the Canadian Pacific Railway Company during the same summer. Exhibiting more unity than the employees of the Maine Central, Canadian Pacific Workers held firm during a bitter seventy-five-day strike and won not only a wage increase but recognition as well. The Canadian Pacific strike had a very salutary effect; unorganized trackmen began to stream into the brotherhood, and the railroads became less rigid in their dealings with the union.

Between 1901 and 1914 the BRTA continued its membership growth and experienced its share of collective bargaining victories as well as defeats, but the continued progress of the union was jeopardized in 1914 by the secession of a substantial portion of its membership. This resulted from intense factional rivalry within the union and the feeling that railroad systems in certain parts of the country were being neglected by the brotherhood. The secessionists formed a rival organization, the Brotherhood of Maintenance of Way Employes. Although the conflict was eventually resolved by an amalgamation on August 15, 1918, the disunity compromised the authority of brotherhood officers during the critical World War I period. At the time of the amalgamation, the name of the organization was changed to the United Brotherhood of Maintenance of Way Employes and Railway Shop Laborers.

As was true of other railroad unions, the BMWE grew tremendously as a result of the nationalization of railroads during World War I. By 1920 it claimed a membership of 200,000. But its rapid growth inevitably brought it into jurisdictional conflicts with other unions. Resulting from these disputes, it was suspended from the AFL from January 1, 1920, until June 12, 1922. In an effort to resolve these annoying jurisdictional problems, the brotherhood gradually restricted its organizing field, and, reflecting this policy, in 1925 it shortened its name to the Brotherhood of Maintenance of Way Employes.

The 1920s and depression years of the 1930s were difficult for the BMWE. Encountering government and employer hostility, challenged by the organization of rival or company unions, and plagued by bitter jurisdictional disputes, it lost many of the gains it had registered during World War I. Moreover, with the enactment of the Railway Labor Act of 1926, political lobbying became almost as important as collective bargaining in the BMWE's efforts to improve the economic condition of its members. The Railroad Retirement Act of 1935, the Fair Labor Standards Act of 1938, and the Railroad Unemployment Insurance Act of 1939 significantly added to the security of railroad workers.

By the mid-1930s the BMWE had begun to recover from the depression, and it prospered organizationally during World War II. In the following years, the union won substantial wage increases, a forty-hour week, and, as a result of an amendment to the Railway Labor Act, union-shop agreements with various railroads. By the mid-1950s the BMWE reached its membership peak of about 250,000. Thereafter, membership began a steady decline as automation and the reorganization and rationalization of the railroad network reduced employment within the BMWE jurisdiction. On February 7, 1965, the BMWE signed an employment stabilization agreement providing greater job security for its members and also gained employment stabilization provisions through railroad merger agreements and the Regional Rail Reorganization Act of 1973. In an attempt to bolster its slipping bargaining position and to coordinate the activities of related unions in legislative and legal matters, the BMWE in 1969 joined the United Transportation Union,* the Brotherhood of Railway and Airline Clerks,* the Hotel and Restaurant Employees Union,* and the Seafarers International Union of North America* to create the Congress of Railway Unions.

The BMWE, which maintains its national headquarters in Detroit, holds quadrennial conventions. The BMWE grand lodge consists of a president, seven vice-presidents (two of whom must be citizens of Canada), a secretary-treasurer, and six members of the executive board (one of whom must be a Canadian citizen). In 1973 the BMWE reported a membership of 142,289 located in 1,080 local unions.

For further information, see the *Brotherhood of Maintenance of Way Journal* published monthly under various titles since 1892. See also D. W. Hertel, *History of the Brotherhood of Maintenance of Way Employes: Its Birth and Growth, 1877-1955* (1955).

MARBLE, SLATE AND STONE POLISHERS, RUBBERS AND SAWYERS, TILE AND MARBLE SETTERS' HELPERS AND MARBLE MOSAIC AND TERRAZZO WORKERS' HELPERS; INTERNATIONAL ASSOCIATION OF (IAMSSP). Several local unions composed of marble workers met in Detroit in 1901 and organized the International Union of Marble Workers (IUMW). On January 11, 1902, the American Federation of Labor* (AFL) issued a national charter to the new union. From its founding, the IUMW emphasized immediate economic objectives. Union leaders were especially interested in ending the growing practice of piecework contracting and the associated introduction of semiskilled workers into the craft. As a consequence, IUMW members were discouraged from accepting piecework, and a four-year apprenticeship became a requirement for union membership. Besides controlling entry into the craft, the IUMW also advocated shorter hours, increased wages, and improved working conditions.

In 1916 when the Bricklayers, Masons and Plasterers' International Union of America* (BMPIUA) affiliated with the AFL, it was given jurisdiction over marble setters. The IUMW was then ordered to transfer all the marble setters it had organized to the BMPIUA. Resulting from its altered jurisdiction, the IUMW was retitled the International Association of Marble, Stone and Slate Polishers, Rubbers and Sawyers on February 2, 1917. Despite the vehement objections of the International Hod Carriers, Building and Common Laborers' Union (later the Laborers' International Union of North America*), the association's trade jurisdiction was readjusted in 1921, when the scope of the organization was expanded to include tile-setters' helpers. This resulted in another name change as the union became the International Association of Marble, Slate and Stone Polishers, Rubbers and Sawyers, Tile and Marble Setters Helpers on July 21, 1921. A decade later the association was given jurisdiction over terrazzo-workers' helpers, precipitating another change in title, and on May 25, 1931, the union became the International Association of Marble Slate and Stone Polishers, Rubbers and Sawyers, Tile and Marble Setters Helpers and Terrazzo Helpers. The listed title was adopted after the AFL-CIO* merger.

The IUMW grew steadily from its chartering until 1914, reaching a membership in excess of 4,000, but it lost heavily in a disastrous jurisdictional war with the BMPIUA; this plus the AFL decision giving the BMPIUA jurisdiction over marble setters decimated the smaller union. By 1916 it paid per-capita taxes to the AFL on only 600 members, but after that date its fortunes improved. Between 1916 and 1930 membership grew from 600 to nearly 7,000, with much of this growth coming during the 1920s when most trade unions suffered substantial membership losses. Although the IUMW did not decline to the extent of most building trades' unions during the Great Depression, the losses it did suffer proved of much greater duration. It was not until the late 1950s that the IAMSSP again attained the enrollment it had in 1932.

The IAMSSP, which maintains its national headquarters in Washington, D.C., holds biennial conventions. Principal officers include a president, ten vice-presidents, and a secretary-treasurer. The general executive council is composed of the above officials. In 1973 the IAMSSP reported a membership of 9,000 located in 120 local unions.

For further information, see *The Marble Worker* published by the IUMW during the period 1907-1915. Since that date, the IAMSSP has not had an official organ. Little published information exists concerning the IAMSSP. A discussion of the IUMW conflict with the BMPIUA can be found in Harry C. Bates, *Bricklayers' Century of Craftsmanship* (1955). Basic information can also be found in *Bulletin No. 618*, Bureau of Labor Statistics, U.S. Department of Labor (1936), and Florence Peterson, *Handbook of Labor Unions* (1944).

MARINE ENGINEERS' BENEFICIAL ASSOCIATION; NATIONAL (MEBA). The early nineteenth century witnessed a tremendous growth in steamboat traffic on the Great Lakes and along the Mississippi River and its tributaries. The poorly constructed steamboats were driven by cheaply built engines employing extremely high boiler pressures to generate greater speeds. The result was frequent explosions, fires, and numerous casualties, especially among those working in close proximity to the engines and boilers. Protests from marine engineers led to a federal steamboat act in 1838, but the legislation provided little relief from hazardous working conditions. Consequently engineers organized associations in cities along the Mississippi transportation network to push for stronger legislation.

This agitation and several spectacular steamboat explosions prompted the U.S. Congress to enact legislation in 1852 requiring the licensing of marine engineers and pilots and providing for the inspection of steamboat machinery. These provisions were extended to ferryboats, tugboats, towboats, and freighters the following decade. During these years engineer associations also developed on the Great Lakes, and these groups played a leading role in the early development of a national organization.

The advantages of a closer relationship between the various city associations became increasingly apparent, and in 1874 the Buffalo Association opened correspondence with other marine engineer societies in an effort to create a national association. Representatives of three associations on the Great Lakes as well as an organization from a river and an ocean port met in Cleveland in February 1875 and organized the National Marine Engineers' Association. The current title was adopted in 1883.

MEBA's leaders devoted much of their efforts during the early years of the association to restricting the use of aliens as marine engineers. Such legislation sponsored by the MEBA was enacted by the U.S. Congress in May 1896. During the agitation, the MEBA gradually transformed itself from a professional and beneficial society into a trade union, and in 1891 it called its first strike to prevent a wage reduction on the Great Lakes.

As was true of most unions, the MEBA grew rapidly during the 1897-1904 period. It reached its early peak in 1908 when it had a membership of nearly 11,000 enrolled in more than 100 local associations. The steady progress of the union was halted and reversed at that time by a successful open-shop offensive launched by the Lakes Carriers' Association. Employers succeeded in eliminating virtually all trade unions in the maritime industry on the Great Lakes, an area that had been the foundation of MEBA's strength since 1874. For many years thereafter the MEBA was confined to activities on the East, West and Gulf coasts.

The MEBA debated affiliation with the American Federation of Labor* (AFL) for many years, but the jurisdictional claims of several AFL craft unions delayed affiliation until 1916. In hopes of protecting its jurisdiction during the critical World War I period, the MEBA affiliated with the AFL after the organization of the rival Ocean Association of Marine Engineers in New York City. Repeated raids by other AFL unions, however, eventually drove the MEBA out of the AFL in 1923. Thereafter it remained independent until affiliating with the Congress of Industrial Organizations* in 1937.

MEBA membership boomed during World War I, increasing from 10,000 in 1916 to more than double that figure by the end of the war. But as it was for most other maritime unions, the postwar period was a difficult one. Drastic reductions in the American merchant fleet created unemployment and great pressures to lower wage rates. These conditions led to the highly publicized maritime strike of May 1, 1922. The strike was broken, in part, when the leadership of the MEBA, against the wishes of the membership, signed an agreement in June. The return to work of the critically important skilled engineers greatly facilitated the employers' efforts to break the strike of less skilled workers, especially during this period of great unemployment.

The years between the two world wars were ones of decline for the MEBA. The 1920 membership of 22,000 declined to 11,000 by 1923 and to less than 5,000 by 1934. World War II temporarily reversed the trend, but the general decline of the American merchant marine continued, until by the early 1970s less than 10 percent of American trade was carried in American hulls. In the midst of these trying times, the MEBA finally managed to consolidate control over its trade jurisdiction. After years of open-shop operation, the Great Lakes' shippers were again organized. The MEBA also succeeded in raising wages, lowering working hours, and establishing the union hiring hall.

The MEBA, which holds biennial conventions, maintains its national headquarters in New York City. Principal officers include a president and secretary-treasurer. The executive committee is composed of the president and representatives of five geographical districts. In 1973 the MEBA reported a membership of 9,500 located in two local unions.

For further information, see the *American Marine Engineer* published monthly. See also the *AFL-CIO American Federationist* (May 1975). For a broader account of maritime affairs, consult Joseph P. Goldberg, *The Maritime Story: A Study in Labor-Management Relations* (1958), and three books by Charles P. Larrowe: *Shape-Up and Hiring Hall: A Comparison of Hiring Methods and Labor Relations on the New York and Seattle Waterfronts* (1955), *Maritime Relations on the Great Lakes* (1959), and *Harry Bridges: The Rise and Fall of Radical Labor in the U.S.* (1972).

MARINE AND SHIPBUILDING WORKERS OF AMERICA; INDUSTRIAL UNION OF (IUMSWA). The Great Depression, which struck the nation in the late months of 1929, caused a severe production curtailment in the American shipbuilding industry, which led to reduced employment and lower wages. When, following several earlier reductions, the New York Shipbuilding Corporation announced a further 15 percent wage reduction in its Camden, New Jersey, shipyard in late 1932, plant employees began organizing, and by

September 1933 an effective independent local replaced the company union, which had previously purported to speak for shipyard workers. Organization quickly spread from the Camden shipyards to nearby Chester, Pennsylvania, and Wilmington, Delaware.

The Camden local struck in March 1934, winning union recognition, a 15 percent increase in wages, and improved working conditions. The successful strike greatly stimulated organizing efforts in the industry, and two paid organizers carried the union message to shipyard employees along the East Coast. Six of these locals met in Quincy, Massachusetts, in September 1934 and organized the Industrial Union of Marine and Shipbuilding Workers of America. Within two years the new, independent union had a membership of 20,000, but realizing only a small percentage of industry workers were organized, union leaders planned a major organizing offensive. Almost simultaneously, the IUMSWA affiliated with the newly organized Congress of Industrial Organizations* (CIO), thereby relinquishing its independent status. Chartering the IUMSWA further exacerbated the tense relationship between the CIO unions and leaders of the American Federation of Labor* (AFL).

The organizing campaign and CIO affiliation quickly paid substantial dividends in the form of a steadily growing membership. These gains, however, did not come without conflict and discord. The 1936-1937 period was rife with industrial strife involving the IUMSWA. Most serious of these conflicts was a strike in New York City concerning union recognition. The strike, which involved all of the IUMSWA's New York City locals, failed due to poor timing and improper planning by strike leaders. Hoping to reverse these losses, IUMSWA leaders pushed a constitutional amendment through the 1937 national convention requiring locals to secure approval from the international office before calling a strike. The IUMSWA also had major jurisdictional problems, not only with AFL craft unions such as the International Brotherhood of Boiler Makers, Iron Ship Builders and Helpers of America,* but also with such CIO unions as the United Federal Workers of America,* which claimed jurisdiction over workers in government naval yards.

After gaining tighter control of union affairs, the IUMSWA leadership initiated a major campaign in 1938 to organize employees of the previously open-shop Bethlehem Shipbuilding Company. Through a combination of National Labor Relations Board representation elections and CIO organizing assistance, the campaign succeeded, and by the end of the decade, the IUMSWA claimed over 100,000 members.

Beginning with the preparedness campaign and followed by the mobilization effort during World War II, a great expansion of shipbuilding activity occurred. Taking advantage of the organizing opportunities created by this increased activity, along with the federal government's favorable policy toward union organization, the IUMSWA grew at a phenomenal pace. By the end of the war, the union had enrolled nearly 250,000 workers in over forty local unions. Moreover, during this period, the IUMSWA became a truly national organization with locals on the Great Lakes and the Gulf and Pacific coasts, as well as the older locals on the East Coast.

The great World War II gains proved largely ephemeral, however, as demobilization after the war and the general decline of the merchant marine ended and reversed the shipbuilding boom. As the shipyards cut back on production, the labor force in the industry also began to shrink. In addition to the economic problems in the industry after the war, the IUMSWA still had to compete with powerful unions in the AFL metal trades department also claiming jurisdiction over the shipbuilding labor force. Resulting from these circumstances, IUMSWA membership dropped sharply in the years immediately following World War II. Thereafter, the large losses ended although a slow decline continued.

The IUMSWA, which maintains its national headquarters in Washington, D.C., holds biennial conventions. Principal officers include a president, vice-president, and secretary-treasurer. The general executive board is composed of the above officers and ten additional members elected by the delegates to national conventions. In 1973 the IUMSWA reported a membership of 21,000 located in thirty-five local unions.

For further information, see *The Shipbuilder* issued bimonthly. See also Lloyd G. Reynolds and Charles C. Killingsworth, *Trade Union Publications* (1944), and *Bulletin No. 618*, Bureau of Labor Statistics, U.S. Department of Labor (1936).

MARITIME UNION OF AMERICA; NATIONAL (NMU). During the 1930s, East Coast seamen were becoming increasingly restive with the conditions of their employment. For years they had worked for less and under less favorable circumstances than their better-organized comrades on the West Coast. Consequently, in December 1935, when leaders of the International Seamen's Union of America* (ISU) signed an agreement with the American Steamship Association extending contracts that continued the East Coast-West Coast discrepancy, it sparked a rank-and-file revolt that eventually destroyed the ISU. Discontented sailors formed a rank-and-file defense committee within the ISU, established their own organ, *The ISU Pilot*, and initiated a series of job action "quickie" strikes against individual ships.

On January 4, 1936, the crew of the SS *Pennsylvania* left their ship in San Francisco and demanded wages equal to those received by West Coast seamen. The protest failed when ISU officials branded their action an outlaw strike and helped recruit replacements. A series of similar protests followed, most of which also failed. Then on March 1, 1936, the crew of the SS *California*, which had docked at San Pedro, California, on its return voyage to New York, employed a new tactic. Under the leadership of Joseph Curran the crew did not leave the ship but remained on board and refused to work. Company representatives immediately labeled their action a mutiny, but the strikers refused to be intimidated and continued their sitdown action. The stalemate was finally broken by Secretary of Labor Frances Perkins, who promised to encourage company officials to negotiate with a committee from the ship's crew upon its return to New York. She also pledged to use the influence of her office to prevent any member of the crew from being "intimidated, coerced or persecuted" when returning to New York. Nevertheless, when the ship returned, Curran and sixty-four other strikers were immediately fired and blacklisted; only Secretary Perkins's active intervention prevented a trial for mutiny.

As a result of the actions taken against the *SS California* crew, a rank-and-file committee headed by Curran led a wildcat strike in New York harbor that detained over twenty ships. The strike was once again broken with the active support of ISU officials. Internal friction in the ISU smoldered through the summer and early fall of 1936, and then in November it once again ignited into open warfare. Angered over provisions of a new contract, Pacific Coast seamen voted to begin a strike on October 29. Rank-and-file leaders in the ISU demanded a simultaneous strike of Atlantic and Gulf coast seamen. The ISU leadership met in New York on October 31, and after refusing to admit the rank-and-file defense committee headed by Curran, voted against the strike. The Curran group then held a rump meeting and issued a strike call for November 6. Their demands included a union hiring hall and complete parity with Pacific Coast seamen. Although the eighty-six day strike resulted in considerable disruption in East Coast shipping, it was broken by a combination of employer resistance, ISU hostility, and the refusal of the International Longshoremen's Association* to honor the rebel's picket lines.

The ISU won yet another battle but decisively lost the war. The ISU's success in crushing the rank-and-file strike only further destroyed any confidence that seamen still had in the old AFL union; conversely, Curran became a hero to many seamen. The final chapter in the internal conflicts of the ISU was written on May 3, 1937, when the National Maritime Union of America was founded at a mass rally of rank-and-file seamen in New York. The new union was an instant success. By its founding convention in July 1937, the NMU had already enrolled over 35,000 members, far surpassing ISU membership at any time since 1920. In a membership referendum shortly after its formation, the NMU voted to affiliate with the Congress of Industrial Organizations* (CIO).

The NMU soon petitioned the National Labor Relations Board (NLRB) for representational elections on most East Coast-based shipping lines. Alarmed by the rapid growth of the NMU, the AFL revoked the charter of the ISU and established its own directly affiliated federal labor union of East Coast seamen. Then, in 1938, the AFL chartered the Seafarers International Union of North America* (SIU) to contest the NMU in the maritime, seagoing jurisdiction. The SIU, which had its greatest strength in the West, had little success when challenging the NMU in the East. By July 1938 the NMU had won sixty-eight NLRB representation elections, the SIU only twelve.

The organizing successes of the NMU were won despite continual internal conflict and turmoil. A strong Communist faction was undoubtedly the most disruptive element in the NMU. The Communists had participated in the early ISU rank-and-file movements and had played an important role in the formation of the NMU. As a result of their long and effective participation in the struggle to organize seamen, Communist organizers had assumed numerous positions of power and influence in the union. The struggle between Communist and non-Communist leaders in the NMU was relatively subdued during World War II as both factions vigorously supported the American war effort. They parted company in the immediate postwar period when the Communists demanded that the wartime no-strike pledge continue to insure an uninterrupted supply line providing material aid to the war-ravaged Soviet Union. Non-Communist NMU leaders pointed to the deterioration of seamen's wages during the war and argued that the union could not afford to abandon the economic necessities of its members in the postwar period while seeking political or ideological objectives. The Communist issue was debated heatedly at the 1947, 1948, and 1949 conventions of the NMU; ultimately Joseph Curran and his followers routed the Communists and other radical splinter groups in several membership referendums. By 1949 the conservatives were strong enough to push through a constitutional amendment barring "Communist, Nazi, Fascist, or other subversive organizations" from membership in the NMU.

While grappling with internal problems, the NMU engaged in constant warfare with the SIU. Moreover, jurisdictional conflicts between the two unions did not subside with the AFL-CIO* merger but continued almost as bitterly as before. In membership terms, the SIU, which started far behind, had the greatest success; by 1971 the SIU reported a membership of 80,250 and the NMU 50,000.

The NMU, which holds triennial conventions, maintains its national headquarters in Washington, D.C. Full-time officers include a president, secretary-treasurer, three vice-presidents, and three national representatives. The above officials constitute the NMU's national council. In 1973 the NMU had a membership of 45,000 located in 333 local unions.

For further information, see the monthly *NMU Pilot* and *On a True Course: The Story of the National Maritime Union AFL-CIO* (1967), both published by the NMU. For a more scholarly treatment, see Joseph H. Ball, *The Government-Subsidized Union Monopoly* (1966), and Joseph P. Goldberg, *The Maritime Story: A Study in Labor-Management Relations* (1958). Walter Galenson's *The CIO Challenge to the AFL: A History of the American Labor Movement, 1935-1941* contains a good treatment of the conflict in the maritime industry between the AFL and CIO, and Max M. Kampelman, *The Communist Party vs. the C.I.O.: A Study in Power Politics* (1957) discusses the ideological conflict.

MASTERS, MATES AND PILOTS OF AMERICA; INTERNATIONAL ORGANIZATION OF (IOMMP). Steamboat pilots, primarily from the Port of New York, met in New York City in 1887 and organized the American Brotherhood of Steamboat Pilots. The new organization listed as its primary objective "the regulation of matters pertaining to our crafts, the elevation of their standing as such, and their character as men." Membership was restricted to "any white person of good moral character, in sound health, and a firm believer in God, the Creator of the Universe, holding a United States license and with 2 years' experience on water craft." Four years after its organization, the scope of the organization was broadened to include captains, and on April 3, 1891, the organization reincorporated under the laws of the state of New York as the American Association of Masters and Pilots of Steam Vessels.

Advances in technology led to further changes in the trade jurisdiction of the pilots' organization and a series of title changes. In 1905 the jurisdiction was expanded to include "officially licensed masters, mates and pilots of lake, bay, river, and ocean steamers and sailing vessels, and operators of motorboats." At the same time the union name became the American Association of Masters, Mates, and Pilots. Another title change in 1916 created the Masters, Mates, and Pilots of America, National Union (MMPANU). On February 26, 1916, The Masters, Mates and Pilots received a charter from the American Federation of Labor* (AFL).

The MMPANU reached an early membership peak of 6,000 in 1910, but after holding at that figure for several years, membership declined to 4,300 before turning upward again during World War I. After attaining a membership in excess of 9,000 by 1921, the MMPANU suffered a steady decline in strength through the 1920s and into the early years of the Great Depression. By 1935 the MMPANU paid per-capita taxes to the AFL on only 2,200 members. An improving economy, the National Labor Relations Act, and the mobilization effort during World War II signaled a substantial recovery for the MMPANU, which regained its previous losses and succeeded in organizing most of the workers within its trade jurisdiction.

On September 23, 1954, the AFL approved a title change and the union became the International Organization of Masters, Mates and Pilots, reflecting the inclusion of Canadian locals. The IOMMP merged with the International Longshoremen's Association* (ILA) on May 12, 1971.

The IOMMP, which maintained its national headquarters in New York City, held biennial conventions. Principal officers included a president, eight vice-presidents, and a secretary-treasurer. The executive council was composed of the above officers, the apprentice vice-president, and three trustees. Shortly before the merger with the ILA, the IOMMP reported a membership of 10,750 located in twenty-five local unions.

For further information, see *The Master, Mate and Pilot* issued monthly by the IOMMP. Scholarly accounts of the IOMMP's history were not found, but information can be found in *Bulletin No. 618*, Bureau of Labor Statistics, U.S.

Department of Labor (1936), and Florence Peterson, *Handbook of Labor Unions* (1944).

MEAT CUTTERS AND BUTCHER WORKMEN OF NORTH AMERICA; AMALGAMATED (AMCBWNA). The hesitant beginnings of union organization among packinghouse workers and retail butchers began shortly after the Civil War. Packinghouse workers responded militantly in May 1886 to a general strike call supporting the eight-hour-day campaign, and several Knights of Labor* local assemblies were organized as a result of the agitation, but these unions disappeared shortly after the strike. Meanwhile retail butchers organized a variety of trade unions and beneficial societies. The panic of 1893 and the following depression, which precipitated a number of strikes, destroyed many of these early organizational gains.

The impulse for a national organization of butcher workmen came primarily from Samuel Gompers, who, acting boldly on instructions from the American Federation of Labor* (AFL) executive council, issued a call for a national convention to meet in Cincinnati in December 1896. Four delegates responded to the convention call and immediately began drawing up a constitution for the new international union, formally chartered by the AFL on January 26, 1897, as the Amalgamated Meat Cutters and Butcher Workmen of North America. The new international union was given a jurisdiction eventually including "all wage earners in any way connected with wholesale and retail markets, slaughtering and packing establishments, sausage makers, poultry, egg and creamery workers, sheep shearers and livestock handlers and those handling fish in wholesale and retail establishments."

The principal officers of the new union were President George Byer of the Kansas City, Missouri, Sheep Butchers' Union and Secretary-Treasurer Homer Call of the Syracuse, New York, Meat Cutters' Union. Along with Michael Donnelly, elevated to the presidency in 1898, Call was the seminal figure in the early history of the union. With Call representing meat cutters and Donnelly packinghouse workers, the two trade union pioneers guided the AMCBWNA through its precarious early years during which it was transformed from a paper organization into a bona fide trade union. By 1904 considerable success had been achieved in the organization of butcher workers in such important packing centers as Chicago, Omaha, and Kansas City.

The new union's first major test came during the summer of 1904, when, under considerable rank-and-file pressure, the Amalgamated's leadership called a national strike. The union narrowly survived; the strike failed and union organization among packinghouse workers disintegrated. The strike also destroyed the effectiveness of Michael Donnelly who shortly thereafter disappeared from the labor scene.

During the 1904-1917 period the AMCBWNA, little more than a skeletal organization, clutched tenaciously to its national AFL charter. With the backing of an insurgent reform element in the Amalgamated, Dennis Lane, a Chicago cattle butcher, replaced Call as secretary-treasurer in 1917 and dominated the affairs of the union for the following quarter century.

Labor organization among butcher workmen revived markedly during World War I. By the end of 1918 the AMCBWNA reported a dues-paying membership of nearly 63,000 as opposed to about 6,000 two years earlier. When the principal meat packers in 1921 repudiated a wartime arbitration agreement, the AMCBWNA faced its second major crisis. A strike was called to protest wage cuts in December 1921. The strike ended two months later in an ignominious defeat that approached the disaster of 1904. National economic conditions, the united strength of meat packers, and its own internal divisions conspired to defeat the Amalgamated. While volatility characterized the attempts to organize packinghouse workers, retail butcher unionism, although limited, was relatively more stable, and this group formed the backbone of the AMCBWNA during the difficult years of the 1920s and the Great Depression.

The Amalgamated confronted the opportunities presented by New Deal labor policies from a position of relative strength. It had a small but secure organizational base in the retail trade, a base greatly expanded as a result of the successful organization of chain stores; it had survived the early years of the depression with relatively few losses; and the authority of national officers had been effectively established by Dennis Lane and Patrick Gorman, who became president in 1922.

Although the Amalgamated had considerable success in the retail field during the 1930s and early 1940s, its efforts to organize packinghouse workers were frustrated once again. As a result of the labor provisions of Section 7(a) of the National Industrial Recovery Act of 1933, large numbers of packinghouse workers and local unions enrolled with the AMCBWNA, but ineffective enforcement of National Recovery Administration codes and a series of indecisive strikes in 1934 effectively ended organizing activities.

The leadership of the Amalgamated sympathized with the objectives of the Committee for Industrial Organization* (CIO) during the mid-1930s and strongly supported the concept of industrial organization. Nevertheless, the Amalgamated remained loyal to the AFL, and, as a result, under the auspices of the Packinghouse Workers Organizing Committee (PWOC), the CIO launched its own organizing drive among packinghouse workers. The United Packinghouse Workers of America* (UPWA), organized from the PWOC, quickly became the dominant organization in the meat packing field. As in the earlier history of the Amalgamated, however, divisiveness and factionalism qualified the UPWA's power and effectiveness.

After World War II, the hostility between the rival unions gradually subsided, although it was briefly rekindled by collective bargaining differences and strikes in 1948 and 1951. A no-raiding clause was included among other items in an agreement signed by the two rival unions in June 1953, and, after protracted negotiations, the Amalgamated and UPWA finally merged in 1968.

Under the leadership of Patrick Gorman, who assumed the office of secretary-treasurer after the death of Dennis Lane in 1942, the AMCBWNA grew steadily in the post-World War II period. A membership of 125,000 in 1944 increased to 327,000 by 1960 and 473,000 by 1972. In part these membership gains resulted from the Amalgamated's expansion into new fields of organization, and in part they resulted from a series of mergers that brought into the Amalgamated fold the Sheep Shearers' International Union (1940), the United Leather Workers International Union* (1951), the Stockyard Workers' Association of America (1955), the International Fur and Leather Workers Union of the United States and Canada* (1955), and the National Agricultural Workers Union (1960).

The AMCBWNA, which maintains its national headquarters in Chicago, holds quadrennial conventions. Full-time officers include a president, nine vice-presidents, and a secretary-treasurer. These officers, all of whom are elected by convention delegates, constitute the Amalgamated's executive board. In 1973 the AMCBWNA reported a membership of 528,631 located in 508 local unions.

For further information, see the *Butcher Workman*, a monthly journal published by the AMCBWNA since 1915. See also David Brody, *The Butcher Workmen: A Study of Unionization* (1964), a valuable analysis of the Amalgamated's history to 1960. Walter Galenson discusses the rival unionism in the meat packing industry in *The CIO Challenge to the AFL: A History of the American Labor Movement, 1935-1941* (1960).

MECHANICS EDUCATIONAL SOCIETY OF AMERICA (MESA). Relatively high wages, seasonal work, transient labor, and employer hostility combined to retard the organization of labor unions in the automobile industry for many years. A further handicap to unionization emanated from certain skilled craft workers within the labor force itself. One such group in the automobile industry was tool and die makers. These well-paid, highly skilled aristocrats of the automobile work force had little in common with the large number of production workers in the industry.

The tool and die makers' enviable position in the work force changed drastically as the Great Depression spread. Unemployment grew, and manufacturers adopted the practice of contracting their tool and die work to the lowest bidder. Soon wages fell to unprecedented levels.

Recognizing their altered economic position, a group of Detroit tool and die makers formed the Mechanics Educational Society of America in February 1933, an organization that rejected militant trade unionism and stressed self-help and educational activities. But the MESA did not long remain a professional and educational association. Economic problems were too pressing, and after the enactment of the National Industrial Recovery Act, its leaders converted the organization into a trade union to take advantage of the collective bargaining provisions of the recovery measure.

Thereafter, organization spread rapidly from Detroit to other automobile production centers in Michigan and the Great Lakes region. Automobile manufacturers and contract jobbers, however, refused to bargain with MESA leaders, and a strike that began in Flint, Michigan, quickly spread to Pontiac and Detroit. Although the six-week strike failed to produce major economic concessions, contract work ended, and the MESA was recognized as the bargaining agent for tool and die makers, thus breaching the automobile industry's trade union barrier.

After the strike, conventions were held in January and May 1934 to adopt a constitution and establish an organizational structure. As a result of these meetings, the MESA emerged as an industrial organization with two classes of membership: skilled workers, such as tool, die, jig, and fixture makers, and semiskilled and unskilled production workers. The new constitution also encouraged rank-and-file participation in union affairs and created a more democratic governing system.

Under the auspices of the MESA, tool and die makers struck again in 1934 in an endeavor to raise wages, but there was less unanimity than in 1933, and few positive gains resulted. While MESA leaders could claim some positive achievements from this strike, even the most optimistic union official could find little consolation in the disastrous strikes at Detroit-Michigan Stove Works and the Burroughs Adding Machine Company. Moreover, the unsuccessful strikes intensified existing internal rivalries, especially between Communist and non-Communist factions, further weakening the union.

The MESA's declining fortunes received another setback in a strike against the Motor Products Corporation. The MESA's defeat in this strike came during a major organizing campaign in the automobile industry launched by the United Automobile Workers Union* (UAW) under the leadership of Homer Martin. The MESA's failures and the spectacular UAW activities led several MESA production locals to join the UAW. The only consolation MESA leaders could find in these events came from the knowledge that the deserting locals contained most of the Communists who had antagonized them since the union's founding.

The long series of MESA defeats finally ended in early 1937 with a successful sit-in strike at the Kelvinator Corporation's principal Detroit plant. When the corporation conceded, the MESA became the bargaining agent for 2,500 Kelvinator employees, thus assuring its continued existence in Detroit. After 1937 the union grew steadily but unspectacularly, increasing its membership annually by 2 to 3 percent. By 1955 the MESA had over 50,000 members, but thereafter declining employment in its trade jurisdiction precipitated a gradual decrease in membership. In 1954 the MESA ended its long career as an independent union and affiliated with the Congress of Industrial Organizations* (CIO). A year later it became an affiliate of the newly merged AFL-CIO.

The MESA, which maintains its national headquarters in Detroit, does not hold national conventions. Regularly scheduled meetings of the national administrative committee, composed of local delegates, are held in lieu of a national convention. The principal MESA officers are a president and a secretary-treasurer, the latter the only full-time official. In 1973 the MESA reported a membership of 26,000 located in approximately 100 local unions.

For further information, see the *MESA Educator* published monthly. See also Harry Dahlheimer, *A History of the Mechanics Educational Society of America in Detroit from its Inception in 1933 through 1937* (1951), and Florence Peterson, *Handbook of Labor Unions* (1944).

METAL ENGRAVERS AND MARKING DEVICE WORKERS UNION; INTERNATIONAL (IME&MDWU). During the early years of the twentieth century, craftsmen skilled in the engraving of metal stamps, dies, hubs, rolls, and similar equipment organized Gravers and Chisel Clubs in several cities throughout the nation. These semisecret clubs were apparently fraternal societies with few economic objectives. Representatives of several of these clubs, however, met in Buffalo, New York, on September 7, 1920, and organized the International Metal Engravers' Union (IMEU).

Unlike the older clubs, the new organization followed strict trade union principles. This is clearly reflected in the organization's statement of purpose:

> Believing it to be the natural rights of those who toil to enjoy to the fullest extent wealth created by their labor and realizing that, under the challenging industrial conditions of our time, it is impossible for us to obtain the full award of our labor except by united action, we pledge ourselves to labor unitedly in behalf of the principles herein set forth.

In an effort to control entry into the trade, the IMEU also adopted a strict apprenticeship system, although it opened union membership to any craftsman "who can command the prevailing rate of wages at any one or more of the various branches of the industry."

The IMEU received a charter from the American Federation of Labor* (AFL) on August 9, 1921, and organized in an extremely limited trade jurisdiction. Moreover, most workers in the trade worked in small shops scattered across the nation and were very difficult to organize in the traditional local union structure. As a result many IMEU members were directly affiliated with the international union. Due to these circumstances, the IMEU never acquired a large membership. During the decade of the 1920s, membership remained fairly constant at about 100, and it did not increase appreciably during the 1930s.

The IMEU was suspended by the AFL executive council on August 16, 1943, for failing to pay per-capita taxes. The small union refused to die, however, and on February 28, 1950, it was reinstated by the AFL under the title International Metal Engravers and Marking Device Workers Union. On September 1, 1956, the IME&MDWU merged with the International Association of Machinists and Aerospace Workers* (IAM).

The IME&MDWU, which maintained its national headquarters in New York City, held biennial conventions. Principal officers included a president, three vice-presidents, and a secretary-treasurer. The above officers also constituted the general executive board. At the time the IME&MDWU merged with the IAM, it paid per-capita taxes to the AFL-CIO* on 300 members.

For further information, see the *Official Bulletin Metal Engravers Union* published monthly by the international union. See also *Bulletins No. 420, 506, 618,* Bureau of Labor Statistics, U.S. Department of Labor (1926, 1929, 1936).

METAL POLISHERS, BUFFERS, PLATERS AND ALLIED WORKERS INTERNATIONAL UNION (MPBPAW). Union organizing activities among metal polishers and brass workers began during the second half of the nineteenth century, but until the emergence of the Knights of Labor* (KofL), little coordinated union activity occurred because unions in the trade remained scattered and retained a local orientation. The character of unionism began to change when the KofL chartered National Trades Assembly No. 252 in the fall of 1888. Assembly 252 constituted the first national union in the trade and was given jurisdiction over all branches of the brass industry.

Two years later eighty local unions sent representatives to Assembly 252's national convention in New Haven, Connecticut. The enthusiasm such remarkable growth should have engendered was qualified by an increasingly devisive struggle between rival factions either supporting continued affiliation with the KofL or urging association with the newly organized American Federation of Labor* (AFL).

Shortly after the New Haven convention, most of the locals west of Philadelphia left Assembly 252 and organized their own national union, the International Brotherhood of Brass Workers. The craft exclusivism exhibited by the AFL soon infected many members of the new union, and various crafts grew increasingly restive and anxious to form their own national union. This they did in the spring of 1892 when delegates representing metal polishers, buffers, and electroplaters met in Toledo, Ohio, and organized the Metal Polishers, Buffers, and Platers' International Union of North America, which on March 8, 1892, received an AFL charter. A few months later, on September

6, the AFL also chartered the older brass workers' union under the title United Brotherhood of Brass Workers.

The process of jurisdictional fragmentation and craft exclusivity, which by 1892 had resulted in the formation of three national unions in a relatively specialized trade, came to an end with the depression of the 1890s. The depression exposed the general weakness caused by such fine craft divisions, and a process of consolidation soon reversed the separatism of the previous few years. In 1895 KofL Assembly No. 252 merged with the United Brotherhood of Brass Workers to create the United Brotherhood of Brass and Composition Metal Workers, Polishers and Buffers. A year later, on July 2, this newly amalgamated union met with the Metal Polishers, Buffers and Platers' International Union in Syracuse, New York, and agreed to a merger creating the Metal Polishers, Buffers, Platers, and Brass Workers International Union of North America. On September 14, 1896, the AFL approved the merger and chartered the new organization.

Thus by the end of 1896 the trade union structure in the industry had come full circle, and the status of unionization was similar to what it had been in 1888 (except that the AFL had replaced the KofL as the national affiliate). Nevertheless, jurisdictional confusion and craft jealousies persisted. In 1911 brass workers were assigned to the International Molders' Union,* and the following year the title was again changed to appease silver workers as the union became the Metal Polishers, Buffers, Brass and Silver Workers Union of North America. Hoping to clarify their trade jurisdiction and avoid conflicts with other craft unions, in 1917 union officials finally confined membership to metal polishing, buffing, and electroplating workers. The AFL approved the new jurisdiction and issued a charter to the renamed Metal Polishers International Union (MPIU) on October 29, 1917. At about the same time, the MPIU absorbed members of the disbanding Pocket Knife Blade Grinders and Finishers National Union, which the AFL had chartered on August 1, 1905.

The Metal Polishers Union, by whatever name, revealed a typical pattern of union growth and decline. It reached an early membership peak of nearly 13,000 in 1904 and then dropped to 10,000 during the later open-shop offensive. Membership expanded once again during the years of World War I, reaching a new peak of almost 15,000 before again declining during the 1920s and the early years of the Great Depression. By 1932, the MPIU paid per-capita taxes to the AFL on only 2,300 members.

As it had done during the 1890s' depression, the MPIU sought to recoup its losses during the 1930s by expanding its jurisdiction. On February 24, 1936, the AFL extended a new charter, under the name Metal Polishers, Buffers, Platers and Helpers International Union, which conferred jurisdiction over "all metal and plastic polishing, buffing, plating, and finishing departments or shops."

The expanded trade jurisdiction, along with New Deal labor legislation and economic recovery during World War II, had a salutary effect on the Metal

Polishers International Union. By the end of World War II its membership surpassed the World War I mark and by mid-century climbed to nearly 20,000 before technological change reduced employment in the trade and initiated a slow decline. Although another title change occured in 1970—Metal Polishers, Buffers, Platers and Allied Workers International Union—the union's trade jurisdiction remained the same, and the membership decline continued.

The MPBPAW, which holds triennial conventions, maintains its national headquarters in Cincinnati. Principal officers include a president-secretary-treasurer and a vice-president. The international executive board consists of five rank-and-file members selected by the president and approved by national convention delegates. In 1973 the MPBPAU reported a membership of 10,000 located in sixty-seven local unions.

For further information, see the *Metal Polisher, Buffer and Plater* published quarterly. See also *Bulletin No. 618*, Bureau of Labor Statistics, U.S. Department of Labor (1936), and Florence Peterson, *Handbook of Labor Unions* (1944).

MINE, MILL AND SMELTER WORKERS; INTERNATIONAL UNION OF (IUMMSW). Aroused by the Coeur d'Alene silver miners' struggle of 1892, delegates representing hard-rock miners in the major districts of the Rocky Mountain West and South Dakota met in Butte, Montana, in May 1893 and formed the Western Federation of Miners (WFM). It had perhaps 2,000 members. Its program differed from trade unionism only in its opposition to written contracts and its belief in inclusive industrial unionism. Not only did the union claim jurisdiction over all of hard-rock mining, milling, and smeltering, but it practiced industrial solidarity. The WFM was also deeply engaged in party politics, sponsoring Populist candidates in the Rocky Mountain states. Until 1896, however, the depression and a succession of ineffective presidents hampered WFM growth.

The 1896 WFM convention elected a forceful president, Edward Boyce, and decided to affiliate with the American Federation of Labor* (AFL). Soon disgusted with what they believed to be conservative, ineffective trade unionism, WFM leaders withdrew from the AFL. Taking advantage of the lack of AFL unions in the West, the next year the WFM played a major part in founding the Western Labor Union, which aimed to affiliate all workers in one regional organization.

Meanwhile, the WFM became involved in one of the most violent series of strikes in American history, lasting from 1894 to 1904. While some WFM leaders saw the strike weapon as a syndicalist device, most WFM strikes were called to close the wage gap between the unskilled and skilled, to protest wage cuts or changes in work procedures, or to provoke showdowns with hostile mine owners. If the union did not deliberately create class warfare, it participated fully in it. Many mine workers and public officials, especially in

Colorado, viewed the WFM as simply a violent, ultraradical conspiracy against the mining interests. Deadly gun battles, bombings, neo-vigilante actions, and mass deportations of strikers, often followed by lockouts of union members, marked the struggles at Leadville, Coeur d'Alene, and Cripple Creek.

As a result of these strikes, the WFM adopted radical unionism. Impressed by the mining corporations' power and angered by the way state officials aligned themselves with the industry, WFM leaders concluded that the struggle could be won only by class-conscious unionism combined with socialism. In response to president Boyce's request, the 1902 convention urged WFM locals to adopt the Socialist Party of America's platform.

By 1904 the WFM had almost 30,000 members, but due to the failure of the American Labor Union* (successor to the Western Labor Union) and hostility toward AFL unions, the WFM found itself isolated. This plus their ideological commitment caused WFM leaders to take a prominent role in founding the Industrial Workers of the World* (IWW) in 1905. Internal IWW bickering, which threatened to disrupt the miners' union, and the Wobblies' failure to attract any large membership other than the hard-rock miners caused the WFM to withdraw from the IWW in 1908. WFM president Charles Moyer probably spoke for the majority when he disavowed all revolutionary intent. Reflecting more a disgust with radical dual unionism than with industrial solidarity, withdrawal nevertheless led to reaffiliation with the AFL in 1911.

WFM governing procedures were notably democratic. Rank-and-file opinions were thoroughly aired in the annual conventions, and after 1903 a membership referendum was required on executive board decisions. The 1912 convention, however, gave the executive board more power at the expense of the locals. At the same time the WFM gave up its opposition to time contracts, reflecting the union's growing moderation. Very early the WFM adopted and adhered to the practice of organizing without regard to race or ethnic origin. In 1916 the union changed its name to International Union of Mine, Mill and Smelter Workers.

From 1914 to 1918 the IUMMSW suffered from IWW raiding of its locals in Arizona and Montana and strike defeats in Upper Michigan and Arizona copper mining, by now the key nonferrous industry. Membership declined to less than 15,000. During the 1920s, the union almost died, having only a few small locals.

By 1934 the IUMMSW had revived itself in the West and gained a foothold on the Mesabi Range and a stronger position in the Alabama iron mines. After trying in vain to merge with the United Mine Workers of America* (UMWA), the IUMMSW became one of the original Congress of Industrial Organizations* (CIO) unions. During the 1940s it expanded its membership in copper and among Canadian nickel miners, and absorbed the Die Casting Workers. In 1948 the union had 114,000 members, its all-time peak.

During his presidency, Reid Robinson had increasingly relied on Communist organizers and advisers, and as the union divided into warring left- and right-wing factions, it became vulnerable to charges of Communist domination. In 1950 it was expelled from the CIO. Six years later fourteen IUMMSW leaders were indicted for falsifying the Taft-Hartley non-Communist affidavit; the last of these cases was not dismissed until 1967.

The United Automobile Workers* and the United Steelworkers of America* (USWA) repeatedly raided the IUMMSW during the 1950s but with scant success. Mine Mill members' loyalty plus the copper firms' preference for a small union incapable of industry-wide bargaining permitted the union to exist. But, as earlier in its history, Mine Mill was again isolated and vulnerable.

More sophisticated raiding by the USWA in the early 1960s made serious inroads, especially in Canada. Membership declined to less than 50,000. Both unions, however, realized the chaotic bargaining situation in nonferrous metals only helped perpetuate the employers' divide-and-rule strategy. In 1965 and 1966 favorable changes in the USWA leadership and bargaining structure made Mine Mill receptive to merger talks. Early in 1967, a special IUMMSW convention voted "organic merger" with the USWA, effective July 1, 1967. Meanwhile Mine Mill president Al Skinner co-chaired the first USWA Nonferrous Industry Conference, which prepared for unified bargaining on behalf of 80 percent of the workers in copper mining and processing. It was perhaps befitting Mine Mill's history that the ensuing copper strike became a long, bitter struggle.

The IUMMSW, which maintained its national headquarters in Denver, held annual conventions. Principal officers included a president, vice-president, and secretary-treasurer. The executive board consisted of the above officers in addition to one member from each geographical district. At the time of the merger with the USWA the IUMMSW had a membership of approximately 35,000.

For further information, see the *Miners' Magazine* and its successor *Mine-Mill Union*, published from 1942 to 1967. Vernon H. Jensen's *Heritage of Conflict: Labor Relations in the Nonferrous Metals Industry up to 1930* (1950) and *Nonferrous Metals Industry Unionism, 1932-1954* (1954) provide an institutional history. See also the chapter on the WFM in John H. M. Laslett, *Labor and the Left: A Study of Socialist and Radical Influences in the American Labor Movement, 1881-1924* (1970). George G. Suggs, Jr., *Colorado's War on Militant Unionism: James H. Peabody and the Western Federation of Miners* (1972), is an interesting study. Melvyn Dubofsky, *We Shall Be All: A History of the IWW* (1969), examines the relationship of the WFM to the IWW. Joseph H. Cash, *Working the Homestake* (1973), a valuable study including the only account of the Lead City Miners' Union.

Donald G. Sofchalk

MINE WORKERS OF AMERICA; PROGRESSIVE (PMA). District 12, Illinois, of the United Mine Workers of America* (UMWA), which traditionally won the highest wage scales in the industry, had long been one of the union's strongest districts. The strength and independence of District 12 proved a major obstacle to UMWA president John L. Lewis in his efforts to destroy district autonomy and centralize collective bargaining power in the national office. Lewis's campaign resulted in numerous conflicts with the leaders of District 12 and bitter intra-union struggles.

The growing depression in the coal industry during the 1920s complicated existing UMWA political divisions by introducing economic problems of major dimensions. As a result of growing unemployment, fuel substitutes for coal, mechanization, and increased production in nonunion mines, Lewis reversed his earlier "No Backward Step" policy of opposing wage reductions and negotiated a contract for the UMWA Central Competitive Field in 1928 that reduced the $7.50 daily wage rate to $6.10. After a vigorous campaign by district officials, miners in District 12 ratified the new contract by a narrow margin, but it did not bring the employment stability promised by union officers. Consequently, when the scale was further reduced to $5.00 in 1932, the miners revolted, rejecting the contract by a four to one margin. Finally relinquishing their cherished autonomy, District 12 officials invited Lewis to assume personal control over negotiations. The new contract Lewis agreed to did not in any significant way differ from the previous contract. Tally sheets from the membership referendum on the new contract, however, were mysteriously stolen, and Lewis assumed unprecedented emergency powers, putting the contract into effect despite overwhelming evidence of the miners' disapproval.

Resistance to Lewis's extraordinary action was immediate and widespread. Mass meetings were held throughout the district as miners attempted to close down the mines rather than accept the $5.00 scale. These efforts in the important Franklin County fields resulted in a violent confrontation between pickets and a large force of county law officers at Mulkeytown. Many miners believed that UMWA officials had actively conspired with law enforcement officials to break the picket line. Shortly after this confrontation, a group of rebel leaders met at Gillespie on September 1, 1932, and, bolting the UMWA, organized the Progressive Miners Union (PMU).

The new union invited coal operators to attend a wage conference at Edwardsville in October 1932. Operators had previously organized the Illinois Coal Operators Association and were almost as divided as the miners. Several companies sent representatives to the PMU conference, and they organized a new trade association, the Coal Producers Association of Illinois. The contracts negotiated between the two secessionist groups were almost identical to those previously rejected by dissident unionists. In reality PMU wage negotiations were irrevocably tied to the UMWA scale. Employers agreed to a check-off of PMU dues and assessments, which, to some extent, ensured the survival of the new union. Out of economic necessity and as a rebuke to the detested

Lewis, PMU miners accepted the new contract (which was not submitted to a membership referendum) without great resistance.

Convinced that a majority of miners in Illinois supported the new union, leaders of the PMU hoped to win collective bargaining rights for miners throughout the state. They sought to wean the coal operators allied with the Illinois Coal Operators Association from the UMWA through the use of strikes and mass picketing. Lewis effectively countered this strategy by meeting with the representatives of the association on December 21, 1932, and negotiating a two-year extension of the "emergency contract" for the period beginning April 1, 1933. The concession Lewis received for agreeing to the extension of the controversial contract was the union shop. Thus Lewis stymied the PMU, and it never effectively penetrated the UMWA's hold in the important coalfields of southern Illinois.

After the enactment of the National Industrial Recovery Act (NRA) in 1933 and the National Labor Relations Act (NLRA) in 1935, the conflict between the two unions was transferred to the offices of federal bureaucrats rather than the Illinois coalfields, but this did little to enhance the PMU's tenuous position. Agencies established under both the NRA and NLRA refused to disturb existing contracts and recognized the legitimacy of bargaining with employer associations. As a result the PMU was closed out of areas where Lewis and the UMWA had negotiated closed-shop agreements.

Following the break between the Congress of Industrial Organizations* (CIO) and the American Federation of Labor* (AFL), the AFL extended a charter to the PMU in the spring of 1938. The union was renamed the Progressive Mine Workers of America and given a national jurisdiction. With some AFL encouragement and assistance, organizing campaigns were launched in West Virginia, Kansas, Kentucky, and Pennsylvania. These campaigns were almost total failures. Again, Lewis checkmated the PMA through the device of negotiating NLRB-sanctioned closed-shop agreements.

Although the PMA had approximately doubled its original membership of 18,000 by the end of World War II, it still remained contained and isolated by the powerful UMWA. Moreover, when the UMWA reentered the AFL in 1946, the PMA was forced out of the federation and found itself also isolated from the national labor movement. Thereafter the PMA entered a long, slow period of decline.

The PMA, which maintained its headquarters in Springfield, Illinois, held biennial conventions. Full-time officers included a president, vice-president, and secretary-treasurer. The executive board was composed of the above officers plus nine additional members elected by PMA districts.

For further information, see Harriet D. Hudson, *The Progressive Mine Workers of America: A Study in Rival Unionism* (1952), and Irving Bernstein, *The Lean Years: A History of the American Worker, 1920-1933* (1960). For several years the PMA also published a weekly organ entitled the *Progressive Miner*.

MINE WORKERS OF AMERICA; UNITED (UMWA). The organization of coal miners began during the first half of the nineteenth century, but efforts to organize a national union were frustrated for several years before a permanent organization was finally established. Organizations such as the American Miners' Association,* begun during the Civil War, and the Workingmen's Benevolent Association* (1869) gave promise of a successful national union, but those hopes never materialized. Employer resistance, volatile economic fluctuations, internal factionalism, and the periodic violence in the coalfields dramatized by the famous Molly Maguires combined to retard the development of a permanent national union.

Events during the decade of the 1880s finally gave rise to the creation of a stable national union of coal miners in the United States. Miners in the Hocking Valley of Ohio, who had organized during the late 1870s, prompted the establishment of a statewide miners' union in 1882, the Ohio Miners' Amalgamated Association. A year later this organization inspired the formation of the Amalgamated Association of Miners of the United States. But the new association's greatest strength remained in the Hocking Valley, and, other than Ohio, only Pennsylvania miners took any significant part in the affairs of the association.

Because of the limited success of the Amalgamated Association and after a long, bitter strike in the Hocking Valley in 1884 and 1885, a new union, the National Federation of Miners and Mine Laborers (NFM&ML), was organized in Indianapolis on September 9, 1885. Thirty delegates from seven coal-producing states attended the organizing conference, giving it a much larger geographical scope than its predecessor had. The secretary of the new federation, Chris Evans, arranged a joint meeting with coal operators in an effort to establish standard prices and wages, thus avoiding costly strikes, lockouts, and other disruptions in the coalfields. Ultimately an agreement was reached in 1886, which lasted until 1888 when Illinois and Indiana operators withdrew.

Meanwhile, the Knights of Labor* (KofL) had established a national miners' union in St. Louis on May 20, 1886, the Mine and Mine Laborers National District Assembly No. 135. In an effort to end dual unionism in the coal industry, a joint conference of the NFM&ML and District No. 135 met at Columbus, Ohio, on December 5, 1888, and organized the National Progressive Union of Miners and Mine Laborers. But the new union was weak, and District Assembly 135 continued to function with considerable independence. Consequently, at a conference in Columbus on January 25, 1890, the National Progressive Union was reorganized into the United Mine Workers of America and received an industrial union charter from the American Federation of Labor* (AFL).

The UMWA made substantial progress until the panic of 1893 signaled the beginning of an industrial depression that nearly destroyed the frail new national union. Unable to reach an agreement with coal operators in the Central Competitive Field (western Pennsylvania, Ohio, Indiana, and Illinois), the location of the UMWA's most significant strength, a strike was called on April 24, 1894. Over 125,000 miners walked off their jobs, but the strike, ended by the negotiation of a weak, unenforceable contract in June 1894, virtually bankrupted the UMWA.

With the beginnings of economic recovery in 1896 and 1897, UMWA leaders moved boldly and aggressively to recover depression losses. Despite a minuscule membership of fewer than 10,000, union leaders demanded higher wages and the establishment of a uniform wage scale throughout the Central Competitive Field. Hoping to end the fierce competition for markets in the industry, many operators agreed, but others refused, and the UMWA struck. The miners' response to the strike call amazed union officials and coal operators alike. With operations in the Central Field virtually at a standstill, the operators conceded. Lengthy negotiations produced an "Interstate Agreement" establishing a standard wage rate and an eight-hour day for miners.

The victory had a dramatic impact on UMWA membership. Within a few years, the 10,000 members of 1897 grew to over a quarter of a million as the UMWA led a tremedous resurgence in the American labor movement. Under the leadership of John Mitchell and buoyed by its new strength, the UMWA turned to the organization of the anthracite coalfields of western Pennsylvania. Union organization in the hard-coal district had disappeared after the "Long Strike" of 1875 and the Molly Maguire trials later in the decade.

Besides bitterly anti-union employers, organizers in the anthracite fields faced the obstacle of attempting to unite more than twenty mutually suspicious nationality groups, many dominated by miners who spoke little or no English. Nevertheless, under the leadership of the patient and persistent Mitchell, the UMWA's campaign was so successful that the UMWA could call a strike in the district in 1900. For both economic and political reasons, anthracite operators made concessions to the union, and the strike ended, but the settlement pleased neither the operators nor the miners. When the UMWA made new demands in 1902, including higher wages, an eight-hour day, and union recognition, a strike resulted, lasting through the summer and into the fall, bringing with it higher coal prices and growing shortages in eastern cities. Through the personal intervention of President Theodore Roosevelt, the famous anthracite strike of 1902 was finally settled by an arbitration commission that gave the miners a 10 percent wage increase and adjusted other grievances. Although union recognition was not won, the UMWA legitimately claimed a stunning victory over a powerful group of anti-union employers.

The UMWA's successes in the Central Competitive Field and among the anthracite miners of western Pennsylvania were not extended to the large and growing coalfields of West Virginia or to miners in many other sections of the nation. Failures in these areas were not the result of a lack of effort, but neither the miners nor the union were a match for the well-armed coal and iron police of the mine owners or the armed force of the state. This combination of public and private police power resulted in such incidents as the murders of unarmed miners in West Virginia and the infamous Ludlow massacre in Colorado. The failure to organize the mine fields outside the Central Field was a major weakness that proved disastrous during the 1920s.

Developments during World War I significantly influenced the industry, the union, and ultimately the miners. Under the direction of the U.S. Fuel Administration, created during the summer of 1918, a settlement was reached (the Washington agreement) establishing a standard wage rate and including the adjustment of various miners' grievances. The agreement was to extend to April 1920, but confronted with rapid increases in the cost of living, miners demanded a new contract after the European armistice of 1919. Owners refused to enter new negotiations until the expiration of the Washington agreement, and a strike spread throughout the nation's coalfields, paralyzing the industry. When a sweeping federal court injunction failed to end the strike, President Woodrow Wilson ordered a temporary 14 percent wage increase preliminary to the announcement of a permanent settlement to be determined by the newly appointed Bituminous Coal Commission. The commission's award included a 27 percent wage increase, but it was the miners' last significant victory for several years.

During the war, UMWA membership had grown beyond the half-million figure, but war-created conditions plagued the union during the following decade. Wartime demands stimulated large increases in coal production, especially in the essentially unorganized southern Appalachian fields. After the war, overproduction, plus the increased use of oil, gas, and electricity, depressed the industry for more than a decade.

Faced with overproduction and falling prices during the postwar years, the coal operators sought to reduce costs, especially those of labor. UMWA president John L. Lewis, who had been elected in 1920, responded with a policy entitled "No Backward Step!" Although the UMWA base rate collapsed in the southern fields, Lewis insisted upon the retention of the $7.50 base rate in the better organized Central Competitive Field and in 1924 negotiated an agreement with the producers in the Central Field (the Jacksonville agreement) to maintain the base. Falling prices soon led the operators to demand modifications in the agreement to enable them to preserve the markets they were losing to lower-priced nonunion coal. Lewis refused to consider any changes in the agreement, and led by the Rockefeller-controlled Consolidated Coal Company and the Mellon-controlled Pittsburgh Coal Company, the operators repudiated the agreement and launched an open-shop drive designed to destroy the UMWA. The campaign began in western Pennsylvania, and within a few years the UMWA's strength had been reduced to the soft coalfields of southern Illinois and the anthracite district of western Pennsylvania.

Meanwhile, in an effort to destroy district autonomy and centralize power in the international office, Lewis further devastated his once-powerful union. Lewis's objectives were generally well within the tradition of most American trade unions: he sought to centralize union power in an effort to establish industry-wide bargaining and a standard wage scale, but his methods and timing were deplorable. Lewis ruthlessly bullied, discredited, and destroyed rivals or perceived rivals (many conscientious and capable persons) within the UMWA whom he felt threatened his absolute control of the union. Lewis survived an internal "Save the Union" campaign led by John Brophy of District 2 (Pennsylvania), who attempted to unseat Lewis in the union elections of 1926, as well as several dual unions such as the Communist-organized National Miners Union,* the Reorganized United Mine Workers Union, the West Virginia Mine Workers Union, and the Progressive Miners Union* (the only one to exhibit any longevity). Unfortunately Lewis was less successful in bringing coal operators to terms; during the first decade of his presidency, UMWA membership fell from over 500,000 to less than 100,000.

The enactment of the National Industrial Recovery Act in June 1933 signaled a significant reversal in the declining fortunes of Lewis and the UMWA. Seizing upon the provisions for union recognition and collective bargaining contained in Section 7(a) of the act, Lewis mounted a major campaign to re-unionize the coal industry, and before the end of the year, over 90 percent of the coalfields were organized.

Convinced of the wisdom of industrial organization and especially desirous of organizing the steel industry to ensure the survival of the recently organized unions in the "captive mines" of the large steel producers, Lewis led a movement within the AFL demanding the organization of mass production industries through industrial unionism. When the craft-oriented leadership of the AFL refused to act, Lewis created the Committee for Industrial Organization, which in 1938 was transformed into the Congress of Industrial Organizations* (CIO), a national federation rivaling the AFL. The UMWA provided much of the leadership and finances for the successful organizing drives that brought many workers in the mass production industries under union control.

The UMWA withdrew from the CIO shortly after Lewis fulfilled his pledge to resign the CIO presidency if Franklin D. Roosevelt won reelection in 1940, and except for a temporary period of AFL affiliation (1946-1947), it has remained independent. Ignoring the no-strike pledges of most American labor leaders during World War II, Lewis led the UMWA in two wartime strikes that brought significant concessions, including a captive mines agreement and portal-to-portal pay, but he also stirred public opinion against organized labor in general and himself in particular.

After the war UMWA strikes in 1946 and 1948 won a royalty on each ton of coal mined to finance the UMWA Welfare and Retirement Fund but at the cost of over $2 million in fines for civil and criminal contempt of court. Following the organization of the Bituminous Coal Operators Association, a National

Bituminous Coal Wage Agreement was reached in 1950 that finally established effective nationwide bargaining and virtually ended strikes in the industry until 1971, but it also provided for the mechanization and modernization of
coal mining operations, resulting in vastly decreased employment for miners.
As a result UMWA membership, 416,000 when the agreement became effective in 1950, dropped to 180,000 by the end of the decade and 130,000 by 1965.

In 1960 John L. Lewis resigned from the presidency of the UMWA, ending
one of the most dramatic chapters in American labor history. The short reign
of his aged and ill successor, Thomas Kennedy, was dominated by W. A.
(Tony) Boyle who officially assumed the presidential office in 1962. Exercising
the enormous power that Lewis had created in the union presidency with little
regard for the miners or for legal niceties, Boyle soon aroused vigorous opposition. A rank-and-file movement organized under the banner "Miners for
Democracy" challenged Boyle's reelection by supporting the candidacy of
Joseph A. Yablonski. Boyle won reelection by a two-to-one margin in a bitterly
contested election. Shortly thereafter Yablonski, his wife, and his daughter
were murdered. Five years later Boyle, among others, was convicted of conspir-
ing to murder Yablonski. Meanwhile the 1969 election was invalidated
through action taken by the U.S. Department of Labor, and in a new election
held in 1972, Boyle was defeated by Arnold Miller, a representative of Miners
for Democracy.

UMWA strikes in 1971 and 1973 illustrated growing rank-and-file militancy
and offered some hope that the union would begin to deal more forcefully with
the legitimate grievances of miners, especially regarding the critical matters of
pneumoconiosis (black lung disease) and mine safety.

The UMWA, which maintains its national headquarters in Washington,
D.C., holds quadrennial conventions. Principal officers include a president, a
vice-president, a secretary-treasurer, three tellers, and three auditors. The executive board consists of the above officers in addition to representatives from
each geographical district. In 1973 the UMWA reported a membership of
213,113 located in 1,329 local unions.

For further information, see the *United Mine Workers Journal*, issued semi-
monthly. Harold W. Aurand, *From the Molly Maguires to the United Mine
Workers: The Social Ecology of an Industrial Union, 1869-1897* (1971), con-
tains good background information. See also Chris Evans, *History of the
United Mine Workers of America* (1918); McAlister Coleman, *Men and Coal*
(1943); Robert J. Cornell, *The Anthracite Coal Strike of 1902* (1957); George S.
McGovern and Leonard F. Guttridge, *Great Coalfield War* (1972); and
Morton S. Baratz, *The Union and the Coal Industry* (1955). Biographies of
UMWA leaders include: Saul D. Alinsky, *John L. Lewis: An Unauthorized
Biography* (1949); James A. Wechsler, *Labor Baron: A Portrait of John L.
Lewis* (1944); Robert Cairns, *John L. Lewis: Leader of Labor* (1941); John
Brophy, *A Miner's Life* (1964); and Elsie Gluck, *John Mitchell, Miner* (1929).

Accounts of more recent UMWA history can be found in Joseph E. Finley, *The Corrupt Kingdom: The Rise and Fall of the United Mine Workers* (1972), and Brit Hume, *Death and the Mines* (1971). An account of the controversial UMWA District 50 can be found elsewhere in this volume.

MINERS' ASSOCIATION; AMERICAN (AMA). A financial panic followed shortly after Abraham Lincoln's election in 1860, and before the end of the year, the panic evolved into a general economic depression. Coal operators in St. Clair County, Illinois, responded to the economic situation by immediately announcing a 10 percent reduction in miners' compensation and a few weeks later ordered a second 10 percent reduction; at this point the miners revolted. Within a few days mines in the area were closed by angry miners who quickly established an organization, the Miners' Association, to direct the strike. Two weeks later the coal operators relented, and the wage reductions were rescinded.

Leaders of the association, many former participants in union activities in the British Isles, soon began extending their organizational activities into nearby counties. Their ultimate ambition is reflected by an 1863 resolution changing the name of the organization to the American Miners' Association. The AMA soon had the distinction of being the first national union in the bituminous coal industry.

The institutional structure of the AMA foreshadowed the organizational style later characterizing trade unions in the industry. The mine fields were generally organized on an industrial basis, and the association was divided into regional districts, each exercising a considerable degree of autonomy. Before the end of the Civil War, the AMA structure had evolved to the extent that various districts within state boundaries organized state branches.

By 1863 the AMA had extended its organizational activities into coalfields throughout Illinois as well as Missouri, Ohio, and western Pennsylvania. The decision to hold the 1864 annual convention in Cincinnati and the 1865 session in Cleveland reflected the extension of the AMA beyond its Illinois base. The AMA encountered increased resistance from employers, who were themselves rapidly organizing, but the union was aided by the growing wartime labor shortage and gained substantial increases in wages and resolved a variety of long-standing grievances. The AMA grew both in membership strength and prestige during the war, and its unprecedented success alarmed employers who were determined to resist any further advances by the association and, in fact, to destroy union organization wherever possible.

Accompanied by a growing labor surplus and lower coal prices, the end of the Civil War facilitated the employers' offensive against the AMA, and developing factional rivalries divided the union and prevented unified action at precisely the time the association faced its most serious challenges. Resulting from factional disputes, the *Weekly Miner*, established in 1863 and edited by the talented John Hinchcliffe, ceased publication in 1865. The weekly newspaper had provided a vital communications link between widely scattered district and local lodges, a link broken just when it was most needed.

The AMA reached the pinnacle of its power and influence in 1865 and disintegrated rapidly thereafter. By the end of 1866, it had largely ceased to exist, although a few AMA lodges continued to function through the remainder of the decade.

The AMA, which maintained its national headquarters in West Belleville, Illinois, held annual conventions. Principal officers included a president, vicepresident, financial secretary, corresponding secretary, and treasurer. The general board consisted of the above officers and a delegate elected from each lodge in the association. Although accurate membership figures are unavailable, at its peak the AMA had approximately 20,000 members.

For further information, see the *Weekly Miner* published between 1863 and 1865. The best scholarly treatment of the AMA is Edward A. Wieck, *The American Miners' Association: A Record of the Origin of Coal Miners' Unions in the United States* (1940). See also Chris Evans, *History of the United Mine Workers of America* (1918), and Andrew Roy, *A History of the Coal Miners of the United States* (1903).

MINERS' UNION; NATIONAL (NMU). Communist and other left-wing radicals had a long history of involvement in the trade union organizing activities of the nation's mining fields. During the 1920s, the activity and influence of left-wing radicals increased dramatically. Those years were filled with violent conflicts between miners and mine operators, as well as factional struggles within the major union in the industry, the United Mine Workers of America* (UMWA). Tenuous labor-management relations were further aggravated by the severe depression that struck the industry during the decade. Moreover, during these same years John L. Lewis conducted his often ruthless campaign to destroy local autonomy and centralize collective bargaining authority in the national office. The result was factional struggles, internal divisions, and secessionist movements that nearly destroyed the once-powerful UMWA by the end of the decade.

This was the state of trade unionism in the industry when the Red International of Labor Unions, meeting in Moscow in 1928, dropped its "boring from within" strategy and ordered its affiliates throughout the world to establish an independent, revolutionary union movement. Communist leaders in the mining fields, battered and beaten by Lewis in their attempts to capture the UMWA, responded to the new policy with alacrity. During the summer of 1928 Communist organizers toured the principal mining areas of the nation, promoting a break with the "reformist" UMWA and the organization of a revolutionary union. Resulting from their labors, a national convention was held in Pittsburgh during the week of September 9-16, 1928, and the National Miners' Union was formed. The new union affiliated with the Communist-organized Trade Union Unity League* (TUUL) after its organization in August 1929.

Although the constitution of the new union firmly established its emphasis on class struggle as the basis for trade unionism, its major immediate demands, including a minimum wage of thirty-five dollars a month, a six-hour day, and a five-day week, union election of checkweighman, and overtime pay, were rather traditional. As a result of organizing activities among metal miners, the union title was changed to Mine, Oil and Smelter Workers Industrial Union (although the older name was still used in the coal mining fields) at the second national convention of the NMU meeting in Pittsburgh in 1930.

Shortly after its organization, the NMU began an active organizing campaign in the coalfields of Pennsylvania, northern West Virginia, Ohio, and Illinois, and made a special but largely unsuccessful appeal to black miners. Although it had been involved previously in a number of local strikes, it was not until 1931 that the NMU dramatically made its presence felt. The NMU's involvement in strikes in Harlan County, Kentucky, and western Pennsylvania illustrate both the successes and failures of the NMU.

Admitting defeat, the UMWA withdrew from a strike in Harlan County in May 1931, and the NMU quickly filled the vacuum. Hoping to use the Harlan strike to dramatize the Communist cause and radicalize the masses, the Communists captured the local miners' union and sent a delegation to the national NMU convention meeting in Pittsburgh in July. If there were any remaining doubts, the Communists openly revealed their involvement in the struggle during an NMU state convention held on August 2. The entrance of the Communist union into the conflict gave mine operators in the area an opportunity to cover their union-busting activities with the cloak of patriotism. Under the guise of protecting the "American way of life," operators unleashed a reign of terror against the strikers that resulted in the destruction of the NMU in the area. Conversely the NMU effort in Harlan County received support from a group of sympathetic writers, including Theodore Dreiser, John Dos Passos, and Sherwood Anderson, who dramatized the struggle with the publication of *Harlan Miners Speak*. Disregarding the welfare of its loyal members, in one last desperate act the NMU called a general strike on January 1, 1932. Mine operators easily broke the strike, drove the NMU out of Kentucky, and blacklisted NMU miners.

The NMU conducted an equally spectacular but equally disastrous organizing effort in the coalfields of eastern Ohio and western Pennsylvania. The NMU's efforts in eastern Ohio lasted throughout the summer and resulted in the death, wounding, or incarceration of several miners, but the strikes in the aera were crushed, and the NMU disappeared. The NMU was stronger in western Pennsylvania where the UMWA had lost much of its influence. In

June 1931 the NMU called a strike in the area characterized by unusual violence even for the mine fields. The violence was further accelerated when the UMWA entered the conflict and negotiated agreements with several operators. Unable to resist the combined power of the mine owners, the state government, and the UMWA, the NMU collapsed, and for its efforts it was awarded a Comintern condemnation for the way in which it had conducted the strike. By the end of 1931, the NMU was shattered and virtually destroyed. Nevertheless, it remained until the Red International of Labor Unions changed its tactics in 1935 and ordered the dissolution of the TUUL and its affiliated unions.

The NMU, which maintained its headquarters in Pittsburgh, held annual conventions. Principal officers included a general secretary and the members of the general executive board. Although accurate membership figures are unavailable, the NMU appears to have been largely a paper organization at the time of its dissolution.

For further information, see Anna Rochester, *Labor and Coal* (1931), a very sympathetic account, and Irving Bernstein's *The Lean Years: A History of the American Workers, 1920-1933* (1960), which contains much valuable information. See also the Rand School of Social Science's *American Labor Year Book*, vols. 11 and 12 (1930, 1931).

MOLDERS AND ALLIED WORKERS UNION; INTERNATIONAL (IMU). Iron molding became an important American industry during the second quarter of the nineteenth century. Foundries producing such items as hollowware, stoves, and machinery sprang up in many American cities, but poor working conditions, long hours, and low wages created worker discontent. As a consequence, labor organization began very early in the industry. The first known molders' union existed in Philadelphia as early as 1833, and by 1836, there is evidence of similar unions in Boston, Pittsburgh, and Albany, Troy, and Schenectady, New York. Most of these unions disappeared during the depression following the panic of 1837. When organization among molders revived during the 1840s, great emphasis was placed on the establishment of cooperative foundries, but most of these ventures failed. Molders then experimented with the creation of fraternal and beneficial societies. Not until the business recessions of the mid-1850s did molders return in large numbers to militant trade union organization. Moreover, unlike the earlier unions those organized after 1855 proved to be stable and permanent.

The panic of 1857 and the economic hard times precipitated by the financial crisis created a general interest in the formation of a national union. In an effort to prevent wage reductions, molders struck in several cities. Most of these strikes were broken by the importation of laborers from neighboring towns, illustrating in a direct and dramatic way the necessity for closer cooperation between molder unions in various cities. Moreover, ominous threats of the organization of a national anti-union employers' association added a sense of urgency to the movement.

It was the Philadelphia local, the strongest molders' local in the nation, that initiated the action leading to the creation of a national union. At the suggestion of William H. Sylvis, a leader of the Philadelphia local and destined to become one of America's most remarkable labor leaders, the Philadelphia union opened a correspondence with molder unions in other cities. Sylvis, serving as secretary of a committee to study the feasibility of organizing a national union, issued a circular in December to all known molders' unions to ascertain their attitude on the subject. A favorable response led the committee to issue a call for a national convention in Philadelphia on July 5, 1859.

Thirty-two delegates representing twelve locals attended the convention; two other unions endorsed the proposal but did not send delegates. As a result of the deliberations, the National Union of Iron Molders was established, a weak organization having little authority over constituent locals. After adopting a provisional constitution, delegates voted to adjourn the convention until the following year when a formal vote would be taken. Forty-six delegates convened at Albany, and on January 11, 1860, the national union was launched officially.

The new national union, renamed the Iron Molders' Union of America in 1861, grew steadily until the outbreak of the Civil War, which nearly destroyed it. Large numbers of molders in cities throughout the North, as well as Sylvis and many of the union's leaders, enlisted in the Union army. Within a few months, molders' unions in many cities began to disintegrate. Alarmed by this development, Sylvis returned to Philadelphia during the summer of 1862 and launched a campaign to rebuild the union.

A national convention meeting in Pittsburgh in January 1863 made several far-reaching decisions. Sylvis was elected president, and, under his urging, the constitution was significantly revised to clearly establish the authority of the national union over constituent locals. Because of the affiliation of Canadian locals, the name of the union was changed by the substitution of "International" for "National."

After the convention adjourned, Sylvis launched a one-man national organizing campaign in an effort to revive older unions and charter new ones. Forced to rely upon his own meager resources and whatever contributions he received from the locals he visited, Sylvis often lived and traveled as a penniless transient in order to complete his mission. Nevertheless the campaign was a remarkable success; the union survived and grew steadily during the next several years.

The molders' union played a significant role in the emergence and development of the American labor movement in the second half of the nineteenth century. The IMU was a charter member of the National Labor Union* in 1866, and Sylvis served as its first president. Although many molders joined

the Knights of Labor* during the 1870s and 1880s, IMU leaders were less enthusiastic about the Knights and never affiliated with it. Conversely they
actively participated in the organization of the American Federation of Labor*
(AFL) in 1886, and the IMU was one of the charter members of the new
federation.

Numerous problems accompanied the progress the IMU made during the
nineteenth century. The premature death of William Sylvis in 1868 robbed the
union of its most dedicated and resourceful leader. Furthermore, the series of
panics, recessions, and depressions during the closing third of the century,
especially the depressions of the 1870s and 1880s, severely tested the viability
of the union.

During this period the union's most cherished economic objective was
industry-wide bargaining. The emergence of an employers' association in
1886, the Stove Founders National Defense Association, facilitated such bargaining even though hostility to unions had partially motivated its organization. By 1890 an agreement for settling disputes had been negotiated between
the union and the Defense Association. The IMU's relationship with two other
employer groups, the National Stove Manufacturers' Association and the
National Founders' Association, proved less cordial. Both associations
adopted essentially open-shop policies, precipitating extended periods of
industrial warfare.

The IMU continued to grow until the post-World War I period, when a renewed open-shop offensive halted and reversed the positive growth pattern of
the union. The collapse of the economy during the early 1930s further depressed both the industry and the union. IMU leaders responded to these troubled
times by radically changing the character of the union. After operating as a
craft union for seventy-five years, in 1934 the IMU extended membership to
non-journeymen, in effect becoming an industrial union. In 1961 jurisdictional lines were further defined:

> This International Union shall have jurisdiction over all workers en-
> gaged in the production, processing and assembling of cast, molded and
> related and/or substituted products and—in process or related to the
> production of castings or their substitutes.

These changes were accompanied by further alterations in the union title:
International Molders and Foundry Workers Union of North America (1934)
and International Molders and Allied Workers Union (1961).

Shortly after the enactment of the National Labor Relations Act in 1935, the
IMU's membership, reversing a decline lasting nearly fifteen years, began to
curve upward, continuing to rise until 1946. Although subject to sharp fluctuations depending upon the state of the national economy, IMU membership
stabilized at about 70,000 after World War II.

The IMU, which maintains its national headquarters in Cincinnati, holds quinquennial conventions. Elected officials include a president, nine vice-presidents, a secretary, a treasurer, two auditors, and an editor. The president and seven trustees constitute the international executive board. In 1973 the IMU reported a membership of 67,000 located in 257 local unions.

For further information, see the IMU's monthly *Journal*, first published in 1864. Frank T. Stockton, *The International Molders Union of North America* (1921), contains valuable information on the early history, governmental structure, and collective bargaining procedures of the IMU. Jonathan Grossman has written a solid biography of William Sylvis, *William Sylvis: Pioneer of American Labor* (1945), and J. C. Sylvis collected *The Life, Speeches, Labors, and Essays of William H. Sylvis* (1872).

MUSICAL ARTISTS; AMERICAN GUILD OF (AGMA). After discussing the idea with numerous individual performers, Lawrence Tibbett and Jascha Heifetz founded the American Guild of Musical Artists on March 11, 1936. Their actions arose from the deep-seated desire of solo musical artists to gain some control over arrangements for their financial compensation and the conditions under which they performed. At the time, musical artists suffered from excessive booking commissions and promotional fees, frequent delinquencies or failures to pay performance fees and expenses, inadequate accounting procedures, and requirements for exclusive contracts with booking agents. Tibbett became the president of the new union and Heifetz vice-president.

The guild remained an independent organization until August 30, 1937, when it affiliated with the Associated Actors and Artistes of America* (AAAA) chartered by the American Federation of Labor.* Under the provisions of its charter, the AGMA received "sole and exclusive jurisdiction in the field of concert, recital, oratorio and grand opera, including jurisdiction over all concert and solo operatic singers, instrumental soloists, dancers and other performers in the field of concert, recital, oratorio and grand opera." At the time of its affiliation with the AAAA, the AGMA merged with the Grand Opera Artists Association, and a year later it absorbed the Grand Opera Choral Alliance. Both groups previously had been chartered by the AAAA.

After receiving its charter from the AAAA, the guild conducted an extensive organizing campaign among artists under its jurisdiction. The AGMA soon had enrolled in membership such well-known artists as George Gershwin, Fred Waring, Efrem Zimbalist, Paul Whiteman, and Lily Pons.

Within a few months of its founding, the new union signed an exclusive bargaining agreement with the Southern California Symphony Association. The contract included provisions for minimum wages and the elimination of booking agent commissions. During the summer of 1938, the AGMA gained recognition as the exclusive collective bargaining agent for all artists engaged by the Metropolitan Opera Association, the San Carlo Opera Company, and the New York Hippodrome Opera Company. Later in the same year, the guild opened negotiations for a similar contract with the National Concert and Artists Corporation (NCAC). After lengthy bargaining sessions, contracts were signed in March 1939 regularizing manager-performer relationships between concert artists and the management companies affiliated with the NCAC.

The AGMA did not survive its early years without difficult jurisdictional disputes, but it resolved those conflicts without excessive bitterness. In 1939 the Actors' Equity Association* and Chorus Equity Association reached a jurisdictional agreement with the AGMA under which the latter received jurisdiction over opera performances in which the intent of the composer was "a dramatico-musico work along classical lines—following historical musical foundations." All three organizations agreed to submit future jurisdictional questions for settlement to the executive board of the AAAA. More serious was the conflict with the powerful American Federation of Musicians* (AFM). In August 1940 AFM president James C. Petrillo claimed jurisdiction over all instrumentalists affiliated with the guild. After eighteen months of difficult negotiations, an agreement was reached in which the AGMA recognized AFM jurisdiction over solo concert instrumentalists and accompanists, and the AFM recognized the AGMA as exclusive bargaining agent for solo concert artists. The two unions agreed to recognize the dual membership of certain solo instrumentalists.

After clarifying its jurisdictional boundaries and gaining recognition as exclusive bargaining agent for concert musical artists, the AGMA devoted much of its time and resources to negotiating collective bargaining agreements and providing a variety of benefits, including a group life insurance plan, welfare fund, and union dental and optical programs.

The AGMA, which maintains its national headquarters in New York City and has branch offices in Toronto, Boston, Los Angeles, Chicago, New Orleans, Philadelphia, San Francisco, Washington, Seattle, and Mesquite, Texas, held regular conventions until 1954. At that time a constitutional amendment eliminated regularly scheduled conventions and substituted a provision that conventions could be called by the board of governors upon written request by at least 10 percent of the active members of each district or 20 percent of all active members. The principal executive officers include a president, five vice-presidents, a treasurer, and a recording secretary. The primary governing agency of the AGMA is a board of governors comprised of a variable number of members chosen by constitutional formula. In 1973 the AGMA reported a membership of 3,500.

For further information, see *Agmazine*, a bimonthly published by the guild, and Abram Loft, "Musicians Guild and Union: A Consideration of the Evolution of Protective Organizations among Musicians" (Ph.D. dissertation, Columbia University, 1950).

MUSICIANS; AMERICAN FEDERATION OF (AFM). Musicians labored under unfavorable conditions throughout much of the nineteenth century. During an age in which most Americans worshipped practicability, their profession was considered frivolous, if not disreputable. To some extent the professional musician's lowly economic position reflected this unfavorable social status. Low wage scales and irregular employment characterized the life of the musician who often competed with unpaid amateurs. As a result, many musicians found it necessary to hold other part-time jobs to earn a living.

Local organizations of musicians began to appear during the third quarter of the nineteenth century, but they were primarily social and beneficial societies that did not attempt to alleviate the economic problems of their members. The first organization of musicians that could legitimately be classified a trade union was organized in New York City in 1863. In the following years musicians' unions appeared in many eastern and midwestern cities. In 1871 a Philadelphia local called a conference of other independent musicians' unions to discuss the feasibility of organizing a national union. The National Musical Association resulted, but it never gained the affiliation of most locals in the trade and failed to survive the decade of its birth.

The second effort to organize a national union of musicians was led by a Cincinnati local that called a meeting of musicians' unions into session in New York City in 1886. At the conference, unions from Cincinnati, New York, Philadelphia, Boston, Chicago, Milwaukee, and Detroit agreed to the formation of the National League of Musicians of the United States (NLM). The NLM grew rapidly, and within a decade claimed a membership of 9,000 located in seventy-nine affiliated locals. Despite its success, advocates and opponents of affiliation with the American Federation of Labor* (AFL) divided the NLM into irreconcilable factions. Beginning as early as 1887, the AFL annually invited the NLM to affiliate, but just as consistently the league spurned the invitation.

Annoyed by the league's actions, the AFL initiated a less conciliatory program. Musicians' unions were organized or granted charters as federal labor unions directly affiliated with the AFL. By the mid-1890s a substantial majority of the local unions affiliated with the NLM also had connections with the AFL. In 1895 the AFL gave the league one last chance to affiliate, and when in a tie vote it failed to do so, AFL president Samuel Gompers issued a call for a national convention of musicians' unions to meet in Indianapolis on October 19, 1896. Twenty-six unions representing 4,000 musicians responded to the call, and the American Federation of Musicians was organized. On November 6, 1896, it received an AFL charter. Although the AFL sought to avoid a jurisdictional war with the NLM, conflict was almost inevitable, and in the struggle that ensued, the AFM vanquished its rival. By 1904 the NLM liquidated its assets and dissolved.

Besides their efforts to organize musicians, leaders of the AFM devoted their efforts to gaining the affiliation of independent musicians' unions and to chartering rival unions when necessary. These efforts were rewarded by a continually growing membership. The 4,000 members of 1896 grew to 22,000 by 1904, 50,000 by 1912, and 70,000 by 1920. Meanwhile the union made some progress in resolving the difficult problem of defining the status of musicians who traveled from one area to another in search of employment. Perhaps most significantly, the AFM succeeded in establishing a closed shop for most of its members during the early years of the twentieth century.

The AFM's success during the first quarter of the twentieth century was predicated to a large extent upon its ability to solve three major problems. The first revolved around the international's effort to establish its authority over constituent locals. The major problem involved the activities of the large, prestigious, but recalcitrant New York Local 310. Ultimately AFM officials revoked the charter of Local 310 and chartered a new new local, 802, over which it assumed complete authority. The AFM's success in effectively resolving the New York situation served definitively to establish the hegemony of the national organization. A second problem concerned the influx of foreign musicians who often worked on a contract basis well below union wage rates. After considerable effort, legislation and the application of economic pressure brought relief to this area. The final problem involved the competition from bands organized by the United States armed services. AFM lobbying efforts achieved a number of reforms, and the problem was finally adjusted by presidential order in 1934.

The AFM grew steadily during the years following World War I, despite the employers' open-shop offensive and the harmful effects of Prohibition. By 1929 the union's membership peaked at 146,326, a figure not reached again until 1944. A number of circumstances contributed to the AFM's decline, which lasted until 1934 when membership had shrunk to 100,000. The depression resulted in reduced employment opportunities for musicians as it did for almost every other occupational group. Even more serious, in the long term, was the challenge produced by technological changes in the industry. The introduction of sound movies eliminated thousands of jobs musicians held in silent movie theaters. Recorded or "canned" music was an even greater threat. Relations with the film industry were largely resolved by a contract negotiated between the AFM and the film industry in 1944 and renegotiated periodically. The issue of musical records was a much more serious problem. After several attempts to resolve the issue, the AFM finally issued a directive under which, after August 1, 1942, union members were prohibited from making records, transcriptions, or any other type of mechanically reproduced music. After a twenty-seven month dispute, the AFM won a royalty on each record union musicians made. The royalty was placed in a trust fund to provide relief for unemployed musicians. The arrangement was revamped after a similar strike in 1948 with the creation of the Music Performance Trust Fund.

Throughout its history the AFM has been involved in relatively few jurisdictional disputes, and when they did occur, the union proved capable of defending itself. It withstood the initiatives of the Congress of Industrial Organizations* during the late 1930s and early 1940s and won a major jurisdictional battle with the American Guild of Musical Artists* in 1940-1941.

The AFM did not make its gains without arousing considerable opposition and, in some cases, the public ire. Much hostility was directed toward the colorful and controversial AFM President James C. Petrillo whose determined efforts to protect the employment opportunities of musicians often seemed arbitrary and dictatorial. This hostility was best reflected in the enactment of the Lea Act in 1946, which, although it did not greatly alter the activities of the AFM, was a precursor of the Taft-Hartley Act.

The AFM, which maintains its national headquarters in New York City, holds annual conventions. Principal officers include a president, a secretary-treasurer, a vice-president, and a five-member executive committee. All of the above officers constitute the international executive board. In 1973 the AFM reported a membership of 315,000 located in 650 local unions.

For further information, see the *International Musician,* a monthly journal published by the AFM. The best account of the history of the AFM is Robert D. Leiter's *The Musicians and Petrillo* (1953). Allen E. Koenig's *Broadcasting and Bargaining: Labor Relations in Radio and Television* (1970) also contains useful information.

NATIONAL LABOR UNION (NLU). Seventy-seven delegates representing thirteen states and the District of Columbia met in the Front Street Theater in Baltimore, Maryland, on August 20, 1866, and created the National Labor Union. John Hinchcliffe, a joint representative of several trade unions, was elected permanent chairman of the convention, and several committees were appointed to establish policy positions on a variety of issues.

Although national trade unions had been instrumental in the convening of the Baltimore Labor Congress that created the NLU, only two of the eighteen existing national unions sent delegates. The convention was dominated by delegates from local trade unions and city trades' assemblies. From the beginning, the NLU was a political, reformist organization. The character of the new national federation appears most clearly in "The Address of the National Labor Congress to the Workingmen of the United States," issued eleven months after the adjournment of the Baltimore Congress. The major labor objective identified in the address was an eight-hour law. Other issues of interest were land reform, anti-monopoly sentiment, prison labor reform, producer and consumer cooperatives, support of trade unionism, and the integration of black workers into existing labor union and reform societies. After the second NLU convention in Chicago in August 1867, the repeal of the Contract Labor Act of 1864 was added to the list of labor reforms.

Although an administrative structure was created, the NLU functioned only sporadically between annual congresses. Always more a forum for labor reformers than a congress of trade unions, in the words of Norman Ware the NLU "was a typical American politico-reform organization, led by labor leaders without organizations, politicians without parties, women without husbands, and cranks, visionaries, and agitators without jobs."

The NLU floundered during its early years, due in part to an economic recession during 1867 and 1868. With the elevation of William Sylvis to the NLU presidency and the return of prosperity in late 1868, however, the union began to flourish. The NLU reached its zenith in 1870 and then began a precipitant decline. The demise of the NLU resulted from varied circumstances--the untimely death of Sylvis in 1869, the growth of the labor movement along more purely economic lines, and controversies over the admission of women and blacks to full membership in trade unions. More important than the above factors, however, was the NLU's increased emphasis on political action, which isolated it more and more from the growing economic trade union movement.

In 1870 the NLU created two separate sections—industrial and political—which resulted in further retardation of the NLU's industrial activities. The political section met in 1872 and organized the Labor Reform Party, which supported the "greenback" monetary reform program. The new party chose David Davis for president. He at first accepted and later rejected the nomination. This fiasco aborted the embryonic labor party. A series of industrial congresses were held during between 1873 and 1875 in an effort to revive the NLU without the political section, but the effort failed.

As a labor federation, the NLU was probably doomed from the beginning; nevertheless it did make important contributions to the labor movement of its day. Under the leadership of Sylvis and Richard Trevellick, it conducted extensive organizing work. The NLU also made important contributions to the eight-hour campaign, including the enactment of an eight-hour law for federal employees, and it accomplished the repeal of the Contract Labor Act. Finally, it furthered the movement toward the eventual establishment of a permanent national federation of labor.

The NLU, which had no permanent national headquarters, held annual conventions. Principal officers included a president, a vice-president at large, one vice-president for each state, territory, and district, a treasurer, four secretaries, and a three-member finance committee. The executive board was composed of the president, recording secretary, corresponding secretary, and vice-president at large. Although reliable membership figures are not available, delegates to the Baltimore Labor Congress of 1866 represented approximately 60,000 workers, and that figure probably grew through 1870.

For further information, see Norman J. Ware, *The Labor Movement in the United States, 1860-1895: A Study in Democracy* (1929); John R. Commons et al., *History of Labour in the United States*, vol. 2 (1918); and David Montgomery, *Beyond Equality: Labor and the Radical Republicans, 1862-1872* (1967).

NATIONAL LABOR UNION; COLORED (CNLU). The Colored National Labor Union (also known as the National Convention of Negro Labor) emerged from the efforts by blacks to join the National Labor Union (NLU). Led by Isaac Myers of Baltimore, who headed the Colored Caulkers Trade Union Society, delegates were selected to represent black labor at the NLU convention by a meeting of black workers held in Baltimore on July 20, 1869. When the NLU would not adopt a policy of racial integration despite Myers's eloquent plea, he called for a convention of Negro labor to be held in the Union League Hall in Washington, D.C., on December 6, 1869. Two hundred fourteen accredited delegates attended the meeting, but because of the poverty of the average black worker, many delegates were lawyers, preachers, politicians, and merchants.

An immediate difficulty arose when John Mercer Langston, a black Virginia politician, objected to the seating of two white labor leaders active in the Democratic party. Myers's efforts permitted the two whites to be seated, but questions of political activity continued to plague the organization. Consolidation with the white NLU was prevented when the NLU refused to call for black admission to factories and apprenticeships and insisted on the need for anti-Republican, independent political action. The NLU supported the Greenbackers and viewed labor and capital as inherently antagonistic. Blacks opposed inflationary currency and felt that although imperfect, the Republican party was more likely to protect southern black laborers from Ku Klux Klan-style terrorism than the Democrats, who would benefit from any independent political action. Myers led the CNLU in calling for open hiring, free public education, staunch support for the temperance movement, and the study of political economy so that both labor and capital might understand the duties and responsibilities growing from their mutually dependent and complementary condition.

The CNLU was a confederation of autonomous state and local unions, including skilled, unskilled, and both male and female agricultural workers. At a large interracial meeting held on February 21, 1870, in Washington, the CNLU appointed its president, Isaac Myers, to the newly created position of organizing agent. He met with some success in Richmond and Norfolk, Virginia, and in Washington, D.C. At the January 9, 1871, convention, Myers warned against the "grand farcial claptrap" of the NLU's chimerical Labor Reform Party. He hoped to maintain cooperation with the NLU but to convince the union to avoid political activity.

Myers failed miserably. Instead of cooperating with the NLU without politics, the CNLU convention elected Frederick Douglass to replace Myers as president. Despite his deep interest in black labor, Douglass's position and tactics were essentially political. He called for the CNLU to meet in concert with the Southern States Convention of Colored Men on October 18, 1871, in Columbia, South Carolina, where the two groups joined, retaining the CNLU constitution and bylaws, but accepting economic concerns viewed from the perspective of Republican party politics, not that of a labor organizing group. The CNLU never met again, although some state groups continued to exist.

For further information, see Philip S. Foner, *Organized Labor and the Black Worker, 1619-1973* (1974), the best account of the CNLU, and Sterling D. Spero and Abram L. Harris, *The Black Worker: The Negro and the Labor Movement* (1931).

Carl S. Matthews

NATIONAL TRADES' UNION (NTU). Trade union interest, which had flamed and then burned out in the backwash of divisive and largely unproductive political activity during the late 1820s, was rekindled in the following decade. The revival was especially obvious in New York City and Philadelphia where two central unions were organized in 1833, the General Trades' Union of New York City and the Philadelphia Trades' Union. The purpose of these central unions was to encourage closer cooperation between the various trade unions in the vicinity, to provide mutual assistance during conflicts with employers, and to create a fund to assist striking laborers.

It soon became obvious that inter-city cooperation could be just as advantageous as intra-city cooperation. Consequently in the summer of 1834, the General Trades' Union of New York City issued an invitation to trade union societies in other cities to meet in conference in New York City to discuss mutual interests. Trade unions in Boston, Philadelphia, Newark, Brooklyn, Poughkeepsie, and New York City sent a combined total of thirty delegates to the conference, representing approximately 21,000 trade union members.

Before the five-day conference ended, the National Trades' Union had been formed, the first national federation of trade unions ever organized in the United States. The constitution of the new union listed as its goals:

> to recommend such measures to the various unions represented herein as may tend to advance the moral and intellectual condition and pecuniary interests of the laboring classes; promote the establishment of Trades' Unions in every section of the United States; and also publish and disseminate such information as may be useful to the Mechanics and Working Men generally; and to unite and harmonize the efforts of all the productive classes of our country.

On a less philosophical and more immediate level, NTU delegates passed resolutions opposing wage reductions, advocating a shorter workday, and favoring the development of a system of manual schools. The delegates elected Ely Moore of the New York General Trades' Union as their first president.

As originally conceived, the NTU was neither an activist nor a forceful organization. Decisions made during the conference sessions were not binding on members, financing was by voluntary subscription, union leaders largely confined their activities to relating the NTU position on various issues, and no provisions were made for the union to function after the adjournment of the first conference. In the words of one student of the NTU, "the main practical result of the first convention seemed to be the calling of a second."

Nevertheless, during its next two conferences (held at New York City in October 1835 and Philadelphia in October 1836) the loose organizational structure of the NTU was changed considerably. The NTU established a treasury, charged regular dues, developed a system of proportional representation to determine the size of delegations from member unions, made provisions to establish a system of communication between annual meetings, and determined that NTU decisions, previously advisory, would henceforth be binding on all members. Although there is little evidence to suggest that the membership of affiliated unions increased dramatically from 1833 to 1836, the geographical distribution of delegates broadened significantly during these years.

Throughout its brief existence, the NTU continued its dedication to broad reform issues such as equal educational opportunities in a public school system, land reform, and restrictions on child labor. Meanwhile it also placed great emphasis on such purely trade union objectives as the recognition of the legality of unions, strikes, boycotts, the ten-hour day, higher wages, equal pay for women, and the strict regulation of prison labor in competition with free labor.

By 1837 the NTU had disappeared from the labor scene in the United States. Although the panic of 1837 and the depression that followed were primarily responsible for the demise of the NTU, other circumstances made the continued survival of the NTU doubtful, even in good times. Little unity existed among workers in the United States during the 1830s. Divisions between skilled and unskilled labor grew during a period in which revolutionary changes in transportation and technology greatly altered usual patterns of labor. Moreover, to the average worker, the NTU was a remote organization that in return for the dues it collected offered little more than altruistic rhetoric and vague promises of future rewards. Finally, many workers, still anticipating becoming shopowners and employers themselves, were distracted by a variety of self-help expedients.

Although obviously a very ephemeral organization, the NTU did play a significant role in the evolution of the American labor movement. It represented the first concerted effort to establish a national federation of trade unions and established the precedent for future organizations of a similar scope. It also greatly encouraged the organization of national unions within various trades. The NTU provides a reflection of labor attitudes during this formative period of union labor thought. A study of the debates, resolutions, and objectives of the NTU suggests the same concern with broad reform issues and immediate trade union objectives that characterized later union labor movements in the United States.

The NTU, which met annually from 1833 to 1836, did not establish a national headquarters. Principal officers consisted of a president and recording secretary. At each annual convention several ad hoc committees were created to study or proselytize for desired reforms. Although accurate membership figures are not available, it is known that thirty-four delegates representing unions in five states attended the 1836 conference.

For further information, see Edward Pessen, *Most Uncommon Jacksonians: The Radical Leaders of the Early Labor Movement* (1967); Philip Taft, *Organized Labor in American History* (1964); John R. Commons et al., *History of Labour in the United States*, vol. 1 (1918); and Walter Hugins, *Jacksonian Democracy and the Working Class: A Study of the New York Workingmen's Movement, 1829-1837* (1969).

NEEDLE TRADES WORKERS INDUSTRIAL UNION (NTWIU). Meeting in Moscow in 1928, the Red International of Labor Unions ordered its affiliates throughout the world to organize independent trade union federations. The new orders reversed the "boring from within" strategy employed since 1921. In the United States the Communists had been especially successful in their efforts to infiltrate needle trades unions. Left-wing radicals eventually seized control of the International Fur Workers' Union* (IFWU) and came very close to capturing the International Ladies' Garment Workers' Union* (ILG).

In response to the new strategy, the Needle Trades Workers Industrial Union was launched in New York City on December 28, 1928. Louis Hyman and Ben Gold, formerly of the ILG and the IFWU, respectively, headed the new dual union. The NTWIU pledged its determination to organize all the workers in the apparel industry into one industrial union. Conflict and inter-union warfare punctuated the six-year history of the NTWIU. Leaders of the American Federation of Labor* (AFL) and its various international union affiliates declared war on the rival union movement and dedicated themselves to the total destruction of the new radical unions; employers also fiercely resisted the efforts of the Communist unions to organize their employees.

Although it launched organizing efforts in such cities as Boston, Chicago, and Philadelphia, the NTWIU had its greatest success in New York City. Within the New York needle trades industry, the Communists were most successful in gaining the allegiance of fur workers and had some influence among bathrobe, knit goods, and custom tailoring workers.

The NTWIU affiliated with the Trade Union Unity League* (TUUL) after its organization in 1929 as a rival to the AFL. The NTWIU, along with the National Textile Workers Union* and the National Miners' Union,* were among the strongest affiliates of the TUUL. Like the TUUL, however, the NTWIU was destined to be short-lived. As a result of international political considerations, the TUUL dissolved and directed the members of its affiliated unions to reenter the established unions in their trades.

The NTWIU, which maintained its national headquarters in New York City, held biennial conventions. Principal officers included a secretary, assistant secretary, and the members of the general executive board. At the time of its dissolution, the NTWIU reported a membership of 30,000.

For further information, see Jack Hardy, *The Clothing Workers: A Study of the Conditions and Struggles in the Needle Trades* (1935), which contains a friendly account of the NTWIU, and Joel Seidman's *The Needle Trades* (1942), and Benjamin Stolberg, *Tailor's Progress: The Story of a Famous Union and the Men Who Made It* (1944), which both treat the NTWIU much more critically.

NEGRO AMERICAN LABOR COUNCIL (NALC). A. Philip Randolph, Cleveland Robinson, and other blacks inspired by the Negro freedom movement led by Martin Luther King, Jr., formed the Negro American Labor Council in 1960 in order to fight racism within the American Federation of Labor-Congress of Industrial Organizations* (AFL-CIO). Such a purpose ensured conflict with George Meany and other AFL-CIO leaders. The NALC was critical of the AFL-CIO's failure to discipline its discriminatory unions, and in October 1961 the AFL-CIO executive council responded by adopting a subcommittee report critical of A. Philip Randolph, the NALC spokesman. The report castigated Randolph for causing "the gap that has developed between organized labor and the Negro Community"; denied Randolph's charge that the AFL-CIO was lax in enforcing its pronounced racial policies; and accused Randolph's Brotherhood of Sleeping Car Porters* of discrimination against whites. The executive council further rejected the NALC proposal that the AFL-CIO adopt a system of penalties against unions that continued to discriminate, alleging that voluntary compliance with the principles of equal rights would produce a more successful solution to the race's problems. In addition, Meany argued that the NALC's attacks had made the AFL-CIO's civil-rights program less effective. Meany moderated his opposition to the NALC after meeting with eighteen delegates from the black group before the AFL-CIO's annual convention in 1961. The NALC delegates and Meany discussed plans for some AFL-CIO action against discriminatory unions and tried to stop the growing breach with Randolph. They also asked Meany to address the 1962 NALC convention.

From 1962 through 1965, Meany and the NALC achieved an uneasy peace. Randolph wooed him by leading the NALC to defend the International Ladies' Garment Workers' Union* against charges of discrimination leveled by the National Association for the Advancement of Colored People (NAACP) and also opposed that group's effort to "decertify" the Atlanta local of the United

Steelworkers* because of its record of discrimination. At the same time the NALC adopted a resolution supporting the NAACP in general.

As the civil-rights movement gained momentum with the murder of Medgar Evers in Mississippi and the long series of demonstrations in Birmingham, Randolph and the NALC recalled the March-on-Washington movement of World War II and joined with King's Southern Christian Leadership Conference (SCLC), the Congress of Racial Equality, the Student Non-Violent Coordinating Committee, and the NAACP in a huge march in Washington, D.C. on August 28, 1963. Its purpose was to pressure the Kennedy administration to move for increased employment for blacks, to end segregation in employment, and to encourage Congress to pass the civil-rights bill submitted by the president. The march was condemned by Meany's executive council but not by Walter Reuther of the industrial union department. Nearly a quarter of the 200,000 marchers were union members. Throughout 1964 and 1965, the NALC, frequently represented by its vice-president Cleveland Robinson, cooperated with the SCLC in civil-rights demonstrations from Selma and Montgomery, Alabama, to Chicago.

In December 1965, at the San Francisco convention, Randolph seemed to lead the NALC away from its course of tough criticism of the AFL-CIO leadership when he declared that although vestiges of discrimination remained, great progress had been made under Meany. In June 1966 Randolph resigned his leadership of the NALC and was replaced by Robinson. Some critics believed that Randolph's moderation toward Meany and the AFL-CIO leadership was caused by his hopes for federation support of the A. Philip Randolph Institute. It may also have come from his fear of growing race consciousness, rather than class consciousness, within the Negro freedom movement, which exploded in the summer of 1966 when Stokely Carmichael called for "black power." After 1966 Randolph and Bayard Rustin, the executive director of the A. Philip Randolph Institute, spoke eloquently for class rather than race consciousness.

Robinson made it plain at the 1966 NALC convention that he planned to continue opposing racism within the AFL-CIO, calling the delegates to "reject compromise and tokenism." Under his leadership the NALC has tried to involve younger workers in organizing drives and has joined the SCLC in struggles of sanitation workers in Memphis and Atlanta and hospital workers in Charleston and Baltimore.

By the end of the decade, however, the NALC was overtaken by the progress of black workers. A Negro American council in an age of black and Afro-American consciousness, it was outstripped in appeal to younger workers by more soulful and radical groups such as the Dodge Revolutionary Union Movement (DRUM) that overwhelmed the Detroit Trade Union Leadership Council, which had been the largest constituent unit of the NALC.

For further information, see Philip S. Foner, *Organized Labor and the*

Black Worker, 1619-1973 (1974), and F. Ray Marshall, *The Negro and Organized Labor* (1965). See also Jervis Anderson, *A. Philip Randolph: A Biographical Portrait* (1972).

Carl S. Matthews

NEGRO LABOR COMMITTEE (NLC). The Negro Labor Committee was formed in July 1935 and led by Frank Crosswaith, a Socialist graduate of the Rand School. The International Ladies' Garment Workers' Union* sponsored the NLC, which held conferences to organize black workers, especially in industries under contract with the affiliates of the American Federation of Labor.* Crosswaith, previously affiliated with the Brotherhood of Sleeping Car Porters,* had made earlier efforts to promote black unionism, most notably the Trade Union Committee for Organizing Negro Workers (TUCONW), supported by the Central Trades and Labor Council of Greater New York, which he began in December 1924. The unwillingness of local unions to accept black members created considerable opposition to the TUCONW by 1926, and it soon died.

The NLC was more successful than its predecessor. As its leader, Crosswaith joined A. Philip Randolph in the March-on-Washington movement, which convinced President Franklin D. Roosevelt to create the Fair Employment Practices Commission. In 1942 New York mayor Fiorello LaGuardia made Crosswaith a member of the New York City Housing Authority after Randolph refused the appointment. Never a national or even statewide organization, the NLC claimed that by 1946 it had changed "Harlem from a community of scabs to a community of labor conscious workers."

For further information, see Frank R. Crosswaith and Alfred B. Lewis, *Black and White Unite for True Freedom* (n.d.); the NLC's *Ten Year Report* (1946); Philip S. Foner, *Organized Labor and the Black Worker, 1619-1973* (1974); F. Ray Marshall, *The Negro and Organized Labor* (1965); and Jervis Anderson, *A. Philip Randolph: A Biographical Portrait* (1972).

Carl S. Matthews

NEW ENGLAND ASSOCIATION OF FARMERS, MECHANICS, AND OTHER WORKINGMEN (NEA). Delegates from several New England states convened in Providence, Rhode Island, on December 5, 1831, to discuss general reform issues affecting the producing classes in American society. Before adjourning, delegates had organized the New England Association of Farmers, Mechanics, and Other Working Men and had issued a call for the association's first convention to meet in Boston the following spring. The object of the meeting was to be the adoption of "mature measures to concentrate the efforts of the laboring classes, to regulate the hours of labor, by one uniform standard, to promote the cause of education and general information, to re-form abuses practiced upon them, and to maintain their rights as American Freemen."

The charge to the Boston convention was clearly a call for the ten-hour day, and to a considerable extent the NEA was a ten-hour organization. Member-ship in the association was open to any individual "of good moral character" who belonged to the producing classes and agreed not to work for more than ten hours a day unless receiving additional compensation. March 20, 1832, was established as the date when the ten-hour system was to begin; anyone working longer than ten hours after that date was subject to expulsion from the associa-tion.

The first annual convention was planned to coincide with the ten-hour dead-line and a ten-hour strike by ship carpenters in the important Boston ship-building industry. An annual membership assessment of fifty-five cents was levied to create a "war chest" to compensate those members losing their jobs for observing the ten-hour resolution. On March 20 employers in the Boston shipyards assumed the offensive and locked out their employees, breaking the strike with relative ease. Because of the strike's defeat and the general ineffec-tiveness of ten-hour agitation elsewhere, delegates to the second annual NEA convention voted to release members from the ten-hour pledge. It was also de-cided to work for the shorter hour reform through political action.

In another important action, the NEA convention endorsed the agitation of Boston workingmen desiring to organize a general trades' union in that city. Such a union, the Boston Trades' Union, began in early 1834 and acquired a membership in excess of 4,000 shortly after its organization. But the Boston Trades' Union had little more success than the NEA in the agitation for a ten-hour day, and following the fate of other labor organizations of the period, it was a short-lived union.

In 1834 the NEA converted itself into a political party advocating hard money, child labor reform, factory legislation, abolition of bank monopolies, and the establishment of public education. The new workingmen's party, how-ever, received an infinitesimal number of votes and soon faded from existence.

Although having a very short life span and largely failing to achieve its major objectives, the New England Association nevertheless earned an important place in American labor history. In many ways it was the first labor organiza-tion in the United States to attempt to organize on an industrial basis. If not a forerunner of the Congress of Industrial Organizations,* it could at least be considered an important antecedent of the Noble Order of the Knights of Labor.* In other ways, the NEA was a unique labor organization. It served as an agency for collecting, disseminating, and publicizing desired labor reforms. It attempted to gain the adoption of these reforms through a combination of economic activism and political agitation. Part political party and part economic trade union, the association pragmatically adopted whatever tactic seemed most appropriate and feasible at the time.

Although the NEA was little more than a series of annual conventions, Boston served as the focal point of association activities. The chief executive position in the association was the president, an office ably filled by Charles Douglas, one of the leading figures in the New England labor movement. Reliable figures on the NEA membership do not exist.

For further information, see the *New England Artisan*, edited by Charles Douglas, which served unofficially as an NEA organ. See also Edward Pessen, *Most Uncommon Jacksonians: The Radical Leaders of the Early Labor Movement* (1967); John R. Commons, et al., eds., *A. Documentary History of American Industrial Society*, vol. 6 (1910) and *History of Labour in the United States*, vol. 1 (1918); and Philip S. Foner, *History of the Labor Movement in the United States*, vol. 1 (1947).

NEWSPAPER GUILD; THE (TNG). The chartering of newswriters' locals began in 1891, when fifteen newswriters in Pittsburgh organized, and on October 13, 1891, they obtained a charter from the International Typographical Union* (ITU) as Pittsburgh Newswriters Union No. 1. The ITU had amended its constitution in 1891 to authorize the chartering of local unions of editors and reporters, and between 1891 and 1923 the union chartered fifty-nine locals in forty cities throughout the United States and Canada. Originally the ITU hoped to eliminate scabbing by reporters who set type, but by 1906 reporters seldom emerged from the ranks of typesetters, and hence ITU interest in organizing reporters diminished markedly. The last wave of newswriters' unionism in which the ITU participated occurred in 1919, when it recognized fifteen news reporters' locals, but in 1923, the ITU officially relinquished jurisdiction over newswriters.

The 1919 movement fared rather poorly, primarily because publishers' opposition, the relative lack of newswriters' union experience, and the 1920-1921 economic recession combined to destroy it. Yet from 1923 to 1933 the American Federation of Labor* (AFL) continued to charter editorial workers' locals. Of the six locals that were organized, three disbanded quickly, while the other three enjoyed only limited success. The situation throughout the first three decades of the twentieth century was additionally exacerbated by the tendency of newspapers to merge and to form local monopolies, effectively restricting the reporters' job opportunities. As a consequence, a reporter frequently was forced to accept any offer an employer made.

After the depression struck the nation in 1929, it became more imperative for newswriters to organize in an attempt to advance their somewhat shaky economic position. The passage of the National Industrial Recovery Act in

1933 spurred unionization, with the result that locals began to appear in major cities throughout the United States. This, together with the impetus provided by Heywood Broun, whose August 7, 1933, column in the *New York World Telegram* called for unionization among newswriters, furnished the immediate background for the organization of the American Newspaper Guild (ANG). On December 15, 1933, representatives from twenty-one local bodies met in Washington, D.C., to form the ANG. Broun and Jonathan Eddy, who both represented the recently organized New York Newspaper Guild, were the moving forces behind the calling of this founding convention. Broun became the guild's first president and guided the union through its first six years.

The ANG's first constitutional convention, held in St. Paul, Minnesota, in June 1934, established the union as a loose association of local bodies. Collective bargaining was conducted locally, and the national guild restricted itself to bargaining with press associations and national syndicates. Throughout 1934 and 1935 the national guild also urged publishers to abide by the National Recovery Administration's (NRA) five-day, forty-hour work week for news staffs. But by mid-1935 the ANG became disenchanted with the NRA and the publisher-dominated Newspaper Industrial Board. Therefore, in order to counter publisher obstinancy and to advance unionism, the guild's 1935 convention turned toward centralization. The general executive board (GEB) was empowered to draft model contracts for the guidance of local guilds. Moreover, it was given authority to disapprove collective agreements that it held to be in violation of both the union's constitution and collective bargaining principles adopted by the convention.

During 1936 and 1937 there was a decided increase in union activity. Two major strikes, one against the *Milwaukee Wisconsin News* and the other against the *Seattle Post-Intelligencer*, occurred in 1936. The *Wisconsin News* strike failed to secure union recognition, but the aid the AFL provided to ANG members contributed to the union's decision to affiliate with the AFL. The *Post-Intelligencer* strike, meanwhile, established a precedent for bargaining with the Hearst chain. In 1937 the guild secured agreements with six Scripps-Howard papers.

But 1937 also witnessed important changes within the ANG. In June the guild voted to affiliate with the Congress of Industrial Organizations,* a decision that marked the ascendency within the union of a leftist-leaning clique based in New York. The 1937 convention altered collective bargaining regulations. Proposed contract changes were to be submitted to the GEB in advance of their presentation to the employer. Any local that accepted contract terms less favorable than the minimum goals of the national guild could be suspended. Furthermore, it was agreed that the entire local, not just the particular newspaper concerned, had to be represented at collective bargaining sessions.

In response to these events, the AFL undertook a drive to organize a rival newswriters' guild. News and editorial employees were invited to join AFL federal locals. After the 1940 defeat of the ANG in a National Labor Relations Board election held to determine the collective bargaining agent for *Chicago Herald and Examiner* newswriters, the AFL formed the American Editorial Association, composed of a national council of fifteen federal locals, but the AFL organization never really offered the ANG any serious opposition.

Overall the guild made notable progress from 1938 to 1941. In 1938 it negotiated its first nationwide contract with the United Press, and in 1940 it entered into a contract with the Associated Press (AP), bringing the New York AP bureau under guild jurisdiction. Meanwhile, membership during these years increased, reaching 17,286 in 1941, a gain of 12,036 over the 1935 number. Additionally, by 1941 the "Communist problem" within the union was solved. The convention that year agreed to the direct (as opposed to convention) election of officers. This move resulted in the defeat of pro-Communist leaders, even in the radical New York local, and the advent of World War II and particularly the Soviet Union's entry into the war helped to further divide Communist leadership within the guild.

Throughout both the immediate postwar period and the 1950s, the ANG continued to seek improvements in wage and hour agreements. Notable among its achievements was the securing of the first minimum weekly salary guarantee for key editorial and advertising personnel (1946). The $100 minimum originally established has risen to $400 secured in 1972. The guild perhaps also changed its image as a leftist-dominated union by withdrawing from the radically oriented International Organization of Journalists (1952) and thereafter helping to form the more conservative International Federation of Journalists. The guild also established a Canadian region in 1951 and intensified its unionizing activities in Canada throughout the 1950s. In 1970 the union title was changed to The Newspaper Guild.

The TNG, which maintains its national headquarters in Washington, D.C., holds annual conventions. Principal officers include a president, thirteen vice-presidents, and a secretary-treasurer. The above officials constitute the international executive board. In 1973 the TNG reported a membership of 32,535 located in eighty-three local unions.

For further information, see *The Guild Reporter* published semimonthly. See also Daniel J. Leab, *A Union of Individuals: The Formation of the American Newspaper Guild, 1933-1936* (1970), the definitive study of the founding of the guild, and Walter Galenson, *The CIO Challenge to the AFL: A History of the American Labor Movement, 1936-1941* (1960).

Marie Tedesco

OFFICE AND PROFESSIONAL EMPLOYEES INTERNATIONAL UNION (OPEIU). The American Federation of Labor* (AFL) issued its first office workers' charter on February 24, 1904, to the Indianapolis Stenographers,

Typewriter Operators, Bookkeepers and Assistants Union No. 11597. The new union, composed primarily of workers at AFL and other international union headquarters offices, was directly affiliated with the AFL as a federal labor union. Later in the same year, the AFL chartered Federal Labor Union No. 1173, a similar local of office workers in Washington, D.C. These two unions eventually became Locals 1 and 2 of the Office and Professional Employees International Union.

Although such federal local unions of office workers appeared in most major American and Canadian cities during the years that followed, membership was largely confined to workers in the bureaucracies of international trade unions. Requests for the chartering of a national union of office and professional workers began during the 1920s, but national AFL officials were annoyed by the militant, left-wing element in the largest of these unions, Bookkeepers, Stenographers, and Accountants' Union, Local 12646 in New York City. AFL officials preferred to keep a tight rein on these unions and continually ignored demands for a national charter.

Beginning with the enactment of Section 7(a) of the National Industrial Recovery Act in 1933 and then the National Labor Relations Act (NLRA) of 1935, white-collar unionism grew substantially. The New York City local alone claimed a membership of 2,500 in 1937. When the AFL at its 1936 convention again refused to act on requests for the chartering of a national union of office workers, the New York City local joined thirteen other AFL-affiliated white-collar unions and several independent locals to form the National Committee of Office and Professional Workers. The AFL immediately suspended the involved unions. The renegade unions then disaffiliated and organized the United Office and Professional Workers of America, International* (UOPWA), and successfully sought a charter from the newly organized Congress of Industrial Organizations* (CIO).

The AFL responded by convening a national conference of office worker unions in Seattle in 1941, and as a result of its organizational activities, the International Council of Office Employees Union was organized in Chicago on July 28, 1942. J. Howard Hicks, head of the Western Council of Office Workers, was elected president of the new organization. Three years later, on Januarty 8, 1945, Cincinnati hosted a constitutional convention during which the AFL officially extended a charter to the Office Employees International Union with a jurisdiction including "all clerical and office employees other than governmental employees (but including employees of government-owned corporations), telegraph employees, and railway and steamship clerks." The union title was changed to Office and Professional Employees International Union in 1965.

Despite the organizing opportunities resulting from the depressed economy, the NLRA, and low salaries and high prices during World War II, the OPEIU, which claimed a charter membership of 22,500, grew very slowly during the

1940s. Meanwhile the rival UOPWA organized aggressively and attained a membership more than twice as large as that of the AFL affiliate. During its early years, the OPEIU appeared satisfied to challenge the UOPWA in National Labor Relations Board (NLRB) representational elections and to offer itself as an anti-Communist alternative to the UOPWA.

The enactment of the Taft-Hartley Labor Act in 1947 proved a disguised blessing to the OPEIU. Its rival, the UOPWA, was severely hampered by the requirement of the new act that trade union officials sign non-Communist affidavits in order to take advantage of NLRB election machinery. Furthermore, the UOPWA was expelled from the CIO as a Communist-dominated union in 1950, thus leaving an organizing field including hundreds of thousands of office and professional workers largely to the OPEIU. Nevertheless, the OPEIU, which negotiated contracts in such varied industries as public utilities, shipbuilding, retail and wholesaling, movies, radio, and television, the New York Stock Exchange, and banking, had only limited organizing success.

The failure to make significant inroads in the organization of white-collar workers was the product of varied circumstances, including the management orientation and identification of many such workers; effective competition from a large variety of independent, semiprofessional associations; jurisdictional disputes with other labor organizations, especially industrial unions; and the failure of the national labor movement to make a sustained effort to organize white-collar workers. Despite these handicaps, the OPEIU has grown steadily, if slowly. Union membership passed the 40,000 figure in the early 1950s and the 50,000 mark in the early 1960s.

The OPEIU holds triennial conventions and maintains its national headquarters in New York City. Full-time officers include an international president and secretary-treasurer. The executive board is comprised of the above officers in addition to the international vice-presidents. In 1973 the OPEIU reported a membership of 82,500 located in 235 local unions.

For further information, see the *Office Worker*, 1943-1944, and *White Collar*, 1945-, both monthly journals published by the OPEIU. See also Albert A. Blum, "The Office Employee," in Blum et al., *White Collar Workers* (1971), and John F. Lubin, "Clerical and Office Unionism in the United States: The Unit for Collective Bargaining" (Ph.D. dissertation, University of Pennsylvania, 1956).

OFFICE AND PROFESSIONAL WORKERS OF AMERICA, INTERNATIONAL; UNITED (UOPWA). Unions of white-collar workers first appeared at the national conventions of the American Federation of Labor* (AFL) shortly after the turn of the twentieth century. These workers were organized into federal labor unions directly affiliated with the AFL. On February 24, 1904, for example, an AFL charter was issued to Stenographers, Typewriter Operators,

Bookkeepers and Assistants Union, No. 11597 in Indianapolis, Indiana. A year later a charter was issued to Local 1173 in Washington, D.C. By 1913 such locals also existed in San Francisco, New York City, St. Louis, Chicago, Denver, and Kansas City, Missouri, and by 1919 at least forty office workers' locals had been founded.

Bookkeepers, Stenographers, and Accountants' Union (BSAU), Local 12646, organized in New York City in 1909, was one of the larger and more influential of these white-collar unions. The BSAU had a strong left-wing element, and when it seemed to be cooperating too closely with the Communist-organized Trade Union Educational League (TUEL), AFL president Samuel Gompers ordered the revocation of its charter. The federal local was then re-chartered under the same title on July 24, 1922. The reorganization, however, obviously did not have the desired effect, for five years later the AFL felt compelled to expel twenty-three BSAU members on charges of TUEL membership.

In 1927 the BSAU attempted to organize insurance workers and chose as its first target the workers and agents of the Metropolitan Life Insurance Company's New York headquarters. Although militantly conducted, the campaign failed to make much progress among Metropolitan's 10,000 employees.

The BSAU, as well as other locals of white-collar workers, grew dramatically during the years of the Great Depression. By 1937 the BSAU alone claimed a membership of 2,500. Dating back to the early 1920s, the growth in white-collar unionism increased demands for a nationally chartered office and professional workers' union. When the AFL, which had continually dismissed such requests, again ignored the office workers at its 1936 convention, BSAU president Lewis Merrill and other white-collar leaders organized the National Committee of Office and Professional Workers.

The AFL responded to the BSAU initiative by threatening its suspension; events then moved quickly. In May 1937 the BSAU met and voted to leave the AFL. On May 30, 1937, the BSAU, along with thirteen other AFL white-collar locals and nine independent unions, met in Philadelphia and created the United Office and Professional Workers of America, International. Lewis Merrill of the BSAU was elected president of the new national union, which claimed a membership of 8,615. The UOPWA immediately sought affiliation with the newly organized Congress of Industrial Organizations* (CIO) and on June 1, 1937, received a CIO charter with a jurisdiction that included stenographers, bookkeepers, bank clerks, artists, typists, insurance workers, and others engaged in similar occupations.

The AFL responded to the UOPWA and CIO challenges by immediately doing what for two decades it had refused to do—it reversed its position on the organization of unions of insurance agents and granted office and professional workers an international charter. The AFL's action, however, was not backed by any vigorous effort to enroll office and professional workers. It apparently wanted to be in a position to challenge the UOPWA if it succeeded in petitioning the National Labor Relations Board (NLRB) for representational elections.

Although chartered with a broad jurisdiction in the white-collar field, the UOPWA concentrated on organizing the agents and office workers in the insurance industry, esepcially the so-called big three of the industry: Metropolitan Life Insurance Co., John Hancock Mutual Life Insurance Co., and Prudential Insurance Company of America. Resulting from its own militant organizing activities and the availability of state and federal election machinery for collective bargaining referendums, the UOPWA's organizing endeavors met with considerable success. During the late 1930 and early 1940s, the UOPWA won representational elections covering the employees of both Metropolitan and John Hancock in the Greater New York City area. The union's greatest achievement, however, came on February 1, 1943, when it signed a national agreement with the Prudential Life Insurance Company covering its employees in thirty-one states.

Besides its involvement in the insurance industry, during the 1940s the UOPWA was able to secure contracts covering the office workers of many banks as well as office employees in such varied businesses as CBS Radio, Arthur Murray Dance Studios, Cutter Laboratories, and Remington Rand. The UOPWA membership, which reached 43,000 in 1944, reflected these organizing achievements.

The UOPWA's success in organizing office and professional employees was qualified by its inability to resolve its own internal conflicts. Dating back to the BSAU period, the UOPWA had always had a substantial left-wing membership, and in 1942 this group gained complete control of the union. Ideological conflicts were restrained during the war as a result of the spirit of wartime cooperation, especially among American Communists, but after the war, the UOPWA leadership, which by this time was closely following the Communist party line, confronted a growing right-wing insurgency. Moreover, the UOPWA leadership in the postwar period devoted more of its attention and energy to national ideological issues and in doing so neglected the militant organizing activities from whence it had originally derived its strength. Meanwhile, UOPWA president Lewis Merrill, who had long supported Communist causes, began criticizing the disruptive Communist influence in the UOPWA in 1946 and a year later was replaced by James H. Durkin whose ideological purity was unquestioned.

The enactment of the Taft-Hartley Labor Act in 1947 was the first in a series of events that reduced the UOPWA to shambles. The new labor law required the leaders of unions desiring to use NLRB election machinery to sign non-Communist affidavits. Although the union had used NLRB elections to build its membership, for obvious reasons UOPWA leaders resolutely refused to sign the oaths. The endorsement of Henry Wallace's presidential candidacy on the Progressive party ticket further antagonized many union members. Dur ing the UOPWA's national convention in 1948, a group of right-wing insurgents challenged the leadership and when defeated began to defect to the United Paperworkers Union,* which had created an autonomous insurance division to accommodate them.

The most serious challenge came in the spring of 1949 when the AFL's National Federation of Insurance Agents' Council won collective bargaining rights for the nearly 9,000 Prudential agents that the UOPWA had represented since 1943. By this time the union's demise was near. The 1949 national convention of the CIO suspended the UOPWA as a Communist-dominated union, and after a lengthy legal battle, it was officially expelled from the CIO on March 1, 1950. Shortly thereafter the UOPWA merged with the Communist-led Food, Tobacco, Agricultural and Allied Workers* and the Distributive Workers Union to create the Distributive, Processing and Office Workers of America.

The UOPWA, which maintained its national headquarters in New York City, held biennial conventions. Its general officers included a president and a secretary-treasurer. The general executive board consisted of the general officers and seventeen additional members elected by convention delegates. At the time of the merger, the UOPWA claimed a membership of 27,000, but actual membership probably numbered no more than 4,000 to 5,000.

For further information, see the UOPWA's monthly, *Office and Professional News* 1935-1948, and *Champion*, 1948-1950. Harvey J. Clermont recounts the UOPWA's involvement in the insurance industry in *Organizing the Insurance Worker: A History of Labor Unions of Insurance Employees* (1966), and Albert A. Blum discusses the economic, political, and sociopsychological factors involved in white-collar unionism in "The Office Employee," Blum et al., *White Collar Workers* (1971). See also Max Kampelman, who has a highly critical account of Communist influences in CIO unions, *The Communist Party vs. the C.I.O.: A Study in Power Politics* (1957).

OIL, CHEMICAL AND ATOMIC WORKERS INTERNATIONAL UNION (OCAW). Merger talks between the Oil Workers International Union* (OWIU) and the smaller United Gas, Coke, and Chemical Workers International Union (UGCCW) began during the spring of 1954. The Congress of Industrial Organizations* (CIO) had chartered the UGCCW in 1942 after a group of local unions, opposing the decision of the United Mine Workers of America* (UMWA) to leave the CIO, withdrew from UMWA District 50.*

An undisciplined and loosely organized union, the UGCCW, which was composed predominantly of low-wage workers living in the eastern states, experienced constant financial stringencies and probably would not have survived without CIO assistance. Like other unions in the petroleum and chemical industries, leaders of the UGCCW encountered great resistance in the effort to organize workers within their jurisdiction. Organizing failures resulted primarily from the effective anti-union tactics of the huge corporations that dominated the industry, but the trade unions themselves further exacerbated the problem through expensive and distracting rivalries that disrupted organizing drives and weakened the union position during collective bargaining negotiations. Consequently most UGCCW leaders were pleased to hear OWIU president O. A. Knight tell the delegates to the 1950 OWIU national convention:

> I think that at this time . . . it behooves us to extend an invitation . . . to the Gas, Coke, and Chemical Union, which is so closely related to ours that you can't tell where theirs stops and our starts, . . . to sit down with us and plan for a united movement in the oil and chemical industry in America.

The first step toward greater unity came in 1951 with the organization of the National Coalition of Oil Unions, a collective bargaining unit that included many independents as well as the OWIU and the UGCCW. Finally, in the late winter of 1955 the two organizations agreed to a merger, creating the Oil, Chemical, and Atomic Workers International Union. Clearly the OWIU was the senior partner in the merger, and its president, O. A. Knight headed the new union.

The UGCCW, which held annual conventions, maintained its international headquarters in Washington, D.C. Full-time officers included a president, vice-president, and secretary-treasurer. The executive council was composed of the full-time officers and members elected from eleven geographical districts. At the time of the OCAW merger, the UGCCW paid per-capita taxes to the CIO on 72,000 members.

During the remaining years of the 1950s, leaders of the OCAW devoted much of their attention to problems emanating from the merger. Both unions had long traditions of rank-and-file participation in decision making, and while the OWIU had gone further toward centralizing authority, advocates of local autonomy in both unions jealousy guarded their prerogatives. While a healthy and desirable condition, this state of affairs complicated the resolution of the inevitable administrative problems following the merger. Disagreements erupted over dues payments, the degree of power to be exercised by the president, collective bargaining policies, procedures for authorizing strikes, representation at conventions, and the election of officers. Although compromises were arranged on most issues, in general terms the positions of the larger OWIU usually predominated.

The merger eliminated existing or potential jurisdictional problems between the OWIU and the UGCCW, but it did not provide the expected organizing gains or improve the collective bargaining positions anticipated by its sponsors. The OCAW steadily added new members but lost almost as many to technological changes, new production methods, craft reclassification, and rival unions. As a result membership fluctuated but has remained fairly constant since 1957. Moreover, the merger movement initiated by the OWIU in 1950 stalled after the formation of the OCAW in 1955. Merger talks with the International Chemical Workers Union* collapsed, and although a few unaffiliated unions joined, most remained independent or merged with other unions.

The OCAW, which holds biennial conventions, maintains its international headquarters in Denver, Colorado. Principal officers include a president, two vice-presidents, and a secretary-treasurer. The executive board consists of sixteen rank-and-file members. In 1973 the OCAW reported a membership of 172,000 located in 596 local unions.

For further information, see the UGCCW *Victory* published semimonthly, and the *Union News* published monthly by the OCAW. Melvin Rothbaum's *The Government of the Oil, Chemical and Atomic Workers Union* (1962) is the best source on the subject. See also Harry Seligson, *Oil, Chemical and Atomic Workers: A Labor Union in Action* (1960).

OIL AND GAS WELL WORKERS; INTERNATIONAL BROTHERHOOD OF (IBOGWW). Organization of oil workers began in western Pennsylvania almost as early as the development of the industry itself. The earliest known union of oil workers organized in Parkers Landing in 1872. Shortly thereafter drillers and tool drivers organized the Oil Well Workingmen's Association in Oil City, and on October 30, 1878, the Oil Well Workers Protective Union appeared at Bradford. By 1889 oil well drillers were organized effectively enough to sign a favorable agreement with the Petroleum Producers Association, but organization remained localized and confined largely to western Pennsylvania.

As the industry expanded beyond its original Pennsylvania base, trade union organization followed. Consequently, in 1899, President Samuel Gompers of the American Federation of Labor* (AFL) invited oil worker locals to send representatives to the forthcoming national AFL convention in Detroit on December 11. Oil workers representing seven locals located in Ohio and Indiana responded to the invitation and heard AFL delegates pledge their assistance to the oil workers in their "earnest endeavor to organize their craft."

Shortly after the convention adjourned, the first national union of oil workers, the International Brotherhood of Oil and Gas Well Workers, was organized. On December 29, 1899, Gompers extended an AFL charter to the new union giving it exclusive jurisdiction over skilled oil field workers.

Although the IBOGWW quickly expanded its membership and extended its organizing activities to the distant oil fields of California, its strength was confined primarily to the Ohio-Indiana area and especially to employees of the

Ohio Oil Company. The loss of a major strike in 1904, the accelerated dispersion of the industry across the country, and the employers' national open-shop
campaign (to which most petroleum companies fervently subscribed) combined to destroy the fledgling IBOGWW, and, on December 9, 1905, the union
surrendered its charter.

The IBOGWW, which established its national headquarters in Bowling
Green, Ohio, held annual conventions. Principal officers included a president,
three vice-presidents, a secretary, and a treasurer. At its peak the IBOGWW
appears to have had between 1,000 and 2,000 members located in approximately twenty-four local unions.

For further information, see Harvey O'Connor, *History of Oil Workers
International Union* (1950), which contains much of the information from
which this sketch was drawn. Other books that discuss union organization in
the petroleum industry include Melvin Rothbaum, *The Government of the
Oil, Chemical and Atomic Workers Union* (1962), and Harry Seligson, *Oil,
Chemical and Atomic Workers: A Labor Union in Action* (1960).

OIL WORKERS INTERNATIONAL UNION (OWIU). Soon after the development of the petroleum industry during the second half of the nineteenth century, oil field workers began organizing in western Pennsylvania. Organization
proceeded rapidly, and by the end of the century the American Federation of
Labor* (AFL) chartered a short-lived national union of oil workers, the International Brotherhood of Oil and Gas Well Workers.* The early twentieth-cen-
tury open-shop campaign and the strong anti-union feelings of the major
employers in the industry, reflected by the Rockefeller interests' murderous
attacks on striking workers at Ludlow, Colorado (1914), and Bayonne, New
Jersey (1915), made union activities very difficult and indicated that the robber
barons in the oil industry would use every expedient from brutality to benevolent paternalism to subjugate their workers and keep trade unionism out. This
was the reality confronting union organizers as they marshalled their limited
financial resources in preparation for a major campaign against the millions of
the Rockefellers, Mellons, and other potentates of the petroleum industry.

Organization in the modern period of the industry began in the Spindletop
Field near Beaumont, Texas, where in 1905 oil workers struck to protest a 12
percent wage reduction. The conflict spread to nearby oil fields, and on December 14, the strikers organized Oil and Gas Well Workers Local 11998,
chartered as a federal labor union by the AFL. Nevertheless, effective large-
scale union organization awaited the World War I period. During the war
crisis, oil workers gained major concessions from the industry, including an
eight-hour day, increased wages, and at least tacit union recognition in California.

The growth of union organization during the war set the stage for another attempt to organize a national union. On June 8, 1918, a delegation of fourteen oil workers from California, Texas, Louisiana, and Oklahoma, meeting with the AFL executive council in St. Paul, Minnesota, requested an international charter. Hopes of obtaining an industrial union charter quickly disappeared. AFL president Gompers made it clear to the delegates "that in issuing a charter to your organization it shall in no way infringe upon the jurisdiction of any existing union or international union." Against the advice of Walter J. Yarrow, who had brilliantly managed the successful organizing effort in California, the delegation accepted the charter, and the International Association of Oil Field, Gas Well and Refinery Workers of America (OFGWRWA) was born. The perverse jurisdictional grant coupled with the continued hostility of the major oil companies doomed the new union to years of inter-union raids, jurisdictional conflicts, and obscurity.

Nevertheless, OFGWRWA began auspiciously enough, chartering over 100 locals and securing a membership of 30,000 by the end of 1919. But this war-time organizing bonanza, like so many others, evaporated quickly after the war. The union's decline began in 1922 and before the nadir was reached in 1933, the 30,000 of 1920 shrank to 300.

OFGWRWA made a remarkable recovery in 1933 and 1934 when President Harvey Fremming gained a thirty-six-hour week and minimum wages of forty-five to fifty-two cents an hour in the new National Recovery Administration (NRA) code for the petroleum industry adopted on August 19, 1933. With renewed faith in the union, oil field workers once again joined in large numbers. Moreover, during this organizing surge, an increasing number of refinery workers enrolled in the OFGWRWA. The climax of this resurgence came in the summer of 1934 when a national agreement was reached with the Sinclair Consolidated Oil Corporation, which, along with fringe benefits and wage concessions, granted a checkoff of union dues.

The OFGWRWA failed to maintain or consolidate its 1933-1934 successes. After a period of indecision inspired by the creation of the NRA with its intended labor safeguards and spurred on by the Supreme Court's invalidation of the NRA, the oil companies unleased a full-scale offensive against the unions. These problems were further complicated by the continual raids of AFL craft unions, which made the industrial union proposals of John L. Lewis especially attractive to OFGWRWA leaders; they became enthusiastic supporters of the movement leading to the creation of the Congress of Industrial Organizations* (CIO).

The year 1937 was a significant one for the OFGWRWA: the awkward union title was changed to the Oil Workers International Union; the Supreme Court upheld the constitutionality of the National Labor Relations Act; and the CIO, which became a functional reality, cooperated with the OWIU to launch the Petroleum Workers Organizing Committee. However, these encouraging developments were seriously mitigated by the unrelenting anti-union campaign of the major oil companies, the economic recession of 1937-1938, and a growing internal struggle between the established OWIU leadership and a rank-and-file revolt that ultimately resulted in a decisive victory for the insurgents. The dissidents succeeded in adopting their "workers' control" program in 1940, drastically reducing the power of elected officials and lodging much of the power in a seven member rank-and-file executive council. The insurgent slate, headed by O. A. Knight, was also elected when the older officers recognized the inevitable and withdrew their names from nomination.

The new regime's victory at the 1940 convention did not end internal conflicts. Critics of the new administration falsely charged that the leadership was dominated by Communists. Moreover, many of the older leaders defected to rival AFL unions (especially the International Union of Operating Engineers*), which exhibited a preference for raiding OWIU members to organizing the unorganized. Despite these difficulties, the union made major gains during World War II, demonstrating through a successful strike in 1945 that the oil companies could no longer unilaterally determine wage patterns in the petroleum industry.

The 1945-1955 period contains many paradoxes for the OWIU. The union made significant advances in organizing the workers within its jurisdiction, but total OWIU membership remained quite stable. Losses due to layoffs, terminations, and raids by other unions usually offset organizing gains as technological changes and an increase in oil imports steadily reduced the work force in the domestic petroleum industry. Moreover, the Operating Engineers, Teamsters,* and the United Gas, Coke and Chemical Workers of America* (UGCCW) were all challenging the OWIU in organizing workers in the petroleum industry. This profusion of unions in the industry and the existence of numerous independent organizations growing from the older company-established unions effectively prevented the development of industry-wide bargaining.

Attempting to cope with this chaotic situation, leaders of the OWIU reluctantly began to centralize an increasing degree of power in the international office. Hoping to resolve the jurisdictional confusion, O. A. Knight inspired the OWIU to initiate plans for the National Coalition of Oil Unions, a loose association of unions in the industry created to coordinate collective bargaining policies. Knight hoped this would be the first step in the merger of all unions in the field, but negotiations between the OWIU and several independent unions eventually failed. Finally, in 1955, the OWIU did succeed in effecting a merger with the UGCCW, resulting in the formation of the Oil, Chemical and Atomic Workers International Union.*

The OWIU, which maintained its national headquarters in Fort Worth, Texas, held annual conventions. Principal officers included a president, two vice-presidents, and a secretary-treasurer. The general executive council was composed of one delegate from each of the seven districts established by the convention, each elected by the district he represented. At the time of the merger with the UGCCW, the OWIU paid per-capita taxes to the CIO on 88,500 members.

For further information, see Harvey O'Connor, *History of the Oil Workers International Union* (1950), a popular history of the union from 1918 to 1950; Harry Seligson, *Oil, Chemical and Atomic Workers: A Labor Union in Action* (1960); and Melvin Rothbaum, *The Government of the Oil, Chemical, and Atomic Workers Union* (1962), a scholarly analysis of trade unionism in the petroleum industry.

ORGANIZACIÓN REGIONAL INTERAMERICANA DE TRABAJADORES (ORIT). At the January 1951 meeting in Mexico City, the American Federation of Labor* (AFL)-oriented Confederación Interamericana de Trabajadores* (CIT) converted itself into the Organización Regional Interamericana de Trabajadores, the Western Hemisphere branch of the International Confederation of Free Trade Unions (ICFTU). Twenty-nine organizations from twenty-one countries were represented. George Meany served as spokesman for the American delegation, and Sir Vincent Tewson, general secretary of the British Trade Union Congress, represented the ICFTU. Elected to posts of leadership were: Arturo Sabroso of Peru, president; Francisco Aguirre of Cuba, secretary; and an executive board broadly representative of the affiliated trade union centers. Serafino Romualdi of the AFL was named an assistant secretary. Headquarters were established at Havana and, in 1953, moved permanently to Mexico City with regional offices scattered throughout the hemisphere.

ORIT followed in succession the Pan-American Federation of Labor* (PAFL) and the CIT through four decades of trade union organizational efforts along hemispheric lines. Where the PAFL, founded in 1918, had concerned itself primarily with workers of Mexico, Central America, the Caribbean, and the United States, the CIT and ORIT were broadly pan-American. Their focus was no longer upon immigrant miners of the American Southwest or Cuban cigarmakers in the shops of Tampa, Key West, and New York City, but upon packinghouse workers in Argentina, garment makers in Colombia, runaway industries, and the competition of "cheap men" throughout the Americas. There were other changes too. Organizers for the PAFL traveled for days in hot and antiquated trains, by automobile and on horseback to remote mining camps of Sonora and Chihuahua or to the plantations of the Mexican South—eating common food and sleeping on the ground or in vermin-infested huts. Representatives of ORIT jetted from Bogotá to Lima and Buenos Aires and Rio de Janeiro, returning to air-conditioned suites in Washington or Mexico City. Gone were the storefront offices, the struggle to pay the printer for the union journal, the calls for working-class solidarity. Founders of the

PAFL had been Socialists or of Socialist background. ORIT was founded as part of an anti-Communist and anti-Socialist counterforce in world labor circles, and its ties to the American government were far more intimate than had been those of the PAFL.

Amid the splendor of the Palace of Fine Arts, Mexican president Miguel Aleman welcomed ORIT delegates to his nation's capital in January 1951. Almost at once, however, hostilities commenced. Fidel Velasquez of the Confederación de Trabajadores de Mexico (CTM), who had been elected permanent chairman of the conference, resigned in a dispute over recognition of Argentina's delegation. Louis Morones, leader of the Confederación Regional Obrero Mexicana (CROM), a co-founder of the PAFL and elder statesman of hemispheric labor, was denied access to the floor; and, as debate continued, the CTM announced its withdrawal from the conference and from the ICFTU. Thus, the major Mexican and Argentine trade union centers remained temporarily outside of ORIT. The Congress of Industrial Organizations* (CIO), the Canadian Congress of Labor, the Confederación de Trabajadores de Colombia, and several other federations affiliated; shortly thereafter, the CTM renewed its affiliation. ORIT soon boasted a membership of some 23 million workers, more than half of them enrolled in the AFL-CIO.*

At Mexico City, ORIT declared for the establishment of strong, democratic, free trade unions, pledging its assistance through educational and organizational programs, which were promptly instituted. The *Inter-American Labor Bulletin* was established as ORIT's official organ. A training center was set up in Mexico City, seminars for trade union leadership were conducted, correspondence courses were created, and organizer/lecturers were dispatched throughout the hemisphere. ORIT also declared its unconditional opposition to Communist aggression (and to leftist trade unions), to dictatorships of the right and left, and to military assistance for totalitarian regimes, and it endorsed the United Nations. Shortly, ORIT became associated with the struggle against oppression in Peru, Venezuela, Colombia, Nicaragua, Haiti, the Dominican Republic, Cuba, Paraguay, and Argentina, but it also became identified with the collapse of the governments of Jacobo Arbenz in Guatemala, Cheddi Jagan in British Guiana, Juan Bosch in the Dominican Republic, and Salvador Allende in Chile. Critics suggested that ORIT was too closely tied to the American Department of State. Indeed, some professed to see ties between AFL-CIO inter-American policy and the Central Intelligence Agency.

Since the early 1940s, Serafino Romualdi had been the dominant personality in inter-American trade union circles. He led the crusade against Perónista trade unions, was the central figure in both the CIT and ORIT and, ultimately, the chief spokesman for the AFL-CIO throughout the Americas. In the early 1960s, Romualdi retired and was replaced as AFL-CIO inter-American representative by Andrew McLellan. Together with William C. Doherty, Jr., Romualdi created the Washington-based American Institute for Free

Labor Development (AIFLD), an autonomous body funded jointly by organized labor, corporate contributions, foundation grants, and other sources. A training school for trade union leaders was established in Washington, D.C., and in Virginia, with subordinate centers in most of the friendly Latin American countries. Doherty headed the social projects division of the AIFLD— public housing, facilities development, and so on—and, for a period, the AIFLD in effect became the labor arm of the Alliance for Progress. While technically independent of ORIT, the work of the AIFLD in many ways paralleled that of ORIT, and there was interlocking leadership, although augmented by corporate and public representatives.

From its foundation, ORIT encountered a fierce intra-labor competition. From the right, the Perónista trade unions organized a counterfederation, the Agrupación de Trabajadores Latino Americano Sindicalizados (ATLAS). Its strength centered primarily in Argentina but drew upon groups throughout the hemisphere, most notably the CROM. Meanwhile, the Confederación de Trabajadores de America Latina (CTAL), founded by Mexican Marxist Vicente Lombardo Toledano in 1938, kept up a left-oriented opposition to ORIT, strengthened by the rise of Fidel Castro in Cuba and the defection from ORIT of the Confederación de Trabajadores de Cuba (CTC) in the late 1950s. Another equally serious challenge to the supremacy of ORIT was the creation of a regional affiliate of the International Federation of Christian Trade Unions (IFCTU), the Confederación Latino Americana de Sindicatos Cristianos (CLASC). Long a force in Europe, the Christian trade union movement had not been active in the Americas, but given the strongly Catholic orientation of the Latin American working classes and the equally strong Yankee-phobia, CLASC seemed a potentially serious competitor to ORIT.

The best study of the ORIT and of the related AIRFLD is Ronald Radosh, *American Labor and United States Foreign Policy* (1967), a highly critical account. See also Serafino Romualdi, *Presidents and Peons: Recollections of a Labor Ambassador in Latin America* (1967).

William G. Whittaker

PACKINGHOUSE, FOOD AND ALLIED WORKERS; UNITED (UPWA). Efforts to organize the meat-packing industry began during the second half of the nineteenth century; packinghouse workers actively participated in the activities of the Knights of Labor* and in the 1886 general strike for the eight-hour day. Nevertheless, a concerted drive to organize such workers did not begin until the Amalgamated Meat Cutters and Butcher Workmen of North America* (AMCBWNA) was chartered in 1897 by the American Federation of Labor* (AFL) with jurisdiction over packinghouse workers. Although the AMCBWNA made a serious effort to organize workers within its jurisdiction, disastrous strikes in 1904 and 1921 left the industry's employees largely unorganized when the Great Depression struck the nation in 1929.

Enactment of the National Industrial Recovery Act (NIRA) with its Section 7(a) labor provisions greatly stimulated interest in organizing packinghouse workers. The packinghouse branch of the AMCBWNA had become insignificant after the failure of the national strike in 1921, but its officials retained their commitment to organize packinghouse workers. They assumed that only renewed government intervention would facilitate a successful organizing campaign and counteract industry opposition. Section 7(a) promised to provide such governmental support.

Within six months of the enactment of NIRA, the AMCBWNA launched an organizing campaign in the nation's meat-packing centers. Packinghouse workers responded favorably, but, as was anticipated, employers resisted. Resorting to the company union tactic, they refused to negotiate with the Amalgamated. After the National Recovery Administration (NRA) proved unwilling or unable to force employer compliance, a number of local strikes were called in the spring and summer of 1934. Although many of these strikes were moderately successful, in most cases neither union recognition nor collective bargaining was achieved. Admitting defeat, by the early months of 1935 AMCBWNA officials dismantled the organizational committee, and the previous gains made in unionization of packinghouse workers quickly evaporated.

Employer resistance again had proven an insurmountable obstacle to organization. Moreover, the NRA period confronted the AMCBWNA with another hurdle: the organization of strong independent unions in several packinghouse districts. Such organizations appeared in Chicago, Austin, Minnesota, and Cedar Rapids, Iowa. These unions were not of great consequence in the industry, but their organization reflected a growing disillusionment with the ability of the Amalgamated to organize meat packers.

When the controversy over industrial unionism erupted in the AFL, the AMCBWNA, long favoring such organization, supported the minority position favored by the Committee for Industrial Organization* (CIO). The Amalgamated continued its support of the CIO even after the suspension of its members and the split in the national labor movement. When the AMCBWNA refused to leave the AFL, however, the CIO began to encourage rival organization. Finally, on October 24, 1937, the CIO announced the formation of the Packinghouse Workers Organizing Committee (PWOC). The independent unions, local industrial unions directly affiliated with the CIO, and a few secessionist AMCBWNA locals formed the nucleus of the new union.

The unionization of packinghouse workers became virtually inevitable after the favorable Supreme Court ruling on the constitutionality of the National Labor Relations Act (NLRA). The only remaining question concerned representation of the meat packers—the AMCBWNA, PWOC, or the semi-independent unions evolving from the company unions organized during the preceding two decades. A series of National Labor Relations Board (NLRB) decisions made it clear that employers would not be able to treat their employees in such a cavalier manner as they had under NRA.

The 1937-1938 recession retarded organizing efforts, but the two rival unions launched vigorous organizing drives among packinghouse workers in 1939. In this conflict, the PWOC's greatest asset was the long history of defeats that characterized its rival's efforts in the meat-packing industry. The reflected glow of the CIO's victories in the steel and automobile industries sparkled on the PWOC. The PWOC also profited from its sensitive efforts among black workers and immigrant groups, its close association with Democratic party organizations (especially in Chicago), and its provision for rank-and-file participation in union affairs. The CIO union had a reputation for militancy that appealed to the impatient packinghouse workers.

The PWOC, however, was not without its difficulties. As in earlier efforts to organize packinghouse workers, the movement was fragmented and splintered by a host of internal grievances and factional rivalries. Moreover local unions were difficult to control, and efforts of national leaders to do so created a full-scale revolt in 1941. As a result, J. C. Lewis replaced Van A. Bittner, the CIO-appointed chairman of the PWOC.

By the end of World War II, the great surge in the organization of the meat-packing industry subsided, and the PWOC could relish its victory. The CIO union won bargaining rights for the employees of the industry's "big four"— Armour, Swift, Cudahy, and Wilson—and most of the larger independent packers. The Amalgamated had its greatest success among medium-sized independents and the smaller production units of the larger packers.

Despite the intense rivalry that developed between the PWOC and the Amalgamated during the organizing wars of the early 1940s, leaders of both unions gradually recognized the interdependence of the two unions in collective bargaining. While inter-union cooperation was not particularly advantageous to either side during the war, the reemployment of the strike as the union's principal weapon after the war virtually necessitated closer cooperation.

The conversion of the PWOC into a fully chartered national union, the United Packinghouse Workers of America (UPWA), enhanced the possibilities of collective bargaining cooperation between the two unions. An agreement to share the national offices between the union's Communist-dominated left wing and the non-Communist administration made possible the organization of the new union. Although the agreement failed to end factional rivalries in the UPWA, there could be little doubt that the UPWA had arrived as a formidable force in the meat-packing industry, one with which the leaders of the AMCBWNA would have to work.

The two unions cooperated to a limited extent during a successful strike in 1946, and their failure to cooperate in a similar strike two years later proved expensive, especially to the UPWA, which lost a bitter ten-week strike and was forced to accept the same terms negotiated without a strike by the AMCBWNA. Furthermore, the strike failure intensified left- and right-wing factional rivalries that nearly erupted into a revolt against the leadership. Although the UPWA quickly recovered from both its external and internal difficulties, the entire 1948 experience illustrated the need for closer cooperation with the Amalgamated. Despite some further acrimony in 1951, an agreement was signed on June 23, 1953, containing the outline for closer negotiating unity and a no-raiding clause to facilitate inter-union cooperation.

A host of technological innovations and new processing and marketing decisions greatly altered the nature of the meat-packing industry during the 1950s. Technological changes sharply increased labor productivity but ultimately reduced employment. The meat-packing industry also became highly decentralized as a result of the dispersion of livestock sources, the increased development of motorized transportation, and changing marketing requirements. Many of these changes worked to the disadvantage of the UPWA, which reached a membership peak during the mid-1950s and then began a slow decline.

As early as 1953 a merger between the two rival unions was discussed by leaders of both unions. The national AFL-CIO* merger in 1955 greatly stimulated this interest, but in 1956 such efforts were frustrated. Nevertheless, the two unions continued their close cooperation in collective bargaining.

After the failure of the merger effort, the UPWA gradually expanded its organizational reach beyond the packinghouse worker jurisdiction. Resulting from this expansion, in 1960 the union title was changed to the United Packinghouse, Food and Allied Workers. Until a merger was finally negotiated in 1968, UPWA continued to lose ground to the AMCBWNA, one of the few unions to expand its membership during the 1950s.

The UPWA, which maintained its national headquarters in Chicago, held annual conventions. Principal officers included a president, two vice-presidents, a secretary-treasurer, and a district director for each geographical district. The UPWA executive board was composed of national officers and district directors. At the time of the merger with the AMCBWNA, the UPWA had a membership of 68,000.

For further information, see *The Packinghouse Worker* published weekly by the UPWA. David Brody's *The Butcher Workmen: A Study of Unionization* (1964) contains a solid analysis of the emergence of the UPWA and its subsequent relationship with the AMCBWNA. Walter Galenson, *The CIO Challenge to the AFL: A History of the American Labor Movement, 1935-1941* (1960), also discusses the early union conflict in the meat-packing industry.

PAINTERS AND ALLIED TRADES OF THE UNITED STATES AND CANADA; INTERNATIONAL BROTHERHOOD OF (IBP&AT). Unionization of house painters reaches back to the early years of the nineteenth century, but leaders of the local unions that periodically appeared in the trade retained an essentially local outlook and exhibited little interest in unifying the scattered locals into a national union. Extensive organizing and the creation of a permanent national union in the painters' trade in the United States awaited the emergence of the Knights of Labor* (KofL). For the first time the painting trade became well organized as workers in the trade flocked into KofL local assemblies; yet the painters had a strong craft orientation and soon became restive in the Knights' heterogeneous assemblies. Consequently a local union of Baltimore painters issued a call for a national conference of painter unions, both independent and KofL, to meet in the Maryland city on March 15, 1887. Delegates representing thirteen local unions with a membership of 600 responded, and as a result of their discussions, agreed to the organization of a national union, the Brotherhood of Painters and Decorators. Three years later leaders of the brotherhood decided to organize paperhangers and changed the union's name to Brotherhood of Painters, Decorators, and Paperhangers of America (BPD&PA).

A regional and geographical schism in the BPD&PA threatened the prospects of the new union. By 1894 the BPD&PA had dissolved into two hostile factions, both claiming to be the legitimate national union. The resulting dual unionism disrupted trade organization in the craft for nearly six years. Conflicts over the location of the permanent national headquarters, which until 1894 had been in the founding city of Baltimore, first signaled the bitterness of the sectional divisions in the union. Ultimately the western group established its headquarters in Lafayette, Indiana, and the original eastern unions continued to recognize Baltimore as their headquarters' city. Both groups sent delegates to the national American Federation of Labor* (AFL) convention in 1894, thus confronting the AFL for the first time in its brief existence with the task of judging the legitimacy of rival claims to union recognition in a single trade jurisdiction. AFL leaders sought to mediate the differences between the two factions but for several years failed to reach a compromise settlement acceptable to both sides. Meanwhile, the Lafayette group, organizing aggressively, soon outgrew the parent organization and increasingly became the dominant union in the industry. Finally through the auspices of the AFL, an agreement was negotiated in 1900 providing for the reunification of the BPD&PA on terms dictated largely by the western insurgents. Reflecting the dominance of the western branch, union headquarters of the reunited union were established in Lafayette.

The BPD&PA affiliated with the AFL on December 1, 1887, and maintained a volatile relationship with federation leaders during its early years. Resulting from a dispute over the organization of paperhangers, the brotherhood withdrew from the AFL in February 1891, but the conflict was resolved the following year and the BPD&PA was reinstated. During the factional struggles of the 1890s, the AFL suspended the eastern BPD&PA (which it had continued to recognize) in accordance with the instructions of the 1899 national convention. After the resolution of the factional conflict, the BPD&PA was reinstated in 1900. Thereafter, relations between the brotherhood and the leadership of the AFL became more amicable.

Following its formation in 1887, the brotherhood continually expanded its jurisdictional reach. Originally established as a union of house painters and decorators, the organizing reach of the BPD&PA was extended to encompass all workers in the painting, paperhanging, and decorative arts trades. Simultaneously the BPD&PA absorbed a number of independent unions, including the United Scenic Artists, National Paperhangers' Association, and the National Union of Sign Painters. On October 1, 1915, the BPD&PA merged with the Amalgamated Glass Workers International Association, a small union of stained and decorative glass workers chartered by the AFL on September 25, 1900. Finally the BPD&PA gained jurisdiction over the unorganized workers employed by paint and varnish manufacturers in 1934 and over linoleum, carpet, and soft tile laying in 1935. The present union title was adopted in 1969.

The Brotherhood of Painters grew spectacularly during the years immediately following its formation. Within a year the original membership of 600 organized into thirteen unions expanded to 7,000 workers in 111 local unions, and by 1890 membership approached 10,000. The depression of the 1890s and the divisive factional conflicts within the brotherhood slowed but failed to halt organizing progress. At the time of the reunification of the brotherhood in 1900, the BPD&PA paid per-capita taxes to the AFL on nearly 30,000 members. Organizing success continued during the first two decades of the twentieth century, and BPD&PA membership surpassed 100,000 by the end of World War I. Although dramatic organizing gains ended during the 1920s, the brotherhood managed to maintain its previous gains and register small membership increases.

The economic consequences of the Great Depression of the 1930s reversed the BPD&PA's growth curve, accomplishing what the employer offensive of the 1920s had failed to achieve. The brotherhood lost nearly half of its membership by the mid-1930s, but beginning in 1936, the BPD&PA growth curve turned upward again, a positive trend that continued until the mid-1950s when membership stabilized at about 200,000.

Although negotiations with employers in the trade were not unusually disruptive, in an effort to provide more orderly bargaining procedures following the depression, the BPD&PA executive board assisted employers in the formation of the Painting and Decorating Contractors of America. The new employer organization established local chapters in each large city, and the BPD&PA recognized these units as the legitimate employers' bargaining agent in the locality. The brotherhood also cooperated with employers in the establishment of local trade boards composed of five employers and five employees, as well as a national trade board also composed of five employer and employee representatives. The trade boards provided a mediational and arbitrational forum for resolving disputes between unions and contractors.

The IBP&AT, which maintains its national headquarters in Washington, D.C., holds quinquennial conventions. Principal officers include a general president, seven vice-presidents, and a secretary-treasurer. The above officials also constitute the general executive board. In 1973 the IBP&AT reported a membership of 207,844 located in 950 local unions.

For further information, see the *Painters & Allied Trades Journal* issued monthly by the IBP&AT. See also Philip Zausner, *Unvarnished: The Autobiography of a Union Leader* (1941), an interesting account of the trials of a union leader written by a former IBP&AT secretary-treasurer. Philip Taft, *The A.F. of L. in the Time of Gompers* (1957), has a good discussion of the dual union period. Information can also be found in *The American Federationist* (September 1950), and *Bulletin No. 618*, Bureau of Labor Statistics, U.S. Department of Labor (1936).

PAN-AMERICAN FEDERATION OF LABOR (PAFL). On November 13, 1918, just two days after the armistice in Europe ending World War I, the founding conference of the Pan-American Federation of Labor convened at Laredo, Texas. Attending were delegates from the United States, Mexico, Guatemala, Costa Rica, El Salvador, Colombia, and Puerto Rico. The Laredo conference established an institutional structure through which inter-American trade union solidarity might be achieved and through which the workers of the Americas might inject a humane influence into inter-American relations, notably the work of the Pan-American Union—and, most significantly, a device through which peace might be maintained among the American nations. The conference elected as the first officers of the PAFL: president, Samuel Gompers, American Federation of Labor* (AFL); vice-president, Luis Morones, Confederación Regional Obrera Mexicana (CROM); English language secretary, John Murray of California, International Typographical Union;* Canuto Vargas of Arizona, International Union of Mine, Mill and Smelter Workers,* Spanish language secretary; and, later by appointment, James Lord, president of the mining department, AFL, as treasurer. Subsequent conferences were held in New York City, 1919; Mexico City, 1921; Mexico City, 1924; Washington, 1927; Havana, 1930; and New Orleans, 1940.

Creation of the PAFL was largely the work of two men: Santiago Iglesias, president of the Federación Libre de los Trabajadores de Puerto Rico, and John Murray—working together with Samuel Gompers. Since 1900, Iglesias had conducted a continuing campaign within the AFL for closer pan-American trade union ties. He wrote, spoke, lobbied within the AFL's executive council and, most important, conveyed to American labor the image of a competent, articulate, immensely talented, "pure and simple" trade unionist who was also Spanish speaking. Iglesias's focus, however, was Puerto Rico, Cuba, and the Spanish-speaking workers of the eastern United States. His contacts were essentially with the eastern trade union establishment.

In 1907 Murray, editor of the Los Angeles Central Labor Council journal *The Citizen*, became involved in the cause of the Mexican exiles, persecuted even within the United States by Mexican dictator Porfirio Díaz. By early 1908, Murray had resigned his editorship to work full time in defense of the exiles. In this effort, he had substantial assistance from others within the western Socialist-trade union community, among them: California Socialist leader and labor lawyer Job Harriman; "Mother" Mary Harris Jones, associated with both the Western Federation of Miners* and the United Mine Workers of America* (UMWA); James Lord, with the UMWA in Illinois; and William B. Wilson, UMWA secretary-treasurer. Murray's focus was Mexican, western and socialist-labor.

While Iglesias was covering the first Pan-American Financial Conference in 1915 for the AFL, he and Murray met and discussed their ideas for a pan-American trade union organization. Together, Iglesias and Murray met with Lord and later with Gompers. The AFL president concurred in the need for such an organization, shared the vision of Murray and Iglesias, and the movement was launched. Systematically Gompers began to collect data concerning conditions in Mexico and Mexican-American relations, then exceedingly strained. Murray traveled to Mexico on a fact-finding mission and to do a series of articles for the *New York Call*, edited by his friend Chester M. Wright. Carefully the foundations for the PAFL were being laid; the eastern and western advocates of pan-American trade union solidarity were now working in tandem.

During the summer of 1916, the potential of Mexican-American trade union cooperation was dramatically demonstrated. In late June an American military force, sent into northern Mexico without legal sanction to capture Pancho Villa, met with defeat at Carrizal, a body of Americans being taken prisoner. War seemed imminent. Murray, working closely with Mexican trade union and political interests, appealed to Gompers to act to save the peace. Following a conference with Woodrow Wilson and others, Gompers cabled Mexican president Venustiano Carranza urging that the Americans be released and war prevented. Within hours, the prisoners were released and Carranza wired the news to Gompers—before advising the Department of State. Whatever the role of labor in averting war with Mexico, American labor believed that Gompers's intervention had been decisive. The thrust was provided to clear away internal AFL opposition to closer ties with Mexican labor (primarily voiced by Catholic trade unionists), and work actively commenced.

Preparations for the Laredo conference moved forward. Two Mexican trade unionists. Baltasar Pages and Carlos Loveira of Yucatán, were dispatched on a goodwill mission throughout the Americas. Late in 1916, a conference committee was appointed with Gompers as chairman and Murray and Iglesias as members. In May 1918 Murray, Iglesias, and Lord were sent to Mexico to consolidate ties between the AFL and the newly formed CROM. Finally in August, *The Pan-American Labor Press* commenced publication in San Antonio, Texas, with Murray as editor—continuing publication through December 1918. Throughout the period leading up to the Laredo conference, Gompers had become increasingly involved in war-related activities and Iglesias with political developments relating to Puerto Rico. Thus primary responsibility rested with Murray.

The six years following the Laredo conference were ones of steady growth. Delegations from the Dominican Republic and Nicaragua came to play an important role in PAFL activities. Peruvian labor affiliated. The PAFL took up the international migration of labor, sought a voice for the workers within the Pan-American Union and other inter-American bodies, opposed American intervention in the internal affairs of the Central American and Caribbean nations, and denounced "dollar diplomacy." It became a continuing force for peace between the United States and Mexico—with serious consequences at the time of the Adolfo de la Huerta revolt in 1923 and 1924. Late in 1924, the AFL convention met in El Paso, the CROM convention across the river in Juarez, Mexico. When the sessions were over, an AFL party of about 300 boarded special trains to visit Mexico City for the inauguration of Mexican president-elect Plutarco Elías Calles. There, Gompers was to preside at the fourth convention of the PAFL. It was the culmination of Gompers's career and the peak of inter-American trade union cooperation.

Taken ill at Mexico City, Gompers died in San Antonio in December 1924. PAFL and AFL leadership fell to William Green of the UMWA, a man of rather limited vision. In early 1925, Vargas became labor attaché at the Mexican embassy in Washington, being replaced as Spanish-language secretary by Iglesias who was already overburdened with his legislative and trade union duties in Puerto Rico. Murray, who had died in 1919, was replaced as English-language secretary by Chester Wright, the one man with the experience, interest, and time to carry on the work Murray, Iglesias, and Gompers had begun. Wright left the AFL early in 1925, shortly after Green assumed control, and resigned his PAFL duties in 1927. Immigration problems, new complications with the Mexican Church, shifts in the Mexican political and trade union power structure, and the deepening depression all added to the decline of the PAFL. The coup de grace was the death of Iglesias in 1939.

The best study of the PAFL is Sinclair Snow, *The Pan-American Federation of Labor* (1964). See also Ethel Duffy Turner, *Ricardo Flores Magón y el Partido Liberal Mexicano* (1960); Harvey A. Levenstein, *Labor Organizations in the United States and Mexico: A History of Their Relations* (1971); and

Moises Poblete Troncoso and Ben G. Burnett, *The Rise of the Latin American Labor Movement* (1960).

William G. Whittaker

PAPER MAKERS; INTERNATIONAL BROTHERHOOD OF. *See* United Paperworkers International Union.

PAPERMAKERS AND PAPERWORKERS; UNITED. *See* United Paperworkers International Union.

PAPERWORKERS INTERNATIONAL UNION; UNITED (UPIU). On August 2, 1972, the United Papermakers and Paperworkers and the International Brotherhood of Pulp, Sulphite and Paper Mill Workers of the United States and Canada* merged to form the United Paperworkers International Union. The merger climaxed a trend toward trade union consolidation in the paper industry initiated shortly after the merger of the American Federation of Labor* (AFL) and Congress of Industrial Organizations* (CIO) in 1955.

A profusion of national labor organizations appeared in the industry beginning in the late 1930s. Overlapping jurisdictions and inter-union rivalries resulted, inhibiting the development of stable trade unionism and detracting from effective collective bargaining. Efforts to rationalize labor organization in the paper industry ultimately led to the merger of the United Paperworkers of America (UPA), CIO, and the International Brotherhood of Paper Makers (IBPM), AFL, on March 6, 1957, creating the United Papermakers and Paperworkers (UPP). The merging unions had waged a bitter struggle for dominance in the paper industry during the 1940s but informal cooperation during the early 1950s eventually led to amalgamation.

International Brotherhood of Paper Makers. Trade unionism in the pulp and paper industry began relatively late. The first known trade organization in the industry was organized by machine tenders in Holyoke, Massachusetts, who organized Eagle Lodge, a fraternal and beneficial society, in 1884. Membership was restricted to machine tenders, the aristocrats of the industry's labor force. The organization gradually assumed more interest in working conditions. Low wages characterized employment in the highly competitive paper industry, but of even greater concern were the long hours of labor. Typically the mills operated two shifts—eleven hours during the day and thirteen hours at night. The mills operated continuously from midnight Sunday until midnight the following Saturday. When efforts to gain some relief from these long hours failed in the state legislature, Eagle Lodge converted itself into an economic trade union and initiated a campaign to organize the trade. Its efforts met with considerable success in New York and Wisconsin, and on May 19, 1893, the organization was chartered by the AFL as the United Brotherhood of Paper Makers. The new union's jurisdiction was limited to machine tenders and beater engineers.

After a few organizing achievements, the UBPM began to disintegrate and by 1897 was reduced to three active locals. In an effort to revive the moribund organization, the UBPM petitioned the AFL for a broader jurisdiction encompassing the entire papermaking trade. The AFL issued the desired charter to the United Brotherhood of Paper Makers of America (UBPMA) on July 10, 1897, but the machine tenders soon became restive in the expanded organization and in 1898 broke with the UBPMA and founded the International Paper Machine Tenders Union (IPMTU). Weakened by its small membership base, the Machine Tenders found it necessary to again expand its jurisdiction. On June 17, 1902, the UBPMA and IPMTU merged and received an AFL charter as the International Brotherhood of Paper Makers.

Meanwhile, organization of semiskilled and unskilled workers in the pulp industry began at Fort Edward, New York, where an AFL federal labor union, Labour's Protective Union No. 9259, was chartered. Organization quickly spread to other areas in New York as well as Massachusetts, Vermont, New Hampshire, and Maine, and by 1903 unionization had expanded so rapidly that an AFL international charter was requested. Doubting the ability of unskilled and semiskilled pulp worker locals to govern themselves, Samuel Gompers and the AFL executive council decided to include the pulp workers in the IBPM, which was then renamed the International Brotherhood of Paper Makers, Pulp, Sulphite and Paper Mill Workers (IBPMPSPMW).

The IBPMPSPMW, however, treated the pulp work locals as second-class members. In 1906 the pulp workers seceded, initiating a two-year war between both factions before a treaty was negotiated in 1909 and a separate AFL charter issued to the International Brotherhood of Pulp, Sulphite and Paper Mill Workers* (IBPSPWM).

As a result of this conflict, both unions were on the verge of collapse when the treaty was signed. A successful twelve-week strike against the International Paper Company in 1910 aided the recuperation of both unions. Nevertheless the IBPM remained a small union largely failing to organize its trade jurisdiction until the post-New Deal years. The IBPM's relations with the International Paper Company, the largest papermaker in the industry, typify the union's problems in the industry. In 1921 the International Paper Company began an open-shop offensive that resulted in a futile five-year strike. The International Paper Company operated as an open-shop employer until 1937.

The Great Depression further plagued the IBPM; by 1932 membership had dropped to 4,000. However, enactment of the National Industrial Recovery Act in 1933 and the National Labor Relations Act in 1935 quickly revived the debilitated union. The International Paper Company recognized the IBPM in

1937, and a year later the union made substantial gains in Canada and launched its first successful foray into the South. The only cloud on the IBPM's horizon was the rivalry of the United Paperworkers of America, an outgrowth of the CIO Paper Workers Organizing Committee established in 1944. The IBPM held its own in the rivalry with the CIO affiliate and continued to expand its membership, reaching 50,000 by the end of World War II and 75,000 by the time of the AFL-CIO* merger in 1955.

The IBPM, which maintained its national headquarters in Albany, New York, held biennial conventions. Full-time officers included a president and secretary-treasurer. The executive board was composed of the full-time officers and seven vice-presidents elected by membership referendums every two years. At the time of the merger with the UPA, the IBPM had a membership of 80,300.

United Paperworkers of America. The large-scale, industrial organizing campaigns the CIO conducted during the second half of the 1930s caught up numerous workers in the paper industry. First assigned to local industrial unions, a steady increase in these members encouraged CIO officials, who were interested in expanding their activities in the pulp and paper industry, to elevate the status of paper workers. Consequently in 1940 the local industrial unions in the paper industry were assigned to the United International Union, Paper, Novelty and Toy Workers (UIUPNTW), which had been chartered two years earlier as the International Union, Playthings and Novelty Workers of America.

Although the UIUPNTW exhibited considerable vitality, doubling its original 1938 base membership of 5,000 by 1940 and redoubling it by 1943, internal conflicts between the toymakers and paper workers convinced CIO officials of the advisability of dividing the workers into two separate unions. Consequently, on January 1, 1944, a charter was issued to the Paper Workers Organizing Committee (PWOC), and it was assigned 12,000 members and seventy-eight local unions previously affiliated with the UIUPNTW. Reflecting the importance with which the CIO viewed the new organizing effort, Secretary-Treasurer James Carey, David J. McDonald of the United Steelworkers,* and Rolland J. Thomas of the United Automobile Workers* were assigned to work with Allan S. Haywood, appointed PWOC organizing director by CIO president Philip Murray.

A few months after its organization the PWOC scored one of its most impressive organizing achievements when it defeated two well-established AFL unions, the IBPM and the International Brotherhood of Pulp, Sulphite and Paper Mill Workers, in an NLRB representation election among the employees of the West Virginia Pulp and Paper Company. The West Virginia victory represented the PWOC's first significant success in the organization of basic pulp and paper workers.

The PWOC, which developed an elaborate system of voluntary organizers, steadily increased its membership, reaching 24,000 in 1946 and nearly 33,000 a year later. By 1946 organization in the industry succeeded to the point that CIO officials rechartered the PWOC as the United Paperworkers of America. Nevertheless, the UPA was a latecomer to the industry, and it generally failed to dislodge the older, well-entrenched AFL, which had already secured contracts with most of the larger corporations in the paper industry before the chartering of the UPA. The UPA was also somewhat limited by the radical reputation of the CIO and the tendency of some companies in the industry to prefer negotiating with more conservative AFL unions.

Like most other unions in the paper industry, the UPA, although willing to strike when necessary, preferred peaceful collective bargaining negotiations. UPA officials also placed considerable interest in political affairs and actively participated in the CIO political action committee. Conversely, the UPA adopted a hard-line, anti-Communist posture in the ideological wars that consumed the CIO during the late 1940s, and UPA president Harry Sayre served on the committees that investigated Communist influence in various CIO unions. On March 6, 1957, the UPA merged with the IBPM to create the United Papermakers and Paperworkers.

The UPA, which held annual conventions, maintained its national headquarters in Cleveland. Full-time officers included the president and secretary-treasurer. The general executive council was comprised of the above officers in addition to six area directors. At the time of the UPP merger, the UPA had a membership of 40,000.

The UPP and IBPSPMW dominated trade unionism in the paper industry from 1957 until their merger in 1972, creating the UPIU. The most significant development during these years was the alienation of many West Coast locals in the pulp and paper industry. The dissident locals organized the Association of Western Pulp and Paper Workers,* which in 1964 won NLRB representational elections in forty-nine western pulp and paper mills.

The UPIU, which maintains its national headquarters in Flushing, New York, holds triennial conventions. Principal officers include the president, secretary, and treasurer. The international executive board is comprised of the above officers in addition to the vice-presidents. In 1973 the UPIU reported a membership of 389,427 located in 1,600 local unions.

For further information, see the *Paper Makers Journal* published bimonthly by the IBPM, the UPA's monthly *Paperworkers News*, and *The Paperworker* issued monthly by the UPIU. The best source on trade unionism in the paper industry is Harry E. Graham, *The Paper Rebellion: Development and Upheaval in Pulp and Paper Unionism* (1970). See also Irving Brotslaw, "Trade Unionism in the Pulp and Paper Industry" (Ph.D. dissertation, University of Wisconsin, 1964); James A. Gross, "The Making and Shaping of Unionism in the Pulp and Paper Industry," *Labor History* (Spring 1964); and the *AFL-CIO American Federationist* (July 1956).

PAPERWORKERS OF AMERICA; UNITED. *See* United Paperworkers International Union.

PATTERN MAKERS' LEAGUE OF NORTH AMERICA (PMLNA). Thirteen pattern makers representing nine Knights of Labor* local unions assembled in Philadelphia on May 18, 1887, and organized the Pattern Makers' League of North America. Claiming jurisdiction over "all practical pattern makers," the new organization grew steadily. The first issue of the *Pattern Makers' Journal*, the title adopted in 1894, was published in 1891. The PMLNA received a charter from the American Federation of Labor* (AFL) on September 4, 1894, and has been continuously affiliated since.

Although exhibiting a healthy growth rate, the PMLNA obviously was destined to remain a small union of specialized workers. Recognizing this fact, its leaders exhibited an unusual interest in developing a federation of related metal trades unions. As a result of PMLNA initiatives, local federations of allied metal trades were established in several cities in 1892, but these organizations failed to survive the depression of the mid-1890s. In 1894 the league joined the National Federation of Metal Trades, but that organization also collapsed, succumbing to lagging interest in 1896. Finally, the PMLNA was a charter member of the AFL metal trades department, organized in 1908, and has played an active role in its affairs through the years.

Other than its interest in such usual trade union activities as higher wages and improved working conditions, which the PMLNA usually sought in conjunction with other metal trades unions, league officials devoted much time to the campaign for a shorter workday. A nine-hour campaign was launched by a strike in Boston in 1898 and quickly spread to other areas. Although this agitation for shorter hours was generally successful, three years after the Boston strike the PMLNA still had seventeen locals on strike for the nine-hour day. The league lost its first extended campaign for an eight-hour day. In cooperation with other metal trades unions, the league struck in Los Angeles after employers refused to institute an eight-hour day. The strike lasted almost two years and ended in total defeat for the unions.

While it conducted militant campaigns for economic concessions from employers, the PMLNA also initiated a number of beneficial programs. Shortly after its founding, the league established tool insurance and strike benefit funds. In 1898 a sickness and death benefit fund was inaugurated, and two years later the PMLNA initiated a retirement pension system, but after several years the costs of the pensions became excessive and the program was abandoned.

After suffering some membership losses resulting from the depression of the

1890s and although still a comparatively small national union, during the first two decades of the twentieth century the PMLNA grew at a rate of approximately 5 percent a year, reaching a membership peak of over 9,000 shortly after World War I. Thereafter, enrollment dropped to slightly over 7,000 where it remained constant through the 1920s and the early years of the Great Depression.

The greatest threat to the PMLNA's existence came with the emergence of the Congress of Industrial Organizations* (CIO) and the inauguration of massive industrial organizing campaigns, especially in the steel and automobile industries. These organizing drives swallowed up numerous workers claimed by the PMLNA. As a consequence, league membership fell to nearly 2,000 in 1937 before again turning upward. Ultimately, however, the PMLNA benefited from the intensified union activity of the late 1930s, and by the end of World War II, its membership stood at 11,000, surpassing its previous World War I high. Thereafter, membership fluctuated slightly from year to year but remained fairly constant near 10,000.

The PMLNA, which maintains its national headquarters in Washington, D.C., holds quinquennial conventions. The president, the only full-time officer, and four other members elected at national conventions constitute the general executive board. In 1973 the PMLNA reported a membership of 11,311 located in eighty-two local unions.

For further information, see the *Pattern Makers' Journal* published bimonthly by the PMLNA. Although the PMLNA has not attracted much scholarly attention, useful information can be found in *Bulletin No. 618*, Bureau of Labor Statistics, U.S. Department of Labor (1936), and Lloyd G. Reynolds and Charles C. Killingsworth, *Trade Union Publications* (1944).

PAVING CUTTERS' UNION OF THE UNITED STATES OF AMERICA AND CANADA (IPCU). Representatives of stone paving block cutters from several cities met in Baltimore in 1887 and organized a national union of paving cutters. Within a few years the new union had thoroughly organized the trade. However, an extensive lockout throughout New England in 1892 plus the beginning of the depression of 1893 combined to destroy the union. After the disintegration of the national union, IPCU locals surviving the imbroglio requested and received charters from the American Federation of Labor* (AFL) as directly affiliated federal labor unions. Several of those federal locals met in Lithonia, Georgia, on August 3, 1901, and reorganized the IPCU.

The IPCU grew steadily in the years following its chartering, reaching a membership peak of 3,500 in 1912 and stabilizing there for several years before beginning a gradual decline. Resulting from a jurisdictional dispute, the IPCU withdrew from the AFL on December 17, 1937, and remained independent thereafter. Changing methods and materials in road and street construction, however, constantly reduced employment in the IPCU trade jurisdiction, and in 1955 it finally disbanded.

The IPCU, which maintained its national headquarters in Rockport, Massachusetts, did not hold national conventions but instead conducted its business through referendum votes. The president was the only full-time official. The board of directors was composed of the president and one representative from each of the union's six districts. At the time it disbanded, the IPCU had fewer than 100 members.

For further information, see the *Paving Cutters' Journal* published by the IPCU from 1912 to 1939. Scholarly accounts of the IPCU's history were not located, but information can be found in *Bulletin No. 618*, Bureau of Labor Statistics, U.S. Department of Labor (1936), and Florence Peterson, *Handbook of Labor Unions* (1944).

PHOTO ENGRAVERS UNION OF NORTH AMERICA; INTERNATIONAL. *See* Lithographers and Photoengravers International Union.

PLANT GUARD WORKERS OF AMERICA; INTERNATIONAL UNION, UNITED (UPGWA). The industrial warfare that gripped mass production industries in the United States during the 1930s created a dilemma for one group of workers, those employed to protect plants and shops. Plant guards often suffered from the same low wages, poor working conditions, job insecurity, and management abuses that had radicalized production workers. Moreover, management considered plant guards to be vital weapons in the effort to crush labor organizations.

Following the example of production workers, within a few years plant guards began to form their own unions, often organized within existing maintenance or production unions. The largest and most militant guard locals were organized by the United Automobile Workers* (UAW). Management's response to the organization of plant guards was even more hostile than its response to the unionization of production workers. Employers argued that as part of the management structure, guards had no legitimate claims to collective bargaining. After the fallacy of this argument was successfully established in the courts, company officials then used a variety of tactics to avoid bargaining in good faith.

Efforts to organize plant guards flagged during World War II, but economic dislocations after the war stimulated renewed interest in organization. Moreover, after considerable indecision, the National Labor Relations Board (NLRB) ruled favorably on the status of guard locals and ordered management to bargain with them. The companies responded in typical fashion by ignoring the NLRB decision and refusing to bargain. A series of strikes resulted in which production workers respected guard locals' picket lines, thus virtually ensuring success.

Just as it appeared that plant guards had finally established their legal authority to organize and had succeeded in gaining recognition, the enactment of the Taft-Hartley Act confused matters. Most plant guard locals had been organized within industrial unions, and under Section 9(B)(3) of the act it became illegal for protection workers to organize in the same unions as production workers. Faced with this new challenge, leaders of various plant guard locals acted quickly. They immediately called a meeting of guard locals with the objective of establishing a national union.

At its November 1947 convention, the UAW, with which most guard locals were affiliated, endorsed the formation of an international union of plant guards within the Congress of Industrial Organizations* (CIO). With the cooperation of the CIO, representatives of locals from New York, Michigan, Indiana, California, and Maryland organized the Plant Guards Organizing Committee (PGOC) in February 1948. The PGOC then sought recognition from the NLRB as the collective bargaining agent for plant guards. But disaster struck again. In a case involving the Cadillac Division of the General Motors Corporation, the NLRB ruled that as a CIO affiliate, the PGOC was indirectly affiliated with production unions, and, therefore, under the provisions of the Taft-Hartley Act, it could not be certified as a collective bargaining unit by the NLRB.

The decision left the guard locals more isolated and their legal status more confused than at any other time since organizing began nearly a decade earlier. Refusing to be stopped by legal technicalities, local leaders immediately set about the difficult task of founding an independent international union of plant guards. Forty-eight hours before the NLRB decision was published, a new constitution was written, membership cards were issued, and PGOC locals were polled to secure their approval of the new union. Consequently at the time the NLRB publicly issued its decision killing the PGOC, James McGahey, newly elected president of the 1,250-member United Plant Guard Workers of America, formally requested NLRB recognition. This was granted a day later on June 4, 1948.

Within sixty days of its formation, the new union confronted its first major crisis. Ignoring the UPGWA's NLRB certification, the Briggs Manufacturing Company of Detroit refused to bargain with the plant guards' union. UPGWA president McGahey called the guards out on strike and established a picket line. The success of the strike was ensured when UAW production workers refused to cross the picket line. Before Briggs agreed to bargain sixteen days later, over 200,000 workers had been idled by the strike.

Although the UPGWA needed to resort to strikes in later years, the Briggs victory convinced most employers that collective bargaining was the most practical method of dealing with their protection workers. At the same time, the UPGWA gradually expanded its original stronghold in the automotive industry to include protection workers in such industries as steel, chemicals, and rubber. In 1950 the UPGWA signed its first major agreement with contract guard agencies, and in 1958 it organized its first Canadian locals.

The UPGWA, which holds conventions every five years, maintains its national headquarters in East Detroit. The principal officers include a president, vice-president, and secretary-treasurer. The international executive board consists of the above officers and nine regional directors nominated and elected by local unions from designated regions. In 1973 the UPGWA reported a membership of 20,000 located in 140 local unions.

For further information, see the *Guard News* issued bimonthly and *UPGWA*, a short history of the union published by the International Union.

PLASTERERS' AND CEMENT MASONS' INTERNATIONAL ASSOCIATION OF THE UNITED STATES AND CANADA; OPERATIVE (OP&CMIA). Local unions of plasterers began to appear in American cities at least as early as the 1820s and early 1830s. Most of these unions disappeared during the depression following the panic of 1837, but organization resumed on a broad scale during the 1850s. Shortly before the end of the Civil War the first national union of plasterers, the National Plasterers' Organization of the United States, made its debut on the American labor scene. But after nearly a decade of activity, the Plasterers' Organization, victimized by the depression of the 1870s, disintegrated. The union reorganized during the following decade and in 1889 adopted the title Operative Plasterers International Association of the United States and Canada (OPIA).

Besides gaining union recognition and winning bargaining concessions from employers, one of the more perplexing problems the plasterers' national union encountered involved the obscure jurisdictional division separating the bricklayers and plasterers. During the decade of the 1860s, the National Plasterers' Organization reached an agreement with the National Union of Bricklayers, a forerunner of the Bricklayers, Masons and Plasterers' International Union of America* (BM&PIUA), whereby the two unions accepted dual membership and agreed to recognize each others' traveling cards. Both unions generally respected the agreement until 1910 when a series of disputes between the two old building trades' unions threatened to evolve into open warfare. An agreement, however, was reached again; the interchange of cards continued, and the legitimacy of the BM&PIUA's practice of organizing plasterers into mixed locals was reaffirmed.

Meanwhile, the OPIU had affiliated with the American Federation of Labor* (AFL) on November 14, 1908. A few years later (August 30, 1915) the OPIU merged with another small AFL national union, the American Brotherhood of Cement Workers, chartered by the AFL on September 22, 1903. The union title was then changed to Operative Plasterers' and Cement Finishers' International Association of the United States and Canada (OP&CFIA). While the merger ended jurisdictional conflicts with the Cement Workers, it only added to reoccurring problems with the BM&PIUA.

Although experiencing a sharp membership decline during the depression of the 1890s, the OP&CFIA grew steadily during the early decades of the twentieth century. A membership of 6,000 in 1900 doubled before 1910 and redoubled by the early 1920s. The OP&CFIA continued to grow, reaching nearly 40,000 before the devastating effects of the Great Depression pushed unemployment rates in the building trades down to unprecedented levels. Membership fell below the 20,000 figure by the mid-1930s before moving upward, a positive trend that continued until the mid-1950s. In 1950 another name change resulted in the adoption of the listed title.

The OP&CMIA claims jurisdiction over interior and exterior plasterers, concrete construction and finishing, and model making and maintains a four-year apprenticeship system. Collective bargaining agreements are normally negotiated on a local basis, but all agreements require the approval of the OP&CMIA general executive board before taking effect.

The OP&CMIA, which maintains its national headquarters in Washington, D.C., holds quadrennial conventions. Principal officers include a general president, an executive vice-president, fifteen vice-presidents, and a secretary-treasurer. The general executive board consists of the president, the secretary-treasurer, and five vice-presidents, at least two of whom are cement masons and two plasterers. In 1973 the OP&CMIA reported a membership of 68,000 located in 450 local unions.

For further information, see *The Plasterer and Cement Mason* issued monthly by the OP&CMIA. See also *Bulletins No. 420, 506,* and *618,* Bureau of Labor Statistics, U.S. Department of Labor (1926, 1929, 1936). Harry C. Bates, *Bricklayers' Century of Craftsmanship: A History of the Bricklayers, Masons and Plasterers' International Union of America* (1955), contains a discussion of the jurisdictional problems between the plasterers' and bricklayers' unions.

PLATE PRINTERS', DIE STAMPERS' AND ENGRAVERS' UNION OF NORTH AMERICA; INTERNATIONAL (IPPDSEU). The first local union of plate printers appeared in the Philadelphia and Washington, D.C., areas during the second half of the nineteenth century. Seeking an alliance with a national labor organization, most of these plate printer locals affiliated with the Knights of Labor* (KofL) during the 1880s. In 1892 several unions affiliated with the KofL, and many unaffiliated locals met in Boston and organized the National Steel and Copper Plate Printers of the United States of America. On July 2, 1898, the new national union affiliated with the American Federation of Labor* (AFL) and was granted jurisdiction over plate printing.

When a local was organized in Ontario, Canada, in 1901, the union title was changed by the substitution of "International" for "National." The extension of the union's organizing jurisdiction to include die stampers necessitated another name change, and in 1921 the union officially became the International Plate Printers and Die Stampers Union of North America. A merger with the International Steel and Copper Plate Engravers' League, chartered by the AFL in 1918, resulted in the adoption of the present title in 1925.

The IPPDSEU, which announced as one of its major objectives the effort "to secure a more equitable share of the wealth which we create," established a four-year apprenticeship for plate printers and die stampers and a five-year apprenticeship for engravers as a requirement for full membership. During its early years, the new national union grew steadily, but it continued its organizing activities in an extremely limited trade jurisdiction. Membership did not reach 1,000 until 1904, and it peaked at 1,500 at the end of World War I. Although membership dipped to 1,200 during the early 1920s, the IPPDSEU had organized virtually all eligible workers in its trade jurisdiction, and for nearly a half-century membership remained relatively stable, usually fluctuating between 1,000 and 1,200 annually. During the decade of the 1960s, however, technological changes reduced employment, and the IPPDSEU's small membership base shrank even further.

The IPPDSEU, which maintains its national headquarters in Ridley Park, Pennsylvania, holds biennial conventions. Full-time officers include a president and a secretary-treasurer. The executive council consists of the president, two vice-presidents, and a representative from each local. In 1973 the IPPDSEU reported a membership of 400 located in thirteen local unions.

For further information, see *The Plate Printer* published by the IPPDSEU from 1902 until 1932. Since 1932 the IPPDSEU has not issued an official organ. Additional information can be found in *Bulletin No. 618*, Bureau of Labor Statistics, U.S. Department of Labor (1936).

PLAYTHINGS, JEWELRY AND NOVELTY WORKERS' INTERNATIONAL UNION (PJNWIU). A group of local industrial unions organized by the Congress of Industrial Organizations* (CIO) met in conference in 1938 and organized the International Union, Playthings and Novelty Workers of America (IUPNWA). Beginning with a base membership of 5,000 and a rather limited jurisdictional grant, the new union's future did not appear too promising, especially when it lost nearly half of its original membership within a year of its chartering. In 1940, however, the CIO expanded the IUPNWA's jurisdiction to include "paper and paper converting industry and such other trades and industries and branches thereof as the General Executive Board may designate from time to time." The CIO then assigned several local industrial unions it had organized in the paper-converting industry to the struggling union, which was renamed the United, International Union, Paper, Novelty and Toy Workers (UIUPNTW). The addition of the paper workers greatly stimulated the membership drive of the CIO union. By 1944 it reported a membership in excess of 50,000. Nevertheless, paper workers and toy workers had little in common, and friction between the two almost inevitably arose as each sought to assert its own identity and its own claim to recognition. Consequently, the CIO on January 1, 1944, chartered the Paper Workers Organizing Committee and assigned to it 12,000 members and seventy-eight locals previously affiliated with the UIUPNTW.

With the reorganization of the union, it was given jurisdiction over jewelry workers and the union title was changed to Playthings, Jewelry and Novelty Workers' International Union. The PJNWIU remained a small union in the specialty trades and largely failed to expand upon its immediate post-World War II membership. On May 24, 1954, it merged with the Retail, Wholesale and Department Store Union* (RWDSU).

The PJNWIU, which maintained its national headquarters in New York City, held annual conventions. Full-time officers included a president and a secretary-treasurer. In addition to all paid officers and representatives, the general executive board included sixteen rank-and-file members elected on a regional basis. Shortly before the merger, the PJNWIU reported a membership of 30,000 located in seventy-five local unions.

For further information, see the *Union Voice* published monthly by the PJNWIU. Harry E. Graham, *The Paper Rebellion: Development and Upheaval in Pulp and Paper Unionism* (1970), also contains some information on the PJNWIU.

PLUMBING AND PIPE FITTING INDUSTRY OF THE UNITED STATES AND CANADA; UNITED ASSOCIATION OF JOURNEYMEN AND APPRENTICES OF THE (UA). Trade unionism among pipe craftsmen dates as far back as the Jacksonian period. The first known strike of workers in the trade occurred in Philadelphia when a union of journeymen plumbers joined other building trades' unions in a ten-hour strike in 1835. Unions of plumbers are also known to have existed in various cities, including Chicago and New York, during the decade preceding the Civil War, but none of these antebellum unions appears to have been long-lived, and there is no evidence of any attempt by them to form a national union in the trade.

Trade unionism in the pipe trades surged forward again during the late years of the Civil War, but until the emergence of the Knights of Labor* (KofL), organization remained scattered and little intercity cooperation existed. As unions of plumbers, gas fitters, and steam fitters joined or were organized by the KofL, the advantages of a national organization became readily apparent. Consequently in the fall of 1884, leaders of several local trade assemblies met in New York City to discuss the possibilities of organizing a national union. Before the meeting adjourned, the National Association of Plumbers, Steam Fitters and Gas Fitters had been organized, and the KofL petitioned for a national trade assembly charter. Within a year the National Association had secured the affiliation of nineteen local unions with a total membership in excess of 2,000. But the KofL general assembly was reexamining the status of national trade assemblies within the organization and delayed action on the association's application for such a charter. Because of this action, as well as a growing disenchantment with the KofL, the National Association (renamed the International Association of Journeymen Plumbers, Steam Fitters, and Gas Fitters [IA] in 1885) established itself as an independent international union.

The newly autonomous organization grew steadily following the 1885 convention but suffered a major setback when the New York City and Brooklyn locals, remaining faithful to the KofL, withdrew from the IA. The dissident New York locals then secured a national trade assembly charter from the KofL in June 1886 as the United Progressive Plumbers, Steam- and Gas-Fitters, National Trade Assembly No. 85. At a joint convention of the two organizations, the possibilities of amalgamation were discussed, but a merger agreement was not reached, and Assembly No. 85 soon suffered defeat in a major New York City strike and ceased to be an effective organization. Meanwhile, the IA leadership devoted an increasing percentage of its time and the organization's resources to a cooperative venture in Milwaukee. The failure of the cooperative destroyed the IA.

The necessity of controlling entry into the trade, a growing trend toward subcontracting, and increasing specialization in the trade soon led to renewed efforts to create an effective national union to provide job security and establish a high level of craftsmanship. These efforts proved successful when forty delegates representing twenty-three local unions, most of them previously affiliated with the KofL, assembled in Washington, D.C., on October 7, 1889, and organized the United Association of Journeymen Plumbers, Gas Fitters, Steam Fitters and Steam Fitters Helpers of the United States and Canada. The union title was modified in 1913, and the present title was adopted in 1947. The UA affiliated with the American Federation of Labor* (AFL) on October 30, 1897.

The new national union that appeared in Washington in the fall of 1889 was a loose federation of largely autonomous local unions. The weak national union office had few financial resources and little power to impose its will on constituent local unions. The UA grew rapidly from its founding until the depression of the 1890s signaled a significant decline in membership. The UA encountered serious intercraft jurisdictional problems, as well as the economic consequences of the depression. Technological change, especially regarding the nature of pipe and the manner in which it was joined, made differentiation between plumbing and steam and gas fitting increasingly difficult. As a result the UA soon found itself locked in a bitter struggle with the International Association of Steam and Hot Water Fitters (IASHWF), which had been organized as a national union in 1888 and was chartered by the AFL in 1898 against the wishes of the UA.

From 1898 to 1914, a self-styled period of UA nationalization, several important developments occurred, firmly establishing the foundation for later union growth and development. During these years the UA tightened and centralized its organizational and governmental structure, facilitating the development of a strong national union. Most large employers extended union recognition without a struggle, thus permitting a concentration on economic benefits in negotiations with employers. Although locally controlled and administered, a strict and arduous apprenticeship program provided control over entry into the trade.

The long and bitter jurisdictional war with the steam fitters finally came to a head in 1912 when the AFL ordered the IASHWF to merge with the UA. The leadership of the IASHWF refused, and the UA then launched a ruthless and frequently violent campaign to exterminate its old rival. Within two years the steam fitters' organization was reduced to a memory, but in the process, the UA seriously antagonized building contractors, other national unions in the building trades, and the general public. Nevertheless, victory had its own rewards as the UA, which previously had gained jurisdiction over sprinkler fitters, established its hegemony over all branches of the pipe trades.

The UA's growth after World War I depended to a considerable extent upon national economic conditions. The union prospered during the construction boom years of the early 1920s, suffered through much of the depression-plagued 1930s, and grew steadily in the years following American involvement in World War II. Unlike many other craft unions, the UA profited greatly from technological innovation. Refrigeration, air conditioning, developments in the oil, chemical, and atomic energy fields, and the emergence of the aerospace industry opened significant new employment opportunities for plumbers and pipe fitters. Because of the union's success in organizing these workers, by mid-century the UA had become one of the most powerful unions in the American labor movement.

The UA, which maintains its national headquarters in Washington, D.C., holds quinquennial conventions. Principal officers include a president, six vice-presidents, and a secretary-treasurer. The executive board is composed of the vice-presidents. In 1971 the UA reported a membership of 297,023 located in 700 local unions. (The UA failed to report its membership figures in 1973.)

For further information, see the *United Association Journal* published monthly by the UA. See also Martin Segal, *The Rise of the United Association: National Unionism in the Pipe Trades, 1884-1924* (1970), an exceptionally valuable study of the early history of the UA. See also Lloyd Ulman, *The Rise of National Trade Unionism: The Development and Significance of Its Struc-*

ture, Governing Institutions, and Economic Policies (1966), and Philip Taft, *The A.F. of L. in the Time of Gompers* (1957).

POST OFFICE AND GENERAL SERVICE MAINTENANCE EMPLOY-EES; NATIONAL ASSOCIATION OF. *See* American Postal Workers Union.

POST OFFICE CLERKS; NATIONAL FEDERATION OF. *See* United Federation of Postal Clerks.

POST OFFICE CLERKS; UNITED NATIONAL ASSOCIATION OF. *See* United Federation of Postal Clerks.

POST OFFICE MOTOR VEHICLE EMPLOYEES; NATIONAL FEDERATION OF. *See* American Postal Workers Union.

POSTAL CLERKS; UNITED FEDERATION OF (UFPC). Organization of postal clerks began during the labor upheavals of the last quarter of the nineteenth century. Many clerks in New York City, Chicago, and other large cities secretly joined assemblies of the Knights of Labor.* Secrecy was necessitated by the U.S. Post Office Department's hostility to any type of collective action by government employees. Postal employees who criticized the department usually had very short tenures in the postal service. The first public organization of postal clerks, the National Association of Post Office Clerks, came into existence in 1890, but it accomplished little; consequently a group of clerks unhappy with the conservative and ineffective leadership of the National Association seceded and organized the United National Association of Post Office Clerks. Resolving their differences in 1899, the two groups effected a merger in New York City on November 14 creating the United National Association of Post Office Clerks (UNAPOC).

Meanwhile, a group of Chicago post office clerks, angry about deplorable working conditions and skeptical of the ability of existing national associations to act, organized a union and took the then revolutionary step of seeking an American Federation of Labor* (AFL) charter. Approving the proposal, AFL president Samuel Gompers issued a charter to the Chicago unions as Federal Labor Union 8703. Theodore Roosevelt's infamous "gag rule" prohibiting federal employees from any type of legislative lobbying and the continued ineffectiveness of the supervisor-dominated UNAPOC resulted in the formation of AFL-chartered federal labor unions in other large cities. On August 27,

1906, delegates from six of these unions met in Chicago and organized the National Federation of Post Office Clerks (NFPOC). The AFL issued a charter to the new postal union on November 17, 1906.

The NFPOC in 1907 considered a reclassification bill its first significant achievement. The bill provided for an increase in wages, protection from indiscriminate dismissals, and established an eight-hour day for postal clerks, but supplied no relief from the seven-day work week or from the gag rule.

The legislative victory quickly made the NFPOC the dominant union of post office clerks. The UNAPOC, which not only failed to support the reclassification bill but actively worked to undermine the NFPOC's efforts on its behalf, lost many members to the more militant and effective NFPOC. Three years later the NFPOC established its national headquarters in Washington, D.C., with Secretary-Treasurer Thomas F. Flaherty serving as the union's full-time legislative representative.

The eight years of Woodrow Wilson's administration were trying times for employees of the Post Office Department. Postmaster General Albert S. Burleson determined to make the post office a profit-making venture and instituted ruthless economy measures: superannuated employees were terminated without pensions; hours and terms of employment were altered to the advantage of the government and the disadvantage of employees; efficiency programs were introduced to increase productivity without increasing wages; and employees were reclassified downward.

Although the NFPOC continued to grow during the 1920s and 1930s, expanding its membership from 16,000 in 1920 to 30,000 in 1925, 36,000 in 1932, and nearly 50,000 by 1940, the union scored few dramatic legislative victories. A retirement plan was secured in 1920 and a salary reclassification measure in 1927, but legislative representatives of the NFPOC found themselves spending much of their time opposing hostile legislation rather than supporting favorable legislation. The NFPOC also had to contend with rival unions seeking to undermine their organizational and lobbying efforts. Although merger discussions with the UNAPOC were held in 1917 and again in 1933, they failed to provide any unity between the old rivals. To further complicate matters, in the early 1930s the Communist-organized Trade Union Unity League formed the National Association of Substitute Postal Employes and the Postal Workers Union of America. Finally, the Congress of Industrial Organizations* also established a rival union, the United Federal Workers of America.* The NFPOC, however, survived all these challenges and remained the dominant union of postal clerks.

Although failing to win many dramatic legislative victories, through the years the NFPOC gained substantial improvements in wages, conditions of employment, pension and welfare benefits, and job security of postal clerks. However, dissatisfied with the conservative leadership of the NFPOC and the inability to gain desired reforms, a group of postal clerks seceded from the

NFPOC in 1958 and formed a rival organization, the National Postal Clerks Union (NPCU). The new union, which rejected craft organization in favor of industrial organization, started with a base of 15,000 members and within a decade had achieved a membership of 80,000.

The proliferation of organizations representing postal clerks had long been considered a serious liability to effective collective action. Merger proposals, however, made little progress until the elevation of E. C. Hallbeck to the NFPOC presidency. Hallbeck initiated merger discussions with the UNAPOC, the NPCU, the National Alliance of Postal Employees, the National Postal Transport Association (NPTA), and the locals of the United Postal Workers in Boston and Pittsburgh. Ultimately a merger of the NFPOC, the UNAPOC, the NPTA, and the United Postal Workers in Boston was consummated in the summer of 1961 creating the United Federation of Postal Clerks.

The NPTA, the oldest of the merging unions, had been established in October 1874 as the Railway Mail Mutual Benefit Association (RMMBA). Initially it had been exclusively a beneficial society organized to provide employees of the railway mail service with inexpensive insurance. As it evolved, the RMMBA began to advocate wage increases and improved working conditions through legislation. As the original objectives of the association changed, the necessity of a complete reorganization became apparent. Consequently a meeting was held in Cincinnati on July 15, 1891, at which the National Association of Railway Postal Clerks was founded. The RMMBA's title was changed to the Railway Mail Association (RMA) in 1904. In 1917 the RMA suddenly reversed its previously negative position on AFL affiliation and was granted a jurisdiction covering all railway postal clerks. The RMA grew slowly through the years. After the Post Office Department combined the railway, air, and highway post office service into the Postal Transportation Service in 1949, the RMA name was changed to the National Postal Transport Association.

After successfully negotiating the merger creating the UFPC, E. C. Hallbeck, the architect of the merger, immediately set about arranging a further merger of post office unions. Although he died before it was completed, Hallbeck's efforts resulted in the creation of the American Postal Workers Union* in 1971 through a merger of the UFPC, the NPU, the National Association of Post Office and General Service Maintenance Employees, the National Federation of Motor Vehicle Employees and the National Association of Special Delivery Messengers.

The UFPC, which maintained its headquarters in Washington, D.C., held biennial conventions. Full-time officers included a president, a legislative representative, a secretary-treasurer, an assistant secretary-treasurer, and nine vice-presidents. The above officers constituted the executive council. Shortly before the merger, the UFPC reported a membership of 166,000 located in 6,800 local unions.

For further information, see the *Union Postal Clerk* issued monthly by the NFPOC, the *Post Office Clerk* published quarterly by the UNAPOC, *The Progressive* published monthly by the NPU, the NPTA's monthly *Postal Transport Journal*, and the *Union Postal Clerk and Postal Transport Journal* issued monthly by the UFPC. See also Karl Baarslag, *History of the National Federation of Post Office Clerks* (1945).

POSTAL AND FEDERAL EMPLOYEES; NATIONAL ALLIANCE OF (NAPFE). The organization of postal workers during the late nineteenth and early twentieth century was fraught with danger for the thousands of black employees in the United States Post Office. Controlled by whites, many of the new postal unions actively discriminated against black workers and wrote provisions into their constitutions prohibiting Negro membership. This was the prevailing atmosphere when Woodrow Wilson and a new Democratic administration came into office in the spring of 1913. Besides his political affiliation, Wilson's southern upbringing and the segregationist activities of a number of his appointees to federal office worried many black workers in the federal civil service. Concern turned to alarm when the Atlanta postmaster discharged thirty-five Negro workers from the postal service, apparently with the full approval of the postmaster general of the United States, Albert S. Burleson, an anti-union Texan.

In an effort to gain some security in these unsettling conditions, twenty-six railway mail service employees, representing black workers throughout the South as well as in Missouri, Kansas, and Indiana, met in Chattanooga, Tennessee, and on October 6, 1913, 'organized the National Alliance of Postal Employees. The new postal union at first restricted its membership to railway mail service workers barred from membership in the Railway Mail Association,* but in 1923 the scope of the organization was expanded to include all black workers in the United States Postal Service. In 1965 the organizing jurisdiction was further expanded to include "All Postal, Federal, State, County, Municipal, Commercial and Industrial Employees," and the name of the organization was changed to National Alliance of Postal and Federal Employees.

The alliance grew steadily during the years following its founding, but like so many other unions, its organizing activities were greatly affected by World War I, the anti-union 1920s, and the Great Depression. By 1936 the NAPFE reported a membership of nearly 5,000, and at the end of World War II, that figure had more than doubled. The alliance continued to grow thereafter, reaching a membership of 15,000 in 1950 and 18,000 in 1960.

The NAPFE, which holds biennial conventions, maintains its national headquarters in Washington, D.C. Principal officers include a president, two vice-presidents, a secretary, a treasurer-comptroller, and an editor. The national executive board consists of the above officials and the president of the auxiliary who serves as an ex officio member. The NAPFE has not reported its membership to the Bureau of Labor Statistics since 1969 when it claimed 45,000 members, but in 1973 it reported 146 local unions.

For further information, see the *National Alliance* issued monthly. Philip S. Foner, *Organized Labor and the Black Worker, 1619-1973* (1974), and Sterling D. Spero and Abram L. Harris, *The Black Worker: The Negro and the Labor Movement* (1931), both contain valuable information on the organization of black workers. See also *Bulletin No. 618*, Bureau of Labor Statistics, U.S. Department of Labor (1936).

POSTAL SUPERVISORS; NATIONAL ASSOCIATION OF (NAPS). At the time of its organization in 1906, the founders of the National Federation of Post Office Clerks* (NFPOC) inserted a provision in the constitution barring supervisors from membership. Realizing that as many of their members rose to supervisory grades they would be deprived of trade union affiliation, NFPOC officials invited supervisors all over the United States to send delegates to meet simultaneously with the national NFPOC convention in Louisville, Kentucky, in 1908. Fifty postal supervisors from thirteen states responded, and under the sponsorship of the NFPOC, the National Association of Postal Supervisors was organized on September 7, 1908.

Postal supervisors had a variety of grievances primarily revolving around working conditions and wages. The establishment of a standard workday and work week along with provisions for sick leave, retirement annuities, overtime pay, and increased salaries constituted the early legislative objectives of the NAPS. Shortly after its organization, the new union launched a campaign to gain one of the supervisors' most desired reforms, the elimination of long hours and Saturday and Sunday work. In association with other postal workers' unions, in 1912 the NAPS successfully lobbied a Sunday closing and eight-hour law for postal workers through the U.S. Congress. The following year a new salary law provided substantial wage increases.

Despite these accomplishments, the early years of the NAPS were characterized more by hardship and frustration than achievement. Albert S. Burleson, Woodrow Wilson's postmaster general, was determined to operate the post office as a' profit-making business. He instituted sweeping economy and efficiency measures, altered working conditions, terminated superannuated employees without a pension, and initiated a variety of other measures having the effect of forcing postal employees to subsidize operations of the U.S. Postal Service. Moreover, Burleson was an implacable foe of union organization in the post office, and through a number of devices, he attempted to undermine the effectiveness of the unions.

Enactment of the Lehlback-Sterling retirement and reclassification act of 1920 was one of the postal unions' most significant victories. The act created a pension system, provided for sick leave, and established a standard salary classification system. In the following years these benefits were gradually increased and expanded through congressional action. The Ramspeck Retirement Act of 1942, which recognized the larger contributions supervisors made to the retirement fund by providing higher benefits, especially pleased NAPS officials.

With the exception of the 1948-1955 period when it was affiliated with the American Federation of Labor,* the NAPS functioned as an independent organization. Nevertheless, in legislative lobbying NAPS cooperated closely with other postal unions, many of them affiliated with the AFL-CIO.*

The NAPS vigorously opposed the Postal Reorganization Act of 1970, but to no avail. The union, however, was able to retain provisions in the law entitling the NAPS to "participate directly in the planning and development of pay policies and schedules, fringe benefit programs, and other programs relating to supervisory and other managerial employees." Postal officials lobbied vigorously but unsuccessfully against recognition of the supervisors' association, and after the act became effective, they simply ignored the provisions for consultation. The issue came to a head in the spring of 1973 when, without consulting the NAPS, the Postal Service initiated a job evaluation program of supervisory and other positions. Claiming a violation of the Postal Reorganization Act, the union immediately sought an injunction in federal court to prevent the Postal Service from implementing the program. Ultimately the case was settled out of court when postal officials agreed to provide a program of consultation and granted the NAPS the right to "participate directly in the planning and development of pay policies and schedules, fringe benefit programs, and other programs relating to supervisory employees." Nevertheless, the problem of downgrading and eliminating supervisory positions instituted under the job evaluation program continues to plague the NAPS and its members.

The NAPS, which maintains its national headquarters in Washington, D.C., holds biennial conventions. Principal officers include a president, an executive vice-president, an administrative vice-president, a secretary, a treasurer, five national vice-presidents, and fifteen area vice-presidents. The NAPS executive committee consists of the above officers. In 1974 the NAPS reported a membership of 34,533 located in approximately 500 local unions.

For further information, see *The Postal Supervisor* published monthly by the NAPS and the biweekly *NAPS News*. See also Florence Peterson, *Handbook of Labor Unions* (1944).

POSTAL UNION; NATIONAL. *See* American Postal Workers Union.

POSTAL WORKERS UNION; AMERICAN (APWU). During the early summer of 1971, postal workers throughout the United States voted their approval of a proposed merger of five postal unions. As a result the American Postal Workers Union, the largest postal union in the world, was formed in Washington, D.C., on July 1, 1971. Those combining in the new union were the: United Federation of Postal Clerks* (UFPC); National Postal Union (NPU); National Association of Post Office and General Service Maintenance Employees (NAPOGSME); National Federation of Post Office Motor Vehicle Employees (NFPOMVE); and National Association of Special Delivery Messengers (NASDM). The combined membership of the five unions at the time of the merger was 280,000.

The UFPC was the largest of the combining unions and had a 1971 membership of 166,000. The United Federation began in 1961 when the National Federation of Post Office Clerks initiated merger discussions with the National Postal Transport Association, the United National Association of Post Office Craftsmen, and the United Postal Workers of Boston. (For a further discussion of the merger, see the UFPC sketch in this volume.)

Frustrated with their inability to gain the type of reforms they felt necessary, a group of "progressives" disaffiliated from the National Federation of Post Office Clerks after its 1958 national convention in Boston. The dissidents organized the National Postal Clerks Union, which rejected the principle of craft unionism and organized on an industrial basis. Starting with a base of 15,000 members, the new union grew steadily, and at the time of the merger, it had a membership of 80,000. At its second national convention, the union title was shortened to the National Postal Union.

The National Association of Post Office and General Service Maintenance Employees organized in Cincinnati on August 23, 1948, by a merger of the National Association of Post Office Mechanics and Maintenance Employees (NAPOMME) and the National Association of Post Office Custodial Employees (NAPOCE). The earliest organization in the field, the National Association of Post Office Mechanics, was organized in Minneapolis in 1937. In 1945 it established an office in Washington, D.C., employed a full-time legislative representative, and changed its name to the National Association of Post Office Mechanics and Maintenance Employees.

Meanwhile a second organization in the same general field of employment, the National Association of Post Office Custodial Employees, had been organized on October 23, 1938. Merger discussions between the NAPOMME and the NAPOCE began during the spring of 1947, and the merger proposal growing from these discussions was approved in a membership referendum. The merging unions adopted the title of the National Association of Post Office Maintenance Employees. In 1950 the association expanded its jurisdiction to include the maintenance employees of the Public Building Services of the General Services Administration. Reflecting this decision, the name of the association was changed to the National Association of Post Office and General Service Maintenance Employees. In April 1966 the NAPOGSME affiliated with the American Federation of Labor-Congress of Industrial Organizations* (AFL-CIO). It had a membership of 13,175 at the time of the APWU merger.

A bill was introduced in the U.S. Congress in 1924 to reclassify the salaries of postal workers. Wages of motor vehicle employees would fall substantially below those of clerks and carriers if this reclassification passed. In an effort to defeat or amend the bill, motor vehicle employees in Chicago banded together into a loosely knit organization, the National Association of Post Office Chauffeurs and Mechanics Union, and raised enough money to send three representatives to Washington. When this action failed to alter the proposed bill and recognizing the need for a national organization to better represent their interests, in 1924 motor vehicle employees organized the National Federation of Post Office Motor Vehicle Employees in Chicago. The new union, however, had a small membership and lacked the financial resources to maintain a full-time legislative representative in the nation's capital. It was not until 1939 that the NFPOMVE had a permanent representative in Washington during sessions of Congress. After establishing its national headquarters in Washington, D.C., in 1941, the NFPOMVE maintained full-time legislative representatives. At the time of the merger creating the APWU, the NFPOMVE, which affiliated with the AFL-CIO in 1958, had a membership of 8,000.

Until 1945 the special delivery messenger had one of the most precarious occupations within the U.S. Postal Service. The post office officially classified the special delivery messenger as a private contractor, and, as such, he was neither covered by civil service regulations nor included in government-sponsored pension and welfare systems. In an effort to protect their interests, special delivery messengers met in Cleveland in 1932 and organized the National Association of Special Delivery Messengers. The NASDM affiliated with the AFL in 1937 and was a charter member of the AFL government employees council. The union scored its first important victory in 1942 when messengers were brought into the Civil Service Retirement System. As a result of the enactment of Public Law 79-134, three years later special delivery messengers came fully under the civil service, although their wages were substantially lower than those of carriers and clerks. Finally, in 1955 special delivery messengers were reclassified and acquired the same status as carriers and clerks. At the time of the APWU merger, the NASDM had a membership of 2,605.

Because normal collective bargaining and such traditional labor devices as the strike and boycott were foreclosed to the employees of the U.S. Post Office Department, postal union officials traditionally devoted much of their time and energy to the task of representing the interests of postal workers before the U.S. Congress. Wages, hours, conditions of employment, job security, sick leave, pensions, and other benefits all were determined by legislation. However, after the creation of the United States Postal Service as a semi-autonomous postal corporation in 1970, postal unions have devoted more time to the traditional methods of collective bargaining and less to legislative lobbying.

The APWU is divided into four sections: the clerk craft, maintenance craft, special delivery craft, and motor vehicle craft. Permanent officers include a general president, presidents of each craft division, a legislative director, an executive vice-president, and a general secretary-treasurer. The APWU, which maintains its national headquarters in Washington, D.C., holds biennial conventions. In 1973 the APWU reported a membership of 238,763 located in 6,500 local unions.

For further information, see the *American Postal Worker* published monthly by the APWU; the weekly *APWU News Service*; the *Maintenance News* (bimonthly) and the *News Bulletin* (weekly) published by the NAPOGSME; the *Rotor* issued monthly by the NFPOMVE; the *Union Postal Clerk and Postal Transport Journal* published monthly by the UFPC; and *The Progressive* issued monthly by the NPU.

POTTERY AND ALLIED WORKERS; INTERNATIONAL BROTHER-HOOD OF (IBPAW). The first known union of pottery workers appeared in Trenton, New Jersey, in 1868. This union and other locals that appeared from time to time were ephemeral organizations that made no effort to create a national union. A sustained effort to organize pottery workers in the United States was not made until the emergence of the Knights of Labor* (KofL). During 1882 local trade assemblies of pottery workers were organized in East Liverpool, Ohio, and in Trenton. The two trade assemblies in East Liverpool, however, were destroyed by a lockout by employers who demanded that their employees disaffiliate with the KofL and sign yellow dog contracts. In their efforts to break the lockout, the East Liverpool workers received little assistance from the Knights, creating among these workers a lasting skepticism of the KofL.

Hoping to rebuild its membership in the pottery industry in 1886, the KofL created a district assembly exclusively for pottery workers—the Operative Potters National Union, National Trades District Assembly, Number 160. Although theoretically a national union, much of the new union's strength was based in the Trenton district. Western pottery workers, especially in the Ohio district, became increasingly disenchanted with the KofL, arguing that they were constantly assessed for funds but received no assistance in return. Finally, in 1890, they led a movement to withdraw from the Knights, and when a resolution to that effect was defeated in a close vote at the annual convention of the Potters National Union, western pottery workers withdrew and created their own national union, the Brotherhood of Operative Potters (BOP). Although their association with the KofL ended in 1892-1893, the eastern organization maintained a separate organization until 1897, when they affiliated with the BOP.

Employer resistance, the depression of the 1890s, and an unsuccessful strike in 1894 nearly destroyed the brotherhood in infancy, but in 1897 it won recognition from most western manufacturers. The affiliation of the eastern locals in 1897 made the BOP the only significant national union in the trade. In the spring of 1900, when it signed an agreement with the United States Potters Association establishing a national wage scale, the brotherhood fulfilled an ambition dating back to the early days of organization in the industry. The agreement, however, created considerable unhappiness in the East where pottery workers had traditionally maintained comparatively higher wage rates. Although several eastern locals withdrew from the national union as a result of this discontent, within a few years most of the eastern pottery workers had returned to the fold. The BOP was further consolidating its strength in the West and making some inroads in the organization of women and unskilled workers in the industry.

With the national agreements in effect, the period between 1905 and 1922 was one of peace and development for the BOP. Only in the chinaware division did the union fail to establish firm control over the work force. During these years membership grew from 5,600 to over 9,000; however, national strikes in the autumn of 1922 signaled a general decline in the national union and in the industry. Although the general wares division won its strike, the sanitary ware division lost not only its strike but its national contract as well. Even though the brotherhood maintained control over most general ware plants (except the sanitary ware division), a general depression in the industry and an accelerated decline in the East reduced the BOP's membership to 6,000 by 1930.

The general decline of the BOP continued during the early years of the Great Depression, but the enactment of the National Industrial Recovery Act and the National Labor Relations Act inspired a reversal in the brotherhood's previously downward membership curve. By 1937 the BOP surpassed the 10,000 membership figure, and at the end of World War II, it had more than 20,000 members. In 1968 the national union changed its title to the International Brotherhood of Pottery and Allied Workers.

The IBPAW, which maintains its national headquarters in East Liverpool, Ohio, holds annual conventions. Full-time officers include a president, a vice-president, and a secretary-treasurer. The above officers plus seven other vice-presidents constitute the union's national executive board. In 1973 the IBPAW reported a membership of 18,209 located in 108 local unions.

For further information, see *The Potters Herald* issued monthly by the IBPAW. See also David A. McCabe, *National Collective Bargaining in the Pottery Industry* (1932).

PRINTING AND GRAPHIC COMMUNICATIONS UNION; INTERNATIONAL (IPGCU). On October 2, 1973, the International Printing Pressmen and Assistants' Union of North America (IPPAU) and the International Stereotypers', Electrotypers', and Platemakers' Union of North America

(ISE&PU) merged to form the International Printing and Graphic Communications Union. The merger, which represented a further manifestation of the trade union consolidation in the printing industry, brought together two of the older unions in the American labor movement.

International Printing Pressmen and Assistants' Union of North America. In 1852 the oldest national union in the American labor movement, the International Typographical Union* (ITU), organized as a craft union of journeymen printers. Technological advances during the second half of the nineteenth century, however, gradually shattered the homogeneity of the printing craft causing internal conflicts, especially between compositors and pressmen. Moreover, the development of commercial presses apart from newspaper printing, the object of the ITU's earliest organizing efforts, created further antagonism. Although the ITU made concessions to job printers, power printers, and other emerging craft divisions, typesetters clearly dominated the national union and most affiliated locals, often subjecting workers in the new crafts to an inferior membership status.

Resulting from these conditions, the New York Adams and Cylinder Press Printers' Association, a strong independent union that had refused to join New York Typographical Union No. 6, issued a call for a national conference of pressmen's unions to meet in New York City on October 8, 1889. Delegates representing thirteen unions responded and organized the International Printing Pressmen's Union of North America. Seven years later the union title was adjusted to incorporate press assistants.

Ignoring both the enticements and threats of the ITU, the IPPAU vowed to remain a permanent union in the printing trades. In their rivalry with the ITU, IPPAU officials saw as one of their major problems the traditional supervision of the pressroom by compositor foremen. Not only were compositors considered unqualified to supervise pressmen, but they could use their position to force pressmen out of the IPPAU. An agreement reached after a bitter inter-union struggle at the large Werner Printing Company in Akron, Ohio, the so-called St. Louis agreement, signed in August 1894, stipulated that each union would recognize the legitimacy of the other; the IPPAU would have sole jurisdiction over pressmen and the ITU would retain jurisdiction over "all compositorial branches of the printing trades." ITU officials, however, apparently entered into the agreement with the intention of sabotaging it at the ITU national convention of 1894. Thus the inter-union warfare continued until the developing depression that first struck the nation in 1893 convinced the ITU to reconsider its position. As a consequence, a tripartite agreement (similar to the earlier settlement), which included the secessionist International Brotherhood of Bookbinders,* was negotiated.

The new agreement initially worked quite well, but disagreements soon arose over the use of the union label, and in 1901 the ITU again abrogated the agreement. After another period of intermittent warfare, a new settlement was

reached, which resulted in the International Allied Printing Trades Association, thus effectively eliminating inter-union rivalries in the industry.

The same technological changes leading to the secession of pressmen, stereotypers and electrotypers, bookbinders, and photoengravers from the ITU
soon created dissension within the IPPAU, as different classes of craftsmen,
such as newspaper web pressmen, web press brakemen, and press feeders, considered organizing their own unions. Secessionist movements, charter
revocations, and reordered jurisdictional lines punctuated the conflict; but the
IPPAU had learned from its conflicts with the ITU and usually exhibited a tol-
erance that defused antagonisms and restored union solidarity.

Meanwhile, the IPPAU gradually regularized collective bargaining relations with employers. Union officials early adopted the policy of working hard
to maintain harmonious relations with employers and attempted to substitute
conciliation and mediation for strikes. In 1899 the IPPAU negotiated the first
industry-wide agreement in the printing industry when it signed a contract
with the United Typothetae of America, a national employers' association,
calling for the introduction of the nine-hour day for compositors and bookbinders, as well as for printers. In 1902 the IPPAU negotiated a long-lived arbitration agreement with the American Newspaper Publishers' Association, and
a few years later it negotiated a similar agreement with another large employer
organization, the Printing Industry of America.

The IPPAU's future took a significant turn in 1907 with the election to the
union presidency of George Berry, then twenty-four years old, who dominated
affairs of the IPPAU for the next forty-one years. During that period, the union
created Pressmen's Home, Tennessee, as a home for ill and aged members and
a technical training school providing members and apprentices with training
in changing printing techniques. Death benefits were increased, and an
old-age pension system was established. Finally a service bureau was created to
counsel and advise local unions in collective bargaining, and a systematic
apprenticeship program was initiated.

Under Berry's direction, the IPPAU experienced a remarkably consistent
pattern of growth. Exhibiting neither the dramatic membership gains during
World War I nor the losses in the following years that characterized so many
American unions, the IPPAU grew consistently from the turn of the century
until the Great Depression struck the nation during the 1930s. A membership
of 9,000 in 1900 doubled in 1910 and again in 1920. Through the 1920s,
IPPAU membership grew slowly, surpassing the 40,000 figure by the end of the
decade. Although the IPPAU lost strength during the depression, its growth
curve turned upward again before World War II and continued to climb
through the 1950s.

The continual growth of the IPPAU in part resulted from its flexibility in
coping with technological changes in the printing industry. The printing
pressmen, for example, established control over workers in the offset printing

and specialty printing establishments long before these trades had made a significant impact on the industry. On October 2, 1973, the IPPAU merged with the International Stereotypers', Electrotypers', and Platemakers' Union of North America to create the International Printing and Graphic Communications Union.

The IPPAU, which maintained its national headquarters in Washington, D.C. held quadrennial conventions. Principal officers included a president, four vice-presidents, and a secretary-treasurer. The board of directors included the above officers and a president emeritus. In 1971 the IPPAU reported a membership of 127,887 located in 711 local unions.

International Stereotypers', Electrotypers', and Platemakers' Union of North America. During the second half of the nineteenth century the International Typographical Union organized stereotypers and electrotypers. By the end of the century, these workers had acquired considerable independence within a partially autonomous ITU trade district union. Nevertheless, following the precedent set by the printing pressmen and bookbinders, in 1898 stereotypers and electrotypers began demanding a separate organization. The ITU resisted at first, voting down independence in 1900; but in 1902 the ITU agreed to an amicable separation. As a result an organizing convention met in Cincinnati in August 1902 and created the International Stereotypers and Electrotypers' Union of North America (IS&EU). The new union received an American Federation of Labor* (AFL) charter on January 23, 1903.

Although a highly specialized trade jurisdiction determined that it would remain a small international union, the IS&EU grew steadily and avoided the great fluctuations exhibited by most American trade unions during the first two decades of the twentieth century. An original IS&EU membership of 1,800 grew to 5,400 by 1920. Moreover, the IS&EU's steady growth continued throughout the 1920s, reaching nearly 8,000 by the end of the decade.

The IS&EU's success during the 1920s, a decade of hard times for most other labor unions in the United States, was largely the product of a conciliation and arbitration agreement reached with most large employers in the commercial branch of the printing trades. Resulting from a developing employee-employer spirit of cooperation in the printing trades industry, the IS&EU largely avoided industrial conflict, strikes, and lockouts. Although the International maintained its previous gains during the Great Depression, membership stabilized for several years at about 8,000 before beginning to move upward again after World War II.

Reflecting the large number of platemakers organized by the IS&EU, the union title was changed to International Stereotypers', Electrotypers', and Platemakers' Union of North America. On October 2, 1973, the ISE&PU merged with the IPPUA to create the IPGCU.

The ISE&PU, which maintained its international headquarters in Chicago, held annual conventions. Principal officers included a president, three vice-presidents, and a secretary-treasurer. The above officers comprised the executive board. At the time of the IPGCU merger, the ISE&PU reported a membership of 8,800 located in 170 local unions.

The IPGCU, which maintains its national headquarters in Washington, D.C., holds quadrennial conventions. Principal officers include a president, eight vice-presidents, and a secretary-treasurer. The above officials also constitute the IPGCU board of directors. In 1973 the IPGCU reported a membership of 123,000 located in 683 local unions.

For further information, see the *American Pressman Reports*, issued quarterly, and *News and Views* published monthly by the IPPAU, and the *I.S.E.U. Journal* issued monthly by the ISE&PU. See also Elizabeth F. Baker's fine study, *Printers and Technology: A History of the International Printing Pressmen and Assistants' Union* (1957), and Jacob Loft, *The Printing Trades* (1944).

PRINTING PRESSMEN AND ASSISTANTS' UNION OF NORTH AMERICA; INTERNATIONAL. *See* International Printing and Graphic Communications Union.

PUBLIC WORKERS OF AMERICA; UNITED (UPWA). Divisions within the American labor movement resulted in the presence of two rival national federations, the older American Federation of Labor* (AFL) and the secessionist Congress of Industrial Organizations* (CIO). This had almost an immediate impact on unions of federal, state, county and municipal employees. Before the end of 1937, the CIO had chartered two dual unions, the United Federal Workers of America (UFWA), which rivaled the American Federation of Government Employees* (AFGE), and the State, County and Municipal Workers of America (SCMWA), a competitor of the American Federation of State, County and Municipal Employees* (AFSCME). The CIO devoted considerable time, attention, and money to these organizations, but they proved to be among the least successful organizing efforts of the CIO.

United Federal Workers of America. The CIO chartered the UFWA in June 1937. Its organization resulted from differences within the AFGE beginning shortly after its chartering in 1932. During the summer of 1934, General Hugh S. Johnson, administrator of the National Recovery Administration (NRA), dismissed the president of the AFGE's NRA local for "inefficiency and insubordination." It was a blatant case of dismissal because of union activity, and NRA local members immediately went to the defense of their president, publishing broadsides critical of Johnson and the NRA and picketing NRA headquarters. The episode was a great embarrassment to the Roosevelt administration and the NRA, both of which were attempting to convince private employers to abide by the labor provisions of the National Industrial Recovery Act.

After an appeal to the National Labor Relations Board, the dismissed union leader was reinstated.

Although the protests proved successful, AFGE leaders disapproved of the tactics employed, arguing that they would ultimately be more harmful than beneficial. Consequently the AFGE leadership pushed through an amendment to the union's constitution in 1935 that forbade picketing, strikes, and delegations to government offices of more than five persons. Many AFGE members, reading the lessons of the NRA case much differently, opposed the conservative, "responsible" image fostered by the AFGE leadership. Concluding that more militant tactics would bring faster results, they attempted to gain control of the AFGE. But the rebels had little success; by the time of the 1936 convention eleven lodges had been suspended on charges of violating the provisions of the AFGE constitution.

The dissidents, however, had not been completely routed, and when Franklin Roosevelt threatened another economy drive in early 1937, government workers feared a repetition of the Economy Act of 1933, and some of them pressed AFGE leaders to pursue more militant tactics. When AFGE officials ignored these critics, seven lodges formed a "Committee Against False Economy" and sponsored a mass rally in Washington, D.C., directly violating established AFGE policy. The rebellious locals were then suspended and successfully petitioned for a CIO charter as the United Federal Workers of America.

CIO officials had great hopes for the UFWA. They selected the national officers of the new union, provided generous organizing support, and conducted a massive publicity campaign. Yet the UFWA made little headway in organizing federal employees; it found itself in the position of projecting a radical image but in some instances pursuing policies more conservative than those of its rivals. The founders of the new CIO union had included in the UFWA constitution all the provisions against picketing, striking, and mass demonstrations they found so objectionable in the AFGE. Moreover, in an effort to keep wages commensurate with industrial standards, the UFWA asked for minimum wage scales lower than those of the AFGE.

The failure of the UFWA to build a mass membership disappointed the founders of the new union and their CIO supporters. By the end of World War II, a period of great growth and expansion for most labor unions, the UFWA had only slightly more than 12,000 members. Finally in April 1946, the UFWA was absorbed by its more successful CIO sister union, the SCMWA.

The UFWA, which maintained its national headquarters in Washington, D.C., held annual conventions. Full-time officers included a president and secretary-treasurer, both appointed by the CIO. The national executive board consisted of the above officers and fourteen other members elected from six geographical regions. At the time of the merger with the SCMWA, the UFWA paid per-capita taxes to the CIO on 12,700 members.

State, County and Municipal Workers of America. The evolution of the SCMWA had a similar history. Shortly after the chartering of the American Federation of State, County and Municipal Employees by the AFL in 1936, factional divisions, centering upon differences over craft and industrial unionism, disrupted the new union. These differences resulted in a split during the summer of 1937, with a seceding faction joining the CIO as the SCMWA. Arguing that the AFL's craft structure resulted in the constant diffusion of government workers, SCMWA leader Abram Flaxer secured a charter from the CIO that included jurisdiction over "all men and women employed by the state, county, municipal and other local government units." This service-wide jurisdiction enabled the SCMWA to avoid the organizing difficulties encountered by its AFL rival when AFL unions were continually claiming craft workers organized by the AFSCME.

Although both AFSCME and SCMWA originally opposed strikes in the public service (the SCMWA included a no-strike clause in its original constitution), both unions soon recognized the necessity of retaining the right to strike as a last resort. Both unions also came to a recognition of the importance of collective bargaining agreements, although in this instance the AFSCME at first relied almost exclusively upon legislative lobbying to secure desired economic concessions. Thus few economic differences separated the two rival unions of government employees; but they were nevertheless bitter antagonists, primarily because of sharp ideological and political differences. While the AFSCME had a generally "liberal" leadership, the SCMWA contained a strong Communist segment and resided on the far left of the political spectrum.

The SCMWA never surpasséd the AFSCME, but it proved much more successful in rivaling an AFL affiliate than the UFWA. By 1945 the SCMWA paid per-capita taxes to the CIO on 50,400 members, while the AFSCME paid dues to the AFL for 61,000 members. Both unions exhibited approximately the same growth rate, and they were similarly successful in their collective bargaining efforts. In April 1946 the SCMWA absorbed the UFWA, which resulted in an expanded jurisdictional field, the acquisition of about 12,000 new members, and a new union title—the United Public Workers of America. The merger, however, strengthened the left-wing faction in the union, which had major repercussions in the future.

The SCMWA, which maintained its national headquarters in New York City, held biennial conventions. Full-time officers included a president and secretary-treasurer. The national executive board was composed of the above officials and the representatives of eleven geographical regions. At the time of the merger with the UFWA, the SCMWA paid per-capita taxes on 50,400 members.

Delegates to the merger convention that resulted in the formation of the UPWA made two significant decisions affecting its future development: the adoption of a resolution endorsing a pro-Soviet foreign policy position, and a hazy policy statement apparently authorizing strikes by federal employees. Although UPWA leaders quickly "clarified" the union's position, emphasizing that it had no intention "of striking against the Government of the United States," the uproar over the strike issue along with the UPWA's left-wing reputation had a disastrous effect on union membership, which declined rapidly, virtually eliminating UPWA members in the federal civil service.

As a result of these events, a rival faction emerged within the UPWA bearing the title, "Build the Union Committee." The dissidents promised to avoid divisive ideological conflicts, adhere to official CIO policy positions, and reverse the UPWA's pro-Soviet foreign policy stance. Factional conflicts and the controversial policies of the UPWA leadership virtually destroyed the CIO affiliate; at the time of the UFWA-SCMWA merger, membership had exceeded 60,000, but it fell below 15,000 by 1949. On March 1, 1950, the CIO expelled the UPWA as a Communist-dominated union. Thereafter the UPWA hung on for several years in Hawaii under the suzerainty of Harry Bridges and the International Longshoremen's and Warehousemen's Union.*

The UPWA, which held biennial conventions, maintained its national headquarters in Washington, D.C., until 1948, when it moved to New York City. Principal officers included a president and a secretary-treasurer. The national executive board included the above officers and representatives from various geographical regions. Shortly before its expulsion from the CIO, the UPWA claimed a membership of 14,000.

For further information, see the *News of State, County, and Municipal Workers*, published monthly by the SCMWA, the *Federal Record*, issued monthly by the UFWA, and the *Public Record* issued monthly by the UPWA. See also Sterling D. Spero, *Government as Employer* (1948); Max M. Kampelman, *The Communist Party vs. the C.I.O.: A Study in Power Politics* (1957); and David J. Saposs, *Communism in American Unions* (1959).

PULP AND PAPER WORKERS; ASSOCIATION OF WESTERN (AWPPW). During the week of September 14-21, 1964, a majority of workers in forty-nine West Coast pulp and paper mills went to the polls in a National Labor Relations Board (NLRB) representational election and chose to support the newly organized Association of Western Pulp and Paper Workers. This action climaxed one of the more significant rebellions to occur in the American labor movement since the mid-1930s.

For many years western pulp and paper workers had been represented by two firmly established international unions, the International Brotherhood of Pulp, Sulphite and Paper Mill Workers of the United States and Canada* (IBPSPMW) and the United Papermakers and Paperworkers* (UPP). The two unions had established cordial relations with the Pacific Coast Association of Pulp and Paper Manufacturers (PCAPPM), a group of eighteen different companies owning forty-nine mills in Oregon, California, and Washington. The two international unions and the PCAPPM periodically negotiated a uniform labor agreement (ULA) binding upon both unions as well as on the companies the PCAPPM represented. Although labor-management disagreements and disputes occurred periodically, relatively harmonious industrial relations prevailed, and contracts had been negotiated for over thirty years without a strike. Most competent observers considered the West Coast contract to be the best in the industry. Because of these conditions, the extent of worker dissatisfaction with their unions was unexpected and unfathomable to many union leaders.

A dispute over negotiating procedures during contract talks in the spring of 1964 sparked the revolt. Negotiations were carried on by a bargaining board elected by union delegates to a pre-wage conference; a similar board was elected by the members of the PCAPPM. Custom and practice, well established over the years, guided bargaining methods and procedures. After a minor dispute in 1963, however, employers demanded the negotiation of a formal set of bargaining rules. In response, representatives of the two international unions and the PCAPPM met in February 1964 and agreed upon a set of rules to be used during upcoming contract negotiations in Portland, Oregon. The elected union bargaining board objected to several of the rules established at the February conference; especially odious was a procedure in which the international office appointed the ULA labor co-chairman rather than leaving the choice to the election of union delegates as had been customary. As a consequence, bargaining board members wrote their own set of negotiating rules, which were introduced at the Portland contract talks.

Hoping to resolve the intra-union dispute, Vice-President Ivor D. Isaacson of the IBPSPMW, selected by the international office as labor co-chairman, sought guidance from international headquarters. He was informed that three international vice-presidents would assume full authority over collective bargaining, thus ending the bargaining authority of the elected union delegates. Seventy-three of the 138 union delegates, led by William R. Perrin who had previously been elected chairman of the union caucus expressed their disapproval by walking out of the caucus and boycotting the negotiations.

Efforts to effect a settlement between the rebels and the international officers failed, and on May 9 leaders of the revolt met in Olympia, Washington, and organized the AWPPW. Several weeks were devoted to a successful campaign to secure the rejection by membership referendum of the contract negotiated by international officers at Portland. After a second referendum, which the rebels boycotted, the AWPPW devoted its energies to the pending NLRB representational election.

The AWPPW's success in that election was the product of several relatively minor grievances rather than the result of a single, dramatic issue. Western pulp and paper workers perceived a steady erosion of democracy within the established international unions. Eastern leaders who controlled both international unions were also thought to be insensitive to the problems of western locals, and the refusal of union leaders to change the method of electing regional vice-presidents further antagonized the westerners. (Majority voting prevailed at international conventions rather than voting by delegates from each particular region.) Finally, a growing feeling that international officers worked too closely with employers and failed to bargain aggressively contributed to the dissatisfaction; but perhaps most importantly, there was widespread unhappiness with the international officers' inability to resolve local grievances. Although carefully itemized during pre-wage conferences, these grievances were largely neglected during ULA negotiations.

After winning the NLRB election, the AWPPW entered contract discussions with the PCAPPM. In those negotiations economic issues were relatively insignificant. The major obstacles to a settlement were AWPPW demands for a union shop and the employer's insistence upon the inclusion of a statement of management's rights in the contract. Confronting the hostility of the two respected international unions as well as the powerful AFL-CIO,* AWPPW leaders considered the union shop essential if they were to avoid a long, bitter struggle to maintain AWPPW membership and bargaining rights. Intransigence on both sides resulted in a strike beginning on November 11, 1964, which ended after thirteen days when both sides accepted a compromise proposed by the Federal Mediation and Conciliation Service. Although the union failed to achieve everything it wanted in the new settlement, by April 1965 contract provisions had enabled the AWPPW to establish the union shop in forty-seven of forty-eight mills.

The AWPPW confronted a critical challenge in January 1967 when the IBPSMW and UPP requested a ULA representational election. The challenge by the international unions proved ill advised, however, as the AWPPW carried 85 percent of the vote. The most serious internal problem with which AWPPW leaders had to contend was the resolution of local grievances, the same issue that created so much dissatisfaction with the older internationals. Two-level bargaining appeared the most effective solution, but employers objected and ultimately withdrew from the ULA. Thereafter bargaining was carried on at the mill level, and local issues ceased to be a significant problem for association officials. Strikes became much more frequent with the resumption of local bargaining, but the AWPPW continued to exhibit considerable success in collective bargaining negotiations. Conversely a southern organizing campaign launched in 1966 by the AWPPW proved much less successful and was abandoned a year later.

The AWPPW, which maintains its headquarters in Portland, holds annual conventions. Major elected officials include a president, executive vice-president, general vice-president, secretary-treasurer, six area representatives, and six trustees. The executive board is composed of all the above officials but the area representatives. In 1973 the AWPPW reported a membership of 20,202 located in sixty local unions.

For further information, see *The Rebel* published semimonthly by the AWPPW. A special tenth anniversary edition contains much historical information. Two fine scholarly studies are also available: Harry E. Graham, *The Paper Rebellion: Development and Upheaval in Pulp and Paper Unionism* (1970), and Paul L. Kleinsorge and William C. Kerby, "The Pulp and Paper Rebellion: A New Pacific Coast Union," *Industrial Relations* (October 1966).

PULP, SULPHITE AND PAPER MILL WORKERS OF THE UNITED STATES AND CANADA; INTERNATIONAL BROTHERHOOD OF (IBPSPMW). The first union of pulp mill workers in the United States appeared at Fort Edward, New York, in the summer of 1901, and it received an American Federation of Labor* (AFL) charter as a federal labor union, Fort Edward Labour's Protective Union No. 9259. The new union quickly expanded its organizing activities to other mills in the area, and within a year, unions appeared in other New York mills as well as in those of Massachusetts, New Hampshire, Vermont, and Maine.

More than 5,000 pulp workers had been organized by 1902. Growth of federal labor unions throughout the Northeast led union leaders to seek an AFL charter as a national union, but President Samuel Gompers and the AFL executive council doubted the ability of the unskilled pulp workers to run their own union. Consequently they assigned the pulp worker locals as a subordinate division to the International Brotherhood of Paper Makers* (IBPM). The AFL then rechartered the IBPM as the International Brotherhood of Paper Makers, Pulp, Sulphite, and Paper Mill Workers (IBPMPSPMW).

It quickly became apparent that the highly skilled paper makers looked upon the pulp workers as second-class members, and when they voted in 1905 to restrict eligibility for election to the union presidency to highly skilled machine tenders, the pulp workers revolted. Pulp worker locals met in convention at Burlington, Vermont, on January 12, 1906, voted to secede, and organized their own union. An extended period of conflict, decimating both unions, resulted. The unions scabbed on each other's strikes and generally attempted to create dissension and discord within the ranks of their rivals. The two rivals nearly destroyed each other before negotiating a treaty in the early summer of 1909, which, among other settlements, defined the jurisdiction of the two unions and included provisions for mutual assistance. Confirming the arrangement, on July 2, 1909, the AFL issued a charter to the International Brotherhood of Pulp, Sulphite and Paper Mill Workers of the United States and Canada, and the title of the IBPMPSPMW reverted to the original International Brotherhood of Paper Makers.

Working together, the two unions recovered much of their lost strength. A successful twelve-week strike against the International Paper Company, the largest in the industry, reversed a defeat suffered two years earlier. The IBPSPMW continued to grow, reaching a membership approaching 15,000 by the end of World War I. The union's accomplishments included victory in a long, drawn-out strike against the St. Regis Paper Company.

Victories, however, dissolved into defeats during the repressive decade of the 1920s. On July 5, 1921, the International Paper Company announced its intention to operate on an open-shop basis. A disastrous five-year strike resulted, and International Paper continued to operate as an open-shop employer until 1937. Although the IBPSPMW made some gains in the organization of Canadian mills, membership plummeted. By 1926 only 6,000 pulp workers paid per-capita taxes to the IBPSPMW. The Great Depression further weakened the already troubled unions in the paper industry. By 1932 the IBPSPMW had fewer than 5,000 members and seemed on the verge of collapse.

Labor provisions of the National Industrial Recovery Act of 1933 and the National Labor Relations Act of 1935 stimulated a remarkable recovery. By the end of 1933 IBPSPMW membership was up nearly 30 percent, and it almost doubled by the end of 1934. The IBPSPMW's fortunes were further raised when the various branches of the International Paper Company recognized the union during the 1937-1938 period. The IBPSPMW's initiatives included successful inroads into the organization of southern pulp mills and significant forays into the Great Lakes area.

The organization of Paper Workers Organizing Committee (PWOC) by the Congress of Industrial Organizations* (CIO) in 1944 represented a threat to the IBPSPMW. The effort of the PWOC (which in 1946 became the United Paperworkers of America*) to organize unskilled and semiskilled workers on an industrial basis appeared especially threatening when the PWOC won bargaining rights for 4,000 employees of the West Virginia Pulp and Paper Company in 1946, but the older AFL unions, already having acquired bargaining rights in many larger companies in the industry, effectively contained the CIO threat.

Despite the competition, the IBPSPMW exhibited a rapid growth. A 1945 membership of 80,000 doubled during the following decade and continued to grow, reaching over 180,000 by 1970. The most significant reversal during these years was the loss of most West Coast locals as a result of the organization of a secessionist union, the Association of Western Pulp and Paper Workers.* (For details, see the association sketch in this volume.) On August 9, 1972, the IBPSPMW merged with the United Papermakers and Paperworkers* to create the United Paperworkers International Union* (UPIU).

The IBPSPMW, which maintained its national headquarters in Fort Edward, New York, held triennial conventions. Full-time officers included a president-secretary, first vice-president, and treasurer. The executive board was composed of the above officials in addition to six vice-presidents elected by majority vote at regular conventions. Shortly before the UPIU merger, the IBPSPMW reported a membership of 193,174 located in 770 local unions.

For further information, see the *Pulp and Paper Worker* issued monthly and the *Canadian Pulp and Paper Workers Journal* published bimonthly by the IBPSPMW. The best scholarly study of trade unionism in the paper industry is Harry E. Graham's *The Paper Rebellion: Development and Upheaval in Pulp and Paper Unionism* (1970). See also Irving Brotslaw, "Trade Unionism in the Pulp and Paper Industry" (Ph.D. dissertation, University of Wisconsin, 1964), and James A. Gross, "The Making and Shaping of Unionism in the Pulp and Paper Industry," *Labor History* (Spring 1964).

RADIO ASSOCIATION; AMERICAN (ARA). Radio operators employed on United States flagships first organized trade unions during the early years of the Great Depression. The steady reduction of wage rates and deteriorating working conditions during the depression led radio operators based in New York City to organize the American Radio Association in 1931. Shortly after its organization, the new union merged with a similar group on the West Coast and was renamed the American Radio Telegraphists Association (ARTA). The union, which conducted a militant campaign to organize radio operators, succeeded in achieving increased wages and improved working conditions for radio operators by striking when necessary.

After a proposed merger with the Commercial Telegraphers Union of America (CTUA) failed, ARTA affiliated with the Congress of Industrial Organizations* (CIO) in 1937. Hoping to establish their own national organization in the telegraph industry, CIO officials gave the ARTA, renamed the American Communications Association* (ACA), a broad jurisdictional grant extending far beyond radio operators and making it the CIO's rival to the American Federation of Labor's CTUA.

As a result of growing left-wing influence in the ACA, radio operators became increasingly restive in the organization, especially in the postwar, cold war years. CIO officials were also becoming concerned about the alleged Communist-dominated leadership of many CIO unions, including the ACA. CIO officials were especially upset by the refusal of this union to support the CIO's official position favoring the Marshall Plan for European recovery and for its endorsement of Henry Wallace's candidacy on the Progressive party ticket, despite the CIO's endorsement of Harry Truman, the Democratic party nominee. In an effort to confine and reduce suspected Communist influence within its ranks, the CIO redefined jurisdictional boundaries of offending unions, and then, accelerating inter-union warfare, expelled the alleged Communist-dominated unions and chartered rival organizations.

It was in this context that in late 1948 the CIO separated radio operators from the ACA and issued them a charter in the name of the American Radio Association. At its first national convention held in San Francisco in January 1949, the new organization established itself as a national union and adopted a constitution and bylaws that won approval in a membership referendum. The new association adopted the slogan, "Democracy has to be more than a word for trade unions," and the officers immediately set about winning concessions for its members through collective bargaining. During its early years, the ARA won a pension and welfare plan, a comprehensive vacation plan operated under joint union-management supervision, higher wages, and improved working and living conditions on board ship.

Besides its primary interest in the economic conditions under which radio operators labored, the ARA also took great interest in safety and apprenticeship training. The ARA strongly opposed efforts by marginal operators to relax the sea-safety radio requirements that had been written into law during the 1930s. Recognizing the safety features implicit in the new innovations and technology in electronics, the ARA also resolved to promote the training or retraining of radio operators in the use and maintenance of the increasingly sophisticated electronic machinery being employed by the merchant marine. To this end, at its 1958 national convention, the ARA adopted a program entitled, "Technical Investigation of Maritime Electronics," or "TIME." The program included four elements:

1) A program of research and development to investigate and evaluate new techniques and innovations and to survey the methods and techniques employed by existing electronic installations.

2) A program to inform radio operators of the result of the research and development effort.

3) A program for orderly introduction of new electronic technology in the industry.

4) A training program to provide for the continuing education of radio officers in the uses and applications of technological changes in the electronics industry.

Although industry representatives were unenthusiastic about the first three parts of the program, the ARA did gain an industry commitment to the training phase. Both the industry and the ARA agreed to using reserve funds from the jointly administered ARA welfare plan to establish a training program. The result was ARA "TIME," which updated and upgraded the skills of hundreds of radio officers by providing instruction in the circuitry of modern electronics and in circuit analysis. As a result of this intensive training, the industry created a new designation, the radio-electronics officer, a position for which one qualified by successfully completing the ARA TIME program.

The ARA, which established its national headquarters in New York City, holds quadrennial conventions. Full-time officers include a president, vice-president, and secretary-treasurer. In 1973 the ARA reported a membership of 700.

For further information, see the *ARA Log*, published quarterly, the *ARA Free Press*, issued weekly, and *Link to the Future*, produced by the ARA in 1964. See also Vidkunn Ulriksson, *The Telegraphers: Their Craft and Their Unions* (1953), which contains background information previous to the organization of the ARA.

RAILROAD SIGNALMEN; BROTHERHOOD OF (BRS). A small group of signal maintenance workers on the Pennsylvania Railroad met in the signal tower of the Altoona, Pennsylvania, railroad yards in 1901 and organized the first lodge of the Brotherhood of Railroad Signalmen. Although desirous of providing illness and death benefits, the organizers also exhibited an interest in such traditional trade union objectives as wages, hours of labor, and working conditions.

The Altoona union remained largely local until 1908, when it established relations with other local organizations in New England. These groups met in New York City and agreed to organize a grand lodge, which they did at a Philadelphia meeting on August 16, 1908. Nevertheless, in its endeavor to organize the signal workers on all American railroads, the new union encountered great resistance from railroad corporations, and when the United States entered World War I, it still had a membership of fewer than 1,000.

The BRS remained a small, ineffective national union until William G. McAdoo, director general of railroads during the World War I period of government control, issued his "freedom of association" directive in 1918. Taking advantage of this opportunity, the BRS quickly organized signal workers on railroads throughout the United States. A membership of 1,000 in 1918 jumped to over 7,000 in 1919 and to nearly 15,000 in 1920. Although the BRS suffered a substantial loss in membership during the 1920s and the Great Depression of the early 1930s, it did succeed in extending its organization to Canadian railroads.

On March 11, 1914, the BRS affiliated with the American Federation of Labor* (AFL) and received a charter conferring exclusive jurisdiction over railroad signal workers but specifically excluding telegraph operators, train dispatchers, levermen, train directors, and station agents. In 1924 the BRS affiliated with the Canadian Labor Congress and two years later was a charter member of the Railway Labor Executives' Association. The BRS's association with the AFL ended in 1927, when it was suspended for failing to comply with an AFL decision in a bitter jurisdictional conflict precipitated by an attempt of the International Brotherhood of Electrical Workers* to raid the BRS membership. Thereafter it remained independent until reaffiliating with the AFL on October 6, 1946.

Over 95 percent of the signal workers on American and Canadian railroads held BRS membership cards in the years following World War II. The brotherhood's membership then stabilized at about 15,000 for several years before beginning a slow decline during the late 1950s because of railroad consolidation and technological innovation.

Throughout its history the BRS avoided strikes when possible, preferring mediation and arbitration; however, it exhibited a willingness to strike when necessary. In 1971, for example, it called a nationwide strike that tied up the railroad industry for several days. A long-standing wage controversy, ultimately resolved by congressional intervention, precipitated the conflict. Besides such traditional collective bargaining items as wages, hours, working conditions, and fringe benefits, the BRS has also placed great emphasis on improved safety standards for signal workers. One of the most significant achievements along these lines came with the enactment of the Federal Signal Inspection Act in the early 1930s.

The BRS, which maintains its headquarters in Mount Prospect, Illinois, holds triennial conventions. Principal officers include a president, secretary-treasurer, seven vice-presidents, and a three-member board of trustees (one vice-president and one trustee to be elected from Canada). The grand executive council is composed of the above officials.

For further information, see *The Signalman's Journal* issued ten times a year. See also J. O. Fagan, *Confessions of a Railroad Signalman* (1908), and *50 Years of Railroad Signaling: A History of the Brotherhood of Railroad Signalmen of America* (n.d.) published by the BRS.

RAILROAD TELEGRAPHERS; ORDER OF (ORT). Railroad telegraphers first began trade union activities during the Civil War when they joined with their commercial counterparts to create the National Telegraphic Union in 1863 and the Telegraphers' Protective League in 1866. Both organizations were short-lived, however, and it was not until the great surge of the Knights of Labor* in the early 1880 that large-scale organization took place. In 1882 the Brotherhood of Telegraphers of the United States and Canada was formed as District 45 of the Knights. Growing rapidly, the brotherhood had 150 lodges and a membership of 18,000 within a year, but the union disintegrated after a premature strike against the Western Union Telegraph Company in the summer of 1883.

Two years after the collapse of the Brotherhood of Telegraphers, a group of railroad telegraphers met in Cedar Rapids, Iowa, and on June 9, 1886, agreed to form a secret organization, the Order of Railway Telegraphers of North America. Membership in the new organization was restricted to telegraph employees in the railroad industry, and by constitutional provision strikes or strike agitation were strictly prohibited. The order did have economic objectives that it hoped to accomplish through controlling entry into the telegraph trade, and to that end, its members were prohibited from teaching telegraphy except under defined circumstances.

Despite its stated objectives of improving wages and working conditions, the ORT was primarily a fraternal organization. As this became clear, an early membership surge, which increased from 2,250 in 1887 to 9,000 in 1889, was replaced by a gradual decline. Moreover, the Brotherhood of Railway and Commercial Telegraphers, a rival organization that adopted militant trade union principles, began to attract ORT members. Responding to these conditions, ORT's leadership reversed its previous position and in 1891 by constitutional revision converted the renamed Order of Railroad Telegraphers of North America into a protective trade union similar in form and structure to other railroad brotherhoods. The change had the desired result as membership curved sharply upward and doubled within two years. Considerable success in collective bargaining added to the growing prestige of the organization.

The economic depression that began in 1893, the rise of the American Railway Union*, the unsuccessful Pullman strike, and a series of largely unsuccessful strikes in 1892 and 1893 once again halted and reversed the growth of the ORT. Membership, which had approached 18,000 two years earlier, was down to 5,000 by 1895. Recovery began in 1896, but due to unwise or mismanaged strikes, it was not until 1901 that the Order regained its strength of 1893. Between 1901 and 1907, however, the ORT grew dramatically, reaching a membership of 37,500. The panic of 1907 and the recession following halted but failed to reduce the ORT's previous gains; moreover, the order successfully resisted wage reductions sought by most railroad lines.

The ORT's achievements in building membership and in collective bargaining were not equaled by progress in acquiring reform legislation. Too often in the quest for major legislation the ORT failed to cooperate with other railroad brotherhoods, and its officers preferred to lobby independently for laws specifically applying to railroad telegraphers. ORT's isolation proved disastrous when the train service brotherhoods' national campaign for an eight-hour law came to fruition with the passage of the Adamson Act in 1917. Telegraphers were not included in the provisions of the Adamson Act, and their own eight-hour bill was stalled in committee.

World War I and the period of federal control of the railroads contributed much to the growth and effectiveness of the telegraphers' union. By 1920 the ORT had a membership of 78,000, which represented nearly all workers in its jurisdictional field. Unlike many other unions during the postwar years, the ORT maintained much of this membership as well as many of the improved working rules and conditions instituted by federal authorities. Perhaps most significantly, the eight-hour day and the substitution of national for local collective bargaining was preserved after the railroads were returned to private control.

Nevertheless the ORT had reached its organizational pinnacle in 1920 and thereafter underwent a slow decline. Although it continued to represent nearly all workers in a jurisdiction expanded to include a variety of employees concerned with railroad communications and traffic control, changes in railroad technology, organization, and structure continually contracted its organizing field. Thus by the 1940s ORT membership had dropped to about 40,000, where it remained for several years. In 1965 the ORT changed its name to the Transportation-Communication Employees Union, and on February 21, 1969, it merged with the Brotherhood of Railway, Airline and Steamship Clerks, Freight Handlers, Express and Station Employees* (BRAC).

The ORT, which held triennial conventions, maintained its national headquarters in St. Louis. Full-time officers included a president, a secretary-treasurer, and six vice-presidents. The board of directors consisted of five members elected to six-year terms by the delegates to the national conventions. At the time of the merger with the BRAC, the ORT had a membership of 30,000.

For further information, see *The Railroad Telegrapher* published monthly by the ORT. See also Archibald M. McIsaac, *The Order of Railroad Telegraphers: A Study in Trade Unionism and Collective Bargaining* (1933), and Vidkunn Ulriksson, *The Telegraphers: Their Craft and Their Unions* (1953).

RAILROAD TRAINMEN; BROTHERHOOD OF (BRT). The disrupting and violent conditions prevailing among the nation's railroads during the 1870s inspired accelerated organizing activities among several classifications of railroad workers. These laborers protested wage rates averaging little more than a dollar a day, long workdays ranging from twelve to eighteen hours, unsafe working conditions that left many railroad workers either dead or disabled, blacklistings, and a variety of other grievances. Although many railroad organizations began as death-and-disability beneficial societies, most quickly evolved into economic trade unions. Such was the case with the organization of railroad trainmen. The first known association of railroad brakemen organized during the early months of 1883 in Albany, New York, and was created primarily to provide sickness and disability insurance.

Inspired by the Albany organization, a group of brakemen working on the Delaware and Hudson Railroad in Oneonta, New York, quickly laid plans to form a similar association. In the early summer of 1883, they met in a Delaware and Hudson Railroad caboose and organized the Oneonta Lodge of the Brotherhood of Railroad Brakemen (BRB). Actions of the Oenonta brakemen sparked the interest of railway trainmen throughout the country. Although un-expected, the response encouraged the Oneonta Lodge to issue a call for a convention to create a national brotherhood. The resulting meeting convened in Oneonta on September 23, 1883, and the Grand Lodge of the Brotherhood of Railroad Brakemen was formed. The new union grew rapidly, and when the first annual convention of the BRB was held in October 1884, ninety-four delegates assembled representing thirty-nine lodges and 900 members. The following year 160 lodges with 4,500 members attended the annual convention. During 1885 the BRB organized its first Canadian local at Moncton, New Brunswick.

Although the BRB increasingly concerned itself with a wide range of labor grievances, the beneficial aspects of the organization remained important. Reflecting this interest, delegates to the BRB's 1885 convention voted to create an insurance department and increased the $300 insurance benefit to $600. In the following years benefits were again raised to $800 in 1886 and $1,200 in 1893.

The decade of the 1890s was a momentous period for the BRB. It organized such diverse railroad workers as conductors, brakemen, roadmen, yardmen, dining car stewards, yardmasters, switchtenders, and baggagemen and in 1890 changed its name to the Brotherhood of Railroad Trainmen. But a new name did little to resolve the problems of the union: a growing internal factionalism (especially an East-West split), which threatened to disrupt the organization; the threat of Eugene Debs's American Railway Union*, and the loss of membership and near financial bankruptcy resulting from the depression of the 1890s. Nevertheless, under the forceful leadership of P. H. Morrissey, the BRT survived the decade and grew steadily during the early years of the new century.

The elevation of William G. Lee as president in 1909 signaled a twenty-year period of conflict and acrimony in the internal affairs of the BRT. An economic and political conservative, Lee's autocratic, uncompromising leadership and his perceived reluctance to pursue aggressively the economic interests of railroaders aroused opposition both from subordinate officers in the BRT and among the rank and file. The leadership conflict was most obviously manifested in a long rivalry between Lee and Alexander F. Whitney. Whitney first challenged Lee for the BRT presidency in 1913, and the two men engaged in close, bitter election contests until Whitney finally defeated the cancer-plagued Lee in 1928. The two men disagreed about the advisability of social legislation, government ownership of the railroads, the La Follette Progressive party candidacy in 1924 (Lee supported Coolidge), and a variety of other issues. The rank-and-file opposition to Lee was reflected by large-scale unauthorized strikes in 1920. Lee ruthlessly broke the strikes, revoked the charter of ninety-two local lodges, and in effect expelled 30,000 members.

Like so many other unions, the BRT's membership grew substantially during World War I, declined during the 1920s and the early years of the Great Depression, recovered in the late 1930s, and grew substantially during World

War II. The BRT reached its peak in 1956 when it enrolled over 217,000 rail-roaders. Thereafter it slowly began to lose members as a result of declining employment on the nation's railroads.

Whitney tolerated little opposition to his leadership and was a domineering figure not unlike Lee, but he always operated within the letter (if not the spirit) of the brotherhood's constitution. During his presidency, Whitney effected several governmental and insurance reforms that tightened the organizational structure of the BRT and placed its insurance program on a sound financial basis. Whitney gained the loyalty of rank-and-file trainmen primarily through his militant and effective collective bargaining methods. Perhaps the most striking example of Whitney's bargaining militancy occurred in 1946 when he and Alvanley Johnston of the Brotherhood of Locomotive Engineers led their unions into a national railroad strike. The conflict began when the trainmen and engineers refused to arbitrate their differences over wages and work rules with railroad managers. The railroads were then seized by the federal government upon orders of President Harry S. Truman. When Truman's compromise proposal proved unacceptable to the two brotherhoods, a strike was called for May 23. It ended two days later when Truman asked Congress to enact drastic, punitive legislation to break the strike.

After eliminating a racial exclusion clause in its constitution, in 1957 the BRT affiliated with the American Federation of Labor-Congress of Industrial Organizations* and the Canadian Labour Congress. Prior to this date the brotherhood had remained independent for over seventy years. Faced with a declining membership and finding its bargaining position weakened accordingly, the BRT negotiated a merger with the Brotherhood of Locomotive Firemen and Enginemen* and the Order of Railroad Conductors,* which took effect on January 1, 1969. Creation of the United Transportation Union* resulted from the merger, and BRT president Charles Luna became the first president of the new transportation union.

The BRT maintained its national headquarters in Cleveland and held quadrennial conventions. Principal officers included a president, a secretary-treasurer, and fifteen vice-presidents. The general board of directors was composed of eleven members, including the president, assistant to the president, and secretary-treasurer. At the time of the merger, the BRT had a membership of 185,000 of which about 40,000 were retired trainmen.

For further information, see the *Trainmen News* published weekly by the BRT. See also Walter F. McCaleb, *Brotherhood of Railroad Trainmen: With Special Reference to the Life of Alexander F. Whitney* (1936); Joel Seidman, *The Brotherhood of Railroad Trainmen: The Internal Political Life of a National Union* (1962); and Willington Roe, *Juggernaut: American Labor in Action* (1948).

RAILROAD YARDMASTERS OF AMERICA (RYA). Local associations of yardmasters sprang up at railroad terminals across the United States after the federal government assumed control of the nation's railroads during World War I. Several of these local assemblies sent representatives to a national organizing convention meeting in Cincinnati on December 2, 1918. Before the delegates departed, the Railroad Yardmasters of America had joined the American labor movement. Within a few years of its formation, the new national railroad union had gained the affiliation of most local associations that had been organized on railroads throughout the United States.

The original RYA constitution limited membership to "any male white person of good moral character actually employed as general yardmaster, assistant general yardmaster, yardmaster, assistant yardmaster, and station masters." At the time of its formation, leaders of the RYA adopted as the union's primary objectives the acquisition of the universal eight-hour day, two days of rest monthly, an annual two-week vacation, increased wages, and improved working conditions.

The RYA's limited trade jurisdiction assured that it would remain one of the smaller unions in the American trade union movement. Moreover, the RYA confronted other problems shortly after its formation, further contracting its limited membership base. The open-shop offensive launched by employers shortly after the railroads were returned to private control eliminated many wartime organizing gains. Another problem occurred when yardmasters on the New York Central Railroad seceded from the RYA. The New York Central yardmasters then met in Buffalo, New York, on January 10, 1925, and organized a rival national organization, the Railroad Yardmasters of North America. The new yardmaster union, however, never expanded far beyond the New York Central system, although it exhibited a surprising longevity before finally succumbing.

The Great Depression further contributed to the RYA's problems. Membership fell to almost 1,000 by 1936, but with the demise of the rival Railroad Yardmasters of North America and economic recovery, especially during World War II, the RYA regained much of its membership loss. By the end of World War II, the RYA enrolled nearly 4,000 where it has remained steadily. After remaining independent for nearly three decades, on November 25, 1946, the RYA affiliated with the American Federation of Labor.*

The RYA, which maintains its national headquarters in Park Ridge, Illinois, holds quadrennial conventions. Principal officers include a general president, eighteen vice-presidents, and a general secretary-treasurer. The general executive board is comprised of the president, secretary-treasurer, and seven other members, not fewer than five of whom must be vice-presidents. In 1973 the RYA reported a membership of 5,302 located in 81 local unions.

For further information, see *The Railroad Yardmaster* published eight times a year by the RYA. Little scholarly work has been completed on the RYA, but some information can be attained from *Bulletin No. 618*, Bureau of Labor Statistics, U.S. Department of Labor (1936), and Florence Peterson, *Handbook of Labor Unions* (1944).

RAILWAY, AIRLINE AND STEAMSHIP CLERKS, FREIGHT HAND-LERS, EXPRESS AND STATION EMPLOYEES; BROTHERHOOD OF (BRAC). Protesting low wages and oppressive working conditions, thirty-three railroad clerks employed by the Missouri Pacific and Missouri, Kansas and Texas railroads met in Sedalia, Missouri, on December 31, 1899, and organized the Order of Railroad Clerks of America (ORC). Two years later fourteen delegates representing various newly formed lodges attended the first national convention of the ORC in St. Louis. The new railroad union was chartered by the American Federation of Labor* (AFL) in 1900 and given a broad jurisdiction covering clerical personnel employed in the transportation industry.

The early history of the ORC was characterized by a desperate struggle to survive in the face of the hostile, anti-union campaigns of the railroads. Nevertheless, they were not unproductive years. The ORC called its first strike in 1906 against the Southern Pacific Railroad, which, although eventually lost, revealed the growing strength of the union. Later the same year, the New Orleans lodge gained recognition from the Illinois Central Railroad and negotiated the order's first working agreement. In 1909 the first system-wide agreement was negotiated with the New York, New Haven and Hartford Railroad. During these years it also broadened its jurisdiction to include freight handlers, but the ORC's greatest accomplishment was simply surviving, thus placing itself in a position to take advantage of the opportunities for organization that accompanied the nationalization of the railroads during World War I.

Under the provisions of General Order No. 8 issued shortly after the government assumed control of the railroads, the new government-appointed railroad administrators were instructed to avoid discriminating against union members. Taking advantage of the tolerant attitude of these administrators, the ORC greatly expanded its membership during the war years. Prior to the war, membership had never reached 6,000; by 1920 it stood at 186,000. Before the end of the war, the ORC held contracts with more than forty railroads. The ORC also expanded its reach into Canada in 1918 and, reflecting its growing jurisdiction, in 1919 changed its name to the Brotherhood of Railway and Steamship Clerks, Freight Handlers, Express and Station Employees (BRC).

The BRC's wartime gains proved somewhat illusory, however. The 1921-1922 depression, the railroad shopmen's strike of 1922, and the employers' open-shop offensive combined to drastically reduce BRC membership. By 1927 half of the 1920 membership had been lost, and the outbreak of the Great Depression in 1929 further contracted membership; by 1932 the brotherhood received dues from only 60,800 members. The most significant development in BRC history during the late 1920s was the unanimous election of George M. Harrison to the BRC presidency. Harrison was destined to play an influential role not only in the BRC but in the labor movement nationally and internationally, as well as in national political affairs.

The Railway Labor Act of 1926, its amendment in 1934, and New Deal labor policies combined to provide BRC officials an opportunity to rebuild their shattered union. Their success is reflected in the BRC membership figures: 90,000 in 1937, 204,000 in 1944, and 350,000 in 1955. These were also years of significant collective bargaining advances, including a forty-hour week (1949), a health and welfare program (1955), and the first contract in the airline industry negotiated with Northeast Airlines in 1945.

Resulting from its increased membership in the airline industry, the BRC changed its name again in 1967 to the Brotherhood of Railway, Airline and Steamship Clerks, Freight Handlers, Express and Station Employees. The BRAC's jurisdiction was also expanded through the negotiation of several mergers. During 1969 the Transportation-Communication Employees Union, the Railway Patrolmen's International Union, and the Federation of Business Machine Technicians and Engineers all merged with the brotherhood. Three years later the United Transport Service Employees* voted to affiliate. The BRAC also played an instrumental role in the creation of the Congress of Railway Unions, a federation of railroad service unions.

Beginning in May 1969, the BRAC began a bitter eighteen-month contract dispute with the railroad industry and the government. In the spring of 1969 the BRAC presented its demands to the railroad industry. After fifteen months of frustrating negotiations, the brotherhood called a series of brief, selective strikes. The BRAC rejected the recommendations of a federal investigative board, which attempted to resolve the dispute, and after the expiration of the thirty-day cooling-off period provided under the Railway Labor Act, called a strike for December 10, 1970. Once again the government intervened in the dispute—this time through emergency legislation. After briefly resisting the government-imposed interim settlement, the BRAC bowed to government pressure and cancelled the strike. Six weeks later a new contract acceptable to the BRAC was finally signed.

The BRAC, which maintains its national headquarters in Chicago, holds quadrennial conventions. Full-time officers include an international president, eleven vice-presidents, and a secretary-treasurer. The international executive council is composed of the above officials. In 1973 the BRAC reported a membership of 238,355 located in 1,250 local unions.

For further information, see the *Railway Clerk Interchange* published monthly by the BRAC. See also Harry Henig, *The Brotherhood of Railway Clerks* (1937), the best available account of the brotherhood.

RAILWAY CARMEN OF THE UNITED STATES AND CANADA; BROTHERHOOD (BRCA). Railway car repairers and inspectors worked under very trying conditions during the early years of the railroad industry in the United States. Low wages, long hours, numerous work-related accidents, and little job security characterized employment. Yet unlike many other railroad crafts, trade union organization began relatively late among these workers. Even the Knights of Labor* had little success in enrolling railway carmen. The absence of trade union activity in part reflects the very tenuous nature of employment; agitating for or organizing a union was one of the better ways to lose a job.

Much of this changed, however, on the evening of October 27, 1888, when seven car inspectors met in a Burlington, Cedar Rapids and Northern Railway car parked on a track in Cedar Rapids, Iowa. The meeting climaxed several weeks of discussion concerning the need for some type of organization and resulted in the founding of the Brotherhood of Car Repairers of North America (BCRNA). Brothers Frank and W. H. Ronemus had provided much of the inspiration for the new union, and W. H. Ronemus was elected grand chief car repairman. Officials of the new union did not immediately launch an effort to improve the economic conditions of workers, feeling the trade needed to be better organized before this would be possible. By 1890 a sister lodge had been established in Clinton, Iowa, and other locals were begun in Topeka and Wichita, Kansas, Pueblo, Colorado, and Fairbury, Nebraska.

Unknown to the BCRNA founders, the Carmen's Mutual Aid Association was organized in Minneapolis on November 23, 1888. Shortly after leaders of the two groups learned of the other's existence, they held merger talks, and on September 9, 1890, the two organizations amalgamated to form the Brotherhood Railway Carmen of America. A year later another independent association organized in Indianapolis, the Car Inspectors, Repairers and Oilers Mutual Benefit Association, merged with the BRCA. Through these mergers and with vigorous organizing activities the BRCA grew to sixty lodges by June 1891. Amalgamation with the Brotherhood Railway Carmen of Canada, which had been organized the previous year, further complemented this growth.

The BRCA played an important role in the organization of Eugene V. Debs' American Railway Union* (ARU). The brotherhood's secretary-treasurer and journal editor, Sylvester Keliher, was especially active and eventually resigned his BRCA office to accept a similar post with the ARU. Few in the BRCA hierarchy shared Keliher's enthusiasm for the ARU, however, and a split developed among executive board members concerning the union's relationship with the ARU. When board members ultimately voted against ARU affiliation, many lodges returned their BRCA charters and joined the ARU. The brotherhood had 143 chartered lodges in 1893, but the number shrank to thirty-eight by its convention in June 1894. The ARU, the Pullman strike, and the depression of the mid-1890s reduced the BRCA to little more than a paper organization by 1896.

Beginning in 1899, however, the brotherhood made a remarkable recovery and began an amazing growth. By 1904 over 30,000 members enrolled in at least 400 lodges. The chartering of a rival organization, the International Association of Car Workers, by the American Federation of Labor* (AFL) in 1901 was the only cloud on the BRCA horizon. The AFL acted after the brotherhood had voted against affiliation several times. This problem was largely resolved in 1910 when the BRCA affiliated with the AFL, and the following year the AFL suspended the charter of the International Association of Car Workers.

The BRCA grew at a tremendous rate during the first two decades of the twentieth century. Although making significant gains while the federal government controlled the railroads during World War I, the brotherhood in fact had experienced a steady growth since 1899. By 1921 it reported a membership of 200,000 in 1,465 lodges.

Throughout its early history the BRCA exhibited little strike militancy, preferring to resolve problems through negotiations, mediation, and, when necessary, arbitration. Employer action following the return of the railroads to private control after World War I, however, forced brotherhood officials to break with their usual conservative policies. In a membership referendum, the BRCA voted overwhelmingly to join the railroad shop craft strike of 1922. Confronted by the combined hostility of the railroads and the federal government (as well as many state governments), the strike proved a disaster. As a consequence, brotherhood officials enthusiastically endorsed the conciliation and arbitration policies established in the Railway Labor Act of 1926.

The anti-union offensive during the 1920s and the depression that ushered in the following decade took its toll on the BRCA. Membership declined to almost 100,000 in the early 1930s and continued downward until 1936 when the brotherhood claimed fewer than 60,000 members. Reduced employment, great pressures to lower wages, and threats against other concessions gained by labor over the years filled the depression years. Conversely, it was a period of significant legislative accomplishment, highlighted by the enactment of the Railroad Retirement Act.

Beginning in the late 1930s and accelerating during World War II, the BRCA recovered many of its previous losses. Union membership continued to grow until the mid-1950s, but railroad consolidation and substantial reductions in the work force gradually reduced the membership potential in the BRCA's trade jurisdiction. These circumstances have produced a slow decline in the brotherhood's membership since the late 1950s.

The BRCA, which maintains its national headquarters in Kansas City, holds quadrennial conventions. Principal officers include a general president, twelve vice-presidents, a secretary-treasurer, and the editor-manager of the brotherhood's *Journal*. The general executive board is composed of five members elected at national conventions. In 1973, the BRCA reported a membership of 103,992 located in 705 local unions.

For further information, see the *Railway Carmen's Journal* published monthly by the BRCA. See also Leonard Painter, *Through Fifty Years with the Brotherhood Railway Carmen of America* (1941), and Robert H. Zieger, *Republicans and Labor, 1919-1929* (1969).

RAILWAY CONDUCTORS AND BRAKEMEN; ORDER OF (ORC).
Amboy, Illinois, was the site of the first known association of railroad conductors. In the spring of 1868, several conductors working on the Illinois Central
Railroad met there and formed The Conductor's Union. As news of the
venture reached conductors working on the Chicago, Burlington and Quincy
Railroad, they responded by organizing Galesburg (Illinois) Division No. 2 of
the Conductor's Union. On July 6, 1868, representatives of the two organizations met in Mendota, Illinois, to form a central body, which they named Conductors' Union. Later in the same year conductors on the Pittsburgh, Fort
Wayne and Chicago Railroad, in concert with the Conductors' Union, issued a
call for a national convention to meet in Columbus, Ohio, on December 15,
1868, to organize a brotherhood of railway conductors. It was entitled the Conductors' Brotherhood until 1878, when the name was changed to the Order of
Railway Conductors of America.

Founders of the ORC had no intention of organizing an economic trade
union; instead, they created a temperance and benevolent society, which emphasized fraternal and ritualistic activities. During the first twenty years of its
existence, the order threatened to expel any member participating in labor
strikes. With the exception of the period of recession during the 1870s, the
ORC grew slowly until the early 1890s. A founding membership of less than
100 increased to 1,000 by 1872, 2,000 by 1882, and 14,000 by 1890.

During these years, the ORC underwent a fundamental transition from a
fraternal and beneficial society into an economic trade union. Despite its conservative philosophy, the ORC encountered substantial hostility from railroad
owners and managers. Moreover as a result of its anti-strike policy, other railroad brotherhoods denounced the ORC as a strike-breaking organization.
Finally an increasing number of conductors themselves grew impatient with
the principles of the order's founders. In 1885, the first changes in its original
objectives were instituted, when convention delegates instructed ORC officials
to assist members in resolving disputes with railroad managers; however, this
change did not go far enough for one group of conductors who organized a
rival Brotherhood of Conductors in September 1889. In 1890 an insurgent
group replaced the older officers of the order, repealed the constitutional anti-
strike clause, and adopted aggressive trade union principles. Shortly thereafter, the Brotherhood of Conductors merged with the ORC. Obviously approving of the changes in the order, railroad conductors began joining the
union in large numbers; membership jumped from 14,000 in 1890 to 20,000 in
1893. The panic of 1893 and the following depression temporarily stalled the
ORC's membership offensive, but membership turned upward again in 1898,
reached nearly 48,000 by 1912, and continued to grow through World War I.

The public nature of the railroad industry inevitably forced the ORC into
politics. The order maintained a representative in Washington, D.C., to lobby
for favorable railway labor legislation. Cooperating with other railroad broth-

erhoods, the ORC successfully lobbied for a bill in 1907 limiting the hours a railroader could work to sixteen out of twenty-four. In 1917, the eight-hour day bill for railroaders, the Adamson Act, became law. In the following years, the ORC was involved in such legislative affairs as the campaign for government ownership of railroads (the Plumb Plan), the Railway Labor Act of 1926, and the Railroad Retirement Act of 1937. In an effort to strengthen the influence of railroad labor, in 1926 the ORC participated in the creation of the Railway Labor Executives' Associaton and played an active role in the association.

Although experiencing its share of internal conflicts, jurisdictional disputes (primarily with the Brotherhood of Railroad Trainmen* (BRT)), and economic problems during the 1920s and the Great Depression, the ORC faced its greatest threat from technological and organizational changes taking place in the railroad industry in the post-World War II period. As a result of protracted and sometimes bitter negotiations, the ORC won substantial wage concessions, cost-of-living adjustments, and rules changes in 1954 and again in 1965-1966. The ORC's membership reached approximately 50,000 by the end of World War II, but because of declining employment in the railroad industry, its membership decreased steadily during the 1950s and 1960s.

In an effort to broaden its membership base in the early 1930s, the ORC expanded its jurisdiction to include brakemen, and in 1942 it absorbed the Order of Sleeping Car Conductors. Reflecting these changes, the union title was changed in 1954 to the Order of Railway Conductors and Brakemen. In a further effort to bolster its slipping bargaining position, in 1969 the ORC combined with the BRT, the Switchmen's Union of North America,* and the Brotherhood of Locomotive Firemen and Enginemen to create the United Transportation Union.*

The ORC, which maintained its national headquarters in Cedar Rapids, Iowa, held quadrennial conventions. Full-time officers included a president, eight vice-presidents, and a secretary-treasurer. The general board of directors consisted of the above officials in addition to three members who consistituted the ORC board of trustees. At the time of the 1969 merger, the order had a membership of 13,700.

For further information, see the *Railway Conductors' Monthly* published by the ORC, and Edwin C. Robbins, *Railway Conductors: A Study in Organized Labor* (1914).

RAILWAY MAIL ASSOCIATION. *See* United Federation of Postal Clerks.

RAILWAY UNION; AMERICAN (ARU). Eugene Debs addressed the annual convention of the Brotherhood of Locomotive Firemen* in Cincinnati in September 1892 and announced his resignation as grand secretary and treasurer.

He revealed his intention to devote himself to the task of establishing a comprehensive railroad union open to all railroad laborers, skilled and unskilled. The following months were spent in general preparations preliminary to the launching of the new union. Finally, on June 20, 1893, fifty railroaders met at Ulrich's Hall in Chicago and formally created the American Railway Union. Debs served as president.

The new union was meant to be an inclusive organization of railroad workers, and membership was open to any worker employed in any capacity by the railroads. The only exception to the ARU's open membership policy was a whites-only constitutional provision reaffirmed at the first annual convention by a 113 to 102 vote. The ARU advocated traditional trade union objectives: higher wages, shorter hours, improved and safer working conditions, adequate compensation for injured workers, and inexpensive insurance. ARU locals were organized on the basis of craft, with locals of each major system divided into systems federations. The national organization was composed of the systems federations. Although craft skills were emphasized in the formation of locals, the ARU assumed many attributes of an industrial union. Notably it adopted a policy of united action in response to the violation of an individual's rights.

The ARU grew rapidly. Within six months of its organization, it had eighty-six lodges and by the end of 1893, 125 affiliated lodges. The ARU successfully organized the employees of the Union Pacific, the Denver and Rio Grande, and the Rio Grande and Western and also had great strength on both the Northern and Southern Pacific railroads. While previously unorganized, unskilled workers constituted much of the ARU's membership, some locals and many members of the older railroad brotherhoods joined the new union.

Within a year of its organization, the ARU registered its first collective bargaining success as a result of a dramatic strike against the Great Northern Railroad. Demonstrating the power of unified action, the ARU tied up transcontinental runs for a period of eighteen days before James J. Hill of the Great Northern conceded to most of the union's demands. In a paradoxical sense, however, the Great Northern victory was both a blessing and a curse. ARU membership grew dramatically, and by early summer 1894 the union had 425 local lodges and a membership of between 125,000 and 140,000. Conversely the ARU's comparatively easy victory created a sense of overconfidence and impatience among rank-and-file railroaders as well as many ARU leaders. Moreover, the ARU's success and dramatic growth alarmed both the railroads and the older railroad brotherhoods.

This was the situation when the employees of George Pullman's Pullman Palace Car Company voted to strike in May 1894. The Pullman employees had been organized by the ARU, and Debs attempted to mediate an adjustment of the dispute. Pullman, however, closed his Chicago plant and resolutely refused to negotiate with his employees or ARU officials. The ARU then decided to institute a boycott of all Pullman sleeping cars.

When railroad officials refused to detach the Pullman cars, the conflict evolved into a national strike. The General Managers' Association (GMA), a combination of Chicago-based railroads, assumed control of the strike for the railroad corporations, and its objective was not only to crush the strike but also to destroy the ARU. The strike quickly spread to all sections of the country, and Pullman traffic through Chicago was halted. The GMA's attempt to import strikebreakers had little effect on the strike, but the decision of the older railroad brotherhoods to continue normal operations, despite the fact that many of their members and locals supported the ARU, was a serious blow.

The GMA, which had been unable to break the strike, turned to the government for help. With the assistance of the attorney general of the United States, Richard Olney, a former railroad lawyer, an injunction obtained under the provisions of the Sherman Anti-Trust Act and alleged interference with the mails virtually prohibited any type of union action in support of the strike. When the ARU ignored the injunction, federal troops were sent into Chicago "to restore order." The presence of the troops and the arrest of ARU leaders for contempt of court effectively crushed the strike. Debs and his fellow officers were sentenced from three to six months in prison, and the ARU disintegrated.

The ARU, which held annual conventions, maintained its headquarters in Chicago. Its principal officers consisted of a president, vice-president, and secretary. At the height of its success during the early summer of 1894, the ARU had a membership of approximately 150,000.

For further information, see the *Railway Times* published biweekly by the ARU. See also Almont Lindsey, *The Pullman Strike* (1942), and Philip S. Foner, *History of the Labor Movement in the United States*, vol. 2 (1955).

RETAIL CLERKS INTERNATIONAL ASSOCIATION (RCIA). Efforts to reduce the hours of labor motivated the earliest organizing activities among retail clerks. In the years prior to the Civil War, a number of early-closing societies sprang up on the East Coast, and, after the war, the early-closing movement spread throughout the country, but intercity cooperation did not begin until the emergence of the Knights of Labor.* Assuming that their problems were different from those of other workers and consequently could best be alleviated by their own organization, the clerks were never entirely happy with the Knights. Conversely, the craft-conscious policies of the newly organized American Federation of Labor* (AFL) proved much more attractive, and as early as 1888, many associations of clerks began to affiliate with the AFL as directly chartered federal labor unions.

The AFL had issued over eighteen charters to local clerks' unions by 1890, and during the federation's annual convention of that year, a successful resolution was introduced to charter a national union of retail clerks to be called the

Retail Clerks National Protective Association. ("National" was changed to "International" in 1899, and "protective" was eliminated from the union title in 1943.)

The struggle for early closing dominated the activities of the RCIA during its first two decades. Local unions found boycotts and adverse publicity the most effective weapons in gaining early-closing agreements. Eventually agitation extended beyond early closing to include Sundays and holidays. Surprisingly, it was not until the 1909 convention of the RCIA that the union adopted the eight-hour day reform.

The early-closing and shorter-hours campaign of the RCIA struck a responsive chord among retail clerks, and the union's membership grew dramatically. In 1890 when the union was chartered, it had 3,000 members; a dozen years later it claimed 50,000 (a figure that was probably somewhat inflated). Following its initial successes, however, the RCIA experienced nearly thirty years of decline only slightly interrupted by World War I and the immediate postwar period.

The RCIA's success in gaining shorter hours without resorting to strikes had stimulated organizing activities, but as the major issue began to change from hours to wages, it became increasingly necessary to withhold service to force employer concessions. The RCIA's first authorized strike occurred in Lafayette, Indiana (then union headquarters), in 1912 and was followed by major strikes in Buffalo (1913), Memphis (1917), and St. Louis (1918). Although the union did gain some concessions from these strikes, in general they were disasters for the union, and membership declined steadily.

The RCIA reached its nadir in 1933, when it represented only 5,000 clerks. Although the upsurge of trade unionism precipitated by the labor provisions of the National Industrial Recovery Act and the National Labor Relations Act reinvigorated the RCIA, its revival was slow and painful. The RCIA was hampered by a timid, conservative leadership either unwilling or unable to take advantage of the organizing opportunities that existed after 1933. Moreover, with the increased development of the department store method of merchandising, organization along strictly craft lines became less rational. Opposition to the policies of the RCIA leaders began to grow, especially among several New York City locals, and with the organization of the Congress of Industrial Organizations*(CIO), dissident factions in the union seceded and organized the CIO-affiliated Retail, Wholesale and Department Store Union* (RWDSU).

The secession of the disaffected locals was a severe blow to the RCIA, but other developments held great promise for its future. During the late 1930s and early 1940s, the RCIA made significant inroads in the organization of chain store employees, and this, along with the continued growth of organization of grocery store employees, compensated for the loss of members of the RWDSU. Moreover, a militant organizing campaign on the West Coast, where the RWDSU was inactive, enlarged RCIA membership. Finally, James A. Suffridge, who had led the West Coast campaign, was elected president in 1944 and secretary-treasurer (then the chief administrative officer) in 1947. Under Suffridge's aggressive leadership, the RCIA reorganized and reinvigorated its organizing effort.

Reversing the trend of many modern labor unions, the RCIA grew steadily during the twenty-five years following World War II. The RCIA reported 100,000 members in 1943, 246,500 in 1954, 400,000 in 1960, and 605,202 in 1970. In part these membership advances resulted from a more expansive and aggressive jurisdictional policy. Under Suffridge's leadership, the RCIA became a less craft-conscious, white-collar union, and increasingly organized along industrial lines. These changes intensified long-standing jurisdictional conflicts with such unions as the International Brotherhood of Teamsters,* the Amalgamated Clothing Workers of America,* and the Amalgamated Meat Cutters and Butcher Workmen.* But the RCIA continued to hold its own in this inter-union competition and constantly expanded its membership base.

The RCIA, which maintains its national headquarters in Washington, D.C., holds quadrennial conventions. Principal officers include a president, a secretary-treasurer (until 1955 the chief administrative officer of the union), and a number of vice-presidents representing regional divisions. The international executive board consists of the above officials. In 1973 the RCIA reported a membership of 633,221 located in 215 local unions.

For further information, see the *Retail Clerks Advocate* issued monthly. See also Michael Harrington, *The Retail Clerks* (1962), a fine study of the structure and government of the RCIA, and George G. Kirstein, *Stores and Unions: A Study of the Growth of Unionism in Dry Goods and Department Stores* (1950), an older study with valuable historical information. Marten Estey, in a number of essays, has contributed significantly to an understanding of unionism among retail clerks. See his "The Retail Clerks" in Albert A. Blum et al., *White-Collar Workers* (1971); "Patterns of Union Membership in the Retail Trades" (July 1955) and "The Strategic Alliance as a Factor in Union Growth" (October 1955), *Industrial and Labor Relations Review*; and "Early Closing: Employer-Initiated Origins of the Retail Labor Movement," *Labor History* (Fall 1972).

RETAIL, WHOLESALE AND DEPARTMENT STORE UNION (RWDSU). The resurgence of trade unionism following the enactment of the National Industrial Recovery Act of 1933 had a profound impact on union organizations of retail store employees. Local unions of retail clerks proved much more aggressive in taking advantage of the new organizing opportunities than their parent body, the Retail Clerks International Association* (RCIA). As these differences grew, local leaders became increasingly critical of the timid and conservative RCIA leadership. Much of the unhappiness was centered in New York City where RCIA locals took advantage of New Deal legislation and conducted a militant organizing campaign. Tensions between the New York locals and the RCIA increased to such an extent that in 1935 the locals refused to forward per-capita taxes to the International, and eleven of the fourteen locals constituting the New York Joint Board demanded that regional RCIA officials be removed from office. The hostile response of Secretary-Treasurer C. C. Coulter, chief administrative officer of the RCIA, further exacerbated the situation, and the dissident locals demanded the calling of the first general convention since 1926. The locals were again chastised for their indiscretion, and their demands were ignored. Unhappy local leaders then appealed unsuccessfully to the American Federation of Labor* for a federal union charter.

Responding to the presistent criticism of the New York locals, Coulter finally agreed to an election of officers in 1937, although he still refused to issue a call for a general convention. When a full opposition slate was nominated, however, Coulter responded by disqualifying all opposition candidates. New York locals had previously organized the "New Era Committee," and dissident locals from other cities joined with the New York groups to push for union reform. The New Era Committee applied for and on May 19, 1937, received an international union charter from the newly organized Congress of Industrial Organizations* (CIO). The new CIO affiliate was titled the United Retail Employes of America (UREA).

Later the same year, the CIO established the Department Store Organizing Committee (DSOC) under the chairmanship of Sidney Hillman. The DSOC, however, was never a very active organization and was administered primarily from UREA offices. In 1940 it was dissolved, and its jurisdiction was assumed by the UREA, which then changed its name to the United Retail, Wholesale and Department Store Employes of America (later shortened to Retail, Wholesale and Department Store Union).

The RWDSU made dramatic membership gains during the 1937-1940 period, especially in New York City. A strike at Gimbels in New York City won the forty-hour week not only for Gimbels workers but for most other New York store workers. But the Gimbels strike exposed a problem of great significance for the future of the RWDSU. A militant, left-wing leadership had assumed control of many New York locals, and as they began to criticize RWDSU president Samuel Wolchok, friction grew between local and international leaders. The conflict temporarily subsided during World War II as the RWDSU left wing adopted a united front policy.

The dramatic strike against Montgomery Ward & Company highlighted the RWDSU's history during World War II. The energies and resources of the union were depleted by the long struggle to gain union recognition from the contumacious Sewell Avery, board chairman of Montgomery Ward. The government had to seize the company because of the strike, and U.S. Army troops physically removed Avery from his office. The strike also refueled simmering ideological differences when the left wing characterized RWDSU officers as treasonous for calling the walkout.

The smoldering hostility between left-wing local leaders and international officers flamed into a full-scale rebellion in 1948 when the RWDSU general executive board passed a resolution requiring local officers to file the non-Communist affidavits required under the provisions of the Taft-Hartley Act. Their failure to do so previously had resulted in the forfeiture of the right to appear on the ballot of National Labor Relations Board representational elections. As a result the rival RCIA had made significant inroads into RWDSU membership. RWDSU president Wolchok suspended the officers of the New York locals who failed to comply with the directive, and they in turn seceded. At this point CIO president Philip Murray intervened. After failing in an effort to force Wolchok's resignation, Murray temporarily awarded jurisdiction over department and men's wear stores to the Amalgamated Clothing Workers of America.*

Having lost much of its jurisdiction and debilitated by secession, the RWDSU appeared to have suffered a terminal ideological illness. Wolchok took a leave of absence and eventually resigned. The union refused to die, however, and in effect was reborn in 1954 when it absorbed two other unions, the Distributive Processing and Office Workers of America and the Playthings, Jewelry and Novelty Workers International Union.* Although failing to keep pace with the dramatic growth of the RCIA, which had profited from the RWDSU's troubles, the RWDSU nevertheless became a stable and effective trade union. Extended merger discussions between the RCIA and RWDSU were held but failed to produce an amalgamation. Moreover, in 1969, RWDSU District 65 seceded and formed a new national organization, the Distributive Workers of America.

The RWDSU, which maintains its national headquarters in New York City, holds quadrennial conventions. The RWDSU has only two international officers—a president and a secretary-treasurer. These officers govern the union between conventions in association with a variable numbered international executive board and general counsel. In 1973 the RWDSU reported a membership of 197,840 located in 315 local unions.

For further information, see the *RWDSU Record* issued monthly. See also George G. Kirstein, *Stores and Unions: A Study of the Growth of Unionism in Dry Goods and Department Stores* (1950); Marten Estey, "The Retail Clerks," in Albert A. Blum et al., *White-Collar Workers* (1971); and *The American Federationist* (July 1959).

ROOFERS, DAMP AND WATERPROOF WORKERS ASSOCIATION; UNITED SLATE, TILE AND COMPOSITION (USTCRD&WWA). Delegates representing the International Slate and Tile Roofers Union of America (ISTRUA) and the International Brotherhood of Composition Roofers, Damp and Waterproof Workers of the United States and Canada (BCRD&WW) met in Pittsburgh on September 8, 1919, and agreed to a merger creating the United Slate, Tile and Composition Roofers, Damp and Waterproof Workers Association. Organized in 1902, the ISTRUA affiliated with the American Federation of Labor* (AFL) on June 5, 1903. The BCRD&WW had been organized as the International Brotherhood of Composition Roofers, Damp and Waterproof Workers and affiliated with the AFL on November 6, 1906. Three years later the words "of the United States and Canada" were added to the union title.

The AFL approved the merger of the two unions on December 17, 1919, and issued a charter to the USTCRD&WWA conferring jurisdiction over "roofing (slate, tile, asbestos, plastic, slag, gravel, asphalt, composition, etc.) except shingles of wood and metal tile; also waterproofing and damp resisting preparations when applied in or outside of buildings." The organizers of the merger identified as one of their major objectives "to confederate as far as possible our somewhat spasmodic individual efforts into one continuous collective undertaking for the upbuilding and improvement of this association." Local unions determined apprenticeship, and skilled or apprentice roofers were eligible for membership. At the time of the merger, the ISTRUA paid per-capita taxes to the AFL on 600 members and the BCRD&WW on 1,000 members.

The newly amalgamated union grew steadily during the 1920s, reaching a membership of 3,000 by 1922 and 4,000 by 1927. Although organizing initiatives ended during the years of the Great Depression, the USTCRD&WWA held its previous gains throughout the decade of the 1930s. The membership curve then started upward again during the 1940s, reaching 12,000 by mid-century and continuing to rise slowly but steadily thereafter.

The USTCR&WWA, which maintains its national headquarters in Washington, D.C., holds triennial conventions. Principal officers include a president, ten vice-presidents, and a secretary-treasurer. The above officials also constitute the general executive board. In 1973 the USTCRD&WWA reported a membership of 26,448 located in 211 local unions.

For further information, see the *Journeyman Roofer & Waterproofer* issued monthly by the USTCRD&WWA. Published accounts of the union's history were not located, but basic information can be found in *Bulletins No. 420, 506,* and *618*, Bureau of Labor Statistics, U.S. Department of Labor (1929, 1929, 1936).

RUBBER CORK, LINOLEUM AND PLASTIC WORKERS OF AMERICA; UNITED (UR).

Low wages and poor working conditions characterized employment during the last quarter of the nineteenth century in the rapidly growing American rubber industry. Because of these conditions, labor organization began early in the industry, but the anti-union sentiment of major rubber producers retarded the development of effective unionism. Utilizing a private, well-armed police force, company spies, and company unions and the incentive of welfare capitalism, employers maintained the open-shop in the rubber industry for several years.

The Knights of Labor* conducted the earliest organizing effort in the industry but accomplished little. During the 1890s, the American Federation of Labor* (AFL) began chartering federal labor unions for rubber workers employed in the eastern states. On November 6, 1902, these federal locals merged to form the Amalgamated Rubber Workers' Union of North America (ARWU), the first national union of rubber workers. The new union, however, had the misfortune of arriving on the labor scene just as anti-union employers launched a vigorous, well-financed national open-shop campaign. The ARWU's efforts to penetrate the expanding rubber industry in Akron, Ohio, came to naught, and this, along with a disastrous strike in Trenton, New Jersey, destroyed the neophyte union.

Taking its turn at challenging the barons of the rubber industry, in 1913 the Industrial Workers of the World* led a dramatic six-week strike of rubber workers in Akron, but a combination of company resistance and the anti-union activities of public officials broke the strike. Similar efforts by an organizer for the International Association of Machinists* to build a union of rubber workers in Akron also ended in failure.

Enactment of the National Industrial Recovery Act (NIRA) in June 1933 stimulated a great revival of union activity not only in Akron but in rubber plants throughout the nation. Rubber workers organized AFL federal labor unions, and by the end of 1933 approximately seventy-five of these federal locals enrolled as many as 50,000 workers. Responding to increasing demands for the organization of a national union, in 1934 the AFL established the Rubber Workers' Council but antagonized rubber workers by ordering the federal labor unions to surrender skilled tradesmen and maintenance men to appropriate craft unions. Meanwhile, the Rubber Manufacturers Association, an organization of rubber companies, refused to bargain with the Rubber Workers' Council, and individual companies organized company unions to subvert the intent of the NIRA. The AFL's actions and the inability of rubber worker unions to gain recognition from employers resulted in disillusionment and demoralization as the surging union tide in the industry crested and began to ebb.

In a halfhearted effort to revive trade union organization in the industry, AFL president William Green issued the call for a national convention of rubber worker locals to meet in Akron on September 12, 1935. The organization of the United Rubber Workers of America (URWA) resulted, and events during the convention presaged the future of relations between the new union and the

AFL. Despite Green's threat to withdraw all AFL financial and organizational assistance, delegates rebelled against Green's attempt to install his own candidates in URWA offices. Moreover, objecting to the proffered AFL jurisdictional grant limiting the URWA to unskilled production workers, the delegates instructed URWA representatives to the AFL 1935 national convention to introduce a resolution granting the URWA an industrial union charter. During debate on this resolution the famous altercation occurred between John L. Lewis and William Hutcheson of the United Brotherhood of Carpenters.*

The year 1936 was the year of the strike for the UTWA. Rubber workers began employing the sitdown tactic, many unauthorized, as a means of forcing management to discuss grievances and grant union recognition. The most dramatic strike occurred at the Goodyear plant in Akron, reputed to be the largest rubber plant in the world. In successfully resolving the grievances precipitating the strike, the URWA won a symbolic victory after a month-long strike that attracted national publicity and support from organized labor throughout the nation. Nevertheless Goodyear still refused to extend union recognition.

On July 1, 1936, the URWA withdrew from the AFL and received an industrial union charter from the Congress of Industrial Organizations* (CIO). the URWA's first major breakthrough in the organization of the rubber industry came a few months later when Local 7 signed a collective bargaining agreement with the Firestone Rubber Company. The Firestone contract and the Supreme Court's favorable decision on the constitutionality of the National Labor Relations Act signaled the beginning of the end of the open shop in the rubber industry. The URWA won National Labor Relations Board representation elections at Goodyear, Goodrich and U.S. Rubber.

Continued employer resistance, the decentralization of the rubber industry, and the 1937-1938 economic recession, however, slowed organization until 1939 when the URWA began a rapid growth that lasted through the years of World War II. The URWA also expanded its organizing activities to include cork, linoleum, and plastic workers, and its success among these workers led to a change in the union title in 1945 to the United Rubber, Cork, Linoleum and Plastic Workers of America.

The UR's major objective in the postwar period was company-wide bargaining. Such an agreement was reached with the U.S. Rubber Company in 1946, and within two years similar agreements were signed with Goodyear, Goodrich, and Firestone. In a further effort to acquire uniform agreements, after 1947 local unions were required to submit contracts to the general president for review and approval. Shortly thereafter a contract department was established at international headquarters to analyze all proposed agreements.

Growing intra-union factionalism and conflict seriously jeopardized the UR's postwar progress. By 1946 a left-wing faction formed a majority on the general executive board and in 1948 nearly won complete control of the union. In the elections of that year, the incumbent president and vice-president were reelected by a vote of 810 to 808 and 811 to 807.

The final showdown came in 1949 in what became popularly known as the Pottstown affair. UR president Leland S. Buckmaster, concerned about the activities of Local 336, Firestone-Pottstown (Pennsylvania), called a special meeting of the local on March 13, 1949. Under the UR constitution, the general president had the right to preside over such special meetings, but Local 336 officials insisted upon conducting the meeting themselves and physically removed Buckmaster from the platform. Buckmaster responded by suspending the president of Local 336, who in turn proffered charges against Buckmaster before the general executive board. After a lengthy trial, the board sustained the charges against Buckmaster and removed him from office. Buckmaster announced his intention to appeal the decision at the national convention meeting later the same year and to offer himself as a candidate for the union presidency. Convention delegates upheld Buckmaster's appeal by a substantial margin and reelected him as president. The repudiation of the left wing and the vindication of Buckmaster greatly reduced the factionalism that had plagued the UR for several years.

A growing internal and external stability characterized UR affairs during the 1950s. Union leaders accepted the provisions of the Taft-Hartley Act, a "no-raiding pact" was negotiated with the International Association of Machinists* with whom the UR had fought numerous bitter jurisdictional wars, and organization was extended to most of the workers in the union's trade jurisdiction, especially the expanding plastics industry. Union membership, which had reached nearly 150,000 by the end of World War II, continued to rise until the early 1950s when it stabilized before again turning upward in the mid-1960s.

The UR, which maintains its national headquarters in Akron, holds biennial conventions. Principal officers include a general president, vice-president, and secretary-treasurer. The general executive board is composed of the above officers and eight additional members elected at national conventions. In 1971 the UR had a membership of 216,259 located in 549 local unions.

For further information, see the *United Rubber Workers* published monthly by the UR. Unfortunately, a full-scale scholarly study of the UR still needs to be written. Nevertheless, much useful information can be found in Harold S. Roberts, *The Rubber Workers: Labor Organization and Collective Bargaining in the Rubber Industry* (1944), and John N. Thurber, *Rubber Workers' History, 1935-1955* (1955).

SCREEN ACTORS GUILD (SAG). On June 30, 1933, a nonprofit organization, the Screen Actors Guild, filed articles of incorporation in Sacramento,

California. Creation of the SAG followed a short but turbulent history of efforts to organize motion picture actors. In March 1920 Associated Actors and Artistes of America* (AAAA), the American Federation of Labor* (AFL) union covering all actors, had granted jurisdiction of screen actors to an affiliate, the Actors' Equity Association* (AEA). The AAAA's action meant the eventual demise of two smaller unions, the Screen Actors of America and the Motion Picture Players Union. AEA organizers, however, found little union sentiment among Hollywood actors and little was accomplished. After the organization in 1924 of the western affiliate of Will Hays's Association of Motion Picture Producers and Distributors of America, AEA president Frank Gillmore hoped to negotiate a minimum standard contract with the new trade association. But his overtures were coolly ignored. The Equity then launched a vigorous but again unsuccessful organizing drive in Hollywood.

Meanwhile organizing efforts among other groups in the entertainment industry met with greater success. Producers responded to the challenge in 1927 by creating an employee-representation organization, the Academy of Motion Picture Arts and Sciences (AMPAS). With a rival in the field, the AEA decided to launch yet another organizing drive. This time a 10 percent salary reduction for nonunion labor announced by the producers' association in the summer of 1927 made it a most propitious time for organizing screen actors. Although the AEA's initial efforts met with a positive response from actors, just as it appeared that the AEA might be successful in establishing an Equity shop, the AMPAS suddenly reversed its previous position and protested the salary cut. Producers immediately agreed to bargain with the AMPAS. Exhibiting little unity or foresight, most screen actors accepted the arrangement, leaving the AEA isolated.

Although the AEA had failed again, the development of sound motion pictures quickly revived its organizing effort. Sound movies required trained voices, which brought to Hollywood many actors from the legitimate and musical comedy stage previously organized by the AEA. With this growing nucleus of members in the motion picture industry, AEA leaders felt strong enough on June 5, 1929, to announce that members would neither work without Equity-negotiated contracts nor work with nonunion actors. In the resulting strike, the AEA demanded a standard contract and an Equity shop. Once again, the AEA was defeated by effective producer resistance, internal dissension, and the lack of support from organized labor.

Failure of the 1929 strike signaled the end of the AEA's organizing efforts in Hollywood. During the following years AMPAS served as the principal bargaining agent for motion picture actors. However, AMPAS's hegemony in the field ended in 1933 when it accepted a 50 percent salary reduction and agreed to a producer-controlled licensing agency. The resulting unhappiness among actors was further accelerated when the National Recovery Administration's (NRA) code for the industry was published in September 1933. The code, which AMPAS approved and had helped draft, incorporated salary control and agency-licensing provisions disliked by actors.

This was the situation that led to the formation of the SAG, which quickly began a campaign against the producer-written NRA code. After SAG president Eddie Cantor met with Franklin D. Roosevelt at Warm Springs, Georgia, in late 1933, the president suspended the salary-control and agent-licensing provisions of the code. The victory quickly elevated the SAG into the forefront of employee organizations, and its membership expanded rapidly. In negotiating a new NRA code, however, the SAG and the producers failed to reach an agreement on the union's insistence on recognition and the establishment of a guild shop. This deadlock continued until the Supreme Court declared the National Industrial Recovery Act unconstitutional in 1935.

Meanwhile, in an effort to gain allies during its battle for NRA recognition, the SAG opened negotiations with the AEA, which still held AFL jurisdiction over screen actors. On November 15, 1934, AEA agreed to surrender its jurisdiction over motion picture actors on the condition that the AAAA award the jurisdiction to the SAG. With the consummation of the arrangement, the SAG became an affiliate of the AAAA and hence the AFL. The SAG and AEA also agreed to a dual membership arrangement for actors working on both the stage and in motion pictures.

The effort to gain recognition and the establishment of a guild shop dominated the early history of the SAG. After resisting for four years and faced with the threat of a well-organized, unified strike of actors, producers finally relented, and on May 15, 1937, recognized the SAG and accepted the guild shop. The resulting 1937 guild contract provided for minimum wage rates, guaranteed employment, a twelve-hour rest period between calls, and conciliation and arbitration machinery to resolve disputes growing from the contract. Through subsequent contracts, conditions of employment were vastly improved, especially for low-salaried players. The SAG also successfully negotiated contracts for actors playing in television motion pictures, and in 1960, it conducted a six-week strike to ensure actors adequate compensation for movies sold to television.

The SAG, which maintains its national headquarters in Hollywood, California, is administered by eight national officers: a president, five vice-presidents, a recording secretary, and a treasurer. These officers constitute the executive committee, which, along with the seventy-three-member national board of directors, is the chief governing agency of the guild. The SAG had a 1973 membership of 26,610.

For further information, see the *Screen Actor* published bimonthly by the SAG. See also Murray Ross, *Stars and Strikes: Unionization of Hollywood* (1941), and Alfred Harding, *The Revolt of the Actors* (1929).

SEAFARERS INTERNATIONAL UNION OF NORTH AMERICA (SIU).

Unusually divisive repercussions in the maritime industry resulted from the split in the American labor movement that saw the creation of the Congress of Industrial Organizations* (CIO) as a rival to the American Federation of Labor* (AFL). Following its usual policy of dividing workers in an industry into craft specialties, on September 8, 1893, the AFL issued a charter to the International Seamen's Union of America* (ISU) covering the merchant seamen's jurisdiction. With the notable exception of the World War I period, however, the ISU was not successful in organizing seamen, especially the large number of sailors on the Atlantic Coast. After the enactment of the National Industrial Recovery Act and the National Labor Relations Act, the ISU continued to be ineffective, and this led to further disintegration and disorganization within the union.

In 1936 the ISU suspended its oldest and strongest affiliate, the Sailors' Union of the Pacific (SUP), after it affiliated with the Maritime Federation of the Pacific, an association of maritime unions on the West Coast. The situation was complicated further in 1937 when the CIO issued a charter to the National Maritime Union of America* (NMU). The new CIO union, which launched a vigorous organizing drive on the East and Gulf coasts, absorbed a number of disaffected ISU locals.

Confronted with the potential loss of its seagoing jurisdiction on both the West and East coasts, the AFL leaders responded by suspending the ISU charter and creating in its place a federal labor union of seamen directly administered by AFL officials. Meanwhile, under the leadership of Harry Lundeberg the SUP became increasingly restive in the Maritime Federation of the Pacific, especially when its leader, Harry Bridges, sided with the NMU in a jurisdictional dispute with the SUP. Although Lundeberg had originally favored affiliation with the CIO, he took the SUP out of the Maritime Federation of the Pacific and opened negotiations with both the AFL and CIO, seeking the most advantageous affiliation terms. Seeing an opportunity to reestablish its seagoing jurisdiction, the AFL executive council revoked the charter of the ISU on October 14, 1938, and the same day issued a charter to the SUP as the Seafarers International Union of North America. Under the terms of the agreement, the SUP was to remain strictly a West Coast organization, and the federal labor union of seamen that the AFL had created in 1937 was to be constituted as a semi-autonomous East Coast division.

The SIU immediately launched a vigorous organizing drive, which by 1939 increased membership to over 15,000. On the East Coast the SIU organized along industrial lines similar to the NMU. As a result of aggressive organizing campaigns and raids on (or the absorption of) smaller independent unions, the SIU grew dramatically during World War II. By the end of the war, the SIU had established its hegemony on the West Coast. Moreover, when the rival NMU became embroiled in a bitter and divisive struggle over Communist domination, the SIU made significant inroads on the East and Gulf coasts.

By the end of the 1940s, the SIU had equalled the membership of the rival

NMU and during the 1950s and 1960s surpassed it. Unlike the NMU, which emphasized social welfare concerns, political activity, and trade union educational programs, the SIU emphasized militant business unionism, relied on individual job actions for organizing, and exhibited little concern about pacifying public opinion. Unlike the case with many other unions, the AFL-CIO* merger did not end the bitter rivalry between the SIU and the NMU, and AFL-CIO leaders have had little success in negotiating an armistice between the two old rivals.

The SIU is composed of thirty-eight semi-autonomous affiliated unions. Besides the SUP and the Atlantic, Gulf, Lakes and Inland Waters District, SIU affiliates include such unions as the Inland Boatmen's Union of the Pacific, which had been organized in 1918 and claimed a jurisdiction including "persons employed on or in connection with the towing operation of ferries, tugboats, freight boats, passenger or other crafts commonly known as inland crafts"; the Pacific Coast Marine Firemen, Oilers, Watertenders and Wipers Association, organized in 1883 and continuing as an independent union until 1953 when it affiliated with the Pacific District of the SIU; and the Marine Cooks and Stewards' Union, organized by the SIU in 1951 to enlist members of the National Union of Marine Cooks and Stewards expelled by the CIO in 1950 as a Communist-dominated union.

The SIU, which maintains its national headquarters in Brooklyn, holds biennial conventions. Full-time officers include a president, executive vice-president, secretary-treasurer, and additional vice-presidents representing each affiliated union having 500 or more members in good standing. The SIU executive board is composed of the above officials. In 1973 the SIU reported a membership of 80,000 located in thirty-eight affiliates.

For further information, see the *International* published monthly by the SIU plus the publications of affiliates such as the *West Coast Sailors* (SUP), the *Seafarers Log* (Atlantic, Gulf, Lakes and Inland Waters District), *The Nor'wester* (Inland Boatmen's Union of the Pacific), and *Stewards News* (Marine Cooks and Stewards' Union). Joseph P. Goldberg, *The Maritime Story: A Study in Labor-Management Relations* (1958), and Joseph H. Ball, *The Government-Subsidized Union Monopoly* (1966), have material on the SIU. Walter Galenson, *The CIO Challenge to the AFL: A History of the American Labor Movement, 1935-1941* (1960), provides a good discussion of the early AFL and CIO rivalry in maritime unionism.

SEAMEN'S UNION OF AMERICA; INTERNATIONAL (ISU). Living and working under deplorable conditions, West Coast seamen revolted in March 1885 after the announcement of a further reduction in already depressed wages. On March 7 a large group of sailors convened in San Francisco and organized the Coast Seamen's Union (CSU). Their efforts represented the climax of attempts to organize seamen that had begun shortly after the end of the Civil War. On January 11, 1866, a group of San Francisco seamen had organized the Seamen's Friendly Union and Protective Society, but having no permanent officers or financial resources, the union accomplished little before disappearing. The next organizing effort came in conjunction with anti-Chinese agitation on the West Coast. During the summer of 1880, the Pacific Mail Steamship Company began discharging regular seamen and replacing them with Chinese sailors. In response to these activities a meeting of steamship sailors and firemen was held in San Francisco on August 31, 1880, which resulted in the founding of the Seamen's Protective Association of San Francisco. Although better organized and better led than its predecessor, the Seamen's Protective Association never acquired a large membership and disintegrated shortly after the treasurer absconded with union funds.

The fact that labor organization in the industry began on the West rather than on the East Coast was not incidental; several circumstances favored West Coast organization. The relative isolation of the Pacific Coast and the small number of ports brought sailors in the area into much closer contact than on the East or Gulf coasts. There was also a high degree of racial homogeneity, fewer sailors, and relatively better conditions of employment due to the absence of a large group of potential strikebreakers.

Within a year of the CSU's organization, the deck crews on steamships organized the Steamshipmen's Protective Union in San Francisco. The two unions soon engaged in bitter jurisdictional quarrels that ultimately led to the Steamshipmen's expulsion from the Federated Trades and Labor Organizations of the Pacific Coast. The continual intramural conflicts obviously weakened both unions; consequently, early in 1891 the Steamshipmen proposed an amalgamation of the two unions under a new name and constitution. The CSU agreed, and on July 29, 1891, the unions merged as the Sailors' Union of the Pacific (SUP).

The greatest achievement of the SUP during its early years was simply remaining organized. Although concerned with the traditional problems of wages and hours, because of the peculiar nature of the seamen's vocation the union devoted considerable attention to living conditions aboard ship, relationships between sailors and officers, and methods of hiring. Shortly after its organization, the SUP attempted to gain control of the seamen's labor market through the establishment of a union shipping office, but the effort proved premature, and traditional methods of securing employment continued for some time.

Recognizing that the lack of organization on other coasts threatened their efforts to increase wage rates and improve working conditions, West Coast seamen led the movement to establish a worldwide organization of seamen. As early as 1890 a delegation was sent to the convention of the British Seamen's Union meeting in Glasgow to promote an international federation of seamen, but the effort failed. After this rebuff, the SUP concentrated on the formation of a national union of seamen. These efforts reached fruition when a national convention of seamen's unions met in Chicago on May 11, 1892, and formed the National Seamen's Union. The new union, which adopted the title International Seamen's Union of America in 1895, consisted of the SUP and seamen's unions on the Great Lakes, the Gulf Coast, and the Atlantic Coast. Other than the West Coast, only in the Great Lakes area had any significant organization of sailors been maintained. There a significant degree of organization had been achieved by the Lake Seamen's Union, a charter member of the Federation of Organized Trades and Labor Unions* and the American Federation of Labor* (AFL).

The ISU was organized along particularistic lines. Not only was the union divided into semi-autonomous geographic regions, but within the regions the union was further subdivided into separate deck, engine, and steward's departments. The centrifugal organizational structure prevented effective unified action and often led to internal conflicts, jurisdictional squabbles, or simple inertia.

The ISU's early organizing efforts were concentrated on the East Coast where, in comparison to the West Coast, three times as many potential members lived. The numerous ports, the heterogeneous work force, and the structural deficiencies of the ISU, however, combined to frustrate these efforts. By 1900 the ISU had a membership of only 3,400, most of which was concentrated on the West Coast and Great Lakes.

While failing to make any significant gains on the East or Gulf coasts, the ISU lost much of its strength in the Great Lakes as a result of a successful open-shop offensive launched by the Lake Carriers' Association in 1908. After losing its foothold on the Great Lakes, only the ISU's West Coast division, the SUP, continued to carry on significant collective bargaining negotiations with employers.

The ISU's organizing and collective bargaining failures were to some extent mitigated by successes in the political arena. The enactment of the La Follette Seamen's Act of 1915 climaxed nearly a quarter of a century of agitation, primarily by Andrew Furuseth, for protective seamen's legislation. The law abolished imprisonment for desertion and reduced penalties for disobedience aboard ship. Provisions were also included to improve working conditions and to reform the methods of wage payment. Although unfavorable economic conditions and the disorganization of seamen circumscribed many of the protective features of the law, at least it gave seamen the same freedom available to other laborers to work or resign.

Although the seamen and the unions that represented them experienced a period of relative prosperity during World War I, the war period created conditions that resulted in the virtual destruction of unionism in the industry in the postwar period. ISU membership peaked in 1920 at 115,000, including over 80,000 East Coast seamen, but a severe depression in merchant shipping in 1921, increased foreign competition, and the growth of the seamen labor force resulted in a confrontation among the government-owned U.S. Shipping Board, private operators, and the unions. Employers demanded wage reductions ranging from 20 to 30 percent, elimination of overtime pay, and the open-shop. In the struggle that resulted from these demands, trade unionism in the industry was crushed.

By 1923 ISU membership had dropped to prewar levels, and its power and influence declined even further. Moreover, during the following years the ISU's jurisdiction was challenged by the Marine Transport Workers' Industrial Union (MTWIU), organized by the Industrial Workers of the World* (IWW), and during the 1930s by the Marine Workers' Industrial Union (MWIU), organized by the Communist Trade Union Unity League.* The MTWIU was organized in 1912 to accommodate Spanish firemen who objected to the treatment they received from the "Anglo-Saxon" leadership of the Atlantic Coast Firemen's Union. The IWW union had its greatest strength in Philadelphia where a black local of longshoremen maintained a strong organization for several years. It was not until the collapse of the ISU in 1921 that the MTWIU made any significant inroads in the industry. The MTWIU, like the IWW, emphasized industrial organization and eschewed political action. Although it precipitated much militant activity, the MTWIU accomplished few permanent improvements in working conditions; it did, however, highlight the seamen's growing dissatisfaction with both the arrogance of the employers and the inability of the hapless ISU to protect them.

The Communist activity in the industry coincided with the increasingly desperate economic conditions growing from the Great Depression. The MWIU, which was organized in 1930, attacked both the ISU and the MTWIU. Emphasizing the individual job action tactic, the MWIU concentrated its effort on the organization of the Munson Line. Similar to the MTWIU, however, the MWIU never became a mass movement. After the enactment of the National Industrial Recovery Act, seamen tended to affiliate with the ISU rather than with the more radical unions.

Nevertheless, ISU leaders failed to take advantage of organizing opportunities or to channel the growing rank-and-file militancy to their purposes. In 1935 the ISU lost its largest and strongest affiliate, the SUP, when it violated orders of national headquarters and joined the Maritime Federation of the Pacific. Shortly thereafter, East Coast seamen began repudiating the ISU, many of them enrolling in the National Maritime Union* chartered by the Congress of the Industrial Organizations* in 1937. Recognizing the hopelessness of the situation, the AFL executive council dropped the charter of the ISU on October 14, 1938, and on the same day, issued a charter covering the old ISU jurisdiction to the Seafarers International Union of North America.*

The ISU, which held annual conventions, maintained its national head-quarters in Washington, D.C. Full-time officers were the president, the secre-tary-treasurer, and vice-presidents representing the various geographic and craft divisions. The executive council was composed of the above officers. At the time its charter was withdrawn, the ISU had a membership of approxi-mately 14,000.

For further information, see the *Seamen's Journal* published monthly by the ISU. Joseph P. Goldberg, *The Maritime Story: A Study in Labor-Management Relations* (1958), provides a good survey of union development in the maritime industry. Paul S. Taylor, *The Sailors' Union of the Pacific* (1923), covers the Pacific Coast, and Charles P. Larrowe, *Maritime Labor Relations on the Great Lakes* (1959), the Great Lakes.

SERVICE EMPLOYEES INTERNATIONAL UNION (SEIU). The organiza-tion of custodial and service employees in public buildings and such other edifices as office complexes, apartment houses, hotels, and hospitals began in Chicago during the early years of the twentieth century when the American Federation of Labor* (AFL) chartered the Chicago Flat Janitors as a federal labor union. As the organization of federal locals in the trade expanded, de-mands for a national union charter grew, and on April 23, 1921, the AFL re-sponded by issuing an international union charter to the Building Service Employees International Union (BSEIU).

The new national union came into existence at a very inopportune period in the history of the American labor movement. The open-shop campaign initi-ated by employers during the early 1920s, the general antipathy of government at all levels, and the outbreak of the Great Depression in the early 1930s effec-tively checked and then reversed the growth pattern of organized labor. Given these circumstances and despite a large potential membership in its trade jurisdiction, the BSEIU grew slowly, with much of its strength concentrated in the metropolitan Chicago area.

Improving economic conditions and the election of sympathetic govern-mental officials encouraged the officers of BSEIU Local 32B, New York City, to launch a major organizing campaign in 1934. When employers refused to bargain with the union, an unusually violent strike resulted when employers, who assumed they had bought impunity from strikes by paying large bribes to union labor racketeers, employed thousands of scabs to replace the striking workers. The union, however, won the strike and soon became the largest local in the international union, accounting for nearly one-third of the BSEIU mem-bership.

The greatest threat to the BSEIU's future was neither irascible employers nor the Great Depression but rather the nearly successful effort of the criminal underworld to seize control of the international union as a means of extorting money from employers and stealing from the membership. In 1937 George Scalise, a former pimp with extensive underworld connections, was appointed to the international union presidency by the BSEIU executive board after the death of President Jerry J. Horan. With firm control over the international union office, the racketeers proceeded to extort hundreds of thousands of dollars from employers while looting the union treasury.

The major source of resistance to the racketeers came from Charles Hardy, an international vice-president for the West Coast, who charged Scalise with several financial irregularities. For his efforts, Hardy was suspended from union office, and Scalise, representing the international office, attempted to take control of Hardy's San Francisco Local 9. Hardy took the controversy to court where he successfully prevented the international officers from taking control of Local 9.

The court action proved Scalise's undoing. In 1940 he was convicted of extorting money from Chicago property owners, stealing union funds, and evading federal income taxes. He spent the following years in a federal penitentiary. William L. McFetridge replaced Scalise in the union presidency and over the next twenty years rebuilt the BSEIU into a solid, respected international union. In 1942 Charles Hardy regained his international vice-presidency.

Despite the dangers to the union inherent in the underworld's great influence, the BSEIU experienced significant organizing success during Scalise's three-year presidency. Union membership, which had risen steadily after its founding in 1921, virtually exploded after World War II, a period during which the BSEIU greatly extended its organizing reach from the original Chicago and New York strongholds. At the end of World War II, the BSEIU paid per-capita taxes on 94,800 members. By 1940 that figure had jumped to nearly 180,000, and a decade later to 270,000. On February 19, 1968, the union title was changed to Service Employees International Union.

During these years collective bargaining negotiations with employers, which were conducted on a local level, became much more regularized and less acrimonious. A death gratuity system was established in 1943, and several years later a college scholarship program was begun to provide financial assistance for the continuing education of selected sons and daughters of SEIU members.

The SEIU, which maintains its national headquarters in Washington, D.C., holds quadrennial conventions. Principal officers include a president, nine vice-presidents, a secretary-treasurer, and an executive secretary. The general executive board is comprised of twenty-four members elected during regular conventions. In 1973 the SEIU reported a membership of 484,000 located in 364 local unions.

For further information, see the *Service Employee* issued monthly by the SEIU. Information can also be found in James J. Bambrick, *The Building Service Story* (n.d.), and *Going Up!* (1955), a history of Local 32B published by the union. The story of racketeering and corruption is told by John Hutchinson,

The Imperfect Union: A History of Corruption in American Trade Unions (1970).

SHEET METAL WORKERS' INTERNATIONAL ASSOCIATION (SMWIA). Delegates representing local unions of tin and sheet iron workers met in Toledo, Ohio, on January 25, 1888, and organized the Tin, Sheet Iron and Cornice Workers' International Association (TSI&CWIU). On April 23, 1889, the new union received a national union charter from the American Federation of Labor* (AFL). Organizers of the new union hoped to secure adequate wage compensation, end piecework, control entry into the trade, and gain the eight-hour day and five-day week.

Although the union met with early organizing success, the outbreak of depression in 1893 halted and reversed organizing initiatives, and in 1896 the AFL recalled its charter. But economic recovery by the end of the decade led to the rejuvenation of the renamed Amalgamated Sheet Metal Workers' International Association, and the union received a new AFL charter on March 23, 1899. A secessionist movement shortly thereafter, however, resulted in the organization of a rival national union, the Sheet Metal Workers National Alliance. The two competitive unions merged in 1903, creating the Amalgamated Sheet Metal Workers' International Alliance.

The Sheet Metal Workers steadily expanded its jurisdictional reach during the early years of the twentieth century but restricted membership to those craftsmen able to command the established wage scale in the trade. Black workers were to be organized in separate locals with the consent and under the jurisdiction of white local unions in the area. In 1907 the Coppersmiths International Union amalgamated with the Sheet Metal Workers, and in 1924 the association's jurisdiction was further expanded when chandelier, brass, and metal workers joined. The listed title was adopted in 1924.

Despite a long, bitter jurisdictional struggle with the United Brotherhood of Carpenters and Joiners* over the organization of metal trim workers, the SMWIA grew steadily during the first two decades of the twentieth century. Membership, which only slightly exceeded 1,000 at the beginning of the century, surpassed the 20,000 figure by the end of World War I. Although failing to make substantial new membership advances during the 1920s, a period of decline for many American trade unions, the SMWIA held its previous gains as membership stabilized at about 25,000 for several years. The coming of the Great Depression, however, debilitated the SMWIA as it did most other unions in the building trades. By 1933 the association had lost over one-third of its membership, and organization did not turn upward again until the late 1930s. Thereafter the SMWIA grew steadily, reaching 65,000 by mid-century and surpassing 100,000 by 1960.

The SMWIA, which maintains its national headquarters in Washington,

D.C., holds quadrennial conventions. Principal officers include a president, ten vice-presidents, a vice-president of railroads, and a secretary-treasurer. The general executive council is composed of the above officers. In 1973 the SMWIA reported a membership of 153,000 located in 462 local unions.

For further information, see the *Amalgamated Sheet Metal Workers' Journal*, 1895-1924, and the *Sheet Metal Workers' Journal* issued monthly by the SMWIA. Little published information on the history of the SMWIA was located, but basic information can be found in *Bulletin No. 618*, Bureau of Labor Statistics, U.S. Department of Labor (1936), and Florence Peterson, *Handbook of Labor Unions* (1944).

SHINGLE WEAVERS UNION OF AMERICA; INTERNATIONAL. *See* International Union of Timber Workers.

SHOE WORKERS OF AMERICA; UNITED (USWA). Dual unionism and the organization of many local unions in different trade centers has characterized trade unionism in the American shoe industry. Much of this early splintering and localism resulted from dissatisfaction with the organizing and collective bargaining policies of the American Federation of Labor's* (AFL) major national union affiliate in the boot and shoe industry, the Boot and Shoe Workers' Union* (BSWU). After losing several major strikes in the decade following its founding, the BSWU abandoned militant organizing campaigns and strikes in 1899 and adopted the tactic of promoting the union label in an effort to secure union recognition and collective bargaining concessions. As a condition for gaining a closed-shop agreement from these employers desiring to use the label, BSWU officers agreed to use binding arbitration to resolve all disputes over wages, hours, and working conditions.

Irritated and angered by these unaggressive and often unproductive BSWU policies, more activist shoe workers and union leaders organized a variety of independent unions, which usually exhibited a much more militant approach to trade unionism but had considerably less longevity. Among the independent unions, some with national ambitions, organized in the shoe industry before 1937 were the

Laster Protective Union, 1879-1895.
Shoe Workers Protective Union, 1898-1900.
National Assembly Boot & Shoe Cutters, 1903-1913.
United Shoe Workers of America, 1909-1923.
Allied Shoe Workers Union, 1912-1923.
Amalgamated Shoe Workers of America, 1923-1925.
Associated Slipper Workers Union of New York, 1928-1929.

United Shoe Workers of America, 1929-1930.
Independent Shoe Workers Union, 1929-1931.
Shoe and Leather Workers Industrial Union, 1929-1931.
National Shoe Workers Association, 1932-1933.
United Shoe and Leather Workers Union, 1933-1937.
Brotherhood of Shoe and Allied Craftsmen, 1933-.

In February 1933 several of these unions, including the National Shoe Workers Association (Lynn), the Shoe Workers Protective Union (Haverhill), and the Shoe and Leather Workers Industrial Union (New York), amalgamated to form the United Shoe and Leather Workers Union (USLWU). Although the new union had a founding membership in excess of 50,000, it not only failed to expand upon its original membership but lost many members as shoe manufacturers migrated from Massachusetts and other organized trade centers into nonunion locations.

The founding of the Congress of Industrial Organizations* (CIO) inspired another amalgamation of independent shoe worker unions. In 1937 the CIO chartered an industrial union bringing together the USLWU, the St. Louis branch of the Shoe Workers Protective Union, which had refused to join the earlier amalgamation, and several local independent unions. The new CIO affiliate, the United Shoe Workers of America, received a trade jurisdiction including "all employees engaged in manufacture of boots, shoes, slippers, component parts and those engaged in the rebuilding of shoes . . . and orthopedic workers."

Beginning with a relatively large, well-organized membership and motivated by the dynamic CIO organizing drives, the USWA appeared likely to bring the first effective union organization to the labor force of the boot and shoe industry. But a disastrous strike in the spring of 1937 against shoe manufacturers in Auburn, Maine, prevented union organizers from taking advantage of favorable organizing conditions elsewhere in the industry, drained the USWA treasury, and dispelled much of the optimism engendered by the chartering of the new CIO affiliate. Soon the same localism, craft jealousy, and factionalism so characteristic of trade unionism in the industry began to hamper USWA activities.

Nevertheless, by the end of World War II, USWA membership was again approaching 50,000. The postwar years, however, were filled with conflict and discord as Communists in control of the general executive board and non-Communist officers struggled for union control. Ultimately the Communists were dislodged, and the USWA avoided the fate of many other Communist-dominated unions that were expelled from the CIO. The long struggle consumed much time and energy of leaders from both factions, with the result that little effective union organizing was accomplished. When the American Federation of Labor* and CIO merged in 1955, USWA membership was only slightly larger than at the end of World War II. Thereafter technological changes in production and the constant relocation of shoe factories precipitated a slow decline in membership.

The USWA, which holds biennial conventions, maintains its national headquarters in Boston. Full-time officers include a president, a secretary-treasurer, and vice-presidents from each geographical district with more than 10,000 members. The general executive board is composed of twelve elected members other than officers. In 1973 the USWA reported a membership of 40,000 located in 131 local unions.

For further information, see the *United Shoe Worker* issued monthly. See also Horace B. Davis, *Shoes: The Workers and the Industry* (1940), an analysis of unionism in the shoe industry from a left-wing perspective, and Max M. Kampelman, *The Communist Party vs. the C.I.O.: A Study in Power Politics* (1957), an unsympathetic account of Communist influence.

SIDEROGRAPHERS; INTERNATIONAL ASSOCIATION OF (IAS). Siderographers, plate printing artists employed almost exclusively in the printing of paper money, bonds, securities, and similar documents, first began organizing in Washington, D.C., where on January 11, 1899, the first national union of siderographers, the Steel Plate Transferrers' Association, was organized. Six years later, on June 22, 1906, the new national union received an American Federation of Labor* (AFL) charter. The listed title was adopted in 1921.

The IAS emphasized both professional and economic objectives and established a five-year apprenticeship for senior members and a two-year apprenticeship for junior members. The small specialty union functioned in an extremely limited trade jurisdiction, and although it quickly organized all of the craftsmen in the trade, IAS membership rarely exceeded a hundred. Moreover, unlike most trade unions, the IAS is composed predominantly of government workers and makes no attempt to negotiate collective bargaining agreements.

The IAS, which maintains its national headquarters in New Milford, New Jersey, holds biennial conventions. The union does not have any full-time officers. The executive board consists of a president, two vice-presidents, a secretary, and a treasurer. In 1973 the IAS reported a membership of nineteen located in two local unions.

For further information, see *Bulletins No. 420, 506*, and *618*, Bureau of Labor Statistics, U.S. Department of Labor (1926, 1929, 1936), and Florence Peterson, *Handbook of Labor Unions* (1944). The IAS has never published an official journal, and other than the basic information contained in the above sources, little published information exists on the IAS.

SLEEPING CAR PORTERS; BROTHERHOOD OF (BSCP). Led by Asa Philip Randolph, Ashley L. Totten, W. H. Des Verney, and Roy Lancaster, black Pullman porters met at Elks Hall in Harlem on August 25, 1925, to found a union. Those attending the meeting called for recognition of the BSCP and the end of Pullman's Employee Representation Plan, a company union and the only type of organization that had existed theretofore. The founders also wanted a near doubling of porters' average monthly wages to $150, the elimination of tipping, a 240-hour work month, and pay for the time spent preparing cars in the yards. The Pullman Company bitterly opposed the BSCP, discharging any porters it could identify as members and refusing them pensions. In the South, Ku Klux Klan opposition was added to that of the company, thus forcing the BSCP to operate unsuccessfully underground. Conservative black newspapers opposed the union editorially, especially Chicago's *Whip* and *Defender* and the *St. Louis Argus*. Large Pullman advertisements were most notable in the *Argus*. Perry W. Howard, a Republican national committeeman from Mississippi and holder of a patronage position in the Department of Justice, was hired by the company to oppose the union, but publicity and Justice Department embarrassment forced him out of the contest. Melvin J. Chisum, Booker T. Washington's sometime spy and agent provocateur, who, by the 1920s was operating out of Chicago, replaced Howard. Chisum's basic pro-employer, anti-union conservatism had been deepened by his observation of white-only American Federation of Labor* (AFL) affiliates eliminating black jobs in Gulf Coast shipyards following World War I.

Randolph, who became president and organizer of the BSCP although he had never worked for the Pullman Company, was able to counter Chisum's anti-union publicity by his own media campaign in the New York press and in his own magazine, *The Messenger*. Randolph was depending for success upon government action by either the Interstate Commerce Commission or the Railroad Mediation Board, but neither would enter the fray. In an effort to force the Mediation Board ruling, Randolph called for a strike vote in 1927. The board would have to act if there was a threat to essential services, and Randolph hoped the vote itself would constitute such a threat. He carefully warned his membership that "a strike vote doesn't mean that the porters will necessarily strike." Apparently convinced that the vote was a moral gesture rather than a tactical decision, the membership voted 6,053 to 17 to allow Randolph to call a strike. Faced with the probability that few porters would actually walk out, certain that those who did would be fired, and realizing that many blacks would prefer the ease and cleanliness of the porter's work to other hard and dirty jobs, Randolph decided against calling the strike. Foreseeing no serious interruption of essential services, the Mediation Board refused to order the company into mediation.

Randolph attempted to overcome his loss in the strike ploy by entering the AFL and gained President William Green's support. But BSCP entry into the AFL was not easy. The opposition of whites to an all-black national union was strong, and the Hotel and Restaurant Employees International* claimed jurisdiction over the porters as workers on wheeled hotels. Green managed to steer the granting of federal charters to thirteen divisions of the BSCP through the executive council, and Randolph accepted the segregated status as a beachhead within the AFL. The BSCP finally received an international charter in 1936. A year later, its membership rebuilt after the drop that followed the strike-vote fiasco, the union took advantage of New Deal requirements for collective bargaining and signed its first contract with the Pullman Company. The contract called for a 240-hour work month, a wage hike amounting to $1.25 million, job security, and union representation.

The BSCP's greatest importance lies outside its normal activities as a union representing its members. As the first successful organizing program among Negroes, it paved the way for union consciousness among blacks. Its members were often influential people in their home communities, as was E. D. Nixon, the Montgomery, Alabama, porter who organized the bus boycott that catapulted Martin Luther King, Jr., to national prominence, initiating the civil-rights movement of the 1950s and 1960s. A. Philip Randolph became the AFL's resident black spokesman, as he introduced the Randolph clause, which urged the elimination of racial exclusion clauses, and at every convention from 1934 Randolph asked all AFL unions to integrate themselves. As late as 1959, Randolph blasted unions applying for membership in the AFL-Congress of Industrial Organizations* for discriminating against blacks. A year later he led other black unionists in founding the Negro American Labor Council.* As technological changes after World War II, especially the growth of air travel, resulted in constant loss of jobs for Pullman porters, the influence of the BSCP's leader was more related to the civil-rights movement than to the union.

The BSCP, which maintains its national headquarters in Oakland, California, holds triennial conventions. Principal officers include a president, four vice-presidents, and a secretary-treasurer. The international executive board is composed of the above officers in addition to seven members elected at regular conventions. In 1973 the BSCP reported a membership of 1,500 located in twenty-two local unions.

For further information, see *The Black Worker*, which was published for several years by the BSCP. See also Brailsford R. Brazeal, *The Brotherhood of Sleeping Car Porters* (1946); Philip S. Foner, *Organized Labor and the Black Worker, 1619-1973* (1974); F. Ray Marshall, *The Negro and Organized Labor* (1965); Sterling D. Spero and Abram L. Harris, *The Black Worker: The Negro and the Labor Movement* (1931); and Jervis Anderson, *A. Philip Randolph: A Biographical Portrait* (1972).

Carl S. Matthews

SONS OF VULCAN. *See* Amalagamated Association of Iron, Steel, and Tin Workers.

SPECIAL DELIVERY MESSENGERS; NATIONAL ASSOCIATION OF.
See American Postal Workers Union.

SPINNERS UNION: INTERNATIONAL (ISU). The textile industry in the United States fell upon hard times during the winter of 1850. As a result employers instituted a series of wage reductions further depressing the paltry salaries textile workers earned. In response to these conditions, mule spinners in Fall River, Massachusetts, organized and struck in hopes of preventing the reductions. The strike lasted nearly six months and ended in total defeat for the workers, but it had significant ramifications. Because of blacklisting and other forms of discrimination, the Fall River mule spinners, who were primarily of British origin, scattered throughout the New England textile industry, carrying with them the idea of a permanent national organization.

Trade unionism in the textile industry revived with the recovery of the economy after the depression of 1857. Revival of the Fall River union stimulated organization throughout New England under the title Benevolent and Protective Association of the United Operative Mule Spinners. Workers were generally successful in petitioning their employers for increased wages during the 1858-1860 period, but the outbreak of the Civil War disrupted the organization.

With the end of the war, the Mule Spinners (renamed the Amalgamated Mule Spinners Association) resumed demands for higher wages and a ten-hour day. Agitation for higher wages generally succeeded, but demands for a shorter day were less successful. Finally a convention was called in Biddeford, Maine, in 1868 where delegates resolved to launch an offensive to win the ten-hour day. Although many employers acceded to their demands, others resisted, and strikes called to enforce the demands were miserable failures. Once again trade unionism in the industry was shattered, and by 1870 the national organization had ceased to exist.

The Fall River mule spinners' organization revived as a result of the conditions precipitated by the panic of 1873. The mule spinners resolved to oppose wage reductions, and once again, unionism quickly spread throughout the industry. When employers refused to retract an announced reduction, the workers struck. After nearly a month, a temporary settlement was reached when employers promised a partial restoration of wages, but, when the reductions were reimposed during the spring and summer of 1875, the strike resumed. The conflict evolved into a general strike and lockout in the Fall River vicinity, which the workers dubbed the "Great Vacation" of 1875. Once again employers emerged victorious. Of all the various crafts involved in the strike, only the mule spinners' organization survived the debacle.

Fall River mule spinners struck again in 1879, and, although unsuccessful, the effort promoted a feeling of solidarity among the workers, and during the following years, the national organization grew steadily stronger. Despite the growing maturity of mule spinner unions, an unsuccessful strike in 1884 again shattered the union. Phoenixlike, the mule spinners' organization rose again in 1886, this time as a national assembly of the Knights of Labor.* A year later a convention of New England mule spinners was held in Fall River, and as a result the National Mulespinners Union (NMU) was formed. This title was retained until 1898, when, for a short time, it was changed to the National Spinners Union to permit the admission of ring spinners.

After 1886 mule spinners faced increased competition from ring spinning machines, and union leaders placed less emphasis on higher wages and concentrated on working conditions and job security. The NMU reached its membership pinnacle in 1894 when it had over 4,000 members located in forty local unions. During the closing years of the nineteenth century and early years of the twentieth century, mule spinning machines were gradually displaced by ring spinning machines, and the NMU declined.

In 1901 the NMU negotiated a merger with the newly organized United Textile Workers of America* (UTWA). At this time the NMU had shrunk to 2,500 members, and leaders agreed that if the new union succeeded, the NMU would disband and its locals would affiliate directly with the UTWA. However, when the UTWA made concessions on autonomy to the weavers and loomfixers to gain their affiliation, the mule spinners were reluctant to give up their separate identity. UTWA officials hestiated to press the matter until 1914 when the per-capita tax paid by the mule spinners was raised. The NMU then withdrew from the UTWA. When its efforts to effect a reconciliation failed, the American Federation of Labor* (AFL) revoked the NMU charter on December 31, 1919. Thereafer the NMU remained a small, independent union until it was rechartered by the AFL on September 20, 1937, as the International Spinners Union. On August 10, 1950, the ISU's charter was suspended for nonpayment of per-capita taxes.

The ISU, which held annual conventions, maintained its national headquarters at Holyoke, Massachusetts. The general secretary was the only full-time officer, and government was vested in a president, vice-president, secretary-treasurer, and executive council of nine members elected annually. At the time of its suspension in 1950, the ISU had fewer than 500 members.

For further information, see Robert R. R. Brooks, "The United Textile Workers of America" (Ph.D. dissertation, Yale University, 1935); George E. McNeill, *The Labor Movement: The Problem of Today* (1887); and *The American Federationist* (1902).

STATE, COUNTY, AND MUNICIPAL EMPLOYEES; AMERICAN FEDERATION OF (AFSCME). Administrators and clerical, fiscal, and technical employees of the state government of Wisconsin met in a hearing room of the state capitol on May 10, 1932, and organized the Wisconsin State Administrative Employees Association. Six days later the new union received an American Federation of Labor* (AFL) charter as Federal Labor Union 18213. This action was an outgrowth of talks between the president of the Wisconsin State Federation of Labor Henry Ohl, Jr., and Colonel A. E. Garey, Wisconsin director of personnel. The two men discussed the need for a union of state employees, and when Governor Phillip LaFollette gave his support, they scheduled the meeting that led to the union's formation.

Besides the necessary organizational work required to establish such a union, delegates at the founding meeting of the Wisconsin Association made two decisions that had significant impact on the union and the labor movement. The first involved a commitment to establish a national union of state employees, and the second was the election of Arnold S. Zander as financial secretary. Zander quickly assumed leadership of the association and soon converted the hopes and plans of the union founders into concrete realities.

Under Zander's leadership, the association immediately launched an organizing drive to enroll state employees. The campaign brought large numbers of new members, but the election of a new Democratic administration in 1932 threatened to disrupt and alter the entire concept of state employment in Wisconsin. Billed as an economy measure, the new governor sponsored legislation that would have destroyed Wisconsin's civil service system, the second oldest and probably best administered system in the nation. The association's role in defeating the measure proved the utility and necessity for union organization of state employees. Despite threats emanating from government officials during the early 1930s, the state's progressive tradition and the heritage of the "Wisconsin idea" provided a hospitable environment for the development of public service unionism in Wisconsin.

The Wisconsin Association ultimately provided the nucleus for a national union of public service employees, but it was not the first state employee organization to appear in the United States. By 1935 at least fourteen such associations existed, and the New York association had been organized as early as 1910. The uniqueness of the Wisconsin Association centered upon its affiliation with the AFL. Following the Wisconsin example, local associations in Colorado, Ohio, and Virginia requested and received AFL federal charters, but the largest associations of state employees, especially those in New York and California, remained independent.

Inspired by visions of a national union of public employees, Arnold Zander opened an extensive correspondence with both leaders of the independent associations and AFL officials concerning the future of public service unionism. At the same time the Wisconsin Association dropped its reference to state employees and expanded the scope of the organization to include municipal workers. But Zander's hopes for a national union charter received a serious setback in 1935 when the AFL granted the American Federation of Government Employees* (AFGE) jurisdiction over the civilian employees of state, county, and municipal governments.

Zander traveled to the Atlantic City convention of the AFL in October 1935, determined to reverse the AFL decision. But AFL convention delegates and leaders were embroiled in a controversy over industrial unionism and had little time to consider the affairs of an obscure federal local. During the convention, however, Zander conducted extensive negotiations with AFGE leaders and secured an arrangement whereby the state, county, and municipal employees were to form a largely autonomous union within the AFGE. Although still committed to the idea of a separate national union, Zander issued the call for a constitutional convention of state, county, and municipal unions to meet in Chicago in December 1935 to organize the union provided for in the AFGE agreement. As a result the American Federation of State, County, and Municipal Employees was organized on December 9, 1935. Attended by thirty-two delegates representing approximately 5,500 members in fourteen associations, the convention was chaired by an AFGE vice-president. The constitutional committee, under the chairmanship of Arnold Zander, simply proposed the adoption of the AFGE constitution. The document approved by convention delegates essentially provided for the creation of a completely autonomous international union. Reflecting that fact, delegates also voted to request an AFL charter.

The constitutional convention left the relationship between the AFSCME and AFGE more confused than ever. Soon an intense rivalry between the two unions disrupted organizing in the public service sector. Ultimately a truce was arranged pending final disposition of the dispute by the AFL executive council. Before the council met, however, a newly installed AFGE leadership adopted significant policy changes. Meeting in the fall 1936, the AFGE executive council passed a resolution urging the AFL to grant a separate charter to the AFSCME, and on October 16, 1936, the AFL chartered AFSCME as an independent international union.

AFSCME quickly proved one of the most dynamic unions in the American labor movement. A membership of 10,000 at the end of 1936 surpassed the 50,000 figure before the end of World War II and reached 100,000 before the AFL-Congress of Industrial Organizations* (CIO) merger in 1955. Moreover, AFSCME continued to grow at a more accelerated pace during a period when most American unions found their membership either stabilizing or declining. During the mid-1960s, AFSCME attained a membership in excess of a quarter-million workers and more than doubled that figure by 1973. In the process, AFSCME became the fifth largest AFL-CIO* affiliate and the seventh largest union in the American labor movement.

A variety of circumstances help explain AFSCME's organizing successes. The union was organizing in an extraordinarily large trade jurisdiction; by 1960 at least 2 million eligible workers existed in its jurisdiction, and the figure continued to grow. Under the presidencies of Arnold Zander (who served until 1964) and Jerry Wurf, the union also was blessed with resourceful and enlightened leadership. An unusual degree of democracy and local autonomy has characterized AFSCME governance, and this has encouraged local initiative and rank-and-file participation in union affairs. Finally, reoccurring periods of inflation have served to constantly reinforce the advantages of collective action by public employees.

Nevertheless, AFSCME also encountered obstacles that easily could have offset the above advantages. State, county, and municipal governments are essentially open-shop employers; public employees are not recognized under the provisions of the National Labor Relations Act. Consequently voluntarism has been a constant factor in AFSCME membership. Although a few states enacted collective bargaining laws for public employees during the post-World War II period, the right to strike is still highly restricted in most states. AFSCME, moreover, has encountered considerable opposition within the labor movement itself. During its early years it had to compete with a rival national union, the State, County and Municipal Workers of America,* chartered by the CIO, and throughout its history various AFL and AFL-CIO craft unions have claimed jurisdiction over a variety of public employees. Finally AFSCME also faces competition for a large number of independent organizations of government employees.

Although opinions differed within AFSCME councils from its inception through 1954, union leaders emphasized the extension of the civil service and the acquisition of improvements in merit systems primarily through legislative and administrative lobbying. As a result of an internal insurgency led by Jerry Wurf, after 1954 AFSCME placed greater emphasis on collective bargaining, union recognition, checkoff of union dues, and signed agreements. A decade later Wurf and his followers gained control of the international union and strongly reaffirmed the commitment to a collective bargaining strategy. Moreover, the new AFSCME leaders changed the union's strike policy to give locals complete autonomy in making decisions concerning strikes. Nevertheless, because of varying legislation (or its paucity) in different states and localities, little uniformity exists among AFSCME locals either in the semantics or the realities of collective bargaining. Considerable uniformity does exist, however, concerning the objectives of trade unionism, not only among AFSCME bargaining units but between AFSCME and other AFL-CIO unions.

AFSCME, which maintains its national headquarters in Washington, D.C., holds biennial conventions. Principal officers include a president, twenty-two vice-presidents elected by geographical district, and a secretary-treasurer. The international executive board is composed of the above officials. In 1973 AFSCME reported a membership of 529,035 located in 2,289 local unions.

For further information, see *The Public Employee* published monthly by AFSCME. See also Leo Kramer, *Labor's Paradox—The American Federa-*

tion of State, County, and Municipal Employees, AFL-CIO (1962), the best book on the subject. Information can also be found in J. Joseph Loewenberg and Michael H. Moskow, *Collective Bargaining in Government: Readings and Cases* (1972); Daniel H. Kruger and Charles T. Schmidt, Jr., eds., *Collective Bargaining in the Public Service* (1969); and Sterling D. Spero, *Government as Employer* (1948).

STATE, COUNTY AND MUNICIPAL WORKERS OF AMERICA. *See* United Public Workers of America.

STEELWORKERS OF AMERICA; UNITED (USWA). The Committee for Industrial Organization* (CIO) and the Amalgamated Association of Iron, Steel, and Tin Workers* (AA) reached an agreement in 1936 leading to the creation of the Steel Workers Organizing Committee (SWOC). The AA had failed to unionize a substantial proportion of the steelworkers, and by organizing basic steel, John L. Lewis, who headed both the CIO and the United Mine Workers of America* (UMWA), hoped to strengthen his bargaining position with the managers of the captive mines owned by the steel industry. Although the 1936 agreement gave SWOC the right to organize on behalf of the AA, in effect SWOC was the nucleus of a new industrial union.

To head it, Lewis appointed UMWA vice-president Philip Murray. Well supplied with UMWA funds, Murray sent a large number of organizers into all the steel-making areas in the summer of 1936. The main target was the U.S. Steel Corporation, which since 1909 had refused to deal with organized labor. SWOC strategy was to capture or disrupt the company unions fostered by U.S. Steel. Although this worked, actual acceptance of SWOC emerged from the secret discussions of Lewis and the board chairman of U.S. Steel. In March 1937 the corporation's subsidiaries signed a contract recognizing SWOC as representative for its members. The union claimed a total of 200,000 members. When the independent steel producers refused to sign during May, SWOC reluctantly called a strike. One of the most violent of the period, the Little Steel strike and the depression of 1937-1938 stopped the union. Thereafter SWOC combined a new organizational thrust with National Labor Relations Board procedures to bring Little Steel to the negotiating table in 1941 and 1942.

Shortly before Pearl Harbor, Murray, by then president of the CIO and a firm supporter of President Franklin Roosevelt's foreign and domestic policies, extended a no-strike pledge. In turn Roosevelt established the National War Labor Board in 1942; the board's award in the Little Steel case enabled the union to obtain wage increases and union security maintenance of membership provisions throughout the industry. Thus by the end of World War II, the union had a strong foothold not only in basic steel but in iron ore mining (except in the South), and much of steel fabricating. In 1944, the steel union expanded its jurisdiction by absorbing the Aluminum Workers of America. With 800,000 members, the new steel union was one of the largest CIO affiliates.

In 1942 the first constitutional convention dissolved the AA and transformed SWOC into the United Steelworkers of America. The USWA constitution centralized authority over finances, bargaining in basic steel, and strike policy, but the wage policy committee, originated under SWOC, retained power to ratify contracts. Although dissidents demanded local or regional autonomy, Murray prevailed, arguing the need for a strong international to achieve industry-wide bargaining.

After emerging from its first industry-wide strike in 1946 with a large wage increase, the USWA leadership focused on fringe benefits and wage rate standardization. As a result of persistent bargaining and strikes in 1949 and 1952, the union won a non-contributory pension, the union shop, elimination of the southern wage differential, and in 1955, a supplemental unemployment benefit plan. Thus USWA played a leading role in developing fringe programs that were extended to a growing segment of American workers. Such benefits, however, did not automatically extend to all USWA members outside basic steel. In steel fabricating, contracts were negotiated separately, the basic steel settlement serving only as a model, with the result that fabricators' benefits tended to lag behind those of the steelworkers.

When Philip Murray died in 1952, Secretary-Treasurer David J. McDonald became president. Under McDonald, membership increased to 1.2 million in 1956, the union achieved industry-wide bargaining in basic steel, and it fought the basic steel industry's attempt to change work rules in the long, costly strike of 1959, only to be confronted with chronic unemployment among steelworkers. Membership dipped to 960,000. McDonald's solutions were the creation of a union-management human relations research committee (1960) to have continuous discussions of new issues and the negotiation of contracts providing only modest wage hikes. Membership continued to decline, while discontent mounted. It surfaced not only among rank-and-file members but in a powerful group of district directors. In the only previous contest for the USWA presidency, the challenger in 1957 had been an obscure local union leader. This time the challenge came from within the top level of the international, when Secretary-Treasurer I. W. Abel defeated McDonald in 1965.

Abel relaxed his predecessor's tight grip on power within the international, provided ways for rank-and-file members to be heard on local issues, and worked to end racial job discrimination. USWA's new leaders altered the bargaining structure by creating industry conferences in containers, aluminum, nonferrous, and basic steel, and each bargained separately on an industry-wide basis. While the wage policy committee still made broad wage policies, the industry conferences ratified contracts and authorized strikes, subject to membership approval. To end employment fluctuations caused by stockpiling in anticipation of steel strikes, in 1973 USWA and basic steel entered into a novel Experimental Negotiating Agreement providing for arbitration of unresolved national contract issues. By absorbing the International Union of Mine, Mill and Smelter Workers* in 1967 and District 50, Allied and Technical Workers* in 1972 and conducting organizing drives in fabricating, USWA became the second largest American union, but less than half of the members were basic steelworkers.

The USWA, which maintains its international headquarters in Pittsburgh, holds biennial conventions. Principal officers include a president, vice-president, and secretary-treasurer. The executive board is composed of the above officers, the national director of the union in Canada, and twenty-four district directors. In 1973 the USWA reported a membership of 1.4 million located in 5,675 local unions.

For further information, see *Steel Labor*, a monthly published since 1936. It has excellent coverage of union affairs. Essential for understanding the background of SWOC is David Brody's *Steelworkers in America: The Nonunion Era* (1960). For a scholarly account of SWOC, see chapter 2 of Walter Galenson, *The CIO Challenge to the AFL: A History of the American Labor Movement, 1935-1941* (1960). Lloyd Ulman's *The Government of the Steel Workers' Union* (1962) is the best source on the subject. U.S. Department of Labor, *Collective Bargaining in the Basic Steel Industry: A Study of the Public Interest and the Role of Government* (1961), provides a history of the union's negotiations from 1937 to 1959. For recent USWA affairs, see John Herling's *Right to Challenge: People and Power in the Steelworkers Union* (1972); John A. Orr, "The Steelworker Election of 1965," *Labor Law Journal* (February 1969).

Donald G. Sofchalk

STEREOTYPERS', ELECTROTYPERS', AND PLATEMAKERS' UNION OF NORTH AMERICA; INTERNATIONAL. *See* International Printing and Graphic Communications Union.

STONE AND ALLIED PRODUCTS WORKERS OF AMERICA; UNITED (USAPWA). Stone and quarry workers were among the first craftsmen in the United States to organize on a local basis, but a permanent union of quarry workers did not appear until the twentieth century. The American Federation of Labor* (AFL) chartered two short-lived national unions of such workers during the late years of the nineteenth century—the Quarrymen's National Union of the United States of America (1890-1900) and the National Slate Quarrymen's Union (1895-1898). An effective national union was not organized until delegates representing several federal labor unions directly affiliated with the AFL met in Washington, D.C., on September 8, 1903, and founded the Quarry Workers' International Union of North America (QUIUNA). The major objectives of the new union included efforts to preserve the integrity of the craft, to reduce the hours of labor, and to gain increased wage compensation. The QUIUNA received a trade jurisdiction that included

> quarrymen, quarry and paving-cutter blacksmiths, derrickmen, engineers and firemen, steam-drill and air-drill runners, laborers, softstone quarrymen and channelers, rubbers, lumpers, and boxers, riggers of derricks, cranes, or other devices used in handling stone, and stone-derrick men wherever employed.

As originally organized the international union office was very weak in comparison to local unions that retained the power to determine membership qualifications, to establish apprenticeship terms, and to conduct collective bargaining negotiations.

The QUIUNA had a chartering membership of 1,200 and grew steadily until 1910 when more than 5,000 quarry workers held membership cards. Thereafter the QUIUNA underwent a decade of decline before its membership stabilized at about 3,000 during the 1920s. The Great Depression initiated another decline in enrollment as membership dipped to 2,000.

The emergence of the Congress of Industrial Organizations* (CIO) breathed new life into the small specialty union. The QUIUNA had long supported the concept of industrial unionism and had organized common laborers along with skilled quarrymen; consequently it withdrew from the AFL on January 6, 1938, and received a CIO charter. The CIO expanded the QUIUNA organizing jurisdiction to include "all operations of every kind and nature in the quarrying and processing of stone, allied and competitive products, and all work and processes connected to or in relation therewith, other than those over which jurisdiction has been conceded by agreement." Reflecting its expanded organizing reach, in 1941 the union title was changed to United Stone and Allied Products Workers of America.

CIO affiliation reversed the twenty-five years of decline that had plagued the QUIUNA. By the end of World War II membership surpassed 5,000 and when the AFL-CIO* merged in 1955, it exceeded 12,000. Nevertheless, the USAPWA still organized in a relatively limited trade jurisdiction, compromised even further by rival AFL unions and by technological change that constantly reduced employment in the trade. On January 1, 1971, the USAPWA merged with the United Steelworkers of America* (USWA).

The USAPWA, which maintained its national headquarters in Barre, Vermont, held triennial conventions. The only full-time officer was a secretary-treasurer. The executive council was composed of the president, vice-president, secretary-treasurer, and four additional members elected at national conventions. Shortly before merging with the USWA, the USAPWA reported a membership of 11,085 located in 130 local unions.

For further information, see the *Quarry Workers' Journal* published monthly by the QUIUNA from 1904 to 1938, and *The Beacon News* issued by the USAPWA. Information can also be found in *Bulletin No. 618*, Bureau of Labor Statistics, U.S. Department of Labor (1936).

STONECUTTERS' ASSOCIATION OF NORTH AMERICA; JOURNEYMEN (JSCA). Stonecutters were one of the first groups of craftsmen to begin organizing activities in the United States. As early as the 1820s unions of stonecutters began to appear, and these unions played a prominent role in the Jacksonian labor movement. The first national union of stonecutters, the Journeymen Stone Cutters Association, was organized in 1853, and it was one of the few unions to survive the panic of 1857 and the depression that followed. While exhibiting great resilience, the JSCA maintained a limited organizing jurisdiction and never acquired a large membership. As a result of the depression following the panic of 1873, the Stone Cutters Association disintegrated, although several local stonecutter organizations survived.

On December 5, 1887, representatives of twenty of these local organizations from cities scattered throughout the nation met in Chicago and reorganized the Journeymen Stone Cutters' Association of North America. Organizers of the rejuvenated union were particularly anxious to eliminate piecework and the subcontracting of stonecutting and stone carving. The JSCA considered any member performing such work an employer and threatened expulsion. As a further means of similarly controlling entry in the craft, the JSCA placed great emphasis on its apprenticeship system requiring a training period of at least four years.

The JSCA was one of the first unions to establish a universal eight-hour day (1904). Three years later, on August 20, 1907, the JSCA affiliated with the American Federation of Labor* (AFL). The JSCA was not without rivals in its trade jurisdiction; the New York Stone Cutters' Society and the Architectural Sculptors and Carvers' Association of New York both challenged the JSCA in the organization of stonecutters and stone carvers. This problem was resolved in 1915 when both organizations merged with the JSCA. As a result of the amalgamation, the JSCA incorporated both stone carvers and cutters, becoming the only union in the trade.

Following the depression of the 1890s JSCA membership grew steadily, reaching a peak of nearly 10,000 in 1912 before beginning a general decline lasting until the mid-1920s. Thereafter membership rose slightly and then stabilized at about 6,000. It remained there for several years until declining sharply during World War II and then again stabilized for a lengthy period at about 2,000. Changing building methods, new construction materials, and the new techniques and machinery used in stonecutting and carving continually reduced employment in the trade. Finally, on February 19, 1968, the old craft union merged with the Laborers' International Union of North America* (LIU).

The JSCA, which maintained its national headquarters in Indianapolis, had no constitutional provisions for regular conventions. The principal officer was a president-secretary-treasurer. The executive board was composed of the above officer, in addition to the international vice-president and representatives elected from the five JSCA geographical districts. Shortly before the merger with the LIU, the JSCA reported a membership of 1,900 located in forty-one local unions.

For further information, see the *Stonecutters Journal* published bimonthly and the *Official Circular* issued periodically by the JSCA. Little published information on the JSCA was located, but basic information can be found in *Bulletin No. 618*, Bureau of Labor Statistics, U.S. Department of Labor (1936), and Florence Peterson, *Handbook of Labor Unions* (1944).

STOVE, FURNACE AND ALLIED APPLIANCE WORKERS' INTERNATIONAL UNION OF NORTH AMERICA (SFAPPWIU). Workers at four Quincy, Illinois, stove companies met on April 24, 1882, and organized the first union of stove mounters in the United States. Soon it became an American Federation of Labor* (AFL) federal labor union entitled the Stove Mounters and Driller's Protective Union, 4006. Organizing activities soon ranged to cities such as St. Louis, Detroit, Belleville, Illinois, and Evansville, Indiana, where other stove mounter locals were established. Because of this expanded organization, the stove mounter locals petitioned the AFL for an international charter, and on January 6, 1894, the Stove Mounters International Union (SMIU) received a charter. It conferred exclusive trade jurisdiction over

> all workmen engaged in mounting, assemblying of stoves, furnaces, heaters, gas and electric heaters, malleable ranges, camp stoves, bake ovens and all parts pertaining thereto, drillers, riveters, machine and bench hands, white metal workers, stove and heater repairmen, cutters, punchers and breakers, press hands, pattern fitters and filers, manifold fitters and testers, gaters and welders, conveyor mounters, grinders, tappers, ware dressers and all enameling pertaining to stove, range and heater parts and all such general workmen that are engaged in the various departments outside of the foundry.

In the years following its chartering, the SMIU grew slowly, reaching an early membership peak of about 2,000 in 1904, but the open-shop campaign initiated by employers affected the union adversely; by 1910 SMIU membership had fallen below 1,000. Although the lost membership was recovered during World War I, employer hostility and the Great Depression once again oppressed the SMIU. By 1932 SMIU membership shrank to a figure approaching its original chartering membership.

The SMIU remained a small, enervate national union during these years, but it was not an uneventful period. The historic Buck's Stove and Range Company case, in which AFL president Samuel Gompers and other AFL leaders were eventually sentenced to prison, evolved from a dispute between the SMIU and the owner of the Buck's Stove and Range Company, James Van Cleave, president of the National Association of Manufacturers. Almost simultaneously, the Stove Mounters became a charter member of the AFL's metal trade department. Meanwhile, the SMIU, always placing great emphasis on the union label, played an active role in affairs of the union label trades department of the AFL.

Enactment of the National Industrial Recovery Act of 1933 and the National Labor Relations Act of 1935 revived the SMIU, which reported a membership in excess of 8,000 by the end of World War II. But technological change confused jurisdictional lines, and the SMIU was often victimized by the larger, aggressive international unions chartered by the Congress of Industrial Organizations* (CIO). As a consequence, the SMIU strongly favored an AFL-CIO merger and was one of the original signers of the 1953 no-raiding agreement. Nevertheless, after reaching a membership high of almost 15,000 in the early 1950s, the SMIU (renamed the Stove, Furnace and Allied Appliance Workers' International Union of North America in August 1962) exhibited a slowly declining enrollment. Although it claimed a much larger membership, in 1973 the SFAPPWIU paid per-capita taxes to the AFL-CIO* on fewer than 4,000 members.

The SFAPPWIU, which maintains its headquarters in St. Louis, holds triennial conventions. Principal officers include a president, three vice-presidents, and a secretary-treasurer. The general executive board is composed of the above officials. In 1973 the SFAPPWIU reported a membership of 9,139 located in fifty-one local unions.

For further information, see the quarterly *Stove & Furnace Workers' Journal* and its predecessor, the *Stove Mounters and Range Workers' Journal*. See also *The American Federationist* (April 1947), and the *AFL-CIO American Federationist* (January 1959).

STREET AND ELECTRIC RAILWAY EMPLOYEES OF AMERICA; AMALGAMATED ASSOCIATION OF. *See* Amalgamated Transit Union.

SWITCHMEN'S UNION OF NORTH AMERICA (SUNA). The first union of railroad switchmen, the Switchmen's Association, appeared in Chicago in 1877. Organizing railroad workers objected to numerous conditions associa-

ciated with their employment. Wages for a twelve-hour, seven-day week usually totaled less than fifty dollars a month; there were no retirement, disability,
or unemployment benefits and little job security. (It was not an unusual practice for railroads to dismiss switchmen at age forty or forty-five.) Working conditions were extremely dangerous, and employers recognized no responsibility
for compensating injured workmen. Moreover, any railroad worker protesting
these conditions could find himself on an employers' blacklist, effectively ending his chances for employment in the railroad industry.

It became obvious that a single local would have little bargaining power in
the railroad industry; consequently a number of switchmen meeting in
Chicago in February 1886 formed the Switchmen's Mutual Aid Association of
the United States of America. The new railroad union was destined to have a
short life, however. Already weakened by a lockout on the Chicago, Northwestern Railroad and the Chicago, Burlington and Quincy Railroad strike of
1888, the new union was further plagued by the embezzlement of funds by its
secretary-treasurer and the rivalry of the American Railway Union.* The
Switchmen's Mutual Aid Association, which had built a membership of over
10,000, went into a precipitant decline and by 1894 had ceased to exist.

A permanent national switchmen's union finally came into existence in
Kansas City, Missouri, on October 23, 1894, when delegates from several local
organizations met and formed the Switchmen's Union of North America. The
new union was immediately tested by the depression of the 1890s, and its
ability to survive those economic hard times forecast its durability. During the
early years of the twentieth century, the SUNA grew slowly but steadily, and on
July 12, 1906, it affiliated with the American Federation of Labor* (AFL). In
the following fifty years, it remained the only operating railroad union to affiliate with the AFL. The SUNA received an AFL jurisdiction including railroad
employees "actually employed in switching service or switchman, switch-
tender, towerman, interlocking man, car retarder operator or yard master."

Like most other trade unions, the SUNA had its share of jurisdictional conflicts, especially with the Brotherhood of Railroad Trainmen,* which claimed
an overlapping jurisdiction. The SUNA also encountered an internal revolt in
1920 when its leadership joined with the Brotherhood of Railroad Trainmen
and called off a planned strike to force a wage increase. As a result an unauthorized strike of switchmen and trainmen began in Chicago on April 1, and
it quickly spread. Encountering great hostility from their international unions,
strikers began forming independent locals, which merged to form the United
Association of Railway Employees of North America. By September the strike
crumbled, and with its defeat the rival railroad union disappeared.

Because of the public nature of the railroad industry, the SUNA, like other
railroad unions, devoted considerable energy to politics. During the early
1920s the SUNA vigorously supported the Plumb Plan, which called for government ownership of railroads. SUNA also endorsed the Progressive party
candidacy of Robert La Follette in 1924.

As a result of the government takeover of the railroads during World War I and its tolerant attitude toward labor organizations, the SUNA grew dramatically during the war. By 1920 it had 14,000 members, virtually doubling its pre-war number. But much of that new membership was lost during the 1920s and the early years of the Great Depression. The membership curve turned up again during the mid-1930s and continued upward until mid-century, when it stabilized between 10,000 and 12,000 members.

In 1926 SUNA became a charter member of the newly organized Railway Labor Executives' Association in which its officers played an active role. Joining with other railroad unions, SUNA was also a founder and owner of *Labor*, an influential railway newspaper, and the Union Labor Life Insurance Company.

As a small union of railroad operatives whose economic bargaining power had been severely restricted by federal legislation, especially the Railway Labor Act, SUNA members found their employment benefits continually faling behind those of other union workers and railroad operatives who were better able to take advantage of technological change. In an effort to improve its bargaining position, on January 1, 1969, the SUNA merged with the Brotherhood of Railroad Trainmen, the Brotherhood of Locomotive Firemen and Enginemen,* and the Order of Railroad Conductors* to create the United Transportation Union.*

The SUNA, which maintained its national headquarters in Buffalo, New York, held quadrennial conventions. Principal officers included a president, seven vice-presidents, and a secretary-treasurer. The international board of directors was composed of five members. At the time of the merger, the SUNA had a membership of 12,000.

For further information, see the *Journal of the Switchmen's Union* published monthly by the SUNA. Information can also be found in *The American Federationist* (November 1955), and Florence Peterson, *Handbook of Labor Unions* (1944).

TAILORS' UNION OF AMERICA; JOURNEYMEN (JTUA). Collective action among tailors to improve their economic condition has had a long history in the United States. Baltimore tailors struck as early as 1795 and again in 1805. Tailor societies are known to have existed in New York, Philadelphia, and Boston in 1806. Although the organization of tailors continued erratically until the Civil War, attempts to organize a national union came to naught. The first recorded national union of tailors appeared in 1865 when The Journeymen Tailors' National Trades Union was formed in Philadelphia. The union held annual conventions from 1865 to 1876 but disintegrated after an officer embezzled the union's funds.

Philadelphia also served as the founding city of the second national union of tailors when a local tailors' union issued a call for a national convention to convene on "the second Monday in August, 1883." Local unions organized in Baltimore, Pittsburgh, and Troy, New York, responded to the call of the Philadelphia union and, as a result of the meeting, created the Journeymen Tailors' National Union of the United States. (The name was later changed to the Journeymen Tailors' Union of America.) The new tailors' union immediately set about organizing the trade and within a decade had 200 affiliated locals with 10,200 members. However, the general economic depression signaled by the panic of 1893 and the loss of many New York members after a disastrous strike in 1894 undercut much of the previous progress. By 1887 membership in the union was about half what it had been four years earlier.

The economic hard times of the 1890s, however, were a relatively minor problem compared to the continuing technological innovations and new methods of production that drastically changed the character of the industry. When it affiliated with the American Federation of Labor* (AFL) in 1887, the JTUA was given a jurisdiction covering custom tailoring. Nevertheless, the improving quality of ready-made clothing and the application of ready-to-wear factory techniques to the manufacture of clothing made to measure (known as the special order trade) made significant inroads into the traditional tailoring trade. Workers employed in the ready-made clothing industry were known as shop tailors, and in 1887 the AFL chartered the Tailors National Progressive Union with jurisdiction in the trade.

Efforts to create a merger of the two unions were frustrated by the JTUA's feeling of trade caste and by political differences: the JTUA was essentially a conservative trade union, while the Tailors National Progressive Union had a strong Socialist influence. Because of the JTUA's continual refusal to broaden its jurisdictional boundaries, two new unions moved into the vacuum: the United Garment Workers of America* (UGW) and the International Ladies' Garment Workers' Union* (ILG). As a result, the JTUA was increasingly isolated in a rapidly declining trade skill.

Although the JTUA and UGW had several jurisdictional problems, the JTUA in 1905 again refused to amalgamate with the UGW. The JTUA repeatedly voted against organizing workers in the less expensive custom trade, but faced with a declining membership, the union reversed its position in 1909 and claimed jurisdiction over "all workers engaged in the manufacture of legitimate custom tailoring, no matter what system of work is used." The JTUA's new claims were immediately challenged by the UGW and the ILG. The AFL called a conference of the three unions in Washington hoping to resolve the jurisdictional matter and to discuss the possibility of amalgamation, but again the JTUA resisted any change in its status.

Faced with a further decline in actual or potential membership because of continued changes in the garment industry, the 1913 JTUA convention proposed a radical policy change. Delegates voted to change the name of the organization to the Tailors' Industrial Union and to claim jurisdiction over all workers in the tailoring industry. These actions were immediately challenged by the UGW and upon appeal to the AFL, the JTUA was instructed to revoke its action upon penalty of suspension from the AFL.

Meanwhile, a group of clothing workers primarily from New York and Chicago bolted the UGW in 1914 and under the leadership of Sidney Hillman made plans to create a new clothing workers' union. The Tailors' Industrial Union immediately entered into negotiations with the seceding faction of the UGW. In December 1914 the two groups agreed to form an amalgamated organization to be known as the Amalgamated Clothing Workers of America* (ACWA). Later the same month the Tailors approved the amalgamation by referendum. But objections to the merger, fears of AFL suspension, and conflicts between clothing worker locals and tailor locals soon led to demands for a reconsideration of the merger vote. In a referendum during the early summer of 1915, the Journeymen Tailors voted not to amalgamate with the ACWA, to resume its old name (Journeymen Tailors' Union of America), and to resume its AFL-approved jurisdiction.

Thereafter the JTUA began its long journey to oblivion. Although temporarily bolstered by organizing gains during World War I, the union never regained the membership (16,000) it had in 1904, and by 1932 it was reduced to fewer than 3,000 members. On December 23, 1937, it was suspended by the AFL executive council, and on October 12, 1938, its charter was revoked.

The JTUA, which maintained its national headquarters in Chicago, held annual conventions. Principal officers included a president, a vice-president, and a secretary-treasurer (the chief administrative officer). The general executive board was composed of five members. At the time of its suspension, the JTUA claimed a membership of approximately 6,000.

For further information, see *The American Tailor and Cutter* published monthly by the JTUA. See also Charles J. Stowell, *The Journeymen Tailors' Union of America: A Study in Trade Union Policy* (1918), and *Studies in Trade Unionism in the Custom Tailoring Trade* (1913).

TEACHERS; AMERICAN FEDERATION OF (AFT). Teacher unionism can be traced back at least to 1897 when Chicago teachers, displeased over salaries and pensions, formed the Chicago Federation of Teachers (CFT). The Chicago group lacked any collective bargaining procedure, and its activities centered on exposing political corruption and alerting city officials to existing funds for school operation. In 1902 Margaret Haley and Catherine Goggin of the CFT conducted an investigation of corporate tax evaders that provided additional tax revenue. When the board of education attempted to divert the money to noneducational purposes, the CFT filed an injunction and secured a victory for the new union. The CFT affiliated with the American Federation of Labor* (AFL) in 1902, following the example of San Antonio Local 10303, which had been chartered two months earlier.

From the initial union efforts in Chicago and San Antonio, teacher unionism was local in nature and weak until 1916. On April 15 of that year, representatives of three Chicago locals and the Gary, Indiana, local met at the call of the Chicago teachers to form a national teacher organization, which affiliated with the AFL. By May 9 the newly formed American Federation of Teachers was launched with eight locals and Charles B. Stillman of Chicago as president.

With the formation of the AFT, teacher unionism spurted forward. In its first four years the AFT claimed 174 locals and approximately 9,000 members, but this growth was short-lived. World War I brought increased calls for budget austerity, and teachers suffered with the rest of labor in the anti-union and red scare campaigns of the 1920s. The lack of teacher tenure laws, yellow dog contracts, laws prohibiting strikes of public employees, and the attitude of many teachers discouraging unionism as unprofessional hindered the growth of the AFT.

By 1930 AFT membership declined to about half of the 1920 figure. Despite the hardships of the depression, AFT organizing surged forward again in the 1930s, quintupling the 1930 membership. Most of this increased membership was in urban areas and coincided with general labor union growth in the cities. The AFL launched a drive to achieve teacher tenure laws and improve academic freedom, which by 1940 resulted in the passage of limited teacher tenure laws in seventeen states. The growing Communist influence within the AFT in the 1930s caused a crisis for teachers torn between a philosophy of academic freedom and those seeking political respectability. In 1939 Dr. George Counts of Columbia University won a bitter struggle for the AFT presidency, and alleged Communists were ousted from the executive board. Two years later the AFT expelled two New York City locals and the Philadelphia union as Communist dominated. In another major struggle within the labor movement, teachers expressed sympathy with the Congress of Industrial Organizations* (CIO) but remained within the AFL. Despite the rapid growth in teacher unionism during the depression decade, AFT membership in 1940 represented only 3 percent of the teaching profession.

During World War II, AFT locals in such cities as Butte, Montana, and Bremerton, Washington, won contracts through the collective bargaining process. In the postwar period the AFT continued to emphasize the need for collective bargaining. In 1946 the St. Paul, Minnesota, AFL local struck for six weeks, closing seventy-seven schools serving 30,000 students. It was the first strike by an AFT local and marked the beginning of a wave of teacher militancy in the postwar period. Although the AFT officially maintained a no-strike policy, teachers in New York, Pennsylvania, Georgia, and Rhode Island struck for increased salaries. In the 1950s teacher discontent increased as wages in private employment continued to outpace teacher salaries. The pivotal battle for collective bargaining in education occurred in New York City.

With strong financial backing from Walter Reuther and the AFL-CIO* industrial union department, Albert Shanker and David Selden brought about a merger of the fragmented New York locals in 1960 under the title of United Federation of Teachers (UFT). In 1960 the UFT won bargaining rights, and after a short strike in 1962, concluded a contract with the board of education. The UFT victory in New York moved it into a dominant position within the AFT. In 1963 the AFT national convention repealed its no-strike policy.

In the 1960s and 1970s organized labor continued to place emphasis on organizing white-collar workers and professionals. Although mergers occurred in some states, among them New York and Florida, attempts to effect a national merger of the AFT and the National Education Association (NEA) collapsed over the issue of AFL-CIO affiliation; the AFT insists on keeping its ties with labor, and the NEA wants to remain an independent professional society. Although NEA membership still exceeds that of the AFT, the federation bargains for over a half-million teachers in nearly every major American city. As states passed public employee bargaining laws in the 1960s and 1970s, the battle for representation spread to colleges and universities as the AFT, NEA, and the American Association of University Professors sought to organize college teachers.

The AFT, which maintains its national headquarters in Washington, D.C., holds annual conventions. Principal officers include a president, thirty vice-presidents, and a secretary-treasurer. The international executive council is composed of the president and vice-presidents. In 1973 the AFT reported a membership of 248,521 located in 1,032 local unions.

For further information, see the monthly *American Teacher* and *Changing Education* issued quarterly by the AFT. See also Robert J. Braun, *Teachers and Power* (1972); *American Federation of Teachers, Commission on Education, Organizing the Teaching Profession* (1955); and Philip Taft, *United They Teach: The Story of the United Federation of Teachers* (1974).

David L. Nass

TEAMSTERS, CHAUFFEURS, WAREHOUSEMEN AND HELPERS OF AMERICA; INTERNATIONAL BROTHERHOOD OF (IBT). Founded at the turn of the century when a few midwesterners turned to Samuel Gompers for assistance in organizing the unskilled and degraded team drivers, the International Brotherhood of Teamsters, Chauffeurs, Warehousemen and Helpers of America was originally not a national union but rather a loose confederation of locals controlled by extremely powerful bosses. The organization grew steadily, responding effectively to changes in the industrial structure of trucking, until it became the largest and most complex single union in the United States.

The American Federation of Labor* (AFL) chartered Team Drivers International Union on January 27, 1899. The organization claimed a membership of 1,700. Conditions at the time were acutely bad, with most team drivers working a fourteen-hour day six days a week and a half-day on Sundays. Also responsible for the grooming of the teams after deliveries, teamsters earned only ten to twelve dollars weekly. Nevertheless, organizing was difficult, and factionalism and animosities plagued early efforts. Chicago locals, more wage oriented than the majority and more fully steeped in the doctrines of trade unionism, took the lead in turning the organization into a true labor union.

In 1902 the Chicago element seceded from the parent organization and forced a restructuring. The dissidents formed the Teamsters National Union, but at a convention in Niagara Falls, New York, in 1903, the Chicago union and the Team Drivers' International Union merged to form the International Brotherhood of Teamsters. The union title was subsequently altered in 1910 and 1940.

The local-market orientation of the industry, stressing competition among employers operating in separate markets rather than in competition with each other, precluded the need for coordinated collective bargaining, with the result that advocates of local autonomy prevailed over supporters of a strong national organization. Throughout the history of the IBT, struggles over the per-capita tax and a death benefit program masked the real issue—the strength of the international union. It was not until long-distance trucking dominated the industry and Dave Beck organized regionally within the IBT structure that local autonomy forces waned.

From the earliest days, teamster locals were involved in corruption, bribery, and collusion with employers. Local leaders often used the dependence of business on the teamsters to extort payments. Strikes were fomented to provide occasion for bribery, but during the presidency of Daniel J. Tobin (1907-1952), the affairs of the IBT were free of this element. Tobin did not control the economic policies or behavior of the locals, however dominant his influence over the national, and corruption continued to be a force in the trucking industry.

Tobin relentlessly pursued a program designed to give stability to this most unstable affiliate of the AFL. He avoided challenging local leaders and intervened only rarely in local affairs. In order to minimize opportunities for factionalism and acrimony, Tobin lengthened the term of office of the national officers by extending the time between conventions to five years. He reduced IBT expenses to the lowest possible level and devoted his energies to creating a powerful place for the IBT in the broader labor scene. The success of Tobin's program is illustrated by his election as AFL treasurer in 1917 over the opposition of Gompers. In 1934 he became ninth vice-president of the AFL and third vice-president in 1955. Tobin also cultivated political power, working closely for and with Presidents Woodrow Wilson and Franklin Roosevelt.

When the motor truck threatened the jurisdictional base of the IBT, Tobin successfully applied to the AFL for expansion of jurisdiction to include truck drivers and also stablemen (later defined to include mechanics), which was granted in 1910. Firmly committed to the craft principles of the AFL, the Teamsters allowed specialized locals by industry in various cities, governed by a joint council when two or more locals operated in one place. This constitutional provision of 1904 was utilized by Dave Beck and others who expanded it to encompass whole sections of a state and, later, regions of the nation, effectively minimizing autonomy of locals and strengthening their personal base of power in the international union.

Processing workers were added to the IBT's jurisdiction when it organized dairy workers in 1918. Such a move was inevitable and led to serious conflicts with other internationals. Teamsters argued that the health and survival of their craft was jeopardized if processors strike or scab. The IBT has been militantly aggressive in pursuing this approach to organization. The bitter and prolonged jurisdictional dispute with the United Brewery, Flour, Cereal, Soft Drink, and Distillery Workers* is the outstanding example of the problem. Beginning at the very foundation of the IBT, the conflict grew to monumental proportions under the leadership of Dave Beck in the 1930s and continued without relief until the merger of the two warring organizations in August 1972. The conflict with Cesar Chavez and the United Farm Workers' Union* over the organization of agricultural workers is only a recent example of this problem.

Corruption in the IBT became acute with the revelations of the McClellan Committee in 1957. Beck, who succeeded Tobin in the presidency, was convicted in federal court, and the AFL ousted the IBT in December 1957. James R. Hoffa was elected to succeed him. Under Hoffa, the union continued to grow along "industrial" lines, until in addition to the traditional trucking related members, its ranks included workers in the automobile, bakery, beverage, cannery, building and construction trades, dairy, general hauling, laundry, log hauling, warehousing, produce, and cold storage industries. It also includes miscellaneous sales drivers as well as department store workers, wholesale optical workers, agricultural workers, and even one local of college professors.

Hoffa also inaugurated the first national contract in the industry in 1964 (renegotiated in 1967), and he worked to expand the health and medical program of the union, which presently constitutes one of the most comprehensive and effective in the nation. Following his conviction for jury tampering in 1963, Hoffa continued to serve as president through the period of appeals until his actual incarceration in 1967, resigning on June 22, 1971. He was succeeded by Frank E. Fitzsimmons who continues in office. In 1968 the IBT formed a short-lived Alliance for Labor Action with the United Automobile Workers,* which left the AFL-Congress of Industrial Organizations* to promote the organization of workers unorganized by established labor unions.

The IBT, which maintains its national headquarters in Washington, D.C., holds quinquennial conventions. Principal officers include a president, fifteen vice-presidents, three trustees, and a secretary-treasurer. With the exception of the trustees, the above officers compose the general executive board. In 1973 the IBT reported a membership of 1,854,659 located in 783 local unions.

For further information, see the *International Teamster* issued monthly by the IBT. The IBT has attracted the attention of numerous scholars and other writers. See, for example, Sam Romer, *The International Brotherhood of Teamsters: Its Government and Structure* (1962); Robert D. Leiter, *The Teamsters Union: A Study of Its Economic Impact* (1957); Walter Sheridan, *The Fall and Rise of Jimmy Hoffa* (1972); Ralph and Estelle James, *Hoffa and the Teamsters* (1965); and James R. Hoffa, *The Trial of Jimmy Hoffa* (1970).

Nuala McGann Drescher

TECHNICAL ENGINEERS; INTERNATIONAL FEDERATION OF PROFESSIONAL AND (IFP&TE). On July 1, 1918, several federal labor unions previously organized by the American Federation of Labor* (AFL) met in convention in Washington, D.C., and organized the International Federation of Draftsmen's Unions. The new national union was given jurisdiction over all classes of technical engineers, architects, draftsmen, and those in related engineering positions. Membership was open to all such craftsmen working in an "employee" capacity.

During the following years the union title was altered several times: International Federation of Technical Engineers', Architects' and Draftsmen's Unions (1919), American Federation of Technical Enginners (1953), and International Federation of Professional and Technical Engineers (1973). But name changes failed to convert the AFL white-collar organization into a successful trade union venture. Instead, the single most significant feature of the union's history was its failure to organize the large number of potential members in its trade jurisdiction.

Varied circumstances explain the IFP&TE's failure to effectively organize engineers, many of whom suffered from relatively low pay, deteriorating working conditions, and the impersonalization and bureaucratization of the profession. The tendency of engineers to identify themselves as "professionals" was reinforced by employers who bombarded engineers with anti-union propaganda, further prejudicing them against affiliating with a "blue-collar" organization. Instead, a number of professional societies emerged (some of them originally organized by employers) to provide engineers an alternative to the IFP&TE. The only consolation available to IFP&TE leaders was that a Congress of Industrial Organizations'* affiliate, the International Federation of Architects, Engineers, Chemists and Technicians, had little more success than their union.

The IFP&TE, which maintains its national headquarters in Washington,

D.C., holds biennial conventions. Principal officers include a president, six or more vice-presidents, and a secretary-treasurer. The above officers constitute the international executive council. In 1973 the IFP&TE reported a membership of 17,700 located in seventy-nine local unions.

For further information, see the *Engineers Outlook* issued monthly by the IFP&TE. The organization of engineers has been widely studied, but few of the studies include any significant account of AFL or CIO unionism in the trade. See, for example, James J. Bambrick and Albert A. Blum, *Unionization Among American Engineers* (1956); Herbert R. Northrup, *Unionization of Professional Engineers and Chemists* (1946); Richard Walton, *The Impact of the Professional Engineering Union* (1961); and James W. Kuhn, "Engineers and Their Unions," in Albert A. Blum et al., *White-Collar Workers* (1971).

TELEGRAPH WORKERS; UNITED (UTW). Seven years after Western Union began operations in 1856, the first labor organization appeared among telegraph workers. On August 26, 1863, a group of telegraphers in Augusta, Georgia, met and formed a group to work toward the reduction of hours. Little is known about the organization, and it was apparently short-lived. Soon after the Augusta meeting, another group of telegraphers gathered in New York City on November 2, 1863, and organized the National Telegraphers Union (NTU). The NTU was essentially a benevolent society, and, while its membership increased in the years immediately following its founding, telegraphers became increasingly militant as Western Union extended its control over the industry. Despite membership pressure the leaders failed to convert the NTU into an effective trade union, and by 1869 the organization had ceased to exist.

The NTU's disintegration was accompanied and to some extent aided by several disaffected NTU members who organized the Telegraphers Protective League in New York City on July 28, 1868. The new organization assumed a militant trade unionist posture and attracted the attention of telegraphers all over the nation. Its membership grew dramatically, but the Telegraphers Protective League failed to survive much longer than the NTU. The new union was crushed as a result of a strike that began after an announced wage reduction in the San Francisco offices of Western Union in early January 1870. The strike quickly spread to other major American cities, but the determined opposition of Western Union and the absence of solidarity among telegraphers doomed the strike and, with it, the Telegraphers Protective League. It also ended union organizing in the telegraph industry for over a decade.

It was not until the emergence of the Knights of Labor* that union organization resumed in the telegraph industry. In March 1882 the Brotherhood of Telegraphers was organized in Pittsburgh as an affiliate of the Knights. Within a year it had 150 locals and over 10,000 members; nevertheless, the new organization of telegraphers soon followed the course of its predecessor. Under the control of Jay Gould, Western Union crushed a national strike during the summer of 1883, and although the brotherhood continued to exist for several years after the strike, it ceased to be an effective trade union organization.

In the following years two more short-lived telegrapher unions appeared. The Triplicate Brotherhood was organized in 1887 and in 1892 joined the American Railway Union* (ARU), changing its name to the Order of Commercial Telegraphers. It disappeared as a result of the unsuccessful ARU Pullman strike and the depression of the mid-1890s. A few years later the Order of Railroad Telegraphers* (ORT) organized the Brotherhood of Commercial Telegraphers as a separate unit. The effort, however, proved more difficult than expected and was soon abandoned.

When organizing efforts among commercial telegraphers resumed and a new organization, the International Union of Commercial Telegraphers, appeared, the ORT revived its commercial unit. Attempting to resolve the confusion of two unions, the American Federation of Labor* (AFL) called a conference of all organized telegraphers, and as a result, the AFL chartered two new organizations, the Commercial Telegraphers Union and the Order of Commercial Telegraphers. On July 19, 1903, the two unions merged to form the Commercial Telegraph Union of America (CTUA).

The CTUA grew steadily during its first years, but as was true of previous telegraph unions, it made little headway in negotiating efforts with Western Union. Growing tensions ultimately led to a strike that began on the West Coast in the summer of 1907 and quickly spread throughout the country. After a bitter eighty-nine-day strike, the company again prevailed; shortly thereafter Western Union launched an intensive anti-union drive. It also initiated a program of welfare paternalism, climaxed in 1918 by the organization of a company union, the Association of Western Union Employees (AWUE). It was to be several years before Western Union was effectively organized.

Unlike many trade unions, the CTUA did not prosper during World War I. After the government took over the telegraph industry, it was administered by Postmaster General Albert S. Burleson, who gave company officials great latitude to continue their anti-action activities. In an effort to force recognition and derail the AWUE, the CTUA conducted another unsuccessful strike in June 1919.

The CTUA did not participate in the general prosperity of the 1920s. It began the decade with a membership of 2,000 and fifteen years later still had 2,000. Moreover, New Deal legislation, especially the National Industrial Recovery Act and the National Labor Relations Act (NLRA), did little to revive the CTUA. Instead, this legislation was used most effectively by the American Communications Association* (ACA), a rival organization chartered in 1937 by the Congress of Industrial Organizations* (CIO). In 1939 the ACA signed a national closed-shop agreement with the Postal Telegraph Company. The ACA then turned to Western Union, where it had successfully prosecuted a

National Labor Relations Board (NLRB) unfair labor practice charge against the Company. As a result the AWUE was declared a company union in violation of the NLRA, and a representational election was called. Profiting from the ACA's efforts, the CTUA launched its most effective counterattack to its CIO rival during the campaign. In the election Western Union employees voted in favor of the CTUA, which effectively exploited the issue of the ACA's alleged Communist-domination. The CTUA's next victory resulted from the merger of Postal Telegraph and Western Union in 1943. A new NLRB representational election was held after the merger to resolve conflicting bargaining rights, and again the CTUA prevailed in all areas except New York City. Projecting itself as the conservative alternative to ACA radicalism, the CTUA effectively capitalized on ACA organizing initiatives. By 1944 its membership, which a few years earlier was less than 2,000, had grown to 20,000.

Soon after the CIO expelled the ACA in 1950 as a Communist-dominated union, the CTUA consolidated its control of trade unionism in the telegraph industry. During the following years, the CTUA successfully organized most potential members within its jurisdiction and on February 19, 1968, changed its title to the United Telegraph Workers.

The UTW, which maintains its national headquarters in Washington, D.C., holds quadrennial conventions. Principal officers include a president, secretary-treasurer, editor, and statistician. The general executive board is composed of nine members elected by majority vote at national conventions. In 1973 the UTW reported a membership of 18,000.

For further information, see the *Telegraph Workers Journal* issued monthly by the UTW. The best account of trade unionism in the industry is Vidkunn Ulriksson, *The Telegraphers: Their Craft and Their Unions* (1953).

TELEPHONE WORKERS; THE ALLIANCE OF INDEPENDENT (AITU). The first national union of telephone workers, the National Federation of Telephone Workers (NFTW), was a highly decentralized melding of autonomous local unions. These unions were extremely jealous of their independence, and many balked when the NFTW was reorganized in 1947 into a more centralized and powerful national union, the Communications Workers of America* (CWA). The dissident locals organized the Eastern Seaboard Group, a loosely-knit association of independent locals of telephone workers. In September 1949 seven independent unions affiliated with the Eastern Seaboard Group met in Pittsburgh and organized the Alliance of Independent Telephone Workers. Organizers hoped that the alliance would bring together "independent labor unions which represent or seek to represent non-supervisory employees in the communications industry within their respective jurisdictions."

Resisting the blandishments of the International Brotherhood of Electrical Workers* and the CWA, the member unions of the alliance determined to protect their local autonomy and maintain their independence. In their publications, alliance members attempted to point out the alleged "weaknesses of international affiliation, with its accompanying high dues rate, subservience to the whim of leaders who had long since lost contact with the feelings and needs of the people they represent, and the feeling of insignificance which characterizes the 'little guy' in a 'big union.'" In a further effort to protect its independent status, the AITU assumed an active role in the National Federation of Independent Unions, an organization of unaffiliated unions proposing, among other things, to provide mutual assistance to independent unions threatened by the raids of unions affiliated with the American Federation of Labor-Congress of Industrial Organizations.*

The improvement of the Bell system pension plan was one of the earliest and most persistent objectives of the AITU. Besides the traditional labor objectives of higher wages, shorter hours, and job security, the AITU also endeavored to gain improvements in vacation benefits, workmen's compensation, and health and life insurance. Using the traditional methods of collective bargaining in their efforts to achieve these objectives, AITU affiliates supported every strike against the Bell system. The AITU also created a legislative department that actively represented the interests of telephone workers in legislative chambers.

The AITU grew steadily, if undramatically, after its founding. The seven local unions that created the AITU in 1949 were joined by nine other unions by 1974. The AITU, however, exists in the shadow of the powerful CWA. Nevertheless, the alliance has proven quite successful in maintaining the affiliation of its constituent locals and, when challenged, defeating the CWA in National Labor Relations Board representational elections.

The AITU, which maintains its headquarters in Hamden, Connecticut, holds semiannual conferences. Principal officers include a president, secretary-treasurer, vice-president, and recording secretary. In 1973 the AITU reported a membership of 50,000.

For further information, see the *Alliance News* published quarterly by the AITU, and other miscellaneous publications of the alliance.

TELEPHONE WORKERS; NATIONAL FEDERATION OF. *See* Communications Workers of America.

TELEVISION AND RADIO ARTISTS; AMERICAN FEDERATION OF (AFTRA). Long hours, low wages, few benefits, and little job security characterized working conditions among radio performers during the early years of the broadcasting industry. New Deal legislation, especially the National Labor Relations Act, inspired radio performers to seek relief from these objectionable conditions through union organization. As a consequence, meetings held in Los Angeles and New York City during the spring and summer of 1937 resulted in the organization of the American Federation of Radio Artists (AFRA). On August 16, 1937, the new union received a charter from the Associated Actors and Artistes of America* (AAAA), a coalition of American Federation of Labor* (AFL) unions in the entertainment industry.

AFRA signed its first collective bargaining agreement with station KMOX, St. Louis, after winning a National Labor Relations Board representational election. The union then moved toward network-wide bargaining as well as securing agreements with those sponsors and advertising agencies employing broadcasting personnel. Within a short time, AFRA was universally recognized as the bargaining agent for broadcasting talent. While emphasizing the organization of national networks, union officials also endeavored to organize individual stations and regional networks. By the time of its second national convention, AFRA was already recognized as the bargaining agent for most radio performers.

The development of television after World War II opened new organizing opportunities but also raised serious jurisdictional problems. The Television Authority, a federation of four AAAA unions—the American Guild of Variety Artists, the American Guild of Musical Artists,* Actors' Equity Association,* and Chorus Equity—had been granted original jurisdiction over television performers. The first network contract was negotiated by the Television Authority and ratified on December 8, 1950. Shortly thereafter, however, the authority and AFRA opened merger discussions, and on September 20, 1952, the two unions officially merged, creating the American Federation of Television and Radio Artists.

The merger did not end jurisdictional problems in the industry, however. A serious dispute developed between AFTRA and the Screen Actors Guild* (SAG) over the representation of performers in television and feature films. Amalgamation again appeared to be the natural solution, but SAG repeatedly rejected AFTRA's merger overtures. Finally the two unions reached an agreement whereby SAG bargained for filmed television performers and AFTRA represented performers on live or videotaped programs.

The blacklisting of performers during the McCarthy red scare of the 1950s was a painful experience for radio and television performers as well as their union. Aware, Inc., one of the more active instruments in creating blacklists of performers and entertainers, was organized by Fordham University professor Godfrey Schmidt, an associate member of AFTRA. Moreover, seven AFTRA members served on the board of directors of Aware. Opposition to Aware's blacklisting activities soon emerged within union ranks, especially concerning the intimate relationship between certain AFTRA officials and Aware. An alternative slate of candidates was nominated for election to the AFTRA board of directors in the union elections of 1954, but the dissidents lost and soon found themselves and their "past associations" listed in "Aware Publication

Number 12." The campaign against the blacklist continued, however, and in the spring of 1955 a membership referendum condemning Aware's blacklisting activities passed by a two to one margin. At the end of the same year, an anti-blacklisting slate, headed by Charles Collingwood, Garry Moore, Orson Bean, and John Henry Faulks, swept most Aware supporters from the board of directors; the insurgents won twenty-seven of thirty-five seats on the board. Thereafter AFTRA joined those forces campaigning against the blacklist.

With the internal controversy over blacklisting resolved, AFTRA again emphasized organizing and collective bargaining during the 1960s. Nevertheless controversy continued to plague the union. In 1962 AFTRA lost a representational election that would have given it bargaining rights for the personnel of noncommercial television stations. Then, in March 1967, the union called its first national network strike. The thirteen-day strike began when the network refused to accept AFTRA's fee and salary schedule at network-owned and -controlled stations. The strike created considerable conflict over the legitimacy of AFTRA, primarily a union of entertainers, acting as a bargaining agent for news personnel. The issue reappeared later the same year when AFTRA voted to honor the picket lines set up by the National Association of Broadcast Employees and Technicians,* which was involved in a collective bargaining dispute with the networks. A few years later right-wing columnist and commentator William F. Buckley challenged the constitutionality of AFTRA's union shop agreements as they affected news broadcasters. He argued that being forced to pay union dues was an "unreasonable restraint" on his freedom of speech. On April 29, 1974, the U.S. Court of Appeals ruled against Buckley, thus resolving the legal status of newsmen in AFTRA.

AFTRA, which maintains its national headquarters in New York City, holds annual conventions. Principal officers include a president, nine vice-presidents, a treasurer, a recording secretary, and a national executive secretary. AFTRA's national board consists of 111 members elected from three different geographical areas. In 1973 AFTRA reported a membership of 23,714 located in forty local unions.

For further information, see *AFTRA Magazine* issued quarterly. See also Allen E. Koenig, ed., *Broadcasting and Bargaining: Labor Relations in Radio and Television* (1970), and "A History of AFTRA," *NAEB Journal* (July-August 1965).

TEXTILE WORKERS OF AMERICA; AMALGAMATED (ATW). The New England textile industry provided the setting for a large and heterogeneous collection of trade unions during the first quarter of the twentieth century. The United Textile Workers of America* (UTWA), the dominant union in the field, was a conservative, craft-conscious organization that largely neglected or ignored the thousands of semiskilled and unskilled workers in the industry. These workers, many of them foreign born, became targets for a rich variety of left-wing, radical unions. The Industrial Workers of the World* (IWW) organized the National Industrial Textile Union in 1908, and the "Detroit Faction" of the IWW also entered the field, organizing the Worker's International Industrial Union (WIIU). Besides the IWW, a number of unions with a radical bent also appeared in different divisions of the textile industry.

Organization of the Amalgamated Textile Workers of America was the direct outgrowth of strikes among the woolen workers of Lawrence, Massachusetts and the workers in the silk mills of Paterson, New Jersey. During the late months of 1918, a general movement for an eight-hour day was initiated by the Amalgamated Clothing Workers of America* (ACWA). Textile unions, including the UTWA, joined the movement, and February 3, 1919, was the deadline for the establishment of the eight-hour day in the textile industry; the situation became confused, however, when the UTWA agreed to accept a reduction in hours without a corresponding increase in the hourly wage rate. It was also unclear whether the unions were demanding a forty-eight-hour or a forty-four-hour week. When the woolen workers of Lawrence learned that the reduction in their hours of labor would result in lower weekly wages, they immediately went on strike; similarly, the UTWA's announcement that it had accepted a forty-eight-hour rather than the forty-four-hour week precipitated a strike of silk workers in Paterson. Neither strike was sanctioned by the UTWA. Meanwhile, the ACWA, which had already won the forty-four-hour week, offered its assistance to the striking workers.

Ultimately the ACWA called a convention of various textile workers from Paterson, Passaic, Lawrence, Hudson County, and New York City to meet in the latter city on April 12, 1919. At that conference the Amalgamated Textile Workers of America was founded. ATW leaders objected to the actions and procedures of the UTWA in several respects: its insensitivity to the rank and file, its autocratic procedures, and its failure to provide full support to strikes while at the same time draining local treasuries by constantly increasing per-capita taxes.

The ATW was organized as an industrial union of textile workers and advanced jurisdictional ambitions making it a full-scale, national rival of the UTWA. The ATW grew at a spectacular rate in the weeks and months immediately following its establishment. Many UTWA locals left their parent union and affiliated with the ATW. Most of the workers organized by the WIIU entered the new union, and they were joined by a variety of previously independent unions.

Alarmed by the rapid membership gains of the ATW, the leadership of the UTWA launched a major propaganda offensive to discredit its new rival, labeling it an un-American union dominated by Jewish foreign workers and led by bolsheviks. The ATW not only survived the fulminations of UTWA propagandists but continued to grow. By the end of 1919, it had approximately 50,000 members.

Although challenged by the UTWA from the right and the IWW from the left, the ATW continued to fare very well during the early months of 1920. The developing depression in the textile industry during 1920, however, soon reversed its success, and it quickly adopted a defensive strategy in an attempt to save previous gains. Recognizing the dangers of employers playing off rival textile unions against one another, the ATW endeavored unsuccessfully to develop a spirit of conciliation and cooperation with the UTWA. The ATW then led in the organization of the Federated Textile Unions of America, a loose federation of independent unions in the textile industry, which formally came into existence in August 1922. Besides the ATW, the federation included the Amalgamated Lace Operatives,* the American Federation of Textile Operatives, the Brussels Carpet Association, and the Tapestry Carpet Weaver's Association. Missing, of course, was the UTWA, and despite numerous conferences, it refused to compromise on issues of local autonomy or per-capita taxes.

In 1924 the ATW, which like other textile unions had gone into a steady decline since 1920, left the federation. Although the ATW experienced a short revival resulting from a successful strike in the Pawtucket Valley of Rhode Island in 1922, the general decline continued, and by the time of the Passaic strike of 1926, the union had disappeared.

For further information, see *The New Textile Worker*, the official organ of the ATW. Jack Hardy and R. W. Dunn's *Labor in Textiles* (1931) contains an account very sympathetic to the radicals. A more balanced analysis is provided by Robert R. R. Brooks, "The United Textile Workers of America" (Ph.D. dissertation, Yale University, 1935).

TEXTILE WORKERS OF AMERICA; UNITED (UTWA). At a conference in Washington, D.C., on November 19, 1901, representatives of the International Union of Textile Workers (IUTW) and the American Federation of Textile Operatives (AFTO) met under the chairmanship of James Duncan, first vice-president of the American Federation of Labor* (AFL), to form the United Textile Workers of America. The event culminated efforts by the AFL leadership to consolidate the various textile unions under the AFL banner.

The IUTW, formed in 1890 and granted an AFL charter in 1896, had jurisdiction over all textile manufacturing occupations except the mule spinners claimed by the Mule Spinners' Union, which held an earlier AFL charter. But the strong textile craft organizations of New England, distrustful of the industrial and centralized character of the IUTW, refused to join the new union. Thus by 1898, IUTW membership was concentrated in the South. Still hoping to unite their southern-based organization with the New England craft unions, representatives of the IUTW met with representatives of the five dominant craft organizations in 1900. Their proposal led only to the formation by these craft unions of their own organization, the AFTO, and application for AFL recognition. The AFL refused to grant a charter, favoring a consolidation of the AFTO and the IUTW. A series of unsuccessful southern strikes during 1900 forced the IUTW to accept the consolidation, which led to the formation of the UTWA in 1901.

Membership of the UTWA in 1902, its first full year of operation, totaled 10,600 in 185 locals. These workers represented only 1.49 percent of all textile workers, and this percentage remained steady until 1919-1920 when wartime gains increased it to approximately 10 percent. During the following two decades, the percentage dropped to 3 percent and stabilized at that figure. The UTWA's inability to gain a more impressive position in the textile industry resulted from the multipartite nature of the textile industry and the heterogeneity of the textile labor force. Additionally, the union had internal difficulties stemming from weak national leadership, the reluctance of craft unions to relinquish their local autonomy, and frequent rebellions against paying per-capita taxes to the national office.

From its founding, the UTWA had to contend with several rival organizations, including such conservative unions as the National Amalgamation of Textile Operatives, the National Mule Spinners' Union, and the American Federation of Hosiery Workers.* These drew their strength from the skilled workers in the craft unions. By 1930 most of the locals in these splinter groups had reaffiliated with the UTWA. On the left, the National Industrial Textile Union established by the IWW, the Amalgamated Textile Workers,* One Big Union, Associated Silk Workers, and the Communist dual union, the National Textile Workers Union,* competed with the UTWA for the unskilled immigrant workers in New England and later for the southern cotton mill operatives. Unable to sustain their membership, these rivals disappeared or by 1930 had been absorbed by the UTWA.

Benefiting from pro-labor legislation and general business improvement in the textile industry, the UTWA experienced substantial growth during the early years of the Roosevelt administration. Although membership fluctuated greatly, the union claimed approximately 350,000 members prior to the outbreak of the general textile strike of 1934. The strike started with the cotton mill workers on Labor Day, 1934, and quickly spread to the rest of the textile industry, involving at its height about half of all textile workers. This strike, the largest of its time, was a particularly violent one. Many workers were killed or wounded, and, in Georgia, strikers were interned in concentration camps established by Governor Eugene Talmadge. Under the leadership of Francis Gorman, chairman of the strike committee, the UTWA demonstrated effective leadership during the strike, which ended on September 22, 1934, after the UTWA executive council voted to accept a compromise settlement. Although the settlement merely promised to establish a board to study the conditions within the textile industry, Gorman and the UTWA proclaimed it a great victory. Many workers were openly disappointed, however, not only by the terms of the settlement but also by the UTWA's proclamation of victory. Thus the union lost much of the goodwill it had established during the strike, especially in the South.

In 1935 the UTWA entered a new era when President Thomas McMahon joined in founding the Congress of Industrial Organizations* (CIO). The AFL suspended the UTWA's charter in 1936 and revoked it in 1938. Early in 1937, the UTWA and the CIO formed the Textile Workers Organizing Committee (TWOC), which was financed and therefore controlled by the CIO. In the fall of 1937, Francis Gorman and supporters in the old UTWA led an unsuccessful bid to gain control of the joint organization. The Gorman faction then set up a rival textile union and applied for the UTWA's AFL charter. The AFL charter was re-invested in February 1939, thus beginning the rivalry between the UTWA-AFL and the Textile Workers Union of America* (TWUA-CIO).

At the time of its re-investment, the UTWA counted only 1,500 members and faced the extremely difficult task of rebuilding the union, which was hampered by internal dissent and financial dependence on the AFL. Externally the union confronted the intense rivalry of the TWUA and the strong opposition of the textile mill owners. Moreover, the migration of the textile industry into the South presented the UTWA with another challenge—the southern textile workers. Unlike their northern counterparts, the southern textile workers did not possess a tradition of craft unionism. Primarily unskilled and skeptical of unions in general, these workers were extremely difficult to organize. Although the UTWA and the AFL made several attempts to unionize the textile workers in the South, including a major organizing drive in 1946, the results were not impressive. In recent years the UTWA has enjoyed more success, as witnessed by the union's significant victory at the Danville, Virginia, mills in 1974, where a long strike ended in higher wages and better fringe benefits for the workers.

The rivalry between the UTWA and the TWUA has always been particularly bitter. In 1952 following an internal dispute within the CIO's Southern Organizing Committee, George Baldanzi of the TWUA switched his allegiance and became director of organization of the UTWA. Baldanzi, who later became president of the UTWA, brought 20,000 members with him to the UTWA, virtually eliminating the TWUA in the South and doubling UTWA membership. The continuing intensity of the rivalry is witnessed by the continued separation of the two rival unions even after the merger of the AFL and CIO. They did, however, sign a no-raiding agreement.

Less than a year after the AFL-CIO* merger, in November 1957 the two top officials of the UTWA, President Anthony Valente and Secretary-Treasurer Lloyd Klenert, were forced to resign under charges of misusing union funds. First Vice-President Francis Schaufenbil became both acting president and acting secretary-treasurer until a convention could be held to elect new officers.

The UTWA, which maintains its national headquarters in Lawrence, Massachusetts, holds triennial conventions. Principal officers include an international president, fourteen vice-presidents, and a secretary-treasurer. The international executive council consists of the above officers in addition to the director of organization. In 1973 the UTWA reported a membership of 52,000 located in 253 local unions.

For further information, see *The Textile Challenger*, a bimonthly newspaper published by the UTWA. See also Robert R. R. Brooks, "The United Textile Workers of America" (Ph.D. dissertation, Yale University, 1935), a history of the early years of the UTWA, and Herbert J. Lahne, *The Cotton Mill Workers* (1944), which includes a discussion of the development of the UTWA to 1944.

Elaine Ross Cline

TEXTILE WORKERS UNION OF AMERICA (TWUA). Organizing activities among textile workers date back to 1834 when 2,000 female textile workers in Lowell, Massachusetts, struck in response to a wage cut, but it was not until the creation of the Textile Workers Organizing Committee (TWOC) on March 9, 1937, that a successful national textile union was established. Textiles, one of America's oldest industries, began to show marked signs of weakness by the beginning of the second decade of the twentieth century. The most persistent malady of the textile industry was its instability. Textile production fluctuated drastically along a boom and bust cycle, which was decidedly more bust than boom. Following World War I, competition from previously non-textile producing nations continually eroded the market for American textiles as had competition from nylon and other synthetic fibers. New enterprises such as the automobile, radio, and household applicance industries challenged textiles for the consumer's dollar with great success. The United Textile Workers of America* (UTWA), formed in 1901 to aid worker security, was soon confronted by a whole range of problems that it was almost entirely unable to overcome.

Since labor costs constitute an unusually high percentage of the total costs of American textiles, it was more profitable for many mill owners to halt production during UTWA organizing drives rather than submit to wage increases. Mill hands, usually from a rural background and suspicious of "foreign" organizers, were slow to see the advantages of union membership. Furthermore, a high percentage of mill workers were women and children, whom the union considered unorganizable. In the Northeast, immigrants contributed a high percentage of the textile work force. These workers were also difficult to organize and occasionally were used as strikebreakers. In addition to these obstacles, internal strife spawned by differences in geographical location, differentials in wages and conditions, and divergent opinions about the proper goals of the textile union and the means of achieving them plagued the UTWA.

The mill environment was not conducive to organizing. Mill owners, particularly in the South, fostered a paternal relationship between themselves and their workers, many of whom lived in company-owned mill villages. Mill owners had absolute power over such workers and used that power to thwart any union activity. Suspected union members were evicted from their homes, set upon by mill-paid deputies, prevented from using the village meeting hall, hounded out of the village church, or jailed for trespassing. In all, the nature of the industry, the social ecology of the mill village, and the nature of the mill worker himself all combined to counteract the organizing and collective bargaining efforts of the UTWA, lower the morale of its organizers, and conservatize its leadership.

The nadir in the struggle for textile unionism came in September 1934 with the ill-fated general textile strike, which was replete with anti-labor violence, the detention of strikers in concentration camp-like enclosures, and massive industry-wide lockouts. Complete ruination of the financially bankrupt and morale-shattered UTWA was averted only when President Franklin Roosevelt demanded the strike be ended. Textile workers again saw their union fail to successfully organize the textile industry.

As the newly formed Committee for Industrial Organization—later the Congress of Industrial Organizations* (CIO)—succeeded in organizing much of the automobile, steel, and rubber industries during between 1935 and 1937, UTWA leaders hoped the CIO could perform the same miracle in textiles. The CIO agreed to try, but remembering the past failures of the UTWA, stipulated in the agreement setting up the organizing machinery (the TWOC) in March 1937 that the UTWA relinquish control of its few remaining locals to the TWOC. The TWOC would direct all organizing activities and control all dues and other acquired revenues. Under the masterful leadership of Sidney Hillman from the Amalgamated Clothing Workers,* the TWOC began a massive organizing drive, which was stunningly successful until the nationwide recession in the fall of 1937. The economic downturn struck the textile industry with special force, drastically curtailing production and nullifying most of the TWOC's hard-won gains. By July 1938 the economy of the nation and the fortunes of the TWOC began to change for the better. Although organizers' reports were still discouraging from the South, traditionally a difficult region to organize, in the Northeast workers were being organized and contracts were being signed at a steady pace.

One problem beginning to plague the TWOC grew from a struggle for leadership between Emil Rieve, president of the American Federation of Hosiery Workers,* a semi-autonomous union affiliated with the TWOC, and Francis Gorman, a long-time UTWA official and director of the 1934 Southern Organizing Drive. Gorman and other UTWA leaders were dissatisfied with the TWOC, especially with wage cuts accepted by Hillman during the 1937-1938 recession. When it became clear that Hillman would not name Gorman his successor as TWOC president, Gorman bolted with eighty-three former UTWA locals, and in early 1939 reaffiliated with the American Federation of Labor* (AFL). Gorman's defection forced the remaining TWOC leaders to realize that as an ad hoc committee that allowed little voice from its rank and file, the TWOC was clearly vulnerable to charges of being dictatorial, a charge Gorman repeatedly made. In response to this realization, on May 15, 1939, delegates representing 100,000 members in 309 locals of the TWOC met in Philadelphia and organized the Textile Workers Union of America, an international union affiliate of the CIO. Emil Rieve was chosen to head the new union.

Rieve entered office at a time when government contracts were drastically increasing the demand for cloth and other textile products, thereby creating vast numbers of new jobs. The wage cuts of 1938, so instrumental in the defection of Gorman and his associates, were restored, and in some areas, wages were even increased. In response to these better times, textile workers flocked to union locals in an effort to protect their jobs and gain higher wages. As a member of the War Labor Board during World War II, Rieve made a patriotic no-strike pledge on behalf of the textile workers, even though it became increasingly evident that while mill workers' wages had been frozen by government controls, profits continued to soar. Upset by the recalcitrance of the War Labor Board in ordering wage increases to offset the disparity between wages and profits, Rieve resigned from the board and revoked the no-strike pledge.

The post-World War II textile industry, overexpanded from war production but no longer supported by government contracts, fell into a long-term slump. As a consequence, the fortunes of the TWUA also turned for the worse. Automation eliminated many jobs and consigned many remaining workers to mere machine tending. Competition from an increasing variety of synthetic fibers bankrupted many of the more traditional mills. Textile employment declined drastically from a high point of some 1.3 million workers in 1942 to a mere 800,000 in 1964. As its membership figures plummeted, the TWUA began to realize that in order to protect its own security, it would have to work toward securing the viability of the textile industry. In this spirit, the TWUA pressed for such industry-supportive measures as protective tariffs, standardized cotton prices, and a federal textile development agency. The TWUA revived its tradition of assisting the industry to develop new ideas in plant efficiency and product marketing.

Paralleling the difficulties of the TWUA and the unstable, ailing industry was a series of internal power struggles between various union factions. The first of these emerged in the early 1950s and involved Emil Rieve and George Baldanzi, then director of southern organizing. Rieve eventually resisted Baldanzi's assault on his office, thus forcing Baldanzi to follow Gorman into the UTWA, which, augmented by the Baldanzi faction, initiated an intensive raiding policy against the TWUA. A later example of internecine warfare centered around a fight for control between Rieve's successor, William Pollack, and a faction within the TWUA executive council. This erupted at the 1964 convention and left much ill feeling on both sides. In 1975 the TWUA entered into merger discussion with the Amalgamated Clothing Workers of America,* but the merger was delayed pending the resolution of disagreements in the unity negotiations.

The TWUA, which maintains its national headquarters in New York City, holds biennial conventions. Principal officers include a general president, twenty vice-presidents, and a secretary-treasurer. The above officers constitute the executive council. In 1973 the TWUA reported a membership of 174,000 located in 718 local unions.

For further information, see the *Textile Labor* issued monthly by the TWUA. See also Esther Thelen, "A Brief History of the Textile Workers Union of America, 1937-1960," in *The Textile Workers Union of America Papers: A Descriptive Guide*, Bulletin #1, John R. Commons Labor Reference Center, The State Historical Society of Wisconsin; *They Said it Couldn't Be Done: A History of the Textile Workers Union of America* (n.d.), an in-house history; and Walter Galenson, *The CIO Challenge to the AFL: A History of the American Labor Movement, 1935-1941* (1960).

Joseph Y. Garrison

TEXTILE WORKERS UNION; NATIONAL (NTWU). The American Socialist movement splintered into three separate groups in 1919. One group supported the traditional goals and tactics of the Socialist Party of America, and the other two groups formed communist parties. A year later the Trade Union Educational League (TUEL), the American arm of the Red International of Labor Unions, was founded with the objective of "boring from within" the established trade unions and converting them to Marxist principles. The TUEL had considerable success in infiltrating unions in the needle trades industry, and as a result of its role in the Passaic strike of 1926 and the strike of textile workers in New Bedford, Massachusetts, in 1928, the TUEL built a substantial rank-and-file constituency among textile workers.

Nevertheless, the hostility of the established, conservative unions and their active campaigns during the late 1920s to eliminate radical influences compromised the success of Communist initiatives. Conflicts over the way in which the United Textile Workers of America* (UTWA) handled the strike in New Bedford led textile workers in that city to call a convention of all left-wing unions to meet in New Bedford on September 22, 1928. During that conference, the National Textile Workers Union was founded.

At the same time that internal conflicts were disrupting textile unions, the Red International of Labor Unions in Moscow changed its tactics. The TUEL was dissolved, the "boring from within" policy discarded, and the Trade Union Unity League* (TUUL) organized as a rival federation of trade unions to the American Federation of Labor* (AFL). The NTWU became the first TUUL affiliate.

The NTWU was organized on an industrial basis. It adopted extremely democratic forms of internal union governance, assessed dues according to wage levels, and conducted an extensive educational campaign condemning any type of "class-collaborationist" tactics. The negotiating demands of the communist union included higher wages, shorter hours, equal pay for equal work, and the abolition of child labor in the textile industry.

The NTWU conducted its major organizing drives in the South, primarily in North Carolina. In conjunction with the AFL, the UTWA also was attempting a southern organizing drive at the time, and the two unions often found themselves in bitter combat with each other as well as also battling employers. The NTWU had its greatest success in Gastonia, North Carolina, where it effectively organized the workers of the Loray Mill of the Manville-Jenckes Corporation. When the company rejected demands for a forty-hour week and other concessions, including increased wages, a strike was called that by April 1929 involved 1,700 of the 2,200 textile workers employed in the mill. The strike was a violent struggle further inflamed by the revolutionary slogans and exaggerated rhetoric of Communist organizers and was brutally crushed by mill owners with the support and assistance of local government officials. The unnecessary brutality that the employers and their allies used aroused widespread sympathy for the embattled and battered workers. Later several NTWU leaders involved in the strike were tried and convicted of conspiracy to murder, charges growing from a confrontation between an overzealous local police official and strikers living in a tent colony after their eviction from company housing.

Ultimately, the Communist southern organizing drive was no more successful than the UTWA and AFL campaigns. Consequently, although it continued to agitate in the South, the NTWU's strength remained largely localized in the southern New England area, the same area that traditionally had been hospitable to left-wing unionism. Then in 1935 the Red International again changed its strategy, reverting to the "popular front," "boring from within" tactic. The NTWU was dissolved and its organizers were ordered to reaffiliate with established AFL unions in the industry.

The NTWU, which maintained its national headquarters in New Bedford, held annual conventions. The union was governed by an executive board, and the secretary was the chief executive official. Reliable membership figures were not located.

For further information, see the Rand School of Social Science, *The American Labor Year Book* (1930-1932); R. W. Dunn and Jack Hardy, *Labor in Textiles* (1931); and Robert R. R. Brooks, "The United Textile Workers of America" (Ph.D. dissertation, Yale University, 1935).

THEATRICAL STAGE EMPLOYEES AND MOVING PICTURE MACHINE OPERATORS OF THE UNITED STATES AND CANADA; INTERNATIONAL ALLIANCE OF (IATSE). The growing maturity of the

American theater during the second half of the nineteenth century was paralleled by the increased organization of local unions of stage employees. Most of these early unions organized as relief and fraternal societies but soon developed an economic orientation. The first such unions of theater stagehands probably appeared in New York City during the early 1870s. Stage employees also joined the Knights of Labor* in large numbers. Their principal grievances included low wages, long hours, and the seasonal or irregular nature of employment in the industry.

The first effort to form a national union of theatrical workers took place in New York City in 1891 when representatives of local unions in the host city, Chicago, and Pittsburgh met to discuss the possibilities for the creation of such an organization. Ultimately the delegates decided to defer organizing a national union until the following year, when it was hoped a better representation of the independent local unions existing in many larger American cities could be assembled. Nevertheless the 1892 meeting also proved abortive, and it was not until 1893 that a central union was formed.

Delegates representing theater workers in New York, Chicago, Pittsburgh, Brooklyn, St. Louis, Denver, Philadelphia, Buffalo, Syracuse, and Boston met in New York City on July 20, 1893, and after three days of deliberation, the National Alliance of Theatrical Stage Employees of the United States assumed its place in the growing American labor movement. Immediately confronted by the depression of the 1890s, the new union not only managed to survive its first test but recorded small membership gains during each of the first forty years of its history.

In July 1894 the alliance was given a charter as a national union by the American Federation of Labor* (AFL). After the chartering of two Canadian locals in 1899, the title of the union was changed by the addition of the words "and Canada," and in 1902 the title was again amended by the substitution of "International" for "National." When the AFL granted the alliance exclusive jurisdiction over motion picture projectionists in 1914, the current title was adopted.

Through the years, changes in the entertainment industry required the IATSE to expand its jurisdiction and alter its organizational structure in order to meet the exigencies resulting from technological innovation. Beginning in 1908 with the organization of projectionists employed in the new film industry, the IATSE expanded its organization to Hollywood studios and the growing network of film exchanges throughout North America. Later, with the development of commercial television, the IATSE also took its place in this area of visual entertainment.

Although originally organized along strict craft lines, changes in the entertainment industry also required changes in organizing tactics. In smaller cities mixed locals of stage employees and moving picture machine operators were formed; the mixed local unit was also used extensively in smaller production centers. In 1937 the IATSE organized the "special department" to represent these mixed locals. Much of the television industry was unionized on an industrial basis with a variety of crafts organized into television broadcasting studio employees' locals in individual cities. In 1951 a radio and television department was created to provide direct IATSE membership where local units did not exist. The organization of shipping, booking, and other distribution employees led to the establishment of a motion picture salesmen department in 1957.

The great variety of craftsmen involved, the evolving character of the entertainment industry, and the IATSE's constant jurisdictional adjustments inevitably brought it into conflict with other unions. The IATSE found itself frequently involved in disputes with such unions as the United Brotherhood of Carpenters and Joiners,* the International Brotherhood of Electrical Workers,* and the International Association of Machinists.*

The IATSE has a long tradition of local autonomy, especially in collective bargaining. Nevertheless, changes in the organizational structure of the union necessitated adjustments in basic policy. Regional bargaining has become increasingly common, and, in some cases, where warranted by the nature of the work, the general officers negotiate nationwide agreements. Although willing to strike when necessary, the IATSE has usually found it possible to negotiate acceptable agreements without resorting to strike activity.

One of the least illustrious chapters of IATSE history occurred during the 1930s when the criminal underworld seized control of the union and extorted hundreds of thousands of dollars from union members as well as from theater and motion picture producers (many of whom willingly paid the bribes as a means of keeping wages low and securing favorable union contracts). Through threats and intimidation, Chicago racketeers succeeded in installing George Browne in the IATSE presidency in 1934, a position he held (under the close supervision of William Bioff, a minor figure in the Capone organization) until convicted of extortion in 1940. Thereafter, under the presidency of Richard Walsh, underworld influence was purged from union councils.

The IATSE, which maintains its national headquarters in New York City, holds biennial conventions. Full-time officers include a president, nine vice-presidents, and a secretary-treasurer. The general executive board consists of the above officers. In 1973 the IATSE reported a membership of 62,000 located in 900 local unions.

For further informaion, see the *Official Bulletin* issued quarterly by the IATSE and "Introduction to the I.A.T.S.E.," also published by the union. The only scholarly account of the IATSE is Robert O. Baker's *The International Alliance of Theatrical Stage Employees and Moving Picture Machine Operators of the United States and Canada* (1933). See also John Hutchinson, *The Imperfect Union: A History of Corruption in American Trade Unions* (1970), and the *AFL-CIO American Federationist* (August 1958).

TIMBER WORKERS; INTERNATIONAL UNION OF (IUTW). The Knights of Labor* first attempted the organization of lumber workers during the 1870-1880 period, but these activities were largely confined to California's redwood region. In 1890 six Washington locals of shingle industry workers organized the West Coast Shingle Workers' Union, but it failed to survive the depression of the 1890s. During the early twentieth century the American Federation of Labor* (AFL) entered the field, chartering federal labor unions composed primarily of shingle workers. Several of these federal locals met in Everett, Washington, in January 1903 and organized the International Shingle Weavers Union of America (ISWUA). On March 3 it was granted an AFL charter.

Lumber producers militantly opposed union organization both individually and by forming employer associations. Consequently the organization of lumber workers was destined to be a chaotic and volatile affair. Seeking higher wages and union recognition, the ISWUA conducted scattered strikes in 1904 and a general strike in the Northwest in 1905. Employers, who responded by organizing the Shingle Mills Bureau and creating a large defense fund, defeated the strike. Six months later the union again threatened to strike for higher wages, and this time employers conceded, but union recognition was not an issue. Another union, the International Brotherhood of Woodsmen and Sawmill Workers, organized earlier the same year and received an AFL charter on August 2, 1905. The new union, however, never proved very effective, and on April 10, 1911, its charter was suspended.

The Industrial Workers of the World* (IWW), which played a significant, if turbulent, role in attempts to organize workers in the lumber industry, appeared in 1905. With the IWW's entrance into the field, an intense struggle developed between the craft-conscious AFL and the IWW, which sought to organize on an industrial basis. Faced with the IWW challenge, the ISWUA, which had managed to survive where other unions failed, asked the AFL for jurisdiction over the entire lumber industry. The AFL agreed and on January 15, 1913, issued a charter to the International Union of Shingle Weavers, Sawmill Workers and Woodsmen (IUSWSWW). In 1914 the new union inaugurated a campaign for an eight-hour day and threatened a May 1 general strike if its demands were not met. Several locals questioned the wisdom of the strike, however. As a result a special convention was convened, where it was decided to seek the eight-hour day through initiated legislation. The defeat of the bill sent the IUSWSWW into a sharp decline. Frustrated and disillusioned in their efforts to organize lumber workers, the shingle workers reorganized as a craft union under their original title, the International Shingle Weavers Union of America, and received a new AFL charter on January 10, 1916.

When employers reneged on a promised wage increase, the ISWUA struck a mill in Everett on May 1, 1916. The ISWUA Everett local contained numerous IWW sympathizers, and the IWW actively intervened in hopes of converting

Everett into a union town. The uninvited IWW involvement led to the infamous Everett massacre in which seven people were killed and fifty wounded.

Along with the newly organized International Union of Timber Workers (IUTW), chartered by the AFL on August 7, 1917, that same year the ISWUA launched a major organizing campaign concurrent with but separate from a similar campaign led by the IWW. After employers rejected demands for an eight-hour day and wage concessions, the IUTW and ISWUA called special conventions during the summer of 1917 to discuss alternatives. Obviously working together, the two organizations set a July 16 strike date if their demands were not met. Choosing to fight, employers formed the Lumberman's Protective Association and resolved to resist the workers' demands and crush the unions.

Meanwhile, the IWW, already involved in strikes in Idaho and Montana, was not anxious to extend the strike into the Northwest fir region. Nevertheless, worker militancy placed IWW leaders in the position of either joining the strike or forfeiting their influence to the AFL. The IWW chose the former course. When in September it appeared as though the strike would collapse, the IWW transformed its strike into a series of "job actions." The AFL unions decided to continue the strike but to permit their members to return to work without penalty. This action ended the AFL's influence in the struggle. Conversely, the IWW's highly successful "strike on the job" and "conscientious withdrawal of efficiency" increased its influence until stymied by federal intervention.

Concerned about the supply of spruce for airplane construction, the War Department dispatched Colonel Bryce P. Disque to investigate. Shortly after his arrival on the scene, Disque organized the Loyal Legion of Loggers and Lumbermen (4L). Although theoretically a creation of the War Department, employers had earlier suggested the creation of such an organization. Accompanied by a large-scale patriotic propaganda offensive, the 4L grew rapidly, reaching a membership of over 70,000 by the spring of 1918.

As it became increasingly obvious that the lumber companies dominated the 4L, its membership declined precipitantly. Nevertheless, 4L organizers decided to maintain the organization after the war in hopes of creating an industry-wide company union. As a result both the IWW and AFL accelerated their activities in the industry. In March 1918 the ISWUA and IUTW merged under the title of the latter. The IUTW then initiated a vigorous organizing campaign that resulted in a membership in excess of 10,000 by the end of 1920. The revival was short-lived. The employers' open-shop offensive, the 1920-1921 economic recession, lost strikes in Bogalusa, Louisiana, and Bellingham, Washington, in 1919 as well as an unsuccessful eight-hour strike in the Great Lakes area in 1920 and a disastrous strike at Klamath Falls, Oregon, in 1922 extinguished whatever spark remained in the IUTW. On March 22, 1923, it disbanded and surrendered its AFL charter.

For further information, see the *Shingle Weaver* and *Timber Worker*. See also Vernon H. Jensen's excellent study, *Lumber and Labor* (1945), and Charlotte Todes, *Labor and Lumber* (1931), an account favoring the IWW. The 4L has been studied by Robert L. Tyler, "The United States Government as Union Organizer: The Loyal Legion of Loggers and Lumbermen," *Mississippi Valley Historical Review* (December 1960), and Harold M. Hyman, *Soldiers and Spruce: Origins of the Loyal Legion of Loggers & Lumbermen* (1963). For IWW activities, see Robert L. Tyler, *Rebels of the Woods: The I. W. W. in the Pacific Northwest* (1967), and Merl E. Reed, "Lumberjacks and Longshoremen: The I.W.W. in Louisiana," *Labor History* (Winter 1972).

TOBACCO WORKERS INTERNATIONAL UNION (TWIU). The American Federation of Labor* (AFL) had directly chartered ten federal labor unions of tobacco workers by 1895. On June 28, 1895, representatives of those unions met at St. Louis and created the National Tobacco Workers Union of America. Four years later, after organizing work had begun in Canada, the union title was changed to Tobacco Workers International Union.

In its early years the TWIU had its greatest success among owners of small concerns who hoped by using the union label to gain a competitive edge on the large tobacco companies in the growing union labor market. Before its dissolution by the Supreme Court, the giant tobacco trust resolutely opposed any type of union organization, and little changed after the trust was dissolved. The hostile attitude toward organized labor was continued by the "big four" that emerged: Liggett & Myers Tobacco Company, American Tobacco Company, P. Lorillard Company, and R. J. Reynolds.

The TWIU's failure to organize any of the large tobacco companies consigned it to the status of a small, marginal union with a large but unfulfilled jurisdictional field. The TWIU did have a membership surge during World War I, reaching 15,200 by 1920, but much of that membership evaporated during the 1920s and early years of the Great Depression. By 1932, the TWIU had shrunk to 2,500 members.

Labor provisions of the National Industrial Recovery Act of 1933 revitalized the TWIU's organizing efforts. Organizational campaigns began in Virginia, North Carolina, and Kentucky, but again the formidable resistance of the large tobacco companies limited the success of the TWIU's campaign. the Union's only major advance during this period was the negotiation of a contract with the Brown and Williamson Tobacco Corporation establishing a union shop, dues checkoffs, and use of the union label.

The TWIU accomplished no further organizing advances until the Supreme Court ruled favorably on the constitutionality of the National Labor Relations Act in 1937. Shortly after the court's decision, three companies—Liggett & Myers, Philip Morris, and American—recognized the TWIU as the bargaining agent for their employees in North Carolina and Virginia. After lengthy litigation, P., Lorillard recognized the TWIU in 1940, leaving only R. J. Reynolds Tobacco Company outside the union fold.

After successfully organizing tobacco manufacturing plants, the TWIU then turned to the seasonal field-workers in the green leaf division of the industry. Besides providing union benefits for those agricultural workers, its success increased the security and stability of the organized workers in manufacturing plants and the organizational stability of the TWIU. The TWIU's effort to have the large tobacco companies use the union label on their products, however, was frustrated.

As it organized an increasing percentage of the workers in the industry, the TWIU had greater success in negotiations with employers. Its collective bargaining achievements resulted in higher wages, shorter hours, and a variety of insurance and pension benefits. Moreover the TWIU's successes came primarily in the South where resistance to organized labor traditionally had been strongest.

The TWIU, which maintains its national headquarters in Washington, D.C., holds quadrennial conventions. Principal officers include a president, senior vice-president, secretary-treasurer, and six general vice-presidents. The general executive board consists of the above officers. In 1973 the TWIU reported a membership of 33,565 located in seventy local unions.

For further information, see the *Tobacco Worker* issued monthly and a historical sketch, *Tobacco Workers International Union,* published by the TWIU. See also *The American Federationist* (December 1954).

TRADE UNION UNITY LEAGUE (TUUL). At the Fourth Congress of the Red International of Labor Unions held in Moscow in the early spring of 1928, American delegates were given radically new instructions concerning the tactics to be used in the United States, especially regarding their relationship with the existing American labor movement. The Trade Union Educational League (TUEL), which had been organized as a propaganda and educational organization, was to be transformed into a trade union central body "uniting all revolutionary unions, minority groups and individual militants." American Communists henceforth were to end their "boring from within" activities and launch a dual union movement.

Faithfully adhering to their new instructions, delegates to the fourth biennial convention of the TUEL held in Cleveland on August 31, 1929, dissolved the TUEL and in its place organized the Trade Union Unity League. The organizing convention of the new labor federation was attended by 690 delegates, most of whom came from the mining fields of the nation. Included among the delegates were seventy-two women, sixty-four Afro-Americans, and 160 persons under twenty-five years of age.

The TUUL constitution stipulated that affiliated unions should levy low initiation fees and dues and permit free transfers within unions; officers' salaries were not to exceed the average wage in the industry. The league was to be governed on the basis of "democratic centralism," and William Z. Foster, long a participant in radical causes and a member of the Communist party in the United States since 1921, was elected general secretary. Between conventions, organization affairs were to be conducted by the national committee, the national executive board, and an executive bureau comprised of the national officers. The TUUL's objectives and demands included organizing the unorganized, developing class-conscious unions, developing a new leadership in the "reformist unions," defending the Soviet Union, working for equal treatment of Negroes, abolishing the "speed-up," establishing a seven-hour day, and supporting the Communist program in America.

At the time of its organization, three national unions had already been organized in response to the new policies of the Red International. They were the National Miners' Union, the Needle Trades Workers Industrial Union,* and the National Textile Workers Union.* Many other unions were established in the years immediately following the formation of the TUUL, including the Auto Workers Industrial Union, Food and Packinghouse Workers Industrial League, Lumber Workers Industrial League, Marine Workers Industrial Union, Metal Workers Industrial League, Railroad Workers Industrial League, and the Shoe and Leather Workers National Committee. Most of these unions were little more than paper organizations having a negligible impact on the industries in which they were organized. Nevertheless, TUUL unions were involved in several violent strikes. Among the more dramatic were the textile strikes at Gastonia and Bessemer City, North Carolina; miners' strikes in Pennsylvania, West Virginia, and Ohio; and agricultural workers strikes in California.

The decision to organize dual unions created a division within the American Communist movement. Led by Jay Lovestone, former general secretary of the Communist party, many Communists preferred to continue working within established unions and objected to the dual union tactic. Although these critics generally joined TUUL affiliates, they continued their criticism within those unions and in a few years led their followers back into the AFL.

The TUUL, however, was destined to be a short-lived dual union. Concerned about the rise of Adolf Hitler in Germany, in 1934 Joseph Stalin ordered the world communist movement to drop the independent tactic and return to the "popular front" strategy. A short time later Communist leaders in the United States began speaking of capturing the "AFL millions"; and in February 1935 the secretary of the Communist party in the United States, Earl Browder, confirmed the new policy. The TUUL was dissolved, and members of its affiliated unions were instructed to rejoin established unions in their industries. Communist trade union work henceforth was to be carried out within the AFL.

The TUUL held biennial conventions. Principal officers included a general secretary, an assistant secretary, an organizer, Negro organizers, and the editor of *Labor Unity*, the official TUUL organ. Although there are no reliable figures, the TUUL reported a membership of 125,000 shortly before its dissolution.

For further information, see *Labor Unity* published by the TUUL. See also Theodore Draper, *The Roots of American Communism* (1957); David J. Saposs, *Communism in American Unions* (1959); and the Rand School of Social Science's *The American Labor Year Book*, vols. 11-12 (1930, 1931). Besides the above sources, most general labor histories have a discussion of the TUUL.

TRAIN DISPATCHERS ASSOCIATION; AMERICAN (ATDA). Despite vehement carrier resistance and threats of blacklisting, a group of train dispatchers met in Spokane, Washington, on November 1, 1917, and organized a local union. The unionization of train dispatchers was obviously an idea whose time had come. Organization spread rapidly through the western states, and within a year of the formation of the original Spokane union, the Western Train Dispatchers' Association was organized. Before the end of 1918, a national union, the American Train Dispatchers Association, was formed. Reflecting the growth and development of the union, in 1920 ATDA national offices were moved from Spokane to Chicago.

The new railroad union, which had both fraternal and economic objectives, limited membership to "any train dispatcher, white, of good moral character, and over 21 years of age." Organization spread rapidly on railroad systems throughout the nation. By the mid-1920s, ATDA membership reached 4,000 where it stabilized for several years before undergoing a gradual decline during the early years of the Great Depression. The ATDA had remained independent since its formation, but in 1957 it requested and received an American Federation of Labor-Congress of Industrial Organizations* charter.

The ATDA, which maintains its national headquarters in Berwyn, Illinois, holds quadrennial conventions. Principal officers include a president, three vice-presidents, and a secretary-treasurer. The above officers comprise the executive board. In 1973 the ATDA reported a membership of 2,817 located in eighty local unions.

For further information, see *The Train Dispatcher* issued eight times annually by the ATDA. Little published information concerning the ATDA exists, but basic information can be found in *Bulletin No. 618*, Bureau of Labor Statistics, U.S. Department of Labor (1936), and Florence Peterson, *Handbook of Labor Unions* (1944).

TRANSIT UNION; AMALGAMATED (ATU). The organization of street railway men began during the Knights of Labor* era in the second half of the nineteenth century, but the unions organized at this time proved weak and short-lived. Organizers from the newly formed American Federation of Labor* (AFL) next entered the field, organizing directly affiliated AFL federal labor unions composed of street railway employees. Their success was such that delegates to the AFL's national convention in 1891 instructed their president, Samuel Gompers, to call a meeting of the street railway unions with hopes of establishing an international union.

After corresponding with several unions, Gompers issued a call for a convention to meet in Indianapolis on September 12, 1892. Fifty delegates from twenty-two locals responded. Although sixteen locals were affiliated with the AFL and only four from the Knights of Labor, the Knights' unions claimed to represent nearly twice as many workers as the AFL unions. Delegates immediately set about the task of writing a constitution establishing the Amalgamated Association of Street Railway Employees of America (AASREA). Much to the shock and anger of Samuel Gompers, the new union voted against affiliating with the AFL. Because of the large Knights' membership that objected to AFL affiliation, the delegates believed harmony could best be preserved by assuming an independent status.

The Amalgamated barely survived its first few years. Shortly after the convention adjourned, the newly elected president, William J. Law, became involved in a heated controversy in his Detroit local over the activities of the American Protective Association. This so consumed his time and attention that he largely neglected the affairs of the AASREA. The national depression of 1893 further disrupted union affairs. The election of William D. Mahon to the AASREA presidency in 1893 represented the most significant event during these early years. Mahon led the union for over a half-century, and during these years it became a large, influential trade union.

Delegates to the Amalgamated's second annual convention (1893) also voted to affiliate with the AFL, to lower dues, and to further centralize authority in the international office. Although the AASREA remained largely a paper organization during the depression years of the 1890s, it did develop the organizational and leadership structure permitting the union to use improved organizing opportunities in the post-depression years.

After an unsuccessful strike in Milwaukee in 1896, surprisingly, AASREA fortunes began to improve. Facing an uncompromising anti-union stand by the management of the Milwaukee Electric Railway and Light Company, workers exhibited great determination and unity of purpose as they conducted their strike with dignity and perseverance. Conversely, the actions of company managers dramatically illustrated the avarice of those controlling the streetcars, not only in Milwaukee but throughout much of the nation.

Although company resistance remained strong, the Amalgamated began to make considerable progress at the turn of the century. Membership grew, and the union became stronger. Numerous strikes were conducted, and while few were totally successful, collective bargaining agreements ceased to be a phenomenal event. Ineffective strikes in Albany and Troy, New York, and St. Louis in 1900 and 1901, however, drained the AASREA treasury and clearly illustrated that the organization of streetcar men was going to be difficult and expensive. Meanwhile, the Amalgamated's jurisdiction was extended in 1903 to include the workers on electric street railways, and the union title was changed to the Amalgamated Association of Street and Electric Railway Employees of America (AASEREA).

Progress was slow during the first two decades of the twentieth century, but it was steady and firm. Fewer than 2,000 members in 1896 became 30,000 in 1904 and continued upward, reaching 60,000 by 1916 and 100,000 in 1921. Moreover, unlike most other unions, the Amalgamated not only retained its World War I membership gains throughout the 1920s but even increased slightly. During the same period, the number of collective bargaining agreements negotiated by the Amalgamated rose from twenty-two in 1901 to over a hundred in 1907, 200 in 1915, and 300 by 1919. The increased strength of the AASEREA was accompanied by a wage rate that rose steadily from 1900 to 1927, the gradual reduction in hours of labor, and improved working conditions, especially concerning safety.

Despite its steady growth during the first quarter of the twentieth century, thousands of streetcar men and hundreds of streetcar systems remained unorganized. Moreover, despite improvements, wages of streetcar men still lagged behind those of workers in comparable occupations. Finally, employers, both private and public, remained hostile to organized labor, fiercely resisting organization, and waiting for an opportunity to break the union.

The Great Depression offered such an opportunity, and despite the provisions of the National Industrial Recovery Act and the National Labor Relations Act, employers succeeded in rescinding trade union gains for the first time in the twentieth century. AASEREA membership fell from a high of 101,300 in 1929 to 65,400 before gradually turning upward in the mid-1930s. It was not until 1944 that the Amalgamated regained its 1929 membership.

While employer hostility and economic conditions do much to explain the AASEREA's hard times during the 1930s and early 1940s, the emergence of the Congress of Industrial Organizations* (CIO) and the introduction of rival unionism created additional problems. In 1937 the CIO chartered the Transport Workers Union of America* (TWUA). The new CIO union originally was composed of many workers withdrawing from the AASEREA, the International Association of Machinists,* and the International Brotherhood of Teamsters* (IBT). Although the TWUA claimed nearly 100,000 members by the end of World War II, much of its early strength was confined to the New York City metropolitan area, and in the rivalry between the two organizations of streetcar employees, the AASEREA held its own until the early 1970s, when the TWUA's membership equaled and then surpassed that of the Amalgamated.

The Amalgamated's membership peaked in the late 1940s when it paid per-capita taxes to the AFL on nearly 200,000 members. Thereafter, membership figures fluctuated considerably, but evidenced a gradual decline precipitated primarily by reduced employment in the Amalgamated's jurisdiction. The AASEREA changed its title to Amalgamated Association of Street, Electric Railway and Motor Coach Employees of America in 1934, but this change was never recognized by the AFL because of objections from the IBT. Again the union changed its name in 1965, becoming the Amalgamated Transit Union.

The ATU, which maintains its national headquarters in Washington, D.C., holds biennial conventions. Principal officers include a president, executive vice-president, and secretary-treasurer. The general executive board includes the above officials in addition to members elected by the delegates to national conventions. In 1973 the ATU reported a membership of 130,000 located in over 300 local unions.

For further information, see *In Transit* published monthly by the ATU. Emerson P. Schmidt, *Industrial Relations in Urban Transportation* (1937), contains a good account of the early history of the union as well as character- istics of the industry. See also *The American Federationist* (September 1952).

TRANSPORT SERVICE EMPLOYEES OF AMERICA; UNITED (UTSE). By the mid-1930s, organizations of railroad redcaps existed in most major railroad terminals in the United States. Many of these unions held federal charters from the American Federation of Labor* (AFL), but prior to 1937 no attempt had been made to organize a national union, which was obviously needed. When confronted with demands for bargaining by organizations of redcaps and station porters, railroad managers declared that redcaps were not railroad employees and therefore were not covered by the collective bargaining provisions of the Railway Labor Act of 1926. If this interpretation stood, such workers would also be excluded from the benefits of other legislation appli- cable to railroad workers. In an effort to unify redcaps before challenging the railroads' actions, the well-organized Chicago porters called a national con- vention of all redcap organizations to meet in Chicago in April 1937. The for- mation of the International Brotherhood of Red Caps (IBRC) resulted from the meeting, and Willard Townsend of the Chicago and Northwestern redcaps was elected president. Dissension erupted shortly after the adjournment of the convention, however, and the new union was almost destroyed when several local organizations withdrew.

In an effort to reunify the IBRC, President Townsend and Secretary T. Wilbur Winchester launched a national tour, visiting many of the local groups throughout the nation. A second convention then met in Chicago on January 14, 1938. With A. Philip Randolph chairing the convention and serving as an impartial arbiter, unity was restored, and Townsend was reelected president.

When their union was firmly established, IBRC officials petitioned the Interstate Commerce Commission (ICC) to rule on the eligibility of redcaps, station porters, and ushers to participate in the rights and benefits accorded railroad workers under the Railway Labor Act. On February 20, 1938, the ICC ruled favorably on the petition. Railroad officials appealed the decision, but it was reaffirmed on September 29. With confirmation of its status under the Railway Labor Act, the IBRC successfully sought National Mediation Board certification as the collective bargaining agent for redcaps and other terminal service personnel.

Through legislation the IBRC also succeeded in eliminating inequities in the Railroad Retirement Act. These problems arose because prior to 1940 most of the remuneration redcaps received was from tips, but retirement benefits under the Railroad Retirement Act were computed on actual wages received. The IBRC amendment stipulated that in computing retirement benefits for redcaps, the wages received during the preceding twelve-month period would be averaged over the entire length of service.

The railroads' response to the Fair Labor Standards Act of 1938 created another problem for the IBRC. The railroads refused to pay the twenty-five cent hourly minimum wage established by the wage and hours provision of the law. Instead, they insisted that redcaps report their tips and pledged to compensate workers for the difference between the tips and the minimum wage. The system was easily abused, and many redcaps justifiably felt that their employment would be terminated if their reported tips did not equal the minimum wage. When the IBRC successfully challenged this action before appropriate government agencies, the railroads resorted to the practice of requiring redcaps to collect ten cents an article from passengers. As a consequence of congressional pressure and threatened legal action by the IBRC, the railroads finally relented and agreed to pay a regular wage.

The IBRC, which had expanded its jurisdiction to include most terminal employees, changed its name in 1940 to the United Transport Service Employees of America. Two years later the UTSE affiliated with the Congress of Industrial Organizations* and received a charter granting it a jurisdiction including "all service employees directly engaged in the transportation industry and such other employees who are denied democratic representation."

The UTSE launched a national organizing campaign to enroll Pullman laundry workers in 1943, and after winning a National Mediation Board representational election, became the collective bargaining agent for these workers. The UTSE had less success in its efforts to organize skycaps in the airport terminals of the nation.

After early organizing successes, the UTSE reached a membership of 12,650 in 1944. Thereafter, as rail passenger service contracted, a slow decline brought membership down to 3,000 in 1955. On October 1, 1972, the UTSE merged with the Brotherhood of Railway, Airline and Steamship Clerks, Freight Handlers, Express and Station Employees.* At the time of the merger the UTSE had a membership of 2,000.

The UTSE, which maintained its national headquarters in Chicago, held biennial conventions. Full-time officers included an international president, a secretary-treasurer, and eight vice-presidents. The executive board consisted of the above officers in addition to fourteen at-large members elected by majority vote of convention delegates.

For further information, see the *UTSE Newsletter* published bimonthly. See also *The American Federationist* (March 1957; June 1958).

TRANSPORT WORKERS UNION OF AMERICA (TWUA). The impetus for organizing workers employed on New York City's Interborough Rapid Transit (IRT) system came directly from the Communist party, which was anxious to organize and control the strategically important workers who operated the city's transportation network. Under the guidance of Communist party organizers, six Irish-American employees of the IRT held a series of meetings during April 1934 and made plans for the organization of the Transport Workers Union. The new union was to be organized on an industrial union basis, and leaders adopted union recognition as their primary objective, assuming that thereafter effective collective bargaining concerning wages, hours, and working conditions would follow.

Organization of workers on New York City's three transit companies, two of which were then privately controlled, was slow and difficult. Management had a long tradition of hostility to independent labor unionism and had erected a well-organized employee representation plan. Despite these obstacles, the Transport Workers made steady if slow progress under the leadership of Michael Quill who quickly assumed a leading role in the organizing effort.

As a result of the August 1935 meeting of the Communist International, the Communist party in the United States reverted to its "boring from within" strategy. Consequently the Transport Workers Union was ordered to affiliate with the American Federation of Labor* (AFL). After unsuccessfully approaching the Amalgamated Association of Street, Electric Railway and Motor Coach Employees,* the Transport Workers finally arranged a merger with the International Association of Machinists* (IAM) and became Lodge 1547. The association with the IAM proved short-lived, however. On May 7, 1937, the Transport Workers voted to affiliate with the Committee for Industrial Organization* (CIO), and the union was given an international charter as the Transport Workers Union of America with jurisdiction over "all workers employed in, on, or about any and all passenger and other transportation facilities and public utilities."

A few days later the union won exclusive bargaining rights for the employees of the IRT subway system. Thereafter, the TWUA, which increased its membership from 16,000 to more than 40,000 in a few months, quickly gained recognition as the bargaining agent for workers on all of New York City's transit systems. Moreover, with the availability of the National Labor Relations Act and the active assistance of the CIO, union organization was extended throughout the United States. Reflecting its new status, the first national convention of the TWUA convened in New York City on October 5, 1937.

Other than its organizing and bargaining activities, the most prominent features of the TWUA's early history were its association with the Communist party and its colorful and bellicose leader, Michael Quill. The Communist party's surprising strength among the predominantly Irish Catholic work force of the New York transit system was largely made possible by Quill, who had acquired a high standing in the Irish-American community. Quill's much publicized (to a considerable extent self-advertised) association with the Irish Republican Army and the Irish Rebellion of 1919-1923, gave him a degree of immunity from political attacks and had the effect of legitimizing the Communist influence in the TWUA.

Quill, however, assumed a proprietary interest in the TWUA and broke with his former Communist associates when forced to chose between union and party loyalty. The close ties between the party and the TWUA, while sometimes troublesome, had been possible during the 1930s and the United Front years of World War II. But in the postwar period, the emerging cold war and the growing anti-Communist hysteria created serious conflicts of interest between trade union activities and party policy. Moreover, the CIO's increased hostility to Communist elements in the labor movement and the controversy over the endorsement of Henry Wallace's Progressive party candidacy in 1948 forced Communists in the labor movement to decide between trade union policy and party loyalty. As a result Quill broke with the party and became as vocal in his criticism of Communist elements as he had once been in their defense. During the 1948 TWUA convention, Quill succeeded in driving most of the left wingers out of union office.

The TWUA membership stabilized near the 100,000 figure during the 1950s and did not turn upward again until the late 1960s and early 1970s. Despite a consistently militant rhetoric, especially by Quill, the TWUA participated in relatively few strikes during the years following World War II. As a result rank-and-file criticism of Quill's bargaining accomplishments grew increasingly severe, especially in New York City, which remained the citadel of TWUA strength. Finally, on January 1, 1966, after years of threats and accommodations, the TWUA struck the New York City Transit Authority, virtually stopping economic activity in the city for twelve days. Quill and other union officials were charged with contempt of court in connection with a court injunction issued in an effort to end the strike, but he suffered a heart attack shortly after his arrest and died soon after a settlement was reached. Quill's death marked the end of a turbulent era in the TWUA's history.

The TWUA, which maintains its national headquarters in New York City, holds quadrennial conventions. Principal officers include a president, vice-president, secretary-treasurer, and editor. The general executive board is composed of the above officers in addition to ten members elected during regular conventions. In 1973 the TWUA reported a membership of 150,000 located in 107 local unions.

For further information, see the *TWU Express* published monthly. See also L. H. Whittemore, *The Man Who Ran the Subways: The Story of Mike Quill* (1968), and Max M. Kampelman, *The Communist Party vs. the C.I.O.: A Study in Power Politics* (1957), which contains a chapter on the TWUA.

TRANSPORTATION UNION; UNITED (UTU). On New Years Day, 1969, four of the oldest unions in the American labor movement ceased to exist: the Brotherhood of Railroad Trainmen* (BRT); the Brotherhood of Locomotive Firemen and Enginemen* (BLFE); the Order of Railway Conductors and Brakemen* (ORC), and the Switchmen's Union of North America* (SUNA). However, the demise of these unions, which ranged from eighty-two to one hundred years of age, resulted in the birth of a new union, the United Transportation Union. The UTU was the largest transportation union affiliated with the American Federation of Labor-Congress of Industrial Organizations* and included all of the railroad operating unions except the Brotherhood of Locomotive Engineers,* which declined to participate in the merger.

Changes in transportation services greatly affecting labor organizations in the railroad industry inspired the merger of the four unions. Employment in the industry had been declining steadily since the mid-1950s because of increased automation, the expanded use of trucks, buses, and airplanes in the transportation of both freight and passengers, and a gradual reorganization and rationalization of the national railroad system. As a result of these changes, union membership gradually declined, and labor's bargaining position underwent a corresponding diminution. It was hoped that the merger would increase the economic power and the political influence of railroad labor and also end craft rivalries.

With a membership of 185,000 the BRT was the senior partner in the 220,000-member UTU, and Charles Luna, who had previously led the BRT, became president of the new union. Leaders of the other unions—Clyde F. Lane of the ORC, Neil P. Speirs of the SUNA, and H. E. Gilbert of the BLFE—became assistant presidents. At the time of the merger the ORC reported a membership of 13,700, and the SUNA and BLFE claimed 12,000 and 69,750, respectively.

In a further effort to expand the political influence of transportation workers, the UTU played a formative role in the creation of the Congress of Railway Unions, a trade union federation consisting of the UTU, the Brotherhood of Maintenance of Way Employes,* the Brotherhood of Railway and Airline Clerks,* the Hotel and Restaurant Employees Union,* and the Seafarers

International Union of North America.* Luna served as chairman of the new federation.

The UTU initially expended its energies primarily in the federal courts and in the U.S. Congress. The UTU successfully gained from the Supreme Court confirmation of the right of railroad workers to strike selectively. The Railroad Safety Act of 1970 and the creation of AMTRAK in an effort to rehabilitate railway passenger service were both considered significant legislative victories by UTU officials. The UTU also claimed a substantial collective bargaining achievement with the negotiation of the 1971 wages and rules agreement with the nation's railroads.

The various insurance and welfare plans of the separate brotherhoods were combined in 1971 under the name of the United Transportation Union Insurance Association, and two years later the association began a college scholarship program for UTU members and their children. The program eventually will provide 200 continuing scholarships of $500 each annually.

The UTU, which maintains its national headquarters in Cleveland, holds quadrennial conventions. Because of arrangements made in the unification agreement, the number of full-time officers will vary over time. Principal officers include a president, a secretary-treasurer, and a variable number of assistant presidents and vice-presidents. Authority is also exercised by an executive board, a board of directors, and a board of trustees. In 1973 the UTU reported a membership of 248,088 located in 1,632 local unions.

For further information, see the *UTU News* issued weekly. See also the sketches of the BRT, SUNA, BLFE, and ORC in this volume.

TYPOGRAPHICAL UNION; INTERNATIONAL (ITU). Workers in the printing industry were among the first laborers in the United States to organize trade unions. As early as 1776, printers struck in New York City, and before the end of the century a number of local unions had been organized in the industry. With the acceleration of trade union activity during the 1820s and early 1830s, a number of local printing unions met in Washington, D.C., in November 1836 and made the first successful effort to form a national union, the National Typographical Society (NTS).

The NTS, which represented unions in at least eight cities, collapsed during the depression following the panic of 1837, but many of the local unions survived. Organizational activities among printers resumed with the end of the depression, and by midcentury interest in the organization of a national union revived. In 1850 a number of local societies met in convention in New York City to discuss standards of craftsmanship, union discipline, and apprenticeship regulations. That conference led to a second meeting a year later in Baltimore, where the delegates resolved to form a national union. Such a union, the National Typographical Union, was formally organized on May 3, 1852, at a convention held in Cincinnati. Local unions from fourteen cities constituted the NTU's initial membership. After the affiliation of Canadian locals, the union was renamed the International Typographical Union in 1869.

Although compositors dominated the membership and affairs of the union, the ITU organized an amalgam of different crafts in the printing trade, including printing pressmen, stereotypers and electrotypers, bookbinders, photoengravers, and journalists (who often worked as typesetters as well as reporters). Beginning during the second quarter of the nineteenth century women were employed in the industry, and in 1870 a local union of women typographers was organized in New York City. Although the female local was chartered by the ITU, the organization of separate female unions soon proved impractical, and women were integrated into regular unions.

During its early years, the ITU could best be described as a loose confederation of largely autonomous local units. Organizers of the new union were primarily interested in establishing apprenticeship standards and in preventing the importation of strike breakers from surrounding areas when a local was on strike. The first significant structural change in the union occurred in 1884 when a more centralized administration was introduced and a full-time national organizer was first placed on the union payroll. The centralizing process was carried further four years later when the president and secretary-treasurer were made full-time, salaried national officers, and an international defense fund was established to assist striking locals. The appointment of a corps of full-time representatives (organizers) during the following years and the ability of international officers to withhold funds from striking locals gave the national union increased authority over local unions, although collective bargaining was still carried on at the local level.

The ITU leadership exhibited an early interest in national labor unity and in 1881 became actively and influentially involved in the formation of the Federation of Organized Trades and Labor Unions of the United States and Canada* and its successor, the American Federation of Labor* (AFL). The growing craft consciousness reflected by the organization of the AFL combined with a feeling among many workers in the printing industry that the dominant compositors controlling the ITU were neglecting the interests of other printing crafts. A fragmentation of trade unionism in the printing industry resulted. In 1889 a group of pressmen locals left the ITU and organized their own national union, and a few years later stereotypers and electrotypers, bookbinders, photoengravers, and eventually journalists did the same. Thus by 1910 the ITU had evolved into a craft union of typesetters.

The ITU adopted its first union label in 1886, and through the years it has placed great emphasis on the utilization of the label. In 1911 the ITU joined with other crafts in the printing industry to form the International Allied Printing Trades Association and adopted its label. During these years, the ITU also developed a number of beneficial plans, including an old age pension and mortuary benefit, and in 1892, the Union Printers' Home was established in Colorado Springs, Colorado. The home was originally designed for aged and indigent members but later was expanded to include a hospital and tuberculosis sanitarium.

The ITU, like most other unions in the American labor movement, did not escape jurisdictional conflicts and rival unionism. The organization in 1873 of the German-American Typographia, a union of printers employed by German-language newspapers, represented one such potential rival. The new ethnically oriented union quickly organized locals in most major cities in the United States having a significant German population; but an amicable relationship soon developed between the two printing unions, and in 1894 the German-American Typographia amalgamated with the ITU under an agreement that permitted it to retain much of its autonomy. A jurisdictional dispute with the International Association of Machinists* (IAM) proved much more difficult to resolve. Shortly after the introduction of typesetting machinery, the IAM claimed jurisdiction over the workers employed as operators. After extended and often bitter conflict, the ITU effectively established its control over these workers.

Beginning in the late years of the nineteenth century, through periods of war, depression, open-shop campaigns, rival unionism, welfare capitalism, and favorable governmental policies, unusual stability characterized the ITU membership pattern. Typically, ITU membership increased at a rate of 3 to 5 percent a year—exhibiting neither the large periodic membership advances nor the losses that characterized so many international unions in the American labor movement.

Although it never affiliated with the Congress of Industrial Organizations* (CIO), ITU president Charles Howard was one of the founders of the CIO and served as its first secretary. Moreover, in a membership referendum, ITU members voted against paying a special AFL assessment to finance an organizing campaign in opposition to the CIO. As a result the AFL suspended the old typographical union in 1939 and did not reinstate it until 1944.

More than almost any other American union, the ITU opposed and resisted the Taft-Hartley Act of 1947. To ITU leaders who had long placed great emphasis on the closed shop and strict enforcement of its seniority system, the Taft-Hartley Act seemed a vital threat to the stability and security of the union. As a consequence, ITU president Woodruff Randolph devoted much of the union's resources to combating the undesirable features of the act.

The ITU is widely considered one of the most democratically governed international unions in the United States. One of the more unique developments to influence ITU governance resulted from the evolution of a two-party system similar in character and function to the national Democratic and Republican parties. Both ITU parties (Progressives and Independents) develop policy positions on pertinent issues and present slates of candidates at biennial ITU conventions.

The ITU, which maintains its national headquarters in Colorado Springs, holds annual conventions. Principal officers include a president, three vice-presidents, and a secretary-treasurer. The above officers constitute the international executive council. In 1973 the ITU reported a membership of 115,273 located in 700 local unions.

For further information, see the *Typographical Journal* (monthly) *Typographical Bulletin* (monthly), and *ITU Review* (weekly), all published by the ITU. See also Seymour M. Lipset, Martin Trow, and James Coleman, *Union Democracy: The Internal Politics of the International Typographical Union* (1956), a landmark study of intra-union politics; George A. Stevens, *New York Typographical Union No. 6: A Study of a Modern Trade Union and Its Predecessors* (1913); and Jacob Loft, *The Printing Trades* (1944).

UPHOLSTERERS' INTERNATIONAL UNION OF NORTH AMERICA (UIU). The organization of upholstery workers in the furniture industry began during the first half of the nineteenth century. The first known strike of such workers occurred in New York City where an upholstery workers' union conducted a successful general strike in 1880. While unionism expanded during the post-Civil War years, an attempt to form a national union was not made until 1882. During February of that year thirteen delegates representing eleven local unions met in Philadelphia and organized a national union in hopes of increasing wages, improving working conditions, and providing greater job security. But the effort proved abortive; within a few years the national union effectively ceased to exist.

A decade after this first attempt to form a national union of upholstery workers, a second organizing convention met in Chicago on August 8, 1892. Delegates from eight local unions attended the meeting and founded the Upholsterers' International Union of America. On September 20, 1900, the new national union received a charter from the American Federation of Labor* (AFL). The present title was adopted in 1922, but beginning in 1929 and for several years thereafter, the UIU operated under the title Upholsterers, Carpet and Linoleum Mechanics' International Union of North America. The AFL, however, never recognized the new name or the jurisdictional expansion implicit in it.

The upholsterers organized in a hostile environment characterized by lockouts, blacklists, and anti-labor injunctions. Moreover, the new national union emerged shortly before the devastating depression of the 1890s, which resulted in increased unemployment, thus compromising the economic leverage of organized labor. Despite employer hostility and costly defeats as well as timely victories on the collective bargaining front, by 1904 the UIU attained a membership in excess of 3,000. Membership remained stable at that figure for several years before turning upward again during World War I. Thereafter, the UIU continued to grow until the years of severe unemployment accompanying the Great Depression of the 1930s.

The decade of the 1930s brought other challenges. Divisions in the national labor movement reflected by the formation of the Congress of Industrial Organizations* (CIO) as a rival to the AFL had its counterpart among furniture workers. Resulting from differences over organizing tactics and political ideology, a group of dissident locals seceded from the UIU and affiliated with the CIO as the United Furniture Workers of America* (UFWA).

Despite the schism in its ranks, the UIU experienced considerable organizing success during the second half of the decade of the 1930s. Moreover, as the UFWA became increasingly distracted by ideological conflicts during the late 1940s, the UIU outstripped its CIO rival in organizing success and collective bargaining achievements.

During the period following World War II, the UIU became more politically conscious. Fed by its rivalry with the UFWA, the UIU adopted a vigorous anti-Communist stance in ideological affairs. Meanwhile, union officials took a greater interest in liberal politics. The UIU was one of the first international unions to establish a formal political education department. It also initiated an extensive social-welfare pension program including the establishment of a retirement village and resort near Palm Beach, Florida.

The UIU, which maintains its national headquarters in Philadelphia, holds quadrennial conventions. Principal officers include a president, six vice-presidents, a treasurer, fifteen members representing nine geographical districts, and nine members at large representing nine branches of the industry. In 1973 the UIU reported a membership of 59,000 located in 176 local unions.

For further information, see the *UIU Journal* published quarterly by the UIU. See also *Bulletins No. 420, 506*, and *618*, Bureau of Labor Statistics, U.S. Department of Labor (1926, 1929, 1936), and *The American Federationist* (February 1952; March 1955).

UTILITY WORKERS UNION OF AMERICA (UWUA). Concluding that the utilities industry was so diverse and widely scattered that it could best be organized and administered by a separate entity, in February 1938 the Congress of Industrial Organizations* (CIO) established the Utility Workers Organizing Committee (UWOC). The United Electrical, Radio, and Machine Workers of America,* the CIO union previously organizing in the industry, was ordered to transfer all of its utility locals to the UWOC. The principal American Federation of Labor* (AFL) competitor in organizing utility workers was the International Brotherhood of Electrical Workers.*

In their previous efforts to avoid union organization, utility companies employed most of the traditional anti-union devices, including the development of elaborate employee representation plans. One of these company unions at

Consolidated Edison Company in New York City, the Brotherhood of Consolidated Edison Employees, after the enactment of the National Labor Relations Act, which prohibited company-dominated unions, gradually converted itself into a strong, militant trade union.

In 1945 the UWOC and the Brotherhood of Consolidated Edison Employees amalgamated, and later that year when converting the UWOC into a national union, the CIO issued a charter to the Utility Workers Union of America. The new national union was given an organizing jurisdiction including all workers employed "in any of the public utilities, embracing gas, electric, water, telephone and rail transportation industries." At the time of its organization, the UWUA had a membership of 20,000, much of it concentrated in the New York City area.

Although encountering bitter resistance from AFL rivals, the UWUA gradually expanded its organizational reach throughout the nation during the first decade of its existence. When the AFL and CIO merged in 1955, UWUA membership reached nearly 75,000, where it remained for several years before beginning a slow decline due primarily to technological changes that reduced employment in the industry.

The UWUA's collective bargaining advances were not made without occasional strikes. Shortly after its organization, the UWUA established the National Union Strike Fund, which provided relief for those workers leaving work to enforce collective bargaining demands. Although the UWUA established a human relations committee to facilitate compliance with Title VII of the Civil Rights Act of 1964, it has been frequently charged as a codefendant with various utility companies in cases of alleged discrimination with regard to minority employment and advancement.

Politically the UWUA usually supported the Democratic party and actively participated in the activities of the CIO political action committee and its AFL-CIO* successor, the committee on political education. In 1972, however, the UWUA executive board, "seriously concerned with the groups that had gained control of the Democratic party," endorsed the reelection of President Richard M. Nixon.

The UWUA, which holds biennial conventions, maintains its headquarters in New York City. Principal officers include a president, executive vice-president, vice-president, and secretary-treasurer. The executive board is composed of five regional representatives and three members elected at large. In 1973 the UWUA had a membership of 60,000 located in 225 local unions.

For further information, see the *Light* published monthly by the UTWU. Other than Florence Peterson's brief discussion of the structure of the UWOC in her *Handbook of Labor Unions* (1944), little published material exists on the UWUA.

WALL PAPER CRAFTSMEN AND WORKERS OF NORTH AMERICA: UNITED (UWPC&WNA). The dynamic activities of the Knights of Labor*

(KofL) during the first half of the decade of the 1880s encouraged workers in various trades throughout the nation to join KofL local assemblies or organize their own locals. One such group of workers in the wallpaper trade in New York City organized the first union in the trade, the Wall Paper Machine Printers' Union, on July 23, 1883. Thereafter, local unions of print cutters appeared in various localities throughout the country and organized a national union, the National Print Cutters Association of America, which was chartered by the American Federation of Labor* (AFL) on September 25, 1902. Meanwhile, machine printers and color mixers began organizing their own local unions, and in 1902 they also organized a national union, the National Association of Machine Printers and Color Mixers, which received an AFL charter on August 13, 1902.

The two national unions grew very slowly during the first two decades of the twentieth century; by 1920 they had fewer than 1,000 members between them. The continued existence of the two small national unions was severely threatened in 1923 when employers initiated an industry-wide lockout of union members. In an effort to survive this critical challenge, the two small unions merged on June 29, 1923, forming the United Wall Paper Crafts of North America (UWPCNA). Although the newly merged union survived the lockout, the UWPCNA remained a small union of 500 to 600 members until the late 1930s when the union's trade jurisdiction was expanded to include unskilled workers in the industry. At the same time the union title was changed to United Wall Paper Craftsmen and Workers of North America, reflecting the expanded trade jurisdiction. Membership immediately jumped to over 3,000 where it remained steadily until reduced employment in the trade precipitated a slow decline during the 1950s. On April 29, 1958, the UWPC&WNA merged with the International Brotherhood of Pulp, Sulphite and Paper Mill Workers of the United States and Canada* (IBPSPW).

The UWPC&WNA, which maintained its national headquarters in York, Pennsylvania, held triennial conventions. Full-time officers consisted of a general secretary-treasurer and a general business agent-organizer. The general executive committee was composed of the above officials in addition to the general president, seven vice-presidents, and four trustees. At the time of the merger with the IBPSPW, the UWPC&WNA paid per-capita taxes to the AFL-CIO* on 1,600 members.

For further information, see *Bulletin No. 618*, Bureau of Labor Statistics, U.S. Department of Labor (1936), and Florence Peterson, *Handbook of Labor Unions* (1944). Other than the basic information contained in the above volumes, little published information exists on the UWPC&WNA. The union never published an official journal.

WESTERN FEDERATION OF MINERS. *See* International Union of Mine, Mill and Smelter Workers.

WIRE WEAVERS PROTECTIVE ASSOCIATION; AMERICAN (AWWPA). Fourdrinier wire weavers, a small group of highly skilled craftsmen who operated machines producing paper in continuous rolls, began organizing during the first half of the nineteenth century. A short-lived national union of such craftsmen was organized shortly after the Civil War but disintegrated during the depression of the 1870s. A second national union appeared in 1882 under the title American Wire Weavers' Protective and Benevolent Association. The association soon discontinued benevolent programs, however, and "Benevolent" disappeared from the union title. On September 11, 1900, the AWWPA affiliated with the American Federation of Labor* (AFL) and was given exclusive trade jurisdiction over fourdrinier wire weavers.

Organizers of the new national union sought primarily to control entry into the trade and to establish standard price lists for the entire industry. AWWPA membership requirements were among the most exclusionist and discriminatory ever adopted by an American trade union. Prospective members had to be "Christian, white, male of the full age of 21, and have served an apprenticeship of four years on a hand or power loom at the fourdrinier wire-weaving trade in a union shop." A foreigner applying for admission had to show proof of application for citizenship and pay a thousand-dollar initiation fee.

Organizers of the AWWPA obviously never intended to build a union with a large membership, and although the trade was virtually completely organized, its membership never exceeded 500 wire weavers. The national executive board negotiated agreements covering the entire industry with paper manufacturers. After over seventy years as an independent national union, on February 16, 1959, the AWWPA merged with the United Papermakers and Paperworkers* (UPP).

The AWWPA, which maintained its national headquarters in Belleville, New Jersey, did not hold national conventions. Although there were no full-time officers, the national executive board elected a president, vice-president, and secretary-treasurer. The executive board was composed of the above officers and representatives from each union division. Shortly before emerging with the UPP, the AWWPA paid per-capita taxes to the AFL-CIO* on approximately 400 members.

For further information, see *Bulletin No. 618*, Bureau of Labor Statistics, U.S. Department of Labor (1936), and Florence Peterson, *Handbook of Labor Unions* (1944). The AWWPA did not issue an official organ.

WOMEN'S TRADE UNION LEAGUE (WTUL). In November 1903 settlement workers William English Walling and Mary Kenny O'Sullivan helped organize the Women's Trade Union League in Boston, Massachusetts. At organizational meetings held in mid-November, national officers and an executive board were chosen, and a constitution was written. Mary Morton

Kehew became the first president, and settlement workers Mary McDowell and Lillian Wald were elected to the executive board. Although the Women's National Union Label League and women's auxiliaries of men's unions were active in 1903, the WTUL became the first national body dedicated to organizing women workers. Because the league derived from a progressive social settlement tradition, it also aimed to promote educational and social activities designed to upgrade the working woman's environment. In its early years, particularly under the presidency of Margaret Dreier Robins (1907-1922), the WTUL was dominated by reformers, not trade unionists. Although trade unionism became dominant in the mid-1920s, the social settlement emphasis persisted throughout the league's existence.

Branches of the WTUL were established in New York, Chicago, and Boston in 1904. The local leagues were closely associated with the settlement movement and became centers for both organizing and "uplifting" women workers by promoting weekly lectures, classes, and recreation. The Chicago League, for example, worked with immigrant women and helped lay the foundations for the Immigrants' Protective League. Additionally, the local leagues served as prime instruments for securing labor legislation at the state level.

The first biennial convention of the National League held in Norfolk, Virginia, in 1907 established the basic organizational framework for the WTUL. There were four classes of membership: local, state, members at large, and affiliated organizations. Local leagues had to consist of at least seven members, and a majority of their executive boards had to be trade unionists in good standing. State leagues were to consist of at least seven local leagues. The national WTUL's executive board contained three national officers and three representatives from each state and local league, two of whom had to be trade unionists. In 1911, however, the league altered its organization by separating the offices of secretary and treasurer and paring the executive board to six officers and six members elected at large at national conventions. Women union members could become WTUL members upon presenting a current union card; conversely, a woman did not have to be a union member to become a WTUL member.

The league first attracted national attention during the 1909-1910 New York City garment strikes. League members picketed with striking garment workers and helped set up strike headquarters and distribute necessary provisions to strikers' families. More importantly, the league set a precedent by securing financial aid from wealthy New York City society women. The league also participated in the 1910 Chicago garment strike and incurred the wrath of American Federation of Labor* (AFL) president Samuel Gompers by refusing to support the United Garment Workers'* settlement.

Relations with organized labor usually were tenuous, so that the WTUL never could rely on either the AFL or individual unions for support. Despite protestations from its leadership, the AFL frequently was lukewarm toward the league. For example, at the 1904 WTUL conference held in New York City, Gompers insisted that he favored the organization of women, but he refused to let WTUL representatives become delegates to AFL conventions. Later in 1922, the AFL denied a WTUL request to charter all-female locals. Although the WTUL preferred integration within the men's locals, it concluded that perhaps female locals would further the unionization of women.

The AFL did provide the WTUL with sporadic financial aid. After the 1912 Lawrence textile strike, the league determined to organize unskilled women, and the AFL executive council allotted it $150 monthly for organizational activities toward this end. The United Mine Workers,* International Boot and Shoe Workers,* and the United Brotherhood of Carpenters and Joiners* contributed fifty dollars per month for one year. The AFL payments stopped in 1915. Fear of the Industrial Workers of the World* (IWW), in part, had induced Gompers to help the league, and waning IWW influence allowed him to end the aid.

The WTUL's relation with city central bodies and state federations of labor varied from region to region. In some cities, such as New York, Boston, and Chicago, each local WTUL sent its delegates to city central bodies, while in other cities, such as St. Louis, the WTUL was not represented on the city central. During Margaret Dreier Robins's presidency, however, the league worked closely with John Fitzpatrick and the Chicago Federation of Labor.

From about 1915 through the 1920s, the national WTUL and the local leagues focused on securing labor legislation. The eight-hour day, elimination of night work for women, abolition of child labor, factory inspection laws, and minimum wage were some of the regulations the league sought. To effect legislation on the national level, the WTUL became a member of the Women's Joint Congressional Committee in the 1920s.

In 1926 the league embarked on a campaign to organize women workers in the South. Focusing on the unionization of textile workers in the Carolinas, Virginia, and Tennessee, the league worked closely with local YWCAs and Leagues of Women Voters in this undertaking. The United Textile Workers* supported the league's efforts, but the AFL ignored the campaign. In the 1930s the WTUL continued its activities among southern textile workers and also participated in strikes in Danville, Virginia (1930), and Huntsville, Alabama (1934). The league favored industrial unionism and, after the formation of the Congress of Industrial Organizations,* decided to aid any union that asked for its assistance despite the AFL's disapproval.

Beginning in the late 1920s the league encountered increased financial difficulties, and from 1929 until 1935 lack of money prevented it from holding a national convention. Financial problems became especially acute after World War II. As labor unions became more established, outside sources refused to contribute monetarily to the league, believing that organized labor should finance the league's activities. Additionally, the passage of much labor legislation made it appear that the WTUL was no longer needed. The league's leaders apparently agreed as national president Rose Schneiderman resigned in 1947. Although a skeletal staff remained in Washington, D.C., until 1950, for all intents and purposes the league died in 1947. The New York league, however, remained active until 1955.

The WTUL, which maintained its national headquarters in Washington, D.C., normally held annual conventions. Principal officers included a president, vice-president, secretary, and treasurer. The executive board was composed of six officers and six members elected at national conventions. Accurate membership figures were not located.

For further information, see the Women's Department of the *Union Labor Advocate* over which the national WTUL assumed responsibility from the Chicago league in 1908. From 1911 to 1922 the WTUL published *Life and Labor*, which was known from 1922 to 1949 as *Life and Labor Bulletin*. For further information, see Gladys Boone, *The Women's Trade Union Leagues in Great Britain and the United States of America* (1942); Alice Henry, *The Trade Union Women* (1915); Allen Davis, "The WTUL: Origins and Organization," *Labor History* (Winter 1964); and William Chafe, *The American Women: Her Changing Social, Economic and Political Roles, 1920-1970* (1972).

Marie Tedesco

WOOD CARVERS' ASSOCIATION OF NORTH AMERICA; INTERNATIONAL (IWCANA). Organized in Philadelphia in 1883, the International Wood Carvers' Association received an American Federation of Labor* (AFL) charter on April 12, 1898. The IWCANA was given exclusive jurisdiction over "hand machine and spindle wood carvers." Never destined to be a large organization, the IWCANA reached its peak in 1903 when slightly over 2,000 wood carvers held membership cards. In the years that followed, the IWCANA began a slow decline. The small national union had fewer than 1,000 members by 1920, the time during which most trade unions increased enrollment because of the labor shortage and favorable governmental policies during World War I.

Due to technological changes and the tendency of wood carvers to join larger, more powerful unions, such as the United Brotherhood of Carpenters and Joiners,* IWCANA membership continued to decline during the following thirty years. By 1936 only 400 wood carvers belonged to the IWCANA, and at the end of World War II, the figure dropped to 300. Finally, on August 16, 1943, the AFL dropped the small union from its rolls for nonpayment of per-capita taxes; shortly thereafter it disbanded.

The IWCANA, which held conventions when requested through membership referendums, maintained its headquarters in Somerville, Massachusetts. The IWCANA had no full-time officers and elected a central committee and board of supervisors by referendum. Shortly before disbanding, the IWCANA had a membership of 300 located in twelve local unions.

For further information, see the *Wood Carver* published quarterly by the IWCANA, and Florence Peterson, *Handbook of Labor Unions* (1944).

WOOD WORKERS' INTERNATIONAL UNION OF AMERICA; AMALGAMATED (AWWIU). Twelve delegates representing sixteen local organizations met in Cincinnati on July 7, 1873, and organized *Der Gewerkschafts Union der Moebel-Arbeiter Nord Amerika*. The new union, which sought to organize cabinetmakers, turners, wood carvers, upholsterers, gilders, and varnishers, barely survived the panic of 1873 and the depression of the 1870s. In the following decade, during which the union was reorganized and renamed the International Furniture Workers' Union of America (IFWUA), it grew rapidly, reaching a peak membership of approximately 10,000 in 1886. A year later it affiliated with the newly organized American Federation of Labor* (AFL).

Leaders of the IFWUA consistently supported the development of a strong centralized union and the amalgamation into one national union of workers in the different woodworking trades. The lower skill level required in machine-produced furniture made these workers especially susceptible to competition from unskilled workers. Amalgamation with the United Brotherhood of Carpenters and Joiners* (UBC) seemed the most natural alliance, but merger discussions collapsed when the UBC refused to consider the admission of IFWUA upholsterers, varnishers, and gilders locals. The UBC maintained that only woodworking locals should be included in the amalgamation.

Refusing to abandon its non-woodworking locals, IFWUA officials opened negotiations with leaders of a newer international union, the Machine Wood Workers' International Union (MWWIU). The use of power machinery and factory production in the woodworking industry produced a growing number of machine workers whose job security was threatened by increasingly specialized divisions of labor. In an effort to protect themselves, these machine operators began to organize on a local basis. Six of these unions responded to a call for a national convention to meet in St. Louis on August 5, 1890. Delegates created the MWWIU, which received an AFL charter on December 22, 1890.

Because of overlapping jurisdictions, the new union found itself almost immediately involved in conflicts with the IFWUA and the UBC. These conflicts plus the disruption caused by the depression of the 1890s enhanced the attractiveness of a merger with the IFWUA. Consequently, after a series of successful preliminary negotiations, a meeting was held in St. Louis on November 11, 1895, to consummate the merger and announce the formation of the Amalgamated Wood Workers International Union of America.

The creation of the AWWIU reduced to two the number of major unions in the woodworking trade: the UBC, which organized outside workers, and the

Amalgamated, which controlled inside factory workers. The AWWIU grew rapidly during the years of the late neneteenth and early twentieth centuries, reaching a membership of 31,230 by 1904, but it declined rapidly thereafter.

The Amalgamated's decline was largely the product of an aggressive raiding policy the UBC adopted in 1898. As technological change altered the nature and character of carpentry, the UBC began to covet the factory workers it had once ignored. Adopting the slogans, "Once carpenter's work, always carpenter's work," and "One craft, one organization," UBC officials recognized that control over the production of building materials would give them considerable leverage in dealing with contractors. The UBC not only refused to recognize the AWWIU's jurisdiction but determined to destroy the smaller union. Despite favorable decisions by impartial arbitrators and the AFL, the Amalgamated found little relief from the UBC's bullying tactics. After a decade of conflict, the AFL leadership caved in to the UBC and reversed its previous position by ordering the AWWIU to amalgamate with the UBC. Confronted with the continued hostility of the powerful UBC along with the AFL's inability or unwillingness to defend or honor the jurisdiction it had granted the Amalgamated, AWWIU officials recognized the inevitable and on May 11, 1912, merged with the UBC.

The AWWIU, which maintained its headquarters in Chicago, held triennial conventions. Principal officers included a general president, secretary, and treasurer. The AWWIU general council consisted of the above officers and four additional members elected simultaneously with the general officers. At its peak the AWWIU had over 30,000 members located in approximately 240 local unions.

For further information, see the *International Wood Workers*, issued monthly from 1895 to 1908. See also Frederick S. Deibler, *The Amalgamated Wood Workers' International Union of America* (1912), and Robert A. Christie, *Empire in Wood* (1956).

WOODWORKERS OF AMERICA; INTERNATIONAL (IWA). On July 19, 1937, 500 members of the Federation of Woodworkers, representing 70,000 workers in sawmills, logging camps, and furniture and plywood plants in the Pacific Northwest and British Columbia, met in Tacoma, Washington, and founded the International Woodworkers of America.

Unionization had first begun fifty years earlier when the American Federation of Labor* (AFL) issued federal charters to locals of the Shingle Weavers' Union.* The Shingle Weavers, organizing on a craft basis, achieved little success and folded in 1923. The militant and colorful Industrial Workers of the World* conducted intensive organizing campaigns among woodworkers in the West and South after 1906 but failed to survive the anti-radical hysteria accompanying World War I.

The AFL returned to the Pacific Northwest in 1933 by granting federal union charters to some 130 locals of the Sawmill and Timber Workers' Union (STWU). In 1935, during a widespread strike in the lumber industry, the highly centralized United Brotherhood of Carpenters and Joiners* (UBC) demanded and secured from the AFL jurisdiction over all workers in the woodworking industry. From the beginning the UBC's heavy-handed methods created rumblings of discontent among the independently minded SWTU members. By September 1936 it became clear that woodworkers would be only inferior members of the Carpenters Union, and representatives from the ten-district council of the STWU met in Portland, Oregon, and created the Federation of Woodworkers, which immediately became the largest union on the West Coast. The federation maintained affiliation with the UBC. Less than a year later, however, the federation changed its name to the International Woodworkers of America and affiliated with the Congress of Industrial Organizations* (CIO).

The IWA was involved in a bitter dispute between the AFL and the CIO. From its beginning the IWA engaged in violent jurisdictional battles with the UBC, one of the oldest and staunchest of the AFL craft unions. The Portland area became the major battleground between the two unions. The UBC boycotted all IWA products and established picket lines around mills under contract with the IWA. This fight, at first a violent one involving gangs armed with clubs and guns, eventually came to the attention of the National Labor Relations Board (NLRB). NLRB elections held in 1938-1939 succeeded in establishing an uneasy balance in the area, with the IWA and UBC having a similar number of locals, but the IWA enjoyed a membership twice that of the Carpenters.

While fighting to survive as a national union, members of the IWA also had to conduct a serious intra-union fight to remove Communists from top leadership positions. Harold Pritchett, formerly president of both the British Columbia District Council of the STWU and the Federation of Woodworkers, was also the first president of the IWA. Pritchett and his faction followed every twist and turn of the Communist party official line. Don Helmick, a leader in the Columbia River district, had opposed the Communist leadership as early as the December 1937 convention, when he accused Pritchett and Vice-President O. M. Orton of playing party politics at the expense of an effective and democratic union. The anti-Communist forces received a boost from the Canadian government when Pritchett was refused permission to enter the United States in December 1940. Unable to defend himself at the upcoming convention in Everett, Washington, Pritchett resigned and named Orton to replace him. The Communists then hurt their cause in 1941 when they tried to oust the effective and popular, but non-Communist, Adolph Germer from his post as organizing director. Delegates to the 1941 convention in Everett voted to exclude Communists, nazis, and fascists from membership and elevated Second Vice-President Worth Lowery, a staunch anti-Communist, to the presidency. For the first time the rank and file controlled the union.

Currently about 75 percent of the IWA's membership is found in the Northwest and in British Columbia, with the remaining divided about evenly between eastern Canada, the Great Lakes states, and the South. Although some locals of the IWA appeared in the Midwest and South as early as 1938, organization on a large scale did not come to these areas and eastern Canada until after World War II. Working with the CIO's "Southern Drive," the IWA won fifty-five NLRB elections in the South in 1946. In eastern Canada, the nucleus of the present Regional Council No. 2 was created in 1947 when the struggling National Union of Furniture Workers and Allied Crafts merged with the IWA.

For over thirty-five years the IWA has fought for higher wages, safer working conditions, elimination of wage differentials between regions, grievance procedures, and shorter hours for persons working in this frontier industry. It is now faced with a rapidly changing job environment—changes with important consequences in terms of the welfare of all woodworkers. Structural changes in the lumber industry to accomplish the integration of radical technological developments have displaced thousands of workers. Total employment in the industry is steadily declining. There are also fewer employers, and more and more of these are multinational corporations with the capacity to bypass American and Canadian woodworkers by shipping logs to Japan, which are returned as plywood. Agreements reached by collective bargaining are placing increasing emphasis on welfare and job security aspects such as pensions, life insurance, health care, long-term disability income supplementation, and reasonable guidelines governing technological change. The IWA is also working for such long-range solutions as the guaranteed annual wage, the thirty-five-hour week, and increased management-government responsibility for retraining workers displaced by automation.

The IWA, which maintains its national headquarters in Portland, holds biennial conventions. Principal officers include a president, two vice-presidents, and a secretary-treasurer. These officials, in addition to five regional directors, constitute the executive board. In 1973 the IWA reported a membership of 105,790 located in 229 local unions.

For further information, see the *International Woodworker* published semimonthly by the IWA. See also Vernon Jensen's classic *Lumber and Labor* (1945), and Walter Galenson, *The CIO Challenge to the AFL: A History of the American Labor Movement, 1935-1941* (1960).

Robert C. Dinwiddie

WORKINGMEN'S BENEVOLENT ASSOCIATION (WBA). Although experimented with previously, the widespread commercial use of anthracite coal as a domestic fuel and the gradual substitution of anthracite for charcoal occurred during the nineteenth century. Most of the nation's anthracite coalfields are located within a 170-square mile area encompassing Lackawanna, Luzerne, Carbon, Schuylkill, and Northumberland counties in western Pennsylvania. Poor working conditions, irregular employment, and low wages, which characterized employment in the anthracite fields, soon led to union organization. Strikes occurred in Minersville as early as 1842 and again in 1844. Four years later, John Bates, an English Chartist, organized a union in Schuylkill County, which acquired a membership of 5,000 miners before collapsing a year later.

Local union organization and sporadic strikes continued throughout the 1850s but inflation accompanying the Civil War spurred labor organization on a large scale. As a result of the labor shortage, the new unions organized during the war flourished, and a few were able to gain union recognition and written contracts. Trade union initiatives were stalled by 1865, and with the demobilization of the army, the unions lost a series of strikes, resulting in the reduction of wages to their lowest level in over a decade.

Recognizing the need to revamp the structure of union organization to prevent further wage reductions and to counter the development of coal operator associations, sixteen miners under the leadership of John Siney met at St. Clair in Schuylkill County and organized the Workingmen's Benevolent Association, which received a charter from the Court of Common Pleas of Schuylkill County on April 6, 1868. Siney was elected its first president.

The WBA faced its first major challenge on July 1, 1868, when a Pennsylvania eight-hour law for miners became effective. In instituting the shorter hours, employers insisted upon a corresponding reduction in wages unless miners waived the eight-hour day. The result was a strike in most of the anthracite fields lasting until August when a compromise agreement was reached. Although the compromise fell well short of the strikers' original demands, it did include a 10 percent wage increase and a return to the ten-hour day, and the WBA grew rapidly as a result of the settlement. In March 1869 the General Council of the Workingmen's Association of the Anthracite Coal Fields of Pennsylvania was created to establish WBA policies and coordinate strikes. The General Council, however, proved a weak instrument dependent upon voluntary compliance by largely autonomous county unions.

Assuming it was the best way to raise wages, one of the WBA's basic objectives was to increase and stabilize coal prices. Coal operators willingly cooperated with the union to control production, but they resisted demands for a closed shop and a local committee system for handling grievances. Between 1869 and 1874 a number of strikes occurred in the anthracite fields, which had the dual purpose of preventing wage cuts and depleting coal reserves to keep prices from falling. Major strikes in 1869 and 1870 were settled by arbitration and the agreement upon a sliding scale pegging wages to the price of coal.

Fearing the WBA was becoming too powerful and was attempting to compromise the owner's exclusive control and management of the mines, coal operators combined into an Anthracite Board of Trade, ended their relationship with the WBA in 1874, and launched a campaign to destroy the union. When contracts expired in late 1874, the operators announced a 10 percent reduction in wages and refused to negotiate or consider arbitration. The famous "long strike" of 1875 resulted. Before the end of the strike, which lasted over six months, the WBA had been crushed.

The failure of the WBA resulted from its inability to resolve several problems peculiar to the anthracite district. Ethnocentrism and regionalism constantly divided miners in the district, and these jealousies contributed to the WBA's failure to effectively establish its authority over constituent unions. Conversely, under the resourceful leadership of Franklin B. Gown of the Reading Railroad, the coal operators resolved their differences and confronted the miners with a united front. Conflicts between wage and contract miners further divided the miners, and the depression following the panic of 1873 greatly weakened the WBA's bargaining position. Finally, the WBA's emphasis on overproduction ignored the basic problem of overcapitalization. Although strikes to reduce production resulted in higher wages, they compounded the problem of irregular employment that had long afflicted the miners.

In their efforts to crush the WBA, coal operators cooperated closely with railroads in the district (many of them also owned anthracite mines) and created a powerful coal and iron police, which operated as a private army in the district. The activities of the coal and iron police initiated the violence in the district needed by employers to convince Pennsylvania authorities to summon the state militia. Coal operators effectively countered WBA appeals to the state legislature and prevented any of the smaller independent operators from negotiating with the union by raising railroad rates to such a point that coal could not be profitably mined. At the same time, coal reserves were pooled, permitting contracts to be filled and eliminating any potential competitive advantage that might accrue to the operator who reopened his mines.

This cordinated assault on the WBA destroyed the union and ended trade organization in the anthracite fields for over a decade. With the collapse of the 1875 strike, a wave of violence erupted, giving rise to the Molly Maguire episode in American labor history. Although it ultimately failed, the WBA did make a contribution to union organization in coal mining. The WBA's failure reinforced the necessity for cooperation between the various ethnic groups in the coalfields, and it left a heritage of successful organization, albeit temporary, that would inspire later efforts to organize the anthracite fields.

The WBA, which maintained its headquarters in St. Clair, Pennsylvania, held annual conventions. Principal officers included a president, a vice-president, and a secretary-treasurer. The WBA general council was composed of the presidents of the various county units. Membership fluctuated wildly, and accurate figures are unavailable.

For further information, see two excellent studies by Harold W. Aurand,

From the Molly Maguires to the United Mine Workers (1971), and "The Workingmen's Benevolent Association," *Labor History* (Winter 1966). See also Edward Pinkowski, *John Siney, The Miner's Martyr* (1963), and Martin W. Schlegel, "The Workingmen's Benevolent Association: First Union of Anthracite Miners," *Pennsylvania History* (July 1943).

WRITERS GUILD OF AMERICA (WGA). Formation of the Writers Guild of America in New York City in 1954 marked the conclusion of over fifty years of organizing activities among authors, dramatists, playwrights, and screenwriters. The earliest such organization, the Authors League of America (ALA), began in New York City in December 1912. Although the ALA stimulated collective action by a variety of writers, the league itself was more a professional organization whose members retained their own copyrights and leased their material rather than acting as a collective bargaining unit.

In 1914 the Photoplay Authors' League, an independent West Coast association of screenwriters, organized in an effort to protect copyrights and expose pseudo-scenario-writing schools. Although the Photoplay Authors' League proved ineffective and soon disappeared, the conditions that inspired its organization remained. Consequently, stimulated by the Actors' Equity Association's* (AEA) success in acquiring a standard contract from Broadway theater managers after a short strike, writers organized the Dramatists Guild in 1920 as an independent branch of the ALA. During the same year, Hollywood screenwriters formed the Screen Writers Guild (SWG). This new organization, which affiliated with the ALA, sought improvements in copyright legislation, freedom from censorship, better recognition through screen credits, better compensation, and legal assistance for its members.

Although the SWG grew rapidly, reaching a membership of 250 within three years of its organization, it failed to accomplish its major goal—a standard contract for writers. For purposes of contract negotiations, the Association of Motion Picture Producers recognized the Academy of Motion Picture Arts and Sciences (AMPAS), a producer-organized and -controlled organization. In 1927 the SWG gained status when it and the AEA forced the cancellation of a threatened 10 percent salary reduction by the studios.

In a surprising reversal, however, SWG officers began actively cooperating with the AMPAS shortly after the salary dispute. As a result, the AMPAS soon supplanted the guild as the principal association of screenwriters. After lengthy negotiations, producers represented by the Association of Motion Picture Producers and writers represented by the AMPAS signed a code of practice for the industry on May 1, 1932. Although limited in its application, the code did eliminate several areas of conflict and provided standard procedures for resolving disputes in other areas. While an inadequate instrument for representing the writers' interests, the AMPAS did provide conciliation machinery through which a number of producer-writer disagreements were resolved.

Nevertheless, the producer-dominated AMPAS failed to take positive steps toward the negotiation of a standard contract. Moreover, as the AMPAS failed to effectively enforce the provisions of the Code of Practice, screenwriters became increasingly restive. The unhappiness exploded into a full-scale revolt in March 1933 when AMPAS acquiesced in a producer-inspired 50 percent reduction in salaries and in the creation of a producer-controlled central employment bureau. The writers immediately withdrew from the AMPAS and restructured the SWG. At this time the SWG also affiliated with the ALA as an autonomous branch.

The revived SWG, however, suffered from internal factionalism and discontent. During 1933 and 1934, it was frustrated by the National Recovery Administration's recognition of the AMPAS as the representative of screenwriters in the formation of an industrial code. Even more frustrating for guild officials was the failure to create an amalgamation of the ALA, the Dramatists' Guild, and the SWG that would have had the economic power to establish a guild shop for all screenwriters. An influential group of SWG scenarists sabotaged the amalgamation and organized the Screen Playwrights as a rival organization in May 1936. Once again, the SWG went into a period of decline, which lasted until the National Labor Relations Act survived its constitutional test in April 1937. Shortly thereafter, the SWG petitioned the National Labor Relations Board for a representational election. After successfully countering the arguments of producers and rival Screen Playwrights' officials who charged that writers were not eligible under NLRA provisions, an election was held on August 8, 1938. The SWG prevailed by a large margin. Producers still proved recalcitrant, however, and it was not until 1941 that a collective bargaining agreement was finally signed.

While employee-employer relations were rationalized by the collective bargaining arrangement, confusion still abounded among writers. The organization of the Radio Writers Guild and the Television Writers of America under the auspices of the ALA created a situation fraught with representational confusion and, not infrequently, conflicts of interest. As a result, eventually an amicable decision was reached to reorganize the writer associations: thus the creation of the Writers Guild of America, a labor union representing writers in motion pictures, television, and radio. Meanwhile, the ALA retained two branches—the Authors Guild and the Dramatists' Guild—both consisting of self-employed independent contractors.

Following the 1954 reorganization, the WGA quickly established itself as the bargaining agent for writers employed by major film producers and broadcasting networks and stations, including theatrical and television film, live and taped television, and documentary film and radio.

The WGA joined with comparable guilds in Great Britain, Canada, and

Australia in 1962 to create an international union of writers in English-speaking countries, and the following year the WGA, along with the British and Yugoslavian guilds, created the International Writers Guild, an international confederation of writer guilds.

The WGA consists of two independent branches—the Writers Guild of America, East, Inc., and the Writers Guild of America, West, Inc. The WGA West has seven officers and a sixteen-member board of directors, while the WGA East also has a sixteen-member board and five regular officers. Delegates from the two branches constitute a national council, which meets twice a year, once each in New York City and Los Angeles, the respective headquarters of the two branches. In 1973 the WGA East had a membership of 1,400 and the WGA West a membership of 2,900.

For further information consult the Authors' League *Bulletin*, 1913-1954; *Screen Writers Magazine*, 1933-1936; the WGA East's *Newsletter* published bimonthly; and the WGA West's *Newsletter* published monthly. Also consult Murray Rose, *Stars and Strikes: Unionization of Hollywood* (1941).

NATIONAL AFFILIATIONS

All national unions chartered by the American Federation of Labor (AFL), Congress of Industrial Organizations (CIO), and AFL-CIO are identified in this appendix. Founded as a national federation of autonomous unions in 1886, the AFL functioned continuously until merging with the CIO in 1955. The CIO, which operated as the ad hoc Committee for Industrial Organization until 1938, evolved into a national federation rivaling the AFL. The AFL-CIO was organized as a result of the merger of the two rival federations.

Charter dates for AFL and CIO unions are provided along with the disposition of those unions failing to survive until the merger. For AFL-CIO unions, previous affiliations, if applicable, are identified along with chartering dates. Significant union title changes are also provided.

AMERICAN FEDERATION OF LABOR

Actors and Artistes of America; Associated
    Originally chartered on January 4, 1896
Agents Association; American
    Originally chartered on August 23, 1895
    Charter revoked on December 14, 1900
Agricultural Workers Union; National
    Originally chartered on August 23, 1946
Air Line Dispatchers Association
    Originally chartered on February 1, 1947
Air Line Pilots Association
    Originally chartered on August 10, 1931
Aluminum Workers International Union
    Originally chartered on February 26, 1953
Asbestos Workers; International Association of Heat and Frost Insulators and
    Originally chartered on September 22, 1904

Automobile Workers; International Union of United
 Originally chartered on August 26, 1935
 Charter revoked on October 12, 1938
Automobile Workers of America; United
 Originally chartered on August 26, 1935
Axe and Edge Tool Makers National Union of America
 Originally chartered on August 27, 1890
 Disbanded in 1892
Bakery and Confectionery Workers' International Union of America
 Originally chartered on February 23, 1887
Barbers, Hairdressers and Cosmetologists' International Union of America; The Journeyman
 Originally chartered on April 10, 1888
Bill Posters, Billers and Distributors of the United States and Canada; International Alliance of
 Originally chartered on January 5, 1903
Blacksmiths, Drop Forgers and Helpers; International Brotherhood of
 Originally chartered on October 30, 1897
 Merged with the International Brotherhood of Boilermakers, Iron Shipbuilders, Blacksmiths, Forgers and Helpers on May 16, 1951
Blast Furnace Workers and Smelters of America; International Association of
 Originally chartered on October 25, 1901
 Disbanded on December 9, 1905
Boilermakers, Iron Shipbuilders, Blacksmiths, Forgers and Helpers; International Brotherhood of
 Originally chartered on August 1, 1887
Bookbinders; International Brotherhood of
 Originally chartered on March 24, 1898
Boot and Shoe Workers' Union
 Originally chartered on April 13, 1889
Brass and Composition Metal Workers, Polishers and Buffers; United Brotherhood of
 Originally chartered on September 6, 1892
 Merged with the Metal Polishers, Buffers, Platers and Helpers International Union on July 5, 1896
Brewery, Flour, Cereal, Soft Drink and Distillery Workers of America; International Union of United
 Originally chartered on March 4, 1887
 Suspended on October 16, 1941
Brick and Clay Workers of America; United
 Originally chartered on February 18, 1896
Bricklayers, Masons and Plasterers' International Union of America
 Originally chartered on October 12, 1916
Bridge and Structural Iron Workers; International Association of
 Originally chartered on June 19, 1901
Broom and Whisk Makers Union; International
 Originally chartered on June 21, 1893
Brushmakers International Union
 Originally chartered on December 9, 1887
 Disbanded on May 22, 1918
Building Employees of America; International Union of
 Originally chartered on March 10, 1904
 Charter revoked on September 18, 1905

Building Laborers International Protective Union of America
    Originally chartered on March 19, 1898
    Dropped in January 1901
Building Service Employees' International Union
    Originally chartered on April 23, 1921
Building and Construction Trades Department
    Originally chartered March 20, 1908
Car Workers; International Association of
    Originally chartered on September 30, 1901
    Charter surrendered on November 28, 1911
Carpenters and Joiners; Amalgamated Society of
    Originally chartered on November 15, 1890
    Merged with the United Brotherhood of Carpenters and Joiners of America in 1914
Carpenters and Joiners of America; United Brotherhood of
    Originally chartered on July 16, 1887
Carriage, Wagon and Automobile Workers of North America; International Union of
    Originally chartered on August 31, 1891
    Suspended on April 1, 1918
Cement Workers; American Brotherhood of
    Originally chartered on September 22, 1903
    Merged with the Operative Plasterers' and Cement Masons' International Association of the
       United States and Canada on August 30, 1915
Cement, Lime and Gypsum Workers International Union; United
    Originally chartered on September 12, 1939
Chainmakers National Union of United States of America
    Originally chartered on September 25, 1900
    Charter surrendered on March 30, 1911
Chemical Workers Union; International
    Originally chartered on September 11, 1944
Cigarmakers' International Union of America
    Originally chartered on March 30, 1887
Circus, Carnival, Fairs and Rodeo International Union
    Originally chartered on February 19, 1940
    Charter surrendered on January 21, 1942
Cleaning and Dye House Workers; International Association of
    Originally chartered on January 21, 1937
    Merged with the Laundry Workers International Union on May 1, 1956
Cloak Makers International Union of America
    Originally chartered on September 28, 1892
    Disappeared in 1893
Cloth Hat, Cap and Millinery Workers International Union
    Originally chartered on June 17, 1902
    Merged with the United Hatters of North America on April 2, 1934
Clothing Makers Union of America; Special Order
    Originally chartered on April 17, 1902
    Merged with the United Garment Workers of America on February 23, 1903
Clothing Operatives National Union
    Originally chartered on November 15, 1890
    Surrendered charter on September 18, 1891
Clothing Workers of America; Amalgamated
    Originally chartered on October 16, 1933
    Charter revoked on October 12, 1938

Compressed Air and Foundation Workers Union of the United States and Canada; International
  Originally chartered on March 26, 1904
  Merged with the International Hod Carriers, Building and Common Laborers Union of
    America on January 1, 1918
Conductors; Order of Sleeping Car
  Originally chartered on November 5, 1919
  Charter returned on June 23, 1942
Coopers' International Union of North America
  Originally chartered on January 16, 1888
Coremakers International Union of America
  Originally chartered on December 29, 1896
  Merged with the International Molders and Foundry Workers Union of North America on
    May 21, 1903
Cutting Die and Cutting Makers; International Union of
  Originally chartered on October 1, 1904
  Disbanded on October 3, 1922
Diamond Workers' Protective Union of America
  Originally chartered on April 12, 1912
  Merged with the International Jewelry Workers Union on December 2, 1955
Distillery, Rectifying and Wine Workers' International Union of America
  Originally chartered on December 20, 1940
Doll and Toy Workers of the United States and Canada; International Union of
  Originally chartered on September 8, 1952
Electrical Workers; International Brotherhood of
  Originally chartered on December 7, 1891
Elevator Constructors; International Union of
  Originally chartered on June 1, 1903
Engineers; Amalgamated Society of
  Originally chartered on June 30, 1898
  Charter revoked on November 22, 1902
Engineers; International Union of Operating
  Originally chartered on May 7, 1897
Engineers; National Brotherhood of Coal Hoisting
  Originally chartered on October 13, 1899
  Charter revoked on December 16, 1903
Engravers; Friendly Society of
  Originally chartered on May 29, 1933
  Withdrew on August 2, 1935
Engravers League; International Steel and Copper Plate
  Originally chartered on July 17, 1918
  Merged with the International Plate Printers, Die Stampers and Engravers Union of North
    America on March 25, 1925
Engravers International Association of America; Watchcase
  Originally chartered on February 1, 1900
  Charter returned on September 16, 1912
Federal Employees; National Federation of
  Originally chartered on September 24, 1917
  Withdrew on December 1, 1931
Fire Fighters; International Association of
  Originally chartered on February 28, 1918
Firemen and Oilers; International Brotherhood of
  Originally chartered on January 11, 1899

Fishermen's International Protective Association; Lobster
    Originally chartered on February 6, 1907
    Suspended on June 3, 1909
Flight Engineers' International Association
    Originally chartered on December 7, 1948
Flour and Cereal Mill Employees; International Union of
    Originally chartered on October 4, 1902
    Charter revoked on March 30, 1911
Foundry Employees; International Brotherhood of
    Originally chartered on March 26, 1904
    Charter revoked on October 9, 1939
Fruit and Vegetable Workers of North America; International Union of
    Originally chartered on July 1, 1921
    Disbanded on July 27, 1922
Fur and Leather Workers Union; International
    Originally chartered on July 1, 1913
    Withdrew on December 28, 1937
    Merged with the Amalgamated Meat Cutters and Butcher Workmen of North America on
        February 22, 1955
Furniture Workers Union; International
    Originally chartered on June 11, 1887
    Merged with the Machine Woodworkers International Union of America on January 1, 1896
Garment Workers of America; United
    Originally chartered on May 1, 1891
Garment Workers' Union; International Ladies'
    Originally chartered on June 23, 1900
Glass Bottle Blowers Association of the United States and Canada
    Originally chartered on August 9, 1899
Glass Cutters and Flatteners Association of America; Window
    Originally chartered on November 6, 1925
    Merged with the Window Glass Cutters League of America on April 22, 1930
Glass Cutters League of America; Window
    Originally chartered on May 24, 1898
    Amalgamated with the Window Glass Cutters and Flatteners Association of North America
        on April 22, 1930
Glass Employees Association of America
    Originally chartered on July 25, 1890
    Dropped in 1896
Glass Flatteners Association of North America; Window
    Originally chartered on April 27, 1898
    Suspended in 1902
Glass House Employees; International Association of
    Originally chartered on January 7, 1903
    Charter surrendered on September 6, 1907
Glass Snappers National Protective Association of America; Window
    Originally chartered on September 19, 1902
    Suspended on March 4, 1908
Glass Workers; National Window
    Originally chartered on April 13, 1918
    Disbanded on July 1, 1928
Glass Workers International Association of America; Amalgamated
    Originally chartered on September 25, 1900

Merged with the Brotherhood of Painters, Decorators and Paperhangers of America on October 1, 1915

Glass Workers of America; Federation of Flat
Originally chartered on August 7, 1934
Charter revoked on October 12, 1938

Glass Workers Union; American Flint
Originally chartered on July 27, 1887
Withdrew on January 30, 1903
New charter issued on October 21, 1912

Gold Beaters National Union of America; United
Originally chartered on October 20, 1897
Suspended in 1900
New charter issued on February 28, 1906
Suspended on June 3, 1909

Glove Workers Union of America; International
Originally chartered on December 23, 1902

Government Employees International Union; American Federation of
Originally chartered on August 18, 1932

Grain Millers; American Federation
Originally chartered on July 26, 1948

Granite Cutters' International Association of America; The
Originally chartered on November 9, 1888

Grinders and Finishers National Union; Pocket Knife Blade
Originally chartered on August 1, 1905
Suspended on September 29, 1917

Grinders National Union; Table Knife
Originally chartered on October 14, 1889
Suspended on August 1, 1911

Hatters, Cap and Millinery Workers International Union; United
Originally chartered on April 2, 1934

Hod Carriers, Building and Common Laborers Union of America; International
Originally chartered on April 28, 1903

Horse Collar Makers National Union
Originally chartered on April 18, 1888
Last paid per-capita tax in February, 1893

Horseshoers of the United States and Canada; International Union of Journeymen
Originally chartered on July 1, 1893

Hosiery Workers; American Federation of
Originally chartered on August 8, 1951

Hotel and Restaurant Employees and Bartenders International Union
Originally chartered on April 24, 1891

Insurance Agents International Union
Originally chartered on May 15, 1951

Iron, Steel and Tin Workers; Amalgamated Association of
Originally chartered on December 13, 1887
Charter revoked on October 12, 1938

Jewelry Workers' Union; International
Originally chartered on September 17, 1900

Knife Makers National Protective Union of America; Spring
Originally chartered on August 9, 1892
Withdrew in 1895

Lace Operatives of America; Amalgamated
 Originally chartered on November 28, 1894
 Suspended on December 31, 1919
Lasters Protective Union of America
 Originally chartered on December 7, 1887
 Merged with the Boot and Shoe Workers Union on April 10, 1895
Lasters Protective Union; New England
 Originally chartered on December 17, 1887
 Merged with the Boot and Shoe Workers Union on April 10, 1895
Lathers; International Union of Wood, Wire and Metal
 Originally chartered on January 15, 1900
Laundry Workers International Union
 Originally chartered on November 19, 1900
Leather Goods, Plastics and Novelty Workers' Union; International
 Originally chartered on March 5, 1937
Leather Workers of America; Amalgamated
 Originally chartered on July 18, 1901
 Charter surrendered on September 6, 1913
Leather Workers International Union of America; United
 Originally chartered on August 12, 1889
 Merged with the Amalgamated Meat Cutters and Butcher Workmen of North America on
  September 24, 1951
Letter Carriers; National Association of
 Originally chartered on September 20, 1917
Letter Carriers; National Federation of Rural
 Originally chartered on January 9, 1920
 Merged with the National Association of Letter Carriers on October 23, 1946
Lithographic Press Feeders of United States and Canada; International Protective Association of
 Originally chartered on July 26, 1909
 Suspended on March 17, 1914
Longshoremen—AFL; International Brotherhood of
 Originally chartered on September 25, 1953
Longshoremen's Association; International
 Originally chartered on July 25, 1893
 Charter revoked on September 22, 1953
Machinists; International Association of
 Originally chartered on June 5, 1895
Machinists Union of America; International
 Originally chartered on June 26, 1891
 Last paid per-capita taxes in January, 1896
Maintenance of Way Employes; Brotherhood of
 Originally chartered on February 5, 1900
Marble, Slate and Stone Polishers, Rubbers and Sawyers, Tile and Marble Setters Helpers and
Terrazzo Helpers; International Association of
 Originally chartered on January 11, 1902
Marine Engineers' Beneficial Association; National
 Originally chartered on July 12, 1916
 Withdrew on February 28, 1923
Marine Water Tenders, Oilers and Firemen of America; Amalgamated Association of
 Originally chartered on March 12, 1894
 Charter revoked in 1902

Maritime Trades Department
   Originally chartered on August 19, 1946
Masters, Mates and Pilots of America; International Organization of
   Originally chartered on February 26, 1916
Master Mechanics and Foremen of Navy Yards and Naval Stations; National Association of
   Originally chartered on May 3, 1933
Mattress, Spring and Bedding Workers; International Union
   Originally chartered on May 18, 1904
   Disbanded on December 9, 1905
Meet Cutters and Butcher Workmen of North America; Amalgamated
   Originally chartered on January 26, 1897
Metal Engravers and Marking Device Workers Union; International
   Originally chartered on August 9, 1921
Metal Mechanics; International Association of Allied
   Originally chartered on December 30, 1896
   Merged with the International Association of Machinists on November 1, 1904
Metal Polishers, Buffers, Platers and Helpers International Union;
   Originally chartered on March 8, 1892
Metal Trades Department
   Originally chartered on July 2, 1908
Metal Workers Union of North America
   Originally chartered on July 5, 1887
   Disbanded on December 31, 1889
Metal Workers International Union; United
   Originally chartered on September 24, 1900
   Suspended on March 29, 1905
Mine Managers and Assistants Mutual Aid Association; National
   Originally chartered on May 1, 1902
   Suspended on February 26, 1902
Mine Workers of America; United
   Originally chartered on January 25, 1890
   Charter revoked October 12, 1938
   Reaffiliated on January 25, 1946
   Withdrew on December 12, 1947
Mine Workers of America; Progressive
   Originally chartered on April 28, 1938
   Withdrew on February 25, 1946
Mine, Mill and Smelter Workers; International Union of
   Originally chartered on July 7, 1896
   Charter revoked on October 12, 1938
Mineral Mine Workers of North America; United
   Originally chartered on December 3, 1895
   Withdrew on May 7, 1904
Miners and Mine Laborers; National Progressive Union of
   Originally chartered on January 4, 1889
   Last paid per-capita taxes in October 1889
Mining Department
   Originally chartered on January 8, 1912
   Disbanded on July 25, 1922
Molders and Foundry Workers Union of North America; International
   Originally chartered on December 14, 1887

Musicians; American Federation of
    Originally chartered on November 6, 1896
Office Employes International Union
    Originally chartered on January 8, 1945
Oil Field, Gas Well and Refinery Workers of America
    Originally chartered on July 2, 1918
    Charter revoked on October 12, 1938
Oil and Gas Well Workers; International Brotherhood of
    Originally chartered on December 29, 1899
    Disbanded on December 9, 1904
Painters, Decorators and Paperhangers of America; Brotherhood of
    Originally chartered on December 1, 1887
Paper Box, Bag and Novelty Workers International Union
    Originally chartered on January 19, 1904
    Suspended on August 29, 1907
Paper Makers; International Brotherhood of
    Originally chartered on May 19, 1893
Pattern Makers' League of North America
    Originally chartered on September 4, 1894
Pavers, Rammermen, Flag Layers, Bridge and Stone Curb Setters and Sheet Asphalt Pavers; International Union of
    Originally chartered on August 28, 1905
    Merged with the International Hod Carriers, Building and Common Laborers Union of
        America on February 9, 1937
Paving Cutters' Union of the United States of America and Canada
    Originally chartered on August 3, 1901
    Withdrew on December 29, 1937
Photo Engravers Union of North America; International
    Originally chartered on May 19, 1904
Piano and Organ International Union of America
    Originally chartered on December 28, 1901
    Suspended on August 17, 1936
Pilots Association; International
    Originally chartered on September 16, 1903
    Charter revoked on September 15, 1904
Pilots Protective Association of the Great Lakes; Lake
    Originally chartered on January 17, 1906
    Suspended on March 29, 1907
Plasterers' and Cement Masons' International Association of the United States and Canada; Operative
    Originally chartered on November 14, 1908
Plumbing and Pipe Fitting Industry of the United States and Canada; United Association of Journeymen and Apprentices of the
    Originally chartered on October 30, 1897
Post Office and Postal Transportation Service Mail Handlers, Watchmen and Messengers; National Association of
    Originally chartered on November 11, 1937
Postal Supervisors; National Association of
    Originally chartered on July 12, 1946
    Withdrew on February 28, 1955
Postal Transport Association; National

Originally chartered on December 22, 1917
Potters; International Brotherhood of Operative
    Originally chartered on March 14, 1899
Potters National Union of America
    Originally chartered on March 23, 1895
    Merged with the International Brotherhood of Operative Potters in 1904
Powder and High Explosive Workers of America; United
    Originally chartered on December 16, 1901
    Disbanded on February 15, 1943
Printers Association of America; Machine Textile
    Originally chartered on March 10, 1903
    Withdrew on March 13, 1907
Printers, Die Stampers and Engravers Union of North America; International Plate
    Originally chartered on July 2, 1898
Printing Pressmen's and Assistants' Union of North America; International
    Originally chartered on November 3, 1895
Pulp, Sulphite and Paper Mill Workers of the United States and Canada; International Brotherhood of
    Originally chartered on July 2, 1909
Quarrymen's National Union of the United States of America
    Originally chartered on August 21, 1890
    Suspended in 1900
Quarrymen's Union; National Slate
    Originally chartered on November 15, 1895
    Disbanded in 1898
Quarry Workers International Union of America
    Originally chartered on September 8, 1903
    Withdrew on January 6, 1938
Radio and Television Directors Guild
    Originally chartered on September 11, 1946
Railroad Employes' Department
    Originally chartered on February 19, 1909
Railroad Patrolmen; Brotherhood of
    Originally chartered on August 19, 1919
    Suspended on February 24, 1923
Railroad Signalmen; Brotherhood of
    Originally chartered March 11, 1914
Railroad Telegraphers; Order of
    Originally chartered on October 31, 1899
Railway Carmen of America; Brotherhood
    Originally chartered on August 9, 1910
Railway Clerks; Brotherhood of
    Originally chartered on November 17, 1908
Railway Clerks of America; Order of
    Originally chartered on October 21, 1900
    Suspended in 1902
Railway Clerks; International Association of
    Originally chartered on April 29, 1903
    Withdrew on January 16, 1905
Railway Employees of America; Amalgamated Association of Street and Electric
    Originally chartered on November 8, 1893

Railway Express Messengers of America; Brotherhood of
    Originally chartered on June 15, 1912
    Disbanded on December 15, 1913
Railway Expressmen of America; Brotherhood of
    Originally chartered on May 14, 1903
    Disbanded in 1905
Railway Freight Handlers; Brotherhood of
    Originally chartered on January 13, 1903
    Merged with the Brotherhood of Railway Clerks on January 20, 1915
Railway Patrolmen's International Union
    Originally chartered on July 7, 1949
Railway Postal Clerks; Brotherhood of
    Originally chartered on June 1, 1914
    Merged with the National Federation of Post Office Clerks on April 25, 1917
Retail Clerks International Association
    Originally chartered on December 24, 1890
Roofers, Damp and Waterproof Workers Association; United Slate, Tile and Composition
    Originally chartered on June 5, 1903
Rubber Workers of America; United
    Originally chartered on September 12, 1935
    Charter revoked on October 12, 1938
Rubber Workers Union of America; Amalgamated
    Originally chartered on November 10, 1902
    Suspended on December 9, 1905
Sailors and Firemen; International Amalgamated Association of
    Originally chartered on November 12, 1889
    Last paid per-capita taxes in April 1891
Saw Smiths Union of North America
    Originally chartered on June 18, 1902
    Suspended on August 22, 1924
Seafarers' International Union of North America
    Originally chartered on October 14, 1938
Seamen's Union; Lake
    Originally chartered in 1887
    Merged with the International Seamen's Union of America in 1892
Seamen's Union of America; International
    Originally chartered on September 8, 1893
    Dropped on October 14, 1938
Sheep Shearers Union of North America
    Originally chartered on July 25, 1932
    Dropped on August 12, 1942
Sheet Metal Workers International Association
    Originally chartered on April 23, 1889
Shingle Weavers Union of America; International
    Originally chartered on March 3, 1903
    Merged with the International Union of Timber Workers on April 12, 1918
Shipwrights, Joiners and Caulkers of America; International Union
    Originally chartered on October 25, 1902
    Suspended on March 30, 1911
Siderographers; International Association of
    Originally chartered on June 22, 1906

Silk Workers; National Federation of
    Originally chartered on May 16, 1889
    Last paid per-capita taxes in April 1892
Slate Workers; American Brotherhood of
    Originally chartered on July 1, 1903
    Disbanded on May 30, 1916
Sleeping Car Porters; Brotherhood of
    Originally chartered on June 2, 1936
Special Delivery Messengers; National Association of
    Originally chartered on November 19, 1937
Spinners Union; International
    Originally chartered on January 9, 1889
    Suspended on August 10, 1950
Stage Employes and Moving Picture Machine Operators of the United States and Canada; International Alliance of Theatrical
    Originally chartered on July 20, 1894
State, County, and Municipal Employees; American Federation of
    Originally chartered on October 16, 1936
Steam and Hot Water Fitters and Helpers of America; International Association of
    Originally chartered on November 6, 1898
    Charter revoked on November 22, 1912
Steam Shovel and Dredgemen; International Brotherhood of
    Originally chartered on January 13, 1915
    Merged with the International Union of Operating Engineers on April 1, 1927
Stereotypers and Electrotypers Union of North America; International
    Originally chartered on January 23, 1902
Stonecutters' Association of North America; Journeymen
    Originally chartered on August 20, 1907
Stove Mounters International Union
    Originally chartered on January 6, 1894
Street and Electric Railway Employees of America; Amalgamated Association of
    Originally chartered on November 8, 1893
Switchmen's Union of North America
    Originally chartered on July 12, 1906
Tackmakers International Union
    Originally chartered on October 3, 1903
    Disbanded on December 9, 1905
Tailors National Progressive Union
    Originally chartered on October 28, 1887
    Last paid per-capita taxes in February 1890
Tailors' Union of America; Journeymen
    Originally chartered on October 15, 1887
    Charter revoked on October 12, 1938
Tanners and Curriers of America; United Brotherhood of
    Originally chartered on August 19, 1891
    Last paid per-capita taxes in December 1895
Teachers; American Federation of
    Originally chartered on May 9, 1916
Teamsters, Chauffeurs, Warehousemen and Helpers of America; International Brotherhood of
    Originally chartered on January 27, 1899
Technical Engineers; American Federation of
    Originally chartered on July 1, 1918

Telegraphers' Union; The Commercial
    Originally chartered on February 16, 1894
Textile Workers of America; United
    Originally chartered on June 4, 1896
Textile Workers Progressive Union; National
    Originally chartered on September 22, 1888
    Withdrew in 1891
Tile Layers and Helpers International Union; Ceramic, Mosaic and Encaustic
    Originally chartered on February 4, 1890
    Suspended on September 20, 1918
Timber Workers; International Union of
    Originally chartered on August 7, 1917
    Disbanded on March 22, 1923
Tin Plate Workers International Protective Association of America
    Originally chartered on January 18, 1899
    Merged with the Amalgamated Association of Iron, Steel and Tin Workers on August 1, 1913
Tip Printers; International Brotherhood of
    Originally chartered on August 21, 1903
    Merged with the International Brotherhood of Bookbinders on December 31, 1918.
Tobacco Workers International Union
    Originally chartered on June 28, 1895
Travelers' Goods and Leather Novelty Workers International Union of America
    Originally chartered on August 4, 1898
    Merged with the Leather Workers on Horse Goods to form the United Leather Workers
        International Union on July 24, 1917
Tube Workers; International Association of
    Originally chartered on March 17, 1902
    Disbanded in 1905
Tunnel and Subway Constructors International Union
    Originally chartered on January 19, 1910
    Merged with the International Hod Carriers, Building and Common Laborers Union of
        America on May 7, 1929
Typographia; German-America
    Originally chartered on April 17, 1887
    Merged with the International Typographical Union on July 1, 1894
Typographical Union; International
    Originally chartered on December 31, 1888
Union Label and Service Trades Department
    Originally chartered on April 2, 1909
Upholsterers' International Union of North America
    Originally chartered on September 20, 1900
Varnishers' National Union of North America; Hardwood Furniture and Piano
    Originally chartered on January 31, 1893
    Last paid per-capita taxes in September 1894
Wall Paper Craftsmen and Workers of North America; United
    Originally chartered on September 25, 1902
Watch Case Makers Union; International
    Originally chartered on February 15, 1901
    Merged with the International Jewelry Workers Union on September 15, 1903
Weavers; Amalgamated Association of Elastic Goring
    Originally chartered on October 5, 1888
    Disbanded on February 17, 1927

Wire Drawers of America; Federated Association of
    Originally chartered on July 1, 1916
    Disbanded on February 16, 1899
Wire Weavers Protective Association; American
    Originally chartered on September 11, 1900
Wood Carvers Association of North America; International
    Originally chartered on April 12, 1898
    Dropped on August 16, 1943
Woodsmen and Saw Mill Workers; International Brotherhood of
    Originally chartered on August 2, 1905
    Suspended on April 10, 1911
Woodworkers International Union of America; Amalgamated
    Originally chartered on January 1, 1896
    Merged with the United Brotherhood of Carpenters and Joiners on March 11, 1912
Woodworkers International Union of America; Machine
    Originally chartered on December 23, 1890
    Merged with the International Furniture Workers Union to form the Amalgamated Wood-
    workers International Union of America on January 1, 1896
Yardmasters of America; Railroad
    Originally chartered on November 25, 1946

AMERICAN FEDERATION OF LABOR-CONGRESS OF INDUSTRIAL ORGANIZATIONS

Actors and Artistes of America; Associated
    Charter union, AFL, 1955
Agricultural Workers Union; National
    Charter union, AFL, 1955
    Merged with the Amalgamated Meat Cutters and Butcher Workmen of North America on
    August 16, 1960
Air Line Dispatchers Association
    Charter union, AFL, 1955
Air Line Pilots Association
    Charter union, AFL, 1955
Aluminum Workers International Union
    Charter union, AFL, 1955
Asbestos Workers; International Association of Heat and Frost Insulators
    Charter union, AFL, 1955
Automobile, Aerospace and Agricultural Implement Workers of America, International Union;
United
    Charter union, CIO, 1955
    Disaffiliated on July 1, 1968
Automobile Workers of America, International Union; United
    Charter union, AFL, 1955
    Title changed to Industrial Workers of America, International Union; Allied on May 1, 1956
Bakery and Confectionery Workers International Union; American
    Originally chartered on December 12, 1957
    Merged with the Bakery and Confectionery Workers' International Union of America on De-
    cember 4, 1969
Bakery and Confectionery Workers' International Union of America
    Charter union, AFL, 1955

Expelled on December 12, 1955

Merged with the American Bakery and Confectionery Workers International Union on December 4, 1969

Barbers and Beauty Culturists Union of America

Charter union, CIO, 1955

Reaffiliated with the Journeymen Barbers, Hairdressers and Cosmetologists' International Union of America on July 1, 1956

Barbers, Hairdressers and Cosmetologists' International Union of America; Journeymen

Charter union, AFL, 1955

Bill Posters, Billers and Distributors of the United States and Canada; International Alliance of

Charter union, AFL, 1955

Charter surrendered on October 31, 1971

Boiler Makers, Iron Shipbuilders, Blacksmiths, Forgers and Helpers; International Brotherhood of

Charter union, AFL, 1955

✓ Bookbinders; International Brotherhood of

Charter union, AFL, 1955

Merged with the Lithographers and Photoengravers International Union on September 4, 1972, to create the Graphic Arts International Union

Boot and Shoe Workers' Union

Charter union, AFL, 1955

Brewery, Flour, Cereal, Soft Drink and Distillery Workers; International Union of United

Charter union, CIO, 1955

Charter revoked October 19, 1973

Bricklayers, Masons and Plasterers' International Union of America

Charter union, AFL, 1955

Brick and Clay Workers of America; United

Charter union, AFL, 1955

Broadcast Employees and Technicians; National Association of

Charter union, CIO, 1955

Broom and Whisk Makers Union; International

Charter union, AFL, 1955

Disbanded, August 1962

Building Service Employees' International Union

Charter union, AFL, 1955

Title changed to Service Employees International Union, AFL-CIO, on February 19, 1968

Carpenters and Joiners of America; United Brotherhood of

Charter union, AFL, 1955

Cement, Lime and Gypsum Workers International Union; United

Charter union, AFL, 1955

Chemical Workers Union; International

Charter union, AFL, 1955

Charter revoked, October 3, 1969

Charter reinstated, May 12, 1971

Cigarmakers' International Union of America

Charter union, AFL, 1955

Merged with the Retail, Wholesale and Department Store Union on August 6, 1974

Clothing Workers of America; Amalgamated

Charter union, CIO, 1955

Commercial Telegraphers' Union; The

Charter union, AFL, 1955

Title changed to United Telegraph Workers on February 19, 1968
Communications Workers of America
    Charter union, CIO, 1955
Coopers' International Union of North America
    Charter union, AFL, 1955
Distillery, Rectifying, Wine and Allied Workers International Union of America
    Charter union, AFL, 1955
Dolls, Toys, Playthings, Novelty and Allied Products of the United States and Canada, AFL-CIO;
International Union of
    Charter union, AFL, 1955
Electrical, Radio and Machine Workers; International Union of
    Charter union, CIO, 1955
Electrical Workers; International Brotherhood of
    Charter union, AFL, 1955
Elevator Constructors; International Union of
    Charter union, AFL, 1955
Engineers; International Union of Operating
    Charter union, AFL, 1955
Engravers and Marking Device Workers Union; International Metal
    Charter union, AFL, 1955
    Merged with the International Association of Machinists and Aerospace Workers on
        September 1, 1956
Farm Workers of America; United
    Chartered on February 21, 1972
Fire Fighters; International Association of
    Charter union, AFL, 1955
Firemen and Oilers; International Brotherhood of
    Charter union, AFL, 1955
Flight Engineers' International Association
    Charter union, AFL, 1955
Furniture Workers of America; United
    Charter union, CIO, 1955
Garment Workers of America; United
    Charter union, AFL, 1955
Garment Workers' Union; International Ladies'
    Charter union, AFL, 1955
Glass and Ceramic Workers of North America; United
    Charter union, CIO, 1955
Glass Bottle Blowers Association of the United States and Canada
    Charter union, AFL, 1955
Glass Cutters League of America; Window
    Charter union, AFL, 1955
    Merged with the Glass Bottle Blowers Association of the United States and Canada on
        August 1, 1975
Glass Workers' Union; American Flint
    Charter union, AFL, 1955
Glove Workers Union of America; International
    Charter union, AFL, 1955
    Merged with the Amalgamated Clothing Workers of America on December 6, 1961
Government Employees; American Federation of
    Charter union, AFL, 1955

Grain Millers; American Federation of
    Charter union, AFL, 1955
Granite Cutters' International Association of America; The
    Charter union, AFL, 1955
Graphic Arts International Union
    Chartered on September 4, 1972
Hatters, Cap and Millinery Workers International Union; United
    Charter union, AFL, 1955
Hod Carriers, Building and Common Laborers Union of America; International
    Charter union, AFL, 1955
    Title changed to Laborers' International Union of North America on September 20, 1965
Horseshoers of the United States and Canada; International Union of Journeymen
    Charter union, AFL, 1955
Hosiery Workers; American Federation of
    Charter union, AFL, 1955
    Merged with the Textile Workers Union of America on April 28, 1965
Hotel and Restaurant Employees and Bartenders International Union
    Charter union, AFL, 1955
Industrial Workers of America; International Union, Allied
    Charter union, AFL, 1955
    (Titled the United Automobile Workers of America, International Union until May 1, 1956.)
Insurance Agents International Union
    Charter union, AFL, 1955
    Merged into the Insurance Workers International Union, AFL-CIO on May 18, 1959
Insurance Workers of America
    Charter union, CIO, 1955
    Merged into the Insurance Workers International Union, AFL-CIO on May 18, 1959
Insurance Workers International Union, AFL-CIO
    Chartered on May 18, 1959
Iron Workers; International Association of Bridge and Structural
    Charter union, AFL, 1955
Jewelry Workers Union; International
    Charter union, AFL, 1955
Laborers' International Union of North America
    Charter union, AFL, 1955
    (Titled the International Hod Carriers, Building and Common Laborers Union of America
        until September 20, 1965)
Lathers International Union; Wood, Wire and Metal
    Charter union, AFL, 1955
Laundry, Dry Cleaning and Dye House Workers' International Union
    Charter union, AFL, 1955
    Expelled, December 1957
Laundry and Dry Cleaning International Union, AFL-CIO
    Chartered on May 12, 1959
Leather Goods, Plastics and Novelty Workers' Union; International
    Charter union, AFL, 1955
Leather Workers International Union of America
    Charter union, CIO, 1955
Letter Carriers of the United States of America; National Association of
    Charter union, AFL, 1955
Lithographers and Photoengravers International Union

Chartered on September 7, 1964
Merged into Graphic Arts International Union on September 4, 1972
Lithographers of America; Amalgamated
    Charter union, AFL, 1955
    Disaffiliated, January 1, 1960
    Merged into the Lithographers and Photoengravers International Union on September 7, 1964
Locomotive Firemen and Enginemen; Brotherhood of
    Chartered on August 29, 1956
    Merged into the United Transportation Union on December 16, 1968
Longshoremen; International Brotherhood of
    Charter union, AFL, 1955
    Merged with the International Longshoremen's Association, AFL-CIO on November 17, 1959
Longshoremen's Association, AFL-CIO; International
    Chartered on November 17, 1959
Machinists and Aerospace Workers; International Association of
    Charter union, AFL, 1955
Maintenance of Way Employes; Brotherhood of
    Charter union, AFL, 1955
Marble, Slate and Stone Polishers, Rubbers and Sawyers, Tile and Marble Setters Helpers' and Marble Mosaic and Terrazzo Workers' Helpers; International Association of
    Charter union, AFL, 1955
Marine and Shipbuilding Workers of America; Industrial Union of
    Charter union, CIO, 1955
Marine Engineers' Beneficial Association; National
    Charter union, CIO, 1955
Maritime Union of America; National
    Charter union, CIO, 1955
Masters, Mates and Pilots; International Organization of
    Charter union, AFL, 1955
    Merged with the International Longshoremen's Association, AFL-CIO, on May 12, 1971
Master Mechanics and Foremen of Navy Yards and Naval Stations; National Association of
    Charter union, AFL, 1955
    Withdrew, April 1, 1964
Meat Cutters and Butcher Workmen of North America; Amalgamated
    Charter union, AFL, 1955
Mechanics Educational Society of America
    Charter union, CIO, 1955
Metal Polishers, Buffers, Platers and Allied Workers International Union
    Charter union, AFL, 1955
Molders' and Allied Workers' Union; International
    Charter union, AFL, 1955
Musicians; American Federation of
    Charter union, AFL, 1955
Newspaper Guild; The
    Charter union, CIO, 1955
Office and Professional Employees International Union
    Charter union, AFL, 1955
Oil, Chemical and Atomic Workers International Union
    Charter union, CIO, 1955

Packinghouse, Food and Allied Workers; United
    Charter union, CIO, 1955
    Merged with the Amalgamated Meat Cutters and Butcher Workmen of North America on
        July 9, 1968
Painters and Allied Trades of the United States and Canada; International Brotherhood of
    Charter union, AFL, 1955
Paper Makers; International Brotherhood of
    Charter union, AFL, 1955
    Merged into the United Papermakers and Paperworkers on March 6, 1957
Paperworkers of America; United
    Charter union, CIO, 1955
    Merged into the United Papermakers and Paperworkers on March 6, 1957
Paperworkers International Union; United
    Chartered on August 9, 1972
Papermakers and Paperworkers; United
    Chartered on March 6, 1957
    Merged into the United Paperworkers International Union on August 9, 1972
Pattern Makers' League of North America
    Charter union, AFL, 1955
Photo Engravers Union of North America; International
    Charter union, AFL, 1955
    Merged into the Lithographers and Photoengravers International Union on September 7,
        1964
Plasterers' and Cement Masons' International Association of the United States and Canada;
Operative
    Charter union, AFL, 1955
Plate Printers', Die Stampers' and Engravers' Union of North America; International
    Charter union, AFL, 1955
Plumbing and Pipe Fitting Industry of the United States and Canada; United Association of Jour-
neymen and Apprentices of the
    Charter union, AFL, 1955
Post Office Clerks; National Federation of
    Charter union, AFL, 1955
    Title changed to United Federation of Postal Clerks on December 6, 1961
Post Office and General Service Maintenance Employees; National Association of
    Chartered in April 1966
    Merged into American Postal Workers Union on July 1, 1971
Post Office Mail Handlers, Watchmen, Messengers and Group Leaders; National Association of
    Charter union, AFL, 1955
    Merged with Laborers' International Union of North America on April 20, 1968
Post Office Motor Vehicle Employees; National Federation of
    Chartered in 1958
    Merged into American Postal Workers Union on July 1, 1971
Postal Transport Association; National
    Charter union, AFL, 1955
    Merged into United Federation of Postal Clerks on December 6, 1961
Postal Clerks; United Federation
    Chartered on December 6, 1961
    Merged into American Postal Workers' Union on July 1, 1971
Postal Workers Union; American
    Chartered on July 1, 1971

Pottery and Allied Workers; International Brotherhood of
    Charter union, AFL, 1955
✓Printing and Graphic Communications Union; International
    Chartered on October 17, 1973
✓Printing Pressmen and Assistants' Union of North America; International
    Merged into the International Printing and Graphic Communications Union on October 17,
      1973
Pulp, Sulphite and Paper Mill Workers of the United States and Canada; International Brother-
hood of
    Charter union, AFL, 1955
    Merged into the United Paperworkers International Union on August 9, 1972
Radio and Television Directors Guild
    Charter union, AFL, 1955
    Disaffiliated, January 1, 1960
Radio Association; American
    Charter union, CIO, 1955
Railroad Signalmen of America; Brotherhood of
    Charter union, AFL, 1955
Railroad Telegraphers; Order of
    Charter union, AFL, 1955
    Title changed to Transportation-Communications Employees Union on February 25, 1965
Railroad Trainmen; Brotherhood of
    Chartered in 1957
    Merged into the United Transportation Union on December 16, 1968
Railway Carmen of the United States and Canada; Brotherhood
    Charter union, AFL, 1955
Railway, Airline and Steamship Clerks, Freight Handlers, Express and Station Employees;
Brotherhood of
    Charter union, AFL, 1955
Railway Patrolmen's International Union
    Charter union, AFL, 1955
    Merged with the Brotherhood of Railway, Airline and Steamship Clerks, Freight Handlers,
      Express and Station Employees on January 1, 1969
Railway Supervisors Association; American
    Chartered in 1958
Retail Clerks International Association
    Charter union, AFL, 1955
Retail, Wholesale and Department Store Union
    Charter union, CIO, 1955
Roofers, Damp and Waterproof Workers Association; United Slate, Tile and Composition
    Charter union, AFL, 1955
Rubber, Cork, Linoleum and Plastic Workers of America; United
    Charter union, CIO, 1955
Seafarers International Union of North America
    Charter union, AFL, 1955
Service Employees International Union, AFL-CIO
    Charter union, AFL, 1955
    (Titled the Building Service Employees International Union until February 19, 1968)
Sheet Metal Workers' International Association
    Charter union, AFL, 1955
Shoe Workers of America; United
    Charter union, CIO, 1955

Siderographers; International Association of
 Charter Union, AFL, 1955
Sleeping Car Porters; Brotherhood of
 Charter union, AFL, 1955
Special Delivery Messengers; National Association of
 Charter union, AFL, 1955
 Merged into the American Postal Workers Union on July 1, 1971
Stage Employes and Moving Picture Machine Operators of the United States and Canada; International Alliance of Theatrical
 Charter union, AFL, 1955
State, County and Municipal Employees; American Federation of
 Charter union, AFL, 1955
Steelworkers of America; United
 Charter union, CIO, 1955
Stereotypers', Electrotypers', and Platemakers' Union; International
 Charter union, AFL, 1955
 Merged into the International Printing and Graphic Communications Union on October 17, 1973
Stone and Allied Products Workers of America; United
 Charter union, CIO, 1955
 Merged with the United Steelworkers of America on January 1, 1971
Stonecutters Association of North America; Journeymen
 Charter union, AFL, 1955
 Merged with the Laborers' International Union of North America on February 19, 1968
Stove, Furnace and Allied Appliance Workers of North America
 Charter union, AFL, 1955
Street and Electric Railway Employes of America; Amalgamated Association of
 Charter union, AFL, 1955
 Title changed to Amalgamated Transit Union on February 25, 1965
Switchmen's Union of North America
 Charter union, AFL, 1955
 Merged into the United Transportation Union on December 16, 1968
Teachers; American Federation of
 Charter union, AFL, 1955
Teamsters, Chauffeurs, Warehousemen and Helpers of America; International Brotherhood of
 Charter union, AFL, 1955
 Expelled, December 1957
Technical Engineers; American Federation of
 Charter union, AFL, 1955
 Title changed to International Federation of Professional and Technical Engineers in May, 1973
Technical Engineers; International Federation of Professional and
 Charter union, AFL, 1955
 (Titled the American Federation of Technical Engineers until May, 1973)
Telegraph Workers; United
 Charter union, AFL, 1955
 (Titled the Commercial Telegraphers' Union until February 19, 1968)
Textile Workers of America; United
 Charter union, AFL, 1955
Textile Workers Union of America
 Charter union, CIO, 1955
Tobacco Workers International Union

Charter union, AFL, 1955
Train Dispatchers Association; American
    Chartered in 1957
Transit Union; Amalgamated
    Charter union, AFL, 1955
    (Titled the Amalgamated Association of Street and Electric Railway Employes of America
        until February 25, 1965)
Transport Service Employees of America; United
    Charter union, CIO, 1955
    Merged with the Brotherhood of Railway, Airline and Steamship Clerks, Freight Handlers,
        Express and Station Employees on October 1, 1972
Transport Workers Union of America
    Charter union, CIO, 1955
Transportation-Communication Employees Union
    Charter union, AFL, 1955
    (Titled the Order of Railroad Telegraphers until February 25, 1965)
    Merged with the Brotherhood of Railway, Airline and Steamship Clerks, Freight Handlers,
        Express and Station Employees on February 21, 1969
Transportation Union; United
    Chartered on December 16, 1968
Typographical Union; International
    Charter union, AFL, 1955
Upholsterers' International Union of North America
    Charter union, AFL, 1955
Utility Workers Union of America
    Charter union, CIO, 1955
Wall Paper Craftsmen and Workers of North America; United
    Charter union, AFL, 1955
    Merged with the International Brotherhood of Pulp, Sulphite and Paper Mill Workers of the
        United States and Canada on April 29, 1958
Wire Weavers Protective Association; American
    Charter union, AFL, 1955
    Merged with the United Papermakers and Paperworkers on February 16, 1959
Woodworkers of America; International
    Charter union, CIO, 1955
Yardmasters of America; Railroad
    Charter union, AFL, 1955

CONGRESS OF INDUSTRIAL ORGANIZATIONS

Aluminum Workers of America
    Charter union, 1938
    Merged with the United Steelworkers of America in 1944
Architects, Engineers, Chemists and Technicians; International Federation of
    Charter union, 1955
    Merged with the United Office and Professional Workers of America in 1946
Automobile, Aircraft and Agricultural Implement Workers of America; United
    Charter union, 1938
Barbers and Beauty Culturists Union of America
    Chartered in 1943

Brewery, Flour, Cereal and Soft Drink Workers of America; International Union of United
    Chartered in 1946
Broadcast Employees and Technicians; National Association of
    Chartered in 1951
Cannery, Agricultural, Packing and Allied Workers of America; United
    Charter union, 1938
    Title changed to Food, Tobacco, Agricultural and Allied Workers Union of America in 1946
Clothing Workers of America; Amalgamated
    Charter union, 1938
Communications Association; American
    Charter union, 1938
    Expelled, 1950
Communications Workers of America
    Chartered in 1949
Department Store Workers of America; United
    Chartered in 1951
Die Casting Workers; National
    Charter union, 1938
Electrical, Radio and Machine Workers; International Union of
    Chartered in 1949
Electrical, Radio and Machine Workers of America; United
    Charter union, 1938
    Expelled, 1949
Farm Equipment and Metal Workers of America; United
    Chartered in 1942
    Expelled, 1949
Federal Workers of America; United
    Charter union, 1938
    Merged into the United Public Workers of America in 1946
Fishermen and Allied Workers of America; International Union of
    Charter union, 1938
    Expelled, 1950
Flat Glass Workers; Federation of
    Charter union, 1938
    Title changed to Federation of Glass, Ceramic, and Silica Sand Workers of America in 1940
Food, Tobacco, Agricultural and Allied Workers Union of America
    Charter union, 1938
    (Titled the United Cannery, Agricultural and Allied Workers Union of America until 1946)
    Expelled, 1950
Fur and Leather Workers Union; International
    Chartered in 1939
    Expelled, 1950
Fur Workers Union of the United States and Canada; International
    Charter union, 1938
    Merged into the International Fur and Leather Workers Union in 1939
Furniture Workers of America; United
    Charter union, 1938
Gas, Coke and Chemical Workers of America; United
    Chartered in 1942
    Merged into the Oil, Chemical, and Atomic Workers International Union in 1955
Glass, Ceramic, and Silica Sand Workers of America; Federation of

Charter union, 1938
(Titled the Federation of Flat Glass Workers until 1940)
Inlandboatmen's Union of the Pacific
Charter union, 1938
Merged with the Seafarers' International Union of North America, AFL, in 1948
Insurance Workers of America
Chartered in 1953
Iron, Steel, and Tin Workers; Amalgamated Association of
Charter union, 1938
Dissolved, 1942
Leather Workers Association; National
Charter union, 1938
Merged into the International Fur and Leather Workers Union in 1939
Leather Workers International Union of America
Chartered in 1955
✓ Lithographers of America; Amalgamated
Chartered in 1946
Longshoremen's and Warehousemen's Union; International
Charter union, 1938
Expelled, 1950
Marine Cooks' and Stewards' Association of the Pacific Coast
Charter union, 1938
Expelled, 1950
Marine Engineers' Beneficial Association; National
Charter union, 1937
Marine and Shipbuilding Workers of America; Industrial Union of
Charter union, 1938
Maritime Union of America; National
Charter union, 1938
Mechanics Educational Society of America
Chartered in 1954
Mine, Mill and Smelter Workers; International Union of
Charter union, 1938
Expelled, 1950
Mine Workers of America; United
Charter union, 1938
Withdrew, 1942
Newspaper Guild; American
Charter union, 1938
Office and Professional Workers of America, International; United
Charter union, 1938
Expelled, 1950
Oil, Chemical and Atomic Workers International Union
Chartered in 1955
Oil Workers International Union
Charter union, 1938
Merged into the Oil, Chemical and Atomic Workers International Union in 1955
Optical and Instrument Workers of America
Chartered in 1947
Merged with the International Union of Electrical, Radio and Machine Workers in 1954
Packinghouse Workers of America; United
Chartered in 1944

Paper, Novelty and Toy Workers International Union; United
    Chartered in 1939
    Title changed to International Union, Playthings, Jewelry and Novelty Workers in 1944
Paperworkers of America; United
    Chartered in 1946
Playthings, Jewelry and Novelty Workers' International Union
    Chartered in 1944
Playthings and Novelty Workers of America International Union
    Chartered in 1938
    Title changed to United Paper, Novelty and Toy Workers International Union in 1939
Public Workers of America; United
    Chartered in 1946
    Expelled, 1950
Quarry Workers International Union
    Charter union, 1938
    Title changed to United Stone and Allied Products Workers of America in 1941
Radio Association; American
    Chartered in 1948
Railroad Workers of America; United
    Chartered in 1946
    Merged with the Industrial Union of Marine and Shipbuilding Workers of America in 1948
    Rechartered in 1951
    Merged with the Transport Workers Union of America in 1954
Retail, Wholesale and Department Store Employees of America; United
    Charter union, 1938
Rubber Workers of America; United
    Charter union, 1938
Shoe Workers of America; United
    Charter union, 1938
State, County and Municipal Workers of America
    Charter union, 1938
    Merged into the United Public Workers of America in 1946
Steelworkers of America; United
    Chartered in 1942
Stone and Allied Products Workers of America; United
    Charter union, 1938
    (Titled Quarry Workers International Union until 1941)
Textile Workers Union of America
    Chartered in 1939
Transport Service Employees of America; United
    Chartered in 1942
Transport Workers Union of America
    Charter union, 1938
Utility Workers Union of America
    Chartered in 1945
Woodworkers of America; International
    Charter union, 1938

CHRONOLOGY

In the listing that follows, the founding dates of national unions included in this volume are arranged chronologically by year. A perusal of the appendix not only reveals periods of accelerated union activity but also indicates the periods during which particular types of workers began to organize. The years used represent the earliest date that a particular organization functioned as a national union.

An Asterisk(*) indicates that the date used was the year in which the union was chartered by a national federation, such as the American Federation of Labor.

1831
New England Association of Farmers, Mechanics and Other Working Men
1834
National Trades' Union
1844
Lowell Female Labor Reform Association
1852
International Typographical Union
1859
International Molders' and Allied Workers' Union
National Union of Machinists and Blacksmiths
1861
American Miners' Association
1862
Sons of Vulcan
1863
Brotherhood of Locomotive Engineers
1864
Cigar Makers' International Union of America

Operative Plasterers' and Cement Masons' International Association of the United States and Canada

1865

Bricklayers, Masons and Plasterers' International Union of America

1866

National Labor Union

1867

Knights of St. Crispin

1868

Glass Bottle Blowers Association of the United States and Canada.

Order of Railway Conductors and Brakemen

1869

Colored National Labor Union

Noble Order of the Knights of Labor

1873

Brotherhood of Locomotive Firemen and Enginemen

1874

International Union of Journeymen Horseshoers of the United States and Canada

1875

Marine Engineers' Beneficial Association

1876

Amalgamated Association of Iron, Steel, and Tin Workers

1877

Granite Cutters' International Association of America

1878

American Flint Glass Workers' Union of North America

International Labor Union

1881

Federation of Organized Trades and Labor Unions of the United States and Canada

United Brotherhood of Carpenters and Joiners of America

1882

American Wire Weavers Protective Association

1883

Brotherhood of Railroad Trainmen

International Wood Carvers' Association of North America

Journeymen Tailors' Union of America

1886

Amalgamated Lithographers of America

American Federation of Labor

Bakery and Confectionery Workers' International Union of America

International Union of United Brewery, Flour, Cereal, Soft Drink and Distillery Workers of America

Order of Railroad Telegraphers

1887

Brotherhood of Maintenance of Way Employes

International Brotherhood of Painters and Allied Trades

International Organization of Masters, Mates, and Pilots

International Spinners Union

Journeymen Barbers, Hairdressers, Cosmetologists and Proprietors' International Union of America

Journeymen Stonecutters' Association of North America

Pattern Makers' League of North America
1888
Brotherhood Railway Carmen of the United States and Canada
International Association of Machinists and Aerospace Workers
Sheet Metal Workers' International Association
1889
Boot and Shoe Workers' Union
International Brotherhood of Blacksmiths, Drop Forgers and Helpers
International Printing Pressmen and Assistants' Union of North America
National Association of Letter Carriers of the United States of America
United Association of Journeymen and Apprentices of the Plumbing and Pipe Fitting Industry of the United States and Canada
1890
Coopers' International Union of North America
International Brotherhood of Pottery and Allied Workers
Retail Clerks International Association
United Mine Workers of America
1891
Hotel and Restaurant Employees and Bartenders International Union
International Brotherhood of Electrical Workers
United Garment Workers of America
1892
Amalgamated Lace Operatives of America
Amalgamated Transit Union
International Brotherhood of Bookbinders
International Longshoremen's Association
International Seamen's Union of America
Upholsterers' International Union of North America
1893
American Railway Union
International Alliance of Theatrical Stage Employees and Moving Picture Machine Operators of the United States and Canada
International Broom and Whisk Makers Union*
International Brotherhood of Boilermakers, Iron Shipbuilders, Blacksmiths, Forgers and Helpers
International Brotherhood of Paper Makers
International Union of Mine, Mill and Smelter Workers
1894
Stove, Furnace and Allied Appliance Workers International Union
Switchmen's Union of North America
United Brick and Clay Workers of America
Window Glass Cutters League of America
1895
Amalgamated Wood Workers' International Union of America
Tobacco Workers International Union
1896
American Federation of Musicians
International Association of Bridge, Structural and Ornamental Iron Workers
International Union of Operating Engineers
Metal Polishers, Buffers, Platers and Allied Workers International Union
United Hatters of North America

1897

Amalgamated Meat Cutters and Butcher Workmen of North America

1898

American Labor Union

International Brotherhood of Firemen and Oilers

1899

Brotherhood of Railway, Airline and Steamship Clerks, Freight Handlers, Express and Station Employees

Federación Libre de los Trabajadores de Puerto Rico

International Association of Siderographers

International Brotherhood of Oil and Gas Well Workers

International Brotherhood of Teamsters, Chauffeurs, Warehousemen and Helpers of America

United National Association of Post Office Clerks

Wood, Wire and Metal Lathers International Union

1900

International Ladies' Garment Workers' Union

Laundry, Dry Cleaning and Dye House Workers' International Union*

1901

International Association of Marble, Slate and Stone Polishers, Rubbers and Sawyers, Tile and Marble Setters' Helpers and Marble Mosaic and Terrazzo Workers' Helpers

International Union of Elevator Constructors

Paving Cutters' Union of the United States of America and Canada

United Textile Workers of America

1902

International Glove Workers Union of America

International Plate Printers', Die Stampers' and Engravers' Union of North America

International Stereotypers', Electrotypers', and Platemakers' Union of North America

1903

International Alliance of Bill Posters, Billers and Distributors of America*

International Shingle Weavers Union of America

Laborers' International Union of North America

National Rural Letter Carriers' Association

United Stone and Allied Products Workers of America

United Telegraph Workers

Women's Trade Union League

1904

International Association of Heat and Frost Insulators and Asbestos Workers*

International Photo Engravers Union of North America

1905

Industrial Workers of the World

1906

International Brotherhood of Pulp, Sulphite and Paper Mill Workers

National Federation of Post Office Clerks

1908

Brotherhood of Railroad Signalmen

National Association of Postal Supervisors

1909

Hebrew Butcher Workers of America

1913

Actors' Equity Association

International Fur and Leather Workers Union
National Alliance of Postal and Federal Employees
1914
Amalgamated Clothing Workers of America
1915
American Federation of Hosiery Workers
1916
American Federation of Teachers
International Jewelry Workers Union
1917
American Train Dispatchers Association
Leather Workers' International Union of America
Loyal Legion of Loggers and Lumbermen
National Federation of Federal Employees
1918
American Federation of Technical Engineers
International Association of Fire Fighters
Oil Workers International Union
Pan-American Federation of Labor
Railroad Yardmasters of America
1919
Amalgamated Textile Workers of America
Associated Actors and Artistes of America
United Slate, Tile and Composition Roofers, Damp and Waterproof Workers Association
1920
International Metal Engravers and Marking Device Workers Union
1921
Service Employees International Union
1923
United Wall Paper Craftsmen and Workers of North America
1924
National Federation of Post Office Motor Vehicle Employees
1925
Brotherhood of Sleeping Car Porters
1928
National Textile Workers Union
National Miners' Union
Needle Trades Workers Industrial Union
1929
Trade Union Unity League
1931
American Communications Association
International Air Line Pilots Association
1932
American Federation of Government Employees
National Association of Special Delivery Messengers
Progressive Mine Workers of America
1933
Mechanics Educational Society of America
National Association of Broadcast Employees and Technicians
Screen Actors Guild

The Newspaper Guild
United Electrical, Radio, and Machine Workers of America
1934
Industrial Union of Marine and Shipbuilding Workers of America
Southern Tenant Farmers Union
United Glass and Ceramic Workers of North America
United Hatters, Cap and Millinery Workers' International Union
1935
Congress of Industrial Organizations
United Automobile, Aerospace and Agricultural Implement Workers of America, International Union,
Negro Labor Committee
American Federation of State, County, and Municipal Employees
United Rubber, Cork, Linoleum and Plastics Workers of America
1936
American Guild of Musical Artists
District 50, Allied and Technical Workers of the United States and Canada; International Union of
United Cement, Lime and Gypsum Workers International Union
1937
American Federation of Television and Radio Artists*
Food, Tobacco, Agricultural and Allied Workers Union of America
International Leather Goods, Plastics and Novelty Workers' Union
International Longshoremen's and Warehousemen's Union
International Woodworkers of America
National Maritime Union of America
Retail, Wholesale and Department Store Union
State, County and Municipal Workers of America
Transport Workers Union of America
United Federal Workers of America
United Furniture Workers of America
United Office and Professional Workers of America, International
United Packinghouse, Food and Allied Workers
United Shoe Workers of America
United Transport Service Employees of America
1938
Playthings, Jewelry and Novelty Workers' International Union
Seafarers International Union of North America
1939
Allied Industrial Workers of America, International Union
Communications Workers of America
Textile Workers Union of America
1940
Distillery, Rectifying, Wine and Allied Workers International Union of America
International Chemical Workers Union
1941
Foreman's Association of America
1942
United Farm Equipment and Metal Workers of America
United Gas, Coke and Chemical Workers of America
United Steelworkers of America

1944
United Paperworkers of America
1945
Office and Professional Employees International Union
Utility Workers Union of America
1946
Major League Baseball Players Association
United Public Workers of America
1948
American Federation of Grain Millers International Union
Confederación Interamericana de Trabajadores
International Union, United Plant Guard Workers of America
National Association of Post Office and General Service Maintenance Employees
1949
American Radio Association
International Union of Electrical, Radio and Machine Workers
The Alliance of Independent Telephone Workers
1951
Insurance Agents International Union
Organizacion Regional Interamerica de Trabajadores
1953
Aluminum Workers International Union
Insurance Workers of America
1954
Writers Guild of America
1955
American Federation of Labor-Congress of Industrial Organizations
Oil, Chemical and Atomic Workers International Union
1957
United Papermakers and Paperworkers
1958
Laundry and Dry Cleaning International Union
National Postal Union
1959
Insurance Workers International Union
1960
Negro American Labor Council
1961
United Federation of Postal Clerks
1962
United Farm Workers' Union
1964
Association of Western Pulp and Paper Workers
Lithographers and Photoengravers International Union
1967
National Hockey League Players' Association
1969
United Transportation Union
1970
National Football League Players Association

1971

American Postal Workers Union

1972

Graphic Arts International Union
United Paperworkers International Union

1973

International Printing and Graphic Communications Union

UNION
GENEALOGIES

This appendix contains a description of the historical evolution of each national union included in the volume. The genealogies include changes in union title, mergers, and amalgamations that significantly changed the character or jurisdictional scope of the union and, if relevant, an explanation of the union's demise.

Indented entries preceded by a ")" indicate that those unions merged to create the union listed immediately below.

Actors and Artistes of America; Associated
　　　　)Actors National Protective Union, 1896-1910
　　　　)White Rats Actors Union, 1900-1910
　　　White Rats Union of America, 1910-1919
　　　Associated Actors and Artistes of America, 1919-
Actors' Equity Association
　　　Actors' Society of America, 1896-1913
　　　Actors' Equity Association, 1913-
Air Line Pilots Association; International
　　　Air Mail Pilots of America, 1919-1926
　　　Professional Pilots Association, 1926-1928
　　　National Air Pilots Association, 1928-1931
　　　International Air Line Pilots Association, 1931-
Allied Industrial Workers of America; International Union
　　　United Automobile Workers of America, 1939-1956
　　　International Union, Allied Industrial Workers of America, 1956-
Aluminum Workers International Union
　　　Aluminum Workers International Union, 1953-
American Federation of Labor
　　　Federation of Organized Trades and Labor Unions of the United States and Canada, 1881-1886
　　　American Federation of Labor, 1886-1955
　　　(Merged into the American Federation of Labor-Congress of Industrial Organizations)

American Federation of Labor-Congress of Industrial Organizations
)American Federation of Labor, 1886-1955
)Congress of Industrial Organizations, 1938-1955
    American Federation of Labor-Congress of Industrial Organizations, 1955-
American Labor Union
    Western Labor Union, 1898-1902
    American Labor Union, 1902-1905
    (Reorganized as the Industrial Workers of the World)
Asbestos Workers; International Association of Heat and Frost Insulators and
    National Association of Heat, Frost, General Insulators and Asbestos Workers of America,
       1904-1910
    International Association of Heat, Frost, General Insulators and Asbestos Workers of
       America, 1910
    International Association of Heat and Frost Insulators and Asbestos Workers, 1910-
Automobile, Aerospace and Agricultural Implement Workers of America; International Union,
United
    National Council of Automobile Workers' Unions, 1934-1935
    United Automobile Workers of America, 1935-1941
    International Union, United Automobile, Aerospace, and Agricultural Implement Workers
       of America, 1941-
Bakery and Confectionery Workers' International Union of America
    Journeymen Bakers' National Union of North America, 1886-1903
    Bakery and Confectionery Workers' International Union of America, 1903;
)American Bakery and Confectionery Workers' International Union, 1957-1969
         (Merged)
Barbers, Hairdressers, Cosmetologists and Proprietors International Union of America; Journey-
men
    Journeymen Barbers' International Union of America, 1887-1941
    Journeymen Barbers, Hairdressers and Cosmetologists' International Union of America,
       1941-1957
)Barbers and Beauty Culturists Union of America, 1943-1956 (Merged)
    Journeymen Barbers, Hairdressers, Cosmetologists and Proprietors' International Union of
       America, 1957-
Baseball Players Association; Major League
    Major League Baseball Players Association, 1946-
Bill Posters, Billers and Distributors of the United States and Canada; International Alliance of
    National Alliance of Bill Posters and Billers of America, 1903-1908
    International Alliance of Bill Posters and Billers of America, 1908-1940
    International Alliance of Bill Posters and Distributors of the United States and Canada,
       1940-1971
    (Surrendered charter)
Blacksmiths, Drop Forgers and Helpers; International Brotherhood of
    International Brotherhood of Blacksmiths, 1889-1919
    International Brotherhood of Blacksmiths, Drop Forgers and Helpers, 1919-1951
       (Merged with the International Brotherhood of Boilermakers, Iron Shipbuilders, Black-
         smiths, Forgers and Helpers)
Boilermakers, Iron Shipbuilders, Blacksmiths, Forgers and Helpers; International Brotherhood
of
    National Boilermaker and Helpers Protective and Benevolent Union, 1881-1883
)International Brotherhood of Boilermakers and Iron Ship Builders, Protective and
         Benevolent Union of the United States and Canada, 1883-1893

)National Brotherhood of Boilermakers, 1888-1893
International Brotherhood of Boilermakers and Iron Ship Builders of America, 1893-1912
International Brotherhood of Boilermakers, Iron Ship Builders and Helpers of America, 1912-1951
International Brotherhood of Boilermakers, Iron Shipbuilders, Blacksmiths, Forgers and Helpers of America, 1951-

Bookbinders: International Brotherhood of
International Brotherhood of Bookbinders, 1892-1972
(Merged into the Graphic Arts International Union)

Boot and Shoe Workers' Union
)Boot and Shoe Workers International Union, 1889-1895
)Lasters' Protective Union, 1887-1895
Boot and Shoe Workers' Union, 1895-

Brewery, Flour, Cereal, Soft Drink, and Distillery Workers of America: International Union of United
Brewery Workers National Union, 1887-1890
National Union of United Brewery Workmen of the United States, 1890-1902
International Union of United Brewery Workmen, 1902-1917
International Union of United Brewery and Soft Drink Workers of America, 1917-1918
International Union of United Brewery, Flour, Cereal, Soft Drink and Distillery Workers of America, 1918-1972
(Merged with the International Brotherhood of Teamsters, Chauffeurs, Warehousemen and Helpers of America)

Brick and Clay Workers of America; United
National Brick Makers' Alliance, 1896-1901
)International Alliance of Brick, Tile, and Terra Cotta Workers, 1901-1917
)United Brick and Clay Workers, 1915-1917
United Brick and Clay Workers of America, 1917-

Bricklayers, Masons and Plasterers' International Union of America
Bricklayers International Union of the United States of North America, 1865-1868
National Union of Bricklayers of the United States of America, 1868-1887
Bricklayers and Masons International Union of America, 1887-1910
Bricklayers, Masons and Plasterers' International Union of America, 1910-

Broadcast Employees and Technicians; National Association of
Association of Technical Employees, 1933-1940
National Association of Broadcast Engineers and Technicians, 1940-1951
National Association of Broadcast Employees and Technicians, 1951-

Broom and Whisk Makers Union; International
International Broom Makers Union, 1893-1905
International Broom and Whisk Makers Union, 1905-1962
(Disbanded)

Butcher Workers of America; Hebrew
Hebrew Butcher Workers of America, 1909-1921
(Became a local of the Amalgamated Meat Cutters and Butcher Workmen of North America)

Carpenters and Joiners of America; United Brotherhood of
Brotherhood of Carpenters and Joiners, 1881-1888
United Brotherhood of Carpenters and Joiners of America, 1888-

Cement, Lime and Gypsum Workers International Union; United
National Council of United Cement Workers, 1936-1939
United Cement, Lime and Gypsum Workers International Union, 1939-

Chemical Workers Union; International
    International Council of Chemical and Allied Industries Union, 1940-1944
    International Chemical Workers Union, 1944-
Cigarmakers' International Union of America
    National Union of Cigar Makers, 1864-1865
    Cigarmakers' International Union of America, 1865-1974
    (Merged with the Retail, Wholesale and Department Store Union)
Clothing Workers of America; Amalgamated
    Amalgamated Clothing Workers of America, 1914-
Communications Association; American
)American Radio Association, 1931-1932
)Commercial Radiomen's Protective Association, 1931-1932
    American Radio Telegraphists Association, 1932-1937
    American Communications Association, 1937-1966
    (Merged with the International Brotherhood of Teamsters, Chauffeurs, Warehousemen
    and Helpers of America)
Communications Workers of America
    National Federation of Telephone Workers, 1939-1947
    Communications Workers of America, 1947-
Congress of Industrial Organizations
    Committee for Industrial Organization, 1935-1938
    Congress of Industrial Organizations, 1938-1955
    (Merged into the American Federation of Labor-Congress of Industrial Organizations)
Coopers' International Union of North America
    Coopers of North America, 1870-1888
    Coopers National Union, 1888-1891
    Coopers' International Union of North America, 1891-
Distillery, Rectifying, Wine and Allied Workers' International Union of America
    Distillery, Rectifying and Wine Workers International Union, 1940-1962
    Distillery, Rectifying, Wine and Allied Workers' International Union of America, 1962-
District 50, Allied and Technical Workers of the United States and Canada; International Union of
    National Council of Gas and By-Product Coke Workers, 1935-1936
    District 50, United Mine Workers of America, 1936-1968
    International Union of District 50, Allied and Technical Workers of the United States and
    Canada, 1968-1972
    (Merged with the United Steelworkers of America)
Electrical, Radio and Machine Workers; International Union of
    International Union of Electrical, Radio and Machine Workers, 1949-
Electrical, Radio, and Machine Workers of America; United
    American Federation of Radio Workers, 1933
    Radio and Allied Trades National Labor Council, 1933-1936
    United Electrical and Radio Workers of America, 1936-1937
    United Electrical, Radio, and Machine Workers of America, 1937-
Electrical Workers; International Brotherhood of
    National Brotherhood of Electrical Workers of America, 1891-1905
    International Brotherhood of Electrical Workers, 1905-
Elevator Constructors; International Union of
    National Union of Elevator Constructors, 1901-1903
    International Union of Elevator Constructors, 1903-
Engineers; International Union of Operating

National Union of Steam Engineers, 1896-1897
International Union of Steam Engineers, 1897-1912
International Union of Steam and Operating Engineers, 1912-1927
International Union of Operating Engineers, 1927-
Farm Equipment and Metal Workers of America; United
Farm Equipment Workers Organizing Committee, 1938-1942
United Farm Equipment and Metal Workers of America, 1942-1949
(Merged with the United Electrical, Radio, and Machine Workers of America)
Farm Workers' Union; United
National Farm Workers' Association, 1962-1966
United Farm Workers Organizing Committee, 1966-1972
United Farm Workers' Union, 1972-
Farmers Union; Southern Tenant
Southern Tenant Farmers Union, 1934-1937
(Merged with the United Cannery, Packing, and Allied Workers of America, 1937-1939)
Southern Tenant Farmers Union, 1939-194?
(Disappeared)
Federal Employees; National Federation of
National Federation of Federal Employees, 1917-
Federation of Organized Trades and Labor Unions of the United States and Canada
Federation of Organized Trades and Labor Unions of the United States and Canada, 1881-1886
(Merged into the American Federation of Labor)
Fire Fighters; International Association of
International Association of Fire Fighters, 1918-
Firemen and Oilers; International Brotherhood of
International Brotherhood of Stationary Firemen, 1898-1919
International Brotherhood of Firemen and Oilers, 1919-
Food, Tobacco, Agricultural and Allied Workers Union of America
United Cannery, Agricultural, Packing and Allied Workers of America, 1937-1946
Food, Tobacco, Agricultural and Allied Workers Union of America, 1946-1950
(Merged with the Distributive, Processing and Office Workers of America)
Football League Players Association; National
)NFL Players Association, 1956-1970
)AFL Players Association, 1962-1970
National Football League Players Association, 1970-
Foreman's Association of America
Foreman's Association of America, 1941-195?
(Disappeared)
Fur and Leather Workers Union; International
Furriers Union of the United States of America and Canada, 1892-1904
International Association of Fur Workers of the United States and Canada, 1904-1913
International Fur Workers Union of the United States and Canada, 1913-1939
International Fur and Leather Workers Union, 1939-1955
(Merged with the Amalgamated Meat Cutters and Butcher Workmen of North America)
Furniture Workers of America; United
United Furniture Workers of America, 1937-
Garment Workers of America; United
United Garment Workers of America, 1891-
Garment Workers' Union; International Ladies'
International Ladies' Garment Workers' Union, 1900-

Glass Bottle Blowers Association of the United States and Canada
United Green Glass Workers Association, 1890-1895
Glass Bottle Blowers Association of the United States and Canada, 1895-
Glass and Ceramic Workers of North America; United
Federation of Flat Glass Workers of America, 1934-1940
United Glass and Ceramic Workers of North America, 1940-
Glass Cutters League of America; Window
Local Assembly No. 300, Knights of Labor, 1880-1894
Window Glass Cutters' League, 1894-1902
Window Glass Cutters and Flatteners' Association of America, Inc., 1902-1930
Window Glass Cutters' League of America, 1930-1974
(Merged with the Glass Bottle Blowers Association of the United States and Canada)
Glass Workers' Union of North America; American Flint
United Flint Glass Workers, 1878-1912
American Flint Glass Workers' Union of North America, 1912-
Glove Workers Union of America; International
International Glove Workers' Union of America, 1902-1961
(Merged with the Amalgamated Clothing Workers of America)
Government Employees; American Federation of
American Federation of Government Employees, 1932-
Grain Millers International Union; American Federation of
Grain Processors Council, 1936-1939
National Council of Grain Processors, 1939-1948
American Federation of Grain Millers International Union, 1948-
Granite Cutters' International Association of America; The
National Union of Granite Cutters, 1877-1905
The Granite Cutters' International Association of America, 1905-
Graphic Arts International Union
)International Brotherhood of Bookbinders, 1892-1972
)Lithographers and Photoengravers International Union, 1964-1972
Graphic Arts International Union, 1972-
Hatters, Cap and Millinery Workers International Union; United
)United Hatters of North America, 1896-1934
)Cloth Hat, Cap and Millinery Workers International Union, 1901-1934
United Hatters, Cap and Millinery Workers International Union, 1934-
Hatters of North America; United
United Hatters of North America, 1896-1934
(Merged into the United Hatters, Cap and Millinery Workers International Union)
Hockey League Players' Association; National
National Hockey League Players' Association, 1967-
Horseshoers of the United States and Canada; International Union of Journeymen
Journeymen Horseshoers' National Union of the United States of America, 1874-1893
International Union of Journeymen Horseshoers of the United States and Canada, 1893-
Hosiery Workers; American Federation of
American Federation of Full Fashioned Hosiery Workers, 1915-1922
(Affiliated with the United Textile Workers of America and the Textile Workers Union of America, 1922-1948)
American Federation of Hosiery Workers, 1948-1965
(Merged with the Textile Workers Union of America)
Hotel and Restaurant Employees and Bartenders International Union
Waiters and Bartenders' National Union, 1891-1892

Hotel and Restaurant Employees' National Alliance, 1892-1898
Hotel and Restaurant Employes' International Alliance and Bartenders' International
League of America, 1898-1929
Hotel and Restaurant Employes and Beverage Dispensers International Alliance, 1929-1935
Hotel and Restaurant Employes' International Alliance and Bartenders' International
League of America, 1935-1947
Hotel and Restaurant Employees and Bartenders International Union, 1947-
Industrial Workers of the World
Western Labor Union, 1898-1902
American Labor Union, 1902-1905
Industrial Workers of the World, 1905-
Insurance Workers International Union
)Insurance Agents International Union, 1951-1959
)Insurance Workers of America, 1953-1959
Insurance Workers International Union, 1959-
International Labor Union
International Labor Union, 1878-1887
(Disintegrated)
Iron, Steel, and Tin Workers; Amalgamated Association of
)United Sons of Vulcan, 1862-1876
)Associated Brotherhood of Iron and Steel Heaters, Rollers and Roughers of the United
States, 1872-1876
)Iron and Steel Roll Hands Union, 1873-1876
Amalgamated Association of Iron and Steel Workers of the United States, 1876-1897
Amalgamated Association of Iron, Steel, and Tin Workers, 1897-1942
(Dissolved)
Iron Workers; International Association of Bridge, Structural and Ornamental
International Association of Bridge and Structural Ironworkers, 1896-1957
International Association of Bridge, Structural and Ornamental Iron Workers, 1957-
Jewelry Workers' Union; International
International Jewelry Workers' Union, 1916-
Knights of Labor; Noble Order of the
Noble Order of the Knights of Labor, 1869-1917
(Disintegrated)
Knights of St. Crispin; The
The Knights of St. Crispin, 1867-1878
(Disbanded)
Laborers' International Union of North America
International Hod Carriers and Building Laborers' Union of America, 1903-1912
International Hod Carriers' and Common Laborers' Union of America, 1912
International Hod Carriers', Building and Common Laborers' Union of America, 1912-1965
Laborers' International Union of North America, 1965-
Lace Operatives of America; Amalgamated
Amalgamated Lace Curtain Operatives of America, 1892-1912
Charter Society of Amalgamated Lace Operatives of America, 1912-c. 1925
Amalgamated Lace Operatives of America, c. 1925-
Lathers International Union; Wood, Wire and Metal
The Wood, Wire and Metal Lathers International Union, 1899-
Laundry, Dry Cleaning and Dye House Workers' International Union
Shirt, Waist and Laundry Workers International Union, 1900-1909
Laundry Workers International Union, 1909-1956
)International Association of Cleaning and Dye House Workers, 1937-1956

Laundry, Dry Cleaning and Dye House Workers' International Union, 1956-1962
  (Merged with the International Brotherhood of Teamsters, Chauffeurs, Warehousemen
    and Helpers of America)
Laundry and Dry Cleaning International Union
  Laundry and Cleaning Trades International Council, 1958-1959
  Laundry and Dry Cleaning International Union, 1959-
Leather Goods, Plastics and Novelty Workers Union; International
  International Ladies' Handbag, Pocketbook and Novelty Workers Union, 1937-1942
  International Ladies' Handbag, Luggage, Belt and Novelty Workers Union, 1942-1946
  International Handbag, Luggage, Belt and Novelty Workers Union, 1946-1951
  International Leather Goods, Plastics and Novelty Workers Union, 1951-
Leather Workers International Union; United
)United Brotherhood of Leather Workers on Horse Goods, 1896-1917
)Travelers' Goods and Leather Novelty Workers International Union of America,
      1915-1917
  United Leather Workers International Union, 1917-1951
  (Merged with the Amalgamated Meat Cutters and Butcher Workmen of North America)
Letter Carriers of the United States of America; National Association of
  National Association of Letter Carriers of the United States of America, 1889-
Letter Carriers' Association; National Rural
  National Rural Letter Carriers' Association, 1903-
Lithographers and Photoengravers International Union
)Amalgamated Lithographers of America, 1915-1964
)International Photo Engravers of North America, 1904-1964
  Lithographers and Photoengravers International Union, 1964-1972
  (Merged into the Graphic Arts International Union)
Locomotive Engineers; Brotherhood of
  Brotherhood of the Footboard, 1863-1864
  Brotherhood of Locomotive Engineers, 1864-
Locomotive Firemen and Enginemen; Brotherhood of
  Brotherhood of Locomotive Firemen, 1873-1906
  Brotherhood of Locomotive Firemen and Enginemen, 1906-1969
  (Merged into the United Transportation Union)
Longshoremen's Association; International
  National Longshoremen's Association of the United States, 1892-1895
  International Longshoremen's Association, 1895-1902
  International Longshoremen, Marine and Transport Workers' Association of North and
    South America and the Island Possessions, 1902-1908
  International Longshoremen's Association, 1908-
)International Brotherhood of Longshoremen, 1953-1959
Longshoremen's and Warehousemen's Union; International
  International Longshoremen's and Warehousemen's Union, 1937-
Lowell Female Labor Reform Association
  Lowell Female Labor Reform Association, 1844-1846
  Labor Reform League of New England, 1846-1847
  Lowell Female Industrial Reform and Mutual Aid Society, 1847-1848
  (Disbanded)
Machinists and Aerospace Workers; International Association of
  Order of United Machinists and Mechanical Engineers, 1888-1889
  National Association of Machinists, 1889-1891
  International Association of Machinists, 1891-1964
  International Association of Machinists and Aerospace Workers, 1964-

Machinists and Blacksmiths' National Union
    Machinists and Blacksmiths' National Union, 1859-1879
       (Disintegrated)
Maintenance of Way Employes; Brotherhood of
)Order of Railroad Trackmen, 1887-1892
)Brotherhood of Railway Section Foremen of North America, c. 1888-1892
    Brotherhood of Railway Track Foremen of America, 1892-1896
    Brotherhood of Railway Trackmen of America, 1896-1918
)Brotherhood of Maintenance of Way Employees, 1914-1918
    United Brotherhood of Maintenance of Way Employes and Railway Shop Laborers, 1918-1925
    Brotherhood of Maintenance of Way Employes, 1925-
Marble, Slate and Stone Polishers, Rubbers and Sawyers, Tile and Marble Setters' Helpers and Marble Mosaic and Terrazzo Workers' Helpers; International Association of
    International Union of Marble Workers, 1901-1916
    International Association of Marble, Stone and Slate Polishers, Rubbers and Sawyers, 1916-1921
    International Association of Marble, Slate and Stone Polishers, Rubbers and Sawyers, Tile and Marble Setters Helpers, 1921-1931
    International Association of Marble Slate and Stone Polishers, Rubbers and Sawyers, Tile and Marble Setters Helpers and Terrazzo Helpers, 1931-1955
    International Association of Marble, Slate and Stone Polishers, Rubber and Sawyer Tile and Marble Setters' Helpers and Marble Mosaic and Terrazzo Workers' Helpers, 1955-
Marine Engineers' Beneficial Association; National
    National Marine Engineers Association, 1875-1883
    National Marine Engineers' Beneficial Association, 1883-
Marine and Shipbuilding Workers of America; Industrial Union of
    Industrial Union of Marine and Shipbuilding Workers of America, 1934-
Maritime Union of America; National
    National Maritime Union of America, 1937-
Masters, Mates and Pilots of America; International Organization of
    American Brotherhood of Steamboat Pilots, 1887-1891
    American Association of Masters and Pilots of Steam Vessels, 1891-1905
    American Association of Masters, Mates, and Pilots, 1905-1916
    Masters, Mates, and Pilots of America, National Union, 1916-1954
    International Organization of Masters, Mates, and Pilots, 1954-1971
    (Merged with the International Longshoremen's Association)
Meat Cutters and Butcher Workmen of North America; Amalgamated
    Amalgamated Meat Cutters and Butcher Workmen of North America, 1897-
Mechanics Educational Society of America
    Mechanics Educational Society of America, 1933-
Metal Engravers and Marking Device Workers Union; International
    International Metal Engravers' Union, 1920-1950
    International Metal Engravers and Marking Device Workers Union, 1950-1956
    (Merged with the International Association of Machinists)
Metal Polishers, Buffers, Platers and Allied Workers International Union
    International Brotherhood of Brass Workers, 1890-1892
)Metal Polishers, Buffers, and Platers' International Union of North America, 1892-1896
)National Trades Assembly No. 252, Knights of Labor, 1888-1895
)United Brotherhood of Brass Workers, 1892-1895

United Brotherhood of Brass and Composition Metal Workers, Polishers and Buffers, 1895-1896

Metal Polishers, Buffers and Platers' International Union, 1896-1912

Metal Polishers, Buffers, Brass and Silver Workers Union of North America, 1912-1917

Metal Polishers International Union, 1917-1936

Metal Polishers, Buffers, Platers and Helpers International Union, 1936-1970

Metal Polishers, Buffers, Platers and Allied Workers International Union, 1970-

Mine, Mill and Smelter Workers; International Union of

Western Federation of Miners, 1893-1916

International Union of Mine, Mill and Smelter Workers, 1916-1967

(Merged with the United Steelworkers of America)

Mine Workers of America; Progressive

Progressive Mine Workers of America, 1932-

Mine Workers of America; United

)National Federation of Miners and Mine Laborers, 1885-1888

)Mine and Mine Laborers National District Assembly No. 135, Knights of Labor, 1886-1888

National Progressive Union of Miners and Mine Laborers, 1888-1890

United Mine Workers of America, 1890-

Miners' Association; American

Miners' Association, 1861-1863

American Miners' Association, 1863-c. 1866

(Disintegrated)

Miners' Union; National

National Miners' Union, 1928-1935

Molders and Allied Workers Union; International

National Union of Iron Molders, 1859-1861

Iron Molders' Union of America, 1861-1863

Iron Molders' International Union, 1863-1874

Iron Molders' Union of North America, 1874-1907

International Molders' Union of North America, 1907-1934

International Molders and Foundry Workers Union of North America, 1934-1961

International Molders and Allied Workers Union, 1961-

Musical Artists; American Guild of

American Guild of Musical Artists, 1937-

Musicians; American Federation of

American Federation of Musicians, 1896-

National Labor Union

National Union, 1866-1872

(Disintegrated)

National Labor Union; Colored

Colored National Labor Union, 1869-1871

(Merged with the Southern States Convention of Colored Men)

National Trades' Union

National Trades' Union, 1834-1837

(Disintegrated)

Needle Trades Workers Industrial Union

Needle Trades Workers Industrial Union, 1928-1935

(Disbanded)

Negro American Labor Council

Negro American Labor Council, 1960-

Negro Labor Committee
    Negro Labor Committee, 1935-?
New England Association of Farmers, Mechanics, and Other Working Men
    New England Association of Farmers, Mechanics, and Other Working Men, 1831-1834
        (Disintegrated)
Newspaper Guild; The
    American Newspaper Guild, 1933-1970
    The Newspaper Guild, 1970-
Office and Professional Employees International Union
    International Council of Office and Employees Union, 1942-1945
    Office Employees International Union, 1945-1965
    Office and Professional Employees International Union, 1965-
Office and Professional Workers of America, International; United
    United Office and Professional Workers of America, International, 1937-1950
        (Merged into the Distributive, Processing and Office Workers of America)
Oil, Chemical and Atomic Workers International Union
)Oil Workers International Union, 1937-1955
)United Gas, Coke, and Chemical Workers International Union, 1942-1955
    Oil, Chemical and Atomic Workers International Union, 1955-
Oil and Gas Well Workers; International Brotherhood of
    International Brotherhood of Oil and Gas Well Workers, 1899-1905
        (Disintegrated)
Oil Workers International Union
    International Association of Oil Field, Gas Well and Refinery Workers of America, 1918-1937
    Oil Workers International Union, 1937-1955
        (Merged into the Oil, Chemical and Atomic Workers International Union)
Packinghouse, Food and Allied Workers; United
    Packinghouse Workers Organizing Committee, 1937-1943
    United Packinghouse Workers of America, 1943-1960
    United Packinghouse, Food and Allied Workers, 1960-1968
        (Merged with the Amalgamated Meat Cutters and Butcher Workmen of North America)
Painters and Allied Trades; International Brotherhood of
    Brotherhood of Painters and Decorators, 1887-1890
    Brotherhood of Painters, Decorators, and Paperhangers of America, 1890-1969
    International Brotherhood of Painters and Allied Trades, 1969-
Paper Makers; International Brotherhood of
)United Brotherhood of Paper Makers of America, 1893-1902
)International Brotherhood of Paper Makers, 1898-1902
    International Brotherhood of Paper Makers, 1902-1903
    International Brotherhood of Paper Makers, Pulp, Sulphite and Paper Mill Workers, 1903-1909
    International Brotherhood of Paper Makers, 1909-1957
        (Merged into the United Papermakers and Paperworkers)
Papermakers and Paperworkers; United
)International Brotherhood of Paper Makers, 1893-1957
)United Paperworkers of America, 1946-1957
    United Papermakers and Paperworkers, 1957-1972
        (Merged into United Paperworkers International Union)
Paperworkers of America; United
    Paper Workers Organizing Committee, 1944-1946

United Paperworkers of America, 1946-1957
(Merged into the United Papermakers and Paperworkers)
Paperworkers International Union; United
)United Papermakers and Paperworkers, 1957-1972
)International Brotherhood of Pulp, Sulphite and Paper Mill Workers, 1909-1972
United Paperworkers International Union, 1972-
Pattern Makers' League of North America
Pattern Makers' League of North America, 1887-
Paving Cutters' Union of the United States of America and Canada
Paving Cutters' Union of the United States of America and Canada, 1901-1955
(Disbanded)
Plant Guard Workers of America; International Union, United
Plant Guards Organizing Committee, 1948
United, International Union, Plant Guard Workers of America, 1948-
Plasterers' and Cement Masons' International Association of the United States and Canada;
Operative
National Plasterers' Organization of the United States, 1864-1889
Operative Plasterers International Association of the United States and Canada, 1889-1915
Operative Plasterers' and Cement Finishers' International Association of the United States
and Canada, 1915-1950
Operative Plasterers' and Cement Masons' International Association of the United States
and Canada, 1950-
Plate Printers', Die Stampers' and Engravers' Union of North America; International
National Steel and Copper Plate Printers of the United States of America, 1892-1901
International Steel and Copper Plate Printers of North America, 1901-1921
International Plate Printers and Die Stampers Union of North America, 1921-1925
International Plate Printers, Die Stampers and Engravers' Union of North America, 1925-
Playthings, Jewelry and Novelty Workers' International Union
International Union, Playthings and Novelty Workers of America, 1938-1940
United, International Union, Paper, Novelty and Toy Workers, 1940-1944
Playthings, Jewelry and Novelty Workers' International Union, 1944-1954
(Merged with the Retail, Wholesale and Department Store Union)
Plumbing and Pipe Fitting Industry of the United States and Canada; United Association of Jour-
neymen and Apprentices of the
National Association of Plumbers, Steam Fitters and Gas Fitters, 1884-1885
International Association of Plumbers, Steam Fitters and Gas Fitters, 1885-1889
United Association of Journeymen Plumbers, Gas Fitters, Steam Fitters and Steam Fitters
Helpers of the United States and Canada, 1889-1913
United Association of Plumbers and Steam Fitters of the United States and Canada, 1913-
1947
United Association of Journeymen and Apprentices of the Plumbing and Pipe Fitting Indus-
try of the United States and Canada, 1947-
Postal Clerks; United Federation of
)National Federation of Post Office Clerks, 1906-1961
)United National Association of Post Office Clerks, 1899-1961
)National Postal Transport Association, 1874-1961
United Federation of Postal Clerks, 1961-1971
(Merged into the American Postal Workers Union)
Postal and Federal Employees; National Alliance of
National Alliance of Postal Employees, 1913-1965
National Alliance of Postal and Federal Employees, 1965-

Postal Supervisors, National Association of
    National Association of Postal Supervisors, 1908-
Postal Workers Union; American
)United Federation of Postal Clerks, 1961-1971
)National Postal Union, 1958-1971
)National Association of Post Office and General Service Maintenance Employees, 1937-
        1971
)National Association of Special Delivery Messengers, 1932-1971
)National Federation of Post Office Motor Vehicle Employees, 1920-1971
    American Postal Workers Union, 1971-
Pottery and Allied Workers; International Brotherhood of
    Brotherhood of Operative Potters, 1890-1899
    National Brotherhood of Operative Potters, 1899-1952
    International Brotherhood of Operative Potters, 1952-1957
    International Brotherhood of Pottery and Allied Workers, 1957-
Printing and Graphic Communications Union; International
)International Printing Pressmen and Assistants' Union of North America, 1889-1973
)International Stereotypers', Electrotypers', and Platemakers' Union of North America,
        1903-1973
    International Printing and Graphic Communications Union, 1973-
Public Workers of America; United
)United Federal Workers of America, 1937-1946
)State, County and Municipal Workers of America, 1937-1946
    United Public Workers of America, 1946-?
    (Disappeared)
Pulp and Paper Workers; Association of Western
    Association of Western Pulp and Paper Workers, 1964-
Pulp, Sulphite and Paper Mill Workers; International Brotherhood of
    International Brotherhood of Pulp, Sulphite and Paper Mill Workers, 1909-1972
        (Merged into the United Paperworkers International Union)
Radio Association; American
    American Radio Association, 1931
    American Radio Telegraphists Association, 1931-1937
    American Communications Association, 1937-1949
    American Radio Association, 1949-
Railroad Signalmen; Brotherhood of
    Brotherhood of Railroad Signalmen, 1901-
Railroad Telegraphers; Order of
)Order of Railway Telegraphers of North America, 1886-1891
)Brotherhood of Railway and Commercial Telegraphers, c. 1890-1891
    Order of Railroad Telegraphers, 1891-1965
    Transportation-Communication Employees Union, 1965-1969
        (Merged with the Brotherhood of Railway, Airline and Steamship Clerks, Freight Hand-
        lers, Express and Station Employees)
Railroad Trainmen; Brotherhood of
    Brotherhood of Railroad Brakemen, 1883-1890
    Brotherhood of Railroad Trainmen, 1890-1969
        (Merged into the United Transportation Union)
Railroad Yardmasters of America
    Railroad Yardmasters of America, 1918-

Railway, Airline and Steamship Clerks, Freight Handlers, Express and Station Employees;
Brotherhood of
    Order of Railroad Clerks of America, 1899-1919
    Brotherhood of Railway and Steamship Clerks, Freight Handlers, Express and Station Em-
       ployees, 1919-1967
    Brotherhood of Railway, Airline and Steamship Clerks, Freight Handlers, Express and
       Station Employees, 1967-
Railway Carmen of the United States and Canada; Brotherhood
)Brotherhood of Car Repairers of North America, 1888-1890
)Carmen's Mutual Aid Association, 1888-1890
    Brotherhood Railway Carmen of the United States and Canada, 1890-
Railway Conductors and Brakemen; Order of
)The Conductors Union, 1868
)Conductors' Union, 1868
    Conductors' Brotherhood, 1868-1878
    Order of Railway Conductors of America, 1878-1954
    Order of Railway Conductors and Brakemen, 1954-1969
    (Merged into the United Transportation Union)
Railway Union; American
    American Railway Union, 1893-1897
    (Disintegrated)
Retail Clerks International Association
    Retail Clerks National Protective Association, 1890-1899
    Retail Clerks International Protective Association, 1899-1943
    Retail Clerks International Association, 1943-
Retail, Wholesale and Department Store Union
    United Retail Employes of America, 1937-1940
    United Retail, Wholesale and Department Store Employes of America, 1940-1954
    Retail, Wholesale and Department Store Union, 1954-
Roofers, Damp and Waterproof Workers Association; United Slate, Tile and Composition
)International Slate and Tile Roofers Union of America, 1902-1919
)International Brotherhood of Composition Roofers, Damp and Waterproof Workers of
          the United States and Canada, 1906-1919
    United Slate, Tile and Composition Roofers, Damp and Waterproof Workers Association,
       1919-
Rubber, Cork, Linoleum and Plastics Workers of America; United
    Rubber Workers' Council, 1934-1935
    United Rubber Workers of America, 1935-1946
    United Rubber, Cork, Linoleum and Plastics Workers of America, 1946-
Screen Actors Guild
    Screen Actors Guild, 1933-
Sailors' Union of the Pacific
    Sailors' Union of the Pacific, 1891-1892
    (Merged into the National Seamen's Union)
Seafarers International Union of North America
    Seafarers International Union of North America, 1938-
Seamen's Union of America; International
)Coast Seamen's Union, 1885-1892
)Steamshipmen's Protective Union of San Francisco, 1886-1892
    National Seamen's Union, 1892-1895

International Seamen's Union of America, 1895-1938
   (Disintegrated)
Service Employees International Union
   Building Service Employees International Union, 1921-1968
   Service Employees International Union, 1968-
Sheet Metal Workers' International Association
   Tin, Sheet Iron and Cornice Workers' International Association, 1888-1896
)Amalgamated Sheet Metal Workers' International Association, 1896-1903
)Sheet Metal Workers National Alliance, 1902-1903
   Amalgamated Sheet Metal Workers' International Alliance, 1903-1924
   Sheet Metal Workers' International Association, 1924-
Shoe Workers of America; United
   United Shoe and Leather Workers Union, 1933-1937
   United Shoe Workers of America, 1937-
Siderographers; International Association of
   Steel Plate Transferrers' Association, 1899-1921
   International Association of Siderographers, 1921-
Sleeping Car Porters; Brotherhood of
   Brotherhood of Sleeping Car Porters, 1925-
Spinners Union; International
   National Mulespinners Union, 1887-1898
   National Spinners Union, 1898-1900
   National Mulespinners Union, 1900-1937
   International Spinners Union, 1937-1950
      (Dissolved)
State, County, and Municipal Employees; American Federation of
   American Federation of State, County and Municipal Employees, 1935-
Steelworkers of America; United
   Steel Workers Organizing Committee, 1936-1942
   United Steelworkers of America, 1942-
Stone and Allied Products Workers of America; United
   Quarry Workers' International Union of North America, 1903-1941
   United Stone and Allied Products Workers of America, 1941-1971
      (Merged with the United Steelworkers of America)
Stonecutters' Association of North America; Journeymen
   Journeymen Stonecutters' Association of North America, 1887-1968
      (Merged with the Laborers' International Union of North America)
Stove, Furnace and Allied Appliance Workers International Union
   Stove Mounters International Union, 1894-1962
   Stove, Furnace and Allied Appliance Workers International Union, 1962-
Swtichmen's Union of North America
   Switchmen's Mutual Aid Association of the United States of America, 1886-1894
   Switchmen's Union of North America, 1894-1969
      (Merged into the United Transportation Union)
Tailor's Union of America; Journeymen
   Journeymen Tailors' National Union of the United States, 1883-1887
   Journeymen Tailors' Union of America, 1887-1913
   Tailors' Industrial Union, 1913-1915
   Journeymen Tailors' Union of America, 1915-1938
      (Dissolved)

Teachers; American Federation of
American Federation of Teachers, 1916-
Teamsters, Chauffeurs, Warehousemen and Helpers of America; International Brotherhood of
Team Drivers International Union, 1899-1903
International Brotherhood of Teamsters, 1903-1910
International Brotherhood of Teamsters, Chauffeurs, Stablemen and Helpers of America, 1910-1940
International Brotherhood of Teamsters, Chauffeurs, Warehousemen and Helpers of America, 1940-
Technical Engineers; International Federation of Professional and
International Federation of Draftsmen's Unions, 1918-1919
International Federation of Technical Engineers', Architects' and Draftsmen's Unions, 1919-1953
American Federation of Technical Engineers, 1953-1973
International Federation of Professional and Technical Engineers, 1973-
Telegraph Workers; United
)Commercial Telegraphers Union, 1902-1903
)Order of Commercial Telegraphers, 1902-1903
Commercial Telegraph Union of America, 1903-1968
United Telegraph Workers, 1968-
Telephone Workers; The Alliance of Independent
National Federation of Telephone Workers, Eastern Seaboard Group, 1947-1949
The Alliance of Independent Telephone Workers, 1949-
Television and Radio Artists; American Federation of
American Federation of Radio Artists, 1937-1952
American Federation of Television and Radio Artists, 1952-
Textile Workers of America; Amalgamated
Amalgamated Textile Workers of America, 1919-1926
(Disappeared)
Textile Workers of America; United
)International Union of Textile Workers, 1890-1901
)American Federation of Textile Operatives, 1900-1901
United Textile Workers of America, 1901-
Textile Workers Union of America
Textile Workers Organizing Committee, 1937-1939
Textile Workers Union of America, 1939-
Textile Workers Union; National
National Textile Workers Union, 1928-1935
(Disbanded)
Theatrical Stage Employees and Moving Picture Machine Operators of the United States and Canada; International Alliance of
National Alliance of Theatrical Stage Employes of the United States, 1893-1899
National Alliance of Theatrical Stage Employes of the United States and Canada, 1899-1902
International Alliance of Theatrical Stage Employes of the United States and Canada, 1902-1914
International Alliance of Theatrical Stage Employees and Moving Picture Machine Operators of the United States and Canada, 1914-
Timber Workers; International Union of
International Shingle Weavers Union of America, 1903-1913
International Union of Shingle Weavers, Sawmill Workers and Woodsmen, 1913-1916

International Shingle Weavers Union of America, 1916-1918
International Union of Timber Workers, 1918-1923
(Disbanded)
Tobacco Workers International Union
National Tobacco Workers Union of America, 1895-1899
Tobacco Workers International Union, 1899-
Trade Union Unity League
Trade Union Unity League, 1929-1935
(Disbanded)
Train Dispatchers' Association; American
American Train Dispatchers' Association, 1917-
Transit Union; Amalgamated
Amalgamated Association of Street Railway Employees of America, 1892-1903
Amalgamated Association of Street and Electric Railway Employees of America, 1903-1934
Amalgamated Association of Street, Electric Railway and Motor Coach Employees of America, 1934-1965
Amalgamated Transit Union, 1965-
Transport Service Employees of America; United
International Brotherhood of Red Caps, 1937-1940
United Transport Service Employees of America, 1940-1972
(Merged with the Brotherhood of Railway, Airline and Steamship Clerks, Freight Handlers, Express and Station Employees)
Transport Workers Union of America
Transport Workers Union of America, 1937-
Transportation Union; United
)Brotherhood of Railroad Trainmen, 1883-1969
)Brotherhood of Locomotive Firemen and Enginemen, 1873-1969
)Order of Railway Conductors and Brakemen, 1868-1969
)Switchmen's Union of North America, 1886-1969
United Transportation Union, 1969-
Typographical Union; International
National Typographical Union, 1852-1869
International Typographical Union, 1869-
Upholsterers' International Union of North America
Upholsterers' International Union of America, 1892-1922
Upholsterers' International Union of North America, 1922-
Utility Workers Union of America
)Utility Workers Organizing Committee, 1938-1945
)Brotherhood of Consolidated Edison Employees, 1940-1945
Utility Workers Union of America, 1945-
Wall Paper Craftsmen and Workers of North America; United
)National Association of Machine Printers and Color Mixers, 1902-1923
)National Print Cutters Association of America, 1902-1923
United Wall Paper Crafts of North America, 1923-1938
United Wall Paper Craftsmen and Workers of North America, 1938-1958
(Merged with the International Brotherhood of Pulp, Sulphite and Paper Mill Workers of the United States and Canada)
Wire Weavers Protective Association; American
American Wire Weavers Protective Association, 1882-1959
(Merged with the United Papermakers and Paperworkers)

Women's Trade Union League
    Women's Trade Union League, 1903-1947
      (Dissolved)
Wood Carvers' Association of North America; International
    International Wood Carvers' Association of North America, 1883-1945
      (Disbanded)
Wood Workers' International Union of America; Amalgamated
    Der Gewerkschafts Union der Moebel-Arbeiter Nord Amerika, 1873-1882
)International Furniture Workers' Union of America, 1882-1895
)Machine Wood Workers' International Union, 1890-1895
    Amalgamated Wood Workers' International Union of America, 1895-1912
      (Merged with the United Brotherhood of Carpenters and Joiners)
Woodworkers of America; International
    International Woodworkers of America, 1937-
Workingmen's Benevolent Association
    Workingmen's Benevolent Association, 1868-1875
      (Disintegrated)
Writers Guild of America
    Writers Guild of America, 1954-

EXECUTIVE LEADERSHIP
(selected unions)

In the following appendix the chief executive officers of selected national unions are identified. Although in most instances those listed were union presidents, it was not unusual during the late nineteenth and early twentieth centuries for the secretary, who was often the only full-time officer, to be the chief executive officer of a union. A number of unions, especially in the early years of the labor movement, also used elaborate fraternal titles for union officials.

In cases where the names and effective dates of union leaders were not located or where the union continued to exist primarily as a paper organization, ellipses enclosed by parentheses and followed by the pertinent dates are used: (. . . . .), 1900-1910.

Actors' Equity Association
> Francis Wilson, 1913-1920
> John Emerson, 1920-1928
> Frank Gilmore, 1928-1937
> Arthur Byron, 1937-1940
> Bert Lytell, 1940-1946
> Clarence Derwent, 1946-1952
> Ralph Bellamy, 1952-1964
> Frederick O'Neal, 1964-1973
> Theodore Bikel, 1973-

Air Line Pilots Association; International
> David Behncke, 1931-1951
> Clarence W. Sayen, 1951-1962
> Charles H. Ruby, 1962-1970
> John J. O'Donnell, 1970-

American Federation of Labor
> Samuel Gompers, 1886-1924
> William Green, 1924-1952
> George Meany, 1952-1955

American Federation of Labor-Congress of Industrial Organizations
 George Meany, 1955-
American Labor Union
 Daniel MacDonald, 1898-1905
Automobile, Aerospace and Agricultural Implement Workers of America; International Union, United
 Warren H. Martin, 1936-1939
 Roland J. Thomas, 1939-1946
 Walter P. Reuther, 1946-1970
 Leonard F. Woodcock, 1970-
Bakery and Confectionery Workers' International Union of America
 (. . . . . .), 1886-1907
 Andrew A. Myrup, 1907-1943
 Herman Winter, 1943-1950
 William F. Schnitzler, 1950-1952
 James G. Cross, 1952-1960
 Daniel E. Conway, 1960-
Baseball Players Association; Major League
 Marvin Miller, 1966-
Boilermakers, Iron Shipbuilders, Blacksmiths, Forgers and Helpers; International Brotherhood of
 Lee Johnson, 1893-1897
 John McNeil, 1897-1906
 George F. Dunn, 1906-1908
 J. A. Franklin, 1908-1944
 Charles J. MacGowan, 1944-1954
 William A. Calvin, 1954-1962
 Russell K. Berg, 1962-1970
 Harold J. Buoy, 1970-
Bricklayers, Masons and Plasterers' International Union of America
 John A. White, 1865-1867
 John S. Front, 1867-1869
 Samuel Gaul, 1869-1870
 John O'Keefe, 1870-1871
 Meredith Moore, 1871-1872
 James T. Kirby, 1872-1874
 Stephen A. Carr, 1874-1875
 Lewis Carpenter, 1875-1877
 Charles H. Rihl, 1877-1878
 Lewis Carpenter, 1878-1879
 Thomas R. Gockel, 1879-1881
 E. J. O'Rourk, 1881-1882
 Henry O. Cole, 1882-1884
 John Pearson, 1884-1885
 Thomas R. Gockel, 1885-1886
 Alexander Darragh, 1886-1890
 Alfred J. McDonald, 1890-1891
 John Heartz, 1891-1894
 William Klein, 1894-1901
 George P. Gibbins, 1901-1904
 William J. Bowen, 1904-1928
 George T. Thornton, 1928-1935

Harry C. Bates, 1935-1967
Thomas F. Murphy, 1967-

Carpenters and Joiners of America; United Brotherhood of
Peter J. McGuire, 1881-1901
William Huber, 1901-1912
James Kirby, 1912-1915
William L. Hutcheson, 1915-1952
Maurice A. Hutcheson, 1952-1972
William Sidell, 1972-

Chemical Workers Union; International
H. A. Bradley, 1940-1954
Edward R. Moffet, 1954-1956
Walter R. Mitchell, 1956-1968
Thomas E. Boyle, 1968-

Cloth Hat, Cap and Millinery Workers' International Union
Maurice Mikol, 1901-1904
Max Zuckerman, 1904-1919
Max Zaritsky, 1919-1925
(Interim Committee), 1925-1927
Max Zaritsky, 1927-1934

Clothing Workers of America; Amalgamated
Sidney Hillman, 1914-1946
Jacob S. Potofsky, 1946-1972
Murray H. Finley, 1972-

Communications Workers of America
Joseph A. Beirne, 1943-1973
Glenn E. Watts, 1973-

Congress of Industrial Organizations
John L. Lewis, 1938-1940
Philip Murray, 1940-1952
Walter P. Reuther, 1952-1955

Electrical, Radio and Machine Workers; International Union of
James B. Carey, 1949-1965
Paul Jennings, 1965-

Electrical, Radio, and Machine Workers of America; United
James B. Carey, 1935-1941
Albert J. Fitzgerald, 1941-

Electrical Workers; International Brotherhood of
Henry Miller, 1891-1893
Quinn Jansen, 1893-1894
H. W. Sherman, 1894-1897
J. A. Maloney, 1897-1899
Thomas Wheeler, 1899-1901
W. A. Jackson, 1901-1903
Frank J. McNulty, 1903-1919
J. P. Noonan, 1919-1929
H. H. Broach, 1929-1933
Daniel W. Tracy, 1933-1940
Edward J. Brown, 1940-1947
Daniel W. Tracy, 1947-1954
J. Scott Milne, 1954-1955

Gordon M. Freeman, 1955-1968
Charles H. Pillard, 1968-
Elevator Constructors; International Union of
    F. W. Doyle, 1901-1916
    Frank Feeney, 1916-1938
    John MacDonald, 1938-1955
    Edward A. Smith, 1955-1959
    Thomas Allen, 1959-1962
    John Proctor, 1962-1966
    R. Wayne Williams, 1966-
Engineers; International Union of Operating
    C. J. DeLong, 1896-1897
    Frank Bowker, 1897-1898
    Frank Pfohl, 1898
    S. L. Bennett, 1898-1899
    P. A. Peregrine, 1899-1900
    Frank B. Monaghan, 1900-1901
    George Lighthall, 1901-1903
    Patrick McMahon, 1903-1904
    John E. Bruner, 1904-1905
    Mat Comerford, 1905-1916
    Milton Snellings, 1916-1921
    Arthur Huddell, 1921-1931
    Dave Evans, 1931
    John Possehl, 1931-1940
    William E. Maloney, 1940-1958
    Joseph J. Delaney, 1958-1962
    Hunter P. Wharton, 1962-
Farm Equipment and Metal Workers of America; United
    Grant W. Oakes, 1942-1954
Farm Workers' Union; United
    Cesar F. Chavez, 1972-
Farmers Union; Southern Tenant
    Harry L. Mitchell, 1934-1944
Fire Fighters; International Association of
    Thomas G. Spellacy, 1918-1919
    Samuel A. Fink, 1919
    Fred W. Baer, 1919-1946
    John P. Redmond, 1946-1957
    William D. Buck, 1957-1968
    William H. McClennan, 1968-
Food, Tobacco, Agricultural and Allied Workers Union of America
    Donald Henderson, 1937-1950
Football League Players Association; National
    Edward R. Garvey, 1970-
Fur and Leather Workers Union; International
    Albert W. Miller, 1913-1918
    Morris Kaufman, 1918-1925
    Oizer Shachtman, 1925-1929
    Morris Kaufman, 1929-1932
    Ben Gold, 1937-1955

Furniture Workers of America; United
    Morris Muster, 1937-1946
    Morris Pizer, 1946-1970
    Carl Scarbrough, 1970-
Garment Workers of America; United
    Charles F. Reichers, 1890-1896
    Henry White, 1896-1904
    Thomaš A. Rickert, 1904-1941
    Joseph P. McCurdy, 1941-
Garment Workers' Union; International Ladies'
    Herman Grossman, 1900-1903
    Benjamin Schlesinger, 1903-1904
    James McCauley, 1904-1905
    Herman Grossman, 1905-1907
    Mortimer Julian, 1907-1908
    Abraham Rosenberg, 1908-1914
    Benjamin Schlesinger, 1914-1923
    Morris Sigman, 1923-1928
    Benjamin Schlesinger, 1928-1932
    David Dubinsky, 1932-1966
    Louis Stulberg, 1966-
Glass Bottle Blowers Association of the United States and Canada
    Samuel Simpson, 1876-1880
    Louis Arrington, 1880-1894
    Joseph D. Troth, 1894-1896
    Denis A. Hayes, 1896-1917
    John A. Voll, 1917-1924
    James Maloney, 1924-1946
    Lee W. Minton, 1946-1971
    Newton W. Black, 1971-1972
    Harry A. Tulley, 1972-
Glove Workers Union of America; International
    George H. Taylor, 1902-1906
    B. M. Lowe, 1906-1913
    Agnes Nestor, 1913-1915
    Thomas H. Mahoney, 1915-1931
    Harry Paxton, 1931-1937
    Thomas Durian, 1937-1954
    Joseph C. Goodfellow, 1954-1961
Government Employees; American Federation of
    David R. Glass, 1932
    E. Claude Babcock, 1932-1936
    Charles E. Stengle, 1936-1938
    Cecil E. Custer, 1938-1939
    James B. Burns, 1939-1948
    James G. Yaden, 1948-1950
    Henry Ihler, 1950
    James A. Campbell, 1950-1962
    John F. Griner, 1962-1972
    Clyde M. Webber, 1972-
Graphic Arts International Union
    Kenneth J. Brown, 1964-

Hatters, Cap and Millinery Workers International Union; United
    Michael F. Greene, 1934-1936
    Max Zaritsky, 1936-1950
    Alex Rose, 1950-
Hatters of North America; United
    Edward Bennett, 1896-1898
    John A. Moffitt, 1898-1913
    John W. Sculley, 1913-1918
    Michael F. Greene, 1918-1934
Hockey League Players' Association; National
    R. Alan Eagleson, 1967-
Hotel and Restaurant Employees and Bartenders International Union
    (. . . . .), 1891-1899
    Jere L. Sullivan, 1899-1928 (Secretary)
    Edward Flore, 1911-1945 (President)
    Hugo Ernst, 1945-1954
    Edward S. Miller, 1954-1973
    Edward T. Hanley, 1973-
Industrial Workers of the World
    Charles O. Sherman, 1905-1906
    William Trautmann, 1906-1908
    Vincent St. John, 1908-1915
    William D. Haywood, 1915-1921
    (. . . . .), 1921-
International Labor Union
    George E. McNeill, 1878-1881
    F. A. Sorge, 1881-1887
Knights of Labor; Noble Order of the
    Uriah S. Stephens, 1869-1881
    Terence V. Powderly, 1881-1893
    James R. Sovereign, 1893-1897
    (. . . . .), 1897-
Knights of St. Crispin; The
    William J. McLaughlin, 1868-1871
    Thomas Ryan, 1871-1872
    James P. Wright, 1872-1873
Laborers' International Union of North America
    Herman Lilien, 1903-1904
    Michael Knipfer, 1905
    August Palutze, 1905-1906
    John Breen, 1906-1908
    Domenico D'Alessandro, 1908-1926
    Joseph V. Moreschi, 1926-1968
    Peter Fosco, 1968-
Lathers International Union; Wood, Wire and Metal
    E. J. Bracken, 1900-1901
    A. H. McFall, 1901-1902
    J. W. L. Clark, 1902-1903
    John E. Toale, 1903-1904
    William J. McSorley, 1904-1926
    John E. Bell, 1926-1929
    William J. McSorley, 1929-1955

Lloyd A. Mashburn, 1955-1963
Sal Maso, 1963-1970
Robert A. Georgine, 1970-1971
Kenneth M. Edwards, 1971-
Letter Carriers of the United States of America; National Association of
William H. Wood, 1889-1890
John J. Goodwin, 1890-1893
John W. Parsons, 1893-1899
James C. Keller, 1899-1905
J. D. Holland, 1905-1907
William E. Kelley, 1907-1915
Edward J. Gainor, 1915-1941
William C. Doherty, 1941-1962
Jerome J. Keating, 1962-1968
James H. Rademacher, 1968-
Lithographers of America; Amalgamated
Frank Gehring, 1915-1917
Philip Brock, 1917-1930
Andrew Kennedy, 1930-1939
William J. Riehl. 1939-1947
John Blackburn, 1947-1955
George Canary, 1955-1958
Patrick Slater, 1958-1960
Kenneth Brown, 1960-1964
Lithographers and Photoengravers International Union
Kenneth Brown, 1964-1972
Locomotive Engineers; Brotherhood of
William D. Robinson, 1863-1864
Charles Wilson, 1864-1874
Peter M. Arthur, 1874-1903
A. B. Youngson, 1903
Warren S. Stone, 1903-1924
Alvanley Johnston, 1924-1950
J. P. Shields, 1950-1953
Guy L. Brown, 1953-1960
Roy E. Davidson, 1960-1964
Perry S. Heath, 1964-1969
C. J. Coughlin, 1969-1974
B. N. Whitmire, 1974-
Locomotive Firemen and Enginemen; Brotherhood of
Joshua A. Leach, 1874-1876
William R. Worth, 1876-1878
Frank B. Alley, 1878-1879
William T. Goundie, 1879-1880
Frank W. Arnold, 1880-1885
Frank P. Sargent, 1885-1902
John J. Hannahan, 1902-1908
William S. Carter, 1908-1922
David B. Robertson, 1922-1953
Henry E. Gilbert, 1953-1969
Longshoremen's Association; International
Daniel J. Keefe, 1892-1908

Thomas V. O'Connor, 1908-1921
Anthony Chlopek, 1921-1927
Joseph P. Ryan, 1927-1953
William V. Bradley, 1953-1963
Thomas W. Gleason, 1963-

Longshoremen's and Warehousemen's Union
Harry Bridges, 1937-

Lowell Female Labor Reform Association
Sara Bagley, 1846
Mary Emerson, 1846-1848

Machinists and Aerospace Workers; International Association of
Thomas W. Talbot, 1888-1889
J. J. Creamer, 1889-1892
John O'Day, 1892-1893
James O'Connell, 1893-1911
William H. Johnston, 1911-1926
Arthur O. Wharton, 1926-1938
Harvey W. Brown, 1938-1945
Albert J. Hayes, 1945-1965
P. L. Siemiller, 1965-1969
Floyd E. Smith, 1969-

Maintenance of Way Employes; Brotherhood of
John T. Wilson, 1887-1908
A. B. Lowe, 1908-1914
T. H. Gerrey, 1914
Allan E. Barker, 1914-1920
E. F. Grable, 1920-1922
Frederick H. Fljozdal, 1922-1940
Elmer E. Milliman, 1940-1946
Thomas C. Carroll, 1947-1958
Harold C. Crotty, 1958-

Marine and Shipbuilding Workers of America; Industrial Union of
John Green, 1935-1951
John J. Grogan, 1951-1968
Eugene L. McCabe, 1968-

Maritime Union of America; National
Joseph E. Curran, 1937-1973
Shannon J. Wall, 1973-

Meat Cutters and Butcher Workmen of North America; Amalgamated
Michael Donnelly, 1898-1907
Homer Call, 1897-1917
Dennis Lane, 1917-1942
Patrick E. Gorman, 1942-

Mine, Mill and Smelter Workers; International Union of
Edward Boyce, 1896-1902
Charles H. Moyer, 1902-1926
James B. Rankin, 1926-1936
Reid Robinson, 1936-1946
Maurice E. Travis, 1946-1947
John Clark, 1947-1963
Albert C. Skinner, 1963-1967

Mine Workers of America; United
    John B. Rae, 1890-1892
    John McBride, 1892-1895
    P. H. Penna, 1895-1897
    Michael D. Ratchford, 1897-1898
    John Mitchell, 1898-1908
    Thomas L. Lewis, 1908-1911
    John D. White, 1911-1917
    Frank J. Hayes, 1917-1920
    John L. Lewis, 1920-1960
    William A. Boyle, 1960-1972
    Arnold Miller, 1972-
Miners' Association; American
    Thomas Lloyd, 1861-c. 1862
    Ben Barstow, c.1862-1863
    James W. Thorley, 1863-?
Musicians; American Federation of
    Owen Miller, 1896-1900
    Joseph N. Weber, 1900-1914
    Frank Carothers, 1914-1915
    Joseph N. Weber, 1915-1940
    James C. Petrillo, 1940-1958
    Herman D. Kenin, 1958-1970
    Hal C. Davis, 1970-
National Labor Union
    J. C. C. Whaley, 1866-1868
    William Sylvis, 1868-1869
    Richard Trevellick, 1869-1872
National Labor Union; Colored
    Isaac Myers, 1869-1871
    Frederick Douglass, 1871
National Trades' Union
    Ely Moore, 1834-1835
    Alexander Ferral, 1835-1836
    J. W. Jackson, 1836-1837
Negro American Labor Council
    A. Philip Randolph, 1960-1966
    Cleveland Robinson, 1966-
New England Association of Farmers, Mechanics and Other Working Men
    Charles Douglas, 1832-1834
Newspaper Guild; The
    Heywood C. Broun, 1933-1939
    Milton Murray, 1939-1947
    Harry L. Martin, Jr., 1947-1958
    Arthur Rosenstock, 1958-1966
    James B. Woods, 1966-1968
    Charles A. Perlik, Jr., 1968-
Office and Professional Employees International Union
    Paul R. Hutchings, 1945-1953
    Howard Coughlin, 1953-
Office and Professional Workers of America, International; United
    Lewis Merrill, 1937-1947

James H. Durkin, 1947-1950

Oil, Chemical, and Atomic Workers International Union
Orie A. Knight, 1955-1965
A. F. Grospiron, 1965-

Oil Workers International Union
Grant G. Jacobs, 1918-1919
Robert E. Evans, 1919-1920
Grant G. Jacobs, 1921
H. L. Hope, 1921
John Sheehan, 1921-1925
R. H. Stickel, 1925-1926
Walter Yarrow, 1926-1939
Harvey C. Fremming, 1939-1940
O. A. Knight, 1940-1955

Parkinghouse, Food and Allied Workers; United
Van A. Bittner, 1937-1941
J. C. Lewis, 1941-1942
Sam Sponseller, 1942-1943
Lewis J. Clark, 1943-1946
Ralph Helstein, 1946-1968

Paper Makers; International Brotherhood of
(. . . . .), 1893-1905
J. T. Carey, 1905-1924
F. P. Barry, 1924
W. R. Smith, 1924-1929
Matthew J. Burns, 1929-1940
Arthur Huggins, 1940-1943
Matthew J. Burns, 1943-1947
Paul L. Phillips, 1948-1957

Paperworkers International Union; United
Joseph P. Tonelli, 1972-

Plumbing and Pipe Fitting Industry of the United States and Canada; United Association of Journeymen and Apprentices of the
Patrick J. Quinlan, 1889-1891
John A. Lee, 1891-1892
Patrick H. Gleason, 1892-1893
John A. Lee, 1893-1894
M. J. Moran, 1894-1896
William P. Redmond, 1896-1897
Thomas H. O'Brien, 1897
John J. Kelley, 1897-1901
William M. Merrick, 1901-1906
John P. Alpine, 1906-1919
John Coefield, 1919-1940
George Masterton, 1940-1943
Martin P. Durkin, 1943-1953
Peter T. Schoemann, 1953
Martin P. Durkin, 1953-1955
Peter T. Schoemann, 1955-1971
Martin J. Ward, 1971-

Post Office Clerks; National Federation of
Edward Goltra, 1906-1910

Oscar F. Nelson, 1910-1923
Leo E. George, 1923-1956
J. Cline House, 1956-1960
Elroy C. Hallbeck, 1960-1961
Postal Clerks; United Federation of
Elroy C. Hallbeck, 1961-1969
Francis S. Filbey, 1969-1971
Postal Supervisors; National Association of
L. E. Palmer, 1908-1909
George A. Gasman, 1909-1910
Ernest Green, 1910-1915
William Sansom, 1915-1916
J. J. Fields, 1916-1920
V. C. Burke, 1920-1921
H. M. Tittle, 1921-1923
Peter Wiggle, 1923-1924
Harry Folger, 1924-1929
W. Bruce Luna, 1929-1930
M. F. O'Donnell, 1930-1931
Herschel Ressler, 1931-1937
M. F. Fitzpatrick, 1937-1941
John J. Lane, 1941-1945
John McMahon, 1945-1950
M. C. Nave, 1950-1958
Fred J. O'Dwyer, 1958-1970
Donald N. Ledbetter, 1970-
Postal Workers Union; American
Francis S. Filbey, 1971-
Printing and Graphic Communications Union; International
Sol Fishko, 1973-
Printing Pressmen and Assistants' Union; International
Thomas F. Mahoney, 1889-1890
C. W. Miller, 1890-1892
Theodore F. Galoskowsky, 1892-1897
Jesse Johnson, 1897-1898
James H. Bowman, 1898-1901
Martin P. Higgins, 1901-1907
George L. Berry, 1907-1948
J. H. de la Rosa, 1948-1952
Thomas E. Dunwody, 1952-1960
Anthony J. DeAndrade, 1960-1970
Alexander J. Rohan, 1970-1973
Pulp and Paper Workers; Association of Western
William R. Perrin, 1964-1968
Hugh Bannister, 1968-
Pulp, Sulphite and Paper Mill Workers; International Brotherhood of
James F. Fitzgerald, 1906-1908
J. T. Carey, 1908-1910
John Malin, 1910-1918
John P. Burke, 1918-1965
Joseph P. Tonelli, 1965-1972

Railroad Telegraphers; Order of
    A. D. Thurston, 1886-1892
    D. G. Ramsay, 1892-1894
    Walker V. Powell, 1894-1900
    M. M. Dolphin, 1900-1901
    H. B. Perham, 1901-1919
    E. J. Manion, 1919-1937
    W. H. Robinson, 1937-1939
    Vernon O. Gardner, 1939-1946
    George E. Leighty, 1946-1965
Railroad Trainmen; Brotherhood of
    George Hudson, 1883-1884
    James Grimer, 1884-1885
    S. E. Wilkinson, 1885-1895
    P. H. Morrissey, 1895-1909
    William G. Lee, 1909-1928
    Alexander F. Whitney, 1928-1949
    William P. Kennedy, 1949-1962
    Charles Luna, 1962-1969
Railway Carmen of the United States and Canada; Brotherhood
    W. H. Ronemus, 1888-1891
    W. S. Missemer, 1891-1894
    F. A. Symonds, 1894-1896
    W. H. Ronemus, 1896-1901
    Joseph B. Yeager, 1901-1902
    Frank L. Ronemus, 1902-1909
    Martin F. Ryan, 1909-1935
    Felix H. Knight, 1935-1947
    Irvin Barney, 1947-1957
    A. J. Bernhardt, 1957-1967
    George L. O'Brien, 1967-1971
    Anthony L. Krause, 1971-
Railway Conductors and Brakemen; Order of
    J. C. Coleman, 1868
    A. R. Church, 1868-1869
    A. G. Black, 1869-1870
    C. S. Moore, 1870-1871
    I. N. Hodges, 1871-1872
    J. W. Silsbee, 1872-1873
    G. Z. Cruzen, 1873-1875
    William L. Collins, 1875-1878
    John B. Morford, 1878-1880
    C. S. Wheaton, 1880-1890
    E. E. Clark, 1890-1906
    Austin B. Garretson, 1906-1919
    L. E. Sheppard, 1919-1934
    James A. Phillips, 1934-1941
    Harry W. Fraser, 1941-1950
    Roy O. Hughes, 1950-1958
    J. A. Paddock, 1958-1960
    Louis J. Wagner, 1960-1964

G. H. Harris, 1964-1966
Clyde F. Lane, 1966-1969
Railway Union; American
Eugene Debs, 1893-1897
Retail Clerks International Association
W. S. Pitman, 1891-1892
Ed Mallory, 1892-1909
H. J. Conway, 1909-1926
C. C. Coulter, 1926-1947
James A. Suffridge, 1947-1968
Vernon A. Housewright, 1968-1969
James T. Housewright, 1969-
Retail, Wholesale and Department Store Union
Samuel Wolchok, 1937-1949
Irving Simon, 1949-1954
Max Greenberg, 1954-
Rubber, Cork, Linoleum and Plastics Workers of America; United
Sherman H. Dalrymple, 1935-1941
Leland S. Buckmaster, 1941-1949
H. R. Lloyd, 1949
Leland S. Buckmaster, 1949-1962
Peter Bommarito, 1962-
Screen Actors Guild
Ralph Morgan, 1933
Eddie Cantor, 1933-1935
Robert Montgomery, 1935-1938
Ralph Morgan, 1938-1940
Edward Arnold, 1940-1942
James Cagney, 1942-1944
George Murphy, 1944-1946
Robert Montgomery, 1946-1947
Ronald Reagan, 1947-1952
Walter Pidgeon, 1952-1957
Leon Ames, 1957-1958
Howard Keel, 1958-1959
Ronald Reagan, 1959-1960
George Chandler, 1960-1963
Dana Andrews, 1963-1965
Charlton Heston, 1965-1971
John Gavin, 1971-1973
Dennis Weaver, 1973-
Seafarers' International Union of North America
Harry Lundeberg, 1938-1957
Paul Hall, 1957-
Seamen's Union of America; International
Andrew Furuseth, 1892-1938
Service Employees International Union
William F. Quesse, 1917-1927
Jerry J. Horan, 1927-1937
George Scalise, 1937-1940
William L. McFetridge, 1940-1960
David Sullivan, 1960-1971

George Hardy, 1971-
Sleeping Car Porters; Brotherhood of
Asa Philip Randolph, 1925-1968
C. L. Dellums, 1968-
Special Delivery Messengers; National Association of
Gilbert Mantor, 1932-1940
George L. Warfel, 1940-1965
Michael J. Cullen, 1965-1971
State, County, and Municipal Employees; American Federation of
Arnold S. Zander, 1935-1964
Jerry Wurf, 1964-
Steelworkers of America; United
Philip Murray, 1942-1952
David J. McDonald, 1952-1965
I. W. Abel, 1965-
Teachers; American Federation of
Charles B. Stillman, 1916-1923
Florence Rood, 1923-1926
Mary C. Barker, 1926-1931
Henry R. Linville, 1931-1934
Raymond F. Lowry, 1934-1936
Jerome Davis, 1936-1940
George S. Counts, 1940-1942
John M. Fewkes, 1942-1943
Joseph F. Landis, 1943-1948
John M. Eklund, 1948-1952
Carl J. Megel, 1952-1964
Charles Cogen, 1964-1968
David S. Selden, 1968-1972
Albert Shanker, 1972-
Teamsters, Chauffeurs, Warehousemen and Helpers of America; International Brotherhood of
George Innis, 1899-1903
Cornelius P. Shea, 1903-1907
Daniel J. Tobin, 1907-1952
Dave Beck, 1952-1957
James R. Hoffa, 1957-1971
Frank E. Fitzsimmons, 1971-
Textile Workers of America; Amalgamated
A. J. Muste, 1919-1921
Textile Workers of America; United
J. Tansey, 1901-1903
John Golden, 1903-1921
Thomas F. McMahon, 1921-1937
Francis Gorman, 1937-1938
George Baldanzi, 1938-1939
C. M. Fox, 1939-1941
Francis Gorman, 1941-1944
Anthony Valente, 1944-1958
George Baldanzi, 1958-1972
Francis Schaufenbil, 1972-
Textile Workers Union of America
Emil Rieve, 1939-1956

William Pollock, 1956-1972
Sol Stetin, 1972
Trade Union Unity League
William Z. Foster, 1929-1935
Transit Union; Amalgamated
William J. Law, 1892-1893
William D. Mahon, 1893-1946
Abe L. Spradling, 1946-1959
John M. Elliott, 1959-1972
Dan V. Maroney, Jr., 1972-
Transport Service Employees; United
Willard S. Townsend, 1937-1957
Eugene E. Frazier, 1957-1964
George P. Sabattie, 1964-1972
Transport Workers Union of America
Michael J. Quill, 1937-1966
Matthew Guinan, 1966-
Transportation Union; United
Charles Luna, 1969-1972
Al A. Chessar, 1972-
Typographical Union; International
J. S. Nafew, 1852-1853
Gerard Stith, 1853-1854
Lewis Graham, 1854-1855
Charles F. Town, 1855-1856
M. C. Brown, 1856-1857
William Cuddy, 1857-1858
R. C. Smith, 1858-1860
J. M. Farquhar, 1860-1863
Eugene Valette, 1863-1864
A. M. Carver, 1864-1865
Robert E. Craig, 1865-1866
John H. Oberly, 1866-1868
Robert McKechnie, 1868-1869
Isaac D. George, 1869-1870
W. J. Hammond, 1870-1873
W. R. McLean, 1873-1874
William H. Bodwell, 1874-1875
Walter W. Bell, 1875-1876
John McVicar, 1876-1877
D. R. Streeter, 1877-1878
John Armstrong, 1878-1879
Samuel Haldeman, 1879-1880
William P. Atkinson, 1880-1881
George Clark, 1881-1883
M. L. Crawford, 1883-1884
M. R. H. Witter, 1884-1886
William Aimison, 1886-1888
E. T. Plank, 1888-1891
W. B. Prescott, 1891-1899
Samuel B. Donnelly, 1899-1901
James M. Lynch, 1901-1914

James M. Duncan, 1914
M. G. Scott, 1914-1921
John McParland, 1921-1924
Charles P. Howard, 1924-1925
James M. Lynch, 1925-1926
Charles P. Howard, 1926-1938
Claude M. Baker, 1938-1944
Woodruff Randolph, 1944-1958
John Pitch, 1958-1972
A. Sandy Bevis, 1972-

Utility Workers Union of America
Joseph A. Fisher, 1945-1960
William J. Pachler, 1960-1970
William R. Munger, 1970-1971
Harold T. Rigley, 1971-

Women's Trade Union League
Mary Morton Kehew, 1903-1904
Ellen Martin Henrotin, 1904-1907
Margaret Dreier Robins, 1907-1922
Maud Swartz, 1922-1926
Rose Schneiderman, 1926-1947

Woodworkers of America; International
Harold Pritchett, 1937-1940
O. M. Orton, 1940-1941
Worth Lowery, 1941-1946
James E. Fadling, 1946-1951
A. F. Hartung, 1951-1967
Ronald F. Roley, 1967-1973
Keith Johnson, 1973-

Workingmen's Benevolent Association
John Siney, 1868-1874

MEMBERSHIP
(selected unions)

National union membership figures during selected years are provided in the following table. Reliable membership figures are extremely difficult to locate. For various reasons, national union leaders found it expedient at times to either understate or inflate their membership figures. Moreover, some unions counted retired and unemployed members; others did not.

The two most continuous sets of membership figures are those reported to the Bureau of Labor Statistics, U.S. Department of Labor, and the membership upon which the unions paid per-capita taxes to national federations. Membership figures used in the union sketches were those reported or claimed by the various national unions. In this appendix, however, the membership upon which the unions paid per-capita taxes were used whenever possible. While these figures were often deflated, they extend back to an earlier period than those accumulated by the Bureau of Labor Statistics, and they provide a more accurate picture of membership fluctuations during important periods in the history of the modern American labor movement.

Membership of Selected Unions
(in hundreds)

	1897	1904	1912	1920	1924	1930	1935	1939	1945	1955	1965	1975
Actors and Artistes				69	74	112	43	201	243	340	610	760
Air Line Pilots							7	10	60	90	180	460
Allied Industrial Workers								42	534	730	710	930
Aluminum Workers										200	220	270
American Federation of Labor	2,648	16,762	17,701	40,787	28,658	29,611	32,184	38,780	68,904			
AFL-CIO										126,220	129,190	140,660
Asbestos Workers		7	8	22	22	33	25	40	40	90	120	130
Automobile Workers								1,653	8,918	12,600	11,500	14,000*
Bakery Workers	20	162	146	275	222	200	207	692	961	1,360	620*	1,230
Barbers	22	236	299	442	453	512	323	475	500	650	730	420
Baseball Players												10
Bill Posters		13	14	16	16	16	14	18	16	20	20	
Blacksmiths	3	105	93	483	50	50	50	50	100			
Boilermakers	11	180	167	1,030	175	193	153	290	1,616	1,510	1,080	1,230
Bookbinders	26	65	85	207	134	139	117	177	346	510	510	
Brewery Workers	100	305	625	341	160	160	417	420	644	450	420	
Brick and Clay	8	73	34	52	48	42	16	100	100	230	210	160
Bricklayers	233	563	811	736	700	900	650	650	650	1,200	1,200	1,430
Broadcast Employees								3	N/A	40	40	50
Broom and Whisk	1	11	7	14	7	5	2		4	1		
Cannery Workers								100	400			
Carpenters	282	1,612	1,955	3,719	3,155	3,032	1,288	2,148	4,708	7,500	7,000	7,000
Cement, Lime								132	159	350	300	290
Chemical Workers									244	790	700	580
Cigarmakers	283	468	485	388	277	155	70	70	100	90	40	
Clothing Workers				1,770	N/A	N/A	1,665	2,397	2,215	2,100	2,880	2,320
Communications Association								60	120			
Communications Workers								450	1,760	2,490	2,880	4,760
Congress of Industrial Organizations								18,377	39,279	46,083		
Coopers	15	69	45	43	15	7	29	41	50	30	20	20
Distillery Workers									100	260	240	180
Electrical Workers, International										2,710	2,650	2,550
Electrical Workers, United								478	4,668	1,327	1,650*	1,650*
Elevator Constructors		22	23	31	81	102	102	102	102	100	120	130

Engineers, Operating	7	176	177	320	250	340	350	582	1,353	2,000	2,700	3,000
Farm Equipment Workers												
Farm Workers								175	500		20	140
Federal Employees				385	208	335	560	646	820	813	800*	1,000*
Federal Workers								44	127			
Fire Fighters		180		221	150	180	263	328	441	720	870	1,230
Firemen and Oilers			114	296	90	90	149	268	559	570	440	400
Football Players												10
Foreman's Assoc									300	93		
Fur & Leather Workers	40			121	89	70	30	303	468			
Furniture Workers								161	312			
Garment Workers		457	464	459	475	472	371	400	400	340	320	280
Garment Workers, Ladies'		22	584	1,054	910	508	1,680	2,015	2,731	3,830	3,630	3,630
Gas, Coke & Chemical	40	66	100	100	60	60	55		300			
Glass Bottle Blowers								208	356	470	650	750
Glass and Ceramic								225	300	410	330	280
Glass Cutters							12	12	16	20	10	10
Glass Workers, Flint	72	69	87	99	61	49	61	178	265	280	310	350
Glove Workers		20	11	10	2	8	35	9	31	30		
Government Employees							139	226	309	470	1,320	2,510
Grain Millers										330	250	290
Granite Cutters	45	99			86	85	50	50	40	40	30	10
Graphic Arts			135	105								930
Hatters, Cap and Millinery	56	89			115	115	214	300	320	423	320	150
Hatters of North America			94	105	115							
Hockey Players												3
Horseshoers	20	42	52	54	20	7	1					2
Hotel and Restaurant	15	494	476	604	385	365	821	2,109	2,824	4,116	3,000	4,210
Insurance Workers											210	220
Iron, Steel, and Tin	105	143	55	315	111	79	86	75	944	1,331	1,321	1,600
Iron Workers		115	109	277	177	209	132	388	80	205	140	100
Jewelry Workers				81	12	8	55	40				
Laborers		120	125	420	490	1,027	394	1,575	1,815	4,361	4,030	4,750
Lathers		39	59	59	80	165	53	75	61	168	160	120
Laundry, Dry Cleaning		65	26	67	55	55	60	292	500	724		
Laundry Workers												200
Leather Workers				117	20	50	27	25			220	
Letter Carriers	111	169	269	325	325	508	541	654	643	982	1,300	1,510
Lithographers	15	30	24	61	55	56	67	123	145	280		

Lithographers and Photoengravers	303	500	719	869	N/A	N/A	596	602	766	518	300	390*
Locomotive Engineers	243	544	853	1,259	N/A	N/A	663	825	1,210	953	401*	
Locomotive Firemen	50	500	235	740	305	347	400	663	639	727	410	600
Longshoremen								300	524	556	500	
Longshoremen and Warehousemen											600*	600*
Machinists	140	557	598	3,308	779	780	978	1,780	6,701	7,001	6,630	7,800
Maintenance of Way		123	91	501	383	401	555	878	1,433	1,590	770	710
Marble, Slate and Stone		6	28	12	30	77	55	55	45	60	80	80
Marine Engineers	39	97	95	170	N/A	N/A	54	79	136	86	90	200
Marine and Shipbuilding								350	1,783	271	220	220
Maritime Union								318	610	380	450	350
Masters, Mates	11	344	60	71	41	30	22	30	33	95	90	
Meat Cutters			40	653	115	125	198	629	1,057	2,850	3,300	4,510
Mechanics Educational Society							25	55	364	194	370	230
Metal Engravers					1	4	3	3	3	4		
Metal Polishers	36	128	100	125	60	60	40	70	100	154	110	90
Mine, Mill	80	241	492	211	91	40	146	301	968	271	750*	
Mine Workers, Progressive	97						N/A	142	117	73		
Mine Workers, United	120	2,510	2,893	3,936	4,027	4,000	5,667	4,785	5,021	3,163	4,500*	4,500*
Molders		300	500	573	336	218	118	233	666	747	500	500
Musicians		220	500	700	771	1,000	954	1,273	1,331	2,482	2,250	2,150
Newspaper Guild								144	151	269	230	260
Office and Professional Employees									136	452	520	740
Office and Professional Workers												
Oil, Chemical and Atomic							428	138	315	1,699	1,400	1,450
Oil and Gas Well												
Oil Workers	50			209	220	110		174	453			
Packinghouse Workers			685					394	1,184	1,353	710	
Painters		607		1,031	1,033	1,062	636	1,025	1,376	1,912	1,600	1,600
Papermakers	1	88	28	74	62	40	93	267	479	752		
Papermakers and Paperworkers											1,210	
Papermakers, United										375		
Paperworkers, International									186			2,750
Pattern Makers	10	37	60	90	70	70	25	70	110	135	100	100
Paving Cutters		12	35	26	20	20	21	20	17			
Photo Engravers		17	40	59	68	89	93	106	120	158		
Plasterers	20	124	157	194	300	382	180	194	250	623	680	550
Plate Printers	6	10	12	14	12	11	14	9	16	8		
Playthings								25	133			

Plumbers	40	165	260	750	350	450	354	586	2,100	2,470	2,170	2,280
Post Office Clerks			90	250	200	350	319	437	448	984	1,170	450*
Postal and Federal Employees			N/A	N/A	N/A	N/A	17	25	120	180	260*	330*
Postal Supervisors			N/A	N/A	N/A	N/A	65	88	110	199	280*	
Postal Workers					N/A	N/A						2,490
Potters	5	58	65	80	83	58	113	149	215	241	190	170
Printing and Graphic Communications												1,050
Printing Pressmen	50	160	190	350	387	400	320	396	544	1,001	1,000	
Pulp, Sulphite		45	35	95	50	50	157	435	800	1,601	1,350	
Radio Association			10	123	80	N/A	70	81	100	16	20	10
Railroad Signalmen			250	780	433	410	350	440	488	153	110	110
Railroad Telegraphers	150		287	1,812	1,375	800	584	786	1,279	465		
Railway Carmen	13	177	50	1,860	884	970	724	910	2,250	1,710	840	560
Railway, Airline		29		560	N/A	N/A	338	330	378	3,189	1,860	1,600
Railway Conductors	207	334	479	208	100	100	120	510	968	325	200*	
Retail Clerks	27	500		18	30	40	40	440	600	2,734	4,100	6,020
Retail, Wholesale								395	1,289	1,227	1,140	1,180
Roofers	40					40	40	172	80	178	220	270
Rubber Workers				659	180	150	125	110	375	1,633	1,530	1,730
Seafarers		201		218	62	162	275	623	948	580	800	800
Seamen's Union	10											
Service Employees	10	153	166		250	250	160	200	250	2,157	3,050	4,800
Sheet Metal Workers										885	1,000	1,200
Shoe Workers				1	1	1	1	1	1	431	450	450
Siderographers					N/A	N/A	12	60	95	1	1	1
Sleeping Car Porters				22						100	50	10
Spinners	24	25			N/A	N/A	N/A	5	5			
State, County, and Municipal				59	65	78	2,250	270	610	1,035	2,370	6,470
Steelworkers		24						2,250	7,357	10,158	8,760	10,620
Stereotypers		26		30	29	30	79	83	85	124	110	
Stone and Allied Products	60	80		40	50	58	20	50	50	119	110	
Stonecutters	7	17		19	16	10	57	41	19	19	20	
Stove, Furnace				140	93	92	20	42	88	95	90	30
Switchmen							80	78	97	105	90	
Tailors	50	159		120	100	67	45					
Teachers				93	37	52	137	321	311	460	970	3,960
Teamsters		840		1,108	750	988	1,619	4,416	6,445	12,911	15,067*	19,732*
Technical Engineers				35	6	12	12	19	78	102	110	140
Telegraph Workers				22	37	38	20	35	208	322	290	120

Union												
Textile Workers, Amalgamated	27	105	109									
Textile Workers, United				400	300	300	792	833	2,476	1,975	1,230	1,050
Textile Workers of America				1,049				13	431	481	360	360
Theatrical Stage Employees	20	50	110	196	200	240	240	420	420	452	500	500
Timber Workers		14	15	101	15	24	88	169	334	341	240	260
Tobacco Workers	41	56	37	152			23	28	38	45	30	30
Train Dispatchers			N/A	N/A	N/A	N/A	23	28				
Transit Union	28	300	402	987	1,000	972	734	797	1,687	1,557	980	900
Transport Service								272	50	40	30	950
Transport Workers									317			
Transportation Union										800	800	1,340
Typographical Union	281	462	538	705	688	776	763	842	770	1,040	870	730
Upholsterers		30	28	56	75	107	65	110	250	506	500	500
Utility Workers								90	147	752	500	500
Wall Paper Craftsmen					N/A	N/A	6	31	23	16		
Wire Weavers	2	3	4			4	6	3	4	4		
Wood Carvers	7	16	10	12	10	12	3	4	4	4		
Wood Workers International	33	283										
Woodworkers of America								130	501	893	490	520

Sources: Sources used for the various years are: 1897-1920: Leo Wolman, *The Growth of American Trade Unions, 1880-1923* (1924); 1924-1930: Labor Research Department, Rand School of Social Science, *The American Labor Year Book, 1931* (1931); 1935-1955: Leo Troy, *Trade Union Membership, 1897-1962* (1965); 1965-1975: *Report of the Executive Council of the AFL-CIO* (1975). The asterisk (*) indicates that the figures used were taken from the Bureau of Labor Statistics' *Directory of National and International Labor Unions in the United States, 1973* (1975), or the *World Almanac and Book of Facts* (1975).

GLOSSARY

Anti-Injunction Law. *See* Norris-LaGuardia Act.

Boycott. A concerted effort to reduce the sales of goods and/or services of an employer that fails to reach a satisfactory agreement with employees.

Closed Shop. An employment situation in which a potential employee must be a union member before being hired and must retain union membership throughout the term of employment.

Collective Bargaining. Preliminary negotiations between labor and management prior to the signing of a contract stipulating the conditions of employment during a specified period; includes negotiations resulting from differences growing from divergent interpretations of the terms of the contract.

Company Union. A union organized at the instigation of management and dominated by the company; declared an unfair labor practice under the provisions of the National Labor Relations Act.

Company-Wide Bargaining. Contract negotiations covering all workers employed by a particular company. *See also* Collective Bargaining.

Craft Unionism. The organization of workers, usually skilled or semiskilled, by craft or trade.

Dual Unions. A situation in which two unions function in the same trade jurisdiction. *See also* Trade Jurisdiction.

Employee Representation Plan. *See* Company Union.

Federal Labor Union. A directly chartered local union of the American Federation of Labor which was comprised of a variety of occupational groups. The Federal Labor Union was used as an organizing device, the members usually being distributed to the various international unions holding jurisdiction.

Industrial Unionism. The organization of all workers in a particular industry, regardless of skill or occupation, into one union.

Industry-Wide Bargaining. Contract negotiations covering all employees in a particular industry. *See also* Collective Bargaining.

Injunction. A court order restricting the conduct of individuals and/or unions involved in activities considered detrimental to the property rights of an employer. *See also* Norris-LaGuardia Act.

Jurisdictional Dispute. A situation in which two or more unions claim organizing rights over the workers in a particular trade or industry. *See also* Trade Jurisdiction.
Jurisdictional Raiding. An aggressive effort by one union to organize workers claimed by another union. *See also* Jurisdictional Dispute.

Labor-Management Relations Act. *See* Taft-Hartley Act.
Labor-Management Reporting and Disclosure Act. *See* Landrum-Griffin Act.
Landrum-Griffin Act. The union member's so-called bill of rights; designed to increase internal union democracy and to reform the manner in which union financial affairs were conducted; additional provisions strengthened the secondary boycott and picketing provisions of the Taft-Hartley Act.
Lockout. A situation in which an employer temporarily suspends production in an effort to coerce employees regarding the terms of employment.

Membership Raiding. An aggressive effort by one union to enroll members already organized by another union.
Mohawk Valley Formula. An anti-union tactic developed, by the Remington Rand Corporation in New York, to turn public opinion against trade unionism through threats to move the business; declared an unfair labor practice under the provisions of the National Labor Relations Act.
Molly Maguires. A secret society of Irish anthracite miners in western Pennsylvania which, after the failure of the anthracite miners' strike of 1875, committed numerous acts of violence and destruction; disappeared soon after the conviction of twenty-four members and execution of ten.

National Labor Relations Act. Under the provisions of this measure, which became law in 1935, employees had the "right to self-organization, to form, join or assist labor organization to bargain collectively through representatives of their own choosing, and to engage in concerted activities for the purpose of collective bargaining or other mutual aid or protection;" established a three-member National Labor Relations Board to administer the provisions of the act and conduct representational elections to determine collective bargaining agents.
National Labor Relations Board. *See* National Labor Relations Act.
Norris-LaGuardia Act. An act greatly restricting the conditions under which anti-labor injunctions could be issued and outlawing yellow-dog contracts. *See also* Injunction and Yellow-Dog Contract.

Open Shop. (1) Before the enactment of the National Labor Relations Act, an effort to keep union members out of employment. (2) Since that act, a situation in which both union and nonunion workers are employed.

Preferential Shop. An agreement under which applicants who are union members are given preference in employment over nonunion applicants.
Pure and Simple Trade Unionism. A situation in which reform and political activities are subordinated to the pursuit of the immediate economic needs of workers—wages, hours, and working conditions—through collective bargaining.

Section 7(a), National Industry Recovery Act (NIRA). Section stipulating that each code of industrial self-government drawn up under the provisions of the NIRA must contain provisions for union recognition, collective bargaining, minimum wages and maximum hours, and restrictions on child labor; was declared unconstitutional in 1935, and its labor provisions were thereafter included in and expanded upon in the National Labor Relations Act.

Sit-Down Strike. A work stoppage in which employees remain at their employment stations but refuse to work; used primarily in the drive to organize mass production workers during the late 1930s.

Systems Federation. A situation, occurring most often among railroad unions, where a national union's locals on a particular railroad line form a federated unit for collective bargaining purposes.

Taft-Hartley Act. An anti-labor law prohibiting labor unions from establishing closed or preferential shops, calling jurisdictional strikes and secondary boycotts, and making contributions in primary and national elections; also permitted the president of the United States to secure an eighty-day no-strike injunction in certain situations, provided for the employer's so-called freedom of speech, increased the membership of the National Labor Relations Board to five, and required each national union official to file a non-Communist affidavit.

Trade Jurisdiction. The workers in a particular trade or industry which an international union claims the right to organize.

Union Label. An insignia attached to or imprinted on a product to indicate that it was made by union labor.

Union Shop. An employment situation in which the potential employee agrees to become a union member after being employed.

Wagner Act. *See* National Labor Relations Act.

Yellow-Dog Contract. A pre-employment condition in which the employee agrees not to join a union during the terms of employment; declared illegal under the terms of the Norris-LaGuardia Act of 1932.

INDEX

About the Editor

Gary M Fink, associate professor of history at Georgia State University, specializes in labor history. His previous works include *Biographical Dictionary of American Labor Leaders, Labor's Search for Political Order*, and articles written for many journals. He is currently working on *Essays on Southern Labor History*, which will be published by Greenwood Press in 1977.